MOSCOW
&
ST PETERSBURG

MOSCOW &

BY

MASHA NORDBYE

ST PETERSBURG

PHOTOGRAPHY BY
PATRICIA LANZA

© 1999, 1995, 1991, 1990 Odyssey Publications Ltd
Maps © 1999, 1995, 1991, 1990 Odyssey Publications Ltd

Odyssey Publications Ltd, 1004 Kowloon Centre, 29–43 Ashley Road,
Tsim Sha Tsui, Kowloon, Hong Kong
Tel. (852) 2856 3896; Fax. (852) 2565 8004; E-mail: odyssey@asiaonline.net

Distribution in the United Kingdom, Ireland and Europe by
Hi Marketing Ltd, 38 Carver Road, London SE24 9LT, UK

Distribution in the United States of America by
W.W. Norton & Company, Inc., New York
Library of Congress Catalog Card Number has been requested.

ISBN: 962-217-611-9

Grateful acknowledgment is made to the following authors and publishers:
Peter Owen Ltd for *Adventures in Czarist Russia* by Alexandre Dumas, edited and translated by
Alma Elizabeth Murch; Farrar, Straus and Giroux Inc. and Georges Borchardt Inc. for *In Plain
Russian* by Vladimir Voinovich translated by Richard Lourie, translation © 1979 by Farrar,
Strauss and Giroux Inc.; North Point Press for *The Noise of Time* translated by Clarence Brown
© 1965 Princeton University Press; Princeton University Press for *The Road to Bloody Sunday:
The role of Father Gapon and the Assembly in the Petersburg Massacre of 1905* by Walter
Sablinsky © 1976 Princeton University Press; Random House Inc. and William Heinemann
Ltd for *Among the Russians* © 1983 Colin Thubron; Penguin Books for *Dead Souls* by Nikolai
Gogol, translation © 1961 David Magarshack; Chronicle Books for *White Nights* by Fyodor
Dostoevsky © 1995

Editor: Kevin Bishop
Series Co-ordinator: Jane Finden-Crofts
Design: Kevin Bishop
Maps: Au Yeung Chui Kwai, Philip Choi and Kevin Bishop
Cover Concept: Margaret Lee
Index: Françoise Parkin

Front cover photography: Kevin Bishop
Back cover photography: Keith Macgregor
Photography by Patricia Lanza
Additional photography/illustrations courtesy of Kevin Bishop 455, 466; Patrick Lucero 6–7,
152 178, 179, 194; Keith Macgregor 398–9, 404, 412, 419, 479, 488, 489, 492; Masha
Nordbye 102, 103, 182 (bottom left), 183 (bottom), 190–1, 195, 206, 207, 230, 238, 242–3,
246, 250, 254–5, 260, 264–5, 269, 277, 280, 367, 390, 391, 444, 462, 501, 505, 507, 512; John
Oliver 98; Carolyn Watts 153; Cary Wollinsky, Trillium Studios 42–3, 110, 111, 119, 122

Production by Twin Age Ltd, Hong Kong
Printed in Hong Kong

Special Acknowledgments

We will preserve you Russian speech; keep you alive great Russian word.
We will pass you to our sons and heirs; free and clean, and they in turn to theirs.
And so forever.

Anna Akhmatova

After 20 years of journeying around Russia, with many extraordinary experiences, a multitude of hosts and characters have blessed my path and generously provided assistance, for which I am forever grateful.

I wish to especially thank my friends and family for all their support, patience, help and humor during the many months of writing and research: Eleanor, Leonard and Gorski; Phil Penningroth; Carlichka 'Bogoliubsky' Gottlieb; Jane Brockman; 'Moshka' Lanza; Lyoni Craven and Ina Goff; 'Bashkaus' Bill; Anatoly and Svetlana; the Valushkins and Romashkovis—for their Moscow pad, car and guidance; John 'Bolshoi' Feist for his never-ending hospitality; Stuart and Santa Richardson; Richard 'Great Master' Neill; St Petersburg Circus—Sonin, Natasha, Vladimir Uspensky and the Circus Hotel; 'Stari' and 'Novi' Moscow Circuses; Jando and Lena and the Big Apple Circus; Sasha, Tanya, Andrei, Max 'and Masha'—the Frishkadelkamis; Robert 'the Great' Trent Jones and Gudren; Ivan Ivanovich Sergeev and UPDK and the Moscow Country Club; Isabel Allende and Villie Gordon; Lynda Svendson and Kent 'Mongol' Madin; Alex 'Igor' Gregory; Bob 'Icebreaker' Liljestrand and Val 'Vladivostok' Ossipov; Stefanski Robertson and Jim McCutcheon; Linda Forristal; Vild Le; Gene Sawyer; Alexandra Baker—my first Russian language teacher; all the members of Sweetwater; Yuko, Ari and Aidan; Andy and Gank; Chris Ellis and the Bhutan Bunch; Tom Sopko and Jenny Larchek; Tom Parker at the Emerald Group and Marina Pisklakova for her work at the Moscow Crisis Center; Peggy Burns; Les Mannos and Jerry White—my computer wizards; Ricardo and Vahé—for opening many doors; Vladimir Shetinin and Operation Amba; Viktor Yudin; Andrei Rey; and Jennie Sutton.

A special hail to my Odyssey *Tovarishi* Kevin Bishop, Magnus Bartlett, Jane Finden-Crofts and Margaret Lam; *Na Zdorovye!*

To my instructors and mates on the Flying Trapeze: Great Master Ritchie and Keri Gaona; the one and only Gary Littlejohn; Pam Pam and Tomcat Ventura; Tom 'Sergei-Oleg' Moore; Joey Preston, Scotti, Zak and Terry—catchers extraordinaire; Jackie; Jules; 'Dolgoruky' William; Der Fliegende Fred; Jorg; Steen; Debbi; Fiona; Randy; Marla; Boopski; Uncle Murray and Crystal; the Russian Flying Cranes—the Golovkos and the first quintuple somersault in trapeze history; and lastly, *oy*, but not leastly Sonoma Sami-sambubba Keen!

In special memory of Yuri Nikulin, Schneer, Robert Baker and Sam Orth at Middlebury College—inspirational teachers; Mek Morsey, Brian Seeholzer, Matt Valensic, and the Slavic-blooded Babushki Annas and Dyedushka Mitro.

And a hearty *spasibo* to all those who helped throughout the many years in the ol' *Bolshaya Kapusta*.

Masha Nordbye

CONTENTS

(previous pages) View of Moscow from the National Hotel. (clockwise from left front) The Historical Museum and GUM Department Store overlook Red Square, bordered on its southern side

by St Basil's Cathedral. The Spasskaya (Savior) Clock Tower stands behind the Lenin Mausoleum. Beyond the red fortified walls stand the government buildings and old churches inside the Kremlin.

SPECIAL TOPICS

LITERARY EXCERPTS

MAPS

Eastern Europe

FINLAND

N

0   100   200   300 km
0   100   200 miles

L. Onega
Kizhi
Island

Valaam
Island

L. Ladoga

Helsinki

SWEDEN

Gulf of Finland

Stockholm

St Petersburg

Tallinn

Narva

ESTONIA

Pskov

Novgorod

Volga

Yaroslavl

Rostov

Baltic Sea

Riga

LATVIA

Dvina

Suzdal

Sergiyev
Posad

Vladimir

Moscow

Neman

LITHUANIA

Kaliningrad

(RUSSIA)

Vilnius

Minsk

Smolensk

Oka

R U S S I A

POLAND

Vistula

Bug

Brest

BELARUS

Dnieper

Pripet

Desna

Warsaw

Vistula

Psel

Don

Kiev

Lvov

Donets

SLOVAKIA

Bratislava

Dnestr

UKRAINE

Kharkov

Budapest

Bug

HUNGARY

Siret

MOLDOVA

Dnieper

Rostov-
on-Don

Kishinev

Odessa

Sea of Azov

ROMANIA

FORMER

YUGOSLAVIA

Bucharest

Sava

Danube

Yalta

Sofia

Black   Sea

BULGARIA

ALBANIA

Istanbul

TURKEY

GREECE

© Odyssey Publications Ltd

Introduction

On with the journey!...
Russia! Russia!
When I see you... my eyes
are lit up with supernatural power. Oh, what a
glittering, wondrous infinity of space....What a
strange, alluring, enthralling, wonderful world!

Nikolai Gogol

Perhaps no other destination in the world has captured the traveler's imagination as much as Russia. Throughout the centuries, its visitors have reported phenomenal and fanciful scenes: from golden churches, bejeweled icons and towering kremlins to madcap czars, wild cossacks and prolific poets. Russia was, and remains, an impressive sight to behold. A travel writer in the early 20th century remarked that Russia's capital, Moscow, 'embodied fantasy on an unearthly scale... Towers, domes, spires, cones, onions, crenellations filled the whole view. It might have been the invention of Danté, arrived in a Russian heaven.'

By the 1600s, Russia was already the largest country in the world, stretching from Finland to Alaska. The massive conquests deep into the Siberian wilds by Ivan the Terrible and Peter the Great had created a territory larger than the Roman Empire with the richest resources on Earth. It was so vast that in 1856, when American Perry McDonough Collins arrived in Irkutsk to propose a railway line to link the country, it took him nearly a year to travel the 5,632 kilometers (3,500 miles) to St Petersburg. He had to change horses over 200 times.

After the 1917 Bolshevik Revolution, the countries bordering Russia fell into the Soviet Union's domain. The USSR became the world's largest nation with 15 republics stretching across 11 time zones and two continents, Europe and Asia. Its borders encompassed one-sixth of the planet's total land area with a population of 290 million speaking 200 languages and dialects.

On the historic day of December 21, 1991, after seven decades of Communist rule, the Soviet Union collapsed. The attempted coup in August 1991 was the catalyst that led to the dissolution of one of the most oppressive regimes in history. As one defender of a new and nontotalitarian government exclaimed: 'I have lived through a revolution, two world wars, the Siege of Leningrad and Stalin, and I will not tolerate another takeover; let the people be in peace!' In its place was established the Commonwealth of Independent States (CIS), or the Soyuz Nezavysimeekh Gosudarstv (SNG).

Moscow is the Commonwealth's largest city and the capital of its largest state, the Russian Federation, which occupies 17,070,959 square kilometers (6,591,104 square miles), stretching to the eastern tip of Siberian Kamchatka. There are 1,064 cities, and over 80 percent of the population lives in European Russia to the west of the Ural Mountains. With nearly 150 million people and 130 nationalities and ethnic groups, Russia is truly the core of the Commonwealth. It is impossible to take in the diversity of the entire country during one, two or even three visits. However, there is no better way to learn about the Russian character and way of life than taking a trip to Moscow, St Petersburg and the area of the Golden Ring.

Moscow is the center of politics, industry and culture—the heart of this giant nation—and the source of the Russian spirit, or *dushá*. The Russian poet Alexander Pushkin wrote of his first trip to Moscow: 'And now at last the goal is in sight: in the shimmer of the white walls...and golden domes, Moskva lies great and splendid before us...O Moskva have I thought of you! Moskva how violently the name plucks at any Russian heart!'

The true enchantment of Moscow begins in the city center, where you can gaze upon the gilded domes of the palaces and churches of the former czars, rising up from within the old protective walls of the Kremlin. From the citadel, paths lead out to the fairy-tale creation of Ivan the Terrible, St Basil's Cathedral, which looms up from the middle of Krasnaya Ploshchad or Red Square. *Krasnaya* is an Old Russian word meaning both red and beautiful. The city, which marked its 850th anniversary in 1997, is also a place where frenzied consumerism is coupled with deep spirituality, and golden domes of long-closed churches are gleaming once again. In 1931, Stalin destroyed the immense Cathedral of Christ Our Savior, but in 1997 the next generation helped rebuild it through hundreds of millions of dollars in public subscriptions. Shopping malls have even popped up alongside the Kremlin and in old KGB bunkers. Surely Lenin would not even recognize the place—and large lines no longer wait to enter Lenin's Mausoleum to view the Father of the Great October Revolution.

Like arteries from the heart of the city, long thoroughfares take one through various stages of Moscow's history. These roads, and ringroads, offer an abundance of sights and over 100 museums. The Arbat district, which celebrated its 500th anniversary in 1993, embodies both Russia's history and the changes currently sweeping the country. Here, *babushki* (grandmothers) amble along carrying bags filled with cabbages and potatoes, while long-haired musicians jam on guitars and saxophones. The city offers a wealth of breathtaking and poetic creations, as the famous Russian writer Anna Akhmatova remarked: 'As you stroll through the city, you'll find...all of Moscow is truly soaked with verses, saturated with meter, time after time.'

(following pages) A large stone lion stands above the Neva by the Palace Bridge (Dvortsovy Most). The building across the river with the tower is the Kunstkammer (Cabinet of Curiosities), built in 1714 to house Peter the Great's private collections. It is now the Museum of Anthropology and Ethnography and the Lomonosov Museum. The columned building to the left is the Academy of Sciences.

With the dawn of Gorbachev's 'second revolution' came a virtual explosion in communications, culture and national awareness. In what was termed the new Russian Renaissance, the people experienced greater freedoms than were ever permitted throughout the entire history of socialism. Mikhail Gorbachev's perestroika and glasnost, and Boris Yeltsin's heroic stance became the symbols of the new generation.

When Boris Yeltsin and his followers triumphed over the abortive coups of August 1991 and October 1993, democratic reforms lit up the country. A new constitution and Federal Assembly were created, and a market economy stumbled into action for the first time in the country's existence. New freedoms and opportunities have flowered from the ruins of 70 years of Marxist-Leninist rule. There has never been a more exciting time to visit Russia.

The towns and villages surrounding the city, known collectively as the Golden Ring, reveal a quieter and quainter lifestyle. This area is considered the cradle of Russian culture. The small towns, like Sergiyev Posad (the center of Russian Orthodoxy) and Suzdal (the most ancient Russian town), were built between the 10th and 17th centuries and are magnificently preserved. Antiquated villages, onion-domed churches, frescoes and icons by the 15th-century artist Andrei Rublyov, colorful wooden dacha (country homes) and endless groves of *beryoza* (birch trees) provide a delightful contrast to the bigger cities. These serene sites are reminiscent of a 19th-century Tolstoyan novel, a portrait of Russia's past.

Much more provincial than Moscow, St Petersburg is the legacy of Peter the Great. Images of this astoundingly beautiful city are reflected in the Neva River which winds around the many islands that comprise the area. A stroll along one of the many canal embankments takes in three centuries of ornate architecture glistening under the pastel northern lights. Sights abound: the Hermitage, one of the largest museums in the world; Peterhof Palace, rivaling Versailles in grandeur; Peter the Great's fortress; the golden-spired Admiralty; the statue of the Bronze Horseman; and scenes of numerous revolutions. Throughout the world, every time someone recites Gogol or Dostoevsky, or sees a performance of *Boris Godunov* or *Swan Lake*, St Petersburg's bounty flowers again. Liberated of the name Leningrad (and anything to do with Lenin) in 1991, the city's residents affectionately refer to their city simply as Pieter. They look forward to celebrating St Petersburg's 300th anniversary in 2003.

Compared to even a few years ago, Russian cities and towns now boast scores of entertainment opportunities, places to eat and items to buy, and it is a lot easier to get things done. Many Western-style stores stock most products that you would find at home. In the old Soviet Union, most enterprises, and people for that matter, were strictly insulated and controlled. After years of suppression, it is not hard to imagine how a taste of democracy and individualization first led to an 'anything goes' atmosphere. Because of the whirlwind creation of new businesses and flood of consumer spending, Moscow has been nicknamed *Deeky Zapad*, the Wild West. But this 'baby' country is just experiencing the growing pains of normal adolescence. Once it matures, economists predict that this large powerhouse, with its vast natural resources, new business-oriented generation, and immense desire for success, will become one of the most dynamic marketplaces in the world. But as capitalism takes hold, so unfortunately does poverty, crime and corruption. Today's visitors must be more guarded with their money and valuables.

Many travelers enter the country through a tourist agency, which provides hotels, meals and sightseeing, but there are other ways. Visitors can also enter on individual or business visas, stay in Russian homes or hostels, or even camp. For the more adventurous, biking, climbing, hiking and rafting trips are available.

If you do not read Cyrillic or speak Russian, take a Russian phrase book; a smile, some patience and the knowledge of a few Russian words will be greatly appreciated. So much so, that you may even find yourself invited to someone's home for dinner, where you will quickly discover that Russians are among the warmest and most hospitable people you will ever meet.

Do Svidanya!

PERESTROIKA

On March 11, 1985, 54-year-old Mikhail Sergeyevich Gorbachev was elected the new General Secretary of the Communist Party. Following in the footsteps of such past rulers as Ivan the Terrible, Peter the Great, Stalin and Brezhnev, Gorbachev inherited a stagnating economy, an entrenched bureaucracy and a population living in fear and mistrust of its leaders.

Gorbachev's first actions were to shut down the production and sale of vodka and ardently pursue the anticorruption campaign instituted by a former president, Yuri Vladimirovich Andropov. In 1986, Gorbachev introduced the radical reform policies of perestroika (restructuring), *demokratizatsiya* (democratization) and glasnost (openness), now household words. He emphasized that past reforms had not worked because they did not directly involve Soviet citizens. Perestroika introduced the profit motive, quality control, private ownership in agriculture, decentralization and multi-candidate elections. Industry concentrated on measures promoting quality over quantity; private businesses and cooperatives were encouraged; farmers and individuals could lease land and housing from the government, and keep the profits made from produce grown on private plots; hundreds of ministries and bureaucratic centers were disbanded. A law was passed that allowed individuals to own small businesses and hire workers so long as there was 'no exploitation of man by man'.

In a powerful symbolic gesture, Andrei Sakharov and other political prisoners were released from internal exile. (After winning the 1975 Nobel Peace Prize, Sakharov, the physicist and human rights activist, was banished for nearly seven years to the city of Gorky, the present-day Nizhny Novgorod. He died in Moscow on November 14, 1989.) One hundred Soviet dissidents from 20 cities were allowed to form the Democratic Club, an open political discussion group. Glasnost swept through all facets of Soviet life.

For the 40 million followers of the Russian Orthodox religion, and people of other religious beliefs, Gorbachev stated that 'believers have the full right to express their convictions with dignity'. On December 1, 1989, Gorbachev became the first Soviet leader to set foot in the Vatican, where he declared: 'We need spiritual values; we need a revolution of the mind... No one should interfere in matters of the individual's conscience. Christians, Moslems, Jews, Buddhists and others live in the Soviet Union. All of them have a right to satisfy their spiritual needs—this is the only way toward a new culture and new politics that can meet the challenge of our time.'

As Peter the Great understood, modernization meant Westernization, and Gorbachev reopened the window to the West. With the fostering of private business, about five million people were employed by over 150,000 cooperatives. After April 1, 1989, all enterprises were allowed to carry on trade relations with foreign partners, triggering the development of joint ventures. Multimillion-dollar deals were struck with Western companies, such as Chevron, Pepsi, Eastman-Kodak, McDonald's, Time-Warner and Occidental.

At the 1986 Iceland Summit, Gorbachev proposed a sharp reduction in ballistic missiles, and in December 1987, he signed a treaty with US President Ronald Reagan to eliminate intermediate-range nuclear missiles. In January 1988, the Soviet Union announced its withdrawal from Afghanistan. Nine months later Andrei Gromyko retired and Gorbachev was elected President of the Supreme Soviet.

During a visit to Finland in October 1989, Gorbachev declared: 'The Soviet Union has no moral or political right to interfere in the affairs of its Eastern European neighbors. They have the right to decide their own fate.' And that is what they did. By the end of 1989, every country throughout Eastern Europe saw its people protesting openly for mass reforms. The Iron Curtain crumbled, symbolized most poignantly by the demolition of the wall between East and West Berlin.

In December 1989, Gorbachev met with US President George Bush at the Malta

Summit, where the two agreed that 'the arms race, mistrust, psychological and ideological struggle should all be things of the past'.

ELECTIONS AND ECONOMY

On March 26, 1989, there was a general election for the new Congress of People's Deputies—the first time since 1917 that Soviet citizens had had the chance to vote in a national election. One thousand five hundred delegates were elected together with an additional 750, who were voted in by other public organizations. The 2,250-delegate body then elected 542 members to form a new Supreme Soviet.

Ousted a year earlier from his Politburo post for criticizing the reforms, the Congress candidate Boris Yeltsin won 89 percent of the Moscow district vote. As Moscow crowds chanted 'Yeltsin is a Man of the People' and 'Down with Bureaucrats', a surprising number of bureaucrats had, in fact, lost to members of such groups as the Church Metropolitan of Leningrad. Andrei Sakharov was also elected. An interesting aspect of the election rules was that even candidates who ran unopposed could lose if over half the votes polled showed a level of no confidence, a privilege not enjoyed by voters in most Western countries.

At the beginning of 1990, Soviet citizens once again headed to the polls to elect their own regional and district officials, this time with the additional opportunity of choosing candidates from other independent and pro-democracy movements. Scores of Communist Party candidates were defeated by former political prisoners, adamant reformers, environmentalists and strike leaders. Yeltsin was voted in as President of the Russian Federation, the Soviet Union's largest republic with more than half the country's population and Moscow as its capital. In June 1990, Yeltsin resigned from the Communist Party, declaring that 'in view of my...great responsibility toward the people of Russia and in connection with moves toward a multiparty State, I cannot fulfill only the instructions of the Party'.

Yeltsin's ascent underscored the fact that for all Gorbachev's unprecedented reforms and innovative policies, he had failed to bring the country's economy out of stagnation; because of this he lost his popularity at home. An extensive poll conducted throughout the Soviet Union revealed that more than 90 percent considered the economic situation critical. Some of the disheartened commented that 'glasnost has produced more copies of Solzhenitsyn than salami'. Food and fuel were in critically low supplies, and the population anticipated the worst food shortages since World War II. Ration coupons were issued for meat, sugar, tea and soap. After the launch of a probe to Mars, graffiti in Moscow appeared exclaiming: 'To Mars for Soap!'

Modernization still did not approach Western standards: there were few computers and most areas continued to use the abacus. It was estimated that 40 percent of the crops had been wasted because of poor storage, packing and distribution methods. Many Soviets felt that their living conditions had worsened: 'We live like dogs. The leash has become longer but the meat is a bit smaller, and the plate is two meters further away. But at least we can now bark as much as we want.'

Gorbachev was also faced with a budget deficit of over 100 billion rubles. The severe shortages boosted the black market, which provided goods for up to 85 percent of the population. On November 1, 1989, the government drastically cut the bank ruble exchange rate by 90 percent to curb black-market exchanges (up to 20 times the official rate) and bring the ruble closer to an open exchange on the world market. The prime minister stated that 43 million people (15 percent of the population) were living below the poverty level. There was also an estimated 23 million unemployed, the new paradox of this modern Soviet society.

Compounding failing measures and political contradictions, the nation was rocked by a series of disasters: Chernobyl, the earthquake in Armenia, ethnic unrest and extensive strikes in mines and factories across the country (a 1989 law legalized strikes). But Gorbachev remained confident and pressed on with perestroika: 'This is a turbulent time, a turbulent sea in which it is not easy to sail the ship. But we have a compass and we have a crew to guide that ship, and the ship itself is strong.'

In one of the most important changes in the country's political and economic system since the 1917 Bolshevik Revolution, Mikhail Gorbachev was elected by Congress as the Soviet Union's first executive president. This new post, replacing the former honorary chairmanship of the Supreme Soviet, had broader constitutional powers. The president now had the right to propose legislation, veto bills passed by Congress, appoint and fire the prime minister and other senior government officials, and declare states of emergency (with the approval of the republics).

Gorbachev himself summarized the results of all his policies: 'Having embarked upon the road of radical reform, we have crossed the line beyond which there is no return to the past... Things will never be the same again in the Soviet Union—or in the whole communist world.' Gorbachev's second revolution became one of the most momentous events in the second half of the 20th century.

THE COMMUNIST PARTY

If what the Communists are doing with Russia is an experiment, for this experiment I would not even spare a frog.

Professor I P Pavlov (1918)

The Bolshevik Party, formed by Lenin, began as a unified band of revolutionaries whose 8,000 members organized the mass strike of the 1905 St Petersburg revolt.

By October 1917, the Bolshevik Party (soon renamed the Communist Party) had over 300,000 members, many of whom became the leaders and planners of the newly formed Soviet State.

Before the fall of Communism, there were more than 20 million Party members, a third of them women. Membership was open to any citizens who 'did not exploit the labor of others', abided by the Party's philosophy and gave three percent of their monthly pay as dues to the Party. Members were also required to attend several meetings and lectures each month, provide volunteer work a few times a year and help with election campaigns. Approximately 200,000 of these members were full-time officials, *apparatchiks*, paid by the Party. The Komsomol, or Communist Youth Organization, had 40 million additional members, while 25 million schoolchildren belonged to the Young Pioneers. Eligibility for party membership began at age 18.

On February 7, 1990, after 72 years of Communist rule, the Soviet Communist Party's Central Committee voted overwhelmingly to surrender its monopoly on power. On March 15, 1990, the Soviet Congress of People's Deputies amended Article Six, which had guaranteed the Communist Party its position as the only 'leading authority' in government. In its revised form, Article Six stated that the Communists, together with other political parties and social organizations, had the right to shape State policy. During the 28th Party Congress, the Party voted to reorganize its ruling body, the Politburo, to include Communist Party leaders from each of the 15 republics, in addition to the top 12 Moscow officials. Instead of being selected by the Central Committee, the Party in each republic chose its own leaders, guaranteeing, at the time, a voice in the Party to even the smallest republic.

Other amendments revised the Marxist view that private property was incompatible with Socialism. Individuals could own land and factories as long as they did not 'exploit' other Soviet citizens. New economic policies replaced direct central planning, instituted price reforms, created a stock exchange and allowed farmers to sell their produce on the open market. Additional new laws decreed that 'the press and other mass media are now free; censorship of the mass media is forbidden', and that all political movements had access to the airwaves with the right to establish their own television and radio stations. The monopoly enjoyed by the Communist Party on State-run radio and television ended. Even advertising, long denounced 'as a means of swindling the people' and a 'social weapon of the exploiter's class', became acceptable. These momentous changes paved the way toward a multiparty democracy and a free-market economy.

By the end of August 1991, Boris Yeltsin stood in the Russian parliament building, the White House, and declared: 'I am now signing a decree suspending the activities of the Russian Communist Party!' All Communist newspapers such as *Pravda* were temporarily shut down. Gorbachev followed by issuing decrees to end

Soviet Communist rule. These decrees dissolved the Party's structure of committees and policy-making, which included the Central Committee. Archives of the Party and the KGB were seized, and the government confiscated all of the Party's assets throughout the country. It would take two years before the Communist Party regained some of its powers.

ATTEMPTED COUP OF AUGUST 1991

Gorbachev's vision of a second revolution never included an attempted coup. During his last year in office, many of his actions contradicted all that he had worked toward. After strongly supporting accelerated reforms, Gorbachev suddenly rejected the 500-Day Plan, which proposed converting the sluggish centralized economy into a market-oriented one. Then, in December 1990, he appointed the conservative Boris Pugo as his Minister of the Interior.

On January 11, 1991, Lithuania announced its independence; two days later Pugo sent in troops. Soviet troops were also sent into Latvia to quell demonstrations. This prompted Eduard Shevardnadze, the Foreign Minister, to resign, stating: 'We are returning to the terrible past... reformers have slumped into the bushes. A dictatorship is coming.' During the Gulf War, the Chairman of the KGB, Vladimir Kryuchkov, charged that foreign governments were trying to destabilize Soviet society; the Russian military had become much more sensitive to the reactionary elements gathering force.

Gorbachev banned Yeltsin's rally of support in March 1991 and renewed censorship of the print and television media. The people in Moscow demonstrated anyway and troops were sent in. One of Gorbachev's aides said: 'March 28 was the turning point for Mikhail Sergeyevich. He went to the abyss, looked over the edge, was horrified at what he saw and backed away.' Gorbachev had to move closer to an alliance with Yeltsin to survive.

Those in the government became uneasy with the upcoming republics' treaty; much of Moscow's power would be usurped if it was signed. Leading bureaucrats realized they could lose their jobs and began planning ways to undermine Gorbachev's power. Even though he had created an unprecedented wave of changes, Gorbachev's popularity at home had now fallen to practically zero. After five years of promises, reforms had only made the living standards of average citizens worse. When prices had risen by over 50 percent, the population became increasingly reluctant to trade their goods for worthless banknotes—inflation rose to over 1,000 percent and the ruble collapsed. Despite a grossly dissatisfied population, disjointed government and repeated warnings of a plot against him, Gorbachev left for a vacation in the Crimea to work on the Union Treaty.

On the Sunday afternoon of August 18, 1991, Gorbachev was told that Yuri

Plekhanov, a top KGB official, had arrived to see him. Gorbachev sensed something was wrong and tried to use the telephones; all five lines were dead. Then Valery Boldin, the Chief of Staff, entered the room, saying that Gorbachev had to sign a referendum declaring a state of emergency within the country. If he did not sign, the vice president would take over leadership duties. Since Gorbachev refused to go along with the conspiracy, thousands of troops were sent into Moscow. Ironically, the coup members failed to arrest Boris Yeltsin who, that morning, had rushed off to his office in the parliament building 45 minutes earlier than usual.

The next morning, the coup leaders announced that Gorbachev, 'with serious health problems', could no longer govern. But it became obvious from the outset that the coup was ill-planned. None of the opposition leaders had been arrested. Yeltsin, holed up in the White House, was receiving calls from around the world (from a cellular phone slipped in by the manager of Pizza Hut) and ate take-out pizza. The coup was doomed to fail just from the attention created by all the international media connections. At one point, Yeltsin went outside and climbed on top of a tank in front of 20,000 protesters. He appealed for mass resistance and named himself the Guardian of Democracy. The crowd swelled to well over 100,000. By the end of the day, troops were switching to Yeltsin's side, and many of the elite commando divisions were now protecting the White House.

By August 20, the coup attempt was weakening; many of the planners stayed at home. Crowds of people raised the old white, blue and red Russian flag. The famous cellist, composer and conductor Mstislav Leopoldovich Rostropovich, a survivor of the Siege of Leningrad, even flew in from Paris and played music within the parliament building. Tank divisions descended upon the White House later in the day. Swarms of people blocked their way; after three were killed, the tanks retreated, refusing to fire on their own people.

Three days after the attempted coup, Yeltsin announced its failure. He sent officials to the Crimea to bring Gorbachev safely back to Moscow. The shaken president and his family returned by airplane early the next morning. Seven members of the State Emergency Committee, also called the Gang of Eight, were arrested; the eighth, Boris Pugo, shot himself in the head.

The crowds stood cheering, not so much for Gorbachev's return, but for their savior, Boris Yeltsin. Communism had disintegrated with the attempted putsch. Thousands celebrated as the statue of 'Iron Felix' Dzerzhinsky, the founder of the secret police after the 1917 Revolution, was toppled from its pedestal in front of the KGB building. A Russian flag and crucifix were put in its place—a monument to the millions who had died in prison camps at the hands of the KGB. Unbelievably, a new era had begun.

THE END OF THE SOVIET UNION

The Soviet Union ceased to exist on December 21, 1991. The great ideological experiment begun by Lenin's Bolshevik Revolution, constituted on December 30, 1922, ended nine days short of its 70th year. 'One State has died,' announced Russian television, 'but in its place a great dream is being born.' The birth was of the Commonwealth of Independent States. Four days later, Gorbachev, the eighth and final leader of the Soviet Union, submitted his resignation. He no longer had a Soviet Union to govern. Boris Yeltsin claimed his office in the Kremlin.

BORIS YELTSIN

Boris Nikolayevich Yeltsin was born into a poor family in Sverdlovsk in 1931. He went on to dismantle the entire Soviet empire. In an historic meeting in Alma Ata, the capital of Kazakhstan, Yeltsin convinced the leaders of the former Soviet republics to sign a new treaty forming the 11-member Commonwealth. In February 1992, Yeltsin officially put the Cold War to rest in a meeting with US President George Bush. He proclaimed a 'new era', in which the two nations would join as allies to seek 'an enduring peace that rests on lasting common values'.

By the time Yeltsin took control, the economy was in disarray. Without GOS-PLAN (the former central planning commission) and GOSNAB (the former central supply organization), factories everywhere had no idea what to produce or where to ship their goods. With the help of economic advisor Yegor Gaidar, Yeltsin announced the lifting of price controls. Gradually, over 600 commodities exchanges were formed and the Moscow Stock Exchange building returned to its original function. Russians received government vouchers redeemable for cash, or shares in businesses that were previously State-owned. People in private enterprises began to flourish, from street vendors to entrepreneurs. Newly rich businessmen (nicknamed *Noviye Russkiye* or New Russians) operated with the latest technology and bought expensive cars. (Today Russia is the largest market in the world for luxury cars.) It was possible for some young people to make more money in one day than their parents had in months, or even years. But for many, especially the elderly, the new order meant standing in longer queues and spending hours in the cold trying to sell pitiful possessions to make ends meet.

Newspapers were also freed of censorship. Advertisements interrupted television programs. Soap operas were watched avidly—over 60 percent of the population tuned in to the Mexican series *The Rich Also Cry*. Western imports, including *MTV*, *Santa Barbara* and *Beverly Hills 90210*, deluged Russian television. And foreigners could now travel legally to once-restricted cities.

Yeltsin's biggest crisis since the attempted coup of 1991 arose after he dissolved the obstructionist Russian legislature at the end of September 1993, and moved to replace it with a new elective body. Yeltsin said he was acting to stem a 'senseless struggle that was threatening to lead Russia into a political abyss... the body is an outmoded Soviet-era institution sustained in office by a useless constitution'.

A growing animosity had been brewing between Yeltsin and his opposition, which had tried and failed to impeach him six months earlier in March 1993. Yeltsin had conducted a referendum in April in which Russian voters had expressed their preference for him and his policies. However, the Supreme Soviet instantly claimed Yeltsin's order to dissolve the legislature as null and void. Vice President Alexander Rutskoi, now a Yeltsin rival, was immediately elected acting president and Yeltsin was impeached on a 144–6 vote. The Parliament Chairman, Ruslan Khasbulatov, called on Russian trade unions to go on strike to protest Yeltsin's order. Communist and nationalist leaders appeared on the White House balcony and urged their supporters to stay on. Many were taken with the irony of the gathering, on the very site where Yeltsin, next to Rutskoi, had faced down the right-wing coup plotters in August 1991. But this time Yeltsin was the coup plotter. While both sides waged all-out political warfare, many Muscovites could not care less if there was a coup. One citizen stated: 'We are tired of the political battles and want to live a normal life and earn some decent money.'

About a week after this crisis began, parliament supporters smashed through police lines, stormed the mayor's office and attacked the headquarters of the State television company, which exploded into the worst political violence since the 1917 Bolshevik Revolution. 'There can be no forgiveness for attacking innocent people,' announced Yeltsin. 'The armed revolt is doomed.' Yeltsin then countered by creating a state of emergency and sending in armored personnel carriers, tanks and elite commando units, which fired upon the White House. A new military tactic was also employed—blasting pop group Dire Straits and Russian Rap from loudspeakers near the White House. Thirteen days later, the opposition leaders surrendered after a massive barrage by tanks and paratroopers. The battle left 187 people dead and the White House a blackened shell with nearly every window blown out. Half a year later, the arrested White House hard-liners, who had tried to topple the government in 1991 and 1993, were pardoned by the new Parliamentary Duma.

Yeltsin continued to promise that his struggling nation would not retreat from economic reform. To aid the reform process, many countries pledged financial support to Russia. In January 1994, US President Bill Clinton journeyed to Moscow for a summit with Yeltsin. In an historic meeting, the Ukraine also participated and signed an agreement to disarm all of the 1,800 nuclear warheads that had fallen to it after the collapse of the Soviet Union. Clinton told Yeltsin: 'You are in the process of transforming your entire economy while you develop a new constitution and democracy as well. It boggles the mind and you have my respect.'

In 1992, Yeltsin addressed the US Congress, saying: 'The world can sigh in relief, the idol of Communism has collapsed. I am here to assure you, we shall not let it rise again in our land.'

THE FIRST MULTIPARTY ELECTIONS

Two years after Yeltsin had banned Communist activity on Russian soil, the constitutional court lifted Yeltsin's order, ruling that it violated the constitution. Thus, the Communist Party participated in the country's first true multiparty election on December 12, 1993. In the election, a new Russian constitution was also voted in, which gave the president more power and Parliament less. The constitution granted Russia's 149 million citizens many economic freedoms and civil liberties that had been stifled since the Bolshevik takeover. These included the right to own land, the right not to be wiretapped and the right to travel freely at home and abroad. It also provided for a new Parliament, known as the Federal Assembly, with the Federation Council as its upper chamber and the Duma as its lower. A month after the ballot, those elected assembled in Moscow to launch the new parliamentary democracy. Yeltsin stated: 'We must preserve this for the sake of national peace and to make sure dictatorship never returns to Russia.'

Even though they were no longer the only party, the Communists again became one of the largest political forces in the land. Taking part in the election were other hard-line groups, among them the Agrarian Party, the Centrist Democratic Party and the Women of Russia Party. The pro-reform parties included Russia's Choice, the Yavlinsky Bloc and the Russian Unity and Accord Party. The Beer-Lovers Party was one of many on the fringe. Some of those elected were reactionary journalist Alexander Nevzorov, weightlifting champion Yuri Vlasov, and the psychic healer Anatoly Kashpirovsky.

Although Yeltsin's opponents won the majority of the 450 seats in the Duma, they were forced to compromise with his supporters. The upper chamber, the 178-seat Federation Council, roughly equivalent to the US Senate, met under the new State symbol, the two-headed eagle. First Deputy Prime Minister Vladimir Shumeiko, a close ally of Yeltsin, was elected as the first Speaker.

The ultranationalist Liberal Democratic Party, headed by Vladimir Zhirinovsky, shocked the world by beating Yeltsin's Russia's Choice Party in these first ever parliamentary elections. Zhirinovsky's party won nearly a quarter of the Russian vote, which many saw as a protest by a population feeling the pain of reform. In the three years that this obscure Moscow lawyer rose into the national spotlight, he rashly advocated party dictatorship, Russian military expansion, the expelling of millions of non-Russians and ending payments of foreign debt. Zhirinovsky also threatened to restore Russia's imperial borders, annex Alaska and invade Turkey and Poland.

With this character climbing to the forefront of Russian politics, no wonder the world was greatly concerned for Russia's fragile young democracy and its vulnerability to irresponsible leadership.

THE EFFECTS OF REFORM
A few weeks after Parliament convened, Yegor Gaidar, the architect of Russia's free-market reforms and leader of Russia's Choice Party, unexpectedly quit his post as Economic Minister. As a result the ruble plummeted. (The Russian Central Bank had already pumped more than one billion dollars into the economy—more than a quarter of its hard currency reserves—to stabilize the monetary system.) Launched in January 1992, Gaidar's reforms had freed most prices from State control, privatized a third of State-owned enterprises and created a new class of entrepreneurs.

But since their introduction no more than ten percent of the population seemed better off, while over 50 percent complained of being worse off. The continuing credit squeeze created more unemployment, delayed pay checks and wiped out entire savings accounts of average citizens. The Russian comedian Mikhail Zhvanetsky joked about the economy: 'Much has changed but nothing has happened. Or is that much has happened and nothing has changed.' Many forecast that nearly a century of suppressed initiative combined with a government-controlled lifestyle would take at least a generation to alter.

By 1993, inflation (2,600 percent in 1992 and 900 percent in 1993) became so rampant that savings of 20,000 rubles—that could once buy four cars—was now worth only a few pounds of sausage. One survey concluded that on his monthly salary, an average Russian could only pay rent, consume a daily ration of half a kilogram (one pound) of bread, half a liter (less than one pint) of milk, 100 grams (three-and-a-half ounces) of beef, and five cigarettes. Satire was commonplace: 'What was the nationality of Adam and Eve? Russian, of course—who else would think that being homeless, naked and splitting one apple between them was living in paradise.'

Russians began to augment their diets with vegetables grown in gardens or apartment window boxes. To supplement their incomes, many turned to vending sausages or cigarettes, pawning family goods, collecting bottles for recycling, or working as taxi drivers. An entire generation of educated people could barely afford to live. And one teacher wryly noted: 'We can't even afford to die.' (The cheapest funeral cost over $300, while the average pension was $50 per month—the official poverty level was set at $35). One retiree summarized, 'And what good is freedom to me now? Freedom to buy a pornographic magazine, openly complain all I want, or travel to Cyprus when I can't even afford to eat? I hope and believe that things will get better. But they will never be better for us. I'll simply not live to see those days.'

During the first years of transition, the World Bank estimated that one-third of the population, or nearly 50 million Russians, had an income below the minimum sustenance level. With prices for food, gasoline and consumer goods approaching US levels, average Russian salaries were still only one-tenth of those in the America. Over one-quarter found themselves unemployed and a survey reported that only ten percent of Russian males were capable of fully supporting their families. Russia's life expectancy plummeted so fast in the first half of the 1990s that a British medical journal stated that it was 'without parallel in the modern era'. Due to the severe decline in living standards a Russian man's life expectancy fell to age 58, compared to 72 in Finland. The male incidences of heart disease, suicide and alcoholism are now the highest in the developed world, and the mortality rate exceeds the birth rate. Alarmingly, if the trend continues, the population would be halved to 75 million by the middle of the next century, and in 1,000 years there would only be 150 people left in Russia!

For the first time in Russian history, investment and stock funds, quasi-banks, and joint-stock companies (without insurance protection) filled print advertising and the airwaves with the promise of large returns—in some cases up to 30,000 percent. In a few years alone, over 2,000 banks opened across the country. Many investors never saw their money again. One businessman stated that 'the average Russian is the most unprepared investor in the world. For 70 years all he did was put his money into State-owned banks and was raised to believe that whatever was told over TV or in the newspapers was true.' Scam operations and pyramid schemes flourished, and hundreds of thousands of victims were cheated out of their life savings in the new era of cowboy capitalism.

However, with the explosion of new commercial activities, a new class was created—that of the filthy rich or *Noviye Russkiye* (New Russians). About 60 percent of this group simply turned the socialist empires they managed into their own private companies. Others capitalized on the 'Wild East' state of mind, where practically everything was up for grabs. With both a penchant for entrepreneurship and greed, some became billionaires virtually overnight. Suddenly, the demand for office space, apartments, retail markets and shopping centers was enormous.

Consumption by the nouveaux riches is decadent even by Western standards. Protected by bodyguards, driving armor-plated Land-rovers, building villas in the French Riviera, sending their children to study abroad, wearing designer clothing, this elite class has built an enormous division between the haves and have-nots. One pensioner declared, 'We're back to having two classes again—the aristocrats and the peasants!' Many Russian nightclubs have no foreign customers—they simply cannot afford the prices. Moscow is now one of the most expensive cities to visit in the world, ranking fourth; St Petersburg comes in eleventh.

It is often said that the collapse of Communism has fertilized the ground upon which gangsters and mafia thrive. But the word mafia has a different implication in Russia. It simply defines a broad range of group activity that was already flourishing under Socialism. Since much was illegal during this era—from owning a business to playing rock 'n' roll—most unsanctioned activities were commonplace; a survey in the 1980s indicated that the average Russian dealt daily with black marketeers who provided the economy with most of its goods. In turn, these types had no problem embracing capitalism and finding immediate ways to make money. Even though encountering mafia activity may be the price of doing business in Russia (the chances of experiencing any as a tourist are practically zero)—all in all, violent crime rates are still much lower than in the United States.

In 1994, after two decades of forced exile in the United States, Russia's greatest living writer Alexander Solzhenitsyn was allowed to return to his homeland. The winner of the Nobel Prize for Literature in 1970, Solzhenitsyn was banished by the former Soviet Government in 1974 for writing *The Gulag Archipelago*, which preserved the memory of the Soviet holocaust. (Also in 1994, the long-suppressed 1939 census was finally published: a quarter of the population, over 40 million people, had been lost in this Stalinist year to famine and purges.) But before Solzhenitsyn returned to his homeland, he first wanted to complete his four-volume epic *The Red Wheel*, a history leading up to the 1917 October Revolution that he had worked on for 20 years: 'Our history has been so hidden. I had to dig so deep, I had to uncover what was buried and sealed. This took up all my years.' The work totals over 5,000 pages.

After his exile, Solzhenitsyn declared: 'All of us in prison in the 1940s were certain that Communism would fail. The only question was when... In a strange way, I was inwardly convinced that I would someday return to Russia.' It was not until late 1989 that Gorbachev had finally given permission to publish Solzhenitsyn's works in Russia.

In 1993, a political poll in St Petersburg showed that 48 percent of the respondents wanted Solzhenitsyn as their president. In *The First Circle*, he described that in a tyranny a real writer is like a second government. Even though Alexander Solzhenitsyn has returned home to live, he knows that there is a long road ahead: 'If it took Russia 75 years to fall so far, then it is obvious that it will take more than 75 years to rise back up. I know we are still faced with incredible hardships for years to come.'

THE RESURGENCE OF THE COMMUNISTS

In February 1995, the Commonwealth of Independent States elected Yeltsin as its chairman and moved its headquarters from Minsk, Belarus to Moscow. After celebrating Victory Day, the 50th anniversary of World War II, in May, Yeltsin had to vigorously embark on his reelection campaign—for only six percent of the population approved of the job he was doing. The majority of Russians blamed Yeltsin for the social upheavals, deplorable living conditions and unpopular war in Chechnya. In addition, many civil servants, teachers, and pensioners had not received a government pay check in up to six months. Following his elevation to near sainthood after the 1991 coup attempt, Yeltsin now found himself with single-digit ratings, was in declining health and drinking heavily. He soon suffered two heart attacks and was confined to bed for four months.

But Yeltsin struggled on, stating: 'It is our task to prevent a Communist victory at the polls.' But, in the December 17, 1995 parliamentary elections, the Communists led the field of 43 parties. Gennady Zhuganov, who had taken charge of the reborn Communist Party in 1993, now even welcomed religious members. The Communists and Zhirinovsky's ultranationalists finished first and second, garnering 22 percent and 11 percent of the vote respectively. The astounded world questioned how a country so recently freed from socialist rule could so quickly choose a course back to renewed oppression. With a long tradition of not regarding freedom as a value, the average Russian experienced reform more as hardship than salvation. Even writer Ivan Turgenev expressed this notion after Alexander II agreed to free the serfs in 1861: 'And although you were freed from slavery, you do not know what to do with freedom.'

Foreigners find it difficult to comprehend how Russians can be skeptical of the transition to a Western-style democracy and economy. One must first understand that to them it may only be another short-lived phase in their country's history. So many promises in the past have proven hollow. Even Gorbachev warned: 'If reforms continue pushing people into a dead end, discontent could spring loose and extremism move in.'

1996 PRESIDENTIAL ELECTIONS

The architect of Russia's privatization program, First Deputy Prime Minister Anatoly Chubais, was dismissed in January 1996, but then called back in March to help with Yeltsin's presidential campaign. Yeltsin's daughter Tatyana Dachenko also played a major role. At 65, Yeltsin wanted to prove he was, indeed, capable of a comeback at the June 16 election. A few weeks before the ballot, on May 27, Yeltsin brought Chechen leader Yanderbiyev to the Kremlin to sign a peace treaty after 18 months of war that had left Chechnya ruined and over 40,000 dead. Boris Yeltsin was as determined as ever not to have the Communist Party win: 'Our responsibility to the memory of the millions who suffered in the camps and to our children and descendants is to prevent neo-Stalinists, fascists and extremists from coming to power in Russia. Russia must enter the 21st century without this filth.'

On June 16, 1996, an 11-man race took place for the presidency. Yeltsin captured 35 percent of the vote, and Zhuganov 32 percent. General Alexander Lebed, an ex-paratrooper and decorated hero of Russia's war in Afghanistan, received 15 percent. Zhirinovsky finished seventh with less than six percent of the first round vote. Since no candidate received over 50 percent a national run-off election was scheduled to take place on July 3. In a calculated move, Yeltsin appointed Lebed as his national security chief.

The Communist Party now faced a major identity crisis. People were just as uncertain of Zhuganov's politics as they were of Zhirinovsky's. Gennady Zhuganov, in his 1995 book *I Believe in Russia*, stated that 'if Stalin had lived longer, he would have restored Russia and saved it from the cosmopolitans'. Most of the population, especially the younger generation, were more interested in pay checks than politics. Many also feared that if Zhuganov won, the Communist party would not allow others to exist and would return to monopolizing the State. To the relief of the majority, the election resulted in a stunning victory for Yeltsin: he received 54 percent to Zhuganov's 40 percent.

On August 9, 1996, Yeltsin, with a stiff walk and slowed speech, swore an oath for his second term as president, with his hand held over a red-bound copy of the Russian constitution. By October Alexander Lebed was fired, accused of plotting a military coup. A month later, on November 5, Yeltsin underwent a major coronary bypass operation; he had had another heart attack right before his reelection.

THE LAST YEARS OF THE 20TH CENTURY

By 1997, even though Russia was finally emerging from its post-Soviet economic slump, just six percent of Russians said they were content. Seventy-two percent felt their lives had changed little over the past five years, while 62 percent felt their lives would not get any better. A major role reversal had also taken place within the country. Instead of children having to live with parents (because of housing shortages), parents now found themselves living with their children out of economic necessity. The clash of extraordinary monetary achievement and oppressive backwardness continued to mar the road ahead.

In February 1998, as Russia journeyed through a seventh year of insecurity, Yeltsin felt that the 'nation needed a new strategy for upsurge', and fired three cabinet ministers along with his deputy prime ministers for failing to reverse Russia's economic and social ills. Yeltsin then pressured the Duma into voting in the 35-year-old Sergei Kiriyenko, then Minister of Oil and Energy, into the position of prime minister. Many regarded this merely as a political stunt to shift blame from Yeltsin's own sagging popularity. By May, thousands of striking coal miners, in massive protests, even blocked routes of the Trans-Siberian railway, demanding $600 million in back wages.

By 1998, Yeltsin's government had fallen behind by months, even years, with payments of State wages and pensions, which forced people in many areas to resort to barter and subsistence farming. It was estimated that nearly 70 percent of the population lived mostly off the produce grown in their small garden plots. Many villagers kept a cow, caught and dried fish from the rivers and grew cabbage, beets, potatoes and onions. The result was an almost cashless society where business was transacted and employees paid mainly by trading goods and services. Since most companies and citizens had no money, they could not pay their taxes, meaning the government was constantly short of funds and the deficit continued to grow.

In 1998, Yeltsin implored Russians to pay their taxes. The government claimed that fewer than three percent of Russia's total population had filed income tax declarations the year before. In addition, taxes on alcohol contribute significantly to the federal budget. During Soviet times these taxes constituted nearly one-quarter of all State revenues. With tax evasion prevalent, Yeltsin urged that 'when the people spend their money on vodka, it should go to the treasury, not to swindlers. We want to give this money to our pensioners, soldiers, doctors and teachers. It will help build the economy.' But officials still estimate the State loses as much as 360 million dollars a month from evasion of alcohol taxes alone.

In August 1998, as the country experienced its worst economic crisis since the 1991 Soviet collapse, Yeltsin dismissed the Russian Government, the second time in one year, replacing Prime Minister Kiriyenko with Foreign Minister Yevgeny Primakov (after the government refused to vote in Viktor Chernomyrdin). A new joke circulated in Moscow: 'For too long we have been standing at the edge of the precipice—now we are taking a great leap forward.' With Russia plunging into turmoil, defaulting on its debts and suffering from one of the worse harvests since 1953 (the last year of Stalinist rule), many accused Yeltsin of trying to shift blame away from himself. In October 1998, millions of Russians across the country took part in rallies demanding Yeltsin's resignation. But Yeltsin asserted, 'I am not going to resign. It is very difficult to remove me. And considering my character, it is practically impossible.' The government struggled to pull Russia away from collapse as the ruble plunged to less than a third of its value on the world market. In the midst of uncertainty, US President Clinton journeyed to Moscow to hold a summit with Yeltsin in order to reinforce Russia's path to democracy and economic reform.

Aside from its many troubles, by 1999 the government had once again achieved a modest stabilization indicating that many reforms are working. Thousands of old State-owned companies have been privatized since 1992—nearly two-thirds of

Russia's 450 billion dollar economy is now in private hands. The quality of life of the average Russian is improving, though not as fast as many had hoped. A solid middle class is emerging between the gung-ho millionaires and pensioned elderly who are less adaptable to change. Shops are now teeming with goods from around the world. The youthful professional (who in the past may have been forced to live in a communal flat) now has his own apartment with a television and VCR, refrigerator, phone and fax, access to a computer, better clothing, summer dacha and can regularly vacation abroad: these are the people building Russia's future.

And one of the most meaningful changes (that Westerners so often take for granted) is that a majority of Russians now have the opportunity to try and lead the type of life they dream of—instead of one forced upon them by socialist dictates. Many still find themselves overwhelmed with the simple notion of choice. For the first time in over 1,000 years, a Russian citizen finally has the right to vote (and with more than one person on the ballot).

Who will lead Russia into the 21st century? In August 1998, during a TV address to the nation, Yeltsin announced that he would not run for reelection and would leave office after the next presidential election in the year 2000. From being the country's most popular leader after his heroic role in the 1991 coup attempt, Boris Yeltsin now found himself suffering the same fate as Gorbachev—ending his days in office with only a two percent approval rating. With his health and mental acuity diminishing, many sadly compared him with the Communist leader Brezhnev, who, at the end of his term, served only as a weak puppet figure. At the end of October 1998, Yeltsin was admitted to a sanatorium for rest and treatment for what was termed neuropsychological asthenia. Although no one really knew what this meant, the Kremlin announced that this condition would force the president to relinquish his day-to-day duties, which would be taken over by Primakov. The question asked by Russia and the world was how the country would survive without a strong leader and find a solution to its economic crisis.

Many predict that either Chernomyrdin, Boris Nemtsov or Moscow Mayor Yuri Luzhkov could get Yeltsin's backing as successor. In June 1998, even the President of the World Chess Federation, Kirsan Yulimzhinov, announced his candidacy. Nor can Gennady Zhuganov (in a 1998 presidential poll 21 percent of adults favored this Communist Party leader), Vladimir Zhirinovsky (elected head of his party until 2004), Grigory Yavlinsky, Anatoly Chubais, Boris Berezovsky (financial baron turned politician) and General Alexander Lebed (former national security chief) be counted out of the running.

RUSSIA TODAY

It is nearly a decade since the collapse of the Soviet State and to visit Russia today is to be awestruck by the considerable contrasts. Ideological propaganda has shifted to corporate advertising, and the ruble is freely exchanged on the world market. Moscow's City Hall cannot keep pace with all the name changes throughout the city, and many old aristocratic families have filed suits in Russian courts demanding the return of ancestral lands. While young millionaires live in gated communities and join expensive private clubs (there are now more casinos in Moscow than Las Vegas), the middle class (whose average salary is $150 per month) work second and third jobs to get by in a world of higher prices and fewer social guarantees. State and charity organizations are unable to meet the demands of housing and feeding the millions of newly impoverished citizens. By 1995 over 15,000 vodka lovers had signed up for the Russian branch of Alcoholics Anonymous.

Without lavish State sponsorship, major theaters, such as the Bolshoi and Mariinsky are struggling to survive while others, supported by private donations, are thriving. Commercial factories dramatically underreport profits to avoid paying taxes, while up to 80 percent of private enterprises are said to pay protection money to the mafia, who reportedly now control 40 percent of the country's economy. With an increase in wealth, the number of registered automobiles has doubled in Moscow since 1991 to over two million, but they now add to the city's pollution problem. But, no matter what its achievements and setbacks, Russia can rightfully claim that no other country on earth has made such radical changes in so short a period of time.

Despite the apparent chaos, the Russian spirit remains strong. Few other nations on earth have endured such turmoil throughout their history. The odds are that Russia can survive yet another turbulent period. Once reforms take root, Russia's vast natural resources can be harnessed more effectively and, in turn, the wealth distributed more evenly. Many world economists firmly believe that the current transitions are shaping the country into one of the largest emerging growth markets of the next century—possibly surpassing even China. Liberated by the policies of Gorbachev and Yeltsin, totalitarianism and the masses no longer march to the same tune. The Russian Government has no choice but to move optimistically forward into the next century, this time with its citizens leading the way.

COWS OF MOSCOW

*T*he proceedings of these cows in the early morning in the heart of the city, wandering alone, was a mystery. On inquiring I was told that throughout Moscow various families possess, among their worldly goods, a cow. Vast numbers of the larger houses have considerable spaces enclosed in the rear of their dwellings—gardens, courts, grassy places. Likewise the innumerable cottages in the by-streets have within their gates green plots and outhouses. In very many of these there is a cow. During the summer time, when there is a pasture, the first duty to be observed in all these dwellings is to open the gates and let out the cow. If there is a delay in this performance a loud warning from the outhouse or court awakes the servant to it. The cow let out, he may go to bed again. She knows her way by certain streets towards a certain barrier of the city. As she goes other cows join her from other cottages or houses, and by the time they all arrive near the barrier they are a considerable body. Here they find a man blowing a horn, whose business it is to conduct them to some pasture outside the town, to take care of them during the day, to collect them by his horn in the afternoon, and to bring them back to the barrier at a given time. When he has done this his business is over. Each cow knows her way home, and finds it unmolested up to the very heart of the city, the Kremlin. What a simple and convenient method for insuring good and pure and fresh milk to the family! Each *materfamilias* can water it according to her wants or tastes, and she can omit the chalk—a blessed privilege!

G T Lowth, Across the Kremlin, *1868*

CHRONOLOGY

700–882: The Vikings begin to leave Scandinavia and establish trading settlements with the Slavs in northwestern Russia. Kievan State in the south is formed and named after the Slavic Prince Kii. In 862, the Norseman Rurik defeats the important Slavic town of Novgorod and becomes one of the first Vikings to rule in Russia. In 880, Rurik's successor, Oleg, conquers the Slavic-ruled Kiev, unites the two states and makes Kiev his capital. The ruling class is known as 'Rus', (thought to be derived from the Viking word *ruotsi*, meaning rower or oarsman). This term is later applied to the people of Eastern Europe; eventually the areas are united into the Russian states.

977: Novgorod gains its independence from Kiev.

978–1015: Rule of Prince Vladimir, who introduces Byzantine Christianity into Russia in 988.

1015–1054: Rule of Yaroslav the Wise. Kiev becomes the first center of the Orthodox Church.

1113–1125: Rule of Vladimir Monomakh. The two principalities of Novgorod and Kiev are united again under his rule. The crown of Monomakh is worn by the later rulers of Russia. The decline of Kievan Rus begins after his death.

1147: Prince Yuri Dolgoruky 'Long Arms' founds Moscow. He builds a kremlin and defensive walls around the city.

1169: Prince Andrei Bogoliubsky transfers the capital from Kiev to Vladimir.

1223: First Mongol invasion of Russia.

1237: Batu Khan, grandson of Genghis Khan, invades Moscow and goes on to conquer many of Russia's other regions. The Mongol Tartars dominate Russia for the next 250 years.

1240: The Prince of Novgorod, Alexander Nevsky, defeats the Swedes in an important battle along the Neva River. Nevsky rules as grand prince in Vladimir from 1252–1263.

1299: The Church Metropolitan flees Kiev and takes up residence with the grand prince in Vladimir.

1325–1340: Reign of Ivan I, nicknamed Kalita 'Moneybags' because of his strong economic hold over the other principalities. Ivan is named grand prince in 1328, and chooses Moscow as his residence. The seat of the Orthodox Church is moved from Vladimir to Moscow. In 1337, St Sergius founds the Monastery of the Holy Trinity in Sergiyev Posad.

1353–1359: Reign of Ivan II.

1362–1389: Reign of Dmitri Donskoi. In 1380, the grand prince defeats the Tartars in the Battle of Kulikovo on the Don, becoming the first Russian prince to win a decisive battle over the Mongol army. Two years later the Mongols burn Moscow to the ground.

1389–1425: Reign of Vasily I.

1425–1460: Reign of Vasily II.

1453: The Ottoman Turks conquer Constantinople, which releases the Russian Orthodox Church from Byzantine domination. Less than a decade later, the head of the Orthodox Church takes on the title of Metropolitan of Moscow and All Russia and receives his orders from the grand prince.

1460–1505: Reign of Ivan III (Ivan the Great). He marries Sophia, the niece of the last Byzantine emperor, in 1472 and adopts the crest of the double-headed eagle. Moscow is declared the Third Rome. During his rule, Ivan the Great rebuilds the Kremlin and annexes the city of Novgorod. He refuses to pay any further tribute to the Mongols and defeats their armies. Two centuries of Tartar oppression in Russia come to an end.

1505–1533: Reign of Vasily III, father of Ivan the Terrible.

1533–1584: Reign of Ivan IV (Ivan the Terrible) who is crowned in 1547 in the Moscow Kremlin with the title of Czar (derived from Caesar) of All Russia. He organizes the Oprichniki, a special bodyguard to prosecute the Boyars (landowners). He defeats the Tartars in the far eastern territories. Russia loses the Livonian War and access to the Baltic. St Basil's Cathedral built.

1584–1598: Reign of Fyodor I, son of Ivan IV. Establishment of Moscow Church Patriarch in 1588.

1598–1613: The Time of Troubles. Boris Godunov rules as czar from 1598 to 1605. Claim to the throne by two false Dmitris. Second false Dmitri seizes the throne with Polish support. Battles with Polish armies.

1613–1645: Following the Time of Troubles and the defeat of Polish invaders, Mikhail Romanov (related to Ivan the Terrible) is elected new czar of Russia on March 14, 1613. The Romanov dynasty continues to rule Russia until 1917; there were 18 rulers in all.

1645–1676: Reign of Alexei I, father of Peter the Great. Establishes Russia's first Law Code in 1649. Patriarch Nikon deposed in 1660.

1676–1682: Reign of Fyodor III. When he dies, his feeble-minded brother, Ivan V, and half-brother, Peter (Peter the Great), are proclaimed joint czars. The Streltsy (marksmen) briefly gain control over the government. Sophia, Peter's half-sister, acts as regent until 1689.

1689–1725: Reign of Peter the Great. During his enlightened rule, Peter adopts the Julian calendar, transfers the capital from Moscow to St Petersburg, introduces Western culture and customs to his country and builds the first Russian fleet along the Baltic. In 1721, after the end of the Great Northern War, he assumes the title of Emperor of All Russia.

1725–1727: Reign of Catherine I, the widow of Peter the Great, who becomes czarina with the help of her guard Menschikov.

1727–1730: Reign of Peter II, Peter the Great's grandson.

1730–1740: Reign of Anna Ivanova, daughter of Ivan V and niece of Peter the Great.

1740–1741: Reign of Ivan VI.

1741–1761: Reign of Elizabeth, daughter of Peter the Great and Catherine I. In 1755, the first university is founded in Moscow.

1761–1762: Reign of Peter III, grandson of Peter the Great.

1762–1796: Reign of Catherine II (Catherine the Great), German-born wife of Peter III. The first foreign woman to rule as czarina. Russia becomes a major power. In 1783, Potemkin annexes the Crimea.

1796–1801: Reign of Paul I, son of Catherine the Great.

1801–1825: Reign of Alexander I, son of Paul I. In 1812, Napoleon's armies flee Moscow in defeat. Rise of the Decembrist movement.

1825–1855: Reign of Nicholas I, son of Paul I. On December 14, 1825 the Decembrists attempt to overthrow the czarist autocracy and gain freedom for the serfs. Bolshoi Theater opens in 1825. In 1851, the first railway opens between St Petersburg and Moscow.

1855–1881: Reign of Alexander II, son of Nicholas I. In 1861, Alexander signs a decree to emancipate the serfs.

1867: Sale of Alaska to the United States; Karl Marx's *Das Kapital* is translated into Russian.

1881: Alexander II is assassinated by members of the Peoples' Will group.

1881–1894: Reign of Alexander III. The brother of Lenin, Alexander Ulyanov, along with four others, attempts to assassinate the czar.

1894–1917: Reign of Nicholas II. Nicholas marries the granddaughter of Queen Victoria. In 1895, workers hold public rallies to celebrate May Day, day of worker solidarity. In 1903, the Social Democratic Party splits into two factions: Bolsheviks and Mensheviks. Russo-Japanese War 1904–05. The first revolution takes place in 1905 (known as Bloody Sunday) in St Petersburg. Romanov dynasty celebrates 300th anniversary in 1913. World War I breaks out in 1914. In 1916, Rasputin murdered by Count Yusupov. Second revolution begins in February 1917. Czar Nicholas abdicates and a Provisional government is formed. The prime ministers of the new government are Prince Lvov (Feb–May) and Alexander Kerensky (May–Oct). Lenin and the Bolsheviks overthrow the Provisional Government in October 1917. In 1918, Nicholas and his family are executed in the Ural town of Sverdlovsk (present-day Yekaterinburg).

1918–1924: In 1918, Lenin moves capital from Petrograd to Moscow. Civil war erupts between 1918–20. The Socialist Soviet State is formed in 1922, and the first Soviet Constitution adopted. Switch to Gregorian calendar. The Communist Government nationalizes industry, introduces censorship of the press and forms the Cheka police force. Lenin introduces the New Economic Policy (NEP). When Lenin dies in 1924, St Petersburg (Petrograd) is renamed Leningrad.

1924–1953: Joseph Stalin. In 1927, Trotsky is expelled from the Party. In 1928, Stalin introduces the First Five Year Plan and Collectivization. A widespread famine sweeps the nation, eventually killing ten million people.

1934–1941: Stalin's assassination of Leningrad Party Chief Sergei Kirov signals the beginning of the Great Terror. Half the delegates of the 17th Party Congress are purged, along with 90 percent of the country's generals. Of approximately 20 million people arrested, seven million are shot immediately while the rest are sent to gulag camps for rehabilitation. In 1939, the Nazi-Soviet pack is formed. In 1940, Soviet Union annexes Baltic republics.

1941–1945: World War II. Hitler invades the USSR in 1941, and the siege of Leningrad lasts for 900 days until 1944. The Soviet Union suffers 20 million casualties.

1945–1953: World War II ends in 1945. Yalta and Potsdam conferences. Occupation of Eastern Europe.

1953–1955: Georgi Malenkov is General Secretary of Communist Party.

1955–1964: Nikita Khrushchev becomes leader and founds the KGB, the committee for state security, in 1954. In 1956, at the 20th Party Congress, he denounces Stalin in a secret speech. Two-thirds of the Orthodox churches and monasteries are closed down. In 1961, the Soviets send the first man, Yuri Gagarin, into space, and the Congress votes to remove Stalin's body from its place of honor alongside Lenin in the Kremlin Mausoleum. Berlin Wall is constructed in 1961. In 1962, Cuban Missile Crisis fuels the Cold War.

1964–1982: Khrushchev's forced resignation is engineered by Leonid Brezhnev, who immediately rescinds Khrushchev's Rule 25 restricting Party officials to 15 years in office. The discovery of large gas and oil reserves boosts the economy, but these benefits are undermined by poor planning and lack of incentives. Alcohol consumption quadruples in 20 years. Further repressions stimulate the dissident and Samizdat movements.

1968: Invasion of Czechoslovakia.

1979: Invasion of Afghanistan.

1982–1984: Brezhnev dies and is succeeded by Yuri Andropov, former head of the KGB.

1984–1985: Andropov dies and is succeeded by Konstantin Chernenko, Brezhenev's 72-year old protégé, who dies one year later.

1985–1991: Mikhail Gorbachev

1991: December 21, the Soviet Union ceases to exist.

1992–2000: Boris Yeltsin, President of the Russian Republic, forms the 11-member Commonwealth of Independent States.

(following pages) The Kremlin's Assumption Cathedral. Its spacious interior, lit by 12 chandeliers, is covered with exquisite frescoes and icons that date back to the 15th century. The screen of icons on the front wall were painted in the mid-17th century by monks of the Trinity-Sergius Monastery in the Golden Ring town of Sergiyev Posad.

Facts for the Traveler

Planning Your Trip

Traveling to and around Russia is not as easy as for most Western countries; it requires much more careful and advanced planning. The average tourist still cannot travel freely throughout the country; for the most part, each city you plan to visit needs to be listed on your visa. Read some literature on your destinations and areas of interest and talk to people who have been there. Locate travel agents or other specialist organizations that have experience in dealing with travel to Russia (see Useful Addresses section).

GROUP TOURS

There are a multitude of package and special-interest group tours from which to choose. The advantage of a group tour—especially if it's your first trip and you do not speak the language—is that everything is set up for you. Travel agencies handling Russian excursions have a list of package tours available. Most group tours have preset departure dates and fixed lengths of stay, and usually include visits to Moscow and St Petersburg. The group rate often includes round-trip airfare, visa-processing fees, first-class accommodation, up to three meals a day, transportation within Russia, sightseeing excursions and a bilingual guide. (If you are more of a free spirit, it may be cheaper to book with a tour and then abandon the group for a time once in Russia.) Special interest groups also offer trips that include some sightseeing, but otherwise focus on more specific areas, such as sports, ecology, the arts, citizen diplomacy, religion or world peace.

Adventure tourism has also opened up a whole new array of opportunities, among them rafting, hiking, climbing, biking, kayaking, horseback riding, golfing and even trans-Arctic expeditions. (See Useful Addresses section for listings of travel agencies and adventure travel companies.)

INDEPENDENT TRAVEL

Independent travel to Russia is still difficult. It is not quite as simple as going to a Russian embassy or consulate, filling out a visa form, and taking off. You must first provide proof of a hotel reservation, or business/family sponsorship. The official reason for this visa restriction is that hotel space in Russia is limited. Many hotels tend to be prebooked in high seasons, and the government does not want visitors to arrive with nowhere to stay. The good news is that the old monopoly of mediocre

Intourist hotels has dissolved along with the Soviet Union, and today many new one- to five-star hotels, motels, hostels, bed-and-breakfasts and even campsites have sprung up. Independent travelers can also arrange homestays with a Russian family. Cheap accommodation is in big demand; try and book at least six to eight weeks in advance to guarantee space and the best rates. Today many higher-class hotels, hostels, host family organizations and Russian travel agencies can also provide visa invitations.

VISAS

All travelers to Russia must have a visa. There are three types: tourist, business and visitor.

TOURIST VISAS

If you are with a group or package tour, the company takes care of your visa application. Independent travelers can collect a visa application at a Russian embassy or consulate. (If you telephone, a form can be mailed or faxed to you, along with specific instructions, and there is also a visa-information telephone recording which explains what you need to do.) Three passport-size photographs and a photocopy of the information page of your passport (valid for at least six months) are also required. (Note: On February 1, 1998, Russia increased its costs for American citizens by $25 as tit for tat for the corresponding US price increase; visa prices may change from year to year.) Depending on how quickly you need the visa returned (a visa can be issued within a few hours), a corresponding processing fee is charged, which you must include with your application. (If you need a quick return, include the proper postage for express mailing or a FedEx number.)

If an agency is not taking care of your visa sponsorship, then you must also include a confirmed hotel booking and dates of stay (made through a travel agency or faxed to you from a host hotel or other booking organization.) The visa lasts as long as your confirmed booking, usually up to 30 days. You must engage this process for each city you plan to visit while in Russia. Also note that if St Petersburg, for example, is not listed on your visa, you cannot use this city as your point of entry—you may be turned back at the airport. A way around this complication is to first land in Moscow or wherever you have a confirmed hotel stay. Once there, you can add cities to your visa, arrange visits to other areas, and lengthen your stay. As an alternative to hotels, book a homestay with a Russian family; agencies coordinating stays may also help process visas. Some of Russia's Youth Hostels are now affiliated with the International Youth Hostelling Association. RYH can help students and other members with visa processing, inexpensive hostels, travel tickets and other information. (See Practical Information sections under

(following pages) Even during the cold winter months, people enjoy walking around Red Square. The distinctive onion domes of St Basil's Cathedral gradually evolved from the original Byzantine cube-shaped roofs to withstand the heavy snowfalls. On the right, the Spasskaya (Savior) Clock Tower overlooks Lenin's Mausoleum.

Accommodation for hotel, homestay and hostel contacts.) For other ways for an independent tourist to get a visa, see Business Visas section below.

BUSINESS VISAS

If you are sponsored by a Russian host organization, you can receive a business visa which is good for up to two months. Have them send, fax or e-mail an invitation letter which contains the dates of your visit, and mentions that they are responsible for all your needs, including a place to stay. (The organization must have a registration number with their Ministry of Foreign Affairs.) By giving this, along with your visa application form, to the Russian embassy or consulate, they will then issue a business visa without needing proof of hotel reservations. (Multiple-entry visas, good for up to six months, are also issued with proper papers.) It is also possible for foreign business people to get a one month visa in the consular office at the Moscow or St Petersburg international airports upon arrival in Russia, but this is not recommended unless all documents are in order, otherwise you will not be allowed entry. A passport, three pictures, and an invitation from the host Russian firm are needed. This letter, stating the purpose of the visit, should be written on the firm's official letterhead, and signed with the appropriate signatures and stamps. A fax copy is acceptable.

Nowadays, to procure a visa independent travelers can also contact a specialist visa service company or travel agency in Russia that can provide visa invitations and find places for the traveler to stay within their budget. Fax or e-mail them directly to request help with visa invitations. Often the agency can even issue a business visa; with this type of visa, the traveler is also free to stay with friends or even rent an apartment. These agencies can book places to stay in different areas all around Russia, and take care of other visa and travel needs.

VISITOR'S VISAS

If hosted by a relative or friend, you can enter on a visitor's visa. You must send your host a duplicate of your completed visa application form, not a photocopy. Upon receipt, the host takes it to his own travelers' organization, OVIR, which will issue a visitor's invitation. This you then send to the Russian consulate or embassy, where it may take several months to be processed. The visitor is only allowed to travel to the cities and stay with the persons designated on the visa. Since you must make these arrangements far in advance, try instead to obtain a business visa from a Russian visa agency.

Do not panic if your visa has not arrived as your departure date nears. Russian embassies and consulates are notorious for issuing visas at the last minute. When applying, indicate with an enclosed letter that you absolutely need the visa delivered by a certain date (you must enclose return postage or FedEx number) and follow up with a phone call. Note that visas for Russia are not stamped in your passport. Upon entering the country half of your visa booklet is taken. The other half is then taken when exiting. You must exit the country before the visa expires. (If it has expired, report to a local OVIR office for an extension; you cannot get one at the airport.) You may also need separate visas (and transit visas) to travel to or through other Commonwealth states such as the Ukraine, and some Baltic countries such as Latvia. If you plan to exit the country and then return, you will need a double- or multiple-entry visa.

On arrival, most visitors to Russia must register their visa and passport with OVIR, the Department of Visas and Registration (unfortunately, this policing process is still left over from Socialist days). If staying in a hotel, the registration desk usually does this for you upon check-in. (You may need to give up your visa and passport for several hours to a day—thus, always make sure to have a photocopy of each with you at all times.) If you need to do this on your own, there are numerous district OVIR offices in Moscow (you can also extend your visa here). One central agency is located at 42 Pokrovka Street (Ulitsa Pokrovka), tel. 208-2091; open 10am–7pm (closed 2pm–3pm), closed Wednesdays and weekends. In St Petersburg, 4 Saltykova-Shchedrina Street (Ulitsa Saltykova-Shchedrina), tel. 278-2481. Open 9.30am–5.30pm; closed weekends.

WHEN TO GO

Hotel prices and itineraries of many tour programs change depending on the season. Peak season is from May to September. Alternatives are to go in the spring (April 1–May 15) or fall (September 1–October 31) when prices are lower and the cities less crowded. The summer White Nights in St Petersburg are spectacular, but at the same time the summer in Moscow can be humid and dusty. An Indian summer in the fall can be quite lovely. If you do not mind the cold and snow, the winter season is cheapest and accommodation most readily available (but the number of daylight hours are limited). The rainiest months for both cities are July and August.

TIME ZONES

Russia has 11 time zones. Moscow and St Petersburg are in the same zone. Moscow is 11 hours ahead of the US West Coast, eight hours ahead of the East Coast, three hours ahead of London, two of Central Europe, and one hour ahead of Helsinki. Russia changes its clocks the last Sunday in March (one hour forward) and last Sunday in September (one hour back). Moscow time is five hours behind Hong Kong, seven hours behind Sydney, and nine hours behind New Zealand.

What To Pack

For your convenience, travel as light as possible. Most airlines allow up to two pieces of luggage and one piece of cabin baggage. Luggage allowance tends to be very strict when exiting Russia. Often all bags are weighed, including your cabin baggage. (If this happens, try concealing your carry-ons when you check in.) You may be charged per additional kilogram (2.2 pounds) for luggage weighing over 20 kilograms (44 pounds) in economy class and 30 kilograms (66 pounds) in first or business class. This is usually the procedure for internal flights as well.

DOCUMENTS

Keep your passport, visa, important papers, tickets, vouchers, prescription medications and money in your hand luggage at all times! Also carry a photocopy of your passport and visa, and a few extra passport pictures. Bear in mind that you may need to show identification to get into certain places or exchange money, even if it is a xerox copy of a passport or visa. Know your credit card and pin numbers, and their emergency telephone numbers in case of loss or theft. Bring along a few personal checks; you may need one in order to get cash from a credit card, such as AMEX (see Traveler's Checks and Credit Cards, page 56).

CLOTHES

The season of the year is the major factor in deciding what to bring. Summers are warm, humid and dusty, with frequent thunderstorms, especially in Moscow—bring a raincoat or an umbrella. The White Nights of St Petersburg are delightful in the summer, but occasionally a pullover or light jacket is needed. Winters are cold and damp, with temperatures well below freezing. It can snow between November and April, when cold Arctic winds sharpen the chill. Be prepared with your warmest clothes—waterproof lined boots, hat, gloves, scarf and thermal underwear (surprisingly, it is often colder in Moscow than St Petersburg). Interiors are usually well-heated, so dress in layers. Bring slightly smarter attire for ballets and banquets. A must is a good pair of walking shoes that can get dirty. Wearing shorts or sleeveless shirts may prevent you from entering churches during services.

Even though numerous clothing stores have now opened throughout both cities, Western attire and brand-name fashion is much more expensive than at home, and Russian-made goods do not ensure quality. It is best to buy necessary clothing before you leave, but otherwise you should now be able to find almost anything, especially in Moscow.

MEDICINE

Many more Western medicinal products are available in Moscow and St Petersburg now, but they cost more than at home. Bring along necessary prescription drugs (know generic names) and allergy medications, antibiotics (such as Cipro) and a course of antidiarrhea drugs (such as Lomotil), glasses and contact lenses. Also consider packing a small first-aid kit for cuts and bruises. If you take injections, bring your own needles and syringes. Even though you can now find the following items in various Western-style supermarkets, they may not carry your preferred brands. To save time looking for them, bring some of these with you: aspirin, throat lozenges, cold formulas, vitamins, laxatives, lip salve, dental floss, travel sickness pills, water-purifying tablets, antibacterial handwash, handi-wipes, contact-lens cleaner, mosquito repellent/anti-itch spray and indigestion tablets. Luxury-class hotels usually have a resident nurse on hand. (See Practical Information sections for each city for listings of medical facilities, dentists and pharmacies.)

PERSONAL ARTICLES

One can now find most necessary travel articles that were always lacking in Russia—thus, no one really needs to pack an extra five kilograms of toiletries and toilet paper! Even though many products are available, consider bringing along preferred brands of cosmetics, shampoo, lotions, razors and shaving cream, toothpaste, sanitary towels or tampons, small packets of tissues for restrooms, a water bottle for long trips, money belt, washing powder, an all-purpose plug for bathtubs and sinks, earplugs, a sewing kit, pantyhose, adhesive tape, extra locks for suitcases, sunglasses, pens and note pads, plastic bags and a sturdy tote-style shopping bag. A small flashlight and whistle are good to carry at night. If you are a student bring a student ID—some places offer discounts on fares or admission charges.

GADGETS

Voltage is 220V (and sometimes varies to 127V). Most of the major hotels have plugs for 220/110V. Pack a few adapters (Russia uses the European round two-pin plug). Duel voltage coils are useful for boiling water and brewing tea and coffee in your hotel room, but should be used with caution. A portable cassette or CD music player, as well as a small tape recorder may come in handy. Bring plenty of batteries for your camera, alarm clock and watch. Also useful is a Swiss army knife or penknife that has a bottle opener and corkscrew.

FILM AND PHOTOGRAPHY

Film is available in both cities, but is more expensive than at home. Bring whatever you plan to use, especially slide film. Since using a flash is prohibited in many museums and churches, have some high-speed film on hand. If you can wait, it is advisable to have your film processed at home. (Kodak and Fuji print film centers are in both cities. VHS or Super/Hi-8 cassettes, though available, cost more in Russia.)

In the former Soviet Union there were many photographic restrictions, but these no longer apply. Some places still prohibit cameras (such as the Lenin Mausoleum), and many locals are still uncomfortable with having their picture taken. Understand that people are sometimes sensitive about foreigners photographing what they perceive as backward or in poor condition. Always remain courteous. When passing through airports, photographers with a lot of film, especially high-speed, should have it inspected by hand—Russian X-rays are not always guaranteed film-safe. (Before leaving home, purchase a film shield pouch—lead laminated; the bag protects your undeveloped film against airport X-rays.)

MISCELLANEOUS/SUNDRIES

A Russian phrase book and dictionary really come in handy. Try to master some of the Cyrillic alphabet before you leave. It is especially helpful in places like the Metro. Bring reading material and travel literature—Western books will be more expensive, and most of the Russian-published material is, surprise, in Russian! Gift-giving is part of Russian *gostyepriimstvo* (hospitality). Bring some specialty gift items from home—picture travel books of your country or city, T-shirts, vitamins, sport pins or favorite music cassettes are always appreciated. You can also purchase liquor and other gift items while in Russia.

Getting There

INTERNATIONAL FLIGHTS

Most major airlines fly to Moscow (Sheremetyevo II) and St Petersburg (Pulkovo II). Moscow is connected to over 120 cities in Europe and 70 countries around the world. Inquire at travel agencies and telephone the different airlines to discover the best rates. The advance-purchase (14–21-day APEX) fares usually give the most value for money. From the US West Coast there are now flights to eastern Siberia, such as Vladivostok (where you can pick up the Trans-Siberian Railway), Khabarovsk and Kamchatka on Aeroflot and Alaskan Air. Since flying from points outside Europe can involve large time differences, consider a stay in a European city for a day or two to recover from jet lag. Stopovers are often included or provided for a minimal extra charge.

Aeroflot is one of the largest airlines in the world, carrying 100 million passengers per year. You can also fly to and from a multitude of destinations in Asia and Europe on Aeroflot with stopovers in Moscow. Aeroflot's in-flight conditions have improved and, in 1998, Aeroflot acquired 15 brand-new Western-made planes, introduced a new menu and plans to build its own airport terminal at Sheremetyevo II by 1999. (Today Aeroflot no longer holds the monopoly over air travel within the country; a number of other Russian airlines, such as Transaero, are also operating.)

CONNECTING TRAINS

One pleasant way to travel is to take a train from a European city to Moscow or St Petersburg. In the USA, call Rail-Europe on (800) 848-7245 (web-site: http://www.raileurope.com, you can make reservations and book tickets directly up to 60 days in advance). For example, after a few relaxing days in Helsinki, you can then take the train to St Petersburg or Moscow. There are two daily trains that leave Helsinki for St Petersburg (445 kilometers/278 miles), one Russian and one Finnish. The Russian train number 33 leaves at 3.34pm and arrives at 10.50pm at Finland Station (about a seven-hour trip). The Finnish train number 35 departs at 8.30am and arrives in St Petersburg at 1.30pm; both arrive on the same day as departure with a one-hour time change. First class one-way costs approximately $130 (luxury class $245, second class $83). The Russian train number 34 departs St Petersburg at 7am and arrives in Helsinki at 12.30pm the same day. The Finnish train number 36 leaves at 4.15pm and arrives in Helsinki at 9.34pm.

The Moscow train leaves each day from Helsinki at 5.08pm and arrives the next morning at 9.10am; first class costs $137 (luxury $250, second class $93) each way (double the fare for round-trip). Travel time is 16 hours covering 1,117 kilometers (698 miles). A return train departs Moscow at 6.30pm and arrives in Helsinki at 9.02am the next morning. (Make sure your visa is good for this extra train day.)

Remember to hide or secure your valuables and money, and lock your compartment door; unfortunately, thefts occur, especially on overnight trains. By reserving a lower berth, you can store your luggage in the compartment underneath it. (A tip: both the compartment door lock and second security lock can be opened from the outside. Use a short nylon cord, necktie or belt to tie the door handle at night when sleeping, and/or jam a cork or bottle cap into the second ventilation lock.)

One can also travel by rail from other European cities, such as Berlin (35 hours) or Warsaw (26 hours) which can take from one to two days. (Make sure to check if any countries you pass through require transit visas.) The famous Trans-Siberian, on its western run, starts in Beijing and routes through either Manchuria or Mongolia, then crosses Siberia (one is allowed to get off at various locations along the way) with Moscow as its destination; from here, one can also continue on to other cities in Western Europe. (See Special Topic on page 291.)

BY FERRY AND BUS

Ferries leave for Russia from numerous European countries, such as Sweden, Finland, Latvia and Germany. The journey takes about 14 hours; overnight cabins are available. Ferries arrive and depart St Petersburg from the Sea Passenger Ship Terminal on Vasilyevsky Island. Cruises are also offered that journey along inland waterways with destinations such as Kizhi Island in Lake Ladoga or Valaam Island in Lake Onega, or along the Volga River. Overland round trip bus excursions are also available to Moscow and St Petersburg from European countries, with frequent departures from Helsinki. (See Useful Addresses and Practical Information sections for more details on cruise and bus excursions.)

DRIVING

It is not recommended to drive to Russia in your own car. The highways and border towns are filled with police and smugglers who both make a living out of extortion and theft. Definitely make sure you have proper insurance and contact a tourist information center before you leave to set up precise routes and learn of requirements and official procedures. Once inside Russia, unkept roads make targets for holdups, routes are poorly marked, parts are scarce or expensive and gas stations are often impossible to find.

CUSTOMS AND IMMIGRATION

Visitors arriving by air pass through a passport checkpoint in the airport terminal. Those arriving by train do this at the border. Uniformed border guards check passports and stamp visas. Passports are not stamped, but you can try asking for one when you leave if you wish. One page of the visa is removed upon arrival, the rest is surrendered on departure. Russian custom declaration forms are issued during your flight or train journey, or you can pick them up from stands located near the baggage claim area in the airport. Fill in exactly how much foreign currency you are bringing into the country (both cash and traveler's checks); generous amounts are permitted. Declare your valuables (gold, silver, jewelry, etc.). These valuables could be confiscated when departing with no proof that you brought them into the country! Any cameras, videos, VCRs, personal computers, typewriters, etc. should also be noted on the customs form. You must depart with these items (unless you have official permission to leave them behind) or you could be subject to a duty up to the full worth of the goods in question.

An inspector will check your luggage and stamp your declaration form. Do not misplace it—you need it to leave the country (nowadays it is rarely needed in order to change money, but carry it with you at all times). On departure, another declaration form (same format) must be filled out, which is compared to your original.

Make sure you are not leaving the country with more foreign currency than you declared upon arrival. Even though Russian customs has become considerably easier and faster than in past years, your bags may still be searched when you enter and leave, and everything is X-rayed. Do not overwrap items; these may be selected for inspection.

Drugs, other than medicinal, are highly illegal—one does not want to end up in a Russian jail! Do not try exiting with antiques (made before 1947), old icons or very expensive works of art (even modern) unless you have permission from the Ministry of Culture. (Carry receipts so you can prove their worth if questioned.) Caviar, other than that officially purchased, can also be confiscated (check—there may still be a two-can limit). Beware, metal cans shine like beacons under X-rays! If something is confiscated, and a friend staying behind is with you at the airport, give it to them for safekeeping; otherwise customs may keep it.

Check if you need a visa (or transit visa) before continuing to locations outside of Russia, such as the Baltic, other Commonwealth states or eastern European countries. Customs may review other visas before allowing you to leave.

Money

The Russian currency is the ruble, which became Russia's national currency in 1534. The new bank notes (first circulated in 1998) come in denominations of 5, 10, 50, 100 and 500 rubles; other bills may follow. There are 1-, 2-, 3- and 5-ruble coins. Kopek coins, which originated during the reign of Peter the Great, are circulated in 1-, 5-, 10- and 50-kopek coins (100 kopeks to the ruble).

RUBLE HISTORY
The last ten years have seen a wide fluctuation in the value of the ruble. Before 1989 the Soviets set an exchange rate for the ruble within the country at about US$1.60. But on November 1, 1989, Gorbachev's government devalued the ruble by 90 percent. Soon after, the kopek coin was completely taken off the market, new notes were printed, and the ruble plummeted to less than one American cent. (Russians nicknamed their currency 'wooden money', while the slang for American dollars, real money, became *kapusta* or cabbage.) The intention of devaluation was to bring the ruble closer to its actual value and discourage huge black-market activities. In 1992, the ruble was floated on the world market and on July 25, 1993, new denomination ruble notes were circulated to coincide with soaring inflation. All of these notes are now invalid. By 1997 the world market exchange had risen to 6,000 rubles to US$1. At the beginning of l998, Yeltsin's government decided to reissue new

ruble tender notes, knocking off three zeros. During the country's economic crisis in the fall of 1998, the ruble plunged to over 20 rubles to US$1, falling to less than one third of its value. Make sure you receive the current ruble notes in your money exchange—any note marked prior to 1997 is probably not valid!

CURRENCY EXCHANGE

For information on currency exchange rates (*kypc*, pronounced 'kurs'), dial 008.

Cash is the most acceptable form of currency in Russia (the country still does not have a check system). Traveler's checks are not as widely accepted. You can convert foreign currency to rubles at the airport or in your hotel. In addition, hundreds of exchange kiosks (signs in Russian say **ОБМЕН ВАЛЮТУ**—*Obmen Valyutoo*) also line the streets of big cities. Counterfeit US dollars have flooded Russia, so do not be offended if your dollars are carefully examined. Make sure all bills are in good condition; any torn, taped or marked bills may not be accepted. Also carry the newer $100 Franklin notes, as older $100 bills may not be taken. The exchange rates are now fixed and there is really no reason to seek out black marketeers; besides, it can be risky and is not recommended. Official exchange offices usually ask for ID, such as a passport or visa (showing a photocopy is acceptable), and they may want to stamp your customs declaration form. You can exchange unused rubles at the end of your trip in town at the airport or border. Remember, when you exit your rubles cannot be converted into more hard currency than you entered with! Most shops and restaurants take only rubles, though many now accept credit cards. (Note: by law, only rubles or credit cards are acceptable in most locations. Even though, because of inflation, prices may be stated in dollars, you can still pay in rubles. On the other hand, few places refuse dollars when offered.) Thus, carry rubles, some US dollars and a credit card to be prepared for any circumstance. Carry lower denomination US dollar bills, for many places cannot provide change for larger bills; they are also handy for tipping, cab fares, etc. Tipping is discretionary, depending on the service. Usually about ten percent is acceptable.

TRAVELER'S CHECKS AND CREDIT CARDS

Traveler's checks and credit cards are now accepted at many banks, hotels, restaurants and some shops. Bear in mind that most shops, bars and cafés still only accept rubles. And if you can pay in foreign currency, you will probably get change in rubles, so always have smaller notes available.

Numerous ATMs (Automated Teller Machines) have sprung up in both cities. Many major banks and hotels have ATMs or can give cash advances against credit cards with a commission based on the amount (always carry your passport and a personal check). When using an ATM, check if the machine dispenses dollars or rubles. (Write down all check and credit card numbers in case of loss or theft; be sure to know your international PIN number.)

At American Express offices, you can cash traveler's checks or get cash from your AMEX card (with an approximate 5 percent commission). You also need a personal check to get cash from a credit card. Make sure you can get the exchange in foreign currency and not all in rubles. They also have a full-service travel bureau. AMEX web-site: http://www.americanexpress.com (Also see Post and Mail, page 69.)

Moscow AMEX Office: 21a Sadovaya-Kudrinskaya Ulitsa, tel. 956-9004/05.

The Dialog Bank (Hotel Radisson-Slavyanskaya) at 2 Berezhkovskaya Naberezhnaya (Embankment) near Kievsky Metro station, tel. 941-8434, also gives cash advances from AMEX and other credit cards, and cashes traveler's checks.

St Petersburg AMEX Office: Grand Hotel Europe, 1/7 Mikhailovskaya Ulitsa, tel. 329-6060; fax. 329-6061.

The Industry-Construction Bank, at 57 Nevsky Prospekt (Nevsky Palace Hotel) and 140 Nevsky, both cash traveler's checks and handle credit cards.

Valuables

Hotels usually have safe deposit boxes by the front desk. It is advisable to lock up your valuables, money, passport and airline tickets—thefts have been reported from hotel rooms. In case of loss or theft, notify the service bureau at your hotel immediately. Always put your money in a safe place, carry bags tightly around your shoulder and make sure backpacks are secured. Buy a money belt, so you can carry your money discreetly. Unfortunately, over the last few years the number of crimes against tourists has risen—pockets are picked and bags stolen. Take extra care when in large crowds and markets, or if a band of Gypsies or street urchins approaches. Take the same precautions as you would in any large metropolis.

Health and Emergencies

To call an ambulance in Russia, dial 03. Since a Russian ambulance may take time to arrive, also try calling one of the Western clinics immediately.

Immunizations are not required unless you are coming from an infected area. Russia does not have many health risks, but the main areas of concern are the food, water and cold weather. Some people may have trouble adjusting to Russian cuisine, which can include heavy breads, thick greasy soups, highly salted and pickled foods, smoked fish and sour cream. Familiar vegetables and fruits are often in short supply. (If you do not have an iron constitution, bring indigestion or stomach-disorder remedies.) If you are a vegetarian or require a certain diet, consider bringing some packaged freeze dried or specialty foods and vitamins along. A vegetarian can always find potatoes and cabbage—ethnic restaurants such as Georgian and many Western-style cafés serve nonmeat fare.

DO NOT drink the tap water, especially in St Petersburg, where a virulent parasite *Giardia lamblia* can cause miserable bouts of fever, stomach cramps and diarrhea. If you feel ill, get checked by a doctor. For *Giardia*, some prescribe Metronidazole (available in Russia as Trikapol) 200mg three times per day for two weeks. Local juices or flavored sugar water, along with iced drinks, cannot always be trusted. (Most five-star hotels now have their own water-purifying systems, but you are advised to check.) Stick to bottled mineral water (some old brands of Russian water can be quite salty). In winter be prepared for a cold, and in the spring and summer months possible allergy attacks or mosquito bites.

If staying in Russia longer than a few months you may need to present a negative HIV test. If illness occurs, see Practical Information sections under Medical for hospital/pharmacy/dental locations. Many of these Western clinics can also organize air evacuation in the event of an emergency. It is advisable to purchase travel medical insurance before the trip. In the USA, try Travel Insurance Service, tel. (800) 937-1387; fax. (510) 932-0442; e-mail: info@travelinsure.com; web-site: http://www.travelinsure.com or International SOS Assistance tel. (215) 633-6607; web-site: http://www.insos.com.

Crime, Safety and Hazards

To call Police, dial 02.

The reports of crime in Russia have, for the most part, been overly dramatized by both Russian and Western press. Statistically, Russian streets are as safe as in Paris, London or New York. Even though some areas of Russia are experiencing unrest, it is considered safe to walk around Moscow or St Petersburg at any time during the day or evening, though, as in any big city, use common sense and take care of your valuables. It is highly unlikely for the average tourist to ever cross paths with Russian mafia or organized crime.

As a foreigner, you are automatically assumed to have money. Do not flaunt expensive jewelry and watches or wads of cash, and try to dress inconspicuously. Never exchange a large amount of money at a currency kiosk while walking alone on the street. Pickpocket gangs, often using children to distract their targets, work areas around major hotels, popular restaurants and tourist attractions (thieves come in all denominations—from the well-dressed or the elderly to pretty young women). As one gets your attention, another may try to pick your pocket, cut the strap off your shoulder bag, snatch your camera or open your backpack. If all valuables are secure, then nothing can be stolen. Carry rubles in one place, and dollars in another; place the bulk of foreign cash in yet another safe area. It has been known for thugs to follow big winners home from a casino, or an intoxicated foreign couple leaving a restaurant. Do not walk alone down poorly lit back-alleys late at night or in neighborhoods you are not familiar with. It is safe to ride the Metro, but from the station, make sure you do not have to wait long for a bus or walk a long way to get home. The biggest nuisance is usually inebriated Russians, but aside from a few incoherent mumbles, their incapacitation renders them relatively harmless.

In addition, do not flag down a taxi or private car late at night and ride by yourself to the outskirts of town; if more than two people are in the vehicle and you are alone, do not get in. If staying with friends, never give the driver, or any other stranger for that matter, the entire address. If you should experience a mugging, do not resist—the gun is probably real. It is a good idea to place a small sum of money in one pocket and hide the rest; this way, you can pull out the smaller amount, and say it is all you have. The GAI or Militsia Police wear blue or gray uniforms with red epaulettes and cap bands. Their vehicles are usually navy blue and white. If robbed, report the incident to the police; your hotel can direct you to the nearest police station (you will probably need an official report to file an insurance claim). If something major occurs, also report it to your embassy or consulate.

If someone tries to pick you up in a bar, restaurant, or hotel, remember both men and women work as prostitutes (they now frequent virtually all of Moscow's hotels). Think twice—not only is AIDS (and hepatitis and other venereal diseases) on the rise, but there are many reports of victims being drugged and robbed (prostitutes often work with criminals to target guests). Hotel guests should also never open their doors for unexpected callers. Russia has now become one of the major routes to Europe from the Golden Triangle. Do not even think of purchasing drugs or using them—Russian jails and prisons are awful; remember this country created the gulags.

Beware of fake art works, especially icons and lacquer boxes. A seller will try to charge a foreigner as much as possible. If you think the price is high and you cannot tell an antique from a modern imitation, do not buy it—scams abound. For example, white fish eggs have been blackened with shoe polish to look like expensive black caviar and resealed in official looking cans. This also happens with vodka—homemade brew or *samogon* is poured into empty bottles and resealed with a brand label. Do not buy vodka and caviar off the street or from some alley kiosk; purchase them in larger stores.

If in need of a public toilet, first try finding one in a hotel, restaurant or museum. Otherwise, look on the street for the sign WC or **ТУАЛЕТ** (*tyalet*)—they are hard to find and most are not in good condition. The men's toilet is marked with an M (women should go to the other door). Most train stations now have automated toilets. At the entrance, you may need to pay a small fee to an attendant. Sometimes, a few squares of toilet paper are provided; learn to carry small packets of tissues, they can be very useful.

Do not jaywalk—cross only at appropriate crossings or lights. Drivers do not care what is in front of them (practically no one has car insurance), and many streets are too wide to cross quickly (use underground crossings). Also be cautious when walking on sidewalks. There are many construction sites or deteriorating areas filled with deep holes, uncovered manholes or other hazards.

The hot water supply is often interrupted in summer months, especially in smaller towns. Central power stations usually close down for repairs and cleaning for several weeks during the year. If you arrive and there is no hot water, this may be the reason. Ask for a samovar or tea pot for your room in which to boil water; take a sponge bath or go to one of the numerous local saunas or *banya*. Remember, when in Rome...!

Smoking has reached epidemic proportions in Russia. While tobacco companies are being hounded in the United States, they are welcomed with open arms in Russia where cigarette sales are a goldmine business and advertising abounds. Smokers are everywhere, in restaurants, hotels, trains and museums, and it is legal. A recent survey reported that 57 percent of Russia's adult men and 48 percent of adult women smoke.

If you are susceptible to allergies, springtime can be a problem, especially in Moscow where pollen from trees and plants is a wheezer's anathema; at times, white fuzzy blossoms from poplar trees, called *pukh*, accumulate like snow drifts throughout the city.

Getting Around

Moscow's international airport is 30 kilometers (19 miles), and St Petersburg's 18 kilometers (11 miles) from the city center—about a 30–45 minute drive. (St Petersburg's Pulkovo II was completely renovated in 1996–7, and a Pulkovo III international terminal is planned to open by the year 2000.)

When arriving in Moscow or St Petersburg, group travelers should automatically be taken by bus to their hotel. When booking a hotel, make sure to check if they provide airport or train station transfers. If you are arriving as an independent traveler, try to arrange some service or friend to meet you at the airport. Otherwise, most airport taxis are controlled by a local cartel of drivers who monopolize the service. Thus, rides from the airport into town can cost up to five times more than they cost in the opposite direction.

From Moscow's Sheremetyevo II, a taxi may try to charge up to $100, from St Petersburg's Pulkovo II, over $30; check first to find out what an average fare should be. Offer to share a ride with others into town and split the cost. There are few alternatives. You may be able to find a private driver moonlighting to earn extra cash.

In St Petersburg the so-called Express Bus Service stops at Metro stations. If you do not have a lot of luggage and are on a tight budget, try riding to a station and then taking the Metro to a stop near your hotel or taking a taxi. City bus number 13 runs to Hotel Pulkovskaya and Moskovskaya Metro station.

In Moscow, the Airport Bus stops at Metro Aeroport, Planernaya, and Rechnoi Vokzal. To return to the airport, your hotel can set up a ride or find a taxi which charges a realistic fare.

Remember to reconfirm your departure flight. This can be done through a hotel service desk or by telephoning the airlines directly. Reconfirm internal flights as well, as they tend to be overbooked. Always arrive at the airport at least two hours in advance of your flight time for international travel. Never try to leave with an expired visa or you will be sent back into town to have it extended at an OVIR office.

TRAVEL BETWEEN CITIES
If on a group tour, most of your itinerary has been booked before your arrival. If traveling independently and you would like to extend your visa, make other hotel, train or plane reservations, or simply book a sightseeing excursion within a city or travel to another town, such as in the Golden Ring area, always inquire first at your hotel. If they cannot handle something for you, they will be able to recommend travel organizations that specialize in your area of interest. As these arrangements can take time, never wait until the last minute to make travel plans.

BY AIR
The airports used for internal flights are much more crowded and chaotic than the international airports. Special preference is usually given to foreign groups at check-in and separate waiting areas may also be provided. Passports and visas are required to be presented at check-in. (Take care, often even carry-on luggage is weighed, and any overweight is charged—have someone take your hand luggage aside when you check in.) Boarding passes are issued, either with open seating or with seat numbers, and rows written in Cyrillic! Remember that Russians are quite assertive and can push vigorously to get on the plane which is usually not boarded by row numbers—one

general announcement for boarding is made, often just in Russian. If the flight has open seating, do not be last on the plane—the airlines frequently overbook. On internal flights, there is often just one class of seating, and no nonsmoking sections. Sometimes the only meal consists of soda water, and bread and cucumber sandwiches. Consider taking some drinks and snacks along. There is no airport departure tax. Airline tickets are sold to foreigners in hard currency, but you can try to pay in rubles. You can reserve and buy Aeroflot (and other Russian airlines) tickets at most major hotels, which is a lot easier than going to local overcrowded offices.

You can also reserve and buy airline tickets on foreign airlines at their representative offices (see Practical Information sections for Moscow and St Petersburg airline office locations).

BY TRAIN

Trains are much more fun, efficient and cheaper than flying. The express (taking about six hours) and other commercial trains between Moscow and St Petersburg are a splendid way to travel. Board the sleeper at night and arrive the next morning for a full day of sightseeing. Traveling during daylight hours affords wonderful views of the countryside. Since there are several train stations in each city, make sure you know which one you depart from. In Moscow, trains for St Petersburg leave from the Leningradsky Vokzal (Leningrad Station). In St Petersburg they leave from the Moskovsky Vokzal (Moscow Station). (The word *vokzal* stems from London's Vauxhall Station.) Large boards listing time schedules are posted at each station. Trains always leave on time with a single five-minute warning broadcast before departure—so pay attention!

There are three classes for long-distance travel. Luxury or *lyuks* has two soft berths to a compartment (and often a personal bathroom); first or *coupé* class has four soft berths; *platskart* has either six hard berths or standard seats (try to avoid the latter). Your ticket will indicate the train, wagon (*vagon*), compartment (*kupé*) and berth (*myesto*) number. The lower the wagon number, the closer it is to the front of the train on departure. A personal car attendant (*provodnik*) serves tea, brewed in the car's samovar, and biscuits, and wakes you up in the morning. Remember to turn off the radio at night or it may blast you awake at 6am.

If you are traveling on an overnight train and can afford it, try buying the entire compartment to ensure both privacy and safety. If you share the compartment with strangers, secure your valuables and sleep with money, passport, etc. on your person. Reserve a lower berth, where you can place luggage and other valuables in the storage compartment underneath. During the night, compartment locks can be opened from the outside. Consider securing both locks before retiring to sleep by using cord, belt or necktie to tie around them as an extra precaution. The compartments are not segregated. If there is a problem, the attendant can usually arrange a swap—it is safe traveling alone as a woman. (Carry earplugs in case of snorers!) A minimal fee may be charged for sheets and towels. Tickets are collected at the beginning of the trip and returned at the end. For outstanding service, tipping your attendant is appropriate.

Even though a dining car is usually available (though often crowded), it is fun to bring along your own food, drink, and spirits to enjoy in your compartment (remember a knife, fork and bottle opener). Also bring clothes to sleep in, slippers and toilet paper. Toilets on most trains are without supplies and never cleaned during trips, thus not always a pleasant experience. In summer months, it can be quite hot as compartment windows are sealed shut; hallway windows can be opened. Porters (*nosilshchiki*) are available, but they may try to charge a foreigner more; negotiate a per bag price before starting out (find out from a local what this is). In stations, always keep a watchful eye on your bags and valuables. Do not let just anyone carry your bag—it may be the last you see of it.

The easiest way to purchase train tickets is through your hotel service desk, or an appropriate travel agency. Each city visited must be listed on your visa. Your passport and visa are supposed to be checked with your ticket when boarding the train, so it is best not to buy a scalper's ticket (especially for a long-distance trip) which will be in a different name. In addition, foreigners are still supposed to pay more for a ticket than locals. Try asking a Russian friend to buy a cheaper ticket for you. If discovered, you may be asked to pay the difference (try offering the conductor a few dollars 'service fee' to take the ticket.) Students sometimes get discounted fares.

To purchase a ticket on your own, go to the appropriate ticket counters. (Some may have special counters for foreigners.) Make sure you bring sufficient rubles and your passport and visa. Each city also has several booking offices that sell tickets to most destinations. Longer-distance tickets can be purchased for next day and up to 45 days in advance. (Same-day tickets must be purchased at the station of departure.) In Moscow, rail ticket centers are at 5 Komsomolsky Prospekt (open 24 hours weekdays), 15 Ulitsa Petrovka and 6 Maly Kharitonevsky Pereulok (open daily 8am–7pm; closed 1pm–2pm). For rail information for Moscow stations, tel. 266-9000/09. Also dial 266-8333 to order tickets in advance. They are delivered to a home or office after two or three days, payment on delivery.

St Petersburg's rail ticket center is at 24 Ekaterininsky Kanal (open 8am–8pm Monday to Saturday, 8am–4pm Sundays). For train information, tel. 168-0111; central railway ticket information, tel. 162-3344. For ticket deliveries, call 201.

Local commuter trains (known as *elektrichka*) serve the suburbs of both cities and some Golden Ring towns. (See individual Golden Ring towns for train transportation.) They usually have only hard wooden benches (some have softer first class seats), poor amenities (toilets are dirty), and can be quite crowded on weekends and in summer months. The advantage is that they are cheap and leave frequently. Tickets can be bought the same day at the station of departure; ID is not usually required.

Take note that many train and plane schedules are still listed throughout the country using Moscow time which does make things confusing. If you are traveling in a time zone other than Moscow's, always check to see what time (Moscow or local) is actually indicated on your ticket.

BY BUS AND COACH

Group tourists are shown around Moscow and St Petersburg by coach. Often the buses are not air-conditioned, but all are heated during winter. If you are an individual traveler, you can sign up through a hotel or local travel agency for city sightseeing excursions. Comfortable coach tours are also offered to Golden Ring towns. Always take notice of your bus number, as parking lots tend to fill quickly. For longer rides bring along some bottled water and snacks.

LOCAL BUSES, TRAMS AND TROLLEYS

Local transportation operates from 5.30am to 1am and is charged by either a flat rate or by distance. The front and back of each vehicle is marked in Russian with its destination, and the number of the route. To find a bus or trolley stop (A for *autobus* or T for *trolleybus*), look for numbered route signs on sidewalks. For trams, signs hang on wires by the street adjacent to the tram stop or over tramlines in the middle of the road. As you board, look for a sign near the door which indicates the cost of a ride. Tickets can be bought from the driver, or an attendant who patrols the aisles. You can also prepurchase transportation coupons, called *talony*, at many kiosks and shops. A special ticket machine is mounted inside the vehicle where you punch your coupon. Inspectors sometimes make spot checks on tickets. If the bus is crowded, try to anticipate your stop and inch towards the door. You may hear a voice behind asking, *Vi Vikhoditye?* (Are you getting off now?). If locals think you are not alighting, they may push by; the *babushka*, especially, are superb shovers! Similarly, if trying to board a crowded bus, you may find yourself pushed from the back and packed in like a sardine. Just make sure the door does not close on you.

METRO

The Metro is the fastest and cheapest way to get around Moscow and St Petersburg. More than eight million people ride the Moscow Metro daily. Trains run every 90 seconds during rush hour. Central stations are beautifully decorated with chandeliers and mosaics. Metro stations are easy to spot—entrances on the street are marked with a large M. Even the long escalator rides are great entertainment. Metro maps are posted inside each station, or use the ones in this book (see pages 90–1 for Moscow and page 395 for St Petersburg). To ride the Metro, purchase a token (called *zheton*) at the underground booth or automated machines. Alas, the cost has risen with inflation, from 5 kopeks to about 2 rubles but is a flat rate regardless of where you ride to or how long you remain underground. The token is made from green plastic and is the size of an American quarter. In 1998, Moscow's Metro authority also began selling ten-ride magnetic tickets, which are valid for 30 days from the date of purchase. A monthly pass is also available.

Deposit the token into the turnstile and wait for the green light before passing through (some turnstiles are still archaic and can shut violently). If using a pass, go to the end of the turnstiles and show it to the inspector. All station and transfer areas are clearly marked, but in Russian. If you do not read Cyrillic, have someone write down the name of your destination. People are always helpful and are glad to point you in the right direction. Even though transferring to another station underground can be especially confusing, never forget to relish the adventure and marvel at the beauty of the stations.

TAXIS

You can order a taxi from the taxi desk located in the lobby of most hotels, or call a taxi to come to a specific location; a minimal service fee may be charged. Officially two hours notice is required, but taxis can arrive within minutes. If in a hotel, it may be easier to just go outside and flag one down (the ride is made cheaper by walking a few blocks away from the hotel). There are official and private taxis (which are required to display ID registrations) and private cars. Unlike most other countries, a Russian taxi ride is not as simple as it would seem. Even hailing a taxi can be a problem. Stand with your arm held out, palm slightly down. If a taxi stops, the driver may ask where you want to go before deciding if he wants to take you. If so, the negotiating begins. Be aware that the wealthier you appear, the higher he may bid. Often you can bring the price down by saying it is too much and pretending to walk away.

Many of the official taxis now have meters, but because of inflation and constant monetary devaluation, these may not have kept up with the changes. Taxi fees can be higher in the evening. It is wise to find out the average cost of your journey before you start bargaining. (By law you should pay in rubles, but a driver never usually refuses dollars.) If the driver seems to take a circuitous route, and the meter is running, ask—the driver may not be trying to cheat you. Often direct roads may be closed and under construction.

Hitching is quite common—taxis are not always available and drivers of private cars are often eager to earn some extra cash by picking up paying passengers. Because of recent crime, evaluate the taxi or car before you get in, and never take a ride late at night, especially to an outlying area. If you do not have a good feeling about the driver, do not get in; always use common sense. Never get into a vehicle already occupied by two people.

CAR HIRE

Many hotels offer a car hire service with a driver, and a guide can also be hired for the day. There are now both Russian and Western car services where automobiles, jeeps, mini-vans and buses can be rented, but usually only with an accompanying driver. If new to the city, it is recommended not to drive on your own; public transportation is actually much safer and more convenient. If you do plan on driving, check with your insurance company before leaving home; often Russia is not covered on a policy. If you want to tour an area, many private cars and off-duty taxi-drivers are often open to suggestions. Some can be hired for the day to take you around. Make sure to agree on the amount and payment terms beforehand; gasoline costs are usually extra. ALWAYS wear your seatbelt.

Being There

HOTELS

Intourist, the old Soviet travel dinosaur, no longer monopolizes the Russian hotel system and the *dezhurnaya*, that hawk-eyed hall attendant, is also nearing extinction. Travelers who may have visited during Socialist days, will not believe the changes—hotel staff are actually friendly and most speak English. From foreign-owned luxury palaces and restored privatized State-run hotels to hip hostels and bed and breakfasts, there is something for everyone's budget. Bohemian suites, moderate motels and bargain beds are available in every area of town. However, it is best to find a location as close to the center as possible; taxis can be expensive and public transportation a time-consuming experience. Many establishments also provide visa and other travel services. Check to see if your hotel provides airport or train station transfers. To prevent crime, hotel doormen may require to see a hotel card before allowing you to enter. If you are stopped, state in English that you are staying in the hotel and have forgotten your card, or wish to eat at the restaurant—once recognized as a foreigner, the guards should let you in. (To find out how to book hotel rooms, check Facts for the Traveler/Visas, page 45, and Practical Information sections under Accommodation for more details.)

Most hotels in Russia charge in dollars (or other foreign currency), and accept major credit cards and traveler's checks. Many have restaurants and bars (breakfast is often included in the price), business and fitness centers, shops, post offices and service bureaus, which book travel, sightseeing excursions, theater tickets, train reservations, etc. If you cannot afford to stay in a more expensive hotel, you can still use its amenities—their spa centers usually offer special day-rates, or have an expresso in the coffee shop while reading the *Herald Tribune* to recharge! Especially during low seasons, bargaining for special rates can be attempted.

COMMUNICATIONS

INTERNATIONAL CALLS

Communications has become substantially easier since the Soviet era when placing an international call would take days. Today there are a number of ways of making an international call. If you have an AT&T telephone card, dial one of the following access numbers and an operator provides direct service to the US or elsewhere abroad. (To get an application for an AT&T Global Calling Card while in Moscow, call 974-0074.)

From Moscow: English 755-5042   Russian 325-5555
From St Petersburg: English 325-5042   Russian 325-5555
From other cities
in Russia: English *8 10 800 497-7211 Russian *8 10 800 497-7201
   (*Dial 8, then wait for tone, then dial the rest of number.)

Sprint Express:
From Moscow and
other Russian cities: English 747-3324   Russian 747-3354.
From St Petersburg: English *8 10 800 497-7255 Russian *8 10 800 497-7155.

If you have a different calling card company, check with them before you leave for appropriate access numbers. One can now call collect.

You can also direct dial to the United States and other countries abroad (including areas in the CIS) from a home or business phone. First dial 8 and wait for second dial tone, then dial international code 10, and then the country code and phone number. The call is charged in rubles.

A telephone service is also available from most major hotels but this can be very expensive. (Always check prices and service charges before calling.) It may be easier and cheaper for somebody to call you from abroad if they know your contact number. Many old-style Russian hotels still do not have switchboards. Thus the seven-digit number may connect directly with the phone in your room, and therefore no messages can be taken when you are out. Check before you use a satellite phone—there are often three-minute minimum charges. Business centers in many hotels also provide fax and computer services.

Another method is to call a Russian overseas operator and place a reservation for an international call up to two days in advance. In Moscow, dial 8-194 or 8-190, and in St Petersburg 315-0012 and ask for an English speaking operator. Give the number you are calling and the number where you will be at the time of the call. The operator will go through dates and times available for booking. You are called when the call is ready to be placed. (The call can be canceled at any time for no charge.)

Yet another way is to use Comstar satellite phone booths that stand in numerous locations throughout both cities. You can pay with either a credit or phone credit card. Calls are expensive, costing between $3–$10 per minute, but it is quick and clear.

Several long-distance telephone centers are also located in each city and town. Go to the international desk and give the attendant your telephone number. When the call goes through, you are directed to a numbered booth to take the call. Afterward the charge is usually paid in rubles, but some now take dollars or credit cards. In Moscow, the main communications centers are at the Central Telephone & Telegraph, 7 Tverskaya Ulitsa and 2 Novy Arbat. In St Petersburg one is at 3/5 Bolshaya Morskaya Ulitsa. All are open daily from 9am–9pm.

CALLS WITHIN RUSSIA ·
One can direct dial most cities in Russia from a hotel, home or office phone. From your hotel phone, first dial 8 and wait for a second dial tone. Now dial the city code and then the phone number. Moscow is (095), St Petersburg (812), Kostroma (0942), Suzdal (09231), Vladimir (09222) and Yaroslavl (0852). If you do not know the area code, ask your hotel service desk to find out for you, or dial 07 for an intercity operator. You can also place calls from main telephone centers or special telephone street booths, called *mezhdugorodny*. Unless marked as such, regular pay phones cannot make city to city calls. Most of these phone booths now use plastic phone tokens or cards, which are sold in stores, kiosks and Metro stations around the city (same token as for local calls).

LOCAL CALLS
To use a pay phone, you must buy a token or *zheton*. The phone token, costing about two rubles, is dark plastic and the size of an American penny. Place the

token in the top slot and it then drops down automatically when someone answers. If you plan on speaking more than a few minutes (one token is usually good for 3 minutes), have a few more tokens available to drop in when the allotted time is up, otherwise you will be disconnected. Newer phone booths also take plastic phone cards.

Do not lose your telephone numbers! Russia has still not compiled a telephone directory with resident phone numbers and addresses. For directory assistance, dial 09; you may need the person's full name, including patronymic and address. For information in other cities, dial 07. A number of business directories are now available. Two excellent editions in English and Russian are: *The Traveller's Yellow Pages for Moscow* and *The Traveller's Yellow Pages for St Petersburg*. (To order a copy in the US, see Recommended Reading section, page 572.)

POST AND MAIL

Russia's main post office centers take care of postal service, telegrams, telegraphs and phone calls. Outbound mail to the US and Europe takes about three weeks. Inbound mail can take longer. You can buy postage stamps at most hotels which also provide mail boxes; some even have their own post offices. To send an international or local package, you must first show the contents for inspection. It is then wrapped for you. There are now several express mail services, such as Federal Express and DHL. (See Practical Information sections for locations.) If staying over a longer period of time, letters can be addressed directly to your hotel or other address, or to a poste restante at a post office which holds mail for up to two months. Never send anything of importance. Notice that addresses are written backwards in Russian with zip code first and name last.

The address for the main post office (*glavpochtamt*) in Moscow is: 103009, Moscow, 26/2 Myasnitskaya Ulitsa, Poste Restante (in Russian *Pochta do Vostrebovaniya*), your name. (Open daily 8am–7.45pm.) The St Petersburg main post office is: 19044, St Petersburg, 9 Pochtamskaya Ulitsa, Poste Restante (*Pochta do Vostrebovaniya*), your name. (Open 9am–7.30pm Monday–Saturday; 10am–5.30pm Sundays.)

Privately owned mail services also exist. In Moscow, call Post International (tel. 209-9168; fax. 200-3858). In St Petersburg: Post International, 20 Nevsky Prospekt (tel. 219-4472; fax. 219-4473), and Westpost, 86 Nevsky Prospekt (tel. 275-0784; fax. 275-0806). These hold and forward mail, and receive faxes 24 hours a day.

American Express card holders can have their mail (letters only) sent to them c/o the American Express office in Moscow and St Petersburg. It takes about four days, via Helsinki, to arrive from the US. (For locations, see Facts for the Traveler/Traveler's Checks and Credit Cards, page 56.)

Media

The best places to find newspapers and magazines in English are at news shops in major hotels. Some street kiosks and stores also carry foreign literature. Pick up a free copy of the *Moscow Times* in English, distributed through many restaurants, stores and hotels. Listings in the Friday and Saturday sections, especially, give up-to-date information on concerts, theaters, nightclubs, films, art events, etc. This newspaper is also distributed in St Petersburg. The *St Petersburg Times* is also a good newspaper to check.

There are now about seven non-cable TV channels in Moscow and St Petersburg. Compared to Soviet TV (consumed by boring propaganda news and war musicals), contemporary TV is filled with everything from talk and game shows to New Age healers and soap operas. Many foreign films are broadcast in their original languages or shown with subtitles. To get an idea of how the culture is changing, try watching some TV during your stay. (Most large hotels subscribe to foreign cable networks, such as CNN, BBC and MTV.) A few Russian radio stations broadcast in English, along with airing Voice of America and BBC World Service. Some good FM music stations, such as Moscow's Europa Plus or Radio Rox, broadcast daily.

Addresses

No other place in the world has harder addresses to locate than in Russia. If you are presented with the following address, for example, this is how to decipher it: Tverskaya Ul Dom 33, Korpus 2, Etazh 3, Kvartira 109, (Kode 899). Firstly, street numbers are poorly marked. Once you have found 33 Tverskaya Ulitsa (Street), there may be several different buildings using this one address, which are separated by their *korpus* or block numbers. (One often enters the buildings from the back.) Once you locate Block 2, look for a list of apartment numbers usually indicated on the outside of each building. Make sure your *kvartira* or apartment number is listed; if not, it may be located in a different block. When you enter the security code of 899, the door should open. (If it does not work, a *dezhurnaya* or attendant may live on the first floor, or wait for someone to enter or exit, or shout.) Once you are inside, proceed up to the third floor or *etazh* and look for apartment 109. (109 does not mean it is on the first floor!) The passage to the apartment may be blocked by yet another door that secures the hallway. Look for the appropriate apartment number by this door and ring the buzzer. If there is no answer the buzzer may be broken, so try ringing some of the others so someone else can let you in. Most Russians also have a double door leading into the apartment; and if you knock they will not hear, so ring the bell. Ideally you should make sure somebody knows you are coming so they can look out for you.

Additionally, many apartment block elevators are old and run down and may not be operating; be prepared to walk up. (On a humorous note: during Soviet times, the primo apartment was considered to be on the first floor and not the penthouse. On the first floor, a tenant was assured of getting hot water, and not having to rely on the elevator!) One last point concerning addresses: 3-ya 55 Liniya means 55 Third Liniya Street, for example; this also means that there is a First and Second Liniya Street indicated by 1-ya and 2-ya.

TRAVEL RESTRICTIONS
Officially you cannot venture more than 35 kilometers (22 miles) outside Moscow or St Petersburg. (You can go to towns in the Golden Ring, but you may need more distant towns added to your visa.) Only the cities specified on the visa can be visited (towns can be added while in Russia). Unless the visa is extended, you must exit the country on the date shown on the visa.

ETIQUETTE
Often Russians appear very restrained, formal or downright glum. But there is a dichotomy between their public (where for so many generations they dared not show their true feelings) and private appearances. In informal and private situations or after friendship has been established, the Russian character is charged with emotional warmth, care and humor. They are intensely loyal and willing to help. Arriving in or leaving the country merits great displays of affection, usually with flowers, bear hugs, kisses and even tears of sorrow or joy. If invited to someone's home for dinner, expect elaborate preparations. Russians are some of the most hospitable people in the world. If you do not like drinking too much alcohol, watch out for the endless round of toasts!

The formal use of the patronymic (where the father's first name becomes the child's middle name) has been used for centuries. For example, if Ivan names his son Alexander, he is known as Alexander Ivanovich. His daughter Ludmilla's patronymic becomes Ivanovna. Especially in formal or business dealings, try to remember the person's patronymic. As in the West, where Robert is shortened to Bob, for example, Russian first names are also shortened once a friendship is established. Call your friend Alexander 'Sasha', Mikhail 'Misha', Ekaterina 'Katya', Tatyana 'Tanya' and Mariya 'Masha', or even use the diminutive form 'Mashenka'.

COMPLAINTS
Even today rules, regulations and bureaucracy still play a role in Russian life, with many uniformed people enforcing them. People here are not always presumed innocent until proven guilty. When dealing with police or other officials, it is best

to be courteous while explaining a situation. For example, police in the streets can randomly pull over vehicles to spot-check the car and registration. If you are pulled over, it does not mean you have done anything wrong. If you are kept waiting, as in restaurants, remember everyone else is waiting too. Be patient and remember that you are in a foreign country. Polite humor can often work well. Do not lose your temper, mock or laugh when inappropriate.

A few commonly used words are *nyet* and *nelzya*, which mean 'no' and 'it's forbidden'. The Russian language uses many negations. If people tell you something is forbidden, it may mean that they simply do not know or do not want to take responsibility. Ask elsewhere.

WOMEN AND MINORITIES

There have been reports of some Russian groups, such as skinheads, targeting Asian and African students living in Moscow. These student groups are mainly from Vietnam, Laos or the African continent. An attack on a foreign tourist is very rare. If of Asian or African origin, or a woman, use proper conduct and common sense as you would to ensure your safety in any big city. Do not walk late at night (especially alone) in unfamiliar neighborhoods or get into cars or taxis you are unsure about. (Carry a whistle, flashlight, penknife or small can of pepper spray.) During the day, you may be hassled by the usual array of souvenir-sellers or street urchins pretending to sell something. Secure all valuables, and keep pockets empty. Do not leave purses or backpacks open, or carry money or cameras in obvious view. If nothing is visible, then you are unlikely to be targeted. In the evenings, the only real threat are the numerous intoxicated locals who may try to pick you up or get your attention in a hotel, restaurant, nightclub, or on the street. Even though a nuisance, they can barely focus let alone cause any harm. If they are in a larger group, do not provoke anybody; politely get out of the area. A Russian escort, now drunk, may insist on seeing you home. If uncomfortable with any situation, just say *NYET!*

GAYS AND LESBIANS

One of the last revolutionary fronts formed was the Gay Rights Association. In the early 1990s, Article 121 of the penal code was finally repealed. Under this code, any type of homosexual conduct, even among consenting adults, was punishable by up to five years in prison or a stay in an asylum. The Russian slang for homosexual is *goloboy* (blue boy) and lesbian, *lesbianka*. Even though gay rights have made enormous strides, there is still prejudice, especially among male heterosexuals who have been known to become violent. However, many prominent figures, especially in the art world, are now having the courage to come out and take a stand for homosexual rights. Gay clubs (that include transvestites) have opened in both cities, along with organized special 'gay nights' throughout the year. (See Practical Information sections.)

VISITORS WITH DISABILITIES

Sadly, Russia has never paid special attention to its disabled. (It is rare to see a handicapped person or, for that matter, anyone using a wheelchair or crutches.) It is nearly impossible to use public transportation, and there are no street access elevators to get down to a Metro station. Street curbs are not built for wheelchairs. It is really only the new international hotels who offer any assistance for disabled people.

Food

Russian cooking is both tasty and filling. In addition to the expected borsch and beef stroganov, it includes many delectable regional dishes from the other Commonwealth states, such as Uzbekistan, Georgia or the Ukraine.

The traditions of Russian cooking date back to the simple recipes of the peasantry, who filled their hungry stomachs with the abundant supply of potatoes, cabbages, cucumbers, onions and bread. For the cold northern winters, they would pickle the few available vegetables and preserve fruits to make jam. This rather bland diet was pepped up with sour cream, parsley, dill and other dried herbs. In an old Russian saying, peasants described their diet as *Shchi da kasha, Pishcha nasha* (cabbage soup and porridge are our food). The writer Nikolai Gogol gave this description of the Russian peasant's kitchen: 'In the room was the old familiar friend found in every kitchen, namely a samovar and a three-cornered cupboard with cups and teapots, painted eggs hanging on red and blue ribbons in front of the icons, with flat cakes, horseradish and sour cream on the table along with bunches of dried fragrant herbs and a jug of *kvas* [a dark beer made from fermented black bread].' Russians remain proud of these basic foods, which are still their staples today. They will boast that there is no better *khleb* (bread) in the world than a freshly baked loaf of Russian black bread. In 1996, the Russian samovar celebrated its 250th birthday. Stemming from *sam* (self) and *varit* (to boil), the samovar came to represent the warmth of the Russian soul and was even given a place of honor in the household. It is used to boil up water for the favorite national pastime—drinking a cup of *chai* or hot tea. Samovars were fashioned mainly from copper, silver, platinum and porcelain, and decorated in the style of the times. One made from gold won a grand-design prize at the Vienna World's Fair in 1873.

Raisa Gorbachev once presented Nancy Reagan with a cookbook containing hundreds of potato recipes. The potato has long been a staple food of most Russian families. Legend has it that Peter the Great brought back the potato from Holland and ordered it planted throughout Russia; it was called 'ground apple'. During these times, so many changes were being implemented upon the peasantry that many, particularly Old Believers, refused to eat what they considered the 'devil's apple'. But, by 1840, after the government decreed that peasants had to plant the potato on all common lands, this 'second bread' soon became the staple food for most of the poorer population. During the lean times of revolution and war, potatoes fed entire armies. Since soldiers did not have time to cut and clean them, they would first boil the potato whole and then eat them with the skin. To this day, unpeeled cooked potatoes (with grated cheese, mayonnaise, or minced garlic added) are known as 'Potatoes in Uniform'.

Peter the Great also introduced French cooking to his empire in the 18th century. While the peasantry had access only to the land's crops, the nobility hired its own French chefs, who introduced eating as an art form, often preparing up to ten elaborate courses of delicacies. Eventually, Russian writers ridiculed the monotonous and gluttonous life of the aristocrats, many of whom planned their days around meals. In his novel *Oblomov*, Ivan Goncharov coined the term 'Oblomovism' to characterize the sluggish and decadent life of the Russian gentry. In *Dead Souls*, Nikolai Gogol described a typical meal enjoyed by his main character in the home of an aristocrat:

> On the table there appeared a white sturgeon, ordinary sturgeon, salmon, pressed caviar, fresh caviar, herrings, smoked tongues and dried sturgeon. Then there was a baked 300-pound sturgeon, a pie stuffed with mushrooms, fried pastries, dumplings cooked in melted butter, and fruit stewed in honey... After drinking glasses of vodka of a dark olive color, the guests had dessert... After the champagne, they uncorked some bottles of cognac, which put still more spirit into them and made the whole party merrier than ever!

As an old Russian saying goes: 'There cannot be too much vodka; there can only be not enough vodka!' Vodka has always been the indispensable drink of any class on any occasion. Whether rich or poor, no Russian is abstemious. Anton Chekhov wrote of a group of peasants who, 'on the Feast of the Intercession, seized the chance to drink for three days. They drank their way through fifty rubles of communal funds...one peasant beat his wife and then continued to drink the cap off his head and boots off his feet!' The writer also added: even though 'vodka is colorless...it paints your nose red, and blackens your reputation!'

The year 1998 marked the 600th anniversary of vodka. Genoese monks are credited as the first to come up with the distillation process. They were said to have begun shipping distilled grain spirits (then called *aqua vitae* or water of life) to

Lithuania in 1398. Soon after, Russia embraced this new spirit with gusto. The word vodka stems from *voda*, meaning water; *vodka*, means dear or little water. Rye was the favored distilling ingredient, followed by barley, wheat or potatoes. Over the next several centuries, vodka became so popular that Czar Alexis (Peter the Great's father) instituted the famous Law Code of 1649 which decreed that all revenues from vodka sales went directly into royal coffers; this state monopoly lasted over 300 years. Only home brewing, or the making of *samogon*, was permitted without government control. Even today, 100 percent proof amateur spirits are still known as *speert* or *samogon*.

Between national consumption and international sales, the income from vodka was enormous. By the late 1800s, nearly 40 percent of all state revenue came from liquor sales alone, and a typical Russian family spent up to 15 percent of its annual income on alcohol. In 1865, it was the famous scientist, Dmitri Mendeleyev (the inventor of the Periodic Tables) who first recommended from his own studies that the human body could best assimilate alcohol in the proportion of 40 percent spirit. It was during this time that a new reform removed the State's monopoly on vodka supplies. Over the next three decades (before the government again took control), Pierre Smirnoff took advantage of the drinking craze and was able to strike it rich with his enterprising new brand of *Smirnoff* vodka. During World War II, Russian soldiers even received *narkomovskiye sto gram*—an allotted 100 grams (three-and-a-half ounces)—to drink up or use to fashion Molotov cocktails against the enemy. Distilling factories had opened everywhere by the 20th century; the most famous was the Moscow State Warehouse No. 1. Built in 1900 on the banks of the Yauza River over three artesian wells, the factory now produces the elite label of *Christal* vodka.

A typical Russian breakfast or *zavtrak*, consists of tea, coffee, eggs, *kasha* (hot cereal), cheese, cold meats or sausage and a plentiful supply of bread and butter. Most hotels now offer either a Russian or Continental-style breakfast. A Russian *obyed* (lunch) consists of soup, bread, salad and usually a choice of meat, chicken or fish with potatoes, a pickled vegetable and a sweet dessert of cakes or *morozhnoye* (ice cream). Over 170 tons of ice cream are consumed in Moscow and St Petersburg each day. Salads or vegetables include cucumbers, tomatoes, cabbage, beets, potatoes and onions. *Smetana* (sour cream) is a popular condiment—Russians like it on everything—some even drink a glass for breakfast. *Oozhiin* (dinner) is similar to lunch, except vodka, wine, champagne or cognac will usually be served.

Gone are the days when a tourist spent hours searching for something to eat, waited in long lines, or bribed a way into a State-run restaurant. The good news is that both Moscow and St Petersburg are teeming with restaurants, cafés, fast-food centers and food markets. The service has improved so much that it is practically unrecognizable from the old Soviet mediocrity and inefficiency. The not-so-good news is that Moscow, especially, has become one of the most expensive cities in the world. Russians joke that under socialism they had money and there was nothing to buy; but now with democracy, they have practically everything at their disposal, but no money to buy it with. First-class restaurants charge the same as they would in New York, Paris or Tokyo. In one private club, I watched as a large table, filled with Russian *biznissmeny*, charged up $5,000 in appetizers alone! To locate a place to dine check the listings in the Practical Information sections for each city. There are also plenty of restaurant guides available in the city, or just have a local recommend one of their favorite spots. Take a stroll and see what you can find; practically every corner now offers something edible, and there are also plenty of food markets that offer all sorts of groceries.

Hundreds of eating establishments operate throughout both cities—from typical old-style Russian fare to ethnic cuisines from Georgian, Chinese and Italian to fast-food and take-out, for any price and palate. (By the way, *bistro* originates from the Russian word *biistra*, meaning fast. During the 1815 Russian occupation of Paris, cossack soldiers were known to scream out '*biistra, biistra!*' to restaurant waiters; soon the bistro opened—a place where one could get served quickly.) Most establishments now accept rubles, foreign currency and credit cards. Tipping is 10–15 percent (check to make sure a service charge has not already been added to your bill). Most menus are printed in both Russian and English; if you cannot read it, the waiter can usually translate it for you. For more popular places, making a reservation is advisable.

DINING AND DRINKING

The first point to remember when dining out is that most Russians still consider eating out an expensive luxury and enjoy turning dinner into a leisurely, evening-long experience. Many restaurants provide entertainment, so do not expect a fast meal. (Russians can spend a few hours savoring appetizers—if your waiter is not prompt with bringing your entrée, this may only be for a cultural reason.) It is also customary for the waiter to take your entire order, from soup to dessert, at the beginning. Different parties are often seated together at the same table, an excellent way to meet locals and other visitors.

Most restaurants (in Cyrillic **Ресторан**, pronounced 'restoran') are open daily from 11am to 11pm, and close for a few hours in the mid-afternoon. Nightclubs and casinos can stay open all night and also be expensive. For fast foods other than pizza, burgers or hot dogs, be on the look out for specialty cafés, such as *shashliki* (shish kebabs), *blinnaya* (pancakes), *pelmennaya* (dumplings), *pirozhkovaya* (meat and vegetable pastries) and *morozhnoye* (ice cream and sweets). Try to drink only bottled water and beware of iced drinks, homemade fruit juices and *kompot*, fruit in sugared water, which are often made with the local water.

If invited to a Russian home, expect a large welcome. Russians love hospitality, which means preparing a large spread. If you can, take along a bottle of champagne or vodka. Remember, a Russian toast is followed by another toast and so on. This usually entails knocking back your entire shot of vodka each time! Since toasts can continue throughout the evening (and if you want to be able to stand up in the morning), you may want to consider diluting the vodka with juice or water, or just giving up—to the chagrin of your host. Some popular toasts are: *Za Mir I Druzhbu* (To Peace and Friendship), *Do Dnya* (Bottoms Up) and, the most popular, *Na Zdoroviye* (To Your Health).

ON THE MENU

(See page 564 for a useful selection of Russian food and drinks vocabulary.) The Russian menu is divided into four sections: *zakuski* (appetizers), *pervoye* (first course), *vtoroye* (second course) and *sladkoe* (dessert). The order is usually taken all together, from appetizer to dessert. *Zakuski* are Russian-style hors d'oeuvres that include fish, cold meats, salads and marinated vegetables.

Ikra is caviar: *krasnaya* (red from salmon) and *chornaya* (black from sturgeon). The sturgeon is one of the oldest fish species known, dating back over 30 million years. Its lifespan is also one of the longest. No sturgeon is worth catching until it is at least seven years old and *beluga* are not considered adult until after 20 years. The best caviar is *zernistaya*, the fresh unpressed variety. The largest roe comes from the *beluga*, a dark gray caviar appreciated for its large grain and fineness of skin, and the most expensive. Caviar from the *sevruga* is the smallest and has the most delicate taste.

Caviar is usually available at Russian restaurants and can be bought in city stores. It has long been considered a health food in Russia. Czar Nicholas II made his children eat the pressed *payushnaya* caviar every morning. Since they all hated the salty taste, their cook solved the problem by spreading it on black bread and adding banana slices. The caviar-banana sandwich became the breakfast rage for many aristocratic families. Russia is still the largest producer of caviar in the world, processing over 1,000 tons per year; 20 percent of the catch is exported.

Many varieties of Russian soup are served, more often at lunch than dinner. *Borsch* is the traditional red beet soup made with beef and served with a spoonful of sour cream. *Solyanka* is a tomato-based soup with chunks of fish or meat and topped with diced olives and lemon. *Shchi* is a tasty cabbage soup. A soup made from pickled vegetables is *rasolnik*. *Okroshka* is a cold soup made from a *kvas* (weak beer) base.

Russian meals consist of *mya'so* (meat), *kur'iitsa* (chicken) or *rii'ba* (fish). *Bifshtek* is a small fried steak with onions and potatoes. Beef stroganov is cooked in sour cream and served with fried potatoes. *Kutlyeta po Kiyevski* is Chicken Kiev, stuffed with melted butter; *Kutlyeta po Pajarski* is a chicken cutlet; *Tabak* is a slightly seasoned fried or grilled chicken. The fish served is usually *lososina* (salmon), *osetrina* (sturgeon), *shchuka* (pike) or *seld* (herring). Russians are not big vegetable eaters, but *kapusta* (cabbage), *kartoshka* (potatoes) and *gribii s smyetanoi* (mushrooms and sour cream) are always available. Georgian dishes include *khachapuri* (hot bread), *baklazhan* (eggplant), *chakhokhbili* (steamed dumplings) and *tolma* (meat and rice in vine leaves). Desserts include *vareniki* (sweet fruit dumplings topped with sugar), *tort* (cake), *ponchiki* (sugared donuts) and *morozhnoye* (ice cream).

Chai (tea) comes with every meal. It is always sweet; ask for *biz sak'hera*, for unsweetened tea. Many Russians stir in a spoonful of jam instead of sugar. Coffee is not served as often. Alcoholic drinks consist of *pivo* (beer), *kvas* (weak beer), *shampanskoye* (champagne), *vino* (wine) and vodka. Alcoholic drinks are ordered in grams; a small glass is 100 grams and a normal bottle consists of 750 grams or three quarters of a liter. The best wine comes from Georgia and the Crimea. There are both *krasnoye* (red) and *beloye* (white) wines. The champagne is generally sweet. The best brandy comes from Armenia—*Armyanski konyak*. *Nalivka* is a fruit liqueur. Vodka is by far the favorite drink and comes in a number of varieties other than Stolichnaya, Moskovskaya or Russkaya. These include *limonnaya* (lemon vodka), *persovka* (with hot peppers), *zubrovka* (infused with cinnamon, lemon and bison grass), *ryabinovka* (made from ash berries), *tminaya* (caraway flavor), *starka* (apple and pear-leaf), *Okhotnichaya* (Hunter's vodka flavored with port, ginger, pepper, cloves, coffee, juniper berries, star anise, orange and lemon peel, and roots of angelica—it was once customary for hunters to toast with it after returning from a kill), and *zveroboy* (animal killer!). One of the strongest and most expensive is *Zolotoye Koltso*, the Golden Ring.

If you see a Russian smile at you, while flicking the middle finger off his thumb into the side of his neck, your invitation to drink (and drink) has arrived. Normally Russians follow a shot of cold pure vodka (it is, of course, sacrilegious to dilute it with any other liquid) with a mouthful of *zakuska* or hors d'oeuvres, such as smoked salmon, caviar, herring, salami or even a slice of hearty Russian *khleb*, bread. Remember, Russians love to follow toast with toast—*dushá v dúshu*—heart to heart (so make sure you eat something while you drink!). They are quite capable of drinking *do beloi goryachki*—into 'a white fever of delirium' and *na brovyakh*—up to their eyebrows. Their equivalent of 'drinking one under the table' is *napeetsya do polozheniya riz*—literally, drinking till one is positioned very low beneath the icon frame. Never forget that Russians have a millennium of drinking in their blood. In 986, Prince Vladimir rejected Islam as the Russian State religion (he chose Byzantine Christianity) because it prohibited the drinking of alcohol. He reputedly said, 'For the people of *Rus*, drinking is joy; we cannot be without it!'

One note of caution when buying liquor, especially vodka, in Russia. These days, many imitations are being passed off on the market, such as homemade *samogon* poured into brand-name vodka bottles. (If it is *samogon*, you will immediately know the difference!) Do not buy vodka from small kiosks or off the street. Check to make sure the seal is secure and the label not suspiciously attached (horizontal glue lines usually mean factory-produced). Many Russians can tell genuine vodka just by the way bubbles move around in the bottle. Recently the government ruled that bar codes needed to be stamped on all labels, but these are already being faked.

Shopping

Since the fall of the Soviet Union the country has yet to be transformed into a shopper's paradise, but it has come an amazingly long way from the previous offering of half-empty shops and State-run *Beriozka* stores. The market economy, especially in Moscow, is booming, and stores are full of both Russian and Western goods. Pre-perestroika, a traveler had to bring along essential supplies, but today almost anything can be found, from peanut butter to prescription drugs. Not only are there department stores, galleries and boutiques, but the streets are also lined with small shopping kiosks with salespeople hawking everything from T-shirts and videos to condoms and cologne. Specialty shops for antiques, arts and crafts, and other souvenirs also exist for any budget and flea markets are especially fun for bargain hunters. Farmer's markets offer a wide selection of foods at cheaper than store prices.

Traditional and popular Russian souvenirs include the *matryoshka* (the painted set of nested dolls), *khokkhloma* (lacquerware), *dymkovo* (earthenware), *gzhel* (china ornaments), *platki* (shawls), *shapki* (fur hats), wood carvings, jewelry made from amber or malachite, linen, samovars, balalaikas, art books and *znachki* (small pins). Painted lacquer boxes vary in style and price according to which Golden Ring town they were made in. The craftsmen of Palekh, for example, use tempera paint to illustrate elongated figures distinguished by the colors red, black and gold. An authentic box takes up to three months to complete, with the smallest details painted using brushes made from squirrel or mink hair. Many fakes are pasted with colored scenes which are not painted—check to make sure you have an original before buying.

LOCAL STORES

Some of the store designations are: *univermag* (large department store), *kommis-sioniye* (commission or second-hand store), *co-op* (cooperative), *rinok* (farmer's market) and *kiosks*. The opening hours of most local stores vary widely, but they usually have a one-hour afternoon break sometime between 1pm and 3pm, and are shut during holidays. Many of the larger department stores and food stores are also open on Sundays. Expect to pay in rubles for your purchases (make sure you carry some smaller notes—changing large bills can be a hassle), though some also accept credit cards.

SHOPPING TIPS

If you see something you would really like, buy it! Otherwise, the item will proba-bly be gone by the time you return for it. Remember to take along an empty bag—in places such as farmer's markets, you are expected to provide your own. (Otherwise you will be emptying the strawberries into your own pocket!) Some local stores still use the three-line purchasing system (along with the abacus). Firstly, locate the desired item and find out its price. Secondly, go to the *kassa* (cashier's booth) and pay. Thirdly, take the receipt back to the salesgirl, who then wraps and hands over your purchase. If you are buying a number of items, ask or gesture for the salesgirl to write the total amount down (if you are wrong—it is back to the *kassa* all over again!). At times you may still have to stand in a long line or force your way to the counter. If you have any questions, do not be afraid to ask; many Russians know some English and are happy to help. It is illegal to take any item made pre-1947 out of the country. Customs officers are especially on the look-out for antiques and icons, and will confiscate things at the airport. When you buy a more expensive painting or work of art, check to see if you need an exit permit from the Ministry of Culture. The gallery owner or artist can often help with this. Always save receipts to show at customs. Beware of the many fakes, especially icons and lacquer boxes. For more information on shoping and markets, see the listings in the Practical Information sections of each city.

Russian Language

HISTORY

In the late 9th century, two Greek brothers Methodius and Cyril (both renowned scholars from Macedonia) converted vernacular Slavic into a written language so that teachings of Byzantine Orthodoxy could be translated for the Slavs. Many letters were derived from the Greek—the Slavic alphabet was called Cyrillic, after

Cyril. When Prince Vladimir brought Christian Orthodoxy into Kievan Rus in the 10th century, Slavonic became the language of the Church. Church Slavonic, written in the Cyrillic alphabet, remained the literary and liturgical language of Russia for over seven centuries.

In 1710, Peter the Great simplified Church Cyrillic into the 'civil alphabet' (*grazhdansky shrift*), a written form used in secular books. The two types of writing, the older script of the Church and Peter's revised version, were both employed in Russia up to the time of Lomonosov and the poet Pushkin, who were largely responsible for combining the two into a national language for the Russian people. The alphabet that is used today was further simplified after the October Revolution.

LETTERS AND WORDS

Since Russian is not a Romance language, it is more difficult to pick up words compared to French or Spanish. Before leaving for your trip, try to spend some time learning some of the Cyrillic alphabet, in which there are 33 letters compared to the English 26. Most Russian sounds are similar to English, but are just expressed with a different character symbol. For example, a Russian C is pronounced 's', and W is a 'sh' sound. Thus Masha is spelled Mawa and Sasha spelled Cawa. Once you start to recognize letters of the Russian alphabet, it is easy to sound out familiar words posted on the street, such as МЕТРО (Metro), Кафе (café) and Ресторан (restaurant). Besides, it is fun to walk down the street and decipher many of the signs and shop names, and you will feel much more at ease in the new environment.

Once you can recognize Cyrillic letters, work on Russian vocabulary and phrases. As with learning any new language, first try memorizing a few common words, such as 'hello', 'goodbye' and 'thank you', and to count from one to ten. Granted, even though Russian is not an easy language to learn (there are seven cases of conjugation compared with four in English), you will discover that its native speakers appreciate any effort made in using their language and are delighted to help out. Even a few gestures and simple Russian expressions can go a long way and bring smiles to many faces! Purchase an English-Russian dictionary and phrasebook that can be shown to Russian-speaking people when you meet. Before your trip, you may also try one of the numerous Russian language courses for beginners and listen to audio cassettes to get a feel for the pronunciation.

See the Russian Language section on page 558 for a more comprehensive selection of useful everyday vocabulary.

RED SHIRTS AND BLACK BREAD

We plunged into plebeian Moscow, the world of red-shirted work-men and cheap frocked women; low vodka shops and bare, roomy traktirs, where the red-shirted workmen assemble each evening to gossip and swallow astonishing quantities of tea, inferior in quality and very, very weak.

Here was Moscow's social and material contrast to the big houses, with sleeping Dvroniks, and of the silent street of painted house fronts, curtained balconies and all the rest. Though day had not yet dawned for other sections of Moscow, it had long since dawned for the inhabitants of this. Employers of labor in Moscow know nothing of the vexed questions as to eight-hour laws, ten-hour laws, or even laws of twelve. Thousands of red shirts, issuing from the crowded hovels of this quarter, like rats from their hiding places, had scattered over the city long before our arrival on the scene; other thousands were still issuing forth, and stream-ing along the badly cobbled streets. Under their arms, or in tin pails, were loaves of black rye bread, their food for the day, which would be supplemented at meal times by a salted cucumber, or a slice of melon, from the nearest grocery.

Though Moscow can boast of its electric light as well as gas, it is yet a city of petroleum. Coal is dear, and, in the matter of electric lights and similar innovations from the wide-awake Western world, Moscow is, as ever, doggedly conservative. So repugnant, indeed, to this stronghold of ancient and honourable Muscovite sluggishness, is the necessity of keep-ing abreast with the spirit of modern improvement, that the houses are not yet even numbered. There are no numbers to the houses in Moscow; only the streets are officially known by name. To find anybody's address, you must repair to the street, and inquire of the policeman or drosky driver, who are the most likely persons to know, for the house belonging to Mr. So-and-so, or in which that gentleman lives. It seems odd that in a country where the authorities deem it necessary to know where to put their hand on any person at a moment's notice, the second city of the empire should be, in 1980, without numbers to its houses.

T Stevens, Traveling Through Russia on a Mustang

MOSCOW

MOSCOW

For centuries Moscow has been an inseparable part of the life of Russia. Moscow's history dates back to 1147, when Prince Yuri Dolgoruky established a small outpost on the banks of the Moskva River. The settlement grew into a large and prosperous town, which eventually became the capital of the principality of Moscovy. By the 15th century Moscow was Russia's political, cultural and trade center, and during the reign of Ivan the Great, it became the capital of the Russian Empire. Ivan summoned the greatest Russian and European architects to create a capital so wondrous that 'reality embodied fantasy on an unearthly scale', and soon the city was hailed as the 'New Constantinople'. In the next century Ivan the Terrible was crowned the first czar of all Russia in the magnificent Uspensky Sobor (Assumption Cathedral) inside the Kremlin. The words of an old Russian proverb suggest the power held by the Kremlin: 'There is only God and the center of government, the Kremlin.' People from all over the world flocked to witness the splendors in the capital of the largest empire on earth.

In 1712, after Peter the Great transferred the capital to St Petersburg, Moscow remained a symbol of national pride. Many eminent writers, scientists, artists and musicians, such as Pushkin, Tolstoy, Lomonosov, Repin and Tchaikovsky, lived and worked in Moscow, which never relinquished its political significance, artistic merit and nostalgic charm. Even when Napoleon invaded in 1812, he wrote: 'I had no real conception of the grandeur of the city. It possessed 50 palaces of equal beauty to the Palais d'Elysée furnished in French style with incredible luxuries.' After a terrible fire destroyed Moscow during Napoleon's hasty retreat, Tolstoy wrote that:

> It would be difficult to explain what caused the Russians, after the departure of the French in October 1812, to throng to the place that had been known as Moscow; there was left no government, no churches, shrines, riches or houses—yet, it was still the same Moscow it had been in August. All was destroyed, except something intangible, yet powerful and indestructible... Within a year the population of Moscow exceeded what it had been in 1812!

Moscow symbolized the soul of the empire, and Tolstoy later observed that Moscow remains eternal because 'Russians look at Moscow as if she is their own mother.' The name Moskva is said to derive from the Finnish word *maska ava*, meaning mother bear.

Moscow has also played an important role in the country's political movements: the revolutionary writers Herzen and Belinsky began their activities at Moscow

University; student organizations supported many revolutionary ideas, from Chernyshevsky's to Marx's; and Moscow workers backed the Bolsheviks during the October Revolution of 1917 and went on to capture the Kremlin. In 1918, after more than two centuries, Moscow once again became Russia's capital. But this time, the city would govern the world's first socialist state—the Soviet Union. Trotsky, Lenin's main supporter, wrote:

> *...finally all the opposition was overcome, the capital was transferred back to Moscow on March 12, 1918... Driving past Nicholas' palace on the wooden paving, I would occasionally glance over at the Emperor Bell and Emperor Cannon. All the barbarism of Moscow glared at me from the hole in the bell and the mouth of the cannon... The carillon in the Savior's Tower was now altered. Instead of playing 'God Save the Czar', the bells played the 'Internationale', slowly and deliberately, at every quarter hour.*

In 1993, Moscow Mayor Yuri Luzhkov readopted the historic figure of St George as the capital's official coat-of-arms; St George also features on the city's flag. You will notice the dark red shield emblem throughout the city: Georgy Pobedonosets—St George the Victorious, wearing a blue cloak and riding a silver horse, strikes a black dragon with his golden spear. (In 1380, Prince Dmitri Donskoi carried the icon of St George to victory over the invading Mongols, and in 1497, Ivan III had St George's image engraved on Moscow's great seal.) In 1997, Moscow celebrated its 850th anniversary and today is the largest city in the country with a population of over nine million.

It is not only the center of the new Commonwealth, but also the capital of the Russian Federative State. The Kremlin remains the seat of government. With the formation of the Commonwealth of Independent States and the collapse of communist Russia, Moscow is now the hub of an enterprising new democratic metropolis. (Even Alexander Solzhenitsyn, who had lived in exile for more than 20 years, returned to live in Moscow in 1994.) New businesses, co-ops and joint ventures are initiated daily. Democracy and capitalism, along with an ever more influential mafia, have already made a big impression; everybody is trying to find his or her own place in the new society. However, the opportunities and changes have created new extremes: from the unemployed to multimillionaires, the homeless to real-estate moguls, poor borrowers to rich bankers and destitute pensioners to enterprising youth.

Whether the visitor has a few days or several weeks, there is always plenty to do and see. Moscow has over 2,500 monuments, 50 theaters and concert halls, 4,500 libraries, 125 cinemas and 70 museums, visited annually by over 20 million people from 150 countries. Moscow is also rich in history, art and architecture. One of the most memorable experiences of your trip to Russia will be to stand in Red Square

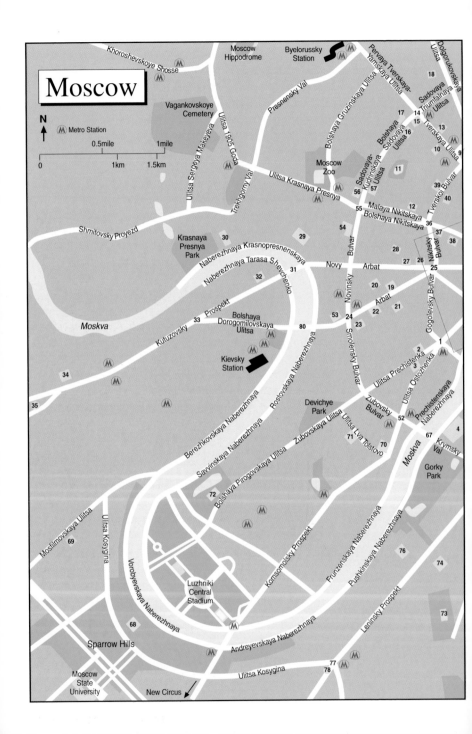

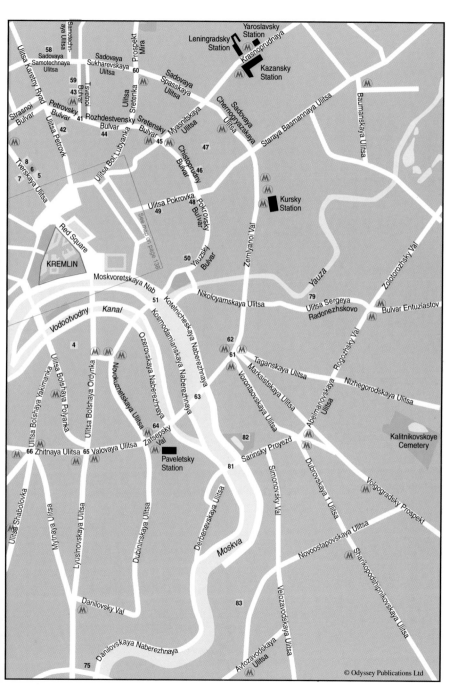

© Odyssey Publications Ltd

Key for Moscow Map:

1 Kropotkinskaya Ploshchad
2 Alexander Pushkin Museum
3 Leo Tolstoy Museum
4 Tretyakov Art Gallery
5 Aragvi Restaurant
6 Tverskaya Ploshchad
7 Moscow City Council
8 Yeliseyev's
9 Pushkin Square
10 Revolution Museum
11 Patriarch's Pond
12 Gorky House Museum
13 Minsk Hotel
14 Triumfalnaya Ploshchad
15 Tchaikovsky Concert Hall
16 Satire Theater
17 Pekin Hotel
18 Glinka Music Museum
19 Vakhtangov Theater
20 Skryabin Museum
21 Melnikov House
22 Pushkin House
23 Ministry of Foreign Affairs
24 Smolenskaya Ploshchad
25 Arbatskaya Ploshchad
26 Church of Simon Stylites
27 Dom Knigi
28 Lermontov Memorial House

29 White House
30 Mezhdunarodnaya Hotel & Sovincenter
31 Kalininsky Most
32 Ukraina Hotel
33 Hero City of Moscow Obelisk
34 Battle of Borodino Museum
35 Triumphal Arch
36 Nikitskaya Ploshchad
37 Mayakovsky Theater
38 Tchaikovsky Conservatory Grand Hall
39 Pushkin Drama Theater
40 Gorky Theater
41 Trubnaya Ploshchad
42 Petrovsky Monastery
43 Old Circus
44 Convent of the Nativity of the Virgin
45 Turgenevskaya Ploshchad
46 Eisenstein's House
47 Vasnetsov Memorial Apartment
48 Apraksin Mansion
49 Church of Saints Cosmas & Damian
50 Church of Saints Peter & Paul
51 Bolshoi Ustinsky Most
52 Krymskaya Ploshchad
53 Belgrad Hotel
54 US Embassy
55 Kudrinskaya Ploshchad
56 Planetarium

57 Chekhov House Museum
58 Obraztzov Puppet Theater
59 Tsentralny Rinok
60 Sukharevskaya Ploshchad
61 Taganskaya Ploshchad
62 Taganka Theater
63 Bolshoi Krasnokholmsky Most
64 Bakhrushin Theater Museum
65 Serpukhovskaya Ploshchad
66 Kaluzhskaya Ploshchad
67 Krymsky Most
68 Trinity Church
69 Mosfilm Studios
70 Church of St Nicholas at Khamovniki
71 Leo Tolstoy Country Estate Museum
72 Novodevichy Convent & Cemetery
73 Donskoi Monastery
74 Church of the Deposition of the Robe
75 Danilovsky Monastery
76 Academy of Sciences
77 Gagarinskaya Ploshchad
78 Yuri Gagarin Monument
79 Spaso-Andronikov Monastery
80 Borodinsky Most
81 Novospassky Most
82 Novospassky Monastery
83 Simonov Monastery

and look out on the golden magnificence of the cathedrals and towers of the Kremlin and St Basil's Cathedral.

Other attractions include the Novodevichy Convent, which dates from 1514, and the Andronikov Monastery, which houses the Andrei Rublyov Museum of Old Russian Art, including the famed iconist's masterpieces. Moscow's galleries and museums, such as the Tretyakov Gallery and Pushkin Museum of Fine Art contain collections of Russian and foreign masters. There are also the fascinating side streets to explore, little changed since the time of Ivan the Terrible. The nighttime reflections of the Kremlin's ancient clock tower and golden onion domes on the Moskva River bring to mind the lyrics of one of Russia's most popular songs: 'Lazily the river like a silvery stream, ripples gently in the moonlight; and a song fades as in a dream, in the spell of this Moscow night.' Moscow has an eternal enchantment that can be felt in the early light of dawn, in the deepening twilight, on a warm summer's day or in the swirling snows of winter.

ARRIVAL

The route from the Sheremetyevo II International Airport into the city center winds along the Leningradsky Highway (Leningradskoye Shosse), linking Moscow with St Petersburg. About 23 kilometers (14 miles) from the airport are large antitank obstacles, **The Memorial to the Heroes** who defended the city against the Nazi invasion in 1941; notice how close the Germans came to entering the city. The highway becomes Leningradsky Prospekt at a place that used to mark the outer border of the city. Here the street was lined with summer cottages. **The Church of All Saints** (1683) stands at the beginning of the prospekt at number 73A. Other sights along the route are Peter the Great's Moorish-Gothic-style **Petrovsky Palace**, built in 1775, and the 60,000-seat **Dynamo Sports Complex**. At number 33 is the **Palace of Newly-weds**, where marriage ceremonies are performed. As you approach the center of Moscow, the Byelorussky Railway Station is on your right. Trains run from here to destinations in Western and Eastern Europe. This station marks the beginning of one of Moscow's main thoroughfares, Tverskaya Ulitsa (Street). A road map of Moscow is made up of a series of rings. The Kremlin and Red Square lie at the center. Five concentric rings circle Red Square, each marking an old boundary of the city, showing its age like a cross-section of a tree.

Centuries ago each ring was fortified by stone, wooden or earthen ramparts, which could only be entered through a special gate. The area around the Kremlin, once known as Kitai-Gorod, formed the original border of the city in the 15th and 16th centuries. Many of the streets and squares in this area carry their original names: Petrovskaya Vorota (Peter's Gate), Kitaisky Proyezd (Kitai Passage), Ulitsa Varvarka (St Barbara Street) and Valovaya Ulitsa (Rampart Street).

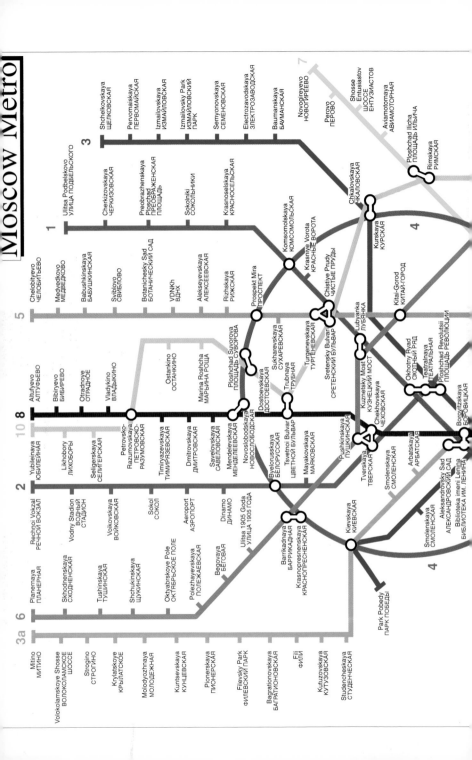

Moscow Metro

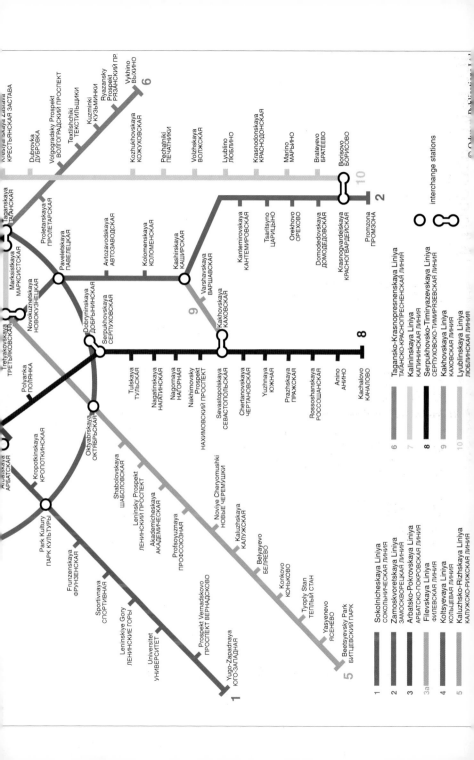

The second ring is known as Bulvarnoye Koltso (Boulevard Ring). The city's suburbs were placed beyond this ring in the 17th century. The Sadovoye Koltso (Garden Ring) is the third ring that runs for 16 kilometers (ten miles) around the city. This is also connected by the Koltso Metro line that stops at various points around the ring. The fourth ring, which stretches for 40 kilometers (25 miles) around the city, was known as the Kamer-Kollezhsky Rampart; it served as a customs boundary in the 18th and 19th centuries. The fifth ring is the Moscow Circular Road, marking the present boundary of Moscow. The area past this ring is known as the Green Belt, a protected forested area where many Muscovites have country and summer houses, known as dacha.

METRO

One of the quickest and easiest ways of getting around Moscow is by Metro. It is also the most popular method of transportation—over ten million people use the Metro daily. Construction began in 1931 under Stalin. Many Soviet and foreign architects and engineers spent four years building the deep stations, which served as bomb shelters during World War II.

The first line was opened on May 15, 1935. Today, ten major lines and nearly 150 stations connect all points of the city. The Metro, with almost 425 kilometers (264 miles) of track, operates daily from 5.30am to 1am; the trains are frequent, arriving every 60 to 90 seconds during rush hour.

Many of the older stations are beautifully decorated with mosaics, marble, stained glass, statues and chandeliers, and are kept immaculate. Some of the more interesting ones are: Okhotny Ryad, Ploshchad Revolutsii, Teatralnaya, Kievskaya, Byelorusskaya, Novoslobodskaya, Mayakovskaya and Komsomolskaya; the latter two even won Grand Prix design awards at the New York International Expositions in 1938 and 1958, respectively. The Moscow **Metro Museum** is at 36 Khamovnichesky Val; near Sportivnaya Metro station. (Open 9am–4pm; Mondays 11am–6pm; closed Saturdays and Sundays.) Tours of the Metro can also be booked through local travel agencies.

The Metro is easy to use by looking at a map. All the color-coded lines branch out from a central point, and are intersected by the brown Koltso (Circle) line. Entrances above ground are marked by a large M. Take the sometimes long and fast escalators down to the station. Maps are located before the turnstiles. From 1935 to 1991, the Metro cost only five kopeks; now the price keeps pace with inflation. You must purchase a plastic token (*zheton*), using only Russian currency, from the ticket booth, *kassa* (касса), inside. (In some stations there are also automatic machines that take ruble notes.) Ten-day or monthly passes can also be purchased at the cashier window; usually on sale the last week of the month. Place the token in the turnstile and wait for the green light; pass through quickly—the heavy stall can close suddenly! If you have a pass, show it to the inspector who stands at the end of the turnstiles. However far you travel while underground you only pay one flat fee.

Since station names are written only in Russian, ask somebody to write down the name of your destination or you can use the Metro map in this book (pages 90–1) to compare the Cyrillic. If you have trouble finding your way, show it to the attendant, who usually stands at the entrance, or ask: people are very helpful to strangers and many understand some English. The trains can be crowded and commuters push to get to where they are going. Stand near a door as your stop approaches. Maps of the route (in Russian) are also posted inside each train car. Changing lines at major stations can be confusing. Look for the word **Переход** (*Perekhod*—Transfer) followed by a list of stations written in Cyrillic. Try to locate your destination and proceed in that direction to a different train line. If exiting the station locate the sign **ВЫХОД В ГОРОД** (*Vwykhod v Gorod*—Exit to Town) and take an escalator up to street level.

Even since the fall of Communism, Muscovites still display a proprietary pride in their Metro; it is clean and graffiti-free, with reserved seats at the front of each carriage for the elderly and disabled. Passages to underground stations, once dark and empty, are now teeming with stores, cafés, money changing kiosks, hawkers, beggars and musicians.

Red Square (Krasnaya Ploshchad)

Most visitors begin their acquaintance with Moscow in Krasnaya Ploshchad, Red Square, the heart of the city. It was first mentioned in 15th-century chronicles as the Veliky Torg, the Great Marketplace and main trading center of the town. From the time of Ivan the Great the square was used as a huge gathering place for public events, markets, fairs and festivals. Many religious processions came through the square led by the czar and patriarch of the Orthodox Church. It was also the scene of political demonstrations and revolts, and the site of public executions. The square received its present name in the 17th century from the old Russian word *krasny*, meaning both red and beautiful. From the Middle Ages it was a popular open-air market and it remained so until GUM, the shopping arcade, was completed in 1893 and the traders moved under cover.

This magnificent square encompasses an area of over 70,000 square meters (almost 84,000 square yards) and is bounded by the Kremlin walls, St Basil's Cathedral, the Lenin Mausoleum, the Historical Museum and the GUM Department Store.

Today national celebrations are held here, especially on May Day when it is filled with huge parades and festivities. The closest Metro stop is Okhotny Ryad.

ST BASIL'S CATHEDRAL

Red Square's most famous and eye-catching structure is St Basil's Cathedral. This extraordinary creation was erected by Ivan IV (the Terrible) from 1555 to 1561, to commemorate the annexation to Russia of the Mongol states of Kazan and Astrakhan. Since this occurred on the festival of the Intercession of the Virgin, Ivan named it the Cathedral of the Intercession. The names of the architects were unknown until 1896, when old manuscripts mentioning its construction were found. According to legend, Ivan the Terrible had the two architects, Posnik and Barma, blinded so they could never again create such a beautiful church. However records from 1588, a quarter of a century after the cathedral's completion, indicate that Posnik and Barma built the chapel at the northeast corner of the cathedral, where the holy prophet Basil (Vasily) was buried. Canonized after his death, Basil the Blessed died the same year (1552) that many of the Mongol Khannates were captured. Basil had opposed the cruelties of Ivan the Terrible, and since most of the population also despised the czar, the cathedral took on the name of St Basil's after Ivan's death.

The cathedral is built of brick in traditional Russian style with colorful, asymmetrical, tent-shaped, helmet and onion domes situated over nine chapels, each dedicated to a saint on whose feast day the Russian army won a victory. The interior is filled with 16th- and 17th-century icons and frescoes, and the gallery contains bright wall and ceiling paintings of red, turquoise and yellow flower patterns. Locals often refer to the cathedral as the 'stone flower in Red Square'. The French stabled their horses here in 1812 and Napoleon wanted to blow it up. Luckily, his order was never carried out.

The interior, now open to the public, has been undergoing a very slow restoration. (The centuries have also taken their toll on the outside of the structure; city and religious officials are trying to raise funds to give the cathedral a much needed facelift.) Inside is a branch of the Historical Museum that traces the history of the cathedral and Ivan IV's campaigns. Under the bell tower (added in the 17th century) is an exhibition room where old sketches and plans trace the architectural history of St Basil's.

The museum is open daily from 10am–4.30pm, except Tuesdays and the first Monday of each month. In 1991, the cathedral was given back to the Russian Orthodox Church to celebrate Russian New Year and Easter services; Yeltsin attended the first Easter service.

In front of the cathedral stands the bronze **Monument to Minin and Pozharsky**, the first patriotic monument in Moscow built from public funding. It originally stood in the middle of the square. Sculpted by Ivan Martos in 1818, the monument depicts Kozma Minin and Prince Dmitri Pozharsky, whose leadership drove the

Named after the Holy Fool, Basil the Blessed, St Basil's Cathedral was built by Ivan the Terrible in 1555. The bronze monument in front is dedicated to Minin and Pozharsky whose leadership united armies to drive Polish invaders out of Moscow during the Time of Troubles in 1612.

Polish invaders out of Moscow in 1612. The pedestal inscription reads 'To Citizen Minin and Prince Pozharsky from a grateful Russia 1818.'

Near the monument is **Lobnoye Mesto**, the Place of Skulls. A platform of white stone stood here for more than four centuries, on which public executions were carried out. Church clergymen blessed the crowds and the czar's orders and edicts were also announced from here.

THE LENIN MAUSOLEUM

By the Kremlin wall on the southwest side of Red Square stands the Lenin Mausoleum. Inside, in a glass sarcophagus, lies Vladimir Ilyich Lenin, who died on January 21, 1924. Three days after his death, a wooden structure was erected on this spot. Four months later, it was rebuilt and then replaced in 1930 by the granite, marble and black labradorite mausoleum, designed by Alexei Shchusev. 'Lenin' is inscribed in red porphyry. For more than 75 years Russians and foreigners have stood in the line that stretches from the end of Red Square to the mausoleum to view the once idolized revolutionary leader and 'Father of the Soviet Union'. Two guards man the entrance but there is no longer a changing of the guard. Photography is prohibited and cameras should be placed out of sight in a bag. Once inside, visitors are still not allowed to pause for long. The mausoleum is usually open 10am–1pm; closed Mondays, Fridays and Sundays.

Once in a while some die-hard Communists and Lenin loyalists will gather at the mausoleum to honor the former leader. But after the attempted coup of 1991, the lines to Lenin's mausoleum have diminished dramatically, and sometimes there is no line at all. In 1994, a German executive tried to purchase the body and take it on a world tour with a final resting place in a Cologne museum. Today there is still a movement within the country to remove Lenin's body from the mausoleum and rebury him elsewhere. Ironically though, with the new wave of capitalism, Lenin souvenirs are now more popular than ever, and Lenin's formaldehyde experts are offering their eternal Lenin Delux preservation techniques for a price of just over a quarter of a million dollars.

Marble reviewing stands on both sides of the mausoleum hold up to 10,000 spectators on national holidays. Atop the mausoleum is a tribune, where the heads of the former Soviet Government and Communist Party once gathered on May and Revolution days.

Behind the mausoleum, separated by a row of silver fir trees, are the remains of many of the country's most honored figures in politics, culture and science, whose ashes lie in urns within the Kremlin walls. They include Lenin's sister and his wife, Sergei Kirov, Maxim Gorky, A K Lunacharsky, the physicist Sergei Korolyov and the cosmonaut Yuri Gagarin. Foreigners include John Reed and William Hayword

(USA), Arthur McManus (England), Clara Zetkin and Fritz Heckert (Germany), and Sen Katayama (Japan). There are also the tombstones of previous leaders of the Communist Party: Sverdlov, Dzerzhinsky, Frunze, Kalinin, Voroshilov, Suslov, Brezhnev, Chernenko, Andropov and Stalin, who was once buried next to Lenin in the mausoleum. Nearby are the granite-framed common graves of 500 people who died during the October Revolution of 1917.

THE HISTORICAL MUSEUM

At the opposite end of the square from St Basil's is a red-brick building, decorated with numerous spires and *kokoshniki* gables. This houses the Historical Museum. It was constructed by Vladimir Sherwood between 1878 and 1883 on the site where Moscow University was founded in 1755 by the Russian scientist Mikhail Lomonosov. When it opened in 1883, the museum had over 300,000 objects and was supported by private donations. Today the government museum contains over four million items in 48 halls that house the country's largest archeological collection, along with manuscripts, books, coins, ornaments and works of art from the Stone Age to the present day. These include birch-bark letters, clothing of Ivan the Terrible, Peter the Great's sleigh, Napoleon's saber and the Decree on Peace written by Lenin. The museum is open daily from 10am–6pm; closed Tuesdays, but is often closed at other times for renovation.

GUM

Next to the Historical Museum, stretching across the entire northeastern side of Red Square, is the three-story State Universal Store, known as GUM. It is the largest shopping center in Russia, with a total length of 2.5 kilometers (1.5 miles), selling half a million items to almost a quarter of a million Russians and 100,000 foreigners every day. GUM's 100th anniversary was celebrated in 1993. The initials GUM stood for Gosudarstvenny Universalny Magazine, the Government Department Store, until 1990, when the Moscow city government turned it into a joint stock company owned mainly by the employees. The initials now stand for Glavny Universalny Magazine, the Main Department Store.

It was designed in 1893 by Alexander Pomerantsev to replace a market destroyed by one of Napoleon's fires in 1812, as his troops were attempting to occupy Moscow. When it was built it was known as the Upper Trading Stalls. It was a showcase for goods and one of the world's most modern commercial areas, built of steel and concrete with ornate glass roofing and even electrical and heating systems. Today the building has been thoroughly renovated, and over 100 shops, both Russian and foreign, along with numerous cafés, line the first and second floors. The grand ceremonial entrance on Red Square, closed since the Bolshevik

Revolution, was reopened in 1992. It is well worth visiting to view the interiors of preserved old Russian shops, ornate bridges, ornamental stucco designs and the large glass roof. It is open daily from 8am–8pm; closed Sundays.

Exiting GUM at the northwest corner (towards the History Museum) brings you to the Kazan Cathedral. The original church was built in 1625 by Prince Pozharsky (whose statue stands in front of St Basil's) in tribute to the Virgin of Kazan icon, whose power

The interior of GUM Department Store, Russia's largest.

was thought to lead Russia in victory over the invading Poles. Stalin had it destroyed in 1936. After the fall of the Soviet Union, private contributions led to the reconstruction of the cathedral. In 1990, a procession led by Boris Yeltsin, the Orthodox Patriarch Alexis II and the Moscow mayor left the Kremlin to lay the foundation stone. The structure was consecrated by the Orthodox Church in 1993. Religious services are conducted daily.

Exiting Red Square to the north takes you through the **Iberian Resurrection Gates**, reconstructed in the early 1990s; the original main entrance gateway and white towers were torn down by Stalin to create more room for mass parades and machinery to enter. On the other side of the arch stands the small **Gate Church of the Iberian Virgin**, also rebuilt. It was once customary for the czar to pray here before he entered the Kremlin.

THE ALEXANDROV GARDENS

The entrance to these charming gardens is opposite the Historical Museum at the Kremlin's wrought-iron Corner Arsenal Gate. On your way there take note of the **Statue of Marshal Georgy Zhukov**, a World War I hero, who gazes proudly from his horse onto Manezh Square. Russia celebrated the 100th anniversary of Zhukov's birth on December 1, 1996. The Alexandrov Gardens were laid out on the banks of the Neglinnaya River by Osip Bovet from 1819 to 1822 for Alexander I. The river was later diverted by a system of pipes to flow beneath the park. An eternal flame burns before the **Tomb of the Unknown Soldier**, who died for his country during World War II. It was unveiled on May 8, 1967, on the eve of Victory Day.

It is a tradition for newlyweds on their wedding day to lay flowers on the tombstone, on which is inscribed: 'Your name is unknown, your feat immortal. To the fallen 1941–45.' Along the alley in front of the tomb are blocks of red porphyry that hold earth from 'Hero Cities' designated after World War II, including Moscow and St Petersburg. Also in the gardens are a memorial to the War of 1812 and a granite obelisk with the names of the world's great revolutionaries and thinkers. The latter was originally erected in 1913 to commemorate the 300th anniversary of the Romanov dynasty. On Lenin's orders in 1918, the double-headed eagle was replaced by the obelisk.

The central alley of the Alexandrov Gardens leads to the Troitsky Bridge that approaches the entrance to the Kremlin.

The Kremlin

The earth, as we all know, begins at the Kremlin. It is the central point.

Mayakovsky

The Moscow Kremlin, an outstanding monument of Russian history, winds around a steep slope high above the Moskva River, enclosing an area of over 28 hectares (70 acres) next to Red Square. The Russian word *kreml* was once used to describe a fortified stronghold that encased a small town. A Russian town was usually built on a high embankment, surrounded by a river and moat, to protect against invasions. The word *kreml* may originate from the Greek *kremnos*, meaning steep escarpment. The medieval kremlin acted as a fortress around a town filled with palaces, churches, monasteries, wooden peasant houses and markets. The Moscow Kremlin was built between the Moskva River and Neglinnaya River (the latter now flows underground). The walls are about one kilometer (half a mile) long, up to 19 meters (62 feet) high and 6.5 meters (21 feet) thick, with 20 towers and gates. Over ten churches and palaces lie inside. The Kremlin is open 10am–7pm (in winter 10am–5pm); closed Thursdays. Ticket offices for the Kremlin can be found near the Kutafya Tower in the Alexandrov Gardens; they usually close around 4.30pm. (Tickets for the Armory Palace museum must be purchased separately, see page 124.) The closest Metro stations are Okhotny Ryad (for Red Square) and Borovitskaya and Aleksandrovsky Sad (for the Gardens and Kremlin museum entrances).

THE BROTHERHOOD GRAVE

*L*ate in the night we went through the empty streets and under the Iberian Gate to the great Red Square in front of the Kremlin. The church of Vasili Blazhenny loomed fantastic, its bright colored, convoluted and blazoned cupolas vague in the darkness. There was no sign of any damage.... Along one side of the square the dark towers and walls of the Kremlin stood up. On the high walls flickered redly the light of hidden flames; voices reached us across the immense place, and the sound of picks and shovels. We crossed over.

Mountains of dirt and rock piled high near the base of the wall. Climbing these we looked down into two massive pits, ten or fifteen feet deep and fifty yards long, where hundreds of soldiers and workers were digging in the light of huge fires.

A young soldier spoke to us in German. 'The Brotherhood Grave,' he explained. 'Tomorrow we shall bury here five hundred proletarians who died for the Revolution.'

He took us down into the pit. In frantic haste they swung the picks and shovels, and the earth-mountains grew. No one spoke. Overhead the night was thick with stars, and the ancient Imperial Kremlin wall towered up immeasurably.

'Here in this holy place,' said the student, 'holiest of all Russia, we shall bury our most holy. Here where are the tombs of the Tsars, our Tsar—the People—shall sleep...' His arm was in a sling from the bullet wound gained in the fighting. He looked at it. 'You foreigners look down on us Russians because for so long we tolerated a medieval monarchy,' he said. 'But we saw that the Tsar was not the only tyrant in the world; capitalism was worse, and in all the countries of the world capitalism was Emperor... Russian revolutionary tactics are best...'

As we left, the workers in the pit, exhausted and running with sweat in spite of the cold, began to climb wearily out. Across the Red Square a dark knot of men came hurrying. They swarmed into the pits, picked up the tools and began digging, digging, without a word.

So, all the long night volunteers of the People relieved each other, never halting in their driving speed, and the cold light of the dawn laid bare the great square, white with snow, and the yawning brown pits of the Brotherhood Grave, quite finished.

We rose before sunrise, and hurried through the dark streets to Skobeliev Square. In all the great city not a human being could be seen; but there was a faint sound of stirring, far and near, like a deep wind coming. In the pale half-light a little group of men and women were gathered before the Soviet headquarters, with a sheaf of gold-lettered red banners, and the dull red—like blood—of the coffins they carried. These were rude boxes, made of unplaned wood and daubed with crimson, borne high on the shoulders of rough men who marched with tears streaming down their faces, and followed by women who sobbed and screamed, or walked stiffly, with white, dead faces. Some of the coffins were open, the lid carried behind them; others were covered with gilded or silvered cloth, or had a soldier's hat nailed on the top. There were many wreaths of hideous artificial flowers.

All the long day the funeral procession passed, coming in by the Iberian Gate and leaving the square by way of the Nikolskaya, a river of red banners, bearing words of hope and brotherhood and stupendous prophecies, against a background of fifty thousand people—under the eyes of the world's workers and their descendants for ever...

John Reed, Ten Days That Shook the World, 1919

After graduating from Harvard University, Reed traveled to Russia to support the Bolshevik Revolution. He was such an ardent supporter of socialism that Lenin penned the introduction to his book.

The 40-ton Emperor Cannon is the largest cannon in the world. Designed in 1586 to protect the Savior's Gate on Red Square, it was never fired—probably because each cannon ball weighed one ton.

The 15th-century Assumption Cathedral in Moscow's Kremlin was modeled after the cathedral of the same name in the Golden Ring town of Vladimir. To its right stands the imposing Bell Tower of Ivan the Great, built in 1505 and once the tallest structure in Russia.

HISTORY

The Moscow Kremlin has a fascinating eight-century history, and is the oldest historical and architectural feature of Moscow. The first written account of Moscow comes to us from a chronicle of 1147, which describes Prince Yuri Dolgoruky of Suzdal receiving Grand Prince Svyatoslav on Borovitsky (now Kremlin) Hill. Nine years later, Dolgoruky ordered a fort built on this same hill, which later became his residence. In 1238, the invading Mongols burned the fortress to the ground. By 1326 the Kremlin had been surrounded with thick oak walls and Grand Prince Ivan I had built two stone churches in addition to the existing wooden ones. During this time the metropolitan of Kiev moved the seat of the Orthodox Church from Vladimir to Moscow. In 1367, Prince Dmitri Donskoi replaced the wooden walls with limestone ones to fortify them against cannon attack; Moscow was then referred to as Beli Gorod (White Town). The Mongols invaded again in 1382; they razed everything and killed half the population. Within 15 years the Kremlin walls were rebuilt and the iconists Theophanes the Greek and Andrei Rublyov painted the interior frescoes of the new Cathedral of the Annunciation.

Ivan III (1460–1505) and his son Vasily III were responsible for shaping the Kremlin into its present appearance. When the Mongols no longer posed a threat to the city, the leaders concentrated more on aesthetic than defensive designs. Ivan the Great commissioned well-known Russian and Italian architects to create a magnificent city to reflect the beauty of the 'Third Rome' and the power of the grand prince and metropolitan. The white stone of the Kremlin was replaced by red-brick walls and towers, and the Assumption and Annunciation cathedrals were rebuilt on a grander scale. During the reign of Ivan IV the architecture took on more fanciful elements and asymmetrical designs with colorful onion domes and tall pyramidal tent roofs, as embodied in St Basil's—a style now termed Old Russian. The Patriarch Nikon barred all tent roofs and ornamental decorations from churches when he took office in 1652, terming the external frills sacrilegious. By 1660 though, the reforms of Nikon had created such schisms in the Church that he was forced to step down. Immediately the old decorative details were again applied to architecture.

Catherine the Great drew up plans to redesign the Kremlin in the new neo-classical style, but they were never carried out. During the War of 1812, Napoleon quartered his troops inside the Kremlin for 35 days. Retreating, he tried to blow it up, but townspeople extinguished the burning fuses, though three towers were destroyed. In the mid-1800s the Kremlin Palace and Armory were built. In 1918, the Soviet Government moved the capital back to Moscow from St Petersburg and made the Kremlin its permanent seat. Lenin signed a decree to protect the works of art and historical monuments and ordered the buildings restored and turned into museums. The Kremlin remains the center of Russian government today.

VIEW FROM RED SQUARE

Ruby-red stars were mounted on the five tallest towers of the Kremlin in 1937, replacing the double-headed eagle. The towers of the Kremlin were named after the icons that used to hang above their gates. The most recognizable tower is the 67-meter-high (220-feet) **Spasskaya (Savior) Clock Tower**, which stands to the right of St Basil's. It used to serve as the official entrance of the czars, who had to cross a moat over an arched stone bridge to reach the gate. It is now the main entrance of government officials, who pull up in black limousines. The Savior Icon once hung above the Spasskaya Gate. Inscriptions in Latin and Old Russian name the Italian Solario as the tower's builder in 1491. In the middle of the 17th century, the Scottish architect Christopher Galloway mounted a clock on its face; this clock was replaced in 1918. Like Big Ben in London, the chimes of the Spasskaya Tower are broadcast over the radio to mark the hour.

The tower behind Lenin's Mausoleum is known as the **Senate Tower**; it stands in front of the Senate building. To the right of the mausoleum stands the **Nikolskaya Tower**, where the Icon of St Nicholas was kept. In 1492, Solario built a corner tower next to a courtyard used by Sobakin Boyars. The Sobakin Tower is now called the **Corner Arsenal Tower**, where munitions were stored.

ENTERING THE KREMLIN

The two main entrances to the Kremlin are through the Kutafya and Borovitskaya towers. Most group tours are taken through the latter gate on the west side, which is closest to the Kremlin Armory. If you are near the Alexandrov Gardens, go through the **Kutafya Tower** and across the Trinity Bridge (which runs through the middle of the gardens). The Kutafya watchtower, built in the early 16th century, was approached by a drawbridge that spanned a moat. The tower was connected by a stone bridge, under which the Neglinnaya River once ran, to the **Troitskaya (Trinity) Tower**. Built in 1495, it was named after the Trinity-Sergius Monastery in Sergiyev Posad. Clergy and military officers entered through the Trinity, the tallest tower at 80 meters (262 feet). There are current plans to erect a statue of Nicholas II near the Trinity Tower.

PALACE OF CONGRESSES

As you enter the Kremlin through the Kutafya and Trinity towers, the modern Palace of Congresses is on your right. Khrushchev approved the plans for this large steel, glass and marble structure. Built by Mikhail Posokhin, it was completed in 1961 for the 22nd Congress of the Communist Party. When no congresses or international meetings are in session, the palace is used for ballet and opera performances. Sunk 15 meters (49 feet) into the ground so as not to tower over the Kremlin, the Palace contains 800 rooms and the auditorium seats 6,000.

(above and top right) The Kremlin's gilded nine-domed Annunciation Cathedral was built in 1482 by Ivan the Great. Once the private church of the royal family, it is now open year-round for visitors.

(bottom right) Built in 1479, the Assumption Cathedral was formerly the coronation church of the czars. Guarding the czar's doors are frescoes of the archangels Michael and Gabriel, and above them stands a row of bishops. The virgin and child at the top symbolizes the virgin's assumption into heaven to which the cathedral is dedicated (also see picture on page 103).

THE ARSENAL

The yellow two-story building to the left of the entrance tower was once used as the Arsenal. Peter the Great ordered its construction in 1702 (completed in 1736), but later turned it into a Trophy Museum. Along the front of the arsenal are 875 cannons and other trophies captured from Napoleon's armies in 1812. Plaques on the wall list the names of men killed defending the arsenal during the Revolution and World War II.

SENATE BUILDING

As you walk through the square, the three-story triangular building of the former Council of Ministers is directly ahead. Catherine the Great had it built in the classical style by Matvei Kazakov in 1787. After Lenin moved the capital from Petrograd (St Petersburg) to Moscow in 1918, the Soviet Government and the Bolshevik Party took up residence in the building. It is now used by the Senate; its large green dome is topped by the national flag. The front wall plaque shows Lenin's portrait and the inscription: 'Lenin lived and worked in this building from March 1918 to May 1923.' The Central Committee of the Communist Party once met in **Sverdlov Hall**. The hall's 18 Corinthian columns are decorated with copies of bas-reliefs portraying czars and princes (the originals are in the Armory). Lenin's study and flat are in the east wing. Special objects stand on his desk, such as the Monkey Statue presented to him by Armand Hammer in 1921. The study leads to a small four-room apartment that Lenin shared with his wife and younger sister. Across from the Senate, near the Spasskaya Tower, is the **Presidium** and the **Kremlin Theater**, which was built between 1932 and 1934. The building has also served as a military school and the former residence of the president of the USSR. The theater seats 1,200. To make room for these buildings, Stalin gave permission to tear down the 14th-century Monastery of the Miracles and Ascension Convent, where female members of the royal family lived and were buried. After the convent was destroyed, the bodies were transferred to the Cathedral of the Archangel Michael. Today these buildings can only be visited with special permission.

PATRIARCH'S PALACE

Opposite the Senate is the four-story Patriarch's Palace and his private chapel, the **Church of the Twelve Apostles** (with the five silver domes), which now house the **Museum of 17th-Century Life and Applied Art** with over 1,000 exhibits. Patriarch Nikon commissioned the palace for himself in 1635. After Nikon banned elaborate decorations on church buildings, he had the architects Konstantinov and Okhlebinin design the structure in simple white Byzantine fashion. The palace was placed near the main cathedral and the Trinity Gate, where clergy formally entered the Kremlin. The vaulted **Krestovskaya Chamber**, the Hall of the Cross, built without a single support beam, was used as a formal reception hall. Every three years the chamber was used for making consecrated oil for the Russian churches. In 1721, Peter the Great gave the palace to the Church Council of the Holy Synod. The museum has an interesting collection of rare manuscripts, coins, jewelry, furniture, fabrics, embroidery and table games. Vestments worn by Patriarch Nikon and the 17th-century golden iconostasis from the Monastery of the Miracles (destroyed to build the Senate) are also on display. The books include an ABC primer written for the son of Peter the Great. Two of the halls are decorated to look like a 17th-century house. Some of the displays in the Church of the Twelve Apostles are wine coffers and ladles, on which Bacchus is carved. These objects belonged to the society of the Highest and Most Jolly and Drunken Council, founded by Peter the Great to make fun of (nonprogressive) Church rituals. The museum is closed on Thursdays.

EMPEROR CANNON

Next to the palace is the 40-ton Emperor Cannon. Its 890mm bore (35 inch caliber) makes it the largest cannon in the world. It was cast in 1586 by Andrei Shchokhov and never fired. A likeness of Fedor I is on the barrel. The decorative iron cannon balls (weighing one ton each) were cast in the 19th century.

Across from the cannon in the southeastern corner of the Kremlin lie the **Tainitsky (Secret) Gardens**. Winter fairs are held here for children during New Year celebrations. A statue of Lenin used to stand on the highest spot, known as **Kremlin Hill**, but was removed in 1997 (see picture on page 455). Nearby is the **Cosmos Oak**, which cosmonaut Yuri Gagarin planted on April 14, 1961. This vantage point affords a good view of the Kremlin and Spasskaya Tower. The **Tsarskaya (Czar's) Tower** stands to the right and is decorated with white-stone designs and a weather-vane. A wooden deck used to stand on top of the tower, from which Ivan the Terrible supposedly watched executions in Red Square. The tower directly behind Lenin is the **Nabatnaya (Alarm) Tower**; the bell that used to hang here is on display in the Armory Museum. Farther to the right is the **Konstantino-Yeleninskaya Tower**, which honors St Constantine and St Helen. In earlier days it was also referred to as the Torture Tower, since it housed a torture chamber. The corner tower is called **Moskvoretskaya**, built in 1487 by Marco Ruffo. It was known as Beklemischevskaya, named after Ivan Beklemisch, whose home stood next to it in the 16th century; his spirit is said to have haunted it. The Mongols broke through this tower to enter the Kremlin in the 17th century.

(above) The Terem Palace was built by Czar Mikhail Romanov to house the children and female relatives of noblewomen. Only the czar's wife, personal confessor and blind storytellers were allowed into the czar's private quarters and royal bedchamber on the top floor. (opposite) Tomb covering dating from 1630.

EMPEROR BELL

The largest bell in the world stands on a stone pedestal by the Secret Gardens. The bell is six meters (20 feet) high and weighs 210 tons. The surface bears portraits of czars and icons. It was designed in 1733 by Ivan Matorin and his son Mikhail, and took two years to cast. An 11.5-ton fragment broke off during the fire of 1737, when water was thrown on it. After the fire the bell was returned to its casting pit, where it lay for a century. The architect Montferrand raised the bell in 1836. It has never been rung.

The square between the Spasskaya Tower and the bell was known as Ivan's Square, along which government offices were located. Here criminals were flogged and officials read the czar's new decrees.

BELL TOWER

Behind the Emperor Bell stands the three-tiered Bell Tower of Ivan the Great. Built between 1505 and 1508, the tower contains 21 bells that hang in the arches of each section, the largest of which is the Uspensky (Assumption) Bell, weighing 70 tons; it traditionally rang three times to announce the death of a czar. The Old Slavonic inscription around the gilded dome notes that it was added to the belfry in 1600 by Boris Godunov. This was once the tallest structure (81 meters, 266 feet) in Moscow and was used as a belfry, church and watchtower. When the enemy was sighted, the bells signaled a warning. The upper tent-roof section, built in the 17th century, was rebuilt after Napoleon partially blew it up. A small exhibition hall is on the ground floor of the belfry showing articles from the Armory Museum.

CATHEDRAL OF THE ASSUMPTION

In front of the bell tower stands the Kremlin's main church, the Assumption Cathedral or Uspensky Sobor. It faces the center of Cathedral Square, the oldest square in Moscow, built in the early 14th century. In 1475, Ivan the Great chose the Italian architect Aristotile Fioravante to design the church. He modeled it on the Cathedral of the Assumption in Vladimir.

This church, also known as the Cathedral of the Dormition of the Virgin, was built on the site of a stone church by the same name, first constructed by Ivan I. For two centuries this national shrine stood as a model for all Russian church architecture. Within its walls czars and patriarchs were crowned. It also served as the burial place for Moscow metropolitans and patriarchs.

Combining Italian Renaissance and Byzantine traditions, the cathedral is built from white limestone and brick with *zakomara* rounded arches, narrow-windowed drums and five gilded onion domes. The ornamental doorways are covered with frescoes painted on sheet copper; the southern entrance is especially interesting, decorated with 20 biblical scenes in gold and black lacquer.

The spacious interior, lit by 12 chandeliers, is covered with exquisite frescoes and icons that date back to 1481. The artists Dionysius, Timofei, Yarets and Kon wove together the themes of heaven and the unity of Russia's principalities, symbolizing the 'Third Rome'. Some of these can still be seen over the altar screen. The northern and southern walls depict the life of the Blessed Virgin. In 1642, more than 100 masters spent a year repainting the church, following the designs of the older wall paintings. These 17th-century frescoes were restored after the Revolution. The elaborate iconostasis (altar screen) dates from 1652. Its upper rows were painted by monks from the Trinity-Sergius Monastery in Sergiyev Posad in the late 1600s. The silver frames were added in 1881. To the right of the royal gates are two 12th-century icons from Novgorod: St George and the Savior Enthroned. A 15th-century copy of the country's protectress, the Virgin of Vladimir, also lies to the left. The original (in the Tretyakov Gallery) was brought to Moscow from Vladimir in 1395 by Vasily I. The icons, Savior of the Fiery Eye, the Trinity, and the Dormition of the Virgin, were specially commissioned for the cathedral in the 14th and 15th centuries. Napoleon's armies used some of the icons as firewood and tried to carry off tons of gold and silver. Most of it was recovered—the central chandelier, Harvest, was cast from silver recaptured from the retreating troops.

The Metropolitan Peter (cofounder of the cathedral) and his successor are buried in the southern chapel. The 15th-century fresco *Forty Martyrs of Sebaste* separates the chapel from the main altar. Other metropolitans and patriarchs are buried along the northern and southern walls and in underground crypts. Metropolitan Iov is buried in a special mausoleum, above which hangs the icon of Metropolitan Peter, the first Moscow metropolitan. The gilded sarcophagus of Patriarch Hermogenes (1606–12) stands in the southwest corner covered by a small canopy. During the Polish invasion Hermogenes was imprisoned and starved to death. After Patriarch Adrian, Peter the Great abolished the position and established the Holy Synod. The patriarch seat remained vacant until 1917. In 1991, Patriarch Alexei was voted in by Church elections. Only after 1991 was the Russian Orthodox Church, headed by the patriarch, allowed to govern itself again.

Ivan the Terrible's carved wooden throne stands to the left of the southern entrance. Made in 1551, it is known as the Throne of the Monomakhs. It is elaborately decorated with carvings representing the transfer of imperial power from the Byzantine Emperor Monomakh to the Grand Prince Vladimir Monomakh (1113–25), who married the emperor's sister. The patriarch's throne can be found by the southeast pier; the clergy sat upon the elevated stone that is decorated with carved flowers. The *Last Judgment* is painted over the western portal. Traditionally the congregation exited through the church's western door. The final theme portrayed was the Last Judgment as a reminder to people to work on salvation in the outside world.

THE MAN IN THE WINDOW

The building stands behind the high red-brick wall known to the entire world. There are many windows in that building, but one was distinguished from all the others because it was lit twenty-four hours a day. Those who gathered in the evening on the broad square in front of the red-brick wall would crane their necks, strain their eyes to the point of tears, and say excitedly to one another: "Look, over there, the window's lit. He's not sleeping. He's working. He's thinking about us."

If someone came from the provinces to this city or had to stop over while in transit, he'd be informed that it was obligatory to visit that famous square and look and see whether that window was lit. Upon returning home, the fortunate provincial would deliver authoritative reports, both at closed meetings and at those open to the public, that yes, the window was lit, and judging by all appearances, he truly never slept and was continually thinking about them.

Naturally, even back then, there were certain people who abused the trust of their collectives. Instead of going to look at that window, they'd race around to all the stores, wherever there was anything for sale. But, upon their return, they, too, would report that the window was lit, and just try and tell them otherwise.

The window, of course, was lit. But the person who was said never to sleep was never at that window. A dummy made of gutta-percha, built by the finest craftsmen, stood in for him. That dummy had been so skillfully constructed that unless you actually touched it there was nothing to indicate that it wasn't alive. Its hand held a curved pipe of English manufacture, which had a special mechanism that puffed out tobacco smoke at pre-determined intervals. As far as the original himself was concerned, he only smoked his pipe when there were people around, and his moustache was of the paste-on variety. He lived in another room, in which there were not only no windows but not even any doors. That room could only be reached through a crawl-hole in his safe, which had doors both in the front and in the rear and which stood in the room that was officially his.

He loved this secret room where he could be himself and not smoke a pipe or wear that moustache; where he could live simply and modestly, in keeping with the room's furnishings—an iron bed, a striped mattress stuffed with straw, a washbasin containing warm water, and an old gramophone, together with a collection of records which he personally had marked—good, average, remarkable, trash.

There in that room he spent the finest hours of his life in peace and quiet; there, hidden from everyone, he would sometimes sleep with the old cleaning woman who crawled in every morning through the safe with her bucket and broom. He would call her over to him, she would set her broom in the corner in business-like fashion, give herself to him, and then return to her cleaning. In all the years, he had not exchanged a single word with her and was not even absolutely certain whether it was the same old woman or a different one every time.

One strange incident occurred. The old woman began rolling her eyes and moving her lips soundlessly.

"What's the matter with you?"

"I was just thinking," the old woman said with a serene smile. "My niece is coming to visit, my brother's daughter. I've got to fix some eats for her, but all I've got is three roubles. So it's either spend two roubles on millet and one on butter, or two on butter and one on millet."

This peasant sagacity touched him deeply. He wrote a note to the storehouse ordering that the old woman be issued as much miller and butter as she needed. The old woman, no fool, did not take the note to the storehouse but to the Museum of Revolution, where she sold it for enough money to buy herself a little house near Moscow and a cow; she quit her job, and rumor has it that to this day she's still bringing in milk to sell at Tishinsky market.

Vladimir Voinovich, A Circle of Friends

Vladimir Voinovich is Russia's greatest living satirist. His other works include Life and Extraordinary Adventures of Private Ivan Chonkin, Ivankiad and the comic masterpiece Moscow 2042.

In October 1989, for the first time in over 70 years, the Soviet Government under Gorbachev allowed a Russian Orthodox service to be conducted within the cathedral. This was a significant act of tolerance, since only three decades earlier Khrushchev had over 10,000 churches closed.

CHURCH OF THE DEPOSITION OF THE ROBE

Next to the Assumption Cathedral is the smaller single-domed Church of the Deposition of the Virgin's Robe, built by Pskov craftsmen from 1484 to 1485. It once served as the private chapel of the patriarch and was linked by a small bridge to his palace. It later became a court chapel in 1653. The iconostasis was executed by Nazari Istomin in 1627. The interior wall paintings are devoted to the Blessed Virgin. The northern gallery displays an exhibition of wooden handicrafts. It is closed on Thursdays.

TEREM PALACE

In the small courtyard next to the church are the Terem Palace and the **Golden Palace of the Czarina**, which served as the reception site for czarinas in the 16th century. The Terem Palace resembles a fairy-tale creation with its checkerboard roof and 11 golden turrets. It housed the children and female relatives of noblewomen, and was built for Czar Mikhail Romanov, whose private chambers on the fourth floor were later occupied by his son Alexei. Many State functions took place here and in the **Hall of the Cross**. The czar received petitions from the population in the Golden Throne Room. Only the czar's wife, personal confessor and blind story-tellers were allowed into the private chapel and Royal Bedchamber, which is whimsically decorated. All the chapels of the Terem were united under one roof in 1681, including the churches of the Resurrection, Crucifixion, Savior and St Catherine.

The adjoining Golden Palace of the Czarina at the eastern end was built in 1526 by Boris Godunov for his sister Irina, who was married to Czar Fedor I. This was her own private reception hall. When Fedor died, Irina refused the throne (the last son of Ivan the Terrible had died earlier in an epileptic attack); her brother Boris Godunov became the first elected czar. Admission to the Terem is by special permission only.

PALACE OF FACETS

Facing the bell tower and on the west side of the square, is the two-story Renaissance-style Palace of Facets, one of Moscow's oldest civic buildings, constructed by Ruffo and Solario between 1487 and 1491. It took its name from the elaborate stone facets decorating its exterior. State assemblies and receptions were held here—Ivan the Terrible celebrated his victory over Kazan in 1532 in this palace, and Peter the Great celebrated here after defeating the Swedes at Poltava in 1709. After Ivan III, all wives including the crowned czarinas were barred from attending State ceremonies and receptions in the Hall of Facets; a small look-out room was built above the western wall, from which the women could secretly watch the proceedings. The **Red Staircase**, which led from the Assumption Cathedral to the palace's southern wall, was reconstructed in 1994; it had been destroyed in the 1930s under Stalin. (Peter acquired his dislike of Moscow when the Streltsy (palace guards) revolted in 1682, and the future czar (then only aged ten) witnessed the murder of family members who were hurled off this staircase onto sharpened pikes below. In 1812, Napoleon also watched his attempted burning of Moscow from here.) Today the Hall is used for State occasions. Entrance to the Palace of Facets is by special permission only.

CATHEDRAL OF THE ANNUNCIATION

This white-stone cathedral, with its nine gilded domes, and jasper floors (a gift from a Persian Shah), stands next to the palace. It was built from 1485 to 1489 by Pskov craftsmen as the private chapel of the czars. After a fire in 1547, Ivan the Terrible rebuilt the cathedral with four additional chapels. Inside, frescoes that date back to 1508 were painted by Theodosius; many were restored in the 1960s. The iconostasis contains icons by Andrei Rublyov, Theophanes the Greek and Prokhor of Gorodets, painted in 1405. Portraits of princes, Greek philosophers and poets, such as Plato, Aristotle and Virgil, can be found on the pillars and in the galleries. It is closed on Thursdays.

CATHEDRAL OF THE ARCHANGEL MICHAEL

The third main cathedral of the Kremlin is the five-domed Cathedral of the Archangel Michael (1505–08), which served as the burial place of the czars; the Archangel Michael was considered the guardian of Moscow princes. It stands directly across from the Annunciation Cathedral. Ivan the Great commissioned the Italian architect Alevisio Novi to rebuild the church that stood here. Novi combined the styles of Old Russian and Italian Renaissance; notice the traits of a Venetian palazzo. The surviving frescos date from 1652 and depict aspects of Russian life. A large iconostasis (1680) is filled with 15th- to 17th-century icons, including the *Archangel Michael* by Rublyov. Nearly 50 sarcophagi line the walls of the cathedral, containing grand princes and czars and some of their sons. All czars and Moscovy princes were buried here up to the 18th century (except for Boris Godunov whose body lies in Sergiyev Posad). White tombstones give their names in Old Slavonic. The first grand prince to be buried here was Ivan I in 1341, who built the original church. After Peter the Great moved the capital to St Petersburg, the czars were buried in the Peter and Paul Fortress, except for Peter II, who died in Moscow. The cathedral is closed on Thursdays.

Behind the cathedral stands **Petrovskaya (Peter's) Tower**, named after the first Moscow metropolitan. The fourth unadorned tower from the corner is the **Tainitskaya (Secret) Tower**, which had an underground passage to the Moskva River. The next one over is the **Blagoveshchenskaya (Annunciation) Tower**, which contained the Annunciation Icon. The round corner tower is called the **Vodovzvodnaya, the Water-Drawing Tower** (1633), in which water was raised from the river to an aqueduct that led inside. This is Russia's first pressurized system; it was used for pumping water to the royal palaces and gardens.

GRAND KREMLIN PALACE

Built from 1838 to 1849, the Grand Palace, behind the Archangel Cathedral, was the Moscow residence of the imperial family. Nicholas I commissioned Konstantin Thon to erect it on the site of the former Grand Prince Palace. There are 700 rooms and five elaborate reception halls; two of these, along the southern wall overlooking the river, were combined to form the Meeting Hall of the Russian Federation. The long gold and white St George Hall has 18 columns decorated with statues of victory. The walls are lined with marble plaques bearing the names of heroes awarded the Order of St George (introduced by Catherine the Great) for service and courage. The six bronze chandeliers hold over 3,000 light bulbs.

This hall is now used for special State receptions and ceremonies; cosmonaut Yuri Gagarin received the Golden Star Hero Award here in 1961. The **Hall of St Catherine** served as the Empress' Throne Room. In October 1994, Britain's Queen Elizabeth II made her first visit to Russia (her grandfather called Nicholas II 'Cousin Nicky') where she met with Boris Yeltsin in the gold and cream splendor of this hall. The Hall of Vladimir connected the Palace of Facets, the Golden Palace of the Czarina and the Terem Palace. The ground floor rooms used to contain the imperial family's bedchambers. Entrance is by special permission only.

AMUSEMENT PALACE

The Poteshny (Amusement) Palace, situated along the west wall behind the Grand Palace, was acquired from a Boyar family in 1652 by Czar Alexis, who turned the building into a residence for his father-in-law. When he died, Alexis turned the palace into the court's first theater. Later, Stalin lived here with his wife and two children. (They had married in 1918 when Stalin was 39 and Nadezhda only 17.) When his wife Nadezhda committed suicide in November 1932 (disillusioned with her husband's ways), the children were moved to other quarters, and Stalin lived separately in another Kremlin apartment.

Two Persian war masks from the 16th century (above)
and a pair of decorative breastplates, on display in the Armory Palace.

ARMORY PALACE

The Oruzheinaya Palata (Armory Palace) is the oldest museum in the country which houses one of the greatest collections of its kind in the world. In 1485, Grand Prince Vasily III, son of Ivan the Great, constructed a special stone building on the edge of the Kremlin grounds to house the royal family's growing collection of valuables. It also contained the czar's workshops and a place to store armor and weapons. In the late 1600s Peter the Great converted it into a museum to house the art treasures of the Kremlin. The present building, designed in 1851 by Konstantin Thon, has nine exhibition halls that trace the history of the Kremlin and the Russian State. It also houses a magnificent collection of Western European decorative and applied art from the 12th to 19th centuries.

Hall I (Halls I–IV are on the first floor) exhibits armor and weaponry from the 13th to 18th centuries. The oldest item is the iron helmet of Yaroslavl the Wise, father of Alexander Nevsky. Hall II has displays of gold and silver from the 12th to 17th centuries, including jewelry, chalices (one belonging to Yuri Dolgoruky), bowls, watches and the Ryazan Treasure collection. Hall III contains gold and silver jewelry from the 18th to 20th centuries, including fabulous Fabergé eggs and jewelry. Hall IV has a collection of vestments, including a robe of the first Metropolitan Peter, Peter the Great, and a coronation robe of Catherine the Great. One robe presented to the metropolitan by Catherine contains over 150,000 semiprecious stones. A silk *sakkos* vestment was embroidered for Patriarch Nikon in 1654; it consists of so many pearls and precious stones that it weighs over 22 kilograms (50 pounds)!

Hall V (Halls V–IX are on the ground floor) exhibits many of the foreign gifts of silver and gold from the 13th to 19th centuries from England, France, Sweden, Holland and Poland. Hall VI is known as the Throne and Crown Room. The oldest throne, carved from ivory, belonged to Ivan the Terrible. A Persian Shah presented Boris Godunov with a throne encrusted with 2,000 precious stones in 1604, and the throne of Czar Alexei Romanov contains over 1,000 diamonds. The most interesting is the Double Throne used by Peter the Great and his half-brother Ivan, when they were proclaimed joint czars. Peter's older half-sister Sophia acted as regent and used to sit in a secret compartment in the throne behind Peter to advise him. The Crown of Monomakh, decorated with precious stones and sable, (first worn by Grand Prince Vladimir Monomakh in 1113) was used by all grand princes and czars until Peter the Great. The room also contains Catherine the Great's petite silver wedding dress, embroidered with imperial eagles (note the size difference between this and Catherine's later gowns). The coronation gown of Alexandra (worn in 1896), the last Romanov empress, is also on display. Halls VII and VIII contain saddles, bridles and sleigh covers. Hall IX is the Carriage Room, containing the world's largest collection of carriages dating back to Boris Godunov. The most elaborate is

FABERGÉ

In 1842, during the reign of Nicholas I, Gustav Fabergé founded the first Fabergé workshop in St Petersburg. His son Peter Carl later extended the French family business to the cities of Moscow, Kiev, Odessa and London. These workshops produced a wealth of exquisite jewelry, clocks, cut glass, and other decorative objects made from gold, silver and semiprecious stones.

For over a century Fabergé crafted unique art objects for the imperial court. Master craftsmen like Mikhail Perkhin, Erik Kollin, Henrik Wigström and Julius Rappoport had their own Fabergé workshops and sometimes spent years designing and crafting a single piece of art.

The fabulous Fabergé eggs were a favorite gift presented by the Romanov family and other members of the aristocracy. The first Fabergé Easter egg was commissioned in 1885 by Alexander III. When Carl Fabergé proposed creating an Easter gift for the Empress Maria Fedorovna, the czar ordered an egg containing a special surprise. On Easter morning, the empress broke open what appeared to be an ordinary egg, but inside a gold yolk contained a solid gold chicken with a replica of the imperial crown. The empress was so delighted by the egg that the czar ordered one to be delivered to the court each Easter. Alexander's son Nicholas II continued the Fabergé tradition and ordered two eggs each Easter, one each for his wife and mother.

On Easter morning 1895, Nicholas gave his mother a Fabergé egg decorated with diamonds, emeralds and a star sapphire. Hand painted miniatures depicting Danish scenes known to the dowager empress (the former Princess Dagmar of Denmark) were hidden inside what became known as the Danish Egg. In 1900, Fabergé presented the imperial family with an egg that contained a golden replica of the Trans-Siberian railroad; the train actually moved and could be wound

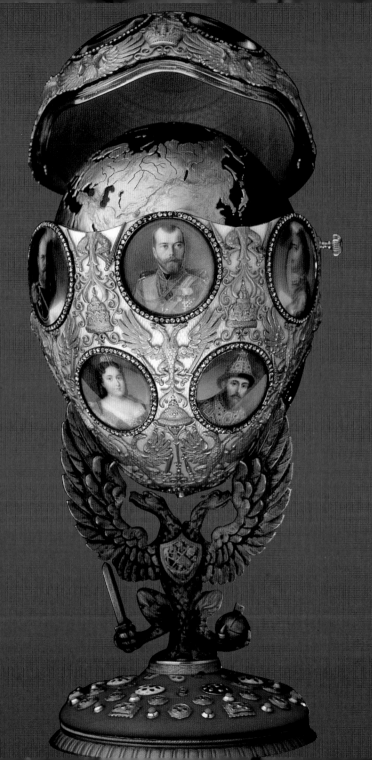

up with a tiny golden key. The 1908 Easter egg had a portrait of Nicholas II on its surface with a model of Alexander I's palace inside. In 1911, eggs were presented for the royals' 15th anniversary. Alexandra received an egg decorated with scenes of the coronation, and the dowager empress was presented with an orange tree egg complete with a golden feathered bird that sang at the press of a button. Other eggs contained flowers that bloomed and a tiny model boat.

When the Russian Exhibition was held in Moscow in 1882, Carl Fabergé received the Gold Medal (in 1887, a Moscow workshop was opened on Kuznetsky Most); later, in 1900, at the Exposition Universelle in Paris, he won the Grand Prix award along with the Legion of Honor. By 1915, there were more than 150,000 Fabergé pieces in circulation around the world; and by 1917 Fabergé had created 54 Imperial Eggs; today 47 survive. Forced to close the company after the Revolution, Carl Fabergé fled Russia and died in Switzerland in 1920. Today, one of the most extensive Fabergé collections in the world can be seen at the Armory Museum in the Moscow Kremlin. (Eleven Imperial Eggs are in the collection of *Forbes Magazine* in New York. The last egg to come onto the market sold for five and a half million US dollars in 1994.) In 1990, the Fabergé Arts Foundation began restoring the master's original workshops at 24 Bolshaya Morskaya in St Petersburg.

One can also pay a visit to the Grand Hotel Europe on Nevsky Prospekt where the Russian jeweler Andrei Ananov, considered Fabergé's contemporary heir, has a showroom with items available for purchase.

A jeweled enameled egg, a gift from Czar Nicholas II to his wife Alexandra in 1913 the coronation coach made for the Empress Elizabeth and most absurd is the miniature coach made in 1675 for young Peter the Great; it was pulled by ponies, and dwarves served as coachmen. The Diamond Fund Exhibit is a collection of the crown jewels and precious gems. These include the Orlov Diamond (189 carats) that Count Orlov bought for his mistress, Catherine the Great. Catherine the Great's coronation crown is covered with pearls and 4,936 diamonds. A new section of the Armory displays gifts to the former USSR from foreign countries.

The Armory is one of the most interesting museums in Moscow and should definitely be visited. Buying an entrance ticket to the Kremlin by the Kutafya Tower is not good for entrance to the Armory. Tickets are on sale either on the ground floor of the Ivan the Great Bell Tower or at the first entrance to the Armory. Only groups are allowed to enter during four separate one-and-a-half-hour daily tours (except Thursdays) at 10am, 12pm, 2pm and 4pm, conducted in English, German, French and Russian. (You can also prebook an excursion through a local travel agency; check at your hotel.) Arrive in advance, there is usually a line. Tickets to view the Diamond Fund (open 10am–5pm) are on sale near the second Armory entrance; sometimes it is only open with special permission.

Old Moscow

The area to the east of the Kremlin is known as **Kitai-Gorod**. *Kitai* is derived from either the Mongolian word for central or the Old Russian *kiti* meaning bundle of stakes. These protective palisades surrounded the area. (One small fragment remaining from the original 16th-century wall is near the northern entrance of the Rossiya Hotel.) *Gorod* is the Russian word for town. (In modern Russian, *Kitai* means China.) Foreign settlements were later established in this area. In the 14th century the central town was surrounded by a protective earthen rampart and served as the central *posad* (market and trade area), where merchants and townspeople lived. Beyond the rampart lay the forest. Later Ivan the Terrible constructed a larger fortified stone wall. The original area of Kitai-Gorod (which formed Moscow's second ring) stretched in the form of a horseshoe from the History Museum on Red Square, along the back of GUM Department Store, and east down to what is now the Rossiya Hotel and the banks of the Moskva River. On each side of GUM are the small streets of Nikolskaya and Ilyinka. The Rossiya Hotel (behind St Basil's) is bordered by Ulitsa Varvarka and Kitaigorodsky Proyezd.

On the opposite side of the square, the Iberian Gates (Iverskiye Vorota) served as the main entrance to Red Square. The Chapel of the Iberian Mother of God once stood atop the gates and contained the Virgin of Iver Icon, said to possess miraculous powers. The gates were also the access route from Kitai-Gorod (China Town) to the Beli Gorod (White Town). Before setting out on long journeys, Muscovites also stopped to pray here.

NIKOLSKAYA ULITSA (STREET)

This street begins at the northeastern corner of Red Square and runs along the side of GUM. After the Revolution until 1991, its name was 25th of October Street, commemorating the first day of the 1917 Revolution. In the 17th century the area was nicknamed the Street of Enlightenment; Moscow's first learning academy, printing yard and bookshops lined the passage. The street was originally named after the nearby Nikolsky Monastery.

The first corner building as you leave the square was the Governor's Office, where the writer Alexander Radishchev was held before his exile to Siberia (by Catherine the Great) in 1790. His book, *A Journey from St Petersburg to Moscow*, described the terrible conditions of serfdom. Behind the Kazan Cathedral stands the **Old Royal Mint** inside the small courtyard. An inscription on the gates shows it was built by Peter the Great in 1697. When he later moved it to St Petersburg, the vice-governor had his office here.

Down the street from the Royal Mint, at number 7, are several buildings that remain from the **Zaikonospassky Monastery** founded by Boris Godunov in the early 1600s. The name means 'Icon of our Savior'; the monastery used to make and sell icons. The red and white **Savior's Church** was built in 1661. The church and adjoining buildings housed the **Slavic-Greek-Latin Academy**, Moscow's first and largest academy for higher education, which operated from 1687 to 1814. Among the first students were the poet Kantemir, the architect Bazhenov and Mikhail Lomonosov (1711–65), who became a renowned poet, historian and educator. Known as the 'Father of Russian Science', Lomonosov established Moscow University under Empress Elizabeth in 1755. (See also St Petersburg pages 365 and 396.)

At number 15 was the first Printing Yard, now the History and Archives Institute. Ivan the Terrible brought the first printing press to Russia in 1553. Still hanging on the Gothic-style aquamarine and white building are the emblems of the old printing yard, a lion and unicorn, together with a sundial, mounted in 1814. The thick black gates lead to the colorfully tiled **Building of the Old Proofreader**, where Ivan Fedorov spent a year printing Russia's first book. Ivan the Terrible visited Fedorov daily until *The Acts of the Apostles* (now in the State Public Library) was completed on March 1, 1564. The first Russian newspaper, *Vedomosti*, was printed here in 1703. The present building was constructed in 1814 and was used as the printing center for the Holy Synod, the council established by Peter the Great that regulated church affairs.

At number 19 is the **Slavyansky Bazaar**, one of Moscow's oldest and most popular restaurants. When it opened in the 1870s, it became a popular meeting place for Moscow merchants who negotiated deals over the delicious *blini* pancakes, and a favorite hangout of Anton Chekhov's when he lived in Moscow. It was here on June 21, 1897, that the stage directors Konstantin Stanislavsky and Vladimir Nemirovich-Danchenko worked out the details for the formation of the Moscow Art Theater over an 18-hour lunch. The restaurant is still being restored after damage from a 1993 fire. If you have an interest in the Russian theater check out the **Stanislavsky House Museum** at number 6 Leontevsky Pereulok (Pushkinskaya Metro station). The dramatist lived here from 1922 to 1938. Open Wednesdays and Fridays 2pm–8pm; Thursdays and weekends 11am–5pm. Nemirovich-Danchenko lived nearby at 5 Glinishchevsky Pereulok. His house museum is open 11am–4pm; closed Mondays.

Opposite the Printing House is the former **Chizhov Coach Exchange**. The Chizhov family hired out horse-drawn carriages and carts as taxis. The Coach Exchange was popular year-round, when Moscow streets were either muddy or frozen. In winter Muscovites could hire a Chizhov troika, or sled (see excerpt from Nicholai Gogol's *Dead Souls* on page 173 for a description of a troika ride). Next door is the one-domed **Church of the Dormition**.

The small passage known as **Tretyakov Proyezd** links Nikolskaya Street with Okhotny Ryad. The wealthy merchant Sergei Tretyakov knocked this passage through the Kitai-Gorod wall in 1871 to gain quick access to the banks along Okhotny Ryad.

Halfway down Nikolskaya Street, take a right on Ilyinka Proyezd. Near the corner, on Bogoyavlensky Pereulok, stands the baroque red-brick 17th-century **Cathedral of Bogoyavlensky** (Epiphany), once part of a monastery established in the 13th century by Prince Daniil in order to protect inhabitants of the then unwalled city. The cathedral stands on the site of Moscow's first stone church, built by Ivan I. Many of the sculptures that were in the church are now on display in the Donskoi Monastery. The wealthy Boyar Golitsyn family had their burial vaults here until the mid-18th century; they were transferred to the Donskoi Monastery outside of the city when a cholera epidemic prohibited burial in the city center.

The pharmacy shop at number 21 is over a century old. The first pharmacy was set up in the Kremlin by Ivan the Terrible in 1581. Beginning in the 1600s, pharmacies sold medicinal herbs in Moscow. Many of the herbs were grown in the area of what is now the Alexandrov Gardens near the Kremlin.

In the small park stands the **Monument to Ivan Fedorov** (1510–83), the first Russian printer. The passage is still lined with small bookshops; a popular one is Knizhnaya Nakhodka at number 23.

The Church of St George on Pskov Hill was built in 1657 from donations given by the community of Pskov merchants who were living in Moscow. The golden Byzantine Orthodox crosses mounted on golden onion domes is a Russian design that dates back to the 15th century.

ULITSA ILYINKA (ILYINKA STREET)

Ilyinka Proyezd (Passage) leads into this street, which begins on Red Square and continues past the south side of GUM. It was once the main thoroughfare of Kitai-Gorod. In 1497, Ivan the Great gave a parcel of land on this street to 500 Novgorod merchant families to establish the Moscow-Novgorod Trade Exchange, at a time when Novgorod was still independent of Moscovy. The wealthy merchants erected **St Ilyia Church**, recognizable by its single dome and *zakomara* gabled arches. From 1935 to 1991 this street was named after the popular revolutionary figure Kuybyshev. The passage was once the busy thoroughfare of Moscow's bank and financial district. At number 6 the classical building of the **Moscow Stock Exchange** or Birzha (1838), with its large Ionic columns, once again bustles with commercial activity.

The wealthy merchant Pavel Riabushinsky commissioned Fedor Shekhtel to build the Riabushinsky Bank in 1904. Shekhtel also designed the nearby Moscow Merchants Building in 1909. Riabushinsky was a highly respected spokesman for the merchant class and chairman of the Moscow Stock Exchange.

As Ilyinka Passage continues across the street of the same name, it becomes Ribny Pereulok (Fish Lane), where many food stalls were once set up. From 1795 to 1805 the Italian architect Quarenghi built the Old Merchant Arcade, **Gostiny Dvor**, which occupied an entire block. This Corinthian-columned white structure was once filled with boutiques; it now mainly serves as an office building.

ULITSA VARVARKA (VARVARKA STREET)

Ribny Pereulok leads into Ulitsa Varvarka, which starts near St Basil's and continues past the Rossiya Hotel. Near the hotel are the remains of the 16th-century brick rampart walls that surrounded Kitai-Gorod; this wall was over 2.5 kilometers (one and a half miles) long and six meters (20 feet) high. One entered Kitai-Gorod through the Vladimirsky Gates; all that remains is a red gate built in 1871. After the Revolution until 1991 the street was known as Razin, named after Stenka Razin, a popular cossack rebel who was executed in Red Square in 1671.

The immense structure behind St Basil's is the **Rossiya Hotel**, completed in 1967 by the architect Chechulin. At the time of its opening the hotel was the largest in the world, with rooms for 6,000 people and a superb view of the Kremlin and the district on the other side of the Moskva River. Go up to the 12th-floor cafeteria where you can snack and take in the view. One of Moscow's largest *Beriozka* gift stores is located at the back of the hotel. It also has many cafés and restaurants, the large Central Concert Hall and the Zariadi Cinema. In Old Russian, *zariadi* means beyond the trading stalls. This area used to lie beyond the old marketplace on the outer fringes of Red Square.

The salmon and white **Church of St Varvara** (Barbara) stands at the beginning of the street, which is named after this saint. The 16th-century church was rebuilt in the 18th century by the architect Matvei Kazakov. It now houses a branch of the All Russia Society for the Protection of Monuments. This passage once stretched from the Kremlin, along the old trade route, to the towns of Vladimir and Kolomna. Prince Dmitri Donskoi used this route to return home after his victorious battle with the Mongols in the Battle of Kulikovo in 1380.

The small cube-shaped and five-domed **Church of St Maxim** stands nearby. Built in 1698 by Novgorod merchants, it held the remains of St Maxim, an ascetic prophet who died in 1433. It now houses branches of the Society for Environmental Protection and the Nobility League Art Salon, which sells souvenirs to do with the last royal family.

Between these two churches, at 4 Varvarka, is the **Old English Inn**, a white-washed house with tiny irregularly placed windows and a steep wooden roof. It originally belonged to a wealthy Russian merchant until, in 1556, Ivan the Terrible presented it to Sir Richard Chancellor, an English merchant who began trade relationships with Russia. Ivan even proposed marriage to Queen Elizabeth I, but she declined and instead offered Ivan asylum in England whenever he might need it. Later the inn was used by English merchants for their stores and living quarters, and English diplomats also stayed here. It has recently been restored and is open 10am–6pm, 11am–7pm Wednesdays and Fridays; closed Mondays.

Next to the Inn, at number 10, is the **House of Boyars Romanov**, now a branch of the State History Museum (also known as the Zaryade Museum) that has displays of life from 17th-century Boyardom. The rich Boyar Nikita Romanov had his home in the center of Kitai-Gorod. Nikita's sister, Anastasia, was married to Ivan the Terrible. Nikita's grandson Mikhail, who was born in the house, was later elected to the throne in 1613 and began the reign of the Romanov dynasty. The house was restored in the 19th century and is furnished to look like an early noble household. Open 10am–5pm, Wednesdays 11am–6pm; closed Tuesdays.

At the back of the Rossiya Hotel is the **Church of St George on Pskov Hill**. The colorful church, with red walls and a blue belfry (1818), was erected by Pskov merchants in 1657 (see picture on page 127). At number 8 is the **Znamensky Cathedral**, built in the 1680s, all that remains of the Nunnery of Our Lady of the Sign. It now houses a small concert hall (with 250 seats), a chapel (which holds services), and an icon workshop.

On the other side of the Rossiya Hotel, on Kitaigorodsky Proyezd by the Moskva River, is the **Church of the Conception of St Anne-in-the-Corner**. The church stood at the corner of the Kitai-Gorod wall and was named after the Virgin's mother, St Anne. The barren wife of Grand Prince Vasily III, Solomonia (whom he later divorced), often prayed here.

KITAI-GOROD SQUARE

Varvarka Street leads east into Kitai-Gorod Square (which has a Metro station of the same name). Kitai-Gorod (China Town) is where the foreign merchants used to live. Following the Bolshevik Revolution, the area was known as Nogin Square, after the revolutionary figure Viktor Nogin. In 1991 it reverted to its original name. The **Church of All Saints on Kulishki** stands here.

After Prince Dmitri Donskoi defeated the Mongols at Kulikovo in 1380, he erected a wooden church on the *kulishki*, marshy land. It was replaced by the stone church in the 16th century, which has been restored. To the left of the church are the gray buildings of the **Delovoy Dvor**, the business chambers. Built in 1913, they were used for the business operations of the city.

Near the square are the **Ilyinsky Gardens**, with a monument to the Russian Grenadiers who died in the Battle of Plevna against Turkey in 1877. Along the small side street called Staraya (Old) Ploshchad, are buildings that were once used by the Central Committee of the Communist Party. A few minutes' walk away at number 3 Nikitnikov Pereulok is a 'jewel of merchant architecture', the Byzantine five-domed **Church of the Holy Trinity in Nikitniki**. In 1620, Mikhail Romanov hired a wealthy merchant from Yaroslavl, Grigory Nikitnikov, to work in the financial administration. (He also served as financial advisor to the first two Romanov czars.)

In Moscow's Church of the Holy Trinity women donate their time to polish the golden iconostasis in preparation for an Orthodox service.

Nikitnikov named the street after himself and later built this church (1635–53) on the site of the wooden Church of St Nikita (his family saint), which burned down. The oldest icon is St Nikita, which Nikitnikov supposedly rescued from the burning church. The icon of the Trinity can be found on the iconostasis, carved in 1640. There are many unique frescoes and wood carvings on the walls.

The burial chapel of the Nikitnikovs lies to the right of the altar. The church now functions as the **Museum of 17th-Century Architecture and Painting**. Open 10am–5pm, 12pm–7pm Wednesdays and Thursdays; closed Tuesdays and the first Monday of the month.

Nearby, Staraya Ploshchad becomes Solyanka Ulitsa (Street). *Sol* means salt, and the old saltyards were along this street in the 17th century. At this time the area was considered the countryside of Moscow; Ivan the Great had a summer palace near the Convent of St John. Farther up the street is the **Church of St Vladimir-in-the-Old Gardens**. Solyanka intersects with Arkhipova Ulitsa, named after the artist who lived here in 1900. Many middle-class artisans lived in this part of the city. The **Moscow Choral Synagogue** is at 8 Bolshaya Spasoglinishchevsky Pereulok; services on Fridays at sunset and Saturdays at 9am.

The Old Marx Prospekt

In 1991, Prospekt Marxa, the city's busiest avenue, was officially divided into three different streets. From Lubyanka Square to Teatralnaya Square, it is Teatralny Proyezd (past the Bolshoi Theater). From Teatralnaya Square to Pushkinskaya Street it is Okhotny Ryad (which leads from the Bolshoi Theater to Tverskaya Street and the National Hotel). The rest of the thoroughfare from the Kremlin to Herzen Street is now called Bolshaya Nikitskaya.

LUBYANSKAYA PLOSHCHAD (LUBYANKA SQUARE)

Teatralny Proyezd (Theater Passage) begins at this square, where a bronze statue of Felix Dzerzhinsky (1877–1926), a prominent revolutionary leader and founder of the Cheka (the All Russia Extraordinary Commission for Combating Counter-Revolution, Sabotage and Speculation), once stood in the center (earlier called Dzerzhinsky Square). The statue was pulled down by crowds on the night of August 22, 1991, after the attempted coup. (It now stands in the Park of the Fallen Idols on the grounds of the State Art Gallery near Gorky Park.) Various graffiti, coup memorabilia and an occasional Orthodox cross decorate the pedestal, which now commemorates all those killed by the KGB. For a century a charming fountain of cherubs, designed by Giovanni Vitali, had stood in the center of the square; in 1932, it was moved to the Academy of Sciences on Leninsky Prospekt. The Dzerzhinsky Monument was erected in its place 26 years later. There is a current movement to bring back the fountain to its original place. In 1991, the square was given back its historical name of Lubyanka. In the 15th century, new settlers from Novgorod named the area Lubyanitsa, after a place in their native city. Also in the square is the great stone from the northern Solovetsky Islands laid in October 1990 by the Memorial Society. It bears an inscription commemorating the victims of the Soviet period.

The Lubyanka Metro station (formerly Dzerzhinskaya) exits on to the square. Original Kitai-Gorod walls were demolished to provide room for the Metro station, designed by Nikolai Ladovsky and opened in 1937. The large department store on one corner is **Detsky Mir** (Children's World), built in 1957, the largest children's store in Russia. More than half a million shoppers visit daily. Behind it is the **Savoy Hotel**. Dzerzhinsky Street has been renamed Ulitsa Bolshaya Lubyanka.

Standing on the northeast side of Lubyanka Square is the infamous former **KGB Building**, constructed in the early 1900s as the headquarters of the Rossiya Insurance firm. It was built on the site of the Royal Secret Dispatch Office, where a dreadful prison was kept in the cellars during the reign of Catherine the Great. After the Revolution, Dzerzhinsky took the building over to house his Cheka police. In the 1930s the building was reconstructed; a new façade was erected, two floors were added and a massive underground prison complex, known as the Lubyanka, was built in the original cellars. (Under Stalin, in five years alone, the secret police or NKVD executed over one million people.) In 1954, after the secret execution of Beria, Khrushchev founded the Committee for State Security—the KGB—to establish party control over the secret police after Stalin. On the left stands another (gray and black) KGB structure, built in 1980, and reputed to have many floors hidden underground. When the Communist Party was banned, the KGB tried to improve its image and even held a Miss KGB contest.

With the fall of the Communist government, the organization of the KGB was disbanded; it was split into five agencies which include the Foreign Intelligence Service (SVRR) and the Federal Counterintelligence Service (SVR). The SVRR now handles all intelligence gathering outside of Russia, including the former Soviet republics. Both divisions handle counterterrorism, illegal arms sales, drug trafficking and smuggling of radioactive materials. It is also now forbidden to use substances (such as poisoned umbrella tips) that could damage human health or to blackmail people into cooperation. After the 1991 attempted coup against Gorbachev, many of the KGB leaders were purged and the agency was turned into the Federal Security Bureau (FSB). In December 1991, shortly after his takeover as president, Yeltsin abolished the Security Ministry and split its functions between the existing agencies. In his decree, Yeltsin harshly spelled out every acronym that the secret police had used since the Bolshevik Revolution: 'The system of the organs of the Cheka-OGPU-NKVD-MGB-KGB-MB turned out to be unreformable.'

Today the agencies are paralyzed with budget crises, massive reorganizations, a 30 percent staff cut, and a severe and disorienting change in mission since the end of the Cold War. A paper shortage in the country is even forcing agents to type reports on the back of old documents; many offices still do not have computers and people are forced to share typewriters. It is now not only difficult to recruit foreigners as (secret) Russian agents, but native Russians as well. The American CIA and FBI were even called in to help revamp their computer systems. The goal of building Communism and the Great Motherland has been usurped by capitalist ideology, and the brightest no longer consider it prestigious to work for intelligence; registration at the Andropov Red Banner Institute, which trains intelligence recruits, has dropped by more than 75 percent.

Three interesting museums are nearby the square. The **Mayakovsky Museum** is on the corner of Myasnitskaya (formerly Kirov) Ulitsa and Lubyansky Proyezd. The popular poet Vladimir Mayakovsky (1893–1930) lived at this address for over a decade, but then, disillusioned with socialism, committed suicide here in April 1930. Many of his works and personal items are on display. Films of Mayakovsky are also shown, along with recordings of him reading his work. The museum is open 10am–5pm, 1pm–8pm Thursdays; closed Wednesdays.

At 12 Novaya Ploshchad (New Square) is the **History of Moscow Museum**, which was founded in 1896. Since 1939, it has been housed in the Church of St John the Divine 'Under the Elm', built in 1825. It has photographic displays of early Kremlin settlements to World War II reconstructions, archeological finds (many from the early 1990s Kremlin Manezh Square excavations for the underground shopping center; other explorations of the Kremlin's honeycomb of tunnels and city sewer systems are also under way) and a waxworks exhibition. The gallery has paintings and prints for sale. Open 10am–6pm, 11am–7pm Wednesdays and Fridays; closed Mondays.

Opposite, at 3/4 Novaya Ploshchad, is the **Polytechnical Museum**. Opened in 1872, it was one of Moscow's first museums. The current building, completed in 1907, has 60 halls containing over 100,000 exhibits that trace the history of Russian science and technology. In the basement is a fabulous collection of old Russian automobiles; the first Russian car was the Pobeda (Victory), manufactured after World War II. Henry Ford also exported his cars to Moscow (through Armand Hammer) until Lenin's death in 1924. On the top floor is an interesting collection of Russian space capsules and an exhibition on the life of the first Soviet cosmonaut Yuri Gagarin. The library has over three million volumes.

The Polytechnical building was also a popular center for local meetings; writers such as Akhmatova, Gorky and Mayakovsky gave readings here, and Lenin often presented lectures. In 1967, the longest telepathic experiment in history took place between the museum and Leningrad. The sender Yuri Kamensky sent telepathic messages from here to the psychic receiver Karl Nikolayev at Leningrad University. From the 1950s until the 1980s, the Soviets vigorously studied parapsychology and aspects of psychic warfare. Today the Central Hall is run by the Znaniye (Knowledge) Society, and lectures and readings are still staged. The museum is open from 10am–6pm; closed Mondays. The Statue of Ivan Fyodorov, the first Russian printer, stands a few minutes walk away along the prospekt.

TEATRALNAYA PLOSHCHAD (THEATER SQUARE)

The next section of the old Prospekt Marxa opens on Teatralnaya Ploshchad (Theater Square). From 1919 until 1991 it was known as Sverdlov Square, after the first president of Soviet Russia, Yakov Sverdlov (1885–1919). The statue of Karl Marx, inscribed with the words 'Workers of All Countries Unite!' stands in the middle of the square. The Metro station is Teatralnaya. From Theater Square to Red Square, Prospekt Marxa is now known as Okhotny Ryad (Hunter's Row—the street once led to the countryside and a popular hunting ground).

On the corner, at 1/4 Teatralny Proyezd, is one of Moscow's finest and most expensive hotels, the **Metropole Hotel**, built between 1899 and 1903 in art-nouveau

style (designed by British architect W F Walcott), and magnificently restored in 1990. The mosaic panels and classical friezes on the front were designed by the Russian artist Mikhail Vrubel. Rasputin once had his headquarters here and entrance plaques honor events of the Revolution. Inside are restaurants, bars and coffee shops, some with excellent all-you-can-eat breakfast and lunch buffets. Next door to the hotel is a fascinating antique shop. Facing the hotel to the right are walls of the 16th-century Kitai-Gorod.

Until 1919 this area was known as Theater Square, because two of Moscow's most prominent theaters were built here, the Bolshoi (Big) and the Maly (Small). One of the world's most famous theaters, **the Bolshoi** was built in 1824 by Osip Bovet and Alexander Mikhailov to stage performances of ballet and opera. It was constructed on the original site of the Royal Peter Theater, built in 1780. After a fire in 1856, the Bolshoi was rebuilt in neoclassical style by Albert Kavos to coincide with Alexander II's coronation. The stately building, with its large fountain in front, is crowned by the famous four bronze horses pulling the chariot of Apollo, patron of the arts. This is the work of sculptor Peter Klodt. The theater's gorgeous interior boasts five tiers of gilded boxes, whose chairs are covered with plush red velvet. The chandelier is made from 13,000 pieces of cut glass. The theater premiered compositions by Tchaikovsky, Glinka, Mussorgsky and Rimsky-Korsakov. After perestroika, it even premiered the Orthodox Church's *Millennium of the Baptism of Rus*. For tickets, inquire at your hotel service bureau, check at theater street-kiosks, or go to the theater's own ticket window. Scalpers are also usually selling tickets outside before performances. Unfortunately, in the last few years prices have gone up considerably.

Opposite the Bolshoi is the light yellow **Maly Drama Theater**. At its entrance stands the statue of Alexander Ostrovsky (1823–86), the outstanding Russian

The Bolshoi Theater stands on Moscow's Theater Square. Built in 1824 to stage performances of opera and ballet, it premiered compositions by some of Russia's greatest composers; (above) Peter Klodt sculpted the four bronze horses that crown the roof; they pull the chariot of Apollo, patron of the arts.

playwright. The theater is nicknamed the Ostrovsky House. Many classic Russian plays are staged here. On the other side of the Bolshoi is the Central Children's Theater, formed in 1921. Across the street from the Maly is the old Mostorg, or Moscow Trade. In 1907, when the building was completed, it housed the English department store Muir and Murrilies.

At the other end of the square is the three-story ornamented brick building of the **Central Lenin Museum** (open 10am–5pm; closed Mondays), which marks the entrance to the old Revolution Square. This building, erected in 1892, once housed the Duma (City Hall) of Moscow. In 1936, its 34 halls were converted into the country's, and world's, largest Lenin museum, displaying nearly a million items associated with the revolutionary leader. After the 1991 attempted coup, there was a movement to close the museum, but it was left open to depict a chapter of Russian history.

Opposite the museum is the **Moskva Hotel** built in constructivist style by architect Shchusev between 1932 and 1935. Note that the top left of the building's façade is different from the right. In the 1930s, when the architect designed two different fronts for the hotel, he asked Stalin, 'Which one do you like best?' 'Yes,' replied Stalin. Afraid to question the Soviet leader again, the architect built the structure asymmetrically, including both designs. In 1998, the Moscow city administration approved a multimillion-dollar plan to turn this Soviet-era behemoth into a high-class hotel.

Located in front of the hotel, in Manezh Square, is the newly constructed 350-million dollar **Manezh Underground Shopping Complex**, opened in 1997. Spot the stained-glass domes and proceed down the bronze-banistered stairwell into the new commercial heart of Moscow. The three-story underground atrium, complete with indoor fountain, holds 86 shops, 26 restaurants, banks and travel agencies. It is amazing to view this enterprising area, considering it was once the center of Bolshevik and Communist activities (which forbade any Western influences) until just a decade ago! The closest Metro station is Okhotny Ryad. Before continuing along the avenue, some old and interesting side streets off Theater Square merit exploration.

ULITSA PETROVKA (PETROVKA STREET)

Ulitsa Petrovka is a small side street that begins in front of the Maly Theater. Three centuries ago, the passage was named after the Monastery of St Peter-on-the-Hill, which also served as a protective stronghold and entrance to the town. The monastery was built by Prince Dmitri Donskoi to honor the Mongol defeat in the Battle of Kulikovo in 1380. In 1682, the future Peter the Great escaped here with his mother, Natalya Naryshkina, during the bloody Streltsy revolts. Today it serves as the patriarch's Department for Religious Education and contains three churches. The Church of the Virgin Icon of Bogoliubovo (1685) was built over the graves of Ivan and Afanasy Naryshkin, killed in 1682 by the Streltsy. The octagonal-drum and helmet-domed Cathedral of Metropolitan Peter was reconstructed between 1514 and 1517. The Baroque-style Refectory Church of Sergius Radonezhsky (founder of Sergiyev Posad Monastery) was commissioned by Peter the Great at the beginning of his reign in 1690; religious services are held here. The **Literary Museum** at number 28 traces the history of Russian literature. Open 11am–5.30pm, 2pm–7pm Wednesdays and Fridays; closed Mondays and Tuesdays.

The street has long been a popular shopping district with stores selling *podarki* (gifts), *bukinisti* (secondhand books) and *almazi* (diamonds). Next to the Maly, at number 2, is the gray four-story neo-Gothic-style building that houses TsUM, the **Central Universal Store**, open 8am–8pm; closed Sundays. The Russkiye Uzory (lace) sells handicrafts, and at number 8 is Zolotoy Klyuchik, one of Moscow's favorite watch stores. The Society of World Art had its first exhibition at number 15, displaying the work of Alexander Benois. The writer Anton Chekhov lived at number 19 for several years. (He also lived by the Garden Ring, at 6 Sadovaya-Kudrinskaya, now the Chekhov House Museum, see page 176.) The **Hermitage Gardens**, at 3 Karetny Ryad, have been here for over a century; open daily 9am–11pm. The Maly Concert Hall is located in the gardens.

KUZNETSKY MOST

Ulitsa Petrovka leads to Kuznetsky Most, a small lane branching to the right. As far back as the 15th century, the area was the popular residence of Moscow's blacksmiths, who lived along the banks of the Neglinnaya River, which at the time flowed through here. Kuznetsky Most means Blacksmith's Bridge.

Almost every building along this steep passage has a fascinating story related to it. It became a highly respected shopping district in the 19th century; items were stamped with 'Bought in Kuznetsky Most'. At number 9 was an ornate and popular restaurant called Yar, which Pushkin and Tolstoy mention in their writings. It was famous for its Gypsy dancers and drunken revelry; Rasputin was thrown out of the restaurant after he got involved in a brawl. Tolstoy listened to one of the world's first phonographs in the music shop that was at number 12, and he wrote of Anna Karenina shopping at Gautier's at number 20. The House of Fashion and many airline agencies are also located along this narrow street. At the end is Kuznetsky Most Metro station.

ULITSA NEGLINNAYA (NEGLINKA STREET)

Kuznetsky Most connects with Ulitsa Neglinnaya, which runs from the old Marx Prospekt to Trubnaya Ploshchad (Square) on the Boulevard Ring. This street also sprang up alongside the banks of the Neglinnaya River, where many popular shops were located. *Neglinnaya* means without clay. Catherine the Great ordered that the

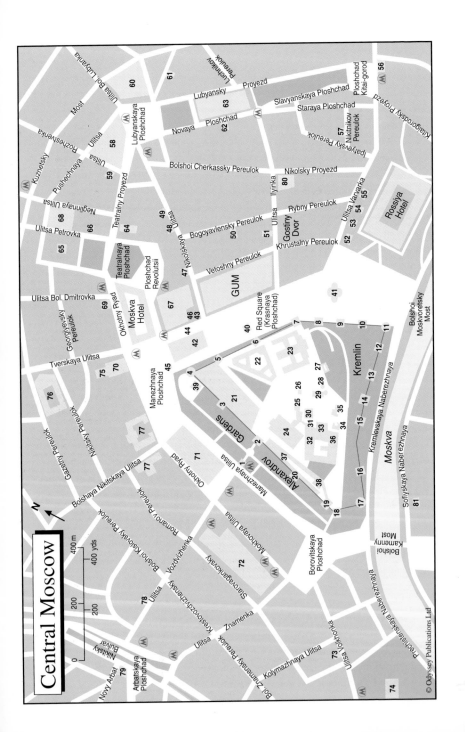

Central Moscow

400 m
400 yds
0   200   200   400

N

© Odyssey Publications Ltd

Ulitsa Bol. Lubyanka
Most
Rozhdestvenka
Kuznetsky
Neglinnaya Ulitsa
Pushechnaya
Ulitsa
Teatralny Proyezd
Ulitsa Petrovka
Ulitsa Bol. Dmitrovka
Georgyevsky Pereulok
Tverskaya Ulitsa
Kislovsky Pereulok
Nizhitsky Pereulok
Gazetny Pereulok
Bolshaya Nikitskaya Ulitsa
Romanov Pereulok
Mokhovaya Ulitsa
Okhotny Ryad
Manezhnaya Ulitsa
Nikitsky Bulvar
Novy Arbat
Bolshoi Kislovsky Pereulok
Vozdvizhenka
Staravagankovsky
Krestovozdvizhensky
Ulitsa
Znamenka
Bol. Znamensky Pereulok
Kolymazhnaya Ulitsa
Ulitsa Volkhonka
Prechistenskaya Naberezhnaya

Lubyansky   Proyezd
Lushnikov Pereulok
Lubyanskaya Ploshchad
Novaya   Ploshchad
Slavyanskaya Ploshchad
Staraya Ploshchad
Ploshchad Kitai-gorod
Kitaigorodsky Proyezd
Nikitnikov Pereulok
Ipatyevsky Pereulok
Bolshoi Cherkassky Pereulok
Nikolsky Proyezd
Ilyinka
Ulitsa
Rybny Pereulok
Bogoyavlensky Pereulok
Khrustalny Pereulok
Gostiny Dvor
Ulitsa Varvarka
Rossiya Hotel
Nikolskaya
Ulitsa
Vetoshny Pereulok
GUM
Red Square (Krasnaya Ploshchad)
Ploshchad Revolutsii
Teatralnaya Ploshchad
Moskva Hotel
Okhotny Ryad
Manezhnaya Ploshchad
Alexandrov
Gardens
Kremlin
Kremlevskaya Naberezhnaya
Moskva
Sofiyskaya Naberezhnaya
Bolshoi Moskvoretsky Most
Borovitskaya Ploshchad
Bolshoi Kamenny Most

60 61 63 62 58 59 64 49 48 47 80 54 55 53 52 51 50 46 43 44 42 45 40 41 57 56
65 66 67 68 69 70 75 76 77 78 79 71 72 73 74 81
1 2 3 4 5 6 7 8 9 10 11 12 13 14 15 16 17 18 19 20 21 22 23 24 25 26 27 28 29 30 31 32 33 34 35 36 37 38 39

Key for Central Moscow Map:

1 Kutafya Tower
2 Troitskaya Tower
3 Srednaya Arsenalnaya
4 Corner Arsenal Tower
5 Nikolskaya Tower
6 Senate Tower
7 Spasskaya Tower
8 Tsarskaya Tower
9 Nabatnaya Tower
10 Konstantino-Yeleninskaya Tower
11 Beklemishevskaya Tower
12 Petrovskaya Tower
13 2-Bezymyannaya Tower
14 1-Bezymyannaya Tower
15 Tainitskaya Tower
16 Blagoveshchenskaya Tower
17 Vodovoznaya Tower
18 Borovitskaya Tower
19 Oruzheynaya Tower
20 Kommendatskaya Tower
21 Arsenal
22 Senate
23 Presidium and Kremlin Theater
24 Patriarch's Palace
25 Church of the Twelve Apostles
26 Emperor Cannon
27 Kremlin Hill

Ⓜ Metro Station

28 Emperor Bell
29 Ivan the Great's Bell Tower
30 Cathedral of the Assumption
31 Church of the Deposition of the Robe
32 Terem Palace
33 Palace of Facets
34 Cathedral of the Annunciation
35 Cathedral of the Archangel Michael
36 Grand Kremlin Palace
37 Amusement Palace
38 Armory Palace
39 Tomb of the Unknown Soldier
40 Lenin's Mausoleum
41 St Basil's Cathedral
42 Historical Museum
43 Kazan Cathedral
44 Iberian Resurrection Gates
45 Statue of Marshal Georgy Zhukov
46 Old Royal Mint
47 Zaikonospassky Monastery
48 History and Archives Institute
49 Slavyansky Bazaar
50 Cathedral of Bogoyavlensky
51 St Ilyia Church
52 Church of St Varvara
53 Old English Inn
54 Church of St Maximus

55 Znamensky Cathedral
56 Church of All Saints on Kulishki
57 Church of the Holy Trinity in Nikitniki
58 Detsky Mir
59 Savoy Hotel
60 Former KGB Building
61 Mayakovsky Museum
62 History of Moscow Museum
63 Polytechnical Museum
64 Metropole Hotel
65 Bolshoi Theater
66 Maly Theater
67 Central Lenin Museum
68 TsUM
69 Dom Soyuzov
70 National Hotel
71 Central Exhibition Hall
72 Russian State Library
73 Pushkin Museum of Fine Arts
74 Cathedral of Christ Our Savior
75 Intourist Hotel
76 Central Telegraph Building
77 Moscow State University
78 House of Friendship
79 Prague Restaurant
80 Moscow Stock Exchange
81 British Embassy

river be diverted underground. In the 19th century, it was redirected to a larger aqueduct where it flows underground to the Moskva River.

The revolutionary Nikolai Schmit had his furniture store at the corner of Kuznetsky Most. The Moorish-style building of the **Sandunovsky Baths** at number 14 was frequented by Chekhov. This is one of the grandest *banya* in town. The building was bought by the actor Sila Sandunov, who turned it into sauna baths in 1896. The *banya* is still a marbled and gilded extravaganza where one can steam, sweat and swim; open 8am–10pm; closed Tuesdays. Another popular *banya* is the Tsentralnaya Banya, the Central Bath House, located off Okhotny Ryad, at 3 Teatralny Proyezd, across from the Metropole Hotel, open 8am–8pm; closed Mondays. A favorite is Krasnopresnenskaya Banya at 7 Stolyarny Pereulok. Open 8am–10pm; closed Mondays; near Ulitsa 1905 Goda Metro station. Try to bring along your own towel, but buy a bunch of birch leaves usually sold seasonally outside; Russians love to swat each other with these while sweating! (See Special Topic on page 340 and Practical Information listings).

Also on Ulitsa Neglinnaya, at number 4, is Moscow's oldest sheet music shop, Nota, opened in 1911, and the Central Bank. At number 29 is the popular Uzbekistan Restaurant.

OKHOTNY RYAD

The continuation of the old Marx Prospekt from Theater Square to the Kremlin is now known as Okhotny Ryad (Hunter's Lane) the name of the old local markets. The main markets of Moscow spread from here to Red Square. Across from the Moskva Hotel is **Dom Soyuzov** (House of Trade Unions) on the corner of Dmitrovka and Tverskaya streets, at number 10. Built in 1784 in Russian classical style by Matvei Kazakov, it used to be the Noble's Club. Its Hall of Columns and October Hall hosted social functions. In 1856, Alexander II addressed the nobility on his desire to abolish serfdom, and the playwright George Bernard Shaw was even honored here on his 75th birthday in 1931. Also past leaders such as Lenin, Stalin and Brezhnev lay in state here before their burials. Next door is the City Duma or Parliament building.

Crossing the prospekt via the underpass brings you out in front of the newly renovated **National Hotel**. Built in 1903, it is still one of Moscow's finest hotels. Lenin stayed in suite 107, marked by a plaque. The famous French restaurant Maxim's opened on the ground floor in 1995. A few doors down, near the corner of Bolshaya Nikitskaya Ulitsa, stands one of the oldest buildings of Moscow University, recognizable by its columned portico and small dome. It was built in classical style, between 1786 and 1793 by Matvei Kazakov. A statue of Lomonosov, who founded the university in 1755, stands in the courtyard. Next door a newer building dating from 1836 now houses the Student Union. In the courtyard are two statues of graduates, Nikolai Ogarev and Alexander Herzen.

MOKHOVAYA ULITSA (STREET)

Running south from the National Hotel to the end of the prospekt at Borovitskaya Ploshchad is Mokhovaya (Moss-Grown) Street. In the center, in Manezhnaya Ploshchad, stands the **Central Exhibition Hall**, which used to be the *manège*, the czar's riding school. It was built in the classical style in 1825 and designed by Augustin Betancourt. Since 1951 Moscow's largest art exhibitions have been shown here. At number 6 is the **Kalinin Museum** (open 10am–6pm; closed Mondays), the former mansion of Prince Shakhovsky, built in 1821. Opened on June 30, 1950, the museum traces the life of Party leader Mikhail Kalinin.

Mokhovaya ends a few minutes' walk farther down by the **Russian State Library** (formerly the Lenin Library), the largest library in Russia with 36 million books. Between 1784 and 1786, the governor of Siberia, P Pashkov, built his neo-classical mansion (to designs by Vasily Bazhenov) with beautiful exotic gardens filled with peacocks that wandered the hills around the Kremlin. It is still referred to as the **Pashkov Dom** and stands on the corner of Mokhovaya and Znamenka streets. Later in 1861, the building housed the famous Rumyantsev collection of over one million books and manuscripts. When Lenin died in 1924, it was renamed the Lenin Library. When the Metro was built in the 1940s, many books were moved into the larger building next door. In 1993, its name was changed once again after extensive restoration. The closest Metro station is Biblioteka Imeni Lenina.

VOLKHONKA AND PRECHISTENKA STREETS

Ulitsa Volkhonka begins at the Kremlin's Borovitsky Tower and runs into Ulitsa Prechistenka. The **Pushkin Museum of Fine Arts** is at 12 Volkhonka, and is a highly recommended stop during your visit. The neoclassical-style building was constructed in 1898 by Roman Klein to house a collection of fine art, which opened in 1912. The museum was initially named after Alexander III, but renamed after Pushkin during the poet's centenary year in 1937. After the Revolution, paintings belonging to two great collectors, Sergei Shchukin (1854–1937) and Ivan Morozov (1871–1921) were nationalized by the State. By 1914, Shchukin had more than 220 French impressionist artworks displayed at his house, the former Trubetskoi Mansion in Moscow. Rooms were filled with Matisse, Gauguin, Cézanne and Picasso. In his mansion at 21 Prechistenka Street, Morozov exhibited more than 100 impressionist paintings and 450 other works by Russian artists, including Marc Chagall. They both fled the country after the Revolution and, until 1948, their paintings were exhibited at Morozov's Mansion, known as the Museum of Western Art.

After this was closed down by Stalin, their collections were kept in storage in the Pushkin Museum. Only after Stalin's death in 1953 were the paintings gradually put back on display. Today the museum boasts one of the world's largest collections of ancient, classical, Oriental and Western European art, with over half a million works. Open 10am–7pm; closed Mondays.

The museum has also expanded to include the **Museum of Private Collections**, located next door at number 14, in the green and white palace. This was once the palace of the aristocratic Golitsyn family, and Catherine the Great stayed here during her coronation in 1762. Today its three floors exhibit private collections, many donated to the state. Open 10am–4pm, 12pm–6pm weekends; closed Mondays and Tuesdays. Behind the museums, along the narrow lane in the last yellow and white mansion, is the **Roerich Museum**, with paintings by artist Nikolai Roerich, an avid Buddhist and mystic. Open 11am–7pm Tuesdays, Thursdays and Saturdays.

Standing beside Kropotkinskaya Ploshchad (Square) is the magnificent and newly reconstructed **Cathedral of Christ Our Savior**. Its history is both long and unbelievably tragic. Founded in honor of the famous Russian victory over Napoleon, it took 45 years to build, but only one day to destroy. Alexander I stipulated that the cathedral was to express the scale of the czar's gratitude to Christ for the country's protection, and selected the site on the bank of the river. But it was not until 1830, under the rule of Nicholas I, that serious planning began. Designed by Konstantin Thon, the czar's favorite architect, its construction then continued through the reigns of yet two more rulers. Alexander III was present during its consecration on May 26, 1883. With a capacity of 15,000, the cathedral was the country's largest and most lavishly decorated shrine, symbolizing the glory of the Russian empire. The cathedral was over 30 stories high, bedecked with over half a ton of gold, and its walls made from 40 million bricks, Altai marble and Finnish granite. The gigantic roof cupola was composed of 176 tons of copper, topped by a cross three stories high. Fourteen bells hung in the four belfries, one weighing 27 tons. The central iconostasis was decorated with bejeweled icons, which reflected thousands of beeswax candles. Hundreds of frescoes were painted along the upper stories, and the lower portion was covered with 177 marble plates, each engraved with particular places, dates and heroes of the battles of Russian armies. This enormous shrine dedicated to the Son of God stood for 48 years; three years longer than it took to build.

Then, in 1931, to perpetuate the glory of the Soviet regime, Stalin decided to build his own glorified House of Soviets and selected the cathedral as its site. (Imagine if Mussolini had ordered St Peter's Basilica in Rome to be razed.) On July 18, 1931, workmen began removing thousands of priceless artifacts; they had four months to complete their assignment. (During this time, ten million would starve to death in the Ukraine, and Stalin started his first purges and labor camps.) Then began the demolition. Finally, on December 5, 1931, after one last detonation, a huge smoking mountain of rubble was all that remained of this wondrous accomplishment.

The final blueprints of 1933 had the planned House of Soviets higher than any American skyscraper at 420 meters (1,380 feet), topped with a 70-meter (230-foot) statue of Lenin (taller than the Statue of Liberty)—130 stories in all. The monument to Socialism was to look like an enormous multitiered wedding cake. But it turned out that the swampy mound of floating bedrock could not support the proposed building. Stalin died in 1953, and in the end it was Khrushchev in 1959 who ordered a pit dug for a swimming pool utilizing the bemired foundation (by then a garbage dump), all that remained of the demolished cathedral. Until 1994 this remained the Moskva Open-Air Pool Complex. With the fall of the Soviet Union, the new government allocated nearly 250 million dollars, underwritten by private donations and nongovernmental funds, to construct a replica of the original cathedral, which opened in 1997.

From the Revolution until 1991, Prechistenka Street was called Kropotkinskaya (the Metro station still is), named after the revolutionary scholar, Pyotr Kropotkin (1842–1921), who lived nearby at 26 Kropotkinsky Pereulok. For centuries the street had been known as Prechistenka (Holy), after the Icon of the Holy Virgin kept in Novodevichy Convent. Many aristocratic families built their residences along this street. In the 18th and 19th centuries the area was one of the most fashionable places to live in Moscow. At number 10 lived Count Mikhail Orlov, a descendant of Catherine the Great's lover, Grigory; the mansion now houses the Peace Commission. Note the outside plaque commemorating the Jewish Committee which worked diligently for the Russian war effort against the Germans. They were later arrested and sent off to gulags by Stalin in 1952. The poets Zhukovsky and Davydov also lived on this street at number 17. Whenever the writer Ivan Turgenev (*Fathers and Sons*) visited Moscow, he stayed at the nearby gray-blue wooden dacha at 37 Ostozhenka Ulitsa with his mother. At 9 Mansurovsky Pereulok (near the Palace of Fine Arts), in the yellow wooden house, another writer, Mikhail Bulgakov (1891–1940) lived for a while in the basement apartment. It is here that, in his famous novel *The Master and Margarita*, the master catches a glimpse of Margarita. (See Patriarch's Pond section on page 151 for more on where Bulgakov also lived.)

The mansion at 12 Prechistenka Street was built by Afanasy Grigorev. It now houses the **Alexander Pushkin Museum**, containing over 80,000 items connected with the celebrated poet. Open 10am–6pm, 11am–7pm Wednesdays and Thursdays; closed Mondays and Tuesdays. Across the street, at number 11, is the **Leo Tolstoy Museum**, which includes a collection of the beloved writer's manuscripts, book editions, literature on his life, a documentary ('Tolstoy Alive') and recordings of his voice. Open 11am–5pm; closed Mondays.

In 1862, Leo Tolstoy (known as Lev Tolstoy in Russian) married Sofia Andreyevna with whom he fathered 13 children. Between 1863 and 1869 he wrote *War and Peace* (his wife hand-copied it over nine times), and between 1874 and 1876 *Anna Karenina*. Two years later, Tolstoy published *Confession*, views on his newly embraced Christian moralities and commitment to individual rights and nonviolence (he even received interested letters from Mahatma Gandhi). The estate-museum, where Tolstoy lived from 1882 to 1901, is at 21 Ulitsa Lva Tolstovo (Leo Tolstoy Street); closed Mondays. (See also Yasnaya Polyana, page 216.)

The **Russian Academy for Arts**, at number 21, was once the residence of Prince Dolgorukov. In 1998, a statue honoring Vasily Surikov (1848–1936) was placed in front of the academy to honor the 150th anniversary of the artist's birth. An entire gallery of busts of outstanding Russian artists will soon join Surikov.

During their brief marriage in 1922, the famous American ballet dancer Isadora Duncan and her husband, Russian writer Sergei Yesenin, lived across the street at number 20. (He spoke no English; she no Russian.) Yesenin, yet another poet who became disillusioned with socialism, committed suicide in 1925. Isadora was strangled two years later in the south of France when her long scarf wrapped itself around the wheel of the car she was driving.

Prechistenka Street ends at the Garden Ring by a statue of Tolstoy. Across the river at number 10 Lavrushinsky Pereulok (Tretyakovskaya Metro station) is the newly renovated **Tretyakov Gallery**. In 1856, the brothers Sergei and Pavel Tretyakov, avid art patrons, began to collect the works of Russian artists. In 1892, they founded Russia's first public museum of national art and donated their collection of 3,500 paintings to the city. Today the gallery houses one of the world's largest Russian and Soviet art collections from the tenth to the 20th centuries with well over 50,000 works. These include the famous 12th-century Byzantine icon Virgin of Vladimir, Rublyov's Old Testament Trinity icon, Ilya Repin's *Ivan the Terrible and His Son*, Vasily Surikov's *Morning of the Execution of the Streltsy*, and the largest painting in the gallery, Alexander Ivanov's *The Coming of Christ*. The shop inside has a collection of books, art and postcards for sale. It is open 10am–8pm; closed Mondays (ticket office closes at 6.30pm). A new branch of the Tretyakov (also closed on Mondays) has opened at 10 Krymsky Val. This is opposite Gorky Park near Oktyabrskaya Metro station.

This area is still known as Zamoskvarechiye—Across the Moskva River. One block east of the Tretyakov Gallery is Bolshaya Ordynka Ulitsa; the medieval name stems from *orda*, which refers to the Mongol Golden Horde. This route once led to the Khan's southern headquarters. Moscow once boasted over 500 churches, and today the city's largest concentration of churches (over 15) is located within this small area. The **Church of Virgin of All Sorrows**, at 20 Bolshaya Ordynka, dates from 1790. When the church was destroyed in the fire of 1812 (which destroyed 80 percent of the city), Osip Bovet designed a new one with a yellow rotunda in empire style in 1836; the Icon of the Virgin is in the left chapel. Orthodox services are held on Sunday mornings. At number 34 is the **Convent of Saints Martha and Mary**, built by the sister of Empress Alexandra in 1908. After her husband Grand Prince Sergei was assassinated, the Grand Duchess Yelizaveta decided to retire to a convent of her own creation. The main Church of the Virgin Intercession was built by architect Alexei Shchusev in 1912, who later designed Lenin's mausoleum on Red Square. The interior frescoes were painted by Mikhail Nesterov; an icon restoration workshop is still on the grounds. After the Revolution Yelizaveta Fedorovna, along with other Romanov family members, was exiled to the Urals. In 1918, they were murdered by Bolsheviks in Alapaevsk (they were thrown down an old mine shaft and grenades were thrown in after them) a day after the royal family's execution in nearby Yekaterinburg. In 1992, the convent reopened in a nearby building.

At number 39 Bolshaya Ordynka a small church now houses the **Art Moderne Gallery** with exhibits by contemporary artists (closed Mondays). The **Church of St Catherine**, at number 60, was also reconstructed after a fire. Catherine the Great had Karl Blank build this church on the original site in 1767. One block west, at number 10 Shchetininsky Pereulok, look for the **Tropinin Museum**. It houses works by 18th-century serf-artist, Vasily Tropinin, as well as other painters who studied at the Academy of Arts. Exhibits include landscape portraits and watercolors of old Moscow. Other churches can be found along the neighboring streets of Pyatnitskaya (numbers 4, 26, 51) and Vtoroy Kadashovsky, where at number 2 stands the five-domed Moscow Baroque **Church of the Resurrection**, built between 1687 and 1713, and funded by donations made from neighborhood weavers.

Nearby, at 9 Malaya Ordynka Ulitsa and behind the whitewashed five-domed **Church of St Nicholas in Pyzhi** (in which services are held), is the **Ostrovsky House Museum** where one of Russia's best-known playwrights was born on March 31, 1823. The small wooden house is filled with photographs and pictures that document Moscow's theatrical history, especially from the Maly Theater where Alexander Ostrovsky worked from 1853 until his death in 1886. Open 1pm–7pm; closed Tuesdays. Further southeast, on the corner of Novokuznetskaya and Vishnyakovsky streets stands the **Church of St Nicholas the Blacksmith** (1681). Rebuilt in the 19th century, it is known as St Nicholas of the Miracles because of its wonder-working icons; many people continue to faithfully pray before them. Running south, Novokuznetskaya ends at **Paveletsky Railway Station** where trains lead to the Ukraine and lower Volga regions.

Tverskaya Ulitsa (Street)

In the 18th century, Tverskaya Ulitsa was the main street of the city; today it is still one of the busiest in Moscow. The passage was named Tverskaya because it led to the old Russian town of Tver (renamed Kalinin) 256 kilometers (160 miles) north; from there it continued to St Petersburg. From 1932 until 1990, the street was called Gorky, after Maxim Gorky, a famous writer during the Stalinist period. In 1990, the Moscow City Council voted to restore the street's old name. From the Kremlin to the Garden Ring, the thoroughfare is known as Tverskaya, and from the Garden Ring to Byelorussky Train Station it is called Tverskaya-Yamskaya (in the 17th century the Yamskaya Sloboda, or settlement, appeared outside the city's ramparts). From the train station it becomes Leningradsky Prospekt, which leads to the international airport, Sheremetyevo II.

In prerevolutionary days the street, once winding and narrow, was known for its fashionable shops, luxurious hotels and grandiose aristocratic mansions. The first Moscow trams ran along this street, and the first movie theater opened here. In 1932 (after being renamed Gorky), the thoroughfare was reshaped and widened, and now retains little of its former appearance.

It takes about an hour and a half to stroll the length of Tverskaya Street. You can also ride the Metro to various stops along it—Pushkinskaya, Mayakovskaya and Byelorusskaya—to shorten the time.

Tverskaya Street begins in front of Red Square at the **Manezhnaya Ploshchad**, known as the 50th Anniversary of the October Revolution Square from 1967 to 1990. The czar had his riding school, the *manège*, in this area. Okhotny Ryad Metro station is at the beginning of the street. On the corner is the newly renovated, elegant **National Hotel** with a splendid view of Red Square. Lenin lived here during the Revolution. The 22-story structure next door is the Soviet-style modern **Intourist Hotel**, built in 1971.

Since the early 1990s many new shops have opened on Tverskaya, including foreign clothing and cosmetic outlets (many now accept credit cards), along with other Russian stores which accept rubles only.

Continuing along the street is the **Yermolova Drama Theater**, named after a famous stage actress, Maria Yermolova. Founded in 1925, the theater moved into the present building at number 5 in 1946. The Meyerhold Theater occupied the building from 1931 to 1938. It has staged everything from *Mary Poppins* to *Heartbreak House*. (For the Yermolova House Museum see page 168.) The **Central Telegraph Building**, with its globe and digital clock, is on the corner of Gazetny Pereulok. The building, designed by Ilya Rerberg in 1927, is open 24 hours a day.

Telegrams, faxes, and long-distance calls can be made here, but there is usually a wait.

Across the street at 3 Kamergersky Pereulok is the **Moscow Arts Theater** (today known as the Chekhov Moscow Artistic Academic Theater), established by Stanislavsky and Nemirovich-Danchenko in 1896. Here Stanislavsky practiced his 'method-acting' and staged many plays by Gorky and Chekhov (see Chekhov House Museum on page 176). After *The Seagull*, the bird was put on the outside of the building as its emblem. Plays such as *The Three Sisters*, *The Cherry Orchard*, *Anna Karenina* and *Resurrection* marked a new epoch in the theater. In 1987, the building was reconstructed and now seats 2,000. Today the theater's repertoire includes such plays as *Uncle Vanya*, *Bondage of Hypocrites* and *Tartuffe*. Next door at 3A is the Moscow Arts Museum, founded in 1923. Another building of the Moscow Arts Theater (under different management) is at 22 Tverskoi.

The **Aragvi Restaurant** (once part of the Dresden Hotel, a favorite of Turgenev and Chekhov), specializing in Georgian cuisine, is on the next corner of Pereulok Stoleshnikov, at 6 Tverskaya. Stoleshnikov is designated to become Moscow's second pedestrian lane (the Arbat is already pedestrianized). Craftsmen embroidered tablecloths for the czar's court in this lane over 300 years ago (*stoleshnik* means tablecloth in Old Russian). The **Stoleshniki Café**, at number 6, is decorated in Old-Russian style. It is affectionately known as *U Gilyarovskovo*, in tribute to one of its past regulars, the writer and journalist Gilyarovsky who wrote the popular *Moscow and the Muscovites*; he lived across the street at number 9 for over half a century. Two rooms have been renovated in the café's 17th-century cellars: the Reporter's and Moscow and Muscovites halls. Here Gilyarovsky medals are awarded annually to the writers of the best articles about Moscow. At number 11, the pastry shop still uses old-fashioned ovens built into the walls, and has some of the best cakes in the city. The lane leads to Petrovka Street, a popular shopping area.

The side street Bryusov Pereulok leads to the terracotta-yellow **Church of the Resurrection** on Yeliseyevsky Lane. The church is said to have been built on the spot where Mikhail Romanov welcomed his father's return in 1619 after Polish imprisonment. It was reconstructed in 1629, and the church even remained open during Soviet years. Its interior is filled with icons, including a 16th-century copy of the Virgin of Kazan (believed responsible for the Russian 1613 victory over the Poles) and the icon of St George, the symbol of the city.

Tverskaya Ploshchad is marked by the equestrian **Statue of Yuri Dolgoruky**, founder of Moscow. It was erected in 1954 to mark the 800th anniversary of the city. The building behind the square, in the small garden, holds Party archives of the Marxism-Leninism Institute. The archives contain more than 6,000 documents of Marx and Engels and over 30,000 of Lenin. In front is a granite statue of Lenin by Sergei Merkurov.

Directly across the street stands the large red-brick and white-columned **Moscow City Council**, the city's legislature. The architect Matvei Kazakov designed the building as the residence for the first governor-general, appointed by Catherine the Great in 1782. Two of Moscow's governors were Prince Dmitri Golitsyn (1820–44), who paved the streets and installed water pipes, and Vladimir Dolgorukov, a descendent of Yuri Dolgoruky. In 1946, the building was moved back 14 meters (46 feet) and two more stories were added.

The north side street of Stoleshnikov leads to the octagonal-drum and small-cupola **Church of Saints Cosmas and Damian** (patron saints of blacksmiths), rebuilt in stone in 1626. Once a factory, it is now slowly being restored.

Farther up Tverskaya is the Tsentralnaya Hotel at number 10, built in 1911 as the Hotel Liuks. In the same building is the most famous bakery in Moscow, formerly known as Filippov's. Next door is another popular food store, Gastronom Number 1, which recently reverted to its original name of **Yeliseyev's** (see Special Topic on page 442). Beautiful white sculptures and garlands line the shopfront, and the gilded interior is filled with stained glass and colorful displays. It is worth a visit just to see the interior. At 14 Tverskaya is the **Ostrovsky Humanitarian Museum**, open 11am–7pm; closed Mondays. Nikolai Ostrovsky (1904–1936) wrote *How the Steel Was Tempered*. The Soviet author's house (where he lived from 1935 to 1936) is now a museum exhibiting his books, photographs and letters. Also in the building is the **Tetris Wax Museum**, open 11am–7pm; closed Mondays. On display are wax figures that include Alexander Nevsky, Ivan the Terrible, Napoleon, Nicholas II and Stalin.

Down the side street, at 6 Leontevsky Pereulok, is the **Stanislavsky Memorial Museum**. The theater director lived here from 1922 until his death in 1938. On display are the living quarters of Stanislavsky and his wife, the opera hall and collections of books, costumes and theatrical props. The ballroom was converted into a theater; the first production was Tchaikovsky's *Evgeny Onegin*. It is open 11am–5pm, Wednesdays and Fridays 2pm–8pm; closed Mondays and Tuesdays. (A museum to Stanislavsky's partner, Nemirovich-Danchenko, is located at 5 Glinishchevsky Pereulok, near Pushkinskaya Metro station; open 11am–4pm; closed Mondays.) Opposite, at number 7, is the **Folk Arts Museum** which exhibits Russian national crafts and decorative art, and has souvenirs for sale. In 1900, the building was bought by art patron Savva Morozov specifically to house this museum. Open 11am–5.30pm; closed Sundays and Mondays. At 17 Tverskaya is the **Konenkov Memorial Studio**, open 11am–6.30pm; closed Mondays and Tuesdays. It displays marble and wooden statues by famous sculptor Sergei Konenkov (1874–1971), who lived here from 1947 until his death.

As Tverskaya crosses the Boulevard Ring, it opens into **Pushkin Square**

Statue of the famous writer Alexander Pushkin which stands on Moscow's Pushkin Square.

(Pushkinskaya Ploshchad). In the 16th century the stone walls of the Beli Gorod (White Town) stretched around what is now the Boulevard Ring; they were torn down in the 18th century. The Strastnoi Convent used to stand on what is now Pushkin Square—the square was originally called Strastnaya (until 1931), after the Convent of the Passion of Our Lord. The convent was demolished in the 1930s and in its place was built the Rossiya Movie Theater and the Izvestia building. In the center of the square stands the **Statue of Alexander Pushkin**, by the sculptor Alexander Opekulin. It was erected in 1880

with funds donated by the public. Pushkin lived over a third of his life in Moscow, where he predicted, 'Word of me shall spread across the Russian land.' Dostoevsky laid a wreath on the statue at its unveiling. Today it is always covered with flowers and is a popular spot for open-air readings and political rallies. In 1999, to celebrate the 200th anniversary of Pushkin's birth, over 100 historical locations connected with the poet's life and work were restored throughout the city. Under the square are the three Metro stations: Tverskaya, Pushkinskaya and Chekhovskaya.

Behind the square is the 3,000-seat Rossiya Movie Theater, built in 1961 for the 2nd International Moscow Film Festival (the festival is held in Moscow every odd year). This area is also Moscow's major publishing center. Here are the newspaper offices of *Izvestia*, *Trud*, *Novosti* (*APN*) and *Moscow News*. Walking down

Malaya Dmitrovka Ulitsa (behind *Izvestia*) leads to the red-green tent-roofed **Church of Nativity of Our Lady in Putniki**, built between 1649 and 1652. Legend has it that a noblewoman gave birth in her carriage as she passed this spot and later commissioned a church to honor the Nativity. When it burned down, Czar Alexei Romanov donated money to have it rebuilt, along with a chapel dedicated to the icon that prevented fires, Our Lady of the Burning Bush, which is in the chapel. Behind it was once a resthouse where travelers or *putniki* stayed; it is currently *na remont* or under restoration.

Across the street from Pushkin Square is the world's largest **McDonald's** fast-food outlet, with 800 seats, 27 cash registers and 250 employees serving up to 50,000 people a day. When the restaurant opened, Russians automatically stood in the longest queue—in Russia a longer queue was indicative of better quality merchandise. Brochures had to be distributed explaining that each queue gave the same service and food. The chain plans to open a total of 20 restaurants in Moscow. As part of an agreement with the Moscow City Council, McDonald's was required to purchase or produce its raw materials in Russia, resulting in a vast production and distribution complex on the outskirts of the city. After decades of waiting hours in long lines, the country enthusiastically embraced fast food. Each month on average Russian customers of McDonald's restaurants consume 1.2 million servings of French fries, 700,000 Big Macs, and 600,000 milk shakes. In 1996, McDonald's opened Moscow's first drive-through restaurant on Leningradskoye Highway on the way to the international airport.

To give an idea of the extent of business enterprise developing in the early 1990s, there was even a black market for hamburgers. Entrepreneurs would stand in line for hours to purchase eight Big Macs each (the maximum allowed per person), ate one, and then sold the rest at a huge profit to those not willing to wait. They earned more in one day than a physicist did in a month. Today black-market burgers are bust and the long lines gone. The grounds surrounding the restaurant are a popular meeting place; small kiosks abound and you can have your picture taken next to cardboard copies of Russian leaders. Bands play here and there are many young people amusing themselves on skateboards and roller blades.

The **Revolution Museum** is at 21 Tverskaya. This mansion was built for Count Razumovsky in 1780 by the architect Manelas. In 1832, it was rebuilt by Adam Menelaws after a fire, and was bought by the Angliisky (English) Club, formed in 1772 by a group of foreigners residing in Moscow. The club's members (all men) were made up of Russian aristocratic intellectuals and included the best minds in politics, science, art and literature. One member of the wealthy Morozov family gambled away one million rubles in a single evening. Tolstoy once lost 1,000 rubles in a card game in the 'infernal' room. Pushkin wrote of the club in his long poem

Evgeny Onegin. When Tatiana arrived in Moscow, Evgeny described 'the two frivolous-looking lions' at the gates. The last *bolshoi* gala at the club was a banquet thrown for Nicholas II to celebrate the 300th anniversary of the Romanov dynasty in 1913. The museum, opened in 1924, exhibits over a million items from the 1905 and 1917 revolutions. It also displays materials on the country's history dating back to 1861. It was called the Central Museum of the Revolution until 1992. A new hall has opened displaying items from the August 1991 coup attempt. The gun outside was used to shell the White Guards in 1917. Also on display here is a tram that burned during the 1991 attempted coup. The museum is open 10am–6pm, Wednesdays 11am–7pm; closed Mondays. Next to the museum, at number 23, is the Stanislavsky Drama Theater. Behind it is the Young Spectator's Theater for children. The Baku-Livan Restaurant, at number 24, serves delicious Azerbaijani food.

Patriarch's Pond—Bulgakov's Haunt

Turn off Tverskaya by McDonald's and into Bolshaya Bronnaya Ulitsa. This leads to Malaya Bronnaya—turn right and at number 30 you will find Patriarch's Pond, one of the oldest and most charming residential areas of Moscow. This land was once known as Patriarskaya Sloboda, the Russian Orthodox patriarch's land in the 17th and 18th centuries. The pond was dug to provide the dining tables with plenty of fish. Later it was occupied by artisans—the *bronnaya* (armorers) and the *kozia* (wool spinners). The writer Mikhail Bulgakov set his well-known masterpiece *The Master and Margarita*, in this neighborhood. Completed in 1938, and about the Devil's influence on corrupt Soviet authorities, it was not allowed to be published until 1966. (Many of the Party elite lived in this area.)

Between 1921 and 1934, Bulgakov lived just around the corner in Bolshaya Sadovaya Ulitsa—in the beige building between numbers 8 and 14. (He describes in his novel, 'it was painted cream, and stood on the ring boulevard behind a ragged garden fenced off from the pavement by a wrought-iron railing.') Go left at the back of the yard and notice the graffiti written by fans on the stairwell—a memorial to the writer who died in disgrace in 1940 and was described in the *Soviet Encyclopaedia* as a 'slanderer of Soviet reality'. There is currently a petition to erect a monument to the author and turn his apartment into a museum.

A monument to Ivan Krylov (1769–1844), a popular children's fabulist, stands in the square. In winter, there is ice-skating and in summer boating. Across the street from the pond, at number 28, is the popular Café Margarita (see Practical Information, page 316). The **Moscow Drama Theater** is at 4 Malaya Bronnaya. Formed in 1950, the theater seats 850.

A few blocks south on Ulitsa Spiridonovka is the newly restored **Morozov Mansion**, a magnificent structure with an incredible history. In April 1893, Zinaida

Morozova, wife of prominent businessman Savva Morozov bought this nobility compound in the upmarket section of the old Arbat. Savva, the grandson of a
serf-peasant, became a millionaire textile merchant and popular patron of the arts.
(Morozov funded Stanislavsky's Moscow Arts Theater.) The Morozovs commissioned the famous architect Fedor Shekhtel to redesign their house in medieval
Gothic style, which was completed in 1898. The attention to detail is astounding—
gargoyles, griffins, stone carvings and cast-iron railings decorate the exterior. For the
interior, Mikhail Vrubel created enormous stained-glass windows. Pavel Schmidt
contributed hand-carved wooden staircases and furniture, and great sandstone fire-
places and crystal chandeliers came from the Zakharov and Postnikov workshops.
The mansion was frequented by the Moscow elite. Savva Morozov, a member of the
Old Believer sect, backed the socialists. He even hid revolutionaries within the many
corners of his home and secretly funded Lenin's newspaper *Iskra* (The Spark). After
the bloody consequences of the 1905 Revolution, Savva Morozov could no longer
live with the conflicts—bouts of industrial strikes in his factories coupled with his
promotion of reforms—he committed suicide by shooting himself in the head.

In 1909 his wife sold the house to Mikhail Riabushinsky, who added art works
by artist Konstantin Bogarevsky. The Riabushinsky family was forced to flee to

Russians love to hang out in their kitchens where they drink chai *(tea)
and snack on freshly baked* khleb *(bread).*

Modern graffiti art on Malaya Bronnaya Ulitsa in the Patriarch's Pond district. Since this was the home of Mikhail Bulgakov, who wrote the famous novel The Master and Margarita, *the colorful mural is entitled Margarita and depicts scenes from the story.*

America in 1918. Under Stalin, the mansion became the People's Commissariat for Foreign Affairs. In 1995, a large fire broke out, and many parts of the structure were severely damaged. For two years the Russian diplomatic firm UpDK painstakingly restored the entire building. Today it serves as the House of Receptions for the Ministry of Foreign Affairs.

Continuing south down Spiridonovka leads to Malaya Nikitskaya and the **Gorky House Museum** at number 6. Maxim Gorky (1868–1936), known as the 'Father of Soviet Literature', lived here for five years before his death. It was Stalin who gave Gorky this house as a meeting place for the union of writers and artists, but the writer felt uncomfortable here, 'like a bird in a golden cage'. The writer's real name was Alexei Maximovich Peshkov; he later adopted the pen name Gorky (meaning bitter). Orphaned in childhood, Maxim was put to work at the age of 11, and attempted suicide eight years later in 1887. He became widely known after writing his 1899 *Sketches and Stories*, and the poem *Song of the Stormy Petrel* in 1901. He followed with the plays *The Lower Depths* (centered in Moscow's destitute Myasnitskaya or Butcher area) and *Summer Folk*. In 1906, to avoid postrevolution crackdowns (he had already been exiled to Siberia in 1901), Gorky journeyed to the United States supported by Mark Twain. While there, he wrote his most famous work, *Mother*, the first example of socialist realist literature. Although it is suspected he was poisoned on Stalin's orders, the dictator still honored Gorky by placing his ashes in the Kremlin wall.

In 1902, the architect Shekhtel was commissioned by a member of the Riabushinsky banking dynasty, Stepan Pavlovich, to design the house in art-nouveau style; it was completed four years later. Encompassing style-moderne themes of nature and fluidity, the mansion was given stained-glass windows, a glass roof and flowered bas-reliefs. The exquisite staircase resembles a giant crashing wave which spills out onto the parquet floors. Today the library has over 10,000 volumes and the parlor looks as it did when Gorky lived here. A superb collection of carved ivory is in the bedroom, and many of the writer's books and letters are on display. The museum is open 10am–4.30pm, Wednesdays and Fridays 12pm–6pm; closed Mondays and Tuesdays. (The Gorky Literary Museum is at 25 Povarskaya Ulitsa, near Barrikadnaya Metro station.)

Next to the Gorky House, at 2/6 Spiridonovka, is the **Alexei Tolstoy House Museum**. This is not the Leo Tolstoy of *War and Peace*, but a distant relative. This Tolstoy wrote *Ivan the Terrible*, *Peter the Great*, and the well-known trilogy about the Revolution, *The Road to Calvary*, completed in 1941; a year later it was awarded the Stalin Prize. His granddaughter Tatyana Tolstaya is a well-recognized contemporary author. Open 1pm–8pm; closed Mondays and Tuesdays.

On the other side of Gorky House stands the white Empire-style **Church of the Ascension**. It was here in February 1831 that Alexander Pushkin married Natalia

Goncharova (who later was the cause of the St Petersburg duel in which Pushkin was killed). It is said that during the ceremony a crucifix fell from a wall and candles mysteriously blew out; an omen not taken lightly. The church, still in the process of being restored, is open for worship. At 12 Malaya Nikitskaya stands the 18th-century classical **Bobrinsky Mansion**, originally built by the Dolgoruky family and inhabited by Catherine the Great's illegitimate son with Grigory Orlov. Bobrinsky's descendants lived here up until the Revolution.

TVERSKAYA-YAMSKAYA ULITSA (STREET)

Passing the Minsk Hotel, whose restaurant specializes in Byelorussian cuisine, brings you to **Triumfalnaya Ploshchad** at the intersection of Tverskaya and the Sadovoye Koltso (Garden Ring). In the 18th century the square was marked by triumphal arches used to welcome czars and returning victorious armies. On the corner of the square stands a large building with ten columns—the **Tchaikovsky Concert Hall** (built for Meyerhold's Theater in the 1930s), where orchestras and dance ensembles perform. The Moscow Stars and Winter Festivals also take place here. The Mayakovskaya Metro station is in front of the Hall. Directly behind it, at number 2, is the circular-domed building of the **Satire Theater**, founded in 1924, whose productions have ranged from *The Cherry Orchard* to the *Three-Penny Opera*. Across the street is the **Peking Hotel**, housing one of the few Chinese restaurants in town.

A statue of the poet Vladimir Mayakovsky (1893–1930) stands in the square at Mayakovskaya Metro station. On the other side of the square is the Sofia Restaurant, which serves Bulgarian food. At number 43 is the House of Children's Books, and at number 46 the Exhibition Hall of Artist Unions. A ten-minute walk north to 4 Ulitsa Fadeyeva is the **Glinka Music Museum**, opened in 1943. The museum has a large collection of musical instruments, rare recordings and unique manuscripts of famous composers, such as Tchaikovsky, Shostakovich and Glinka; open 11am–6.30pm; closed Mondays. Nearby at 3 Delegatskaya Ulitsa is the **Decorative and Folk Art Museum** with displays of Russian jewelry, applied art and handicrafts. Open 10am–6pm, 10am–4pm weekends; closed Fridays.

Tverskaya-Yamskaya Street ends at Byelorusskaya Ploshchad, also called Zastava (Gate) Square, which was the old site of the Kamer-Kollezhsky gates on the road to Tver. At the center of the square is a **Monument to Maxim Gorky** (1868–1935), erected in 1951. Trains from the 120-year-old **Byelorussky Railway Station** journey to points west, including Warsaw, Berlin, Paris and London. The Byelorusskaya Metro station is in front. Here Tverskaya-Yamskaya Street turns into Leningradsky Prospekt, which runs all the way to the international airport, Sheremetyevo II. On the next side street are the offices of the newspaper *Pravda*, whose circulation was once ten million. After the 1991 attempted putsch, the offices were shut down for the first time in its history. There was no money to continue operations (Communist Party funds had been frozen). A few months later the newspaper was back in business, but it was asking for investments and the price of the paper had increased.

Along Begovaya Ulitsa (Running Street) is the **Moscow Hippodrome**, a race course. It was built a century ago in Empire style and frequented by the Russian aristocracy. The Hippodrome is open three or four times weekly, drawing up to 20,000 people for the nine daily races. During off hours, horses can be hired. The **Casino Royale** is now located in the Hippodrome's Central Hall. This was the idea of renowned eye-surgeon Svyatoslav Fyodorov, who developed the famous daisy-wheel operating room technique—operating on up to 10 patients in one room at a time; Fyodorov also breeds horses. In nearby Begovaya Lane, find the small archway designed by Klodt, who also crafted the famous horse sculptures on St Petersburg's Anichkov bridge. A little farther up, at 32 Leningradsky, is the Hotel Sovietskaya and the **Romany Gypsy Theater**. Seating over 800, the theater focuses on gypsy national culture. The Moscow Chamber Musical Theater is at 71 Leningradsky Prospekt.

From here you can take the Metro or a bus to return to the city center.

Ulitsa Vozdvizhenka and Novy (New) Arbat

In 1991, Kalinin Prospekt was divided into two different streets. Vozdvizhenka Street (the name stems from the 16th-century Krestovozdvizhensky or Church of the Exaltation) runs from the Kremlin's Kutafya

The Old Arbat is one of the most popular shopping areas in Moscow. Everything from antikvariant antique stores and portrait painters to McDonald's are found along this pedestrian thoroughfare.

Tower (by the Alexandrov Gardens) to Arbatskaya Ploshchad (Arbat Square). Novy Arbat begins at Arbat Square and continues to the Kalininsky Most (Bridge). Here Novy Arbat becomes Kutuzovsky Prospekt and later the Minsk Highway.

The old route was known as Novodvizhenskaya; it stretched from the Kremlin to the outer walls of the city. A new thoroughfare was built along this former road

and from 1963 to 1991 it was named Kalinin, after a leader of the Communist Party, Mikhail Kalinin. The old section of the prospekt runs from the Kremlin to the Boulevard Ring, where the more modern part begins.

The road starts by a large gray building off Mokhovaya—the Russian State Library (see page 141). The first part of the street still contains a few 18th-century buildings. At number 7 is the former **Monastery of the Holy Cross**. The house at number 9 belonged to Tolstoy's grandfather, Count Volkonsky, upon whom he based a character in *War and Peace*. At the corner of Romanov Pereulok is an early 18th-century mansion that belonged to a member of the wealthy Sheremetyev family. Across the street at number 5 is an old mansion of the Tolyzin estate, built by Kazakov. Many prominent Soviet officials also lived along this street, such as Frunze, Voroshilov, Kosygin and Khrushchev. The nearest Metro station is Alexandrovsky Sad.

At number 16 is the white, medieval former mansion of the merchant Arseny Morozov who, in 1899, hired his friend, the designer Mazyrin, to model his residence after a 16th-century Moorish castle they had seen while visiting Portugal; each room was decorated in a different style from Greek to English Gothic. After the Revolution it was turned over to the Union of Anarchists. In 1959, it became the **House of Friendship**, where delegations of foreign friendship societies meet. Nearby, the eight-story building with one turret was built in the 1920s as the first Soviet skyscraper in constructivist style. Near the Arbatskaya Metro station, on Bolshaya Nikitskaya Ulitsa, is the Journalist Club. Opposite this is a monument to Gogol, standing in front of the house where the writer lived.

STARY (OLD) ARBAT

On the southwest corner of Arbat Square is the Prague Restaurant, marking the entrance to one of the city's oldest sections, the **Arbat**. Long ago the Arbat Gates led into Moscow. *Arbad* is an old Russian word meaning beyond the town walls. Alternatively, some believe the word could stem from the Mongol word *arba*, a sack to collect tributes; the ancient 'Arab' settlements; or the Latin *arbutum*, cherry, because of the cherry orchards that were once in the area. There is one other proposed origin: a creek named Chertory, the Devil's Creek, once meandered or 'hunchbacked' through the vicinity, which was quite damp and boggy. When a small one-kopek candle started a fire in the All Saints Church and burnt it and the rest of Moscow to the ground in 1365, many thought the area cursed. The Russian word *khorbaty* means hunchbacked place.

The area was first mentioned in 15th-century chronicles. It lay along the Smolensk Road, making it a busy trade center. Many court artisans lived here in the 16th century; in the 19th century many wealthy and educated people chose to live in the Arbat. Today the street is a cobbled pedestrian thoroughfare about one kilometer (two-thirds of a mile) long, and one of the most popular meeting and shopping spots in Moscow. Along with its shops, cafés, art galleries, concert and theater halls and a museum tracing the history of the area, are portrait painters, performance artists and even demonstrators. It is also a frequent site for festivals and carnivals. Chekhov once said that 'the Arbat is one of the most pleasant spots on Earth'. It is definitely worth a stroll.

The colorful buildings lining the pedestrian mall and its side streets have a rich and romantic history. Many poems, songs and novels, such as Anatoly Rybakov's *Children of the Arbat*, have been written about this area. The czar's stablemen once lived along Starokonivshenny (Old Stable) Lane. An old church stood on the corner of Spasopeskovsky Pereulok (Savior-on-the-Sand Lane). Other small streets have the names Serebryany (Silversmith), Plotnikov (Carpenter) and Kalashny (Pastrycook). After a leisurely stroll, you will better understand the lyrics to a popular song: 'Oy, Arbat, a whole lifetime is not enough to travel through your length!'

At 7 Arbat is the Literary Café, a favorite of both Mayakovsky and Isadora Duncan's husband, the Russian poet Yesenin, in the 1920s. The niece of Tolstoy, Countess Obolenskaya, lived at number 9; it is now an antique store. Several other *antikvariant*, souvenir shops and book stores are located along the street. After passing the 1,000-seat **Vakhtangov Theater** (founded in 1921), at number 26, turn right up Bolshoi Nikolopeskovsky Pereulok. At number 11 is the **Skryabin Museum**, home of the Russian composer from 1912 to 1915. His concert programs, photographs and books are on display, along with recordings of his music; there is also a chamber concert hall. Open 10am–4.30pm, 12pm–6.30pm Wednesdays and Fridays; closed Mondays and Tuesdays. Walking a few short blocks west to Spasopeskovsky Pereulok leads to the **Spaso House**, part of the US Embassy; it was originally built in neo-Empire style by banker Ftorov in 1913. Along this street notice the **Church of the Savior-on-the-Sand**, built in 1711, and currently under restoration.

Crossing the Arbat, continue a block south down to 10 Krivoarbatsky Pereulok and the **Melnikov House**. In 1927, the renowned architect Konstantin Melnikov built this house in constructivist style for his family, and lived here until his death in 1974. (Melnikov designed Lenin's glass sarcophagus.) The exterior consists of two honeycombed concrete cylinders cut into each other and connected by hexagonal windows, and the inside stories are linked by a spiral staircase. Today his son is restoring the house, and is planning to open it as a museum. One block further south leads to the **Herzen Museum** at 27 Pereulok Sivtsev Vrazhek (*vrazhek* means gully—once the River Sivtsev ran through a gully in this location). The writer

Alexander Herzen (1812–70) lived here from 1843 to 1846. Here he wrote *Dr Krupov*, *Magpie and the Thief* and his famous novel *Who is to Blame?* For these revolutionary views he was exiled in 1847. From London, Herzen wrote his radical political magazine *Kolokol* (The Bell) and smuggled copies into Russia. His *Letters on Nature*, according to Lenin, put him alongside 'the most prominent thinkers of his time'. (Herzen was born in the house at 25 Tverskoi Boulevard.) The museum is open 11am–5.30pm, 1pm–5.30pm Wednesdays and Fridays; closed Mondays.

At 53 Arbat is the blue and white stucco **Pushkin House**. Here, in 1831, the famous writer lived with his new bride Natalia Goncharova. Exhibits are on his marriage and Moscow activities. (Tchaikovsky also lived here in 1875.) Open 11am–5pm; closed Mondays and Tuesdays. In connection with the 200th anniversary of Alexander Pushkin's birth in 1999, the city created a 'Pushkin Path' that leads from this house to the Pushkin Museum on Prechistenka Street.

The Arbat ends at the Garden Ring Road and Smolenskaya Ploshchad where one of Stalin's seven Gothic skyscrapers stands, now the MID or Ministry of Foreign Affairs.

NOVY ARBAT

The avenue from Arbat Square on the Boulevard Ring to the Kalinin Bridge is known as Novy (New) Arbat, the main western thoroughfare of the city. The shops and flats in this area were built during Khrushchev's regime in the 1960s; they were designed by Moscow's chief architect Mikhail Posokhin. Across the street from the Prague Restaurant (one of the oldest in Moscow) is the **Church of Simon Stylites** with colorful *kokoshniki* gables. It was here in 1801 that Prince Nikolai Sheremetyev married serf-actress Praskovia Zhemchugova-Kovalyova. Theirs is one of Russia's most romantic love stories. She, a daughter of a serf blacksmith, worked as an actress on the Sheremetyev estate in Kuskovo. They fell in love in 1789 and ten years later Nikolai granted her freedom. Sadly, two years after the marriage, Praskovia died in childbirth. Today the church has an exhibition hall, and is open for worship.

Heading north, down the side street behind the church, leads to the **Lermontov Memorial House** at 2 Malaya Molchanovka. Mikhail Lermontov (1814–41) lived here with his grandmother from 1829 to 1832, and while studying at Moscow University wrote about 100 poems and plays. He is best known for the 1840 prose-novel *A Hero of Our Time*; the main character Grigory Pechorin is one of the great romantic heroes in modern literature. For a poem criticizing the court's connivance in the death of Pushkin, Lermontov was exiled to the Caucasus by Nicholas I. Like Pushkin, Lermontov also died in a duel—over a trivial quarrel with a fellow infantry officer—he was shot through the heart on July 15, 1841. The museum is open

After the collapse of the Soviet Union people were free to demonstrate. These protesters with the Ukrainian Orthodox Church openly voice their demands in Moscow's Old Arbat Square.

11am–5pm, 2pm–5pm Wednesdays and Fridays; closed Mondays and Tuesdays.

Next to the church, at 8 Novy Arbat, is **Dom Knigi** (House of Books), the city's largest bookstore (closed Sundays). Here books, posters, and even antiques and icons (for rubles only) are for sale. The Malachite Casket Jewelry Shop is also in this building. On the same side of the street is the Melodia Record Shop and the 3,000-seat Oktyabr Cinema at number 24.

A series of shops and cafés line the left side of Novy Arbat. On the second floor of number 19 is the **Irish House**, a hard-currency store where you can find most Western food products and the **Shamrock Bar**. The block ends at the 2,000-seat Tropikana (formerly the Arbat) Restaurant (open 6pm–6am with loud music and floor shows).

Novy Arbat crosses the Garden Ring at Novinsky Bulvar (Boulevard) and ends at the river. The **White House** or Beli Dom, once headquarters of the Russian Parliament, stands to the right. It was the famous scene of two coup attempts. In August 1991, a number of conservative plotters tried to overthrow the Gorbachev government while he was vacationing in the Crimea. Boris Yeltsin, who became the nation's hero, climbed atop a tank in front of the building and rallied thousands of demonstrators to oppose the coup's collaborators. The events of these days led to the fall of the Soviet Union four months later. Then two years later, in September 1993, after Yeltsin suspended the constitution for three months, Parliament mutinied and Yeltsin's deputy Alexander Rutskoi declared himself 'acting president'. For eleven days, Rutskoi and his 300-member unofficial entourage took control of the White House until army tanks shelled them into submission. After the building's restoration, the Moscow patriarch came by and blessed it. It has since been turned into an office block.

Further east, on the same side of the river, is the Sovincenter and the **Mezhdunarodnaya (International) Hotel**, built with the help of Armand Hammer and used by foreign firms. Before more hotels were built in Moscow, the Mezhdunarodnaya was the international businessman's hotel of choice. It has a number of restaurants, cafés and shops, a health center with sauna and pool, a pharmacy, an Aeroflot ticket office and a food store on the second floor. Next door, in the **Sovincenter** office building (also known as the World Trade Center), are many other airline offices and Federal Express is on the ground floor.

Kutuzovsky Prospekt

After crossing the Kalinin Bridge, Novy Arbat becomes Kutuzovsky Prospekt, named after the Russian General Mikhail Kutuzov (1745–1813), who fought against Napoleon. The building on the right with the star-spire is the **Ukraina Hotel**, which celebrated its 40th birthday in 1997. It has a large Ukrainian restaurant with other European-style cafés, a jazz club and disco. (This is one of Stalin's seven Gothic structures.) A statue to the Ukrainian poet Taras Shevchenko stands in front. On the next corner south of the hotel is the **Hero City of Moscow Obelisk**. Troops left from this point in 1941 to fight the advancing German army.

The obelisk stands at the junction with Bolshaya Dorogomilovskaya, along which is the **Kievsky Railway Station** (with a Metro station). Kievsky, which celebrated its 80th anniversary in 1998, was once the largest station in Europe (this honor is now held by Moscow's Kazansky Station), and is still considered the city's most beautiful. The train terminal handles up to 35,000 passengers a day.

Stalin's dacha was in this area, where he died in 1953. At number 26 Kutuzovsky, a plaque marks the 30-year residence of Leonid Brezhnev; Yuri Andropov also lived here. The prospekt ends at the **Triumphal Arch** in **Victory Square** (Ploshchad Pobedy), designed by Osip Bovet in 1829 to honor Russia's victory in the War of 1812. It originally stood in front of the Byelorussky Train Station and was moved to this spot in 1968, when Tverskaya Street was widened. It is decorated with the coats-of-arms of Russia's provinces. Here on Poklonnaya Hill, Napoleon waited for Moscow's citizens to bow to him and relinquish the keys to the city. From the hill is a magnificent view of Moscow—Anton Chekhov once said, 'Those who want to understand Russia should look at Moscow from Poklonnaya Hill.' Between Kutuzovskaya Metro station and the arch is the **Statue of Mikhail Kutuzov** by Nikolas Tomsky and an obelisk that marks the common graves of 300 men who died in the War of 1812.

The large circular building at number 38 is the **Battle of Borodino Museum**, open 10.30am–6pm, 10.30am–4pm weekends; closed Fridays. The 68 cannons in front were captured from Napoleon. In 1912, to commemorate the 100th anniversary of the war, Franz Rouband was commissioned to paint scenes of the Battle of Borodino, which took place on August 26, 1812 (September 7 on the new calendar). The large murals are displayed in the museum, which was constructed in 1962 to honor the 150th anniversary. Behind is the **Kutuzov Hut**. Here on September 1, 1812, as the French invaded Moscow, Kutuzov and the Military Council decided to abandon the city. The cottage is open 10am–5pm, closed Mondays and Fridays. The actual site of the Battle of Borodino is about 120 kilometers (75 miles) outside of Moscow (see Vicinity of Moscow section on page 201).

From here, Kutuzovsky Prospekt becomes the Mozhaiskoye Chausee, the Minsk Highway, which leads to the city of Minsk in Byelorussia.

MOSCOW BURNING

Narye at lunch next day—the Moscow Chief of Police, Schetchinsky by name. Before we had been more than 10 minutes at table a wild-looking police officer rushed in unannounced and uttered one word—"Pajare!"—"Quick!" The Chief of Police sprang from his seat while Narychkine and Jenny, with one voice, exclaimed: "A fire? Where?" A fire is no rare event in Moscow and is always a serious matter, for of the 11,000 houses in the centre of Moscow only 3,500 are of stone, the rest are of wood. Just as St. Petersburg counts its disasters in floods, Moscow numbers the fires that have reduced great stretches of the city to ashes, the most terrible being, of course in 1812, when barely 6,000 buildings remained standing.

I was seized with a sudden urge to see this fire for myself.

"Can I come with you?" I begged the Chief of Police.

"If you promise not to delay me a single second."

I seized my hat as we ran together to the door. His troika, with its three mettlesome black horses, was waiting. We jumped in and shot off like lightning while the messenger, already in the saddle, spurred his own mount and led the way. I had no conception of how fast a troika can move behind three galloping horses, and for a moment I could not even draw breath. Dust from the macadamised country road billowed up in clouds above our heads; then, as we skimmed over the pointed cobbles of Moscow's streets, sparks struck by our flying hooves fell around us like rain and clung desperately to the iron strut while the Chief of Police yelled: "Faster! Faster!"

As soon as we left Petrovsky Park we could see smoke hanging like an umbrella—fortunately there was no wind. In the town there were dense crowds, but the messenger, riding a horse's length ahead, cleared a path for us, using his knout on any bystanders who did not move fast enough to please him, and we passed between ranks of people like lightning between clouds. Every moment I feared that someone would be run over, but by some miracle no one was even touched and five minutes later we were facing the fire, our horses trembling, their legs folding beneath them. A whole island of houses was burning fiercely. By good fortune the road in front of it was fifteen or twenty yards wide, but on every other side only narrow alleys separated it from neighbouring dwellings. Into one of these alleys rushed M. Schetchinsky, I at his heels. He urged me back—in vain. "Then hold fast to my sword-belt," he cried, "and don't let go!" For several seconds I was in the midst of flames and thought I would suffocate. My very lungs seemed on fire as I gasped for breath. Luckily another alley led off to our right. the Chief of Police ran into it, I followed and we both sank on a baulk of timber. "You've lost your hat," he laughed. "D'you feel inclined to go back for it?"

"God! No! Let it lie! All I want is a drink."

At a gesture from my companion a woman standing by went back in to her house and brought out a pitcher of water. Never did the finest wine taste so good! As I drank, we heard a rumble like thunder. The fire-engines had arrived!

Moscow's Fire Service is very well organised, and each of the 21 districts has its own engines. A man is stationed on the highest tower in the area, on the watch day and night, and at the first sign of fire he sets in motion a system of globes to indicate exactly where smoke is rising. So the engines arrive without losing a second, as they did on this occasion, but the fire was quicker still. It had started in the courtyard of an inn, where a carter had carelessly lit a cigar near a heap of straw. I looked into that courtyard. It was an inferno!

To my amazement, M. Schetchinsky directed the hoses not on the fire itself but on the roofs of the nearby houses. He explained that there could be no hope of saving the houses that were actually burning, but if the sheets of iron on neighbouring rooftops could be prevented from getting red hot there might be a chance of saving the homes they covered.

The only source of water in the district was 300 yards away, and soon the engines were racing to it to refill their tanks. "Why don't the people make a chain?" I asked.

"What is that?"

"In France, everyone in the street would volunteer to pass along buckets of water so that the engines could go on pumping."

"That's a very good idea! I can see how useful that would be. But we have no law to make people do that."

"Nor have we, but everyone rushes to lend a hand. When the Théâtre Italien caught fire I saw princes working in the chain."

"My dear M. Dumas," said the Chief of Police, "that's your French fraternity in action. The people of Russia haven't reached that stage yet."

"What about the firemen?"

"They are under orders. Go and see how they are working and tell me what you think of them."

They were indeed working desperately hard. They had climbed into the attics of the nearby houses and with hatchets and levers, their left hands protected by gloves, they were trying to dislodge the metal roofing sheets, but they were too late. Smoke was already pouring from the top storey of the corner house and its roof glowed red. Still the men persisted like soldiers attacking an enemy position. They were really wonderful, quite unlike our French firemen who attack the destructive element on their own initiative, each finding his own way to conquer the flames. No! Theirs was a passive obedience, complete and unquestioning. If their chief had said "Jump in the fire!" they would have done so with the same devotion to duty, though they well knew that it meant certain death to no purpose.

Brave? Yes, indeed, and bravery in action is always inspiring to see. But I was the only one to appreciate it. Three or four thousand people stood there watching, but they showed not the slightest concern at this great devastation, no sign of admiration for the courage of the firemen. In France there would have been cries of horror, encouragement, applause, pity, despair, but here—nothing! Complete silence, not of consternation but of utter indifference, and I realised the profound truth of M. Schetchinsky's comment that as yet the Russians have no conception of fraternity as we know it, no idea of brotherhood between man and his fellows. God! How many revolutions must a people endure before they can reach our level of understanding?

Alexandre Dumas, Adventures in Czarist Russia

The Boulevard Ring

During the 16th and 17th centuries, the stone walls of the Beli Gorod (White Town) stretched around the area now known as the Boulevard Ring. During the 'Time of Troubles' at the end of the 17th century, Boris Godunov fortified the walls and built 37 towers and gates. By 1800 the walls were taken down and the area was planted with trees and gardens, divided by a series of small connected boulevards. Ten *bulvari* make up the Bulvarnoye Koltso, the Boulevard Ring, actually a horseshoe shape that begins in the southwest off Prechistenka Street and circles around to the back of the Rossiya Hotel on the other side of the Kremlin. Some of the squares still bear the name of the old gate towers. Frequent buses run around the ring, stopping off at each intersecting boulevard.

THE TEN BOULEVARDS

The first bears the name of the writer Nikolai Gogol. **Gogolevsky Bulvar** stretches from the Cathedral of Christ Our Savior to Arbat Square. It was known as the Immaculate Virgin Boulevard (Prechistensky Bulvar) until 1924; the first square is still called Prechistenskiye Vorota (Gates) with the Kropotkinskaya Metro station nearby. The right side of the street is lined with mansions dating back to the 1800s. In the 19th century the aristocratic Naryshkin family had their estate at number ten. At number 14 is the Central Chess Club. The next square is Arbatskaya, which leads into the Old Arbat district (see page 158). A side street leading to the Kremlin is Znamenka, which dates back to the 13th century. It means 'the sign', taking its name at the time from the Church of the Virgin Icon. In the 17th century the czar's apothecary was nearby; medicinal herbs were planted on Vagankovsky Hill.

Nikitsky Bulvar extends from Novy Arbat to Bolshaya Nikitskaya Ulitsa. Until 1992, it was named after the famous Russian army commander Alexander Suvorov, who lived at the end of the thoroughfare. The Nikitskiye Gates used to stand at the junction of the boulevard and Bolshaya Nikitskaya Ulitsa, which is named Nikitskaya Ploshchad after a monastery that was in the area. Gogol lived at number seven; increasingly despondent in his later years, Gogol burned the second volume of his novel *Dead Souls* in this house and died here in 1852. A monument to Nikolai Gogol, upon which characters from his books are depicted, stands in front. The Union of Journalists, opened in 1920, is at number eight. The General Lunin House, at number 12, was built by Gilliardi in Russian-Empire style with eight Corinthian columns (1818–22). It is now the **Oriental Art Museum**, open daily 11am–7pm, 11am–4pm Mondays. The museum exhibits Asian art, Siberian shaman artifacts and works by Nikolai Roerich (1874–1946), who studied and traveled in the Himalayas.

Bolshaya Nikitskaya extends from the Kremlin's Manezhnaya Square to the Boulevard Ring. In the 15th century, this was the route to the town of Novgorod. At number 19 is the **Mayakovsky Theater**, home to Meyerhold's Theater of the Revolution in the 1920s. (Meyerhold was later arrested in the 1930s and died in prison.) At number 13 is the **Tchaikovsky Conservatory Grand Hall**, the country's largest music school. The conservatory was founded in 1866 by Nikolai Rubinstein. (His brother Anton founded the St Petersburg Conservatory in 1862.) Tchaikovsky taught here and pupils included Rachmaninov, Skryabin and Khachaturian. The building also has two concert halls; the annual International Tchaikovsky Piano Competition is held in the larger one. A statue of Tchaikovsky stands in front (sculpted by Vera Mukhina in 1954). Notice the musical notes on the cast-iron railings—they come from the famous opus *Glory to the Russian People* from the Glinka opera *Ivan Susanin*. This was once the mid-18th century Moscow home of Princess Ekaterina Vorontsova-Dashkova, a close friend of Catherine the Great's; the czarina made her head of the Russian Academy of Arts and Sciences in 1783.

Nearby, at number 12 Gazetny Pereulok (Lane), is the **Menschikov Mansion**. Popular architect Matvei Kazakov designed the blue and white porticoed residence for Prince Sergei Menschikov (grandson of Alexander, Peter the Great's prime minister). It was restored after the great 1812 fire in Empire style.

Back on Bolshaya Nikitskaya, at number six, is the **Zoological Museum**. Founded in 1791 as a natural history project of Moscow University, it is one of Moscow's oldest museums. It was opened to the public in 1805; the present building was completed in 1902. The museum has a collection of over 10,000 species of animal, bird, fish and insect from around the world. Open 10am–6pm; closed Mondays.

Tverskoi Bulvar begins with the Monument to Kliment Timiryazev, a prominent Russian botanist. Built in 1796, it is the oldest boulevard on the ring, and was once a very fashionable promenade. Pushkin, Turgenev and Tolstoy all mentioned the Tverskoi in their writings. At number 11, where the great Russian actress Yermolova lived during the last half of her life, is now the **Yermolova House Museum**. Maria Yermolova (1853–1928) was the first person in the Soviet era to be awarded the title of 'Peoples' Artist'. The theater hosts a salon where small concerts are also performed. The museum is open 1pm–8pm, 12pm–7pm weekends; closed Tuesdays. At number 23 is the **Pushkin Drama Theater**, and across the street the **Gorky Theater**, built in 1973. The Literary Institute, at number 25, was started by Maxim Gorky in 1933. (The revolutionary Alexander Herzen was born in this building in 1812.) Tverskoi ends at Pushkin Square and the Pushkinskaya Metro station.

The Strastnoi (Passion) Monastery used to be in the area of the **Strastnoi Bulvar**, which begins with the Statue of Pushkin. On Pushkin's birthday, June 6, many people crowd the square to honor the poet. Chekhovskaya Metro station is close to the square. Strastnoi is one of the shortest and widest parts of the Boulevard Ring. It was Catherine the Great who ordered the city's original walls taken down from around the ring area. The city's Catherine Hospital, with its 12 Ionic columns, is at number 15. It was originally built by Matvei Kazakov as a palace for the Gagarin princes, and later housed the English Club from 1802 to 1812.

About one and a half kilometers (one mile) to the north at 2 Ulitsa Dostoevskovo is the **Dostoevsky Apartment Museum**, where the pensive writer lived from 1823–37. The events surrounding this ground floor apartment would greatly affect his later writings—Fyodor's father worked as a surgeon at the Hospital for the Poor next door; his mother contracted consumption and died here. Their windows also faced onto a route that prisoners took on their way to Siberia. The three rooms are open 11am–6pm, 2pm–6.30pm Wednesdays and Fridays; closed Mondays and Tuesdays.

The Petrovskiye Gates used to stand at what is now the beginning of **Petrovsky Bulvar**, which runs from Ulitsa Petrovka to Trubnaya Ploshchad. It is one of the few areas on the ring whose appearance has hardly changed since the 1800s. Some buildings still remain from the 14th century, such as the **Petrovsky (St Peter's) Monastery**, which still stands on the Neglinnaya River (see Ulitsa Petrovka on page 136). Trubnaya originates from the Russian word *truba*, meaning pipe; the river was diverted through a pipe under this square. Many of the old mansions on this boulevard were converted into hospitals and schools after the Revolution. At the end of Petrovsky stands the building of the former Hermitage Hotel; its restaurant was once the most popular in Moscow—Turgenev, Dostoevsky and Tchaikovsky all ate here. After the Revolution it became the House of the Collective Farmer and today is a theater. At 3 Karetny Ryad (Carriage Row) are the Hermitage Gardens.

Branching off north from Petrovsky is Tsvetnoi Bulvar, named after the flower (*tsveti*) market that used to be here. At number 13 is the **Old Circus**, also known as *Tsirk na Tsvetnom Bulvare* or Circus on Tsvetnoi Boulevard (closed Tuesdays). It was established by Salamonsky for his private circus, the first in Moscow. After the Revolution it was turned into the State Circus. In the late 1980s a new circus was built on the site to match the original building. The 'new' Old Circus was reopened in 1989 under independent (non-State) management. Tickets can be purchased at the building itself or at your hotel's Service desk. Some kiosks on the street also sell tickets. Take the Metro to Tsvetnoi Bulvar. Make sure you buy tickets for the Old Circus (Stary Tsirk) since the New Circus (Novy Tsirk) is near Moscow University. (In summer tent circuses are set up in Gorky and Izmailovo parks.) Next to the Old Circus is the Tsentralny Rinok (Central Market), the best stocked *rinok* in the city; open daily.

Rozhdestvensky (Nativity) Bulvar ends at Ulitsa Sretenka, a popular shopping area. On the south side are the 14th-century walls of the **Convent of the Nativity**

of the Virgin. It was founded in 1386 by the wife of Prince Andrei Serpukhovsky, son of Ivan I, as a place for unmarried women and widows to take refuge. The Church of St John Chrysostom was built in the mid-17th century. The white single-domed Cathedral of the Nativity (1501–05) houses the Icon of the Virgin which hangs on the left of the iconostasis; it was discovered in the 1980s by a priest clean-ing an old door. The Refectory Church once housed exhibitions, but the Church is now taking control of the building. Other structures are also used as a refuge by the homeless.

On the corner of the boulevard and Sretenka Street stands the **Printer's Assumption Church**, built with money donated by the printers who lived in the area.

The **Statue to Nadezhda Krupskaya** (1869–1939), Lenin's wife, marks the beginning of **Sretensky Bulvar**, the shortest boulevard with a length of 215 meters (705 feet). The Old Russian word *vstreteniye* means meeting. In 1395, the Vladimir Icon of the Mother of God was brought to Moscow and was met here at the gate of the White Town on its way to the Kremlin. Lining the sides of the boulevard are early 20th-century homes, distinguished by their original façades. In 1885, Moscow named its first public library, located here, after the writer Turgenev. The boulevard ends on Turgenevskaya Ploshchad with a Metro station of the same name.

A statue of the writer Griboedov (1795–1829) marks the beginning of **Chistoprudny Bulvar**. Its name, Clear Pond, comes from the pond at its center, which offers boating and ice-skating in winter. (The Rachka River was diverted underground.) To the right, in Arkhangelsky Pereulok, one can make out the tower of the Church of the Archangel Gabriel. Prince Alexander Menschikov ordered it built on his estate in 1707; he wanted it to be taller than the Kremlin's Ivan the Great Bell Tower. In 1723, the archangel at the top was struck by lightning, so for a while the tower was the second largest structure in Moscow. It was rebuilt in 1780 without the spire, and today it is topped by a golden cupola and known as the **Menschikov Tower**. Next door is the 19th-century neo-Gothic **Church of St Fyodor Stratilit**, used as a winter church. The Sovremennik (Contemporary) Theater (called the Moscow Workers' Theater of the Prolekult in the 1930s) is at number 19. It was originally built as a cinema in 1914. Nearby at 23 Ulitsa Makarenko lived the renowned master of Russian cinema, Sergei Eisenstein. (See Special Topic on page 506.) At number 6 Furmanny Pereulok is the **Vasnetsov Memorial Apartment** where the painter lived from 1903 to 1933. The museum dis-plays his paintings, fairy-tale drawings, watercolors, sketches and lithographs. Open 11am–5pm, 12pm–6pm Wednesdays and Fridays; closed Sundays and Mondays. The closest Metro station is Chistiye Prudy.

Pokrovsky (Intercession) Bulvar begins at Ulitsa Pokrovka. The 18th-century buildings to the east used to serve as the Pokrovsky barracks. The highly decorative rococo-style house at number 14 was known as the Chest of Drawers. Built in 1766, the façade is decorated with many strange beasts and birds. Ulitsa Pokrovka is distinguished by many well-preserved old churches and aristocratic residences. North of the ring, at number 22, is the baroque-style **Apraksin Mansion**, built in 1766. At the south corner of Pokrovka and Armyansky Pereulok stands the classical-style **Church of Saints Cosmas and Damian**, built between 1791–93 by Matvei Kazakov. A Colonel Khlebnikov commissioned the church, and also lived across the street in the palace located behind what is now the Belarus Embassy. Another palace, at 11 Pokrovka, was built in 1790 by Prince Ivan Gagarin, a famous naval captain. Stroll down Armyansky Lane to find the Armenian Embassy at number 2. The wealthy Armenian businessman Lazar Lazaryan came to Moscow from Persia during the reign of Catherine the Great and built this residence. The Lazaryan family later bequeathed the buildings to the Armenian community.

Across the street at number 3 is an old 17th-century manor house which now houses the **Lights of Moscow Museum** with exhibits on the history of Moscow's street lighting from 1730 to present day. Open 9am–4pm weekdays. The city's first kerosene lamps were installed on Tverskaya Street in 1861 (prior to this oil and alcohol-burning street lamps were used), which were soon followed by new gas lights around 1865. In 1883, the invention of electric lights (known as Yablochka's 'electric candle') was put to use during the coronation of Alexander III. The square of the Cathedral of Christ the Savior was lit by these special arc lights. Filament lamps soon followed. The last gas lamp was removed from Moscow in 1932, marking the end of an era—prior to the 18th century, Moscow was draped in winter darkness for over 15 hours a day.

Yauzsky Bulvar is the last and narrowest section of the Boulevard Ring. This ends by Yauzsky Gate Square, where the Yauza River joins the Moskva River. A few 18th-century mansions remain in this area. Branching off to Petropavlovsky Pereulok brings you to the 18th-century baroque **Church of Saints Peter and Paul**. The 17th-century Trinity Church is located to the south in Serebryanichesky Pereulok (Silversmiths' Lane), named after the jewelers' quarter. Across the river lies Moscow's old Zayauzye district, once home to artisans and tailors. Continuing along the banks of the Moskva, past another of Stalin's Gothic skyscrapers, leads you to the back of the Kremlin. One of the best views of the Kremlin is from the **Bolshoi Kamenny Most** (Large Stone Bridge), first constructed in 1692 and rebuilt in 1936.

The czars often took Pokrovsky Boulevard to their estate in **Izmailovo**, now a popular 3,000-acre (over 1,200 hectare) park in the eastern part of the city, with a theater, amusement park and summer tent circus. The estate, situated on an artificial island, dates back to the 14th century, and was the property of the Romanovs.

Later Peter the Great staged mock battle maneuvers here. The 17th-century Churches of the Nativity and Protecting Veil survive along with some of the gates and three-tiered bridges. It is especially worth visiting on weekends when a huge flea market stretches across the park with thousands of people selling a wide variety of goods—a marvelous place to shop and bargain. It can be reached from Izmailovsky Park Metro station.

One Metro stop before this, at Semyonovskaya, leads you to **Nikolsky Old Believers' Commune**. In 1652, the newly appointed Patriarch Nikon sought to reform the Church and remove any traditions from the service that did not follow the original Byzantine beliefs. Many people felt these reforms as an attack on the true Russian Church they had come to honor. Thus, a great schism broke out between Nikon's Orthodoxy and the groups who called themselves the Old Believers. They were even ready to go into exile for the sake of continuing to cross themselves with two fingers instead of with the newly prescribed three. The schism so weakened the independence and wealth of the Church that, after Nikon's death, Peter the Great placed the Church under the governing control of the Holy Synod. When Catherine the Great in 1771 granted Russia's citizens freedom to worship as they pleased, many Old Believers returned to Moscow from as far away as Siberia and continued to live together in community compounds. The Old Believers established this residence in 1790; the red and white Gothic-style church was soon filled with icons and other works of art contributed by wealthy patrons. In the 1800s many aristocratic families such as the Riabushinskys and Morozovs belonged to the Old Believers' sect. Services are held in the church daily at 8am and 6pm, and on Sundays mornings.

Another two Metro stops toward the city is Baumanskaya. Outside on the building to the right is a mosaic that depicts scenes from the Nyemyetskaya Sloboda or German Quarter where, in the 16th and 17th centuries, most foreigners were required to live outside the city walls (so as not to so easily spread Western ideas to the population). It was in this area that Peter the Great was first introduced to his lover Anna Mons by his Swiss friend Franz Lefort, after whom the nearby prison, Lefortovo, is now named. A few minutes walk away is the **Yelokhovsky Cathedral**, at 15 Spartakovskaya Ulitsa. From 1943 to 1988 the complex was the seat of the Russian Patriarchy when it was then transferred to Danilovsky Monastery. The five-domed aquamarine structure, also known as the Church of the Epiphany, was rebuilt between 1837 and 1845 in an eclectic style. The poet Pushkin was baptized in the earlier church. The interior is filled with golden iconostases, and a few Church Patriarchs are buried in the chapel; Patriarch Alexei, who died in 1971, is buried in front of the main iconostasis. Open daily 8am–8pm with services held. At number 11 is Razgulyay Restaurant, a colorful Russian-style cellar eatery with Gypsy music on weekends; open daily 12pm–11.30pm.

THE TROIKA RIDE

*S*elifan sat up and, flicking the dappled-grey on the back with his whip a few times and making him set off at a trot, then flourishing the whip over all the three horses, he cried out in a thin, sing-song voice: 'Gee-up!' The horses roused themselves and pulled the light carriage along as though it were a feather. All Selifan did was to wave his whip and keep shouting: 'Gee-up, gee-up, gee-up!', bouncing smoothly on the box, while the troika flew up and down the hillocks scattered all along the highway that sloped imperceptibly downhill. Chichikov only smiled as he bounced lightly on his leather cushion, for he was very fond of fast driving. And what Russian does not love fast driving? How could his soul, which is so eager to whirl round and round, to forget everything in a mad carouse, to exclaim sometimes, 'To hell with it all!'—how could his soul not love it? How not love it when there is something wonderful and magical about it? It is as if some unseen force has caught you up on its wing and you yourself fly and everything with you flies also; milestones fly past, merchants on the coachman's seat of their covered wagons fly to meet you, on each side of you the forest flies past with its dark rows of firs and pines, with the thudding of axes and the caw-ing of crows; the whole road flies goodness only knows where into the receding distance; and there is something terrible in this rapid flashing by of objects which are lost to sight before you are able to discern them properly, and only the sky over your head and the light clouds and the moon appearing and disap-pearing through them seem motionless. Oh, you troika, you bird of a troika, who invented you? You could only have been born among a high-spirited people in a land that does not like doing things by halves, but has spread in a vast smooth plain over half the world, and you may count the milestones till your eyes are dizzy. And there is nothing ingenious, one would think, about this travelling con-traption. It is not held together by iron screws, but has been fitted up in haste with only an axe and chisel by some resourceful Yaroslav peasant. The driver wears no German top-boots: he has a beard and mittens, and sits upon goodness only knows what; but he has only to stand up and crack his whip and start up a song, and the horses rush like a whirlwind, the spokes of the wheels become one smooth revolving disc, only the road quivers and the pedestrian cries out as he stops in alarm, and the troika dashes on and on! And very soon all that can be seen in the distance is the dust whirling through the air.

Nikolai Gogol, Dead Souls, 1842

The Garden Ring (Sadovoye Koltso)

After much of Moscow burned in the great fire of 1812 (80 percent of the city and over 7,000 buildings were destroyed), it was decided to tear down all the old earthen ramparts and in their place build a circular road around the city. Anyone who had a house along the ring was required to plant a *sad* (garden); thus the thoroughfare was named Sadovoye Koltso (Garden Ring). It is Moscow's widest avenue, stretching for 16 kilometers (ten miles) around the city, with the Kremlin's Bell Tower at its midpoint. It is less than two kilometers (just over one mile) from the Boulevard Ring. The 16 squares and streets that make up this ring each have a garden in their name, such as Big Garden and Sloping Garden. Buses, trolleys and the Koltso Metro circle the route. Along the way, 18th- and 19th-century mansions and old manor houses are interspersed among the modern buildings.

Beginning by the river, near the Park Kultury Metro station and Gorky Park, is Krymskaya Ploshchad (Crimean Square), surrounded by very old classically designed provisional warehouses, built by Stasov between 1832 and 1835. Nearby is the Olympic Press Center, Novosti Press Agency and Progress Publishers, which publishes books in foreign languages.

Zubovsky Bulvar ends at Zubovsky Square, near Devichye Park (Maiden's Field) where carnivals were held and maidens danced to Russian folk tunes. To the right, Prechistenka Street leads to the Kremlin. The area between the Boulevard and Garden rings was once an aristocratic residential district; many old mansions are still in the area. Bolshaya Pirogovskaya (named after Nikolai Pirogov, a renowned surgeon) leads southwest to Novodevichy Monastery. Many of Moscow's clinics and research institutes are located in this area. At number 18 Zubovsky Bulvar is the former estate of the wealthy merchant Morozov.

On **Smolensky Bulvar** (formerly called Sennaya, the Haymarket) is the tall Ministry of Foreign Affairs. The Belgrad Hotel is at number 8.

Novinsky Bulvar begins at Smolenskaya Ploshchad. The great singer Fyodor Shalyapin (1873–1938) lived at number 25 from 1910 to 1922; it is now the **Shalyapin House Museum**. Open 11.30–4pm, 10am–6pm Tuesdays and Saturdays; closed Mondays and Fridays. Fyodor wrote in his autobiography *Pages From My Life* that his childhood was a mixture of beatings, poverty and hunger. At the age of 17, he was taken under the wing of Tbilisi Imperial Theater artist Dmitry Usatov to learn the art of singing. He would soon perform operas in St Petersburg and Nizhny Novgorod where he met Savva Mamontov, who later became his patron. After marrying the ballerina Iola Tornagi, Shalyapin began the 1896 Moscow operatic season as Susanin in *A Life for the Czar*. By training his incredible basso voice, utilizing expressive gestures, exerting strong stage control and using dramatic face make-up, Shalyapin was attracting the attention of the West by the end of the century. After performing on the stages of the Paris Grand Opera and La Scala in Milan, he also continued to tour throughout Russia and played every role imaginable. Later, severely disillusioned with the new Soviet regime, Shalyapin left Russia on July 29, 1922, on a foreign tour which lasted 16 years, until the singer's death. In his other book *The Mask and The Soul* Shalyapin wrote that he was a free man and wanted to live freely; he could not adapt his art to the confines of Soviet realism. Many decades later, upon the request of Shalyapin's five children, their father's remains were transferred from Batignoles Cemetery in Paris and reburied, on October 29, 1984, in Moscow's Novodevichy Cemetery (see page 189).

The boulevard ends at Kudrinskaya Ploshchad, named after the local village of Kudrino. Up until 1992, it was called Vosstaniya (Uprising) Square, named after the heavy fighting that took place here during the revolutions of 1905 and 1917. The US Embassy is just south of the square on Novinsky Bulvar.

Povarskaya Ulitsa, heading southeast from the square, was once one of the most fashionable areas of the city. It was named centuries ago, when the czar's servants and cooks lived in this area; *povarskaya* means cook. (Over 150 court cooks were employed to prepare 3,000 daily dishes for royalty and guests.) Other side streets were Khlebny (Bread), Nozhevoy (Knife), and Chashechny (Cup). The two lanes Skaterny (Tablecloth) and Stolovoy (Table) still branch off the street. In *War and Peace*, Tolstoy described the Rostov's estate at 52 Povarskaya Ulitsa, where there is now a statue of Tolstoy. Next door is the Writer's Club, named after the Soviet writer Alexander Fadeyev. The **Gorky Literary Museum** at number 25, recognizable by the statue of Gorky at the front, chronicles the life of the Russian writer who lived here before his departure abroad in 1921. It is open 10am–4.30pm, 12pm–6.30pm Wednesdays and Fridays; closed weekends. Gorky also spent his last years (1931–6) in a house on the neighboring street of Malaya Nikitskaya, at number 6, which is also a museum. (See page 154.)

On the other side of Kudrinskaya Ploshchad is Barrikadnaya Ulitsa with a Metro station of the same name. The Planetarium and Zoo are in the area. In May 1996 the **Moscow Zoo** was reopened after major reconstruction; open daily 9am–7pm. In the 1990s Moscow Mayor Yuri Luzhkov chose Georgian Zurab Tsereteli as the city's lead architect. Besides remodeling the zoo, he also designed the Manezh outdoor shopping complex, a 50-meter high (164 feet) monument to Peter the Great and a memorial sculpture dedicated to the victims of Stalin's purges. His next project is to construct a Disneyland-like park in Moscow's northwestern suburbs.

Barrikadnaya leads into Krasnaya Presnya, once a working-class district and the scene of many revolutionary battles. Nearby, at number 4 Bolshoi Predtechensky

Pereulok is the **Krasnaya Presnya Museum** which traces the history of the area and revolutions in Russia up to the present day. Open 10am–6pm, 11am–7pm Wednesdays; closed Mondays.

The famous writer Anton Chekhov lived from 1886 to 1890 along the next boulevard, **Sadovaya-Kudrinskaya**, in the small red house at number 6. It is now the **Chekhov House Museum**. Open 11am–6pm, 2pm–7pm Wednesdays and Fridays; closed Mondays. Chekhov was not born into nobility; his grandfather had, only a generation before, purchased the family's freedom from serfdom, and in 1876 the family moved to Moscow. By 1879 Chekhov had entered the Moscow University medical school and supported the family by writing humorous fiction. During his first seven years of literary activity, he published over 400 stories, novellas and sketches, and in 1883 received the Pushkin Prize in Literature. His first full-length play *The Seagull* failed miserably in its 1896 St Petersburg première. However, two years later, under the guidance of Stanislavsky at the Moscow Arts Theater, the production was a triumphant success. The company took the image of a seagull as its symbol, and Chekhov became, in the words of Stanislavsky, 'the soul of the Moscow Arts Theater'. He followed with *Uncle Vanya* in 1899, and while in Yalta wrote *The Three Sisters* (1901) and *The Cherry Orchard* (1903). In 1901, he married Olga Knipper, a leading actress with the Moscow Arts Theater. Chekhov died of tuberculosis on July 2, 1904, at the age of 44. Both Chekhov and Stanislavsky are buried in Moscow's Novodevichy Cemetery (see page 189).

Bolshaya Sadovaya Ulitsa (Great Garden Street) once had a triumphal arch through which troops returned to Moscow. The next boulevard, **Sadovaya-Triumfalnaya Ulitsa**, is followed by **Sadovaya-Samotechnaya Ulitsa**. At number 3 is the **Obraztzov Puppet Theater**, named after its founder. The puppet clock on the front of the building has 12 little houses with a tiny rooster on top; every hour, one house opens. At noon, all the boxes open, each with an animal puppet dancing to an old Russian folk song.

On Tsvetnoi (Flower) Bulvar, branching off to the south, are the Old Circus and popular **Tsentralny Rinok** (Central Market).

To the north of the Garden Ring, in Frunze Central Army Park, is the **Armed Forces Central Museum** with exhibits of the Russian Army during the 1918–22 civil war and World War II. Open 10am–4.30pm; closed Mondays and Tuesdays. Novoslobodskaya is the nearest Metro station. Nearby, at number 12 Ulitsa Sovetskoy Armii is the **Children's Theater Museum** with exhibits on the history of puppets. Open 10am–6pm weekdays.

The next street and square returned to their original names of **Sukharevskaya** in 1992; they are named after Sukharov, a popular commander of the czar's Streltsy guards who were quartered here. After the Revolution the street and square were called Kolkhoznaya (Collective Farm). Peter the Great opened Russia's first naviga-tional school in the center of the square where the Sukharov Tower had stood. Prospekt Mira (Peace Prospekt) leads north to the **All-Russian Exhibition Center** (see page 196). Prospekt Mira's original name was Meshchanskaya Sloboda, Commoners' Quarters; immigrant settlements were concentrated here. At 5 Prospekt Mira is the Perlov House, the former home of an old tea merchant family of the same name. At number 18 is the **Wedding Palace**, an 18th-century structure designed by Bazhenov. Opposite the palace are the headquarters of Vyacheslav Zaitsev, Moscow's top fashion designer. At number 26 are the **Aptekarsky Botanical Gardens**, the oldest gardens in the city. They were started by Peter the Great as medicinal gardens for the court. Today they are still filled with medicinal herbs, along with thousands of types of bushes and trees. Open daily 9am–5pm. (Prospekt Mira Metro station.) Also near the Prospekt Mira Metro station is the Olympic Sports Complex, built in the late 1970s. **The Cosmonauts Memorial Museum** is at 111 Prospekt Mira with exhibits on the history of Russian space exploration. Open 10am–7pm; closed Mondays. VDNKh Metro station.

Returning to the Garden Ring, the next square, **Lermontovskaya**, is named after the Russian poet Lermontov, who was born in a house near the square on October 3, 1814; a plaque on a building marks where the house stood. The plaque is inscribed with Lermontov's words: 'Moscow, Moscow, I love you deeply as a son, passionately and tenderly.' The square was known as Krasniye Vorota (Red Gate) because red gates once marked the entrance to the square. The Metro station was given this name.

Zemlyanoi Val (Earthen Rampart) is the longest street on the ring, once named after the pilot Valeri Chakalov, who made the first nonstop flight over the North Pole from the USSR to America in 1936. At numbers 14 to 16 lived the poet Marshak, the composer Prokofiev and the violinist Oistrach. Tchaikovsky once lived at number 47. Behind the Kursky Railway Station is an 18th-century stone mansion, the Naidyonov Estate. Gilliardi and Grigorev built the estate, whose gar-dens stretch down to the Yauza River; it is now a sanitarium. After crossing the Yauza River, the ring reaches Taganskaya Ploshchad (with a Metro station of the same name), where the popular avant-garde theater **Taganka** is located.

Across the Bolshoi Krasnokholmsky Most (Bridge) that spans the Moskva River and just off Zatsepsky Val, our next stop on the Garden Ring is the **Bakhrushin Theater Museum** at 31 Ulitsa Bakhrushina. Established by merchant Alexei Bakhrushin in 1894, the museum displays over 200,000 items (though not well organized) which illustrate the history of Russian theater and ballet from the clas-sics to the avant-garde. The basement floor is dedicated to the opera singer Fyodor Shalyapin and the art patron Savva Mamontov. Open 1pm–6pm; closed Tuesdays and last Monday of each month. The Paveletskaya Metro station is nearby.

Serpukhovskaya Ploshchad was, until 1992, named Dobryninskaya Square after the 1917 revolutionary. The next square, Kaluzhskaya, leads to the entrance of **Gorky Park**, with two large Ferris wheels. The nearby chocolate factory of Krasny Oktyabr (Red October) has been making chocolate here for over 125 years. Across from the park, at 10–14 Krymsky Val, is the **Tretyakov Art Gallery**; open 10am–8pm; closed Mondays. On the grounds is the evocative **Park of the Fallen Idols**, where statues of revolutionary figures now lie, sit and stand. The statue of Felix Dzerzhinsky, toppled during the 1991 attempted coup, is here along with the statues of Kalinin, Sverdlov, Khrushchev and Stalin. Krymsky Val (Crimean Rampart) is the last section of the ring. It crosses the Moskva River by way of the Krymsky suspension bridge.

When strolling along the Garden or Boulevard rings, pay attention to the traffic. Even 150 years ago, Nikolai Gogol wrote: 'What Russian doesn't like fast driving?' (See Literary Excerpt on page 173.) And this is just as true today. Traffic accidents have multiplied; cars often use sidewalks as passing lanes; and at night, headlights are not normally used. Many *yama* (potholes) are left unrepaired, so that getting splashed with rain and mud during a rainfall is likely.

(above) First appearing in Russia in the 1890s, matryoshka dolls represented peasant girls. Today they are still painted in traditional Russian dress with sarafan jumpers, embroidered blouses and kokoshniki headdresses, and are one of Russia's most popular souvenirs; (opposite) a large variety of items are for sale at the popular weekend Izmailovsky Flea Market, including contemporary cartoons and old religious icons.

Sparrow Hills (Vorobyoviye Gory)

The Sparrow Hills are situated in the southwestern part of the city; they were given this name in the 15th century. From 1935 to 1992, the area was referred to as Lenin Hills. Peter I and Catherine the Great had their country palaces in this area, and today many dachas, or country homes, are still situated here. It remains a favorite place for recreational activities like hiking, picnicking and swimming in summer, and ice-skating, sledding and skiing in winter. This spot is the highest point in Moscow and provides one of the most spectacular views of the city. Currently the Leninskiye Gorii Metro station (with a viewing platform) is closed for repairs. Take the Metro one stop farther to Universitet—the train will ride above ground and cross the Moskva River. After leaving the Metro, stand and face the river; in good weather even the golden domes of the city Kremlin are visible. It is customary for wedding parties to have photographs taken by this spot.

In the opposite direction you can see a massive 36-story building. This is Lomonosov University, more widely known as **Moscow University**, founded in 1755 by Russian scientist Mikhail Lomonosov. This university building was erected between 1949 and 1953 on the highest point of Sparrow Hills by Stalin, who had six other similar Gothic-style skyscrapers built throughout the city. This is the tallest of the seven at 240 meters (787 feet). The top of the university's main tower is crowned by a golden star in the shape of ears of corn. It is the largest university in Russia, with students from over 100 countries. The campus comprises 40 buildings, including sports centers, an observatory, botanical gardens and a park. The Gorky Library has over six million volumes. Gorbachev graduated from Moscow University with a degree in law, and his wife Raisa with a degree in Leninist philosophy. Recently Moscow University became independent from the Ministry of Education. Within the campus stands the green-domed **Trinity Church**, built in 1811 and open for worship.

A few blocks to the east, between Vernadsky and Lomonosovsky prospekts, is the circular building of the **New Circus** (*Novy Tsirk na Vorobyovykh Gorakh* or New Circus on Sparrow Hills); closed Mondays and Tuesdays. The circus is one of the most popular forms of entertainment in Russia, and the Moscow Circus is famous throughout the world. This circus building, opened in 1971, seats 3,400. Its ring has four interchangeable floors that can be switched in less than five minutes. One is the regular ring, another a special ring for magicians, and the others are a pool for the aquatic circus and a rink for the ice ballet. The Universitet Metro station is directly behind the New Circus. The other main circus of Moscow is the **Stary Tsirk** (Old Circus) at 13 Tsvetnoi Bulvar.

In front of the New Circus is the Moscow Palace of Young Pioneers, sometimes referred to as **Pioneerland**. This is a large club and recreational center for children. Before the Communist Party lost its supreme power in 1991, children who belonged to the Communist Youth Organization were known as Young Pioneers. Older members belonged to the Young Komsomol League. During the last years of Communist rule, there were over 25 million Young Pioneers, and over 39 million in the Komsomol. The 400 rooms in the palace include clubs, laboratories and workshops. It also has its own concert hall, sports stadium, gardens and even an artificial lake for learning how to row and sail. There are over 35 youth house branches in Moscow. The entrance to the palace is marked by the Statue of Malchish-Kibalchish, a character from a popular children's book. On the corner is the **Children's Music Theater**. A few minutes' drive away along Mosfilmovskaya Ulitsa is **Mosfilm Studios**, dating from 1927. Here worked many of the great Russian film directors like Pudovkin, Dovzhenko, Eisenstein and Tarkovsky (see Special Topic on Russian Cinema on page 506).

Across the river from the Sparrow Hills are the white buildings of the **Luzhniki Central Stadium** (the largest in Moscow). The complex consists of the stadium (seating 100,000), the Palace of Sport, the swimming and tennis stadiums, the Friendship Hall and the Museum of Physical Culture. Many events of the Moscow 1980 Olympics were held here. The Olympic Village was built behind the University on Lomonosov Prospekt. Glancing to the left of the stadium, you can make out the golden domes of the Novodevichy Convent.

Beyond the stadium, at 2 Lev Tolstoy Street (Ulitsa Lva Tolstovo), is the five-domed and colorfully tiled **Church of St Nicholas at Khamovniki**, built between 1676–1682; services are still conducted here. In the past weavers lived in the area and their guild paid for the construction of this church; the old Russian word for weavers is *khamovniki*. A copy of the Virgin Icon Helper of all Sinners (credited for working a few miracles) rests in the iconostasis left of the royal gates; to the right is an Icon of St Nicholas. Farther along the street, the whitewashed building with steep roof was once the Weaver's Guild House, where material was woven. Also along this street, at number 21, is the 18-room **Tolstoy Country Estate Museum** where the writer lived from 1882 to 1901, the year he was excommunicated from the Orthodox Church. After this act by the Holy Synod, Tolstoy moved to his estate at Yasnaya Polyana (see page 216). A few of the works he wrote while living in this house are *Power of Darkness*, *The Death of Ivan Ilyich*, *The Kreutzer Sonata* and *Resurrection*. The opening hours in summer are 10am–6pm, and in winter 10am–4pm; closed Mondays and last Friday of the month. (Tolstoy's family would often stop by the beer factory next door, which has been brewing for over a century!) Another Tolstoy Museum is located at Ulitsa Prechistenka, see page 143.

SOVIET CIRCUS
СОВЕТСКИЙ ЦИРК

Oleg POPOV
Олег ПОПОВ

(main picture) The Zapashny family is considered a circus dynasty after performing with elephants and tigers for four generations; (above right) the circus always has a variety of acts, such as this bird act performed by a female Lilliputian; (right) a poster shows the face of a young Alexander Popov, known as the Sunshine Clown, one of Russia's most famous clowns; (left) Popov (in blue jacket) as he is today. After performing in the circus for nearly 50 years, he prefers to continue working. 'What happens,' he reflects, 'is that a fine speck of sawdust enters your bloodstream and stays there for life.' (far left) the audience discovers that circus magic never ends.

THE RUSSIAN CIRCUS

'Oh, how I love the circus,' bellows Alexander Frish, a charismatic and eccentric clown, who has been clowning around in the Russian Circus for over 20 years. Frish believes that 'the circus is the universal language of joy and laughter that lets us all become children again'.

The Russian Circus is a world of vibrant artistry, precision and grace. Throughout the country, the circus is a highly respected art form taken as seriously as classical ballet. It is also the most popular entertainment: more than 100 million Russians attend performances each year. The circus employs more than 25,000 people, including 6,000 performing artists and 7,000 animals. Seventy permanent circus buildings, including ice and aquatic circuses, are scattered from Moscow to Siberia—more than in the rest of the world combined. Over 100 circus troupes (many are government regulated, others private collectives) give up to nine performances a week in over 30 countries a year.

The early traditions of the circus go back over three centuries. The first formalized circus was created in England in 1770 by an ex-cavalry officer and showman named Philip Astley. It consisted mostly of trick riding, rope dancers, tumblers and jugglers, staged within a circular ring. In 1793, one of Astley's horsemen and later competitor Charles Hughes introduced this novel form of entertainment to Russia, with a private circus for Catherine the Great in the Royal Palace at St Petersburg. (In the same year, Hughes' pupil John Bill Ricketts introduced modern circus to American audiences in Philadelphia.)

Russia's first permanent circus building was built in St Petersburg in 1877 by Gaetano Ciniselli, an equestrian entrepreneur from Milan. The Ciniselli Circus was the center of performance activitity up to the Revolution, and this classic building still houses today's St Petersburg Circus. The second oldest circus was the Old Circus in Moscow (a new Old Circus has been built on the site where the original once stood). Moscow also boasts the New Circus and summer tent circuses.

Nowhere in Europe were circus performers as politically active as in turn-of-the-century Russia. The circus became a sort of political sanctuary where sketches depicting the tumultuous state of Russia were tolerated. The clowns, especially, took every opportunity to satirize the czars, landowners and merchants. Many of the performers participated in active demonstrations with organized parades through the cities. Lunacharksy, the head of the Circus House that organized performers, encouraged their participation: 'Here it will be possible to have fiery revolutionary speeches, declarative couplets and clowns doing caricatures on enemy forces.' The artists performed on small flatbed stages that were rolled through the streets of Moscow. Vladimir Durov, with trained animals, joined the merry cavalcade, as did the most popular clown of the era, Vitaly Lazarenko, on stilts! Taking up the Bolshevik cause, the acts were now catalysts for social reform. The circus had become a political hotbed.

The poet Mayakovsky wrote for the circus. In one of his most famous skits, Moscow Burning, he wrote: 'Proud of the year 1917/Don't forget about 1905/A year of undying glory and fame/When the dream of the land came alive.../Comrade Circus, where's your grin?/Here's a sight to tickle us/Look and see who's trotting in/The Dynasty of Czar Nicholas !!!'

During these years of intellectual and political intensity, some of Russia's finest writers and directors, such as Gorky, Chekhov and Stanislavsky, turned their attention to the circus. In one of his short stories, Maxim Gorky wrote: 'Everything I see in the arena blends into something triumphant, where skill and strength celebrate their victory over mortal danger.' Later, even Lenin took time off from the Revolution to nationalize the circus—on September 22, 1919, the world's first government circus began its operations.

In order to provide a consistently high standard of training in the circus arts, the government founded the first professional circus

school in 1927. Today at scores of circus schools throughout the country, students train for up to four years, studying all facets of circus life. During the final year, the student creates his own act and utilizes the services of circus producers, directors and choreographers. Once approved by a circus board, the performer's professional career begins.

Sadly, on August 21, 1997, the heart of Russia's most beloved clown, Yuri Nikulin, stopped beating. He had performed in the circus for over 30 years and had acted as the director of the Old Circus on Tvsetnoi Bulvar since 1984. Nikulin always tried to overcome hard times with the help of humor. He had accumulated more than 10,000 jokes since he started collecting them in 1936, which filled two volumes of his books Anekdoti I & II.

'Laughter is beneficial to the human body,' he wrote. 'When smiling, giggling, bursting into laughter (until you drop) a person, without even suspecting it, keeps himself healthy.'

The emblem of the Russian Circus depicts a circus performer reaching for the stars. The language of the circus is without words, as beauty, courage and skill bridge the gap between generations and nationalities. The circus is the universal language of the heart.

(opposite) The famous Flying Cranes trapeze act chalk up before a performance at Moscow's Bolshoi or New Circus on Sparrow Hills. Considered one of the finest aerial acts of our time, the ten flyers rehearsed more than five years together before a single performance was given. They combine extraordinary trapeze and acrobatic skills and perform a breathtaking aerial ballet to classical music. The act was first inspired by a Russian song commemorating the spirits of the fallen soldiers who turn into white cranes and fly away, their souls released to heaven. The only female performer, Lena Golovoko, plays the last of the fallen cranes and is courageously rescued so that peace may prevail. 'When I appear in the arena,' says Lena, 'I immediately forget about everything else. My soul is in it.'

NOVODEVICHY CONVENT

From Universitet Metro station, take the train one stop across the river to Sportivnaya and get off in front of the stadium. Walking a short distance to the northwest will bring you to one of the oldest religious complexes in the city, Novodevichy (New Maiden) Convent, a baroque-style complex of 15 buildings and 16 gilded domes dating from the 16th and 17th centuries. Grand Prince Vasily III founded the convent in 1514 to commemorate the capture of Smolensk from Lithuania, which had controlled the area for over a century (the convent was built on the road to Smolensk). The convent was also one in a group of fortified monasteries that surrounded Moscow. Novodevichy served mainly as a religious retreat for Russian noblewomen. Peter the Great banished his half-sister Sophia and first wife Evdokia to the convent and forced them to wear the veil. Boris Godunov was crowned here in 1598. Napoleon tried to blow up the convent before he fled the city, but a nun pulled out the fuses. The convent was converted into a museum in 1922.

The white-stone five-tiered **Virgin of Smolensk Cathedral** (1524) was the convent's first stone building and lies at its center. It was dedicated to the Virgin of Smolensk, a much revered 16th-century icon, and modeled on the Kremlin's Uspensky Cathedral. Many 16th-century interior frescoes portray the life of Vasily III (the father of Ivan the Terrible). A copy of the Icon of Our Lady of Smolenskaya hangs over the altar, and many of the icons were painted by Simon Ushakov. The beautiful gilded five-tiered iconostasis (1683–86) was presented by Sophia; its wooden columns, decorated with climbing grapevines, are made out of whole tree trunks. Ivan the Terrible's daughter Anna, Sophia and Evdokia are some of the noblewomen in the burial vault.

The baroque **Transfiguration Gate Church** (1687–9) stands above the main northern entrance. To its right are the two-story **Lopukhina Chambers**, where Peter the Great's first wife Evdokia Lopukhina lived. The **Gate Church of the Intercession** (1688) tops the southern entrance, and west of the cathedral is the **Church of the Assumption** (1687), which has been open for worship for over three centuries (a choir sings during Sunday services). Behind it is the 16th-century **Church of St Ambrose**. The small palace next door, along the southern wall, is where Irina Godunova lived out her days. She was the sister of Boris Godunov and the wife of Fyodor I. When the czar died in 1598, Irina refused the throne and her brother Boris was elected ruler during the Time of Troubles. The **Miloslavsky Chambers** are named after Sophia's sister Maria Miloslavskaya, who also lived here until her death. Sophia's chamber-prison is where Peter the Great incarcerated his half-sister (until her death) when he deposed her as regent and took the throne. To further punish Sophia for leading the Streltsy against him in 1698, Peter ordered

that the dead bodies of revolt members be strung up outside her cell. Other structures include the **Refectory Church** (1685–7), the six-tiered octagonal baroque bell
tower (1690), small exhibit halls and four nun's residences (in 1994, Novodevichy
was permitted its first resident nun since 1922).

Many notable Russian personalities are buried in the Novodevichy's two cemeteries. Within the convent grounds are the graves of princes, wealthy merchants,
clergymen and war heroes. Behind the southern wall, the 19th-century cemetery
has been the burial site of many of Russia's most prominent statesmen, artists and
scientists. These include Chekhov, Eisenstein, Gogol, Khrushchev, Mayakovsky,
Prokofiev, Scriabin, Serov, Shalyapin, Shostakovich, Stanislavsky and Stalin's wife
Nadezhda Alliluyeva. The complex is open 10am–5pm; closed Tuesdays. Guided
excursions (in Russian) start from the entrance ticket kiosk every Sunday at noon
and visit most of the buildings.

Nearby, at 4 Novodevichy Pereulok, is **Restaurant U-Pirosmani** with delicious
Georgian food and paintings on the wall by famous Georgian painter Pirosmani,
along with other artists.

GORKY PARK

Gorky Park lies a few minutes walk over the Moskva River from Park Kultury Metro
station in the Frunze district. It can also be reached from the other side of the river,
from Oktyabrskaya Metro station. A large archway marks the entrance to the park.
Named after popular Soviet writer Maxim Gorky, the area was commissioned as a
Park of Culture and Rest in the 1920s. Today there are Ferris wheels and amusement rides, restaurants, boats for hire and the Zelyoni (Green) open-air theater. In
summer the park is teeming with strollers, performance artists and circus performers of the tent circus. In winter the popular ice-skating rink is in operation (made
famous by the book *Gorky Park*), along with cross-country skiing. The park is open
daily 10am–10pm. Also in the park are the Neskuchny Sadi (Not-Boring Pleasure
Gardens), originally part of the Trubetskoi Estate and later bought by Nicholas I in
1826; it is now used by the Academy of Sciences. The estate is part of the Main
Botanical Gardens (with a collection of over 16,000 varieties of roses) that stretch
as far as the river.

DONSKOI MONASTERY

South of Gorky Park, near the Shabolovskaya Metro station, is the Donskoi
Monastery. This monastery and seven churches were founded by Czar Fyodor I and
Boris Godunov in 1591, on the site of the Russian army's line of defense against the
invading Mongols. Legend claims that the city was protected by the Donskaya
Virgin Icon, the icon that Prince Donskoi took for protection against the invading

Tartars during the 1380 Battle of Kulikovo near the River Don. In the 16th century, six fortified monasteries formed a ring to defend the cities from the Mongols. The monasteries were connected by an earthen rampart, today's Garden Ring. By the 18th century, this monastery was one of the most prosperous in all of Russia and owned over 7,000 serfs. After the Revolution, the Donskoi Monastery was opened to the public as a government architectural museum. In the early 1990s the complex was returned to the Orthodox Church and is now a working monastery. (Open 11am–6pm; closed Mondays and Saturdays.) The red and white **Old Cathedral of the Donskaya Virgin** was the first building of the monastery. (This was one of the few churches allowed to conduct services throughout the Soviet period.) The cube roof and onion domes are topped with golden half-moon crosses that symbolize the Christian victory over Islam. A copy of the Donskaya Virgin Icon is on the eight-tiered iconostasis; the original is in the Tretyakov Gallery. Patriarch Tikhon, who was appointed the head of the Orthodox Church on the eve of the October 1917 Revolution, is buried in a marble tomb at the southern wall.

Novodevichy Convent was built in 1524 by Vasily III, and became part of the city's outer defensive ring. In 1598, Boris Godunov was crowned czar in the five-domed Smolensk Cathedral.

The Naryshkin baroque-style **New Cathedral of the Donskaya Virgin** was commissioned a century later by Peter the Great's half-sister Sophia. The interior frescoes were painted by the Italian artist Antonio Claudio between 1782 and 1785. At the southwestern corner of the monastery is the classical **Church of the Archangel Michael**, built between 1806 and 1809. The church served as a memorial chapel for

the Golitsyn family. Mikhail Golitsyn (1681–1764) was Peter the Great's star general who began his career as a service drummer. Fourteen Golitsyns are buried here, including Dmitri and his wife Natalia, who is the subject of Pushkin's novel *Queen of Spades*. Some of the people buried in the cemetery are Turgenev, the architect Bovet, and Zhukovsky, the father of Russian aviation. Other buildings include the Tikhvin Gate Church, the Abbot's residence, a bell tower and the 20th-century Church of St Seraphim, now a crematorium. Outside the gates is the Church of Rizpolozhenie, whose priests also conduct mass in the Old Cathedral on Sundays and holidays.

At 20 Donskaya Ulitsa is the Moscow baroque **Church of the Deposition of the Lord's Robe**, built in 1701. The Church is filled with interesting cherubs and contains a copy of the Icon of the Deposition of the Lord's Robe under a gilded canopy. In 1625, an envoy of a Persian shah presented Czar Mikhail Romanov and the Patriarch Filaret with a fragment of Jesus' robe. Filaret had an icon painted and declared a new Church holiday. The icon shows Romanov and Filaret placing the gold box, containing the piece of cloth, on the altar of the Kremlin's Uspensky Cathedral. The original icon is now in the Tretyakov Gallery.

DANILOVSKY MONASTERY

The Danilovsky Monastery, off Danilovsky Val, is about a 15-minute walk south of the Donskoi Monastery. It was founded in 1276 by Prince Daniil, the youngest son of Alexander Nevsky, who was the only Moscow prince to be canonized by the Russian Church. The monastery's thick walls served as part of the southern defenses of the city. During Stalin's rule the monastery was closed and later served as an orphanage, electronics factory and juvenile prison. Restoration work began in 1983 when the government returned the complex to the Orthodox Church. Two years later the buildings were reconsecrated for religious use. In 1988, to celebrate the Millennium of the Baptism of Rus, Patriarch Pimen chose St Daniil Monastery for the celebrations. It is now the residency of the Moscow patriarch, along with the administrative bodies of the Holy Synod.

The whitewashed **Cathedral of the Holy Fathers of the Seven Ecumenical Councils** was built by Ivan the Terrible in 1565 on the original site of St Daniil's church. Only a few of the 17th-century frescoes remain. St Daniil is buried here within a golden coffin. Services are usually held daily in the mornings and early evenings. Within the building is also the Church of the Protecting Veil, added in the 17th century. The largest structure in the complex is the **Trinity Cathedral**, designed in Moscow classical-style by Osip Bovet in 1833. Standing over the monastery entrance is the pink and white **Belfry Chapel of St Simon Stylites** (1730). New bells were placed in the tower during restoration; the old ones toll at Harvard University. The monastery also has an icon-painting workshop.

The Moscow patriarch has its own hotel near the southern walls of the complex at 5 Starodanilovsky Lane. The **Danilovsky Hotel Complex** has a restaurant, café and bar, and even a swimming pool.

Leninsky Prospekt runs past the Donskoi Monastery and leads out of the city and into Moscow's modern southwestern district, which consists mostly of residential housing. Beginning at Oktyabrskaya Metro station the prospekt passes the Academy of Sciences, formerly Neskuchny Castle, and Gagarinskaya Ploshchad (Gagarin Square). The square (at Leninsky Prospekt Metro station) features a titanium monument of Yuri Gagarin, who made the first manned space flight. At the base of the monument is a replica of the space capsule Vostok (East) in which Gagarin traveled on April 12, 1961. (Gagarin, trained as a test pilot, died in a plane crash in 1968; his ashes lie in the Kremlin Wall in Red Square.) This square used to mark the city limits in the 1950s. The prospekt continues past many department stores to the Lumumba People's Friendship University, with 6,000 students from around the world. It eventually becomes the Kievsky Highway and ends at the Vnukovo local airport.

SPASO-ANDRONIKOV MONASTERY

This monastery, at 10 Andronevskaya Ploshchad, is situated along the Yauza River, a tributary of the Moskva, in the eastern part of the city, not far from Ploshchad Ilicha Metro station. It was founded in 1359 by the Metropolitan Alexei during the reign of Prince Donskoi and has quite an interesting history. After Alexei was confirmed by the Byzantine Patriarch in Constantinople, a heavy storm occurred at sea during his return journey. Alexei promised God that if he should live he would build a monastery dedicated to the saint whose feast day was celebrated on the day of his safe arrival in Moscow. Alexei returned on August 16, the Savior Day, or Vernicle. When the Mongol Khan suddenly summoned Alexei to help his ailing wife in the south, the metropolitan appointed Andronik, a monk at Sergiyev Posad's Trinity-Sergius Monastery, to oversee the complex's construction in his absence. The monastery was named the Spaso-Andronikov after the Savior and its first abbot. It later became the stronghold of the Old Believers.

This is the oldest architectural complex in Moscow after the Kremlin. The white helmet-domed **Cathedral of the Savior** was built between 1420 and 1427, and is considered the oldest building in Moscow. The master iconist Andrei Rublyov, who also trained as a monk at the Trinity-Sergius Monastery, painted many of the interior frescoes (it was here that Rublyov painted his famous Old Testament Trinity icon, now in the Tretyakov Gallery); he is also buried in the monastery. The baroque **Church of the Archangel Michael** (1691–1739) was commissioned by Ustinia Lopukhina in 1694 to celebrate the birth of her grandson Alexei, son of Peter the Great, and her daughter Evdokia. Peter later banished Evdokia to Novodevichy Monastery (a form of divorce in those days) and the Lopukhinas to Siberia. The church is now an icon restoration studio.

The **Andrei Rublyov Museum of Old Russian Art** is housed in three separate buildings in the monastery. They are located immediately beyond the main gate. The former Seminary Building contains many 15th- and early 16th-century icons by Rublyov (many now copies of the originals) and his students. Some of the icons include St Sergius, St George, John the Baptist and the Savior. Many of the icons found in the Monks' Quarters (behind the Savior Cathedral) were painted in Novgorod in the 17th century. Nearby is a new Exhibition Hall of mainly 17th- and 18th-century icons that include Our Lady of Tikhvin. There are also displays of other paintings, sculpture, embroidery, old books and chronicles. The museum complex is open 11am–6pm; closed Wednesdays.

(below) A youthful audience gathered at a rock 'n' roll concert in Moscow's Gorky Park; (opposite) zakomara gold trim decorates the plain walls of a small chapel in Moscow's Novodevichy Convent.

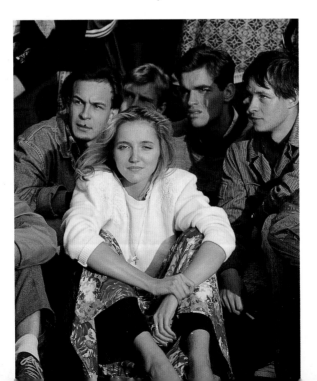

All-Russian Exhibition Center

The former Exhibition of Economic Achievements or VDNKh, was opened in 1959 where nearly 100,000 objects representing the latest Soviet achievements in science, industry, transport, building and culture were exhibited in 300 buildings and 80 pavilions which spread out over an area of 220 hectares (545 acres). Now called the All-Russian Exhibition Center, the park is situated on the opposite side of the street from the **Kosmos Hotel** at the end of Prospekt Mira, near VDNKh Metro station. The first monuments that come into view are the 96-meter high (315-feet) **Sputnik Rocket** (the first Sputnik satellite was launched on October 4, 1957), and the Soviet-realist **Monument to the Worker and Collective-Farm Girl** (Rabotnik i Kolkhoznitsa), sculpted between 1935 and 1937 by Vera Mukhina. In 1998, a Hollywood firm offered to purchase the statue (it has long been a symbol of Mosfilm Studios, as the lion is to MGM), but the government refused the sale. Pavilions include the **Atomic Energy, Agriculture and Culture Pavilions**.

Since many of these halls never exhibited much of interest anyway (the Pig Pavilion had one pig from each of the Soviet republics), a few have now been converted into shopping centers, and hundreds of small shop and food kiosks line the footpaths. The most interesting hall, located at the end of the park, is the **Kosmos Pavilion**. In front of it stands a replica of the Vostok rocket that carried Yuri Gagarin into space in 1961. Inside are displays of rockets and space capsules, including the first Sputnik, Lunnik and Soyuz rockets, and Salyut space stations. A display also honors Konstantin Tsiolkovsky, the father of the Russian space program. He invented the first wind tunnel and outlined the principle of the reactor rocket; he once said, 'This planet is the cradle of the human mind, but one cannot spend one's life in a cradle.' Lining the walls are photographs of Yuri Gagarin, Valentina Tereshkova (the first woman in space), Alexi Leonov (who took the first space walk), and Laika, Belka and Strelka (the first dogs in space). One exhibit chronicles the first joint US–USSR space mission, Soyuz–Apollo, undertaken in July 1975. The first Russian cosmonaut flew in the American Space Shuttle in February 1994 and in 1998, Russians and Americans flew together in the Mir Space Station.

Other buildings include an open-air theater, small zoo, amusement park, shopping centers, the Circorama (standing-only) circular movie theater and restaurants. You can hire boats and go fishing in the ponds; fishing tackle can be rented from booths along the bank. In winter, especially during the Winter Festival, there is plenty of entertainment, including ice skating and troika rides. The park is open on weekdays 10am–10pm, and on weekends 10am–11pm; the pavilions are open from 10am–7pm. A half-hour tour of the park can be taken on electric trams.

OSTANKINO

Not far from VDNKh Metro station near the Exhibition Center, at 5 Pervaya Ostankinskaya Street, is the **Ostankino Palace**. It was built by serf-architect Pavel Argunov between 1792 and 1797 as the summer residence of Nikolai Sheremetyev on the grounds of the family's estate. The palace was built of wood, but painted to resemble bricks and stone. Interesting rooms are the Blue Room, Egyptian Ballroom, Italian Reception Room and the Picture Gallery and Theater, which had over 200 serf actors, dancers and musicians. The palace also houses the **Museum of Serf Art**. The beautiful serf-actress Praskovia Zhemchugova-Kovalyova later became the count's wife (see page 161 and 208). One of the streets in Ostankino bears her name. The Trinity Church adjoins the palace. The museum is open daily, except Tuesdays and Wednesdays, 11am–5pm; in winter 10am–4pm. A beautiful English-landscaped park and gardens are also on the grounds, along with chess pavilions, playgrounds, cafés, skating and ski rentals. A short walk away is the **Ostankino TV Tower**. The tower has an observation deck and a rotating restaurant called Sedmoye Nebo (Seventh Heaven).

Down the Moskva River

The Moskva River is 500 kilometers (300 miles) long, of which 77 kilometers (48 miles) wind their way through Moscow. Fourteen road bridges cross the river. Boat cruises leave at regular intervals (April to October) from various locations on both sides of the river; one of the popular embarkation points is near the Kievsky Railway Station—take the Metro to Kievskaya, not far from the Ukraina Hotel. The boat pier is located on the Berezhkovskaya Naberezhnaya (Embankment) near Borodinsky Most (Bridge). The *Rocket* hydrofoils also leave from beside Gorky Park and the Bolshoi Ustinsky Most where the Yauza and Moskva rivers meet, and continue eastwards down the river to the Novospassky Most. The full cruise takes about two hours, but you can leave the boat at any point. Some sites along the way are the Kremlin, Rossiya Hotel, Cathedral of Christ the Savior, Novodevichy Monastery, Sparrow Hills, Moscow University, Gorky Park, Strelka Rowing Club, Ostankino TV Tower, and many estates, palaces and churches.

The tour ends at the **Novospassky Monastery**, founded in the 15th century by Ivan the Great. The 17th-century Cathedral of the Transfiguration of the Savior became the burial site of the czar's relatives; the inner vaults were painted by masters from the Kremlin armory. The bell tower, gates and stone walls also date from the 17th century. Today the New Monastery of the Savior is a restoration institute. Also lying on the banks of the Moskva River are the 17th-century **Krutitskoye**

Metropolitans' Residence (*krutitsy* are small hills), and the **Simonov Monastery**, founded by the monk Simon in the 14th century; it was built as a defensive fortress to protect the southern end of Moscow from the invading Mongols.

Boats leaving from the same piers also run westward to Kuntsevo-Krylatskoye in Fili-Kuntsevo Park, with a river beach and the swimming island of Serebryany Bor. This trip lasts about an hour.

Vicinity of Moscow

The privileged classes of Russia used to build their summer residences in the countryside around Moscow. Many of these palaces and parks have been preserved and converted into museums. Here are 13 spots that can easily be reached by Metro, bus or car. There are also group excursions (day or overnight) to some of these areas; check at the Service Bureau in your hotel for more information.

ABRAMTSEVO ESTATE MUSEUM (Абрамцево)

The **Abramtsevo Estate Museum** is located along the M8 Yaroslavskoye Highway (a few kilometers west of the 61k signpost) near the town of Sergiyev Posad, about 65 kilometers (40 miles) north of Moscow. It is about an hour's journey by train from the Yaroslavsky Railway Station. (At Abramtsevo station, a left at the main road brings you to the estate.) If driving, try the Russkaya Skazka Restaurant at 43 Yaroslavskoye Highway. Otherwise bring food from Moscow for a picnic lunch. In 1843, the Russian writer Sergei Aksakov bought the country estate (built in the 1770s); over the next 15 years it was frequented by many prominent writers, such as Gogol, Tyutchev and Turgenev. Here Gogol gave a reading of the first chapter from his second volume of *Dead Souls*, which he later burned at his home in Moscow. In 1870, textile millionaire and art patron Savva Mamontov bought the estate and turned it into a popular meeting place and artist colony. Art, theater, writing and pottery workshops were held, and Serov, Vrubel, Repin, Shalyapin and Stanislavsky all lived and worked here. Serov's famous portrait *The Girl with Peaches* hangs in the dining room (the original can be found in the Tretyakov Gallery); it is of Mamontov's daughter Vera, who is buried on the estate. Also gracing the walls are Repin's portraits of Mamontov and his wife Elizaveta. The traditional long timber-framed house with fancy lacework gable was said to be the model for Chekhov's manor house in *The Cherry Orchard*. Mamontov also opened a school for peasant children and taught their parents traditional folk crafts.

The Novgorod 12th-century-style Orthodox church (built in 1882) in the park

View of the Kremlin interior from the Moskva River. In the center stands the great Bell Tower of Ivan the Great and the golden-domed Assumption Cathedral. The eleven small golden turrets on the left belong to the Terem Palace, and the polished silver domes on the right grace the Church of the Twelve Apostles, now housing an art museum.

was designed by Victor Vasnetsov and painted by Polenov and Repin. The ceramic tiles that decorate the exterior were produced at the estate's own ceramic workshop. Icons on the interior iconostasis were painted by Repin, Polenov, and Vasnetsov, who also built the park's Hut on Chicken Legs, based on the popular Baba Yaga fairy tale. The countryside is filled with birch groves, colorful gardens and woods, and greatly inspired the landscape artist Isaac Levitan, who often visited the estate. Abramtsevo is now a museum and displays the rooms as they were used by Aksakov and Mamontov. Paintings and other art work executed on the estate, including many by Vrubel, are exhibited in the art studio. The museum is open from 11am–5pm, closed Mondays and Tuesdays. If the weather is pleasant, take a stroll about a kilometer north to the village of **Khotkovo**, where a convent was founded in 1308 (and later destroyed in the 17th century during the Time of Troubles). The Cathedral of the Intercession holds the remains of the parents of St Sergius who founded the monastery at Sergiyev Posad.

ARKHANGELSKOYE ESTATE MUSEUM   (Архангельское)

This museum lies in the village of Arkhangelskoye, 16 kilometers (ten miles) west of Moscow. Take the Volokolamskoye Highway and then the left road toward Petrovo-Dalniye. The closest Metro station is Tushinskaya; then proceed by bus. The estate is situated along the banks of the Moskva River and took 40 years to complete. Prince Golitsyn originally founded the estate at the end of the 18th century. The mansion and park were designed in French style by the architect Chevalier de Huerne and built by serf craftsmen. In 1810, the estate passed into the hands of the wealthy landowner Prince Yusupov (a descendent of one of the Khans—not the one who killed Rasputin) who was the director of the Hermitage Museum and Imperial Theater. He turned the classical palace into his own personal art museum. Today the palace (made into a State museum in 1919) contains works by such artists as Boucher, Hubert Robert, Roslin and Van Dyck. The rooms and halls are beautifully decorated with antique furniture, marble sculptures, tapestries, porcelain and chandeliers; much of the china and glassware was produced on the estate. The palace is surrounded on three sides by a park, lined with sculptures, pavilions and arbors. The Temple to the Memory of Catherine the Great depicts her as Themis, Goddess of Justice. There is also a monument to Pushkin, who enjoyed visiting the grounds. The triumphal arch over the entrance was built in 1817.

A short distance from the palace is the wooden **Serf Theater**, exhibiting theatrical and original set designs by Pietro Gottardo Gonzaga. Built in 1819 by the serf-architect Ivanov, the theater had one of the largest companies of serf actors. Nearby is the Russkaya Izba (Russian Cottage) Restaurant, fashioned after Russian peasant rooms. The cooking is also Old Russian; the menu offers bear meat and venison along with *kvas*, mead and tea served from a bubbling samovar. Call ahead to make reservations (tel. 561-4244); it is located at Ilyinskoye village, at 1 Naberelikaya Ulitsa, a few kilometers southwest of the estate; open daily 10am–10pm.

Arkhangelskoye is open 11am–6pm; closed Mondays and Tuesdays and the last Friday of each month. Check before you go; Arkhangelskoye has often been closed for restoration (tel. 561-9785/9660). For dining, try the **Arkhangelskoye** restaurant, located on the estate, open 12pm–midnight; (tel. 562-2291/8645). It has Russian and European dishes and wines, and a dining terrace open in summer months. (Live music Thursday–Sunday after 7pm.) For a hotel in the area—one stop past Metro Tushinskaya is Skhodnenskaya. At 10 Skhodnenskaya Lane is the **Hotel Gostiny Dvor** (tel. 492-5315).

BORODINO   (Бородино)

Borodino, site of the most famous battle in the War of 1812, lies on the Moscow–Minsk road, 120 kilometers (74 miles) southwest of Moscow. *Elektrichka* commuter trains run from Moscow's Byelorussky Railway Station. In the late spring of 1812, Napoleon led his massive army of more than half a million men into Russia. Presented with no other option but a bloodbath, the generals of Alexander I's armies ordered a humiliating retreat. But, in August, the czar appointed 67-year-old Prince Mikhail Kutuzov as commander-in-chief to stop Napoleon invading Moscow. On August 26, 1812, the Russians took on the French at Borodino. Napoleon's army numbered over 135,000 soldiers with 600 guns. Remarkably, after 15 hours of fighting (and 75,000 dead from both sides), Napoleon was forced to retreat; the Battle of Borodino marked the turning point of the war. Kutuzov's generals, including Barclay de Tolly, wanted to stage another battle with Napoleon before Moscow, but Kutuzov refused to save his armies from yet another bloody encounter. He argued, 'Moscow will be the sponge that will suck him in.' Meeting no resistance, Napoleon's remaining troops entered the gates of Moscow on September 2 at Poklonnaya Gora (Hill of Greeting) and waited for a formal surrender. No one arrived and the French found Moscow nearly deserted. As Napoleon slowly marched towards the Kremlin, immense fires broke out throughout the city; eventually over 80 percent of Moscow would burn to the ground. By mid-October, with winter approaching and no supplies at hand, Napoleon was forced to abandon Moscow and undertake a long march home during one of the worst winters on record. When he finally released his army only 25,000 Frenchmen remained alive. To celebrate Russia's triumphant victory, Alexander I ordered the Cathedral of Christ the Savior built in Moscow 'in the name of the fatherland to express our thanks and gratitude to all our loyal subjects, true sons of Russia'.

In 1912, to mark the battle's 100th anniversary, 34 monuments were erected throughout the battlefield. The polished granite obelisk (1966) crowned by a bronze eagle is dedicated to Field Marshal Kutuzov. Leo Tolstoy visited the battlefield in 1876 while writing *War and Peace*. Other memorials commemorate World War II battles that took place here in 1941. Every year the anniversary of the 1812 battle is celebrated by a Borodino Field Day, when the battle is actually reenacted. People playing the French and Russian soldiers dress in period uniforms, cannons roar and smoke rises from the battlefield. A religious ceremony is held after the battle to give thanks for Napoleon's defeat.

Filmmaker Sergei Bondarchuk's four-part nine-hour epic *War and Peace* was Russia's longest and most expensive film ever made. Taking five years to produce, it encompassed some of the most spectacular battle scenes ever seen on film. During the recreated Battle of Borodino over 120,000 extras were used from the Soviet army.

The **Borodino Military History Museum**, with exhibits of the Battle of Borodino, is open 10am–5pm; closed Mondays and the last Friday of each month. (Another Battle of Borodino Museum is in Moscow at 38 Kutuzovsky Prospekt, by the Triumphal Arch, see page 163.)

ISTRA RIVER MUSEUM OF WOODEN ARCHITECTURE   (Истра)

The museum is located 56 kilometers (34 miles) west of Moscow, along the M9 or Volokolamskoye Highway. *Elektrichka* trains also run from Moscow's Rizhsky Railway Station. The Museum of Wooden Architecture, in the park along the Istra River, contains a 17th-century wooden church and farmstead, cottages, granaries and windmills brought in from nearby areas. The museum is open 10am–5pm; closed Mondays and the last Friday of each month. (Note that if you wish to visit the New Jerusalem Monastery at the same time, this is also closed on Tuesdays.)

The Novoyarusalimsky or **New Jerusalem Monastery** is situated a few kilometers to the west of Istra (local buses make the short trip). Patriarch Nikon, who caused the great Orthodox schism, began construction of the monastery in 1656. (Ironically, he was later stripped of his position by the czar and exiled here until his death in 1681.) During World War II the Germans blew up the grounds, but today much has been restored. The **Resurrection Cathedral** (1656–85) is modeled after Jerusalem's Holy Sepulcher Church, and the surrounding fortress walls represent the city of Jerusalem with its Zion and Damascus Towers. Many parts of the church (still under restoration) are named after the Stations of the Cross, and are extensively covered by tiles and colorful plasterwork. The most intriguing spot is the Golgotha Chapel where an artificial fissure (representing the earthquake that shook the world when Christ died) cuts across a 17th-century wooden iconostasis with figures of the crucifixion. Nikon is buried beneath in the Chapel of St John the

Many of those decorated for their services during World War II participate in ceremonies on May 9, Victory Day, to honor those who gave their lives for the motherland.

Baptist. A collection of Russian paintings, furniture and porcelain is on display in the refectory and other buildings behind the cathedral. The Gethsemane Park holds a small museum of wooden architecture. The monastery is open 10am–4pm; closed Mondays and Tuesdays, and the last Friday of the month.

KLIN   (Клин)

The old Russian town of Klin, founded on the banks of the Sestra River (a tributary of the Volga) in 1318, is located 80 kilometers (50 miles) northwest of Moscow along the M10 Highway. *Elektrichka* trains also run from the Leningradsky terminal, and take about two hours. Pack a lunch to bring along. The town was the ancestral home of the Romanov dynasty; today only two Naryshkin baroque-style churches remain of the monastery. Klin is more widely known as the home of the great Russian composer Peter (Pyotr) Tchaikovsky (1840–93). The composer who said, 'I find no words to express how much I need the charm and quiet of the Russian countryside', bought the estate in 1885. (Tchaikovsky also yearned for peaceful isolation after the public rebuffed him for his homosexuality, and a number of friends had criticized some of his earlier works.) In the gray-green timber-framed house, at 48 Tchaikovsky Street, the composer went on to score some of his most popular works: the ballets *The Nutcracker* and *Sleeping Beauty*, and his Fifth and Sixth Symphonies. Not long after the première of his *Pathétique* (Sixth) Symphony in St Petersburg, Tchaikovsky died of cholera after ignoring a warning not to drink the water during an epidemic. (Some consider that he committed suicide.) Inside his dacha, portraits of famous musicians hang in the living room, along with a photographic picture of Tchaikovsky's father in the study. On his birthday, May 7, and day of his death, November 6, winners of the Moscow Tchaikovsky International Competition and other virtuosi play works on his grand piano. Concerts are also given year-round in a hall on the grounds. The **Tchaikovsky Memorial House** and estate-museum is open 9am–5pm; closed Wednesdays and Thursdays, and the last Monday of each month.

KOLOMENSKOYE MUSEUM PRESERVE   (Коломенское)

This preserve is on the southern side of Moscow on the banks of the Moskva River at 39 Prospekt Andropova, about a ten-minute walk from Kolomenskaya Metro station. Kolomenskoye was once the country estate of numerous Russian princes and czars, including Ivan the Terrible and Peter the Great. The name of the area dates from the 13th century, when villagers fleeing Mongol attacks on the town of Kolomna settled here.

The area is now an open-air-park museum of 16th- and 17th-century architecture. Visitors enter the park through the whitewashed Savior Gate, which stands on the grounds that were once Czar Alexei's orchards. The czar (father of Peter the Great) was passionate about hunting, and also helped train falcons; more than 300 birds of prey and 100,000 doves were said to have been raised on his estate. Between 1666 and 1667, workers for Alexei constructed a large wooden palace known as the Jewel-Box, complete with 250 rooms, 3,000 windows of glittering mica, and elaborate *kokoshniki* gables. The czar's throne was flanked with a pair of large gilded lions who could roar and roll their eyes with a pull on a hidden mechanism. (A model replica of the throne room, torn down by Catherine the Great, can be seen in the museum.) Alexei's royal palace was joined by a passageway to the 17th-century baroque-style **Church of the Kazan Virgin**; it stands on the left as you walk through the gates. A copy of the famous icon the Virgin of Kazan is located in the main iconostasis. (After the Revolution the original icon disappeared.) Today the church is a busy place of worship, and services are held daily.

Rising high on the banks of the river stands the tent-shaped and elaborately decorated **Ascension Church**. The brick structure was built in 1532 to celebrate the birth of Vasily III's first son, Ivan the Terrible. The building was also the highest structure in all of Moscow at 60 meters (197 feet) and served as a watchtower. From an upper window Ivan the Terrible could observe his soldiers fighting the invading Mongols. Nearby stands the five-domed **Church of St John the Baptist** and 16th-century **St George Bell Tower**, all that remains of the Church of St George the Victorious. Other structures of interest are the Dyakovskaya Church, the red-brick water tower (which brought water up from the river), a Siberian watch tower (1631) and a gatehouse whose clock has been working since the time of Peter the Great. A museum housing religious and royal artifacts is situated in the gatehouse and adjoining building; it was founded in 1923. Of particular interest is the replica of Czar Alexei's wooden palace, made by the carver Smirnov in the 19th century.

From the 1930s to 1950s, monuments of Russian architecture were brought to the park from different regions of the country. These buildings now exhibit 16th- to 19th-century Russian applied and decorative art, including collections of paintings, ceramics, woodcarvings and clocks. Peter the Great's cottage, where he lived in 1702, is from the northern city of Archangel. It is a favorite area for picnics, shaded by oaks, elms and poplars; one of the ancient oak trees is thought to date back to the 14th century, during the rule of Ivan Kalita. The estate-museum is open 10am–5pm; closed Mondays. (In summer months the museum is usually open until 8pm.) To check times or book excursions, tel. 115-2309/112-5217.

Next to the estate is the **Elektron-1 Hotel** (tel. 118-2356, fax 118-2292). In the vicinity, at 19 Borisovsky Lane, is the 40-room **Borisovsky 19 Hotel** with restaurant (tel. 394-4475). The **Elektron-2 Hotel** is at 23 Nagornaya Street (tel. 127-5701); Nagornaya Metro station. (Also check area hotels listed under Tsaritsyno.)

(opposite) In the town of Istra, west of Moscow, an old 17th-century church is exhibited in the Museum of Wooden Architecture, surrounded by beryoza or birch trees; (above) master icon painter Andrei Rublyov painted the Apostle Paul in the early 15th century. Its elongated proportions make the three-meter-long figure look slender and weightless. The blue lapis lazuli was a favorite color used by Rublyov. In 1918 it was discovered in a shed in the town of Zvenigorod where it once hung within the Assumption Cathedral's iconostasis. It now hangs in Moscow's Tretyakov Gallery.

KUSKOVO PALACE MUSEUM   (КУСКОВО)

This estate-museum is located within the city limits to the southwest and can be easily reached from the Ryazansky Prospekt Metro station. From the station, it is a 20-minute walk or shorter bus ride to 2 Yuzhnost Street; pack a lunch to bring along. The lands of Kuskovo were in the Sheremetyev family since the early 17th century. (Boris Sheremetyev fought with Peter the Great against the Swedes in the Battle of Poltava in 1709.) The Sheremetyevs were incredibly wealthy with over three million acres of land holdings and 200,000 serfs. When Boris' son Pyotr Borisovich married a Romanov princess in 1743, they decided to built a summer estate at Kuskovo; it was soon nicknamed the Moscow Versailles. The pink and white wooden mansion (1769–75) was designed by Karl Blank and the serf-architects Alexei Mironov and Fyodor Argunov. It is faced with white stone and decorated with parquet floors, antique furniture, embroidered tapestries and crystal chandeliers; notice the carved initials PS over the front door. The mansion also houses an excellent collection of 18th-century Russian art; a portrait of Catherine the Great hangs in the Raspberry Drawing Room and the White Ball Hall is decorated with rich bucolic scenes painted by Sheremetyev serfs.

Outside, near the kitchen, stands the old estate church and five small pavilions are situated around the pond and grotto. (Pyotr Sheremetyev loved to stage mock military battles on the lake for his friends.) Other garden pavilions include the cross-shaped **Hermitage**, designed by Karl Blank in 1765; the brick-façade **Dutch Cottage** (1749); and the **Swiss House**, built in 1864 by Nikolai Benoit. Beyond the **Italian Cottage**, which also displays a collection of 18th-century paintings and sculpture, is the famous **Open-Air Theater**, where the celebrated company of Sheremetyev serf-actors performed weekly plays. One of the most popular actresses was Praskovia Zhemchugova-Kovalyova, the daughter of a serf blacksmith. In 1789, when she caught the eye of Nikolai Sheremetyev, son of Pyotr, one of Russia's most romantic love stories developed. Creating a major scandal, Nikolai granted her freedom and went on to marry the commoner in 1801. To get away from increasing social gossip, they moved to a palace at Ostankino. (Sadly Praskovia died two years later in childbirth.) In the neighboring **Orangerie** a small display tells their love story, and the **Ceramics Museum** exhibits a fine collection of Russian and European porcelain, faience and glass. The estate and museums are open 10am–3pm from October to March. During other months, it is open 10am–6pm weekdays, and 10am–7pm weekends. It is closed Mondays and Tuesdays and the last Wednesday of each month. To check times or book excursions, tel. 370-0160/0150. In the vicinity, at 10 Second Pyatigorsky Lane, is the **Veshnyaki Hotel** (tel. 174-2500/2545).

MOSCOW COUNTRY CLUB   (Нахабино)

The 142-hectare (350-acre) Moscow Country Club, called Nahabino, with Russia's first 18-hole championship golf course, is located about 30 kilometers (18 miles) northwest of Moscow in the Krasnogorsk district (a 40-minute drive from the city center along the M9 Volokolamskoye Highway or by train from Moscow's Rizhsky Railway Station). Designed by renowned California golf architect Robert Trent Jones II, the course is rated as one of the top ten golf courses in Europe and has an 18-hole, 6,735-meter (7,000-plus-yard) par-72 championship course. The club is owned by GlavUpDK, Russia's Diplomatic Service Administration, and managed by Forte International Hotels.

The golf course construction began in 1987, and took over six years to complete. The first Russian Golf Association was established in 1992. A year later, Moscow held its first Golf Open Championship at Nahabino; the first winner in Russian history was American Steve Schroeder. In September 1996, the club hosted Russia's first international golf tournament as part of the PGA European Challenge Tour, with 100 tour-ranked members, including 20 professionals from 26 countries; ten of the participants were Russian, playing for the first time on home soil.

It took over two decades to negotiate and build Russia's first golf course. The first joint venture planning began in 1974 between Robert Trent Jones Senior and Junior, Armand Hammer and GlavUpDK. Many interruptions (some serious, others wildly amusing) occurred during periods of the Brezhnev stagnation and Afghanistan War. When Trent Jones II submitted some of his first course plans to the US Commerce Department (a mandatory requirement when doing business in Russia at the time), the US Defense Department wanted to immediately halt the progress when they noticed that 'bunkers' had been incorporated into the design! (Later, while building the course in Moscow, Jones' employees actually came across foxholes, dug during World War II as protection against invading Germans.) Russia has come a long way—no golf terminology existed in their language: 'Fore' started out as *Ostarozhno* or 'Look Out!' Today the Reds on the greens now make up over one-tenth of club members and many Russian children come out as part of school curriculums to practice their golf swing.

On the grounds, there is also a driving range, practice greens, and a clubhouse with an extensive restaurant menu and full bar service, and pro-shop, complete with locker room facilities and a computerized golf simulator. The club has a hotel complex and conference center, a ten-million dollar spa and sports club which provides an indoor pool, tennis, squash, basketball, gymnasium, aerobics and fitness training, plus a health spa and beauty salon. Outside, there is also a lakeside beach area, water sports, boating and fishing. Individual luxury homes, modeled on

18th-century wooden dachas, are arranged around a central garden area. In colder months one can try cross-country skiing, snowmobiling, and winter golf on the lake. (Manager tel. 926-5924/564-8390/563-8635.)

The first-class Le Meridien Park Hotel (with four restaurants and bars) is open year-round to tourists. (In Moscow tel. (7-095) 926-5911, fax (7-095) 926-5921 for reservations.) Bookings can also be made by calling Forte Hotels (in the US) at (800) 225-5843. Spa and golf facilities are available for nonmembers.

The golf course was designed to be a very traditional parkland course. From the back tees, it has sufficient length and difficulty to host any type of championship tournament. The deep Russian forest with large evergreens, birch and native wildlife and song birds is a magnificent setting. The concept is classic strategy with hazards placed to create risks and rewards and exciting, enjoyable golf for beginners and proficient golfers of all ages and abilities.

Robert Trent Jones, Jr.

For more information on the Moscow Country Club and a golf or tennis tour, along with sightseeing in Moscow, contact Los Angeles, CA, tel. (310) 306-6262, fax (310) 306-5025.

ZAVIDOVO   (Завидово)

At the confluence of the Volga and Shoshka rivers, 120 kilometers (74 miles) northwest of Moscow (off the M10 Highway north of Klin) is the resort village of Zavidovo. It is managed by Russian firm GlavUpDK (who own the Moscow Country Club and the prestigious apartment/office complex Park Place in southwest Moscow). The year-round moderately priced resort has hotel and cottage accommodation, a health spa, swimming pool and shooting range. Sports include tennis, squash, horse riding and other water activities. Hunting and fishing excursions are also available and a golf course is currently under construction. For information in Moscow tel. (095) 539-2044/2057.

PEREDELKINO   (Переделкино)

Take an *elektrichka* train from Moscow's Kievsky Railway Station for the half-hour ride southwest to Peredelkino in the Solntsevo district. From the station, either take a bus to the end of Pavelyenko Street, or walk 20 minutes to the village. (If driving, take the Mozhaiskoye Highway about 12 miles west out of town.) For decades the Soviet Government granted the Writers' Union land in this area to build resident dachas for their members. Peredelkino became a name synonymous with a writer's and artist's colony. Even Anna Akhmatova and Alexander Solzhenitsyn lived here at one time; the latter lived in a spare room of a writer friend after he had smuggled out *The Gulag Archipelago* to the West. Here you can also visit the estate and grave of the great Russian writer and Nobel laureate Boris Pasternak, who wrote *Dr Zhivago*. (For this novel the disillusioned writer was expelled from the Writers' Union and forced to decline his 1958 Nobel prize.) In 1960, Pasternak died at his dacha, now the **Pasternak House Museum**. (Open 10am–6pm; closed Mondays, Tuesdays and Wednesdays.)

Pasternak wrote of Moscow:

> *For the dreamer and the night-bird*
> *Moscow is dearer than all else in the world.*
> *It is at the hearth, the source*
> *Of everything that the century will live for.*

Above the railway station stands the 15th-century Church of the Transfiguration, whose interior is decorated with a multitude of saints and a fine iconostasis. Following the path to the left of the church brings you to Pasternak's grave, bordered by three pines and usually covered with flowers. Other prominent writers are also buried in the cemetery. It is a fine place to stroll through the countryside; bring a picnic. Nordic skiing and ice fishing are also possible in winter months.

Near the railway station, at 2a Pervaya Chubotovskaya Alley, and housed in what was formerly Brezhnev's daughter's dacha, is the ten-room **Villa Peredelkino Hotel** (tel. 435-8184/1478) **and Restaurant** (tel. 435-8345), open 12pm–midnight (last train to Moscow is at 12.30am). **Setun Restaurant**, at 1 Pervaya Chubotovskaya, also has Russian food. Open 12pm–11pm; tel. 439-0429.

TSARITSYNO (Царицыно)

Tsaritsyno Estate lies in the southern part of Moscow at 1 Dolskaya Street. To get here, take the Zamoskvoretskaya Liniya to Orekhovo Metro station. (Note the line splits at Kashirskaya. If coming from the city center, make sure the destination posted on the front of the train reads Krasnogvardeiskaya, not Kakhovskaya.) In the 16th century Irina, wife of Czar Fyodor Ioannovich, lived at her country estate here and had the Tsaritsyno (Czarina) ponds dug. Later it was the favorite of the Golitsyn princes; in 1712, Peter the Great presented the estate to a Moldavian count.

After Catherine the Great remodeled the Winter Palace and Hermitage in St Petersburg, she turned her attention to Moscow. In 1775, she bought the estate in the wooded countryside south of Moscow, complete with a palace and miniature

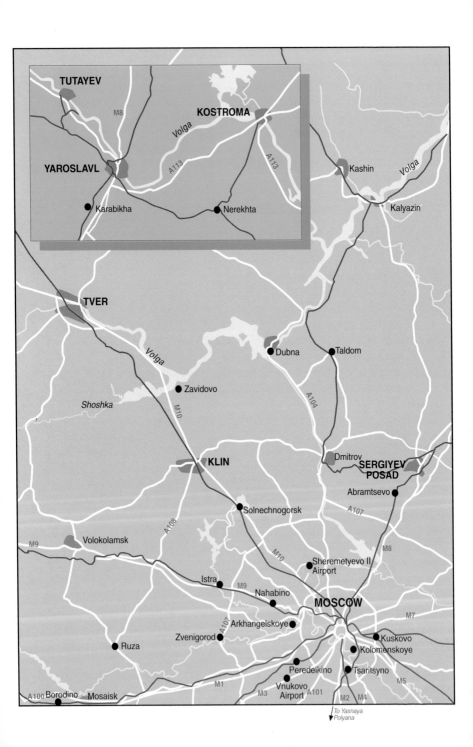

TUTAYEV

M8

Volga

KOSTROMA

A113

A113

YAROSLAVL

Karabikha

Nerekhta

Kashin

Volga

Kalyazin

TVER

Volga

Dubna

Taldom

Shoshka

Zavidovo

M10

A104

KLIN

Dmitrov

SERGIYEV
POSAD

Abramtsevo

Solnechnogorsk

A107

A108

Volokolamsk

M9

M10

M8

Sheremetyevo II
Airport

Istra

M9

Nahabino

MOSCOW

M7

A107

Arkhangelskoye

Kuskovo

Zvenigorod

Kolomenskoye

Ruza

Peredelkino

Tsaritsyno

M5

M1

Vnukovo
Airport

A101

M3

M2 M4

A100 Borodino Mosaisk

To Yasnaya
Polyana

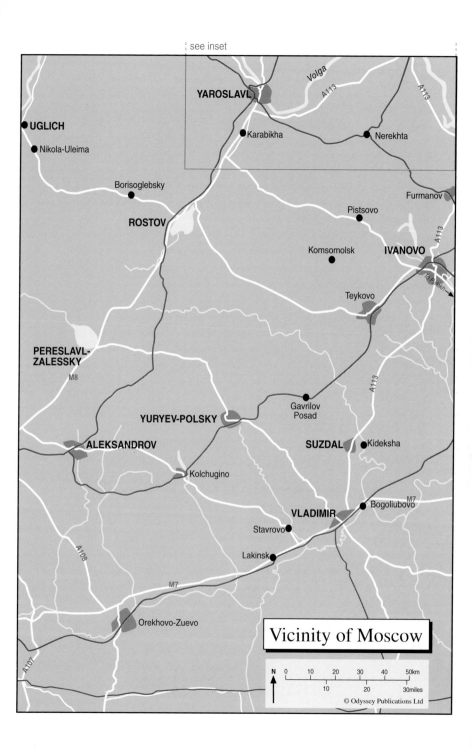

see inset

Volga

A113

A113

YAROSLAVL

● **UGLICH**

● Nikola-Uleima

● Karabikha

● Nerekhta

Furmanov

Borisoglebsky ●

ROSTOV

● Pistsovo

A113

● Komsomolsk

IVANOVO

To Palekh →

Teykovo ●

**PERESLAVL-
ZALESSKY**

M8

A113

● Gavrilov
Posad

YURYEV-POLSKY

SUZDAL   ● Kideksha

ALEKSANDROV

● Kolchugino

M7

● Bogoliubovo

VLADIMIR

Stavrovo ●

A108

Lakinsk ●

M7

A107

● Orekhovo-Zuevo

Vicinity of Moscow

N 0   10   20   30   40   50km

10   20   30miles

© Odyssey Publications Ltd

opera house. It was known as Chornaya Gryaz (Black Mud); Catherine renamed it Tsaritsyno. Her architect Vasily Bazhenov was commissioned to transform the main building into a Moorish-Gothic-style palace, and the 6,200 acres into English-style formal gardens. After ten years of work, Catherine came down from St Petersburg to inspect it. She commanded that all work be stopped and the main palace torn down. In 1786, Bazhenov's pupil and main rival, Matvei Kazakov, was asked to redesign the property; these are the buildings we see today. Some speculate that Catherine had the original palace torn down because she had had it constructed in two parts—one for herself and one for her son Paul—connected by a common corridor. After a decade, however, she had come to abhor her son, who held equal contempt for her, so she no longer wanted anything to do with him. She also came to dislike the Freemasons and hated all freemasonry motifs. The rebuilding was halted at the resumption of the Turkish wars and stopped altogether upon her death in 1796.

Intended as the main entrance to the palace, the **Figurny Bridge** (with stone Maltese crosses—motifs of the Freemasons) separates Tsaritsyno's two lakes. The main building, through the **Grapevine Entrance** gates, looks more like a cathedral than a palace. Its windows are broken and roof crumbling—in the 19th century, a local factory needed roofing materials and raided the roof. At one time it was also used for mountaineering training, and crampon holes are still in the walls. The **Palace** has never been lived in and has stood empty for more than two centuries. Other structures are the **Bakery** (Khlebny Dom); octagonal **Octahedron**, the servants' quarters; **Opera House**; and the small whitewashed church, built in 1722. The strange deserted buildings are fun to explore, and strolling around the grounds is delightful; bring a picnic. (There is talk of restoration and plans for the buildings to house a gallery of modern art.) Boats are available for hire in summer. In winter it is fun to ice-skate, sled or cross-country ski in the area (you need to bring your own equipment).

In 1988, the Russian Church was allowed to build a church in the town of Tsaritsyno to commemorate the Millennium of the Baptism of Rus; it was the first church allowed to be built in Moscow during the Soviet era. The **Museum of History, Architecture, Art and Nature** is open 11am–5pm; weekends 10am–5pm; closed Mondays and Tuesdays. To check times and information, tel. 321-0743.

To dine try the **Country Estate**, open 12pm–11pm, at 10 Dolskaya. Russian food and live music at night (tel. 343-1510/3836). The nearby **Hotel Orekhovo** is located at 39 Shipilovsky Lane with restaurant, bar and fitness room (tel. 343-3681). At 47 Shipilovsky is the smaller **Hotel Tsaritsyno** (tel. 343-4356/63). Near both Kolomenskoye Complex and Tsaritsyno is the large block **Sevastopol Hotel** at 1a Bolshaya Yushunskaya Street (tel. 318-0918/8400); Sevastopolskaya Metro station.

THE CONQUEROR

*A*t ten in the morning of the second of September, Napoleon was standing among his troops on the Poklonny Hill looking at the panorama spread out before him. From the twenty-sixth of August to the second of September, that is from the battle of Borodino to the entry of the French into Moscow, during the whole of that agitating, memorable week, there had been the extraordinary autumn weather that always comes as a surprise, when the sun hangs low and gives more heat than in spring, when everything shines so brightly in the rare clear atmosphere that the eyes smart, when the lungs are strengthened and refreshed by inhaling the aromatic autumn air, when even the nights are warm, and when in those dark warm nights, golden stars startle and delight us continually by falling from the sky.

The view of the strange city with its peculiar architecture, such as he had never seen before, filled Napoleon with the rather envious and uneasy curiosity men feel when they see an alien form of life. By the indefinite signs which, even at a distance, distinguish a living body from a dead one, Napoleon from the Poklonny Hill perceived the throb of life in the town and felt, as it were, the breathing of that great and beautiful body.

Every Russian looking at Moscow feels her to be mother; every foreigner who sees her, even if ignorant of her significance as the mother city, must feel her feminine character, and Napoleon felt it.

"A town captured by the enemy is like a maid who has lost her honor," thought he, and from that point of view he gazed at the oriental beauty he had not seen before. It seemed strange to him that his long-felt wish, which had seemed unattainable, had at last been realized. In the clear morning light he gazed now at the city and now at the plan, considering its details, and the assurance of possessing it agitated and awed him.

Leo Tolstoy, War and Peace, 1869

YASNAYA POLYANA   (Ясная Поляна)

The town lies 200 kilometers (124 miles) south of Moscow along the Simferopolskoye Highway (about a three-hour drive). It is a longer train ride from Moscow's Kursky Railway Station; get off at Tula and take a local bus to the estate. The great Russian writer, Count Lev (Leo) Nikolayevich Tolstoy, was born in Yasnaya Polyana (Clear Glade) on August 28, 1828, and lived and worked here for over 60 years; he inherited the property in 1847. Everything on the estate, situated in a pastoral setting of birch forests and orchards, has been preserved as he left it—his living room (Tolstoy was born on the leather sofa), library (with 22,000 volumes), and parlor (where his wife Sofia Andreyevna meticulously copied his manuscripts). On the Persian walnut desk in the study, Tolstoy wrote *Anna Karenina*, *War and Peace* (which Sofia recopied by hand nine times, when not busy bearing his 13 children!) and chapters of *The Resurrection*. Portraits by Ilya Repin and Valentin Serov decorate the walls. Today the manor house functions as the **Tolstoy House Museum**. The writer also opened a school for local peasant children, and this now houses the **Literary Museum**. Peasants and other followers would gather outside under the Tree of the Poor to ask his advice.

The 445-hectare (1,100-acre) Yasnaya Polyana was the main source of creative inspiration for Tolstoy, and the location is reflected in many of his works. Here he wanted to create a miniature of Russian society. Tolstoy also developed a philosophy of Christianity so potent that the Russian Church excommunicated him. He also became a vegetarian, enjoyed wearing simple peasant attire and worked in the fields alongside his serfs. Tolstoy wrote: 'It is difficult for me to imagine Russia without my Yasnaya Polyana.' On October 28, 1910, at the age of 82, Tolstoy decided to renounce all his possessions and left the estate with his youngest daughter, Alexandra and his doctor to embark on a journey. When they arrived at Astapovo Railway Station almost 320 kilometers (200 miles) away, Tolstoy was stricken with influenza. The great writer died in the station master's hut on November 7; his last words were said to be: 'To seek, always to seek.'

A short walk down a well-worn path leads to Tolstoy's simple grave—a small mound of earth with no headstone (be prepared for mosquitoes in summer). Tolstoy's wife, and then his daughters, managed the estate until 1956, when it was placed under Soviet control. Today Tolstoy's great-great grandson Vladimir (over 200 relatives are scattered around six countries) presides over the daily management. Yasnaya Polyana is open 9am–5.30pm; closed Mondays, Tuesdays and the last Wednesday of each month. In Moscow you can also visit two other Tolstoy museums (see pages 143 and 181).

The great Russian writer Count Leo Tolstoy was born at Yasnaya Polyana, south of Moscow, in 1828. He inherited the estate in 1847 and lived and worked here for more than 60 years. Today this 19th-century estate is known as the Leo Tolstoy Museum where everything of the writer's has been preserved, including the 22,000 tome library and study.

At the Persian walnut desk, inherited from his father, Tolstoy penned his novels, Anna Karenina and War and Peace (see Literary Excerpt on page 215).

ZVENIGOROD   (Звенигород)

Zvenigorod lies about 55 kilometers (33 miles) west of Moscow along the M1/A105/A107 routes. *Elektrichka* trains also run from Moscow's Byelorussky Railway Station; get off at Golitsyno where a small branch line breaks from the main railway. Since commuter trains are infrequent, try taking a local bus or car for the remaining ten kilometers (six miles).

Zvenigorod, standing atop a hill that overlooks the Moskva River and founded in 1339, is known as Moscow's Switzerland. Up in the hills stands the 14th-century single-domed **Cathedral of the Assumption**, built by the son of Dmitri Donskoi; morning services are usually held here. The monk Savva, a disciple of St Sergius, began construction on the **Monastery of Savva-Storozhevsky** in the 14th century. It became the favorite religious retreat of Czar Alexei in the mid-17th century; his white palace is situated across from the cathedral's porch. Over the centuries the monastery grew to one of the richest and most powerful in Russia. Monks led a local revolution against the Bolsheviks in 1918; but a year later the monastery was shut down by the new government.

Today the 15th-century **Cathedral of the Nativity**, decorated with *kokoshniki* and stone carvings, is once again open for religious services. Next to the multi-tiered bell tower (which you can climb) is the **Transfiguration Church**. The 17th-century **Trinity Church** is nearby with the attached Kazan Refectory. It was here that one of Russia's greatest film directors, Andrei Tarkovsky, staged much of his classic film on the life of the famous icon painter Andrei Rublyov, whose icons were discovered within the church in 1918 (now exhibited in the Tretyakov Gallery). Lining the left-hand wall of the fortress is the red and white **Czaritsa's Chambers**, used by the Polish wife of Czar Alexei. On the outside porch, notice the carved double- and single-headed eagles, emblems of Russian and Polish rulers. The **History Museum** is now located within the chambers, and another museum, exhibiting paintings, ceramics and wood carvings by local contemporary artists, is in the nearby two-story monks' quarters. Museums are open 10am–5pm; closed Mondays.

In summer, bring food from Moscow to picnic by the river and have a swim. Take a stroll through the Old Town (uphill from the center), and get swept back a century as you pass old wooden dachas, intricately carved and colorfully painted. In 1884, the writer and physician Anton Chekhov lived in the area and wrote the story *Ward 6* about a doctor who goes mad. During the Soviet era, KGB and military officers kept summer homes here and frequented the nearby health resort.

THE OLD ARISTOCRACY

Wealth was measured in those times by the number of "souls" which a landed proprietor owned. So many "souls" meant so many male serfs: women did not count. My father, who owned nearly twelve hundred souls, in three different provinces, and who had, in addition to his peasants' holdings, large tracts of land which were cultivated by these peasants, was accounted a rich man. He lived up to his reputation, which meant that his house was open to any number of visitors, and that he kept a very large household.

We were a family of eight, occasionally ten or twelve; but fifty servants at Moscow, and half as many more in the country, were considered not one too many. Four coachmen to attend a dozen horses, three cooks for the masters and two more for the servants, a dozen men to wait upon us at dinner-time (one man, plate in hand, standing behind each person seated at the table), and girls innumerable in the maid-servants' room—how could anyone do with less than this?

Besides, the ambition of every landed proprietor was that everything required for his household should be made at home by his own men.

"How nicely your piano is always tuned! I suppose Herr Schimmel must be your tuner?" perhaps a visitor would remark.

To be able to answer, "I have my own piano-tuner," was in those times the correct thing.

"What a beautiful pastry!" the guests would exclaim, when a work of art, composed of ices and pastry, appeared toward the end of the dinner. "Confess, prince, that it comes from Tremblé" (the fashionable pastry cook).

"It is by my own confectioner, a pupil of Tremblé, whom I have allowed to show what he can do," was a reply which elicited general admiration.

As soon as the children of the servants attained the age of ten, they were sent as apprentices to the fashionable shops, where they were obliged to spend five or seven years chiefly in sweeping, in receiving an incredible number of thrashings, and in running about town on errands of all sorts. I must own that few of them became masters of their respective arts. The tailors and the shoemakers were found only skillful enough to make clothes or shoes for the servants, and when a really good pastry was required for a dinner-party it was ordered at Tremblé's, while our own confectioner was beating the drum in the music band.

That band was another of my father's ambitions, and almost every one of his male servants, in addition to other accomplishments, was a bass-viol or a clarinet in the band. Makar, the piano-tuner, alias under-butler, was also a flautist; Andrei, the tailor, played the French horn; the confectioner was first put to beat the drum, but misused his instrument to such a deafening degree that a tremendous trumpet was bought for him, in the hope that his lungs would not have the power to make the same noise as his hands; when, however, this last hope had to be abandoned, he was set to be a soldier. As to "spotted Tikhon", in addition to his numerous functions in the household as lamp-cleaner, floor-polisher, and footman, he made himself useful in the band—today as trombone, tomorrow as bassoon, and occasionally as second violin...

Dancing-parties were not infrequent, to say nothing of obligatory balls every winter. Father's way, in such cases, was to have everything done in good style, whatever the expense. But at the same time such niggardliness was practised in our house in daily life that if I were to recount it, I should be accused of exaggeration. However, in the Old Equerries' Quarter such a mode of life only raised my father in public esteem. "The old prince," it was said, "seems to be sharp over money at home; but knows how a nobleman ought to live."

Prince Peter Kropotkin, Memoirs of a Revolutionist, 1899

The Golden Ring (Zolotoye Koltso)

The ancient towns of the Golden Ring, built between the 11th and 17th centuries, are the cradle of Russian culture. During Russia's early history, the two most important cities were Kiev in the south and Novgorod in the north. They were both situated in what is now western Russia and lay along important commerce routes to the Black and Baltic seas. The settlements that sprang up along the trade routes between these two cities prospered and grew into large towns of major political and religious importance. From the 11th to 15th centuries, the towns of Rostov, Yaroslavl, Vladimir and Suzdal became capitals of the northern principalities, and Sergiyev Posad served as the center of Russian Orthodoxy. In the 12th century Moscow was established as a small protective outpost of the Rostov-Suzdal principality. By the 16th century Moscow had grown so big and affluent that it was named the capital of the Russian Empire. The prominent towns that lay in a circle to the northeast of Moscow became known as the Golden Ring. Each town is a living chronicle documenting many centuries in the history of old Russia.

THE RUSSIAN TOWN

Up to the end of the 18th century, a typical Russian town consisted of a kremlin, a protective fortress surrounding the site. Watchtowers were built in strategic points along the kremlin wall and contained vaulted carriageways, which served as the gates to the city. The timber town within the kremlin contained the governmental and administrative offices. The boyars, or noble class, had homes here too that were used only in time of war—otherwise they lived outside the town on their own country estates, where the peasants or serfs worked the land. The *posad* (earth town) was the settlement of traders and craftsmen. The *posad* also contained the *rinoks*—the markets and bazaars, as well as the storage houses for the town. The merchants and boyars used their wealth to help build the churches and commissioned artists to paint elaborate frescoes and icons. The number of churches and monasteries mirrored the prosperity of the town. The rest of the townspeople lived in settlements known as the *slobody* around the kremlin. The historical nucleus and heart of the town was known as the *strelka*. The regions were separated into principalities with their own governing princes. The ruler of the united principalities was known as the grand prince and later czar. The head of the Orthodox Church was called the metropolitan or patriarch.

The Golden Ring area provides an excellent opportunity to view typical old Russian towns, which are still surrounded by ancient kremlins, churches and monasteries. The towns of Rostov, Vladimir, Suzdal and Pereslavl-Zalessky retain much of their original layouts. Outside Suzdal and Kostroma are open-air architectural museums—entire wooden villages built to typify old Russian life. All the towns of the Golden Ring have been well-restored, and many of the buildings are now museums that trace the history of the area that was the center of the Golden Age of Rus.

RELIGION AND THE CHURCH

Before Prince Vladimir introduced Byzantine Christianity to the Kievan principality in AD 988, Russia was a pagan state; the people of Rus worshipped numerous gods. Festivals were held according to the seasons, planting and harvest cycles, and life passages. Special offerings of eggs, wheat and honey were presented to the gods of water, soil and sun. Carved figures of mermaids and suns adorned the roofs of houses. When Prince Vladimir married the sister of the Byzantine Emperor and introduced Christianity, Russia was finally united under one God and Kiev became the center of the Orthodox Church. But it took almost a century to convert the many pagan areas, especially in the north. Early church architecture (11th-century) was based on the Byzantine cube-shaped building with one low rounded cupola on the roof bearing an Orthodox cross facing east. The domes gradually evolved into helmet drums on tent-shaped roofs. In the 17th century Patriarch Nikon banned the tent-shaped roof because it appeared too similar to the design of Western Lutheran churches. Thus the onion-shaped dome (also more suitable for the heavy snowfalls) became the distinctive design of the Orthodox Church. Nikon also decreed the assembly of five domes (instead of the usual one); the central higher dome symbolized 'the seat of the Lord', while the four lower ones, the four evangelists. The next two centuries witnessed classical and baroque influences, and the onion domes became much more elaborately shaped and decorated. During your tour of the Golden Ring, try dating the churches by the shapes of their domes.

The outer walls of churches were divided into three sections by protruding vertical strips, which indicated the position of the piers inside. A few centuries later churches expanded considerably and were built from white stone or brick instead of wood. (Unfortunately, many of the wooden buildings did not survive and stone churches were built on their original sites.) The main body of the church was tiered into different levels and adjoined by chapels, galleries and porches. A large tent-shaped bell tower usually dominated one side.

During the two and a half centuries of Mongol occupation (beginning in the mid-13th century), Russia was cut off from any outside influence. Monasteries united the Russian people and acted as shelters and fortresses against attacks. They became the educational centers and housed the historical manuscripts, which monks wrote on birch-bark parchment. During this period Russian church architecture developed a unique style. Some distinctive features were the decorative *zakomara*, semicircular arches, that lined the tops of the outer walls where they joined the roof (see picture on page 195). The *trapeza* porch was built outside the western entrance of the church and other carved designs were copied from the decorations on peasant houses. Elaborate carved gables around doors, windows and archways were called *kokoshniki*, named after the large headdresses worn by young married women. Through the years, even though the architecture took on European classical, Gothic and baroque elements, the designs always retained a distinctive Russian flair. Each entrance of the kremlin had its own Gate Church. The most elaborate stood by the Holy Gates, the main entrance to the town. Many cathedrals took years to build and twin churches were also a common sight—one was used in winter and the other, more elaborate, for summer services and festivals.

The interior of the church was highly decorated with frescoes. Images of Christ were painted inside the central dome, surrounded by angels. Beneath the dome came the pictures of saints, apostles and prophets. Images of the patron saint of the church might appear on the pillars. Special religious scenes and the earthly life of Christ or the Virgin Mary were depicted on the walls and vaults. The Transfiguration was usually painted on the east wall by the altar and scenes from the Last Judgment and Old Testament were illustrated on the west wall, where people would exit the church. The iconostasis was an elaborate tiered structure, filled with icons, that stretched behind the altar from the floor toward the ceiling. The top tiers held Christ, the middle the saints and prophets, and the lower tiers were reserved for scenes from church history.

Fresco painting was a highly respected skill and many master craftsmen, such as Andrei Rublyov and Daniil Chorny, produced beautiful works of art. The plaster was applied to the wall of the church and then the artists would sketch the main outline of the fresco right onto the damp plaster. The master supervised the work and filled in the more intricate and important parts of the composition, while the apprentices added the background detail.

The building of elaborate churches and painting of exquisite icons and frescoes reached its zenith in the prosperous towns of the Golden Ring. Even cathedrals in the Moscow Kremlin were copied from church designs that originated in Rostov, Vladimir and Suzdal. Today these churches and works of art stand as monuments to an extraordinary era of Russian history.

RELIGION AFTER THE REVOLUTION

For nearly 1,000 years the Russian Orthodox Church dominated the life of Russia and, as Tolstoy observed, for most of the Russian people 'faith was the force of life'. But after the 1917 Revolution, when Marx proclaimed that 'religion is the opium of

With the new era of religious freedom, many artists practice the trade of fresco restoration and also paint religious art for the many new churches now under construction.

the masses', all churches were closed to religious use and their property confiscated and redistributed by the government—even though Article 124 of the Soviet Constitution stated that 'Church is separate from State' and provided 'freedom of worship for all citizens'. Before the Revolution, Russia had almost 100,000 churches and monasteries; Moscow alone had more than 500. By the time of the purges in the 1930s, the capital had lost over a third of its glorious churches, and less than 100 still functioned officially in the entire Soviet Union. Churches were turned into swimming pools, ice-skating rinks and restaurants. Moscow's Danilovsky Monastery was used as a prison. The Church of St Nicholas became a gas station.

In 1988, the Millennium of Russian Christianity was officially celebrated throughout the former Soviet Union, and government decrees provided a new legal status for the Orthodox Church and other religions. The Russian Orthodox Church remained headed by the patriarch and assisted by the Holy Synod, whose seats are in Sergiyev Posad and Moscow respectively. But the government continued to control and dictate the moves of the Church, while the topic of religion was discussed in meetings of the Supreme Soviet. Positive signs of increased religious tolerance and freedom slowly emerged and a small number of churches were eventually given back for religious use.

During the period of perestroika, the process of renewal of Soviet society brought about major changes in the relations between Church and State and believers and nonbelievers. On April 29, 1988, the eve of the Millennium of Russian Orthodoxy, Gorbachev received the Patriarch of Moscow and All Russia and members of the Synod in the Yekaterinsky Hall in the Kremlin. Gorbachev stated: 'Believers are Soviet people; they are workers and patriots and they have a full right to adequately express their convictions. The reforms of perestroika and glasnost concern them also without any limitations.' On October 13, 1989, a Thanksgiving Service was held in the Kremlin's Assumption Cathedral, the first service to take place there in 71 years. The last Mass held there had been at Easter in 1918. The government also returned the Danilovsky Monastery to the Orthodox Church. In 1988 alone some 900 buildings were returned to the Church, and religious figures were even elected to the Congress of Peoples' Deputies. On December 1, 1989, Gorbachev became the first Soviet leader to set foot in the Vatican.

One well-respected St Petersburg rector of the Orthodox Church and city seminary (who was allowed to visit Rome for an audience with the Pope during perestroika) remarked, 'I am an optimist. People are not only interested in bettering themselves economically, but also morally and spiritually. The powers of the Communist State could never extend to the soul. And in these uncertain times, we would like to help the new generation find its way.'

Since the collapse of the Soviet Union, the Patriarch of All Russia is now the

head of the Russian Orthodox Church and the Church is separate from the State. Since the establishment of Christianity in Russia, the form of Church leadership has changed several times. From AD 988 until 1589, the Church was headed by a metropolitan and from 1589 until 1721, by a patriarch. Peter the Great then dissolved the seat of patriarch and created a governing Church body known as the Holy Synod, a group of 11 of the highest-ranking priests. In November 1917, the Bolshevik government decided to restore the patriarchate; that is, leadership by one supreme individual rather than by a collective body.

In 1992, Boris Yeltsin became the first Russian leader since the 1917 Bolshevik Revolution to attend Easter ceremonies in an Orthodox Church. Yeltsin, who was baptized, told Patriarch Alexei, 'It is time for Russia to return to her strong religious heritage.' On November 4, 1993, Yeltsin attended the consecration of the newly restored Kazan Cathedral in Red Square. During the stand-off siege of 1993 in the White House, the patriarch was called in to help arbitrate between the hard-liners and Yeltsin. However, another battle is being waged: to determine whether the government, museums or the Church owns religious art. In 1993, Yeltsin signed orders to transfer two famous icons by Andrei Rublyov in the Tretyakov Gallery to the Orthodox Church.

After the fall of the Soviet Union more than 10,000 churches were reopened for religious activities. Today the Orthodox Church claims 80 million followers, or more than half of Russia's population. St Petersburg has over 30 places of worship and Moscow supports over 130 active churches. More people, especially the younger generation, are attending religious services and being baptized. Theological seminaries are training monks and priests, and Church charity organizations are now permitted to help the new classes of homeless, poor and unemployed. The Russian Orthodox Church has also embraced the capitalist spirit. Many churches have their own shops, and priests are earning money by blessing businesses and apartments, even cars, bars and casinos.

With Moscow's new 250-million-dollar Cathedral of Christ the Savior (rebuilt on the spot where Stalin destroyed the old one), the Orthodox Church and its patriarch find themselves back at the apogee of political power in the new Russia. During the presidency of Boris Yeltsin a strong partnership, which had not existed for centuries, was formed between the Orthodox Church and the Russian State. While State officials attended Christmas and Easter services, the patriarch was invited to the Kremlin to attend secular ceremonies and treaty signings.

A monk stops to chat with a member of his congregation in front of the Assumption Cathedral in Sergiyev Posad, one of the major centers of the Russian Orthodox Church.

In 1997, to fully cement its dominance, the Orthodox Church sponsored a bill in an attempt to restrict all other faiths in the country. Patriarch Alexei II commented: 'A law on religion is needed to protect Russians from destructive pseudo-religious cults, and foreign false missionaries.' (Ironically, the bill was supported by the Communists.) On September 26, 1997, Yeltsin signed the Freedom of Conscience and Religious Association Acts, which state that only those churches that collaborated with the regime during 1917–91 are recognized by the Russian Government; others may still pray and worship, but only in their homes. Many consider that this new State supervision of religion in Russia is directed as much at internal as well as external enemies of the Russian Orthodox Church. Others cannot miss the irony that the Church, more intent at gaining political power than promoting faith, is not much better than Stalin's old government which conducted devastating campaigns of persecution against Christians and other religions. Today, clashes continue between post-Soviet Church conservatives, members of other religious groups and State reformists.

Also in 1997, the Council of Archbishops of the Russian Orthodox Church bestowed sainthood on metropolitans Pyotr and Sarafim, and Archbishop Faddei, who were all subjected to repression by Stalin in 1937. Even though a St Petersburg burial was approved for the last czar, Nicholas II, and his family (in July 1998), the Chairman of the Holy Synod refrained from canonizing Nicholas. The Commission is still considering the idea of elevating the czar and his family to the status of martyrs.

Many other religious groups are also enjoying a new period of openness. There are one and a half million officially registered Jews (given as their nationality), four million Roman Catholics, five million Uniates (Catholics of Eastern Rite), 800 Protestant congregations, over one million Baptists, two million Lutherans, 250,000 Pentecostalists, and 50,000 each of Mennonites, Seventh-Day Adventists and Jehovah's Witnesses. Other groups such as Scientologists, Sikhs and Hare Krishnas have also established themselves in Russia. There are also half a million Buddhists, five and a half million Moslems and about one million Old Believers, a sect resulting from the 1666 schism of the Orthodox Church. Such religious tolerance in Russia has not been known since Peter the Great.

GETTING THERE

Many travel organizations (both international and local) offer package tours specifically to the Golden Ring area that include stops in Moscow and St Petersburg. Most tour the Golden Ring by bus, which is also an ideal way to see the Russian countryside. (See Travel Agencies and Tour Companies in Moscow Practical Information section, page 334.) Once you are in Russia, a hotel service desk or travel agency can also advise how to book excursions to areas along the Golden Ring route. Towns close to

Moscow such as Sergiyev Posad and Vladimir should not have to be added to your visa, but more distant cities such as Yaroslavl and Ivanovo may. Some places, Aleksandrov and Sergiyev Posad for example, can be visited in a day from Moscow. In others you can stay overnight, but it is advised to reserve a hotel room in advance. (Since the towns are popular, many hotels may be fully booked by groups.) You can travel quite comfortably to the areas by bus, train or car. There are cafés and restaurants along the way, but it is a good idea to take along some food and drink for the journey.

The Golden Ring area is still not easily accessible to independent travelers. To travel off the beaten path, plan an itinerary and figure out how to get there and where to stay. The easiest way is to take the *elektrichka* (electric) commuter trains from Moscow stations. (Dress warmly in winter—many of these trains are not heated!) Some towns are also served by local tour buses. You can also try renting a car and driver, or bargain with a taxi driver or owner of a private car. It is better to go during weekdays since trains and towns are crowded at weekends, especially in summer. A more detailed description on how to get to Golden Ring locations and where to stay is provided under each individual listing. A web-site that includes information on some Golden Ring towns is http://mars.uthscsa.edu/Russia/.

The towns of the Golden Ring are a majestic mirror of Russia's past grandeur. The churches and monasteries are beautifully preserved and their frescoes and icons have been painstakingly restored. Many of the churches hold religious services, which you are welcome to attend. (Do not wear shorts or sleeveless shirts; men should remove hats.) Other religious buildings have been converted into museums that house the art and historical artifacts of the region.

A splendid skyline of golden-domed churches, tent-shaped towers, ornamental belfries, picturesque old wooden buildings and rolling countryside dotted with birch trees greets you—as it did the visitor more than seven centuries ago.

Sergiyev Posad   Сергиев Посад

CENTER OF RUSSIAN ORTHODOXY

A 75-kilometer (46-mile) ride north of Moscow leads to Sergiyev Posad, the most popular town on the Golden Ring route. As soon as the road leaves Moscow, it winds back in time through dense forests of spruce and birch, past old wooden dachas, country homes and farms, and eventually opens onto a magical view upon which fairy tales are based.

You can drive via the M8 Yaroslavskoye Highway (a continuation of Prospekt Mira) or take an inexpensive *elektrichka* train from Moscow's Yaroslavsky Railway Station (Komsomolskaya Metro station), which depart quite frequently during the day; the journey takes about 90 minutes and the stop is called Sergiyev Posad. Departure times are listed on a board in front of the station. Buy your ticket at an inside *kassa* booth; you do not need to show any ID. Usually, only same-day tickets are sold. Get on the train early to secure a window seat. (Before embarking, take

The 18th-century baroque bell tower in Sergiyev Posad

note of departure times of trains back to Moscow and buy a return ticket; you do not want to miss the last train! Or you can continue on from here to the nearby town of Aleksandrov.)

Once at Sergiyev Posad, turn left, walk west down the main road and head for the bell tower, about a 15-minute walk away. Turn right at the Zolotoye Koltso (Golden Ring) Restaurant; the monastery is a few minutes walk from here.

If you are driving, the Russkaya Skazka is at number 43 on the M8 Yaroslavskoye Highway from Moscow (tel. 584-3436; open daily 12pm–10pm). This unique wooden Russian Fairy Tale restaurant offers hearty appetizers, soups and stews. Other small cafés dot the area around the monastery; you can also bring or buy food (at the monastery entrance) and have a picnic by the pond or rivers.

A small fee is charged at the front kiosk to enter the monastery grounds; camera and video permits cost extra. Brochures and books on Sergiyev Posad are available in English. Shops on the premises sell souvenirs, art works and religious items. The grounds and museums are open 10am–5pm; closed Mondays.

HISTORY

In the early 14th century two brothers, Stefan and Varfolomei (Bartholomew), built a small wooden church and monastic retreat in the forests of Radonezh (lands inherited from their father, a pious Rostov boyar). Varfolomei took his monastic vows as Sergius and founded his own monastery in 1345; St Sergius would one day be named the patron saint of all Russia. Sergius and his pupils went on to establish 50 other monasteries across northeastern Russia that also acted as educational centers and regional strongholds during the Mongol occupations. Seventy of St Sergius' disciples attained sainthood.

In 1380, Grand Prince Dmitri Donskoi and his armies were blessed before battle by Sergius Radonezhsky. Outnumbered four to one, they defeated Khan Mamai's hordes—the first major Mongol defeat in over a century. At the monastery, one of St Sergius' pupils, the famous iconist Andrei Rublyov (see Special Topic on page 275), painted the *Old Testament Trinity* (now in Moscow's Tretyakov Gallery) to commemorate this famous battle at Kulikovo on the Don. After the victory, Moscow princes and rich boyars contributed heavily to the establishment of the Troitse-Sergiyev Lavra (Trinity Monastery of St Sergius) until it became not only the wealthiest in all Russia, but also the most revered pilgrimage shrine in Moscovy.

The thick kremlin walls were built around the monastery in 1540 during the reign of Ivan the Terrible to protect it from attack. A half-century later, the *lavra* (monastery) withstood a 16-month siege by Polish forces; it was protected by over 3,000 monks. The monastery complex was such an important center for the Russian people that its fall would have meant the end of Rus. The monastery remained an important fortress that defended Moscow well into the 17th century. Eleven octagonal towers were built into the walls as key defense points. The most famous, the northeast tower, is known as the Utichya (Duck) Tower; the duck atop its spire symbolizes Peter the Great's hunting expeditions in Sergiyev Posad. (He also enjoyed taking shots at the ducks swimming in the pond below.) The place also played an important cultural role; the manuscript-writing and color miniature painting sections date back to the 15th century.

After his death, Sergius was canonized; he is buried in the Holy Trinity Cathedral on the monastery grounds. In 1992, the Orthodox Church celebrated the 600th anniversary of St Sergius' passing. Each year special church processions are held, especially during St Sergius and Holy Trinity Days, New Year's and Easter holidays.

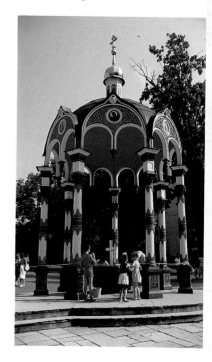

The Chapel-over-the-Well in Sergiyev Posad. It is customary for pilgrims to fill bottles with holy water to take home.

Today the Trinity-Sergius Monastery is the largest *lavra* run by the Orthodox Church, with over 100 monks. The monastery remains a place of devoted pilgrimage, and believers from all over the country continue to pay homage to 'the saint and guardian of the Russian land'.

In 1930, the town's name of Sergiyev Posad (Settlement of Sergius) was changed to Zagorsk, after the revolutionary Vladimir Zagorsk. The monastery was closed down and converted into a State museum by Lenin in 1920 and during the Stalinist era it lost most of its wealth and power. The town officially reverted back to its original name of Sergiyev Posad in 1990, when the monastery was also returned to the Orthodox Church. Sergiyev Posad has a population of over 100,000, but receives nearly a million visitors a year.

The art of carving wooden toys has long been a tradition here; the first toys were made and distributed by St Sergius to the children of the town. Many painters, sculptors and folk artists trace their heritage back to the 17th century, when the first toy and craft workshops were set up in the town. The shop to the left as you pass through the main gates sells many locally made wooden toys.

SIGHTS

The parking square, near the main gates of the monastery complex, looks out over many ancient settlements that dot the landscape and the large kremlin citadel that houses priceless relics of old Russian architecture. Enter the main gates at the eastern entrance; paintings of the Holy Pilgrims depict the life of Sergius Radonezhsky, the 14th-century monk who established the Trinity Monastery of St Sergius. The small **Church of St John the Baptist**, built in 1693 by the wealthy and princely Stroganov family, stands over the main or Holy Uspensky Gates. It now functions as a confessional for Orthodox pilgrims.

The first large structure that catches the eye is the monastery's main **Assumption (Uspensky) Cathedral**. This blue and gold-starred, five-domed church with elegant sloping *zakomara* archways was consecrated in 1585 to commemorate Ivan the Terrible's defeat of the Mongols in the Asian territory of Astrakhan. Yaroslavl artists, whose names are inscribed on the west wall, painted the interior frescoes in 1684. The iconostasis contains the *Last Supper*, a painting by the 17th-century master icon-artist Simon Ushakov. The burial chambers of the Godunov family (Boris Godunov was czar from 1598 to 1605) are located in the northwestern corner. Its design resembles the Kremlin's Uspensky Cathedral. By the south wall is the Sergius Church (1686–92). The first oak coffin of St Sergius is preserved here. Under the cathedral is the Orthodox church crypt where patriarchs Alexis I (1970) and Pimen (1990) are buried. Many of these churches are open for worship and conduct services throughout the day.

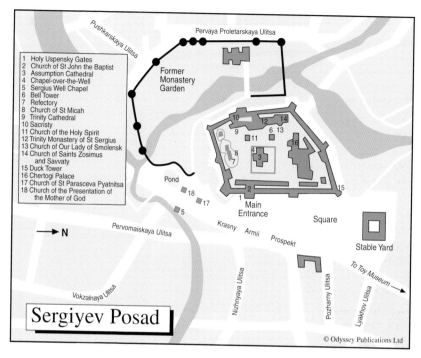

1 Holy Uspensky Gates
2 Church of St John the Baptist
3 Assumption Cathedral
4 Chapel-over-the-Well
5 Sergius Well Chapel
6 Bell Tower
7 Refectory
8 Church of St Micah
9 Trinity Cathedral
10 Sacristy
11 Church of the Holy Spirit
12 Trinity Monastery of St Sergius
13 Church of Our Lady of Smolensk
14 Church of Saints Zosimus
   and Savvaty
15 Duck Tower
16 Chertogi Palace
17 Church of St Parasceva Pyatnitsa
18 Church of the Presentation of
   the Mother of God

Sergiyev Posad

© Odyssey Publications Ltd

Respectfully dressed visitors are welcome. Photography without flash is usually permitted.

The brightly painted **Chapel-over-the-Well**, located outside by the cathedral's west wall, was built in Naryshkin, cube-shaped, octagonal-style at the end of the 17th century. Legend has it that when St Sergius touched a stick to the earth here, a well miraculously appeared, and a blind monk was the first to be healed by the holy water. Near the riverbank stands the **Sergius Well Chapel**. It was customary for small chapels to be built over sacred springs; today, pilgrims still bring bottles to fill with holy water.

Directly beyond the cathedral, standing in the complex center, is the five-tiered turquoise and white baroque **Bell Tower** (88 meters/288 feet high), designed by Prince Ukhtomsky (1740–70) and Rastrelli. Topped with a gilded dome in the form of a crown, it once held 40 bells; the largest weighed 65 tons. The chiming clock of the tower dates back to 1905.

Head directly left of the cathedral to the southern end of the complex. A stroll in this direction to the Refectory may lead past long-bearded monks dressed in the traditional black robes and *klobuki* tall hats. The **Refectory**, rebuilt in 1686, is painted in colorful checkerboard patterns of red, blue, green and yellow. It has a large open gallery with 19th-century paintings and wide staircases, and is decorated with carved columns and gables.

The small chapel at the end of the hall has a carved iconostasis by the altar and a beautiful red jasper inlaid floor. Another quaint church, standing next to the Refectory, is the **Church of St Micah**. In 1379, St Sergius' cell attendant, Micah, witnessed the appearance of the Blessed Mary promising prosperity for the monastery. In 1734, this church was built to hold the relics of St Micah.

Behind the Refectory, in the southwestern corner, is the oldest building in the monastery, the one-domed **Trinity Cathedral**, which the Abbot Nikon erected over the site of the original Church of St Sergius in 1422 (the year Sergius was canonized). Pilgrims still visit the remains of St Sergius of Radonezh, which lie in a silver sarcophagus donated by Ivan the Terrible. An embroidered portrait of St Sergius that covered his coffin is now preserved in the History and Art Museum, a short walk away. In 1425, Andrei Rublyov and Daniil Chorny painted the icons on the cathedral's iconostasis, which include a copy of Rublyov's *Holy Testament Trinity* (the original is now in Moscow's Tretyakov Gallery). The cathedral contains 42 works by Rublyov and is joined by the smaller **Church of St Nikon** (1548), Sergius' first successor. Behind the Cathedral is the **Sacristy**, now a small museum that exhibits early Russian applied art (14th–17th centuries), and includes collections of metalwork, jewelry, icon covers and exquisite embroideries or 'needle paintings'.

Across from the cathedral is the slender **Church of the Holy Spirit** with a tall bell tower under its dome. It was built in 1476 by Pskov stonemasons. Prominent Russian saints are buried here: St Maxim the Greek (1556), a translator of church books; St Innocenti of Moscow (1879), a missionary; and Church metropolitans Platon (1812) and Philaret (1867).

Behind this church in the northwest corner stands the **Trinity-Sergius Monastery**, one of the most important monuments of medieval Russia.

The Metropolitan's House, vestry and adjoining monastery buildings now house the **History and Art Museum**. The museum, which displays gifts in the order presented to the monastery, contains one of Russia's richest collections of early religious art. The exhibits include icons from the 14th to 19th centuries, and portraits, chalices, china, costumes, crowns, furniture, latticework and handicrafts from the 14th to 20th centuries. The museum also has the original 15th-century gates from the iconostasis of the cathedral. In front of the museum is the **Church of Our Lady of Smolensk** (1745–53) with a blue baroque-style rotunda. In 1730, a pious psalm

One of the most outstanding collections of Russian church architecture is to be found in the town of Sergiyev Posad. A monk walks toward the bell tower; beyond stands the blue 18th-century Church of Our Lady of Smolensk. On the left is the Church of Saints Zosimus and Savvaty and in the background stands the Pilgrim Tower, part of the monastery walls.

reader who suffered from paralysis was healed after praying to the Icon of the Mother of Smolenskaya. The building of the church honored this miracle.

The monastery also served as the town's hospital and school. Next to the museum is the red-brick and yellow-and-white sandstone hospital building with the adjoining all-white tent-roofed **Church of Saints Zosimus and Savvaty** (1635).

In the northeastern corner, behind the Duck Tower, is the colorfully painted and tiled **Chertogi Palace**, built at the end of the 17th century for Czar Alexei, who often came to Sergiyev Posad with an entourage of over 500 people. One of the ceilings in the palace is covered with paintings that honor his son's (Peter the Great) victories in battle. It now houses the Moscow Theological Academy and Seminary. The seminary, founded in 1742, and the academy, founded in 1812, now have over 1,000 students. In 1744, the monastery was awarded the title of *lavra*, the country's highest accolade given to a teaching monastery.

Exiting through the main gate, turn right and walk toward the **Kelarskiye Ponds**, situated beyond the southeastern Pyatnitskaya Tower. There you may find artists sketching and people strolling among the old garden walls. Two churches built in 1547 stand outside the walls—the **Church of St Paraskeva Pyatnitsa** and the **Church of the Presentation of the Mother of God**, nearest the pond. The Zolotoye Koltso (Golden Ring) Restaurant is only a few minutes' walk away.

The craft of wood carving remains alive in Sergiyev Posad. The famous *matryoshka*, the nest of carved dolls, has its origins here. First appearing in Russia in the 1890s, the *matryona* doll was later called by its diminutive form, *matryoshka*, representing peasant girls. The dolls were carved from wood and painted in traditional Russian dress, with *sarafan* jumpers, embroidered blouses and *kokoshniki* headdresses. Up to 24 smaller dolls could be nested within the largest, including Russian lads or fairy-tale figures. The doll first attained popularity at the 1900 World Exposition in Paris. Today there are even Yeltsin (containing past leaders from Gorbachev down to Nicholas II) and Clinton *matryoshki*. The history of toys and folk art can be viewed at the **Toy Museum** at 115 Krasny Armii Prospekt. The Art Workshop Collective continues to produce wooden folk art. A special souvenir section contains carved wooden dolls, boxes and jewelry. Open 10am–5pm; closed Mondays.

Aleksandrov   Александров

RESIDENCE OF IVAN THE TERRIBLE ON THE GRAY RIVER

From Moscow, you can travel here directly (120 kilometers/74 miles north) and inexpensively by *elektrichka* train from Moscow's Yaroslavsky Railway Station

(Komsomolskaya Metro station) in about two and a half hours. You can also travel by train from Sergiyev Posad in less than an hour. By car, take the M8 past Sergiyev Posad and then turn east (at Dvoriki) on the P75. (It is possible to cover both towns in one day.) The old town is about a ten-minute ride from Aleksandrov Railway Station. (Inside the station, departure times are posted for both Moscow and Sergiyev Posad.) When exiting the station, walk directly across the street to the bus stop. Take bus number 7 (facing the station, travel right) five stops to 'Museum'. The bus will pass the main square with a statue of Lenin, cross the Gray River and climb up a hill. You will see the old kremlin on your left. If you have time, it is a pleasant half-hour walk through town back to the train station. A number of cafés dot the path, along with markets selling bread, fruit and drinks.

The museum town is currently closed on Mondays and Tuesdays. A small gift shop is located inside the entrance gates on the left. (Patriarchi Dom in Moscow, tel. 926-5680, offers guided tours to Aleksandrov and other Golden Ring areas.)

The **Aleksandrovskaya Sloboda**, packed full of grim history, was once the residence of Ivan the Terrible for 17 years (1564–1581) and headquarters to his police army of ruthless *oprichniki*. (After the suspicious deaths of his wife and first son, Ivan abandoned Moscow for Aleksandrov.) It is from here that Ivan launched his reign of terror over Russia and kept its citizens in the grip of fear. Ivan married six more times in Aleksandrov. (Of his wives, six died mysteriously and one was sent off to a nunnery.) The most unfortunate, Martha Sobakina, whose story is depicted in Rimsky-Korsakov's *The Bride of the Tsar*, lasted a mere two weeks.

The oldest buildings are the (nonfunctioning) convent and white-rectangular one-domed **Trinity Cathedral** that women helped build in the early 15th century. The interior walls are decorated with the Icon of the Virgin Mary, said to be her real portrait from first-century Rome. After Ivan's army sacked Novgorod in 1570 (suspicious of the town's betrayal during a war with Poland, his troops slaughtered 35,000 of its citizens), he brought the golden oak doors from the Hagia Sophia Cathedral to adorn the Trinity's entrance. A covered gallery surrounds the cathedral which contains several coffins of white limestone.

Each morning Ivan climbed the nearby tent-shaped bell tower with it three-tiered layers of arched *kokoshniki*; he enjoyed ringing the bells and giving morning sermons. Adjacent to the bell tower are residential quarters which later housed Marfa, the stepsister of Peter the Great (who forced her to become a nun); she was exiled here between 1698 and 1707. (Two daughters of Czar Alexei, Peters' father, are buried in the Church of the Purification.) The future Empress Elizabeth was also banished to Aleksandrov for nine years.

Opposite the bell tower stands Ivan IV's personal church, the red-brick and green tent-roof **Church of the Intercession**. It was in the adjoining palace (later

In 1885, realist artist Ilya Repin painted Ivan the Terrible and His Son—16 November 1581. *On this date Ivan the Terrible killed his son in a fit of jealous rage. Repin was strongly affected by the execution of the People's Will revolutionary group in 1881. The painting now hangs in Moscow's Tretyakov Gallery.*

destroyed by invading Poles) that Ivan the Terrible committed his last and most atrocious crime—the murder of his own son. The son became enraged one night when finding Ivan in his bedroom with his wife whose dress was in 'slight disarray'. The ensuing fight between father and son ended in Ivan the Terrible beating his son to death with a cane. The czar was so horrified by what he had done that he left Aleksandrov and returned to govern from Moscow, where he died a few years later. (When in Moscow's Tretyakov Gallery, note the famous painting by Ilya Repin, *Ivan the Terrible and His Son—16 November 1581*, the date of the murder.)

Pereslavl-Zalessky Переславль-Залесский

IMPORTANT OUTPOST OF MOSCOVY

The tranquil town of Pereslavl-Zalessky is situated on a hilltop by the southeastern shores of Lake Pleshcheyevo, about 56 kilometers (35 miles) northeast of Sergiyev Posad. Approaching Pereslavl from the road, pleasantly scented by the surrounding groves of pine and birch, you have an enchanting view of the shimmering azure waters of the lake, three old monasteries on the side of the road, and golden crosses on top of painted onion domes that loom up from sprawling green fields dusted with blue and yellow wildflowers. Young boys wave at passersby as they fish in the lake with long reed poles. The River Trubezh meanders through the old earthen kremlin that winds around the center of town. These ramparts date back over eight centuries. One of Russia's most ancient towns, Pereslavl-Zalessky is a charming place, scattered with well-preserved churches and monasteries that once numbered over 50. Take a pleasant walk along the dirt roads and imagine that Peter the Great may have traversed the same footpaths before you.

Tour buses from Moscow stop at Pereslavl-Zalessky, as well as local buses from Sergiyev Posad. There are no trains. The easiest way is to visit by car; it is about a two-and-a-half-hour drive north on the M8 from Moscow. To dine, try the Skazka (Fairy-tale) Restaurant set in a lovely old wooden building near the town's center.

HISTORY

Pereslavl-Zalessky's long and fascinating history can be traced back to the year 1152, when Prince Yuri Dolgoruky (who founded Moscow five years earlier) fortified the small village of Kleschchin on the banks of the Trubezh and renamed it Pereslavl after an old Kievan town. Situated in an area on the *zalasye* (beyond the dense woods of Moscow), it became known as Pereslavl-Zalessky. The area was an important outpost of Moscow; Prince Alexander Nevsky set out from Pereslavl to win his decisive battle against the Swedes in 1240. Since the town also lay on important White Sea trade routes, it quickly prospered. By 1302 Pereslavl had grown large enough to be annexed to the principality of Moscovy.

SIGHTS

Ivan the Terrible later consolidated Pereslavl, along with the nearby village of Aleksandrov, into a strategic military outpost and headquarters for his *oprichniki* bodyguards. In 1688, the young Czar Peter I came here from Moscow to build his first *poteshny* (amusement) boats on Lake Pleshcheyevo. It was in a small shed near the lake that Peter discovered a wrecked English boat, which he learned to sail against the wind. In 1692, Peter paraded these boats (forerunners of the Russian fleet) before members of the Moscow court. One of them, the *Fortuna*, can be found in the **Botik Museum**, which lies about three kilometers (two miles) from Pereslavl, by the south bank of the lake near the village of Veskovo. Other relics from the Russian flotilla are also displayed here. Two large anchors mark the entrance and a monument to Peter the Great by Campioni stands nearby. Open from 10am–4pm; closed Tuesdays.

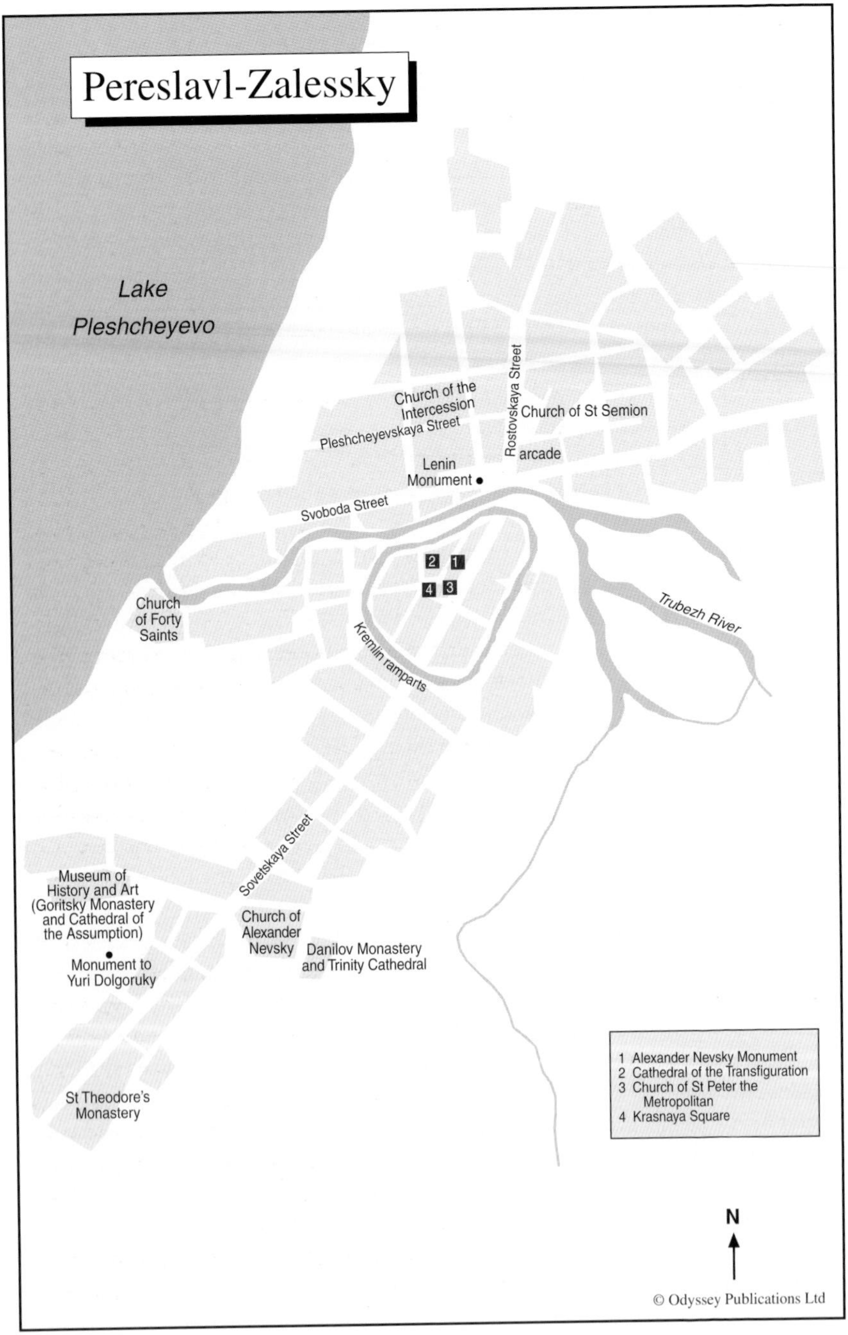

Pereslavl-Zalessky

Lake
Pleshcheyevo

Church of the
Intercession
Pleshcheyevskaya Street

Rostovskaya Street

Church of St Semion

arcade

Lenin
Monument ●

Svoboda Street

2 1

4 3

Trubezh River

Church
of Forty
Saints

Kremlin ramparts

Sovetskaya Street

Museum of
History and Art
(Goritsky Monastery
and Cathedral of
the Assumption)

Church of
Alexander
Nevsky

Danilov Monastery
and Trinity Cathedral

● Monument to
Yuri Dolgoruky

St Theodore's
Monastery

1 Alexander Nevsky Monument
2 Cathedral of the Transfiguration
3 Church of St Peter the
   Metropolitan
4 Krasnaya Square

N
↑

© Odyssey Publications Ltd

Make your way to the central Krasnaya Ploshchad (Red Square). The small grassy hills around you are the remains of the town's 12th-century earthen protective walls. In front of the **Statue of Alexander Nevsky** (who was born in Pereslavl) is the white stone **Cathedral of the Transfiguration**, the oldest architectural monument in northeastern Russia. Yuri Dolgoruky himself laid the foundations of this church, which was completed by his son, Andrei Bogoliubsky (Lover of God), in 1157. This refined structure with its one massive fringed dome became the burial place for the local princes. Each side of the cathedral is decorated with simple friezes. The *zakomara*, the semicircular rounded shape of the upper walls, distinguish the Russian style from the original simpler cube-shaped Byzantine design. Frescoes and icons from inside the cathedral, like the 14th-century *Transfiguration* by Theophanes the Greek and Yuri Dolgoruky's silver chalice, are now in Moscow's Tretyakov Gallery and Kremlin Armory. The other frescoes were executed during the cathedral's restoration in 1894. Across from the cathedral is the **Church of St Peter the Metropolitan**. Built in 1585 (with a 19th-century bell tower), the octagonal frame is topped with a long white tent-shaped roof. This design in stone and brick was copied from the traditional Russian log-cabin churches of the north.

In the distance, over the river, is the **Church of St Semion** (1771). Between this church and the Lenin Monument on Svoboda Ulitsa are the early 19th-century shopping arcades, Gostiny Dvor. Religious services are held at the **Church of the Intercession** on Pleshcheyevskaya Ulitsa.

Take a leisurely stroll towards the river and follow it down to the lake. Scattered along the paths are brightly painted wooden dachas with carved windows covered by lace curtains. Children can be found playing outside with their kittens or a *babushka* hauling water from the well. *Dedushka* may be picking apples and wild strawberries or carving a small toy for his grandchildren out of wood. Stop for a chat; it is amazing how far a few common words can go—an invitation for tea may soon follow. At the point where the Trubezh flows into the lake stands the **Church of the Forty Saints** (1781) on Ribnaya (Fish) Sloboda, the old fish quarter. With a little bargaining or a smile, get a rowing boat to go out on the lake or go out with the fishermen. On a warm day, it is a perfect place for a picnic; you may even want to take a dip.

On a little side trip out of the town are a number of monasteries and chapels that you may have glimpsed if you arrived from Sergiyev Posad. The four monasteries lining the road into Pereslavl also acted as protective strongholds, guarding the town from invasions. The one farthest away is the **Convent of St Theodore**, six and a half kilometers (four miles) south on Sovietskaya Ulitsa. Ivan the Terrible built this convent and the **Chapel of St Theodore** to honor his wife Anastasia, who gave birth to their first son, Fedor (Theodore), in 1557. Ivan often stopped at the shrine to pray when he visited his bodyguard army residing in Pereslavl-Zalessky.

About one and a half kilometers (a mile) closer to the town is the memorial **Church of Alexander Nevsky** (1778). A few minutes' walk from this church, set in a woody rustic setting, is the **Danilov Monastery**. A few buildings remain of this 16th-century structure. The **Trinity Cathedral** was commissioned by Grand Prince Vasily III in 1532. The single-domed cathedral, with 17th-century frescoes by renowned Kostroma artists Nikitin and Savin, was built by Rostov architect Grigory Borisov in honor of Vasily's son, Ivan the Terrible. The Abbot Daniel, who founded the monastery in 1508, was in charge of the cathedral's construction and present at Ivan's christening. The smaller **Church of All Saints** was built in 1687 by Prince Bariatinsky, who later became a monk (Ephriam) at the monastery and was buried near the south wall. Other surviving structures are the two-story Refectory (1695) and the large tent-roofed bell tower (1689), whose bell is now in the Moscow Kremlin's Ivan the Great Bell Tower.

On the other side of the road, behind the Monument to Yuri Dolgoruky, is the Goritsky Monastery, surrounded by a large red-brick kremlin. On the hilltop, a cluster of sparkling onion domes rise up from inside the fortified walls. The monastery is now the **Museum of History and Art** (open from 10am–4pm; closed Tuesdays). The monastery, founded during the reign of Ivan I in the 14th century (rebuilt in the 18th), is a fine example of medieval architecture with its octagonal towers, large cube-shaped walls and ornamental stone entrance gates. The tiny white gate-church next to the gatekeeper's lodge-was once known as the 'casket studded with precious stones', for it was richly decorated with gilded carvings and color-ful tiles. The large seven-domed Cathedral of the Assumption was built in 1757. The exquisite golden-framed and figured iconostasis, designed by Karl Blank, was carved and painted by the same team of artists who decorated the churches in the Moscow Kremlin.

The monastery, with 47 rooms filled with local treasures, is now one of the largest regional museums in Russia. The rooms include a unique collection of ancient Russian art, sculp-tures and rare books. The museum also exhibits the plaster face mask of Peter the Great by Rastrelli (1719) and Falconet's original model of the Bronze Horseman.

In 1147 the Prince of the Rostov-Suzdal principality, Yuri Dolgoruky, erected a wooden fortress overlooking the Moskva River, where the Kremlin stands today, to serve as a defensive outpost. This settlement later became Moscow, the capital of Russia. Five years later Prince Yuri also

The elaborately carved wooden gates from the Church of the Presentation won the Gold Medal at the 1867 Paris World Exhibition. May 2nd is a town holiday, Museum Day, at the Goritsky Monastery.

Heading north toward Rostov and Yaroslavl, you will find the last monument structure of Pereslavl-Zalessky, the 12th-century **Monastery of St Nicetas**, encased in a long white-bricked kremlin. In 1561, Ivan the Terrible added stone buildings and the five-domed cathedral. He intended to convert the monastery into the headquarters of his *oprichniki*, but later transferred their residence to the village of Aleksandrov.

Rostov Veliky   Ростов

THE WEALTHY ECCLESIASTICAL CENTER OF EARLY CHRISTIANITY

Approaching Rostov on the road from Moscow (54 kilometers/34 miles north of Pereslavl-Zalessky), the visitor is greeted with a breathtaking view of silvery aspen domes, white-stone churches and high kremlin towers. Rostov is one of Russia's ancient towns and has stood along the picturesque banks of Lake Nero for more than 11 centuries. It was once called 'a reflection of heaven on earth'. Named after Prince Rosta, a powerful governing lord, the town was mentioned in chronicles as far back as AD 862. Rostov's size and splendor grew to equal the two great towns of Novgorod and Kiev. By the 12th century Rostov was named Veliky (the Great) and became the capital of the Russian north. Rostov later came under the jurisdiction of Moscow and lost its importance as a cultural center by the end of the 18th century.

Today Rostov is the district center of the Yaroslavl region, and considered a historical preserve, heralding the glory of old Russian art and architecture. The town, with a population of about 50,000, has been restored to much of its original grandeur after a tornado destroyed many of the buildings in 1953. The oldest section of the town, set by the lake, is still surrounded by low earthen walls built around 1630. Rostov is about an hour's drive on the M8, north of Pereslavl-Zalessky. Check at Moscow's Yaroslavsky Railway Station; some trains bound for Yaroslavl make stops at Rostov. The main hotel in town is the Krasnaya Palata.

HISTORY

Rostov Veliky was one of the wealthiest towns in all Russia and the most important trade center between Kiev and the White Sea. Rostov became not only the capital of its own principality, but also the northern ecclesiastical center of early Christianity and the seat of the metropolitan, head of the Orthodox Church. In the

fortified the area along the banks of the Trubezh River and named the new town Pereslavl after an old Kievan town. As Prince of the Rostov-Suzdal principality, Yuri received the honorary name of Dolgoruky (Long Arms) for his wide-sweeping territorial conquests.

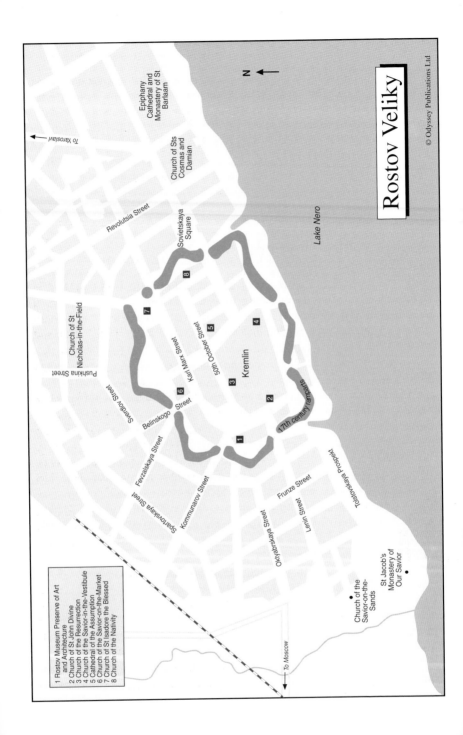

Rostov Veliky

© Odyssey Publications Ltd

To Yaroslavl

N

Epiphany Cathedral and Monastery of St Barlaam

Church of Sts Cosmas and Damian

Revolutsia Street

Sovietskaya Square

Church of St Nicholas-in-the-Field

Pushkina Street

Sverdlov Street

Karl Marx Street

50th October Street

Belinskogo Street

Ferzaliskaya Street

Spartovskaya Street

Kommunarov Street

Oktyabrskaya Street

Frunze Street

Lenin Street

Tolstovskaya prospekt

Kremlin

17th century ramparts

Lake Nero

Church of the Savior-on-the-Sands

St Jacob's Monastery of Our Savior

To Moscow

1 Rostov Museum Preserve of Art and Architecture
2 Church of St John Divine
3 Church of the Resurrection
4 Church of the Savior-in-the-Vestibule
5 Cathedral of the Assumption
6 Church of the Savior-on-the-Market
7 Church of St Isadore the Blessed
8 Church of the Nativity

17th century the metropolitans Jonah and Ion Sisoyevich built a large number of magnificent cathedrals and church residences, decorated with the Byzantine influence of icons and frescoes. The many religious shrines of a Russian town symbolized its wealth and status. Unlike other Russian towns, the Rostov kremlin was not originally built as a protective fortress, but served as a decorative feature that surrounded the palace of the metropolitan. Also the main cathedral stood outside the kremlin walls and not in the town's center.

SIGHTS

The kremlin itself, built in 1670, has 11 rounded towers and encompasses an area of about five acres. At the west gate is the **Church of St John-the-Divine** (1683), whose interior paintings depict the life of this saint. The five-domed **Church of the Resurrection** (1670) at the northern gates is designed with intricate white-stone patterns and the classic Russian *zakomara*, forming the 24 slopes of the roof. The towers on either side of both churches are made from aspen, and sparkle with a silken sheen. Stone iconostasis (instead of traditional wooden ones) inside both churches are decorated with beautiful frescoes painted by the artists Nikitin and Savin from the Golden Ring town of Kostroma. The Church of the Resurrection stands over the Holy Gates, so named because the metropolitan passed through them on the way from his residence inside the kremlin to the main cathedral.

The first stone of the massive **Cathedral of the Assumption** was laid by Prince Andrei Bogoliubsky (son of Yuri Dolgoruky who founded Moscow) in 1162. Bogoliubsky ruled the Russian north from Rostov. The 11th-century Vladimir Virgin hangs to the left of the Holy Doors. A few of the 12th-century frescoes have survived, along with the original lion mask handles that guard the western doors. Rostov frescoes were known for their soft color combinations of turquoise, blue, yellow and white. Five large aspen-hewn onion domes and beautiful white-stone friezes decorate the outside of the structure. The four-tiered bell tower (1687), standing atop the Assumption Cathedral, was the most famous in all Russia. Bells played an important role in the life of Russian towns. The 13 bells (the heaviest, the *Sysoi*, weighs 32 tons) can be heard 15 miles away.

Other churches inside the kremlin include the one-domed **Church of the Savior-on-the-Marketplace** (1690) that is located a few blocks north of the cathedral; it is now the town library. In the northeast corner stands the single-domed **Church of St Isodore the Blessed** (1566), built during the reign of Ivan the Terrible. Directly behind this church, on the other side of the earthen walls, stands the **Church of St Nicholas-in-the-Field** (1830) on Gogol Street. This is one of the few places in town open for religious services. At the eastern end is the **Church of the Nativity**. Gostiny Dvor (Traders' Row) marks the town's center. This long yellow arcade, with its many carved white archways, is still the shopping and market district of Rostov. The southeast part of the kremlin is made up of 17th-century civic buildings and the cube-shaped, single-domed **Church of the Savior-in-the-Vestibule** (1675), whose interior is made up of stone arcades that rest on thick gilded columns; it served as the house chapel of the metropolitan's residence. The walls and stone altar iconostasis are decorated with exquisite frescoes painted by local master artists, and the chandelier and candelabra are also from the 17th century.

The 17th-century Church of St John-the-Divine in Rostov Veliky with its aspen-shingled domes

The large main complex at the western end by the Cathedral of the Assumption is the Metropolitan's Palace (1680), containing the highly decorated Otdatochnaya Hall; here people gathered to pay their respects to the metropolitan. The White Chambers were built for the prince, and later, visiting czars. The Red Chambers accommodated other church and civil dignitaries. This complex of buildings now houses the **Rostov Museum Preserve of Art and Architecture**. The chambers are filled with collections of icons, wood carvings and enamels from the 14th to 20th centuries. Of particular interest is the 15th-century Icon of the Archangel Michael, the carved limestone cross (1458) of the prince's scribe, and the 15th century wooden figure of St George the Victorious. Rostov enamels were famous throughout Russia. Craftsmen painted miniature icons and other decorative enamels for church books and clergy robes. Today Rostov craftsmen still produce elegant enamel jewelry, ornaments and small paintings that are sold in stores throughout Russia.

Heading west out of the kremlin brings you to the small three-domed **Church of the Savior-on-the-Sands**. This is all that has survived of a monastery built by Princess Maria, whose husband was killed by invading Mongols in the 13th century. Princess Maria and other noblewomen of Rostov chronicled many of the events of medieval Russia. During the 17th century the library of Countess Irina Musina-Pushkina was one of the largest in Russia.

On the banks of Lake Nero are the 17th-century remains of **St Jacob's Monastery of Our Savior**; the original walls are still standing. The Immaculate Conception Cathedral (1686) and Church of St Demetrius (1800) are designed in the Russian classical style. Along the water is a park where boats can be rented. Fishing is also possible.

Along the shores of the lake at the eastern end of town is the **Church of Saints Cosmas and Damian** (1775). Next to this small church stands the larger **Epiphany Cathedral** (1553), part of the **Monastery of St Barlaam** (Abraham); this is one of the oldest surviving monasteries in Russia, dating back to the 11th century.

Outside Rostov, in the northwestern suburbs of the village of Bogoslov, is the lovely red **Church of St John upon Ishnya**, one of the last wooden churches left in the region. It stands on the River Ishnya and legend has it that it miraculously appeared from the lake and was washed up on the shores of its present location. It is open daily for visits and closed on Wednesdays.

VICINITY OF ROSTOV VELIKY

About 20 kilometers (12 miles) northwest of Rostov Veliky (on road P153), lies the **Borisoglebsky Fortress-Monastery**. Built in the early 14th century, it was later surrounded by a kremlin during the reign of Boris Godunov to protect it from Polish invasions. Surrounded on three sides by the River Ustye, the fourth was once protected by a moat. The fortifications were as strong as those of Moscow's Kremlin; the walls were 12 meters (40 feet) high and over three meters (ten feet) thick and had 14 observation towers. (The towers were placed the distance of an arrow's flight apart.) The walls also had stone arches that held cannon and archer posts, and the two gateways were fortified with heavy oak and iron doors.

The famous Rostov architect Grigory Borisov built the single-domed **Cathedral of Saints Boris and Gleb** in 1524, and had it decorated with colorful tiles, gables and frescoes. Boris and Gleb, sons of Prince

The ancient walls and towers of the kremlin in the Golden Ring town of Rostov Veliky, built in the 17th century

Vladimir (who introduced Christianity to Russia in AD 988), were the first saints of Russia. As political and religious turmoil swept Kiev, they passively accepted their deaths without fighting, believing in Christ's redemption.

Borisov also built the five-domed **Gate Church of St Sergius** (1545); each narrow window is topped by cylinder-shaped *kokoshniki*. Other buildings inside the monastery grounds include the **Church of the Annunciation** (1526), Refectory, Head Monk's Residence, Dormitory Quarters, Treasury and Wafer Bakery (which once contained the dungeon), all designed by Borisov. The **Church of the Purification** stands over the Water Gates on the north side. The three-tiered bell tower (1680) was the last structure built, with the **Church of St John** on the ground floor.

Nikola-Uleima   Никола-Улейма

About 60 kilometers (37 miles) west of Borisoglebsky, along the P153, lies the quaint **Monastery of St Nicholas-on-the-Uleima**. Founded in 1400 as a lookout post, it was one of the bloodiest sites of the attempted Polish invasions of Moscovy. The monks and village inhabitants fought to their deaths trying to resist the enemy; during the last battle the monastery burnt to the ground. Later, in 1675, the five-domed **Cathedral of St Nicholas** was reconstructed on the old foundation, and the helmet-domed **Church of the Presentation-in-the-Temple** restored. A refectory and bell tower were later added next to its *kokoshniki*-gabled walls. The monastery is surrounded by white birch and dark-green lime trees and its towers are covered with ornamental shapes and colorful pilaster panels.

Uglich on the Volga   Углич

Only 18 kilometers (11 miles) west of Nikola-Uleima along the P153 road lies the town of Uglich. (Trains also stop here on their way to Rybinsk; they depart from Moscow's Savelovsky Railway Station, and it is a half-day's journey.)

In the 16th century the seventh wife of Ivan the Terrible, Maria Nagaya, was banished here to live in a palace within the kremlin walls. Later one of the False Dmitris, who tried to claim the Russian throne during the Time of Troubles, was found dead in the palace garden on May 15, 1591; many believed he was killed by assassins sent by Boris Godunov. Alexander Pushkin wrote of the event in his epic poem *Boris Godunov*.

The **Church of St Demetrius-on-the-Blood** (1630) was built over the spot where Dmitri was murdered. It was replaced in 1692 by a more elaborate red-and-white stone and five-domed church which now functions as a museum. All that remains of the czarina's court is the two-story stone **Palace of Czarevich Dmitri**, built in the 15th century by Prince Andrei Bolshoi. Later, after a feud with his brother Grand Prince Ivan III, Andrei died in prison. The palace walls are decorated with bands of brick terracotta, and the tent roofs with sheets of weathered copper. Outside the kremlin stands the five-domed **Church of St John the Baptist** (1689–1700) with an adjoining octagonal bell tower, made famous by the painting by Russian artist Nikolai Roerich.

Across the street stands the **Monastery of the Resurrection**, ordered built in 1674 by Metropolitan Jonah of Rostov. The enclave is made up of a cathedral, bell tower, refectory and the **Church of Our Lady of Smolensk**. The neighboring **Monastery of St Alexis** is the oldest in Uglich and was founded in 1371 by Alexis, Metropolitan of All Russia. It was burnt to the ground during Polish and Lithuanian invasions, and rebuilt in the 1620s. Next to the two-story Refectory stands the slender triple-spired **Church of the Virgin Dormition** (1628). This church, nicknamed the Divnaya (Wondrous), has long remained dear to the people of Uglich. A few surviving secular structures are also of interest: the two-story wooden **Voronin House**, once owned by the Mekhov family, has a tile stove that is still located on the ground floor. The two-story 18th-century stone houses of the Kalashnikov family (a member of the family invented the famous rifle of the same name) and Ovsiannikov merchants are located nearby.

Yaroslavl Ярославль

JEWEL ON THE VOLGA
The English writer and adventurer Robert Byron wrote of his first visit to Yaroslavl in the early 1930s:

> While Veliki Novgorod retains something of the character of early Russia before the Tartar invasion, the monuments of Yaroslavl commemorate the expansion of commerce that marked the 17th century... The English built a shipyard here; Dutch, Germans, French and Spaniards followed them. Great prosperity came to the town, and found expression in a series of churches whose spacious proportions and richness of architectural decoration had no rival in the Russia of their time.

Today Yaroslavl is still an important commercial center and regional capital with a population of almost a million. Lying 280 kilometers (174 miles) northeast of Moscow on the M8 Highway (and by train from Moscow's Yaroslavl Railway

Station), it occupies the land on both sides of the Volga at its confluence with the River Kotorosl. Yaroslavl, the oldest city on the Volga, will celebrate its millennium in 2010. A monument commemorating its 975th anniversary was placed in the city center in 1985. The seven-ton Ice Age boulder was unearthed on the site of the *strelka* and the inscription reads: 'On this spot in 1010 Yaroslavl the Wise founded Yaroslavl.' Another statue, dedicated to Yaroslavl the Wise in 1983, has him holding a piece of the town's kremlin while gazing toward Moscow. The oldest part of town, located at the confluence of the two rivers, contains many grandiose churches and residences erected by the many prosperous merchants. Not far from the city is the estate-museum of the poet Nekrasov and the Cosmos Museum, dedicated to the first Soviet woman cosmonaut, Valentina Tereshkova.

HISTORY

The bear was long worshipped by pagan inhabitants as a sacred animal. Another legend provides the story of Prince Yaroslavl the Wise who wrestled a bear on the banks of the river and won. On the city's coat-of-arms a bear stands on his hind legs and holds a gold pole-ax, representing the endurance of the Yaroslavl spirit. In the ninth century a small outpost arose on the right bank of the Volga River and became known as Bear Corner, forming the northern border of the Rostov region. When Kievan Grand Prince Yaroslavl the Wise visited the settlement in 1010, its named was changed to honor him. It grew as large as Rostov; an early chronicle entry stated that in one great fire 17 churches burned to the ground. By the 13th century Yaroslavl had become the capital of its own principality along the Volga and remained politically independent for another 250 years.

Barge Haulers on the Volga *was completed by Ilya Repin in 1873, shortly after he graduated from St Petersburg's Art Academy. Besides portraying the brutal reality of hard physical labor, the artist also symbolizes the spiritual strength of man which cannot be broken. The painting now hangs in St Petersburg's Russian Museum.*

The hordes of the Mongol Khan Batu invaded in 1238 and destroyed a great part of the city. In 1463, when Prince Alexander handed over his ancestral lands to Ivan III, the Grand Prince of Moscow, Yaroslavl was finally annexed to the Moscovy principality. For a short time Yaroslavl regained its political importance when it was made the temporary capital during the Time of Troubles from 1598 to 1613.

The city reached the height of its prosperity in the 17th century when it became known for its handicrafts. Located along important trade routes, merchants journeyed from as far away as England and the Netherlands to purchase leather goods, silverware, wood carvings and fabrics. At one time, one-sixth of Russia's most prosperous merchant families lived in Yaroslavl, which was the second most populated city in the country. These families, in turn, put their wealth back into the city. By the middle of the 17th century, more than 30 new churches had been built. During this time the city became an architectural chronicle etched in stone on a scale unmatched anywhere else in Russia. Yaroslavl was also Moscow's Volga port until the Moscow–Volga canal was built in 1937.

The *burlaki* (barge haulers) were a common sight, as portrayed in Repin's famous *Barge Haulers on the Volga*. Merchants would travel along the Volga and Kotorosl rivers to Rostov, and then along a system of rivers and dry land (*volokoi*), on to Vladimir. In 1795, Count Musin-Pushkin discovered in the Savior Monastery the famous 12th-century chronicle *The Lay of Igor's Host*. This text was based on the fighting campaigns of Prince Igor of Novgorod who, in the words of the chronicle, 'did not let loose ten falcons on a flock of swans, but laid down his own wizard fingers on living strings, which themselves throbbed out praises....' Later Borodin composed the opera *Prince Igor* based on this chronicle.

Today there are over 300 historical sites listed in the city, many in need of restoration. But the cash-strapped Orthodox Church and city council have teamed up with international organizations to help revitalize the area. Joint ventures have been established, and Kassel in Germany and Burlington in Vermont were even named sister cities. German architects from Kassel are also helping to build a new hotel complex in the city center, and a local foundation is financing the re-creation of a whole pedestrian street to look like old Rus, with everything from coach inns and trading stalls to craft workshops and eating houses.

SIGHTS

A tour of Yaroslavl, known as the Florence of Russia, begins at the oldest part of town, the *strelka* (arrow or spit of land), lying along the right bank of the Volga, where the Kotorosl empties into it. The Bear Ravine, now Peace Boulevard, once separated the timber town from the *posad*, earth town.

By the Kotorosl, on Podbelskov Ploshchad (Square), is the oldest surviving structure in Yaroslavl, the **Transfiguration of Our Savior Monastery,** founded at the end of the 12th century. Northern Russia's first educational college was set up here, and the monastery library contained a huge collection of Russian and Greek literature. (Today the city remains one of the country's major learning centers.) It also grew into a large feudal power—by the end of the 16th century the monastery was one of the strongest fortresses in the northern states, with a permanent garrison of its own Streltsy, musketeer marksmen, to protect it. The white kremlin walls that dominate the town center were fortified to three meters (ten feet) thick in 1621. During an attack, the defenders would pour boiling water or hot tar on their enemies.

The Holy Gates of the monastery were built at the southern entrance in 1516. The archway frescoes include details from the Apocalypse. The 16th-century bell tower stands in front of the gates; climb up to the observation platform along its upper tier for a breathtaking panorama of the city.

The monastery's gold-domed **Cathedral of the Transfiguration of the Savior** (1506) was one of the wealthiest churches in Russia. The frescoes that cover the entire interior are the oldest wall paintings in Yaroslavl. The fresco of the *Last Judgment*, painted in 1564, is on the west wall; the east side contains scenes of the *Transfiguration and Adoration of the Virgin.* It served as the burial chamber for the Yaroslavl princes. The vestry exhibits icons and old vestments that were used during church rituals and services.

Behind the bell-clock tower are two buildings, the Refectory and the Chambers of the Father Superior and Monks, which now house branches of the **Yaroslavl Museums of Art, History and Architecture**. The museums are open daily 10am–5pm; closed Mondays and the first Wednesday of each month. The Refectory exhibits the history of the Yaroslavl region up to the present day. The monk cells contain collections of Old Russian art, including icons, folk art, manuscripts, costumes, armor and jewelry. Here also is the **Museum of The Lay of Igor's Host**. The story of this famous epic, along with ancient birch-bark documents and early printed books, is on display. Twelve years after Count Musin-Pushkin discovered the epic and other old rare manuscripts in the monastery library, the great fire of Moscow, during Napoleon's invasion, destroyed all the originals. **The Church of the Yaroslavl Miracle Workers** (1827), at the southern end of the cathedral, is the museum's cinema and lecture hall.

The red-brick and blue five-domed **Church of the Epiphany** (1684) stands on the square behind the monastery. The church is open from May 1 to October 1 from 10am–5pm; closed Tuesdays. It is festively decorated with *kokoshniki* and glazed colored tiles, a tradition of Yaroslavl church architecture. The interior is a rich tapestry of frescoes illustrating the life of Christ, painted by Yaroslavl artists in 1692; notice that the faces of the saints appear decidedly more human than in earlier

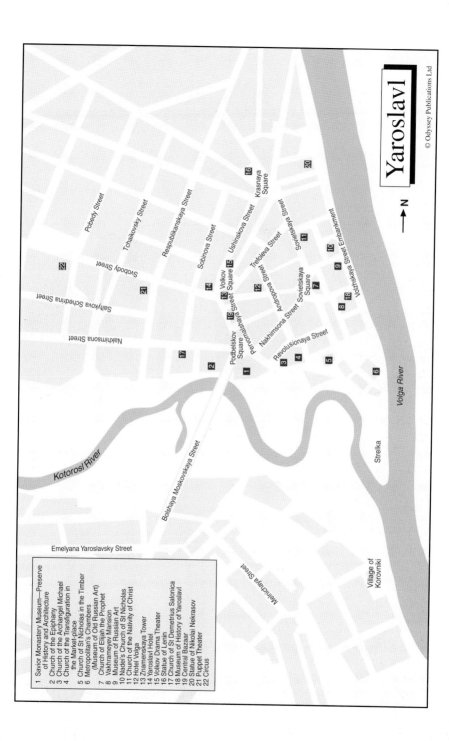

Yaroslavl

© Odyssey Publications Ltd

→ N

Kotorosl River

Volga River

Bolshaya Moskovskaya Street

Emelyana Yaroslavsky Street

Melnichaya Street

Village of Korovniki

Strelka

Pobedy Street

Tchaikovsky Street

Respublikanskaya Street

Svobody Street

Salykova Schedrina Street

Nakhimsona Street

Sobinova Street

Ushinskova Street

Krasnaya Square

Trefeleva Street

Andropova Street

Sovietskaya Street

Sovietskaya Square

Revolusionaya Street

Volzhskaya Street Embankment

Volkov Square

Podbelskov Square

Pervomalskaya Street

1 Savior Monastery Museum—Preserve of History and Architecture
2 Church of the Epiphany
3 Church of the Archangel Michael
4 Church of the Transfiguration in the Market-place
5 Church of St Nicholas in the Timber
6 Metropolitan's Chambers (Museum of Old Russian Art)
7 Church of Elijah the Prophet
8 Vakhrameyev Mansion
9 Museum of Russian Art
10 Nadei's Church of St Nicholas
11 Church of the Nativity of Christ
12 Hotel Volga
13 Znamenskaya Tower
14 Yaroslavl Hotel
15 Volkov Drama Theater
16 Statue of Lenin
17 Church of St Demetrius Salonica
18 Museum of History of Yaroslavl
19 Central Bazaar
20 Statue of Nikolai Nekrasov
21 Puppet Theater
22 Circus

decades. It also has an impressive gilded seven-tiered iconostasis. Across the street is the **Hotel Volga**.

Crossing the square and walking up Pervomaiskaya Ulitsa (away from the Volga) leads to the early 19th-century **Central Bazaar**. Today this area is still a busy shopping district. A short walk behind the walls of the arcade brings you to the Znamenskaya (Sign) Tower of the kremlin. Towers in Russia were usually named after the icon that was displayed over their entrance. This tower once held the icon known as Sign of the Mother of God.

Directly behind the tower on Ushinskov Ulitsa is the **Yaroslavl Hotel**. Here you can stop at the café and have a quick cup of tea or a meal in the Medvyed (Bear) Restaurant. Across from the hotel on Volkov Ploshchad is the **Volkov Drama Theater**, founded by Fyodor Volkov, who opened Russia's first professional theater to the public in 1729; he formed his own drama company in 1748.

At the end of Ushinskov Ulitsa is a statue of Lenin on Krasnaya Ploshchad (Red Square). Circle back toward the Volga on Sovietskaya Ulitsa until it intersects with Sovietskaya Ploshchad. Dominating the town's main square is the **Church of Elijah the Prophet**, now a Museum of Architecture (said to be built over the spot where the prince wrestled the bear). The church is open from May 1 to October 1, 10am–6pm; closed Wednesdays. Built in 1647, the white-stone church is decorated with ornamental tiles and surrounded by a gallery with chapels and a bell tower. The wooden iconostasis is carved in baroque fashion; the frescoes were painted in 1680 by the Kostroma artists Savin and Nikitin. These murals depict Christ's ascension, his life on earth, the lives of his Apostles, and the prophet Elijah. Prayer benches carved for Czar Alexei (father of Peter the Great) and Patriarch Nikon are also to be found inside.

Behind this church, at 23 Volzhskaya Avenue Embankment, is a **Branch Museum of Russian Art** from the 18th to 20th centuries, housed in the former governor's residence. Open 10am–5pm; closed Fridays. Across the street from the museum is **Nadei's Church of St Nicholas** (1620), a gift to the city from a wealthy merchant named Nadei Sveteshnikov. This church is open from May 1 to October 1, 9am–5pm; closed Thursdays. Ten churches in Yaroslavl were dedicated to St Nicholas, the patron saint of commerce.

The impressive **Vakhrameyev Mansion** is also next to the water in the other direction, off Revolution Street. The house was built in the 1780s in the baroque fashion. Members of this wealthy noble family were avid patrons of the arts in Yaroslavl. Behind the mansion (at 17 Volzhskaya Embankment) is a small Branch Museum of Local History. Open 10am–5.30pm; closed Mondays.

Walking directly along the Volga, on Volzhskaya Avenue Embankment, leads to the two-story building of the Metropolitan's Chambers (1690), located in the old

(previous pages) The massive bell cote inside the kremlin at Rostov Veliky. Its 13 large bells can be heard 15 miles away. In ancient times bells played a significant role in village life—sounding as a fire alarm, calling the town to battle, summoning the congregation to church or celebrating a joyous occasion.

timber town. It was originally built to accommodate the Metropolitan of Rostov Veliky when he visited. The chambers are now a **Museum of Old Russian Art**, displaying many icons, paintings and ceramic tiles. The museum is open from 10am–5pm; closed Fridays. Of interest is the icon *The Lay of the Bloody Battle with Khan Mamai*, a portrait of Count Musin-Pushkin and a bronze sculpture of Yaroslavl the Wise.

Making your way back toward the Savior Monastery, along the Kotorosl River, leads past three distinctive churches. The first is the simple white cube-shaped **Church of St Nicholas-in-the-Timber** (1695), built by the local shipbuilders who lived in this part of the timber town. Next is the **Church of the Transfiguration-in-the-Market-Place** (1672). It was built from funds collected by the townspeople in the old marketplace of the original earth town, where the local merchants and artisans lived. In the summer of 1693, 22 Yaroslavl artists helped paint the interior frescoes. The red-brick **Church of the Archangel Michael** (1658), directly across from the monastery, stands on the site of a former palace. It once marked the boundary between the kremlin and the marketplace and is filled with brightly colored frescoes painted by local Yaroslavl artists in 1730.

In the village of Tolchkovo (in the northern part of the city) is the picturesque 15-domed **Church of St John the Baptist** (1671), located at 69 Kotorosl Embankment on the right bank of the river. The five central green domes with a tulip-shaped dome in the middle, gold crosses and ornamental tiles, are prime examples of the architecture of the Golden Age of Yaroslavl. The whole principality of Yaroslavl donated funds to build the church. In 1694, 15 masters from around Russia painted the frescoes and icons that adorn every part of the interior. The baroque-style iconostasis was carved in 1701. The complex also includes a seven-tiered bell tower. The church is open 10am–6pm; closed Tuesdays. In 1992, the **Tolga Convent** and **Tolchkovo Church** were beautifully restored with funds donated by city and local firms. The structures are highly decorated with ornamental bricks, terracotta and colorfully glazed tiles. On Tugova Hill, to the left of the village, looms the single-domed **Church of St Paraskeva**, built over the mass grave of Yaroslavl warriors who were killed in battle against the invading Mongols. To its right stands the **Church of St Theodore**, the **Church of St Nicholas Pensky**, and beyond another **Church of St Nicholas-at-Melenki**.

Just south of the confluence of the Kotorosl with the Volga (at 2 Port Embankment), is a delightful architectural ensemble in the **Village of Korovniki**. The most impressive structure is the five-domed **Church of St John Chrysostom** (1649). Its tent-shaped bell tower is known as the Candle of Yaroslavl. The **Church of Our Lady of Vladimir** (1669) was used as the winter church. Other buildings of interest are the **Church of St Nicholas-the-Wet** and its 'twin' winter

Church of Our Lady of Tikhvin. The Korovnikova Sloboda was built in 1654, and its churches decorated with colored ceramic tiles and faceted tent-shaped roofs and bell towers.

If you have time, take a boat ride along the Volga; cruises last about an hour. For an evening's entertainment, book tickets at your hotel for the Yaroslavl Circus (located at 69 Svobody Street across from Truda Square). The Puppet Theater is at 25 Svobody Street.

Each summer, beginning August 1, the Yaroslavl Sunsets Music Festival is held, which usually opens with the overture to Borodin's *Prince Igor.*

VICINITY OF YAROSLAVL

On the Uglich Highway 29 kilometers (18 miles) southwest of Yaroslavl is the **Cosmos Museum**, dedicated to Valentina Tereshkova, the first female cosmonaut. Valentina's flight, in 1963, lasted 70 hours and orbited the earth 48 times. The museum, near the house where she was born in the village of Nikulskoye, displays her space capsule and the history of Soviet space travel. In 1993, a major auction of Soviet space memorabilia was held in New York at Sotheby's. In 1994, history was made when the first Russian cosmonaut flew in the American space shuttle, and in 1997 Americans joined a flight on the Mir Space Station. The museum is open 10am–5pm; closed Mondays. The service desk at your hotel may arrange excursions to these places.

About 16 kilometers (10 miles) from Yaroslavl, along the Moscow–Yaroslavl M8 Highway, is the **Nekrasov Estate Museum** in the village of Karabikha. The famous Russian writer Nikolai Nekrasov (1821–78) stayed on the estate in the summer months; it retains much of its former appearance. Among his works is the satire *Who is Happy in Russia?* His poems and other works are on display. The museum is open 10am–5pm; closed Mondays. Each summer there is a Nekrasov Poetry Festival at Karabikha.

Tutayev on the Volga   Тутаев

About 40 kilometers (25 miles) northwest of Yaroslavl, on the way to Rybinsk (along the P151 road) lies the village of Tutayev. *Elektrichka* trains also travel here from Yaroslavl. If you have time, and enjoy viewing historical architectural sites, it is a pleasant short trip along the Volga to this quaint town.

In the 13th century when Prince Roman (great-grandson of Grand Prince 'Big Nest' Vsevolod) was granted lands in this area, the village district became known as Romanov-Borisoglebsk. On opposite banks of the Volga, the prince constructed two fortified towns with ramparts and a moat. The prince's troops lived in Romanov, while the townspeople congregated in Borisoglebsk, on the right bank. It was not until 1921 that the town's name was changed to Tutayev, in honor of a Red Army hero.

In the 1670s the five-domed **Cathedral of the Resurrection** was built on the foundations of an older 12th-century church and embellished with a tent-shaped bell tower, elaborate porches and ornamental brickwork and tiling. Yaroslavl artists painted the 17th-century interior frescoes. *The Tower of Babel*, *The Last Judgment*, and *Tortures of Hell* attest to their love of biblical scenes.

Along the left bank, six other churches and their tent-shaped bell towers rise above the maple and birch sprinkled countryside. The oldest is the **Cathedral of the Exaltation of the Cross**, standing on the town's old ramparts. Further up the river is the **Spaso-Arkhangelskaya Church**, the **Church of the Virgin of Kazan** (on the hillside), and the **Church of the Intercession**, all built in the early 18th century.

Kostroma   Кострома

Kostroma, 76 kilometers (47 miles) northeast of Yaroslavl, can be reached by driving the A113 road, or taking a commuter train from Yaroslavl. Kostroma is the only city in Russia which has retained the original layout of its town center; it was founded by Yuri Dolgoruky in the 12th century. Reconstructed in the early 18th century, it is one of the country's finest examples of old Russian classic design; no two houses are alike.

Once a bustling trade center known as the Flax Capital of the North, Kostroma (pronounced with last syllable accented) supplied Russia and Europe with the finest sail cloth. The emblem of this picturesque town set along the Volga River depicts a small boat on silvery waters with sails billowing in the wind. The central mercantile square was situated on the banks of the Volga. The Krasniye (Beautiful) and Bolshiye (Large) stalls were connected by covered galleries where fabrics and other goods were sold. Today the modernized **Arcade** still houses the town's markets and stores. The **Borschchov Mansion** (home of a general who fought in the War of 1812), the largest of the older residential buildings, stands nearby.

The real gem of the town is the **Ipatyevsky Monastery**, founded in the 14th century by the Zernov Boyars, ancestors of the Godunovs. This large structure is enclosed by a white-brick kremlin and topped by green tent-shaped domes. Later the relatives of Boris Godunov built the monastery's golden-domed **Trinity Cathedral**. While Boris Godunov was czar (1598–1605), the Ipatyevsky Monastery became the wealthiest in the country, containing over 100 icons. The Godunov

family had its own mansion (the rose-colored building with the small windows) within the monastery, and most members were buried in the cathedral. The monastery was continually ravaged by internal strife, blackened by Polish invasions, and captured by the second False Dmitri in 1605, who claimed the throne of the Russian Empire. Later the Romanovs who, like the Godunovs, were powerful feudal lords in Kostroma, got the young Mikhail elected czar after the Time of Troubles. In 1613, Mikhail Romanov left the monastery to be crowned in the Moscow Kremlin. Today the famous Ipatyevsky Chronicles are displayed here; this valuable document, found in the monastery's archives, traces the fascinating history of ancient Rus.

The **Church of St John the Divine** (1687), which functioned as the winter church, stands nearby. From the monastery's five-tiered bell tower, there is a pleasing view of the countryside and the **Museum of Old Wooden Architecture**, open daily to the public. Intricately carved old wooden buildings gathered from nearby villages include the **Church of the Virgin** (1552), a typical peasant dwelling, a windmill and a bathhouse.

Other churches on the right bank of the Volga are the **Church of the Transfiguration** (1685), **Church of St Elijah-at-the-Gorodishche** (1683–85) and the beautiful hilltop **Church of the Prophet Elijah**.

The beautiful **Church of the Resurrection-on-the-Debre** is situated on the outskirts of town. In 1652, the merchant Kiril Isakov built this elaborate red-brick and green-domed church from money found in a shipment of English dyes. When informed of the discovery of gold pieces, the London company told Isakov to keep the money for 'charitable deeds'. Some of the bas-reliefs on the outside of the church illustrate the British lion and unicorn. The towering five-domed church has a gallery running along the sides; at the northwestern end is the **Chapel of Three Bishops**, with a magnificently carved iconostasis. The gates of the church are surrounded by ornamental *kokoshniki*, and the interior is ornately decorated with frescoes and icons from the 15th century.

The Kostroma Hotel, with restaurant, overlooks the Volga (request a room on the riverside with balcony). There are paths along the river and even swimming in summer. Try catching a circus performance in the evening.

VICINITY OF KOSTROMA

The areas in and around Kostroma were well known in Moscovy for their production of gold and silver ornaments, and the major jewelry workshops were situated in the village of **Krasnoye-on-the-Volga**. The lands of Krasnoye were once owned by the Godunov family. The oldest building in the village is the white-stone and octagon-shaped **Cathedral of the Epiphany** (1592). Its helmet drum, tented roof (the

In 1652, Kiril Isakov discovered a small barrel of gold pieces in a shipment of English dyes. When reported, the London company requested that the money be put to some charitable use. The merchant built one of the most beautiful structures in Kostroma—the Church of the Resurrection-on-the-Debre, overlooking the Volga River.

tent-shape style became popular in the early 16th century), long gallery, side chapels and decorative *kokoshniki* patterns are similar to Moscow's St Basil's Cathedral, built three decades earlier.

Situated further down the Volga is the small enchanting town of **Plios**. The son of Dmitry Donskoi, Vasily I, founded the village in 1410 as a stronghold and look-out point from the area's *plios*, the straight part of a river between its bends. The fortress protected the region from the Mongols, who had already conquered the Kingdoms of Kazan and Astrakhan further down the Volga. The lovely white five-domed **Church of the Resurrection**, built in the 18th century, stands on a bluff overlooking the water. One of Russia's finest landscape artists, Levitan, was inspired to paint *Golden Plios in the Evening*, one of Anton Chekhov's favorites.

Ivanovo   Иваново

Ivanovo, an industrial and regional center 288 kilometers (180 miles) northeast of Moscow (and about 80 kilometers/50 miles south of Kostroma), began as a small village on the right bank of the River Uvod. (Trains run here from both Yaroslavl and Kostroma, as well as from Moscow/Vladimir. To drive, take the A113 south from Kostroma, or the M7 from Moscow then the A113 north from Vladimir.) The River Talka also crosses the town; both rivers flow into the River Klyazma, a tribu-tary of the Moskva. The village of Voznesensk on the left bank was annexed by Ivanovo in 1871. In 1561, a chronicle mentioned that Ivan the Terrible presented the village of Ivanovo to a powerful princely family. When two centuries later an Ivanovo princess married a Sheremetyev, the town passed over to this powerful aris-tocratic family. In 1710, Peter the Great ordered weaving mills and printing facto-ries built here. Soon the town grew into a major textile and commercial center with little religious significance. Ivanovo calico was famous worldwide; by the mid-1800s, the town was known as the Russian Manchester. Today almost 20 percent of the country's cloth is produced in this city of more than half a million people. Ivanovo is nicknamed the City of Brides—since 80 percent of textile workers are women, many men come here to look for a wife.

Ivanovo participated actively in the revolutionary campaigns and was called the Third Proletarian Capital after Moscow and the former Leningrad. Major strikes were held in the city. In 1897, 14,000 workers held a strike against the appalling conditions in the factories. A 1905 strike, with over 80,000 participants, was head-ed by the famous Bolshevik leader Mikhail Frunze, who established the town's first Workers' Soviet, which provided assistance to the strikers and their families during the three-month protest.

Compared to other Golden Ring towns, Ivanovo is relatively new and modern, with only a few places of particular interest. On Lenin Prospekt, the **Ivanovo Museums of Art and History** portray the city's historical events and display collections of textiles, old printing blocks and other traditional folk arts. Off Kuznetsov Street is the **Museum-Study of Mikhail Frunze**. On Smirnov Street is the 17th-century **Shudrovskaya Chapel**; on nearby Sadovaya Street stands the large red-bricked **House Museum of the Ivanovo-Voznesensk City Council**. Other locations of interest in the city are the circus, puppet theater, a 17th-century wooden church and **Stepanov Park**, with an open-air theater, planetarium and boats for hire. The Zarya Restaurant is on Lenin Prospekt and the Tsentralnaya Hotel on Engels Street.

Palekh   Палех

This village lies 48 kilometers (30 miles) east of Ivanovo and is famous for its colorfully painted lacquer boxes. (Local buses run here from Ivanovo, or drive east along the P152/80.) After the Revolution when icon production was halted, it became popular to paint small miniatures on lacquer papier-mâché boxes, which combined the art of ancient Russian painting with the local folk crafts. Ivan Golivko (1886–1937), the Master of Palekh Folk Art, created many beautiful lacquer scenes drawn from traditional Russian fairy tales, folk epics and songs; he sometimes lined the box interiors with Russian poetry. The **Museum of Palekh Art** displays a magnificent collection of painted boxes and other lacquer art by the folk artists of Palekh. These include works by the master Golivko, who established a shop of ancient folk art in 1924. This included a wide assortment of objects: wooden toys, porcelain, glass and jewelry boxes. The most popular became the lacquered papier-mâché boxes. The **Timber House of Golivko** where he lived and worked, is also open to the public. The best eatery in town is the Palekh Restaurant.

Traditionally, the Palekh box was fashioned from birch wood or linden and varnished black on the outside with a red interior. The artists used special tempera paints and made fine brushes from squirrel tails. After the top of the box was dusted with a special powder, the outline of the painting was sketched on with white paint. After the design was colored in, a series of coats of translucent lacquer was applied, so that the box shone with an unusual brightness. The top was further decorated with gold, silver and mother-of-pearl. A wolf's tooth was used to fine-polish the decorative colors.

The 17th-century **Cathedral of the Exaltation of the Holy Cross**, now a museum, stands in the town center. A plaque on the outside of the west wall shows the

(following pages) Inside Kostroma's Museum of Old Wooden Architecture stands the weathered Church of the Virgin, built in 1552.

builder to be Master Yegor Dubov. Local craftsmen carved and painted the magnificent golden baroque-style iconostasis inside the church, bedecked with nearly 50 icons from floor to ceiling. In front stands a near life-size sculpture of Christ on the cross, with a large intricate chandelier hanging above. The Czar Gates were brought from a church in the town of Uglich. For centuries before the Revolution the highly respected Palekh artists were sent all over Russia to paint beautiful icons and frescoes in the Central Russian style. Today the artists of Palekh carry on the traditions of lacquer design and over 250 craftsmen are employed at the Palekh Art Studio. Palekh lacquerware and jewelry are widely sold throughout Russia and the world. The writer Maxim Gorky, who often asked Golivko to illustrate his texts, wrote: 'The masters of Palekh carry on the icon painting traditions through their boxes... and with these beautiful achievements, win the admiration of all who see them.'

Vladimir   Владимир

THE CENTER OF THE GOLDEN AGE OF RUS

Vladimir lies 190 kilometers (118 miles) northeast of Moscow along the M7 Highway. It is recommended to spend at least a few days in the Vladimir region. Trains depart daily from Moscow's Kursk or Yaroslavl stations and take nearly four hours to Vladimir, passing through the hundred miles of cultivated countryside dotted with farms that raise corn and livestock. The same rural scenes of farmers, dressed in embroidered peasant shirts with wide leather belts and *valenki* (black felt boots), plowing the fertile land, were painted by Russian artists such as Kramskoi, Vrubel and Repin over a century ago. Unfortunately, it is hard to plan a day trip to the area; the first train arrives in the afternoon, and no trains depart to Moscow until well after midnight. (Check current schedules.) By car, take the M7 Highway. Bus tours also run from Moscow. The best way to visit the Vladimir/Suzdal region is to stay overnight; it is easiest to make hotel reservations through a travel agency in Moscow. The best hotel in town is the Zolotoye Koltso (tel. 092-22-48807), which also has a good restaurant. After visiting Vladimir, spend the next day in the ancient town of Suzdal, only 16 miles (26 kilometers) to the north. (Local buses run from Vladimir.) Between these two cities is the historic village of Bogoliubovo and the Church-of-the-Intercession on the River Nerl.

HISTORY

Even though Vladimir is now a bustling city of 325,000 and the administrative head of the region, it is still one of the best preserved centers of 12th- and 13th-century Old Russian architecture. Eight centuries ago Vladimir was the most powerful town of ancient Rus. Located on the banks of the Klyazma River, a small tributary of the Volga, Vladimir was an important stop on the trade routes between Europe and Asia. Greeks from Constantinople, Vikings from the north, Bulgars from the Volga and Central Asian merchants all journeyed through the Vladimir-Suzdal principality.

Vsevolod, the son of Kievan Grand Prince Yaroslavl the Wise, first began to settle the area of Vladimir in northeastern Rus while Kiev was being attacked by numerous hostile tribes in the late 11th century. At this time many Russians began to migrate northward; this exodus is described in one of Russia's earliest epic chronicles, *The Lay of Igor's Host*. With the death of his father, Vsevolod became the most powerful prince in the land. Prince Vsevolod built a small fortress near the village of Suzdal on the road from Kiev. Later a trading settlement was established around the fort by Vsevolod's son, who also built the first stone church. The town was named after Vladimir Monomakh in 1108. After Monomakh's death in 1125, the Kievan states in the south began to lose their political and economic importance; under Monomakh's son Yuri Dolgoruky, the northern territories began to flourish. Vladimir grew so large and prosperous that it became the capital of northern Rus by the middle of the 12th century.

Dolgoruky's heir Andrei Bogoliubsky decided to rule Russia from a more centralized and peaceful area, and transferred the throne of the grand prince from Kiev to Vladimir in 1157, after a vision of the Blessed Virgin directed him to do so. Bogoliubsky (Lover of God) left Kiev under the protection of a holy icon, said to have been painted by St Luke from Constantinople, known as Our Lady of Vladimir. This revered icon became the sacred palladium of the Vladimir region; the prince even took it on his military campaigns. As the protectorate of the city, it became the symbol of divine intervention and power of the grand princes.

Andrei brought in master artists and craftsmen to recreate the splendors of Kiev in the new town of Vladimir. A crowned lion carrying a cross was the town's coat-of-arms. Under his brother Vsevolod III (who ruled from 1174 to 1212) the Vladimir-Suzdal principality, with Vladimir as its capital, reached the zenith of its political power.

When the Mongol Tartars invaded in 1238, Vladimir, like many other towns in Russia, suffered extensive damage. A Novgorod chronicle described the Mongol invasion: 'The Tartars struck the town with their wall-battering weapons; they released endless streams of arrows. Prince Vsevolod saw their fierce battle axes, took fright (because of his youth), and fled forth from the town with his group of men, carrying many gifts and hoping to save his life. Batu Khan [son of Genghis], like a wild beast, did not spare him, but ordered that he be slaughtered before him, and then he slew the rest of the town. When the bishop, with the princess and her children, fled into the church, the godless one commanded it to be set on fire. Thus, they surrendered their souls to God.'

For a brief time, Vladimir retained the seat of the Church Metropolitan, and the grand princes were still crowned in the town's Uspensky Cathedral. But eventually the princes of Moscovy began governing Russia through the Khans. When Vladimir was annexed to the principality of Moscovy, and Moscow became the capital of the country in the 16th century, its importance slowly declined; by 1668, the population numbered only 990. After the Revolution the city grew with industrialization and today it is a large producer of electrical machinery. The Vladimiret tractor, sold around the world, once won a Gold Medal at a Brussels Machinery Exhibition.

SIGHTS

To enter the old part of town along the river, pass through the **Golden Gates** (the only surviving gates of the city), built in 1158 by Prince Bogoliubsky, who modeled them after the Golden Gates of Kiev. The oak doors of the now white gates were once covered with gilded copper; the golden-domed structure on top of the gates was the Church of the Deposition of the Robe. These gates were used as a defense fortification for the western part of town and also served as a triumphal arch— Alexander Nevsky, Dmitri Donskoi in 1380 and troops on their way to fight Napoleon in the Battle of Borodino in 1812 all passed through the arch. The gates were damaged many times through the years, and were reconstructed in the 18th century. Today the Golden Gates house the local **Military Historical Museum**. Next to the Gates, in the red-brick building (formerly a church) and the fire observation tower, are the **Museums of Contemporary Artists and Ancient Town Life**. The latter has many interesting old illustrations and black and white photographs tracing the history of the region.

The oldest buildings of the city were constructed on the hills by the water, which served as a defense. As you walk through the gates, a cluster of golden-domed white churches come into view. In 1158, Andrei Bogoliubsky brought in master craftsmen from all over Russia and Europe to build the triple-domed Uspensky Sobor, the **Assumption Cathedral**. Built to rival Kiev's St Sophia, the cathedral was decorated with gold, silver and precious stones. It was the tallest building in all of Rus. Filled with frescoes and icons, the iconostasis was also the largest of its kind in Russia. A tenth of the grand prince's revenue was contributed to the upkeep of the cathedral. After much of it was destroyed by fire in 1185 (along with 33 other churches), Prince Vsevolod III had it rebuilt with five domes. Since the original walls were encased within a larger structure, the cathedral doubled in size, with an area for a congregation of 4,000 people. The Italian architect Fioravante used it as his model for the Moscow Kremlin's own Assumption Cathedral. After more fires blackened the walls, the famous iconists Andrei Rublyov and Daniil Chorny were sent to restore the interior in 1408 and painted over 300 square meters (3,200 square feet) of wall space; frescoes from the 12th and 13th centuries are still evident on the western and northern walls. Rublyov's and Chorny's frescoes, including scenes from the Last Judgment, decorate two vaults beneath the choir gallery and the altar pillars. The famed icon of the Virgin of Vladimir that once hung by the altar was transferred to Moscow's Assumption Cathedral in 1380; it is now in the Moscow Tretyakov Gallery.

This cathedral was one of the most revered churches in Russia; all the Vladimir and Moscow grand princes were crowned inside it, from the son of Yuri Dolgoruky to Ivan III, in the early 15th century. It was the main center of the Church Metropolitan in the 14th century. The Assumption Cathedral was also the burial place of the princes of Vladimir, including Andrei Bogoliubsky and Vsevolod III. The three-story belfry was built in 1810. The cathedral has been under continuous restoration during the last century. Mass is celebrated on Saturday evenings, Sundays and Orthodox feast days. Visitors are welcome in respectful attire. Flash photography is not permitted.

The Cathedral of St Demetrius in Vladimir, built by Vsevolod III in the 12th century.
More than 1,300 bas-reliefs decorate its outer walls.

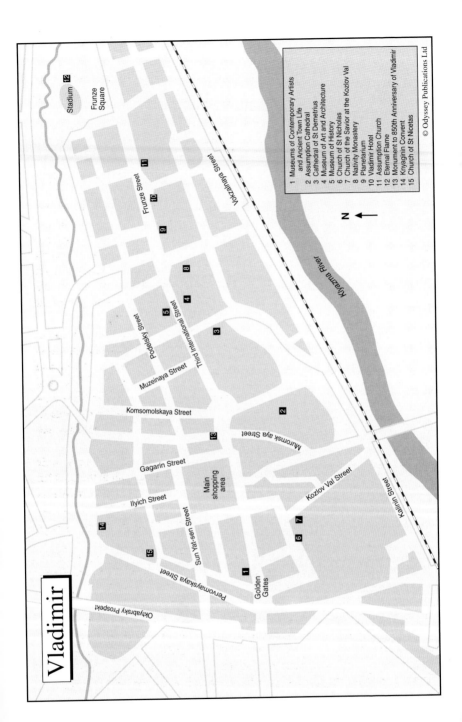

Vladimir

Oktyabrsky Prospekt

Pervomayskaya Street

Ilyich Street

Gagarin Street

Sun Yat-sen Street

Komsomolskaya Street

Main shopping area

Golden Gates

Muromskaya Street

Kozlov Val Street

Kalinin Street

Podolsky Street

Muzeinaya Street

Third International Street

Frunze Street

Vokzalnaya Street

Frunze Square

Stadium

Klyazma River

N

1 Museums of Contemporary Artists
   and Ancient Town Life
2 Assumption Cathedral
3 Cathedral of St Demetrius
4 Museum of Art and Architecture
5 Museum of History
6 Church of St Nicholas
7 Church of the Savior at the Kozlov Val
8 Nativity Monastery
9 Planetarium
10 Vladimir Hotel
11 Assumption Church
12 Eternal Flame
13 Monument to 850th Anniversary of Vladimir
14 Knyaginin Convent
15 Church of St Nicetas

© Odyssey Publications Ltd

A short walk away to the right of the cathedral (with your back to the river) leads to one of the most splendid examples of Old Russian architecture, the **Cathedral of St Demetrius** (1193–97). It was built by Vsevolod III as his court church; his palace once stood nearby. The cathedral, with its one large helmet drum, was named after 'Big Nest' Vsevolod's patron saint (St Demetrius of Thessaloniki) and newborn son Dmitri. (Vsevolod was nicknamed 'Big Nest' because of his large family of 12 children.) It is built from blocks of white lime-stone and decorated with intricate *kokoshniki* along the doorways and arches. Over 1,300 bas-reliefs cover the outer walls: decorative beasts, birds, griffins, saints, prophets, the labors of Hercules and many elaborate floral patterns all glorify the might of Vladimir. The friezes of King David and Alexander the Great symbolize Vsevolod's cunning military exploits. At the top of the left section of the northern façade is Prince Vsevolod seated on the throne with his young son; the other sons are bowing to their father. The interior frescoes date back to the 12th century. In 1834, Nicholas I ordered the cathedral restored; it is now part of the local museum complex.

Across from this cathedral at 64 Third International Street is the **Vladimir Museum of Art and Architecture**, with displays of old religious paintings, manuscripts and architectural designs. Directly across the street is the **Museum of History**. A rich collection of artifacts, archeological materials, old fabrics and weapons, princely possessions and the white-stone tomb of Alexander Nevsky are on display. Another branch of the museum with lacquered art, crystal and embroidery is located at the end of the street past the Golden Gates. The museums are open daily and closed on Thursdays.

Directly behind this last branch museum is the simple white **Church of St Nicholas** and the **Church of the Savior at the Kozlov Val**, both built in the late 17th century. You can climb the Kozlov Val Tower for a great view of the town. Across from them, nearer the water, is the **Church of St Nicholas-at-Galeya**, with its tent-shaped bell tower. The church was built by a wealthy citizen of Vladimir in the early 18th century.

At the opposite end of Third International Street toward Frunze Square is the **Nativity Monastery** (1191–96), one of Russia's most important religious complexes until the end of the 16th century; it was closed in 1744. Alexander Nevsky was buried here in 1263; his remains were transferred to St Petersburg by Peter the Great in 1724. The Nikolskaya Church next door is now the Planetarium.

Next to the Vladimir Hotel (down the street from the Planetarium on Frunze Street) is the brick and five-domed **Assumption Church** (1644), built from donations given by rich local merchants. At the end of Frunze Street is the Eternal Flame, commemorating the soldiers who lost their lives during World War II.

Down the street from the Golden Gates on Gagarin Street is the city's main shopping district, the Torgoviye Ryady. Across the street is the **Monument to the 850th Anniversary of Vladimir.**

Stroll down Gagarin Street and look out over the old section of Vladimir. In the distance are many old squat wooden houses with long sloping roofs and stone floors. Many of the town's inhabitants have lived in these homes for generations. The people enjoy a simple town life. During the day you may see residents hanging out laundry, perhaps painting the lattice work around their windows a pastel blue-green, chopping wood, or gathering fruits and mushrooms. The children enjoy having their pictures taken. Bring a few souvenirs from home to trade.

At the end of Gagarin Street is the **Knyaginin (Princess) Convent,** founded by the wife of Vsevolod III, Maria Shvarnovna, in 1200. The grand princesses of the court were buried in the convent's **Assumption Cathedral,** rebuilt in the 16th century. The cathedral's three-tiered walls are lined with fancy *zakomara* and topped with a single helmet drum. In 1648, Moscow artists painted the colorful interior frescoes. The north and south walls depict the life of the Virgin Mary, and the west wall shows scenes from the Last Judgment. Paintings of Vladimir princesses, portrayed as saints, are on the southwest side, and the pillars recount the lives of the grand princes. The cathedral is the only remaining building of the convent complex and now houses a restoration organization. Next to the convent stands the **Church of St Nicetas** (1762). This green and white, three-tiered baroque church was built by the merchant Semion Lazarev. The interior is divided into three separate churches on each floor. It was restored in 1970. In front of this church is a bust of the writer Gogol. Pervomaiskaya Street leads back to the Golden Gates.

At the end of the day, you may stop at the rustic log-hewn Traktir Restaurant for an enjoyable meal of the local cuisine.

VICINITY OF VLADIMIR

The quaint village of Bogoliubovo lies eight kilometers (five miles) from Vladimir. Group tours sometimes stop here; if not, go by local bus, taxi or car, a short hop along the M7. One legend says that when Prince Andrei was traveling from Kiev to Vladimir, carrying the sacred icon of Our Lady of Vladimir, his horses stopped on a large hill and would move no farther. At this junction, by the confluence of the Klyazma and Nerl rivers, Andrei decided to build a fortress and royal residence. He named the town Bogoliubovo (Loved by God) and took the name of Bogoliubsky; he was canonized by the Church in 1702. Supposedly, after the Virgin appeared to him in a dream, he built the **Nativity of the Virgin Church.** This cathedral was still standing in the 18th century, but when one father superior decided to renovate it in 1722 by adding more windows, the cathedral collapsed; it was partially rebuilt in

Children swim and fish in the Klyazma River in Vladimir. The old Refectory buildings and bell tower of the town stand over the residents' wooden dacha-style homes.

1751. Only a few of the 12th-century palace walls remain, of which chronicles relate: 'it was hard to look at all the gold.' On the staircase tower are pictures depicting the death of Andrei Bogoliubsky—assassinated by jealous nobles in this tower in 1174. The coffins of his assassins were said to have been buried in the surrounding marshes and their wailing cries heard at night. The buildings in Bogoliubovo are now museums, which are closed on Mondays. About one and a half kilometers (one mile) southeast of Bogoliubovo on the River Nerl is the graceful **Church of the Intercession-on-the-Nerl**, built during the Golden Age of Vladimir architecture. Standing alone in the green summer meadows or snowy winter landscape, it is reflected in the quiet waters of the river that is filled with delicate lilies. It has come down from legend that Andrei built this church in 1164 to celebrate his victory over the Volga Bulgars. The Virgin of the Intercession was thought to have protected the rulers of Vladimir. With the building of this church, Andrei proclaimed a new Church holiday, the Feast of the Intercession.

Yuryev-Polsky   Юрьев-Польский

About 65 kilometers (40 miles) northwest of Vladimir (situated halfway to Pereslavl-Zalessky along the P74 road) lies the old town of Yuryev-Polsky. Trains also stop here on the way from Ivanovo. Prince Yuri Dolgoruky founded Yuryev-Polsky in 1152, and named it after himself. Since two other Russian towns were already named Yuryev, Dolgoruky added Polsky, meaning 'Yury's town among the fields'. At the confluence of the Koloksha and Gza rivers, Dolgoruky had a fortress built, complete with moat and rampart walls that stood over six meters (20 feet) high; for a short period the town became the capital of Dolgoruky's principality. During the next several centuries Yuryev-Polsky was taken over by invading Lithuanians and Mongols, and never again regained its status and power. The original Holy Gates had four separate entrances, two for pedestrians and two for carriages. The **Monastery of the Archangel Michael** (1250) was reconstructed at the end of the 17th century. The **Cathedral of the Archangel Michael** and tent-shaped bell tower are decorated with green-glazed tiles. The town's greatest treasure is the limestone **Cathedral of St George** (1234), modeled after Vladimir's Cathedral of St Demetrius. The elegant helmet-shaped dome survived a partial collapse of the walls in the 15th century. Today carved scenes and floral designs are still visible on some of the greenish-yellow walls. Figures include St George, patron saint of Dolgoruky; lions with tails in shapes of trees, masks and emblems; and the fairy-tale bird, Sirin. Burial vaults and the tomb of Grand Prince Svyatoslav (13th century) are situated in the northwest corner.

THE RUSSIAN ICON

The ancient art of icon painting has been a part of Russian life for over 11 centuries and is still being passed on to future generations. The core of this art portrays spiritual and aesthetic ideals, as well as historical events and lifestyles of Old Russia. Soon after Prince Vladimir introduced Christianity in AD 988, Byzantium's art and religious customs were quickly absorbed into Russian culture. The word *icona*, in Russian, stems from the Greek *eikon*, meaning holy image; icons portrayed the likenesses of Christ, the Virgin, saints and martyrs.

Byzantine art dissipated greatly during the Mongol invasions in the mid-13th century, when artistic styles transcended their Byzantine heritage. During Russia's long period of isolation (two and a half centuries of Mongol occupation), several unique types of icon painting were established. The main schools were the Novgorod, Pskov, Moscow and Central Russian. Each retained some of the original elements of color and design from early Byzantium, while adding their own distinctive flair.

The purpose of the icon was to bring spiritual power to light. The icon's own light and color mirrored the sacred qualities of the celestial world. In addition, the icon's impersonation of the divine and earthly planes was based on a hierarchy of colors: the tops were white, purple and gold, which symbolized divine light, purity, salvation and love. Blue and green, the earthy colors, represented heaven, joy and hope; and red portrayed the Holy Spirit's flame, the passions of Christ, and the burning fire of faith and martyrdom. The treachery of Judas was symbolized in yellow. Black was derived from Russia's old folk beliefs: the gloom of the underworld and the emptiness of the nonbeliever; the icon educated the viewer how to overcome this chaos and darkness. Many monks fasted for several days before starting work on an icon, chanted prayers, and wholeheartedly believed in the moral and educational powers of their creations.

The Novgorod school mainly used a symmetrical design and painted in bold and simple outlines using red, white, and black—with a style similar to folklore traditions. The iconographers of Pskov, one of the last remaining regions to be annexed to Moscovy, developed a more dynamic style, using dramatic color schemes of gold, green, red and yellow. The Central Russian school was greatly affected by Moscow and Novgorod, but used blue as its dominant color combined with yellow and white. This style was centered in the Golden Ring towns of Rostov, Pereslavl-Zalessky, Palekh, Yaroslavl, Vladimir and Suzdal.

Icons were painted on panels of wood with tempera paints. Designs were initially sketched with chalk or charcoal and then filled in with colors. First glazes, then a varnish of linseed oil were applied to the completed work. But, after about 80 years, the linseed oil darkened the icon, at which time another artist usually painted over the original design. With some icons, this process was repeated many times. Today, restorers can remove paint layer by layer to recreate many of the original portraits. These efforts have been especially concentrated in churches in Moscow and the Golden Ring area.

Icons were at the center of Old Russian art and kept in churches, chapels and homes. Later the iconostasis, a number of small icons layered together on wooden or stone tiers, were painted as well. This allowed Christ, the Virgin and numerous saints to be brought together as one entity. Icons played an essential role in people's lives; they were given a place of honor in the homes and thought to possess healing powers. The 16th-century icon of the Kazan Virgin was believed to have saved Moscow residents from the plague. Icons were also placed along roads, at the entrances to gates and towers and were even carried on poles high above troops as they entered military campaigns.

By the beginning of the 15th century, Andrei Rublyov was recognized as the Church's foremost artist. The master lived in Moscow, establishing it as the new center of icon painting. No one is quite sure of the year of Rublyov's birth, but his name became a symbol for the highest values in Old Russian art; he eventually painted for all the grand princes of Moscovy. His innovative style, luminous colors, symbolic images, and rhythmical lines had a profound effect on the other schools. In his later life Rublyov became a monk, lived at the Spaso-Andronikov Monastery in Moscow, and painted frescoes in the Cathedral of Our Savior. He died in 1430.

Rublyov's technique was asymmetrical in form, and his colorful images possessed a narrative and harmonious tone. He meticulously individualized

The Virgin of Vladimir is one of Andrei Rublyov's most beautiful icons. Painted in the early 15th century for the Assumption Cathedral in Vladimir and based on the Byzantine Virgin of Eleousa, it can be seen today in the Vladimir-Suzdal Museum of History and Art.

his portraits and gave each figure a life of its own. Instead of the simple Novgorod outline, Rublyov's personages were enveloped with character and movement. Rublyov also used the circle as a symbol for the unity of life, and angels and saints were portrayed in real-life scenes on earth, surrounded by rocks, trees and animals. Allegorical symbols were introduced: Christ wore purple robes; the golden chalice contained a calf's head; and angels held trumpets or swords. Dark and somber colors gave way to vibrant greens, blues and yellows. Attention was paid to background; gems and metal were even added to create a more multidimensional setting.

Both Theophanes, Greek leader of the Novgorod school during the late 14th century, and Rublyov painted frescoes and the iconostasis in the Moscow Kremlin's Annunciation Cathedral. Rublyov and Daniil Chorny painted in Vladimir's Assumption Cathedral, where many of the icons and frescoes are still visible today. In the Trinity-Sergius Monastery, Rublyov portrayed the famous religious figure of Old Russia—St Sergius blessed Dmitry Donskoi before the decisive Battle of Kulikova, where Donskoi destroyed the Mongol-Tatar yoke in 1380. For once, icons not only symbolized God, but also the awesome events of human life. The saint's blessing (as portrayed in the Old Testament Trinity) symbolized Russian's desire for freedom and unity; the Eucharist served as a metaphor to sacrifice in battle and the chalice hope, faith and the common bond of the Russian people.

Many of Rublyov's works were lost through the centuries, destroyed in fires or painted over. But, some of his works, such as the Virgin of Vladimir, can still be found in the Vladimir-Suzdal Museum; the Archangel Michael, the Savior, Apostle Paul and the Old Testament Trinity can be viewed in the Tretyakov Gallery in Moscow. Other works are exhibited at the Rublyov Museum in the Andronikov Monastery. When British travel author, Robert Byron, made his first visit to Moscow and viewed Rublyov's icons, he professed: in Rublyov's masterpieces 'live the eternal sorrows, joys, and the whole destiny of man. Such pictures bring tears to the eye and peace to the soul'.

The genius of Andrei Rublyov can be compared to that of other major artists of Renaissance Europe, such as Giotto and Raphael. He was so revered that a century after his death, the Church Council decreed that

Rublyov's icons were merited as the true standard of artistic Orthodoxy. It was Rublyov's desire in life to help lead the world out of medieval darkness and despair and back into realms of beauty, harmony and love. By capturing infinite goodness on a simple and timeless icon, Andrei Rublyov achieved his own immortality and will always live in the hearts of those who view his work.

By the 17th century, Western European art had greatly influenced Russian religious painting. The icons became smaller and more intricate, decorated with jewels and cloisonné enamels and mosaics. With the reforms of Peter the Great (in the early 18th century) and the subsequent Westernization of Russian society, the popularity of icon painting made a sharp decline. It took several centuries before an interest returned to the old icon masterpieces; the first to be restored was Rublyov's Old Testament Trinity. A leading exhibition of restored medieval icons took place in Russia in 1913; many artists, such as Henri Matisse and Kazimir Malevich were greatly influenced by their beauty. Sadly, during the Communist era, icon painting was banned altogether, and the art of painting lacquered wooden boxes and dolls replaced religious art. Thousands of icons were burnt and destroyed, and many more stolen, smuggled or sold to the West.

Today restoration and icon painting schools are being revived in Russia, and the art of *spiski*, making copies of old icons, is flourishing. Most major monasteries (particularly in Sergiyev Posad) now have their own icon workshops. Many of these incorporate old-style techniques: the icons are painted atop wooden boards which are covered with *levki*, a mixture of linen oil, chalk, glue, bones and sturgeon skin. The color blue, for example, is made by crushing lapis lazuli, and the pigments are then mixed with eggs and water. It usually takes up to three months to create an average icon; generally students paint the nature scenes, architecture and clothing, while the most experienced artists design the faces, hands and feet. The Moscow Icons Workshop is considered one of the best in Russia; one of their most recent creations was the iconostasis for St Nicholas Church on Bersenevskaya Embankment. One private Russian company even presented Boris Yeltsin with the newly created icon, Boris and Gleb (based on the original). Boris and Gleb are patron saints of Russia as well as being the names of Yeltsin's grandsons.

The 15th-century icon by Andrei Rublyov known as the Old Testament Trinity is one of the greatest masterpieces of Old Russian art. Painted for his teacher St Sergius, it once hung as the central icon in Sergiyev Posad's Trinity Cathedral. The three angels represent the harmony of the Father, Son and Holy Spirit. It now hangs in Moscow's Tretyakov Gallery.

Suzdal   Суздаль

Suzdal is a pleasant half-hour journey from Vladimir (26 kilometers/16 miles north along the A113 road) through open fields dotted with hay stacks and mounds of dark rich soil. There are no trains to Suzdal. Take one of the frequent buses leaving Vladimir, or a direct bus also leaves for Suzdal from Moscow's Shchyolkovsky Station. Vladimir was the younger rival of Suzdal which, along with Rostov Veliky, was founded a full century earlier. The town was settled along the banks of the Kamenka River, which empties into the Nerl a few miles downstream. Over 100 examples of Old Russian architecture (in a space of only nine square kilometers/three and a half square miles) attract a half million visitors each year to this remarkable medieval museum.

Just before Suzdal is Kideksha, a small preserved village that dates back to the beginning of the 12th century. On the left bank of the river is the delightful **Suzdal Museum of Wooden Architecture**, portraying the typical Russian life-style of centuries ago. In 1983, the town received the Golden Apple. Awarded by an international jury, the prize symbolizes excellence in historical preservation and local color.

The first view of Suzdal from the road encompasses towering silhouettes of gleaming domes and pinkish walls atop Poklonnaya Hill, rising up amidst green patches of woods and gardens. It is as though time has stopped in this enchanting place—a perfection of spatial harmony. Today Suzdal is a quiet town with no indus-trial enterprises. Crop and orchard farming are the main occupations of the resi-dents who still live in the predominant *izba* (wooden houses). The scenic town is a popular site for film-making. The American production of *Peter the Great* used Suzdal as one of its locations.

Traveling along the Golden Ring route, you may have noticed that the distances between towns are similar. When these towns were settled, one unit of length was measured by how much ground a team of horses could cover in 24 hours. Most towns were laid out about one post-unit apart. So the distance between Moscow and Pereslavl-Zalessky, Pereslavl and Rostov, or Rostov and Yaroslavl could easily be covered in one day. Distances in medieval Russia were measured by these units; thus the traveler knew how many days it took to arrive at his destination—from Moscow to Suzdal took about three days.

The three best places to stay in Suzdal are: the Likhonsky Dom, located in a 17th-century house (tel. 09231-21901 or 20444); Intercession Convent, where you can stay in a moderately priced whitewashed wooden cabin (tel. 09231-20908); or the Main Tourist Complex (tel. 09231-21530/fax 20666). More inexpensive places, such as the Sokol Hotel, are available, but at times they only take in Russians (just try finding someone who speaks Russian). A number of restaurants are in the hotels and numerous cafés are spread around the town.

HISTORY

The area of Suzdalia was first mentioned in chronicles in 1024, when Kievan Grand Prince Yaroslavl the Wise came to suppress the rebellions. By 1096 a small kremlin had been built around the settlement, which one chronicle already described as a town. As Suzdal grew, princes and rich nobles from Kiev settled here, bringing with them spiritual representatives from the Church, who introduced Christianity to the region. The town slowly gained in prominence; Grand Prince Yuri Dolgoruky named it the capital of the northern provinces in 1125. From Suzdal, the seat of his royal residence, he went on to establish the small settlement of Moscow in 1147. His son Andrei Bogoliubsky transferred the capital to Vladimir in 1157.

After the Kievan states crumbled in the 12th century Suzdal, along with Rostov Veliky, became the religious center of medieval Rus. The princes and boyars donated vast sums of money to build splendid churches and monasteries; by the 14th century Suzdal had over 50 churches, 400 dwellings and a famous school of icon painting. No other place in all of Russia had such a high proportion of religious buildings. The crest of Suzdal was a white falcon wearing a prince's crown.

Since the town itself was not situated along important trade routes, the monks (and not the merchants) grew in wealth from large donations to the monasteries. The Church eventually took over the fertile lands and controlled the serf-peasants.

Suzdal was invaded many times, first by the Mongols in 1238, then by Lithuanians and Poles. After the Mongol occupation no new stone buildings were erected until well into the 16th century. When it was annexed to Moscovy in the late 14th century Suzdal lost its political importance, but remained a religious center.

During the 1700s Peter the Great's reforms undermined ecclesiastical power and the Church in Suzdal lost much of its land and wealth. Churches and monasteries were mainly used to house religious fanatics and political prisoners. Many barren or unpopular wives were forced to take the veil and exiled to Suzdal's convents. By the end of the 19th century only 6,000 residents remained, and one account described Suzdal as 'a town of churches, bell towers, old folk legends and tombstones'. Today with a population of well over 12,000, this enthralling poetic spot has been restored to the majesty of its former days. As one 13th-century chronicler observed: 'Oh, most radiant and bountiful, how wondrous art thou with thy beauty vast.'

SIGHTS

Approaching Suzdal from Vladimir, as horse coaches once did, two churches are passed on the right before crossing the Kamenka River. These are the **Church of Our Lady of the Sign** (1749) and the **Church of the Deposition of the Robe** (1777). The former houses the Suzdal Excursion Bureau.

The kremlin was well protected on three sides by the river; along the eastern wall ran a large moat, now the main street. Remnants of the 11th-century earthen walls are still evident today. These ramparts are topped with wooden walls and towers.

A tour of Suzdal begins on the right bank of the river, where much of the old architecture is clustered. Take a moment to gaze out over the fertile plains and meandering waters of the river. The rich arable land in this area first attracted settlers seeking greater freedoms from Novgorod, where pagan priests were still leading uprisings against Kievan attempts to Christianize and feudalize the northern lands. In Old Russian, *suzdal* meant to give judgment or justice. Today several streets still carry the names of Slavic pagan gods, such as Kupala, Netyoka and Yarunova.

As you cross the river a simple white church with red outlines comes into view on the left side of Lenin Street. This was used as the summer church; the slender helmet-domed building behind it was used in winter.

The 13th-century **Korsunsky Gates** lead to the main cathedral and are covered with Byzantine patterns; religious scenes from the New Testament were engraved and etched with acid on copper sheets and then gilded.

Prince Vladimir Monomakh laid the first stone of the town's main **Cathedral of the Virgin Nativity** at the end of the 11th century. This structure was rebuilt many times. In 1528, Grand Prince Vasily III of Moscow reconstructed it from brick and white stone and surmounted it with five helmet-shaped domes. In 1748, the domes were altered to the present blue onion and gold-star pattern.

The southern doors, surrounded by elaborate stone decorations, were the official entrance of the princes. Lions, carved along the portals, were the emblems of the princes of Vladimir. The carved female faces symbolize the Virgin Mary, whose nativity is celebrated. The southern and western doors (1230–33) are made of gilded copper and depict scenes from the life of St George, the patron saint of both Prince Georgi and his grandfather Yuri Dolgoruky.

Early 13th-century frescoes of saints and other ornamental floral patterns are still visible in the vestry. Most of the other murals and frescoes are from the 17th century. Tombs of early bishops and princes from as far back as 1023 are also found inside. The burial vaults of the early princesses are near the west wall. The octagonal bell tower was built in 1635 by order of Czar Mikhail Romanov and repaired in 1967. Old Slavonic letters correspond to numbers on the face of the clock.

The impressive whitewashed Archbishop's Palace, now the **Suzdal Museum**, was built next to the cathedral on the bank of the Kamenka between the 15th and 17th centuries. The main chamber of the palace, a large pillarless hall, held important meetings and banquets. In the 17th century this *krestovaya* (cross-vaulted) chamber was considered one of the most elegant rooms in Russia. The museum contains collections of ancient art and traces the evolution of architecture in the Suzdal region.

Enter the palace chamber through the western entrance. In the center stands a long wooden table, covered with a rich red cloth, once used by the archbishop and his clergy. An 18th-century tiled stove stands in one corner. The walls are decorated with many 15th-century icons. Suzdal developed its own school of icon painting in the early 13th century. Its use of lyrical flowing outlines, detailed facial qualities and soft designs in red and gold, were later adopted by the Moscow school, headed by Andrei Rublyov. Both the Moscow Tretyakov Gallery and the St Petersburg Russian Museum include Suzdal icons among their exhibits.

Pass through the gateway to the left of the palace to reach another art section of the museum. Here are more displays of icons, paintings, sculptures, ivory carvings, embroideries and other crafts.

In front of the palace by the river is the wooden **Church of St Nicholas** (1766). It represents one of the oldest types of Old Russian wooden architecture and is built from logs into a square frame with a long sloping roof. The early architects used only an ax, chisel and plane to build these designs. No nails were needed; the logs were held together by wooden pegs and filled with moss. The church was transferred from the village of Glotovo in 1960. Beside it, in lovely contrast, stands the red-and-white-trimmed **Church of the Assumption** (1732), with its green rounded roof and horseshoe *kokoshniki*.

Residents of Suzdal sell their homegrown vegetables at the local market. Most people living outside the bigger cities grow their own potatoes, cabbage, tomatoes and other vegetables in small garden plots by their homes out of economic necessity.

Farther up the riverbank is the yellow-white brick summer **Church of the Entry into Jerusalem** (1707), surmounted by a half-dome drum and a gilded cross. The whitewashed winter **Church of St Paraskeva** (1772) stands next to it.

Many of the local citizens built their own churches. Across the river are four churches constructed between the 16th and 18th centuries with money raised by the local tanners, who lived and worked by the river near the marketplace. The local blacksmiths, who lived at the northern end of town, built the **Churches of Saints Cosmas and Damian**, the patron saints of blacksmiths.

The long trading stalls of the Torg (marketplace) built in 1806, mark the town's center. During holidays the grounds were opened to fairs and exhibitions, and were filled with jolly jesters, merry-go-rounds and craft booths. Horses were tied up along the arcade. Today the colonnade has over 100 stores where the townspeople congregate, especially around midday.

For a lunch break, try dining at the Trapeznaya Restaurant, located in the Refectory of the Archbishop's Palace (closed on Mondays; sometimes advance reservations are needed). Sample the splendors of ancient Suzdalian monastic cooking—the local fish soup and home-brewed mead are especially tasty. Also try the *medovukha*, an alcoholic beverage combined with honey that is made only in Suzdal. On Lenin Street are the Sokol restaurant and a tearoom. The Suzdal Hotel and Restaurant are near the central square and the Pogrebok (Cellar) Café is on Kremlyovskaya Street.

Suzdal's open-air Museum of Wooden Architecture exhibits old wooden buildings based on architecture dating back to 1238. Using the simplest of tools—chisel, plane and axe— early Russian architects created structures without the use of nails. This log-built church is covered with hand-hewn aspen shingles, an early trademark of the region.

Behind the trading stalls on Lenin Street is the **Church of the Resurrection-on-the-Marketplace**, now a branch of the Suzdal Museum. Here are exhibits of architectural decorations, wooden carvings and colorful tiles used to adorn buildings in the 17th and 18th centuries.

Continuing north along Lenin Street brings you to two other sets of church complexes. Not only did the number of churches in a town symbolize its wealth, but it was also customary in medieval Russia to build twin churches; this added even more to the cluster of religious structures. These twin churches usually stood in close proximity to each other—one cool, high-vaulted and richly decorated was used only in summer; the other, simpler and smaller, held the congregation in winter. The first complex comprises the **Church of the Emperor Constantine** (1707), topped by five slender drum domes, a unique feature of Suzdalian architecture. The glazed green-roofed and white-bricked **Church of Our Lady of Sorrows** (1787), with a large bell tower, was for winter. The next pair consists of the **Church of St Antipus** (1745), recognizable by its unusual multicolored octagonal red-roofed bell tower, and the **Church of St Lazarus** (1667), surmounted with beautiful forged crosses on five domes.

Suzdal had the largest monasteries and convents in the region, which served as protective citadels for the citizens during times of war. These institutions, besides being religious, became the educational centers of the town. Husbands could also force their wives to take the veil as a quick way to divorce. Fathers would also place daughters in a convent until they were married.

In front of the twin churches, by the water, is the **Convent of the Deposition of the Robe**, founded by Bishop John of Rostov Veliky in 1207. The convent was rebuilt in stone in the 17th century. The white Holy Gates are topped with two red and white octagonal towers covered with glazed tile. The convent's church was built by Ivan Shigonia-Podzhogin, a rich boyar who served Czar Vasily III. The citizens of Suzdal erected the 72-meter (236-foot) bell tower in 1813 to commemorate Napoleon's defeat.

The neighboring red-brick **Convent of St Alexander** was built in 1240 in honor of Prince Alexander Nevsky, who defeated the Swedes on the Neva River that same year. After it was burned down by the Poles in the 17th century, the mother superior had Peter the Great rebuild it. In 1682, the Ascension Cathedral was constructed from funds donated by Peter's mother, Natalya Naryshkina. The convent closed in 1764, but the church remains open to the public.

Behind this convent and nestled in the former *posad* is a 17th-century tailor's house with a gabled roof. It now contains a domestic museum with displays of furniture and utensils from the 17th to 19th centuries. The rooms represent a typical peasant hut. Across from the *pechka* (stove), over which the eldest member of the

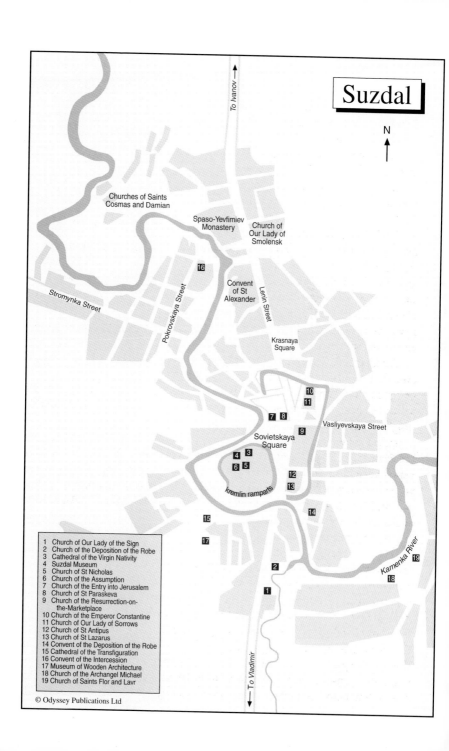

Suzdal

N ↑

To Ivanov →

Churches of Saints
Cosmas and Damian

Spaso-Yevfimiev
Monastery

Church of
Our Lady of
Smolensk

Stromynka Street

Pokrovskaya Street

16

Convent
of St
Alexander

Lenin Street

Krasnaya
Square

Vasliyevskaya Street

10
11
7 8
9

Sovietskaya
Square

4 3
6 5

12
13

kremlin ramparts

14

15

17

Kamenka River

19

18

2

1

To Vladimir ↓

1 Church of Our Lady of the Sign
2 Church of the Deposition of the Robe
3 Cathedral of the Virgin Nativity
4 Suzdal Museum
5 Church of St Nicholas
6 Church of the Assumption
7 Church of the Entry into Jerusalem
8 Church of St Paraskeva
9 Church of the Resurrection-on-
   the-Marketplace
10 Church of the Emperor Constantine
11 Church of Our Lady of Sorrows
12 Church of St Antipus
13 Church of St Lazarus
14 Convent of the Deposition of the Robe
15 Cathedral of the Transfiguration
16 Convent of the Intercession
17 Museum of Wooden Architecture
18 Church of the Archangel Michael
19 Church of Saints Flor and Lavr

© Odyssey Publications Ltd

family slept, was the *krasnaya ugol* (beautiful corner) where the family icons were kept. Usually the *gornitsa* (living area) comprised one or two rooms. Here were found a few beds, chairs, tables and a clothes chest. The kitchen was situated in the corner nearest to the *kamin* (fireplace or stove). A small storage house was also built into the hut. This house stands next to the summer **Church of Our Lady of Smolensk** (1696) on Krasnaya Square.

The largest architectural complex on the right bank of the river is the **Spaso-Yevfimievsky Monastery** (Savior Monastery of St Euthymius), founded in 1350 by a Suzdal prince; the monks eventually owned vast amounts of land and their monastery became the wealthiest in the region. It is enclosed by a massive, one-and-a-half kilometer (one-mile) long, red kremlin that has 12 decorated towers. By the 17th century the monastery controlled over 10,000 serfs. Today film companies often use the high red brick walls to double as Moscow's Kremlin. The five-domed **Cathedral of the Transfiguration** was built in 1594. Both exterior and interior 17th-century frescoes, painted by masters from Kostroma, depict the history of the monastery. Prince Dmitri Pozharsky, hero of the 1612 Polish war and Governor of Suzdal, is buried beside the altar; a monument to him, standing outside the cathedral, is inscribed: 'To Dmitri Mikhailovsky 1578–1642.' Adjoining the cathedral is a small chapel that stands over the grave of the Abbot Yevfim.

The **Church of the Assumption**, built in 1526, was decorated with *kokoshniki* and a large tent-shaped dome. The Kostroma artists Nikitin and Savin painted the frescoes on the outside southern and western walls. At one point, Catherine the Great had it converted into a prison to house those who committed crimes against the Church and State. The Decembrist Shakhovskoi died in this prison. The monk cells contain an exhibit of Contemporary Folk Art that includes works by local painters, potters, sculptors and glass blowers. A particular treat is to listen to the ringing of the bells in the bell tower. On the hour, the bell-ringer ascends the tower and performs a ten-minute concert. It sounds like an entire bell choir, but it is just one man tugging on the multitude of ropes that hold the clappers.

The large complex across the river is the **Convent of the Intercession**, built by Prince Andrei in 1364. Prince Vasily (Basil) III commissioned the convent's churches in 1510 as supplication for the birth of a male heir. The polygonal bell tower, rebuilt in the 17th century, is one of the earliest examples of a brick tower and conical roof design. The white three-domed Cathedral of the Intercession served as the burial place for Suzdal noblewomen. Eventually, in 1525, Vasily exiled his wife Solomonia Saburova to the convent. He wanted to divorce her on the grounds that she was barren; Solomonia accused Vasily of sterility. The metropolitan granted Vasily his divorce and sent Solomonia to the Pokrovsky (Intercession) Convent to live out her life as a nun. Vasily remarried a Polish girl named Elena Glinskaya.

Besides churches, Suzdal is full of historic residential architecture. Children play after school by the elaborately decorated 18th-century wooden house that once belonged to an influential merchant named Bibanov.

Some time later news reached Moscow that Solomonia had given birth to a son. Fearing for her son's life, Solomonia hid him with friends and then staged a fake burial. For centuries this tale was regarded only as legend, but in 1934 a small casket was unearthed beside Solomonia's tomb (she died in 1594). There was no skeleton, only a stuffed silk shirt embroidered with pearls. The small white tomb and pieces of clothing are on display in the Suzdal Museum. Ivan the Terrible (son of Elena Glinskaya) also sent his wife Anna to this convent in 1575. Peter the Great even exiled his first wife Evdokia Lopukhina here in 1698. The convent buildings have been returned to the Orthodox Church; there is also a hotel residence in the complex. For a splendid panoramic view of Suzdal, climb the bank of the river in front of the convent.

At the southern end of town on the left bank of the Kamenka is the **Suzdal Museum of Wooden Architecture**. Old wooden villages were brought in from all around the Vladimir-Suzdal region and reassembled at this location on Dmitriyevskaya Hill, to give an idea of the way of life in a typical Russian village. This open-air museum consists of log-built churches covered with aspen-shingled roofs, residential houses, windmills, barns and bathhouses.

At the end of the day take a walk along the river as the sun sets over the town. Young boys can be seen swimming and fishing in the warmer months or skating in winter. Many small side streets are filled with the local wooden dachas, covered with elaborate wood carvings and latticework. Ask your driver to stop by the **House of Merchant Bibanov**, the most lavishly decorated house in town. If you are lucky, a pink full moon will rise above the magical display of gabled roofs and towers, to signal an end to the delightful Suzdalian day.

VICINITY OF SUZDAL

A few kilometers to the north of Suzdal is the small **Village of Kideksha**. In 1015, according to chronicles, the brothers Boris and Gleb, sons of the Kievan Prince Vladimir who brought Christianity to Russia, had a meeting here where the Kamenka River empties into the Nerl. They were later assassinated by their elder brother Svyatopolk (who was later murdered by a fourth brother, Yaroslav). Boris and Gleb, who died defending the Christian faith, became Russia's first saints. In 1152, Prince Yuri Dolgoruky chose to build his country estate on this spot. Dolgoruky also erected the simple white-stone **Church of Saints Boris and Gleb**, where his son Boris and daughter-in-law Maria are buried. The winter Church of St Stephan was erected in the 18th century.

THE TRANS-SIBERIAN RAILWAY

A lthough today the Commonwealth of Independent States has one of the world's largest rail networks and arguably the most famous of train journeys—the Trans-Siberian—for years it actually lagged behind the railway systems of other European powers. Fourteen years after George Stephenson began building his railway in England from Stockton to Darlington, and eight years after the engineer's locomotive *Rocket*, was built, Czar Nicholas I opened Russia's first railroad. The Tsarskoye Selo to St Petersburg line, inaugurated in 1837, was succeeded by additional tracks including a St Petersburg to Moscow service in 1851. Yet by this date the country could still only boast some 1,240 kilometers (770 miles) of track.

Russia's transport and military supply service was shown to be woefully inadequate in 1854 when British, French and Turkish armies inflicted a humiliating defeat on the country in the Crimean War. More Russian troops died on the freezing march to the Crimea and from disease than perished in battle.

The first proposal of a steam railway through Siberia by the American Perry McDonough Collins in 1857 was rejected. But soon after, the reform-minded Czar Alexander II instituted programs of modernization, often inspired by military campaigns, which included railway building. The St Petersburg to Warsaw line was initiated in 1861; a decade later the rails reached the Volga. At the time of his death in 1881, Russia had 22,500 kilometers (14,000 miles) of track.

Construction of the Trans-Siberian Railroad was ordered by Alexander III and on May 31, 1891, his son Nicholas laid the foundation stone. By 1898 it linked Chelyabinsk in the Ural Mountains to Irkutsk. The last leg to the Pacific port of Vladivostok was finally completed in 1916. At Lake Baikal (until track was laid around the south of it) a ferry carried passengers across in summer, and in winter they were pulled across the frozen lake on horse sleighs to the next depot or track was laid across the ice; it would take over five hours to cross the 48-kilometer (30-mile) wide lake.

The railroads held enormous economic and strategic importance for the country. The Trans-Caspian line to Central Asia was part of a military campaign to conquer the territory. As the rails snaked their way from the Baltic Sea through the rolling heartland of Russia and on across the Siberian wilderness and the deserts of Uzbekistan and Kazakhstan, markets and trade opened up almost overnight. The railways were responsible for Russia's first speculative boom.

Today the CIS's network carries some 11 million travelers every day on some 233,300 kilometers (145,000 miles) of rails. Thanks to Lenin's prognosis that Communism was Soviet power plus the electrification of the whole country, a third of the rail network is now electrified while the rest runs on diesel. (Steam engine production was ceased in 1956.) The most heavily used route is between St Petersburg and Moscow where express trains run the distance in about four hours.

And now, over 100 years after the first tracks were laid, the Trans-Siberian, one of the greatest travel adventures, is still one of the cheapest ways of traveling from Europe to Asia. The main section of the railroad stretches approximately 8,000 kilometers (5,000 miles) from Moscow to Beijing, or 9,342 kilometers (5,805 miles) to Vladivostok. The five-and-a-half-day train via Mongolia departs Moscow at 7.50pm on Tuesdays and arrives in Beijing at 3.33pm on Mondays. The Chinese train via Ulan Bator leaves Beijing at 7.40am on Wednesdays, and arrives in Moscow at 7pm on Mondays. The Trans-Manchurian train via Manzhouli departs Beijing at 8.32pm Fridays and Saturdays and arrives in Moscow at 6.30pm six days later. Trains via Manchuria leave from Moscow at 9.25pm Fridays and Saturdays, and arrive in Beijing at 6.32am six days later after covering 9,052 kilometers (5,625 miles). (With trains covering such large distances, schedules are often delayed.)

The Vladivostok train departs daily from Moscow's Yaroslavsky Station at 2.25pm (and from Vladivostok at 5.55pm) and takes six and a half days. Even though the train usually stops only two or three times a day, it passes by over 800 stations along the route. One can now fly directly to Vladivostok or Khabarovsk from the West Coast of the United States via Alaska and from there, journey westwards on the train to Moscow. On Russian trains the timetable runs according to Moscow time (across 11 time zones), but local time often applies to stations and dining-car hours! Beijing time is the same as Ulan Bator, Mongolia, but is four hours ahead of Moscow summer time or five ahead of Moscow winter time.

A separate branch of the Trans-Siberian is known as the BAM (Baikal Amur Main Line). This railway, running through northeastern Siberia, was completed (for about 60 billion dollars) in 1990 as part of Brezhnev's Fifteen-Year Plan. The task was monumental—seven large tunnels and 2,400 bridges were built across 3,200 kilometers (2,000 miles) of permafrost. Earthquakes, mud flows and avalanches continue to pose additional hazards. There is nothing much but endless taiga to see on the journey; the route was mainly built to stimulate timber, coal and oil production and increase industrial transport. The line begins at Tayshet (slightly west of Irkutsk), continues north to Bratsk (along the Angara River), across the northern end of Lake Baikal (at Severobaikalsk), on to Tynda and Komsolmolsk-na-Amure (north of Khabarovsk), and terminates at Imperatorskaya (formerly Sovyetskaya) Gavan on the Pacific.

Reservations are essential, especially during summer, and should be made at least two months in advance. Many travel agencies, including places in Moscow and Beijing, can book space on the Trans-Siberian.

The Cyrillic on this Trans-Siberian dining car reads RESTORAN and illustrates how a little time spent learning the Cyrillic alphabet can help visitors understand and pronounce many simple words and street names.

Tourists have the option of reserving a berth in a two-, four- or six-berth compartment (the last is not recommended). Compartments are often set aside just for foreigners. If traveling alone, you may be booked into a compartment with local travelers. Avoid buying open tickets, as they are virtually impossible to book and expire after several months. Russian and/or Chinese visas are required for both trains, and an additional Mongolian visa is needed for the Trans-Mongolian, even if only transiting.

From Vladivostok on the Pacific Ocean, a ferry service operates to Niigata, Japan from May to September. Air connections also run between Khabarovsk and Vladivostok throughout the year. There is also a ferry between Sakhalin Island and Hokkaido. You can also stop overnight or spend a few days in Siberian cities, such as Novosibirsk or Irkutsk on Lake Baikal. (If you do get off along the way, make sure you have already prebooked the continuation of your journey.)

Popular connection destinations to the West include: Berlin, which can be reached from Moscow in 24 hours; Budapest (34 hours) and Helsinki (14 hours). If you are a real train fanatic, you can extend the journey all the way to Paris, London or beyond on the East-West Express via Berlin.

Travelers on the Trans-Siberian should always pack basic foods, snacks and drinks, including bottled water and alcohol if so desired. Items such as bread and sweets can be bought at stations along the way. The Russian restaurant car has a tasty enough menu but a limited supply as time goes by. Other handy items to have are earplugs, a Swiss army knife, instant soup, coffee, tea and milk creamer, a large mug, bowl and utensils, Thermos flask, toilet paper and tissues. Hot water is available from each wagon's large titan-samovar usually located at the end of the hallway. Dress appropriately for the season and pack lounging clothes. Bring along plenty of reading material; a Walkman with music can also help pass the time.

FARES (as of summer 1998)

Moscow to Vladivostok (via Khabarovsk)

First class: $1,384   Average travel time: 6 1/2 days
Second class: $705   Distance 9,342 kilometers (5,805 miles)

From Moscow's Yaroslavsky Station, Train number 2 departs daily at 2.25pm and arrives in Vladivostok at 2.45am. From Vladivostok, Train number 1 leaves at 5.55pm and arrives in Moscow at 6.20am.

Moscow to Beijing (via Mongolia or Manchuria)

    First class: approx. $700   Average travel time: 5–6 days

    Second class: approx. $525   Distance: 7,910 or 9,052 kilometers

                                      (4,915 or 5,625 miles)

(*Ticket prices may vary, depending if bought in Moscow, Beijing or from a Western ticket agency. Trans-Siberian packages can also include a night or two in Moscow with hotel accommodation, and additional stops in Novosibirsk and Irkutsk.)

Moscow to Warsaw

    First class: $154   Average travel time: 20 hours

    Second class: $105   Distance: 1,328 kilometers (825 miles)

Trains depart from both Moscow's Belorussky Station and Warszawa Central three times a day.

Moscow to Berlin

    First class: $232   Average travel time: 24 hours

    Second class: $150   Distance: 1,904 kilometers (1,183 miles)

Trains depart from both Moscow (Belorussky Station) and Berlin twice daily.

Moscow to Paris (via Berlin)

    First class: $485   Average travel time: 38 1/2 hours

    Second class: $330   Distance: 3,143 kilometers (1,953 miles)

Departures are up to four times daily from either Paris Nord Station or Berlin Zoologisch.

The interior of GUM Department Store on Red Square. Built in 1893, it is Russia's largest store and has a large glass roof and ornate bridges that lead to over 200 shops on three levels.

Moscow Practical Information

TELEPHONE NUMBERS
Country Code for Russia (7)

CITY CODES

Moscow	(095)	Kostroma	(0942)	Novgorod	(816)
St Petersburg	(812)	Ivanovo	(09322)	Pskov	(81122)
Yaroslavl	(0852)	Vladimir	(09222)		

(Vladimir and Suzdal are Moscow time plus one hour.)

EMERGENCY SERVICES

Fire	01	Ambulance	03 (See also Medical)
Police	02	Gas Leaks	04

TELEPHONE INFORMATION

Time	100		
Moscow City Information	937-9911	Intercity Information	07 or 007
Directory Enquiries	09 or 009	International Calls	8-190

To order an international call dial 8-194
(you can also direct dial with 8—wait for tone—then 10 + area code + number.)

The following are charged calls:

Moscow Addresses/		Weather: Moscow and	
Telephone	943-5001	Vicinity	975-9133
Museum Information	975-9144	Weather: International	975-9111
Theater Information	975-9122		

TAXIS

Central Taxi Bureau	927-0000
ABC Taxi	201-5954
Moscow Taxi	238-1001

ON-LINE SERVICES

Traveller's Yellow Pages for Moscow 1998: http://www.infoservices.com
See Recommended Reading for more Russia information and on-line services.

EXPRESS MAIL/POST

DHL, 11 3rd Samotechny Pereulok. Tel. 956-1000. Other centers at the Mezhdunarodny-1 Hotel (3rd entrance), Slavyanskaya Hotel (2 fl), Park Place Hotel and 2 Novy Arbat.

EMS Garantpost, 37 Varshavskoye Highway. Tel. 117-0040; 114-4755.

Federal Express, 12 Krasnopresnenskaya Nab. (Mezh Hotel) Tel. 253-1641.

Post Internationl, 15 Malaya Dmitrovka Ul. Tel. 733-9278.

TNT Express Worldwide, 3 Baltiisky Lane. Tel. 931-9640; fax 931-9644. 1 Deyezhny Lane. Tel. 201-2585; fax 254-4015. (Also receives faxes for clients.)

USEFUL PUBLICATIONS IN ENGLISH

The best place to find newspapers and magazines from home is to check in the city's main hotel newsstands, or at central kiosks around town. *The Travellers' Yellow Pages of Moscow* contains over 30,000 useful addresses (in English and Russian); on sale in stores throughout the city. Tel. 229-7914; fax 209-5465; e-mail: Moscow@infoservices.com. To order books in the US, see Recommended Reading. *Moscow News* is published daily in Russian and English.

The *Moscow Times* is distributed daily, and, together with the *Moscow Times Weekly*, provide current local and international news, along with listings of events in theaters, concerts, movies, and reviews of restaurants and other shows. Look for both distributed in hotels, restaurants and selected shops. The *Moscow Tribune* also offers news, published daily. *Moscow Magazine* (monthly) is in English and Russian, reports on the city; city guide and information on restaurants, shops, museums. Tel. 924-4280. *What & Where in Moscow* (monthly) provides information for consumers and details of cultural events.

MEDICAL

Most top-end hotels have a resident nurse or doctor. In case of major medical emergencies, contact a clinic below or an embassy; you may need to arrange for evacuation to a foreign hospital. If you have a preexisting condition, consider purchasing travel medical insurance before departing; a medical evacuation can be very expensive, costing up to $10,000!

American Medical Center, 10 2nd Tverskoy-Yamskoy Proyezd. Tel. 956-3366; fax 956-2306. Metro Mayakovskaya. Can be contacted 24-hours a day; it also has a pharmacy, ambulance service, and can arrange medical evacuations.

European Medical Center, tel. 956-7999. Can be contacted 24-hours a day. Also has ambulance services.

Mediclub Moscow Ltd (Canada), 56 Michurinsky Prospekt. Tel. 931-5018/5318; fax 932-8653. Metro Prospekt Vernadskovo. Has pharmacy and ambulance services. Also **Athens Medical Center** at 6 Michurinsky Prospekt. Tel. 143-2503; 147-9121.

DENTAL
US Dental Care, 8 Ulitsa Shabolovka, Bldg 3/1st floor. Tel. 931-9909; fax 931-9910.
MedStar (British-Russian), 43 Lomonovsky Prospekt. Tel. 143-6076/6377. Open Mon–Sat 9am–9pm.
Russian-American Dental Center Corp, 28 Rusakovskaya Ul. Tel. 269-1392. Metro Sokolniki. Open Mon–Sat 9am–6pm.
Mosta (Russian-Japanese), 13 Bolshoi Cherkassky Pereulok. Tel. 923-3169; 927-0747.

OPTICAL
Medstar-Optics, 43 Lomonosovsky Prospekt. Tel. 143-6354. Metro Universitet. Mon–Fri 10am–6:30pm.
Vioptica, 22 Sivtsev Vrazhek. Tel. 241-6093. Metro Arbatskaya. Mon–Sat 10am–7pm.

EMBASSIES
This is a partial listing of foreign embassies in Moscow which are open Monday through Friday and closed on weekends. If needing a visa, call first to find out department hours and locations—the visa department may be in a separate location.
Australia, 13 Kropotkinsky Per. Tel. 956-6070. Metro Park Kultury.
Open 9am–5pm; closed 12:30–1:30pm.
Austria, 1 Starokonyushenny Per. Tel. 201-2166. Metro Kropotkinskaya.
Open 9am–5pm.
Belgium, 7 Malaya Molchanovka Ul. Tel. 291-6018. Metro Arbatskaya.
Open 9:30am–5:30pm; closed 1–2:30pm.
Bulgaria, 66 Mosfilmovksya Ul. Tel. 143-9022. Metro Universitet.
Open 9am–5:30pm; closed 1–2pm.
Canada, 23 Starokonyushenny Per. Tel. 956-6666. Metro Kropotkinskaya.
Open 8:30am–5pm.
China, 6 Druzhbii Ul. Tel. 147-4283. Metro Universitet.
Open 9am–6pm; closed 12:30–3pm.
Cuba, 9 Leontevsky Per. Tel. 290-6230. Metro Mayakovskaya. Open 8:30am–5pm.
Czech Republic, 12/14 Yuliusa Fuchika Ul. Tel. 251-0545. Metro Mayakovskaya.
Open 8:30am–5:30pm.
Denmark, 9 Prechistensky Per. Tel. 201-7860. Metro Kropotkinskaya.
Open 9am–5pm; closed 1–2pm.
Estonia, 5 Kislovsky Malaya Per. Tel. 290-4655. Metro Arbatskaya. Open 9am–6pm.

Finland, 15/17 Kropotkinskaya Ul. Tel. 246-4027. Metro Park Kultury.
Open 9am–5pm; closed 1–2pm.
France, 45 Bolshaya Yakimanka Ul. Tel. 236-0003. Metro Okyabrskaya.
Open 9am–6pm; closed 1–3pm.
Germany, 56 Mosfilmovskaya Ul. Tel. 936-2401. Metro Universitet.
Open 8am–5pm; closed 1–2pm.
Great Britain, 14 Sofiyskaya Nab. Tel. 915-3511. Metro Biblioteka Imeni Lenina.
Open 9am–5pm; closed 1–2pm.
Greece, 4 Leontevsky Per. Tel. 243-3838. Metro Arbatskaya. Open 9am–4pm.
India, 6–9 Ulitsa Vorontsovo Polye. Tel. 917-1841. Metro Kitai-Gorod.
Open 9:30am–6pm; closed 1–2pm.
Israel, 56 Bolshaya Ordynka Ul. Tel. 230-6753. Metro Serpukhovskaya.
Open 9am–5pm; Fri 9am–3pm.
Italy, 5 Denezhny Per. Tel. 241-1536. Metro Smolenskaya.
Open 9am–6pm; closed 1–3pm.
Japan, 12 Kalashny Per. Tel. 291-8500. Metro Arbatskaya.
Open 9am–6pm; closed 1–2:30pm.
Latvia, 3 Chapligina Ul. Tel. 925-2707. Metro Turgenskaya. Open 9am–5pm.
Lithuania, 10 Borisoglebsky Per. Tel. 291-2795. Metro Arbatskaya.
Open 9am–6pm; closed 1–2pm.
Mexico, 4 Bol. Levshinsky Per. Tel. 201-2553. Metro Kropotkinskaya. Open 9am–5pm.
Mongolia, 11 Borisoglebsky Per. Tel. 290-6792. Metro Arbatskaya.
Open 8am–6pm; closed 1–2pm.
Netherlands, 6 Kalashny Per. Tel. 203-1167. Metro Arbatskaya.
Open 9am–6pm; closed 1–2:30pm.
New Zealand, 44 Povarskaya Ul. Tel. 956-3579. Metro Barrikadnaya.
Open 9am–5:30pm.
Norway, 7 Povarskaya Ul. Tel. 290-3874. Metro Arbatskaya. Open 9am–5pm.
Poland, 4 Klimashkina Ul. Tel. 255-0017. Metro Belorusskaya. Open 9am–6pm.
Slovakia, 17/19 Yuliusa Fuchika Ul. Tel. 250-5595. Metro Belorusskaya.
Open 8:30am–5:30pm; closed 12–1pm. Fri 8:30am–5:30pm.
Spain, 50/8 Bol. Nikitskaya Ul. Tel. 202-2180. Metro Arbatskaya. Open 8am–3pm.
Sweden, 60 Mosfilmovskaya Ul. Tel. 956-1200. Metro Universitet.
Open 9am–5:30pm; closed 1–2:30pm.
Switzerland, 2/5 Ogorodnoi Slobody. Tel. 925-5322. Metro Turgenevskaya.
Open 8:30am–4:30pm.
Thailand, 9 Bol. Spasskaya Ul. Tel. 208-0856. Metro Sukharevskaya. Open 9:30am–4pm.
United States, 15–23 Novinsky Bul. Tel. 252-2451/59. Metro Barrikadnaya.
Open 9am–6pm.

CIS EMBASSIES

A foreign visitor may now need a visa to the following areas:

Azerbaijan, 16 Leontevsky Per. Tel. 229-1649. Metro Pushkinskaya.
Open 9am–6pm; closed 1–2pm.

Armenia, 2 Armyansky Per. Tel. 924-1269. Metro Kitai-Gorod.
Open 9am–6pm; closed 1–2pm.

Belarus, 17/6 Maroseika Ul. Tel. 928-8724. Metro Kitai-Gorod.
Open 9am–6pm; closed 1–2pm.

Georgia, 6 Maly Rizhsky Per./Khlebny Per. Tel. 290-6902. Metro Arbatskaya.
Open 9am–5pm; closed 1–2pm.

Kazakhstan, 3a Chistoprudny Bul. Tel. 927-1820. Metro Chistiye Prudy.
Open 9am–5pm; closed 1–2pm.

Kirghizia, 64 Bolshaya Ordynka Ul. Tel. 237-4882. Metro Dobrinskaya.
Open 9am–6pm; closed 1–2pm.

Moldova, 18 Kuznetsky Most. Tel. 924-5342. Metro Kuznetsky Most.
Open 9am–6pm.

Tadzhikistan, 13 Granatny Per. Tel. 290-4186. Metro Barrikadnaya.
Open 9am–6pm; closed 1–2pm.

Turkmenia, 22 Filippovsky Per. Tel. 291-6593. Metro Arbatskaya.
Open 9am–6pm; closed 1–2pm.

Ukraine, 18 Leontevsky Per. Tel. 229-1438. Metro Pushkinskaya.
Open 9am–6pm; closed 1–2pm.

Uzbekistan, 12 Pogorelsky Per. Tel. 230-0054. Metro Okyabrskaya.
Open 9am–6pm; closed 1–2pm.

AIRPORTS

There are five airports around Moscow. Express buses run to each airport from the Aerovokzal Terminal at 37a Leningradsky Prospekt. Metro Aeroport/Dynamo.

Sheremetyevo-II International Airport is 32 kilometers (20 miles) north of the city on Leningradskoye Highway. Tel. 578-9101/956-4666. Take an express bus or go to Metro Rechoi Vokzal, then take bus 551, or to Metro Planernaya and take bus 517. Rides take 30–45 minutes.

Sheremetyevo-I, flights within CIS, Russia and Baltic states.

Vnukovo (flights within CIS and Russia) is 30 kilometers (18 miles) south of the city on Vorovskoye Highway. Tel. 436-2813/8646. Take an express bus (30 minutes) or go to Metro Yugo-Zapadnaya, then take bus 511.

Domodedovo (flights within Russia and the CIS and some charter flights). Tel. 155-0922. Take the Metro to Domodedovskaya or *elektrichka* trains also run from Paveletsky Station. Express bus takes 1 hour 20 minutes.

Vykovo (flights within the CIS, Russia and some charters) is located southeast of the city. Tel. 558-4738. Metro Vykhino.

AIRLINES

This is a partial listing of major airlines. If an airline is not listed below, check at your hotel service desk for telephone number and location.

Central Information Bureau, 37a Leningradsky Prospekt. Tel. 155-0922.
International Information on Arrivals/Departures, daily 9am–8pm. Tel. 156-8019.
Aeroflot, 37/9 Leningradsky Pr. Tel. 155-6648/5045. Mon–Fri 9am–6pm.
Metro Rechnoi Vokzal.
Air France, 7 Kirovy Val. Tel. 237-2325/234-3377. Mon–Fri 9am–6pm.
Metro Oktybrskaya. Sheremetyevo Airport, tel. 578-2757.
Air India, 7 Kirovy Val. Tel. 237-7494. Mon–Fri 9:30am–5pm; closed 1–2pm.
Alitalia, 7 Pushechnaya Ul. Tel. 923-9856/9840. Mon–Fri 9am–5pm;
Sat 9am–12pm. Metro Kuznetsky Most.
All Nippon Airways, Sheremetyevo Airport, tel. 578-5744/2921.
Austrian Airlines, Hotel Mezhdunarodnaya, Rm 1805. Tel. 258-2020.
Mon–Fri 8:30am–6:30pm; Sat 8:30am–1pm. Sheremetyevo, tel. 578-2932/2734.
Balkan Bulgarian Airlines, 3 Kuznetsky Most. Tel. 921-0267; 928-9866.
Mon–Fri 9am–6pm; Sat 9am–2pm. Metro Kuznetsky Most.
British Airways, Hotel Mezhdunarodnaya-Sovincenter Rm 1905. Tel. 258-2492.
Mon–Fri 9am–5:30pm. Sheremetyevo, tel. 578-2923/2736.
Continental Airlines, 15 Neglinnaya Ul. Tel. 925-1291; 921-1674. Mon–Fri
9am–5pm. Metro Kuznetsky Most.
CSA Czech Airlines, 21/27 2nd Brestskaya Ul. Tel. 250-4571.
Mon–Fri 9am–5pm. Metro Belorusskaya.
Delta Airlines, Hotel Mezhdunarodnaya/Sovincenter, Rm 1102. Tel. 258-1288.
Mon–Fri 9am–5:30pm.
El Al, Sheremetyevo Airport, tel. 578-6512.
Estonian Air, Sheremetyevo Airport, tel. 578-9301/2190/2186.
Iberia, 3 Kuznetsky Most. Tel. 921-9293; 923-0488. Mon–Fri 10am–6pm.
Metro Kuznetsky Most.
Finnair, 3 Kuznetsky Most. Tel. 292-1758/1762. Mon–Fri 9am–5pm.
Metro Kuznetsky Most.
JAL Japan Airlines, 3 Kuznetsky Most. Tel. 921-6441/6448/6648. Mon–Fri
9am–6pm. Metro Kuznetsky Most.
KLM Royal Dutch Airlines, 35 Usacheva Ul. Tel. 258-3600. Mon–Fri 9am–5pm.
Metro Sportivnaya.
Lithuanian Airlines, 24 Povarskaya Ul. Tel. 203-7502. Mon–Fri 9:30am–6pm;

closed 1–1:30pm. Metro Arbatskaya.

LOT Polish Airlines, 7 Korovy Val. Tel. 238-0313/0003. Mon–Fri 9am–6pm; Sat 9am–4pm. Metro Dobryninskaya.

Lufthansa, 18/1 Olympisky Pr./Hotel Renaissance. Tel. 975-2501. Mon–Fri 9:30am–6pm. Metro Prospekt Mira. Sheremetyevo, tel. 578-2752/2696.

Malev Hungarian Airlines, 21 Povarskaya Ul. Tel. 202-8416. Mon–Fri 9am–4pm. Metro Arbatskaya.

SAS, 3 Kuznetsky Most. Tel. 925-4747. Mon–Fri 9am–5:30pm. Metro Okhotny Ryad. Sheremetyevo, tel. 578-2727.

Swissair, Hotel Mezhdunarodnaya/Sovincenter. Tel. 258-1888. Mon–Sat 9:30am–5:30pm; closed 12–1pm. Sheremetyevo, tel. 578-2932.

Transaero, 3/4 2nd Smolensky Per. Tel. 241-7390/7676. Daily 9am–8pm. Metro Smolenskaya.

RAILWAYS

See Getting Around section for more details on train travel and buying tickets. To book tickets for home or office delivery, call 266-8333 (takes 2–3 days; pay upon delivery). The Central Railway Ticket offices are at 5 Komsomolskaya (tel. 266-9006), 15 Petrovka, and 6 Malaya Kharitovevsky. For rail information concerning all stations, tel. 266-9000.

Byelorussky, 7 Tverskaya Zastava Pl. Tel. 973-8191. Trains to western Europe eg. Berlin, Geneva, Madrid, Vilnius, Smolensk, Brest, Minsk, Prague and Warsaw. *Elektrichka* run to suburbs of Borodino and Zvenigorod. Metro Byelorusskaya.

Kazansky, 2 Komsomolskaya Pl. Tel. 264-6556. Trains to Siberia and Central Asian States. Metro Komsomolskaya.

Kievsky, 2 Kievsky Vokzal Pl. Tel. 240-1115. Trains to the Ukraine and Eastern Europe. *Elektrichka* run to Vnukovo Aeroport and Vladimir. Metro Kievskaya.

Kursky, 29 Zemlyanoi Val Ul. Tel. 917-3152. Trains to Vladimir, Armenia, Azerbaijan, Crimea and Caucasus. (Soon a $200-million three-year reconstruction is planned.) Metro Kurskaya.

Leningradsky, 3 Komsomolskaya Pl. Tel. 262-9143. Trains to St Petersburg, Murmansk, Finland, Novgorod, Pskov and Estonia. Metro Komsomolskaya.

Paveletsky, 1 Paveletskaya Pl. Tel. 235-0522. Trains to Volgograd region. Metro Paveletskaya.

Rizhsky, 2 Rizhsky Vokzal Pl. Tel. 266-0596. Trains to Baltic areas. Metro Rizhskaya.

Savelovsky, Savelosky Vokzal Pl. Tel. 285-9005. Trains to Uglich and Rybinsk areas. Metro Savelovskaya.

Yaroslavsky, 5 Komsomolskaya Pl. Tel. 921-5914. Trains to the Far East. The Trans-Siberian departs daily. *Elektrichka* also run to Sergiyev Posad and Aleksandrov in the Golden Ring area. Trains also stop at Vladimir and Yaroslavl. Metro Komsomolskaya.

ACCOMMODATION

In the 1990s, a lot of new accommodation, from five-star luxury to bargain rooms opened up throughout the city. One can now select a hotel based on location, budget, service and style. (For more information see Being There/Hotels section, page 66.) Find out what amenities are included such as breakfast, private bath, visa suppor, and airport/town center transportation. How close to a Metro station are they? Cheaper hotels can often be far from the city center; you may consider booking a slightly more expensive and more centrally located hotel to save on travel time.

DELUXE—FIVE STAR

Most luxury hotels provide visa invitation services and airport transportation.

Baltschug Kempinski, 1 Baltchug Ul. by the Moskva River, only a short walk from the Kremlin and Tretyakov Gallery. The hotel dates back to 1898, and has over 200 rooms, two restaurants and café, business center and fitness club with pool and sauna. (The area was once known as the *balchug*, a Tartar word meaning muddy.) Tel. 230-6500 (satellite phone 7-501-230-9500); fax 230-6502 (satellite fax 7-501-230-9502). In the US tel. 800-426-3135. Metro Novokuznetskaya/Tretyakovskaya.

Marriott Grand Hotel, in the center of town at 26 Tverskaya Ul. Has over 350 rooms, three restaurants, business center, sports club and pool. Tel. 935-8500; fax 935-8501. Metro Okhotny Ryad.

Metropole-Intercontinental, originally built in 1903 by a British architect in style-moderne and decorated with a ceramic frieze by Vrubel (Rasputin even had an office here); it was completely restored in 1990. At 1 Teatralny Proyezd (near Bolshoi Theater), it has over 350 rooms, five restaurants, bars, business and fitness centers. Tel. 927-6000; fax 927-6010. In the US, tel. 800-462-6686. Metro Teatralny.

National, built in 1903 in style-moderne and reopened in early 1990s after an $80 million transformation. Check out the historic mosaic-façade. (Lenin lived in Room 107 after moving the capital back to Moscow in 1918.) It has over 200 rooms (some with Kremlin views), four restaurants, bars, nightclub, business center, sports club and indoor heated rooftop pool. On the corner of Tverskaya and Okhotny Ryad near Red Square. Tel. 258-7000/7115; fax 258-7100. Metro Okhotny Ryad.

President, at 14 Yakimanka Bol. Ul., was the hotel for former world Communist Party leaders. Now houses tourists with over 200 rooms, restaurant and bar, sauna, business center. Tel. 238-6558; 239-3800; fax 230-2216. Metro Polyanka/Oktyabrskaya.

Radisson Slavyanskaya, 2 Berezhkovskaya Nab., centrally located on banks of Moskva River across from Kiev Station, with over 400 rooms, restaurants, cafés and bar, casino, business center, health club and pool, shopping mall. Tel. 941-8020; fax 941-8000 (satellite fax 7-502-224-1225). In the US, tel. 800-468-3571. Metro Kievskaya.

Renaissance Olympic, located by the northern ring at 18 Olympisky Pr. Has 475 rooms, restaurants and bars, fitness center and pool, shops, business center. Tel. 931-9000/9833; fax 931-9076. Metro Prospekt Mira.

Savoy, formerly known as Hotel Berlin, built in 1912 and fully restored in 1989. Has over 80 rooms, restaurant and bar, business center, art gallery. At 3 Rozhdestvenka Ul., near the old KGB building within the Garden Ring. Tel. 929-8500/8555; fax 230-2186. Metro Kuznetsky Most/Lubyanka.

Sheraton Palace Hotel, 19/1st Tverskaya Yamskaya Ul. (a five-minute drive from the Kremlin), has over 200 rooms, three restaurants, café and bar, business center, sports center, sauna and marble mosaic of Moscow in the lobby. Tel. 931-9700; fax 931-9708. Metro Belorusskaya.

HIGH-END

In the off-season it is worth trying to negotiate prices.

Agmos, a hotel onboard the Riverboat Valery Bryusov docked at Krymskaya Nab. Has 40 rooms, restaurant, bar and casino. Tel. 956-6508; fax 956-6523. Metro Park Kultury.

Aleksander Blok/Inflotel, a hotel onboard the Riverboat Aleksander Blok docked at 12 Krasnopresnenskaya Nab. Also has a lively casino, restaurant and bar. Tel. 255-9284/9278; fax 253-9578. Not easily accessible by public transport; closest Metro Ulitsa 1905 Goda in the northwest.

Alfa, 71 Izmailovsky Park, in the eastern part of town. It has over 1,000 rooms, restaurant, bar and business center. Close to Izmailovsky shopping market. Metro Izmailovsky Park.

Art-Sport Hotel, 2 Third Peschanaya Ul. (overlooking the stadium), run by former German soccer player, Dieter Fritz. It has over 80 rooms, restaurant and bar, sports club, tennis courts and sauna, art gallery. Tel. 955-2300. Metro Sokol at the northern end of town.

Budapesht, 2/18 Petrovskiye Linii, a 19th-century building transformed into a hotel. A central location (behind Bolshoi Theater and a 15-minute walk to the Kremlin), 100 rooms, restaurant and bar, and popular tavern. Tel. 921-1060; 924-8820; fax 921-1266. Metro Teatralnaya/Okhotny Ryad.

Club 27, 27 Malaya Nikitskaya, by the northwest ring. Exclusive club (over 45 rooms) with Victorian atmosphere. Restaurant and bar, business center. Tel. 202-5650; fax 200-1213 (prior fax reservation only). Metro Barrikadnaya.

Danilovsky, 5 Starodanilovsky Pereulok (a ten-minute walk from the Danilovsky Monastery), run by the Orthodox Church. It has over 100 rooms, restaurant and bar, pool and sauna, business center. Tel. 954-0503; fax 954-0750. Metro Tulskaya.

Intourist, 3 Tverskaya Ul., a Soviet-style complex built in the 1970s, near Red Square. Over 450 rooms, restaurants and bars, casino and slots, business center, shops. Tel. 956-8426; fax 956-8416. Metro Okhotny Ryad.

Kosmos, 150 Prospekt Mira, French-built in 1977, in northern end of town. Over 1,700 rooms, four restaurants and bar, casino, bowling, pool and sauna, business center, shops. Tel. 215-6791, 234-1206; fax 215-8880. Metro VDNKh.

Le Meridien Park Hotel, located inside the Moscow Country Club, 30 kilometers (18 miles) outside the city in Nahabino at 30 Volokolamskoye Highway. Access to tennis courts and the 18-hole/72-par golf course designed by Robert Trent Jones, II. (See Vicinity of Moscow section.) Has restaurants and bars, business center, health club, pool and saunas. Tel. 926-5911; fax 926-5921.

Mezhdunarodaya 1 and 2 (International), 12 Krasnoprenenskaya Nab., over 1,000 rooms, restaurants, cafés and bars, fitness club, pool and sauna, business center, shops, and the Sovin business center. Tel. 253-1316, 253-2378; fax 253-2051. Not easily accessible by public transport. Metro Ulitsa 1905 Goda in the northwest.

Moskva, 2 Okhotny Ryad, near the Kremlin. Built in the 1930s, has over 1,000 rooms, restaurants and bars, casino, fitness center, shops. Tel. 292-1100/1002; fax 928-5938. Metro Okhotny Ryad.

Pallada, 14 Ostrovityanova Ul., in southwest part of city. Has over 20 rooms, restaurants and bar, nightclub, sauna (run by ITT Sheraton). Tel. 336-6566/0545; fax 336-9602. Metro Konkovo.

Pekin, 5/1 Bolshaya Sadovaya. Built in the 1950s in Soviet Gothic-style, has over 200 rooms and Moscow's first Chinese restaurant. Tel. 209-2135/3400; fax 200-1420. Metro Mayakovskaya.

Presnya, 9 Spiridonevsky Per., 2 kilometers (1.25 miles) from Red Square near Patriarch's Ponds. Remodeled in 1991 (originally built for visiting Communist bigwigs), over 65 rooms, restaurant and bar, business center, sauna. Tel. 244-3631; fax 926-5404. Metro Mayakovskaya/Pushkinskaya.

Sofitel-Iris, 10 Korovinskoye Highway, at northern end of town. Over 190 rooms, restaurants and bar, fitness complex, pool and sauna, business center and free shuttle service to downtown. Tel. 488-8000; fax 906-0105. Metro Petrovsko-Razumovskaya.

Tverskaya, 27 1st Tverskaya Yamskaya Ul. (next to Sheraton Palace), opened in 1995. Over 150 rooms, restaurant and business center. Tel. 290-9900, 258-3000; fax 258-3099. Metro Belorusskaya.

Ukraina, 21 Kutuzovsky Pr., across from the White House. One of the Stalinist

Gothic skyscrapers, built in 1957, with over 1,000 rooms, restaurant and bars, business center, shops. Tel. 243-3030, 232-0592; fax 243-2596. Metro Kievskaya, a ten-minute walk from hotel.

MODERATE

Altai, 41 Botanicheskaya Ul., in the northern part of the city. Over 1000 rooms and restaurant. Tel. 482-5703; fax 482-5621. Metro Vladykino.

Apogey, 16 Kostromskaya Ul., in northern part of town. Has both guest and apartment-style rooms, café and bar. Tel. 901-8322. Metro Bibirevo.

Arbat, 12 Plotnikov Per., by the western ring. Over 100 rooms, restaurant and bar, business center. Tel. 244-7636; fax 244-0093. Metro Smolenskaya.

Art-Hotel, 41 Vernadsky Pr., near Moscow University and Bolshoi Circus in Sparrow Hills in southwest part of town. Over 50 rooms, bar, pool, solarium and sauna. Tel. 432-7287; fax 432-2757. Metro Prospekt Vernadskovo.

Belgrad, 8 Smolenskaya Ul., by the western ring. Has 450 rooms, two restaurants and business center. Tel. 248-1643; fax 230-2129. Metro Smolenskaya.

Brighton, at 29 Petrovsko-Razumovsky Pr., in northern end of town. Has a small pool and sauna, and fitness center. Tel. 214-9511; fax 214-9332. Metro Dynamo/Dmitrovskaya.

East-West, 14 Tverskoy Bul. Not advertised—they mainly get guests by word of mouth. Over 25 rooms, restaurant and bar, business center, sauna. (Usually only accepts cash; make reservation by fax.) Tel. 290-0404; fax 956-3027. Metro Pushinskaya.

Globus, 17 Yaroslavskaya Ul., in the northern end of town. Over 350 rooms and apartments, restaurant and bar, fitness complex and sauna, and casino. Tel. 286-4189; fax 286-3514. Metro VDNKh.

Izmailovo, 71 Izmailovo Highway, in four complexes (Beta, Vega, Gamma and Delta) with 7,500 rooms. Restaurants and bars, casinos, sauna, business center. Tel. 166-5272. Metro Izmailovsky Park in eastern part of town.

Leningradskaya, 21/40 Kalanchevskaya Ul., another of Moscow's Stalinist skyscrapers built in 1950s. Near to three major railway stations on the northeast part of the ring. Over 300 rooms, restaurant and piano bar, casino, shops, business center. Tel. 975-1815/1850. Metro Komsomolskaya.

Minsk, 22 Tverskaya Ul., centrally located. Has 500 rooms, restaurant and bar. Tel. 299-1001; fax 299-1300. Metro Pushkinskaya.

Park Hotel Mayak, 25 Bolshaya Filevskaya Ul., in western part of town past Fili. Has a restaurant and bar, sauna. Tel. 142-2117; fax 142-2384. Metro Bagrationovskaya.

Rossiya, 6 Varvarka Ul., next to Red Square. One of the largest hotels in the world, with over 5,500 rooms, 9 restaurants, cafés and bars, pool, shops. Tel. 232-5000; fax 232-6262. Metro Kitai-Gorod.

Royal Zenith, 49B Tamanskaya Ul., about 20 minutes from downtown on the Moskva River set in the Serebryany Bor (Silver Forest) area. Opened in 1993, it has over 30 rooms, restaurant and bar, health center, sauna and pool, and provides free shuttle to/from downtown. Tel. 199-3565/2779; fax 199-8101; e-mail: R.Z@g23. relcom.ru; web-site: http://www.royal-zenith.ru. Metro Polezhaevskaya.

Tsentralnaya, 10 Tverskaya Ul., in center of town. Restaurant and bar. Tel. 229-8589/8957. Metro Pushkinskaya.

Volga, has two complexes at 2 Dokuchaev Lane and 4 Bolshaya Spasskaya Ul., inside the northern ring. It also has rooms for long-term residence. Tel. 207-4553, 280-4434; fax 232-3240. Metro Sukharevskaya.

Vostok, 9a Gostinichnaya Ul., in northern end of town. Over 1,200 rooms, café and bar. Tel. 482-2649/4039. The **Voskhod Hotel** is also nearby at 2 Altufyevskoye Highway. Tel. 401-4183/9822. Both are near Metro Vladykino.

INEXPENSIVE

Many of these were built in old Soviet style and have not yet been renovated, but are conveniently located. Some of the bargain hotels offer rooms only with communal bathrooms/showers; check to find out what amenities are included. Note the location, as some are quite far from the center and may not be close to a Metro station.

Arena, 11a 10-Letiya Oktyabrskaya Ul., near the Bolshoi New Circus. Hotel for circus artists, but takes tourists when rooms are available. Tel. 245-2802. Metro Sportivnaya.

Molodyoznaya (Youth), 27/1 Dmitrovskaya Highway, in north of the city. Over 500 rooms, restaurant and café-bar, fitness center. Tel. 977-3283/4011. Metro Timiryazevskaya.

Orlenok (Eagle), 15 Kosygina Ul., in the south. Has a restaurant and café-bar, fitness center and sauna. Tel. 939-8844/8884; fax 938-2200. Metro Leninsky Prospekt.

Ostankino, 29 Botanicheskaya Ul., in the north. Over 1,700 rooms, restaurant, café-bar. Tel. 219-4526/6590; fax 219-4547. Metro Vladykino.

Salut, 158 Leninsky Pr., in southwest part of town. Has a restaurant and café-bar, fitness center and casino. Tel. 234-9292. Metro Yugo-Zapadnaya.

Tsentralny Dom Turista (Central House of Tourists), 146 Leninsky Pr., near the Salut Hotel, with restaurants and bars, sauna and pool, casino and shops. Tel. 438-9562, 434-9467; fax 438-7756. Metro Yugo-Zapadnaya.

Savastopol, 1a Bolshaya Yushunskaya Ul., a hotel complex at the southern end of the city, has 550 rooms, restaurant, sauna, casino. Tel. 318-0390/6474; fax 318-0918. Metro Sevastopolskaya/Kakhovskaya.

Seventh Floor, 88/1 Prospekt Vernadskovo, a small bed and breakfast hotel in southwest, with restaurant and bar. Tel. 437-9997, 956-6038. Metro Yugo-Zapadnaya.

Sovyetsky Hotel, 32/2 Leningradsky Pr., in the north of town (once the old snoring ground of the Communist Party Central Committee). Has over 100 rooms, restaurant and café-bar, business center. The Gypsy Theater Roman is also located in the complex. Tel. 960-2000, 250-7253; fax 960-2006. Metro Dynamo.

Soyuz-1, 12 Levoberezhnaya Ul., near the Moskva River, in the north of town. Has a restaurant and café. A 15-minute bus ride from Metro Rechnoi Vokzal, the last stop on the line.

Sputnik, 38 Leninsky Pr., in the south of the city, run by the Independent Trade Union. Has 500 rooms, restaurant and café-bar, sauna. Tel. 930-2287, 938-7057; fax 930-6383. Metro Leninsky Prospekt.

Tourist, 17/2 Selskokhozyaystvennaya Ul., in the north of town, near Yauza River. A complex of seven buildings with a restaurant and bar. Ask for an upgraded room. Tel. 187-3894/5211; fax 187-6018. Metro Botanichesky Sad, a five-minute walk away.

Universitetskaya, 8 Michurinsky Pr., in Sparrow Hills, in the southwest. Has over 150 rooms, café-bar and sauna. Tel. 939-9770; fax 956-1155. Metro Universitet.

Vega, 11 Begovaya Alleya, in the northwest, run by the Ministry of Agriculture and Hippodrome. Has 70 double rooms, restaurant and bar, sauna. Tel. 945-5213; fax 946-1537. Metro Begovaya.

Yaroslavskaya, 8 Yaroslavskaya Ul., a complex of seven buildings with over 550 rooms, restaurant and café-bar, sauna. Tel. 217-6643/6695. Metro VDNKh.

Yunost (Youth), 34 Khamovnichesky Val, in the southwest part of the city. Has over 100 rooms, restaurant, sauna. Tel. 242-4860; fax 242-0284. Metro Sportivnaya.

Yuzhny (Southern), 87 Leningradsky Pr., in the southwest, with over 250 rooms, restaurant and café, business center. Tel. 134-3065/3086; fax134-9326. Metro Universitet. Across the street, at no. 90, is the **Sport Hotel**, with over 300 rooms, restaurant and bar, casino, sauna. Tel. 131-3515/4141. Metro Prospekt Vernadskovo.

Zarya (Dawn), 4 Gostinichnaya Ul., in five buildings at the northern end of town. Restaurants and cafés, fitness rooms. Tel. 482-0738/2106; fax 482-0692. Metro Vladykino/Petrovsko-Razumovskaya.

Zolotoy Kolos (Golden Spike), 15 Yaroslavskaya Ul., in six buildings, at the northern end of town. Tel. 217-4251, 286-2703; fax 217-4356. Metro VDNKh.

Zvezdnaya (Star), 2 Argunovskaya Ul., has a café-bar, business center. Tel. 215-4292/4265/4101; fax 215-4013. Metro Alekseevskaya/VDNKh.

HOTELS NEAR INTERNATIONAL SHEREMETEVO-II AIRPORT

Aerostar, 37 Leningradsky Pr., in the northern part of the city halfway from town to the International Airport. Over 400 rooms, restaurants, café and bar, business center. Ask for a room facing Petrovsky Palace. Tel. 213-9000; fax 213-9001. In the US, tel. 800-843-3311. Metro Dynamo/Aeroport. (Another hotel at this location at Complex 5 is the **Aeroflot** used mainly by airport transit passengers. Tel. 151-7543.)

Novotel, located 200 meters from Sheremetevo-II International Airport. Built in 1992 with over 400 rooms, restaurant and bar, business center, fitness complex. Tel. 926-5900; fax 926-5904. In the US, tel. 800-221-4542. Metro Rechnoi Vokzal.

Sheremetevo-II, mainly used by transit passengers. It has a restaurant, gym and sauna. Tel. 578-5794/3464; fax 753-8091. Metro Rechnoi Vokzal.

HOSTELS

Traveller's Guest House/Hostel, 50 Pereyaslavskaya Bol. Ul., 10th floor, located near the northern ring. Over 15 rooms (single, double and dormitory), restaurant and café-bar, kitchen and laundry facilities, visa support and travel bureau (tel. 974-1781). Set up as a partner to Youth Hostel in St Petersburg. Tel. 280-8562, 971-4059; fax 280-7686; e-mail: tgh@glas.apc.org. Metro Rizhskaya.

For bed and breakfasts, host families, homestays, see Useful Addresses on page 550 for contact information.

CAMPING

Most sites are only open in the summer months; some also offer small wooden *domik* structures to rent. (Camping is not advised, due to increased crime.)

Rus-Hotel, Varshovskoye Highway, 21 kilometers (13 miles) from city. Tel. 382-1465; 384-4101; fax 382-1410. Metro Yuzhnaya and bus.

Yut, 5 Butovskaya Bolshaya Ul. Tel. 712-7136/7450. Metro Yuzhnaya and bus.

Dubrava, located in the village of Mytishchi in the Moscow region. Tel. 582-5597. Metro Medvedkovo and bus.

RENTALS

Acme Real Estate, 11 Sadovaya-Kudrinskaya. Tel. 252-7644. Metro Barrikadnaya.

Blackwood, 1/15 Kotelnicheskaya Nab. Tel. 956-3307. Metro Kitai-Gorod.

Claremount Group, 21 Novy Arbat. Tel. 291-2323. Metro Arbatskaya.

Flat Finders, 9/1 Kutuzovsky Prospekt. Tel. 142-1835. Metro Kievskaya.

JAT Ltd, 5 Nikoyamskoi Lane. Tel. 915-0014. Metro Taganskaya.

Noble Gibbons, 20 Pechatnikov Lane. Tel. 258-3990. Metro Turgenevskaya.

DINING

If you haven't visited Russia since the Socialist era, it's time to be flabbergasted at the sight of over 1,000 eating establishments in Moscow alone—from cafés and fast-food to the most elegant restaurants in old palaces and new hotels. If not in the mood for the classic Russian fare, hundreds of ethnic restaurants from Italian to Vietnamese have sprung up throughout the city; many are open well past midnight, and even offer live music or variety shows, and have wine, beer and other alcoholic beverages. Every type of dish imaginable is available, as well as matching prices, which vary from the very cheap to amazingly expensive. The larger hotels all have their own restaurants, bars and cafés; and for many restaurants, reservations are recommended. Besides Russian rubles, many establishments also accept credit cards. Decide what cuisine you're game for, then check the restaurant's location by finding its Metro stop on the map.

So many food stores, supermarkets and mini-malls have opened, just ask the hotel staff to direct you to the nearest one. A few supermarkets can be found in the Ukraina Hotel, the Arbat Irish House at 13 Novy Arbat, and Kalinka Stockman at 2 Zatsepsky Val. A Westerner can now find practically everything in Moscow that is available at home. (See the Menu Vocabulary on page 564.)

ARMENIAN

Dukhan Shavo, 58 Karamyshevskaya Nab. Tel. 197-1975. Armenian, Georgian and Russian food; draft beer. Live music after 8pm. Daily 11am–11pm. Metro Polezhaevskaya.

Elegans, 9 Maly Ivanovsky Per. Tel. 917-3108. Armenian dishes and live music 8pm–12am. Daily 12pm–12am. Metro Kitai-Gorod.

Moosh, 2 Oktyabrskaya Ul. Tel. 284-3670. Traditional Armenian dishes and wines; light music. Daily 10am–11pm. Metro Novoslobodskaya.

U Tigranycha, 13 Lesnaya Ul. Tel. 251-0257. Armenian cuisine and live music. Daily 1–11pm. Metro Belorusskaya.

ARABIC

Flamingo, with Arabic and Russian specialties, has three locations at: 18 Sadovaya-Triumfalnaya Ul. Daily 12pm–12am. Metro Mayakovskaya. 6 Maroseyka Ul. Disco. Daily 12:30pm–6am. Metro Kitai-Gorod. 48 Prospekt Mira. Daily 12:30pm–3am. Metro Prospekt Mira.

AZERBAIJANI

Agdam, 4 Khlebnikov Lane. Tel. 278-7149. Azerbaijani cuisine and live music after 7pm. Daily 12pm–5am. Metro Ploshchad Ilicha.

Farkhad, 4 Bolshaya Marfinskaya Ul. Tel. 218-4136. Azerbaijani and Turkish food. Open 24 hours. Metro Vladykino.

BAKERIES

Moscow has bread and bakery stores practically on every corner. Freshly baked goods abound; a must is trying the traditional Russian brown or black bread. To order in Russian: *khleb* is bread; *baton* (oval white loaf); *bely kirpich* (white brick loaf); *chorny kirpich* (dark brick loaf); *tort* (sweet cake); *bulochki* (sweet rolls). The **French Bakery** is at 3 Boyarsky Per. Daily 8am–9pm. Metro Krasniye Vorota.

CHINESE

Dao, Gorky Park. Chinese food and music. Daily 11am–11pm. Metro Oktybrskaya.
Dinastiya, 29 Zubovsky Bulvar. Tel. 246-5017. Traditional Chinese cuisine. Daily 11:30am–11pm. Metro Park Kultury.
Jonka, 22 Tverskoi Bulvar. Tel. 203-9420. Open 24 hours. Metro Pushkinskaya.
Khram Luny (Temple of the Moon), 1 Bolshoi Kislovsky Per. Tel. 291-0401. Variety of seafood dishes, and Chinese music. Daily 1:30–11pm. Metro Biblioteka Imeni Lenina.
Kitaisky Sad (Chinese Garden), in the Mezhdunarodny Hotel. Daily 12:30pm–12am.
Lili Vong, in the Intourist Hotel. Tel. 956-8301. Daily 12pm–12am. Metro Okhotny Ryad.
Palma, 11 Novy Arbat/2nd floor. Tel. 291-2221. Chinese, Taiwanese and Thai cuisine and karaoke. Daily 11am–11pm. Metro Arbatskaya.
Panda, 3 Tverskoi Bulvar. Tel. 298-6565. Musical ensemble. Daily 12pm–12am. Metro Tverskaya.
Pekin in Moscow, in the Pekin Hotel. Tel. 209-1815. Moscow's first Chinese restaurant. Live music after 7pm. Daily 12pm–4am. Metro Mayakovskaya.
Zolotoy Drakon (Golden Dragon), 64 Plyushchikha Ul. Tel. 248-3602. Chinese chef and Chinese music. Daily 12pm–5am. Metro Smolenskaya.

COFFEE

For over 30 types of coffee, go the the **Coffee Bean**, at 9 Pushechnaya Ul. Metro Pushkinskaya.

ETHIOPIAN

Kantri-bar, 50 Pokrovka Ul. Tel. 917-2882. Ethiopian and European-style dishes and wine. Live music on Thurs and Sat after 9pm. Daily 11–12am; Thurs–Sat 11–2am. Metro Krasniye Vorota.

EUROPEAN AND AMERICAN

Ambassador, 29 Preschistenka Ul. Both Continental and Russian-style fare and piano music. Daily 12–11:30pm. Metro Kropotkinskaya.

Amsterdam, 30 Pyatniktskaya Ul. Tel. 231-4244. Small restaurant offering European cuisine and draft beer. Daily 10am–11pm. Metro Novokuznetskaya.

Angelicos, 6 Bolshoi Karetny Per. Tel. 299-3696. Mediterrenean cuisine and a Swiss management. Daily 11–2am. Metro Tsvetnoy Bulvar.

Burbon and Biifsteaks, 8 Bryusov Per. Tel. 229-7185. In the House of Composers. European and Caucasian dishes and selection of beers. Daily 12pm–12am. Metro Okhotny Ryad.

La Gourmet, 1 Bolshaya Polyanka. Tel. 238-8911. European food, draft beer and homemade ice cream. Open 24 hours. Metro Polyanka.

Le Gastronome, 1 Kudrinskaya Pl. Tel. 255-4554. European food and live music 1–3pm. Daily 12pm–12am. Metro Barrikadnaya.

Nostalgie Art-Cafe, 12a Chistoprudny Bulvar. Tel. 916-9090. European-French food, draft beers and live music after 8pm. Daily 12–11:30pm. Metro Chistiye Prudy.

Sankt Petersburg, in the National Hotel. Mediterranean cuisine and seafood. Piano and violin music after 7pm. Daily 6–11pm. Metro Okhoyny Ryad.

Savoy Hotel, has the Savoy Restaurant with European and Russian dishes, and live jazz and classical music after 7:30pm. Downstairs at the restaurant-bar one can order a quick burger or Russian *blinis* and watch CNN on TV. Metro Lubyanka.

Skandinaviya, 7 Maly Palshevsky Per. Tel. 200-4986. Traditional Swedish dishes, wines and beer. Daily 12pm–12am. Metro Tverskaya.

EASTERN EUROPEAN

Budapesht, 2 Petrovskiye Linii, in the Budapest Hotel. Tel. 924-4283. Hungarian food. Daily 12pm–12am. Metro Kuznetsky Most.

Morova, 3 Sadovaya-Kudrinskaya Ul. Tel. 254-3648. Yugoslavian cuisine and live music Mon–Sat after 8pm. Daily 12–11pm; Sun 12–10pm. Metro Barrikadnaya.

Praga, 2 Arbat. Tel. 291-4185. Czech food and German draft beer. Metro Arbatskaya.

Ukraina, in the Ukraine Hotel. Tel. 243-3297. Live music, disco, jazz club and variety show. Daily 8–11pm. Metro Kievskaya.

FRENCH

Brasserie du Soleil, 23 Taganskaya Ul. Tel. 258-5900. Daily 12pm–12am. Metro Taganskaya.

Klub-T, 21 Krasina Ul. Tel. 232-2778. French food and wines. Live music after 7pm. Daily 12pm–12am. Metro Mayakovskaya.

Maxim's de Paris, in the National Hotel. Tel. 258-7148. Live music after 8pm; jacket and tie. Daily 12pm–12am; closed 3–7pm. Metro Okhotny Ryad.

Reporter-Nostalgie, 6 Gogolevsky Bulvar. Tel. 956-9997. French food and wines, live music after 8pm. Daily 12pm–12am. Metro Kropotkinskaya.

Tri Peskarya, 4 Zubovsky Bulvar. Tel. 201-8738. French and Russian food. European wines. Live classical music. Daily 12pm–12am. Metro Park Kultury.

GEORGIAN

Aist, 1 Malaya Bronnaya. Tel. 291-6692. Small Georgian-Russian restaurant Mon–Sat 12–10pm. Metro Pushkinskaya.

Aragvi, 6 Tverskaya Ul. Georgian musical ensemble after 7pm. Daily 12pm–12am. Metro Okhotny Ryad.

Iberiya, 5 Rozhdestvenka Ul. Tel. 928-2672. Georgian dishes and wines, and live music after 7:30pm. Daily 12pm–12am. Metro Kuznetsky Most.

Pitsunda, 3 Krzhizhanovskaya Ul. Tel. 125-2782. Georgian and European food and wines, and Georgian music. Daily 11am–10pm. Metro Profsoyuznaya.

U Nikitskikh Vorot, 23 Bolshaya Nikitskaya Ul. Tel. 290-2845. Georgian wines and live music 7–11pm. Daily 12–11pm. Metro Tverskaya.

U Pirosmani, 4 Novodevichy Passage. Tel. 247-1926. Overlooks Novodevichy Convent and has Georgian wines, live music and a lovely Tbilisi decor with paintings by Georgian artist Pirosmani. Daily 12:45–10:30pm. Metro Sportivnaya.

INDIAN

Darbar, 38 Leninsky Prospekt in Sputnik Hotel. Tel. 938-8008. Indian Mughlai and South Indian food and live Indian music. Open 12–11pm.

Kohinoor, 101 Prospekt Mira. Tel. 287-8127. Indian food and European wines. Live music after 6pm. Daily 12pm–12am. Metro Alekseevskaya.

Moscow Bombay, 3 Glinishchevsky Per. Tel. 292-9731. Wide choice of Indian, Chinese, European and vegetarian dishes. Oriental dancing. Metro Pushkinskaya.

ITALIAN

Artistichesky, 6 Kamergersky Per. Tel. 292-4042. Has been serving theater stars since before the Revolution. Italian-European cooking. Daily 12pm–12am. Metro Teatralnaya.

Belfiori, 10 Petrovka Ul. 3rd floor. Tel. 924-9658. Italian dishes, French wines and live music after 6pm. Daily 12–11pm. Metro Kuznetsky Most.

Bella Napoli, 30 Leningradsky Prospekt. Tel. 214-7311. Italian dishes, pizza, Austrian beer and live music on Thurs–Sat nights. Daily 12pm–12am. Metro Belorusskaya.

Dolce Vita, 88 Taganskaya Pl. Tel. 915-1130. Italian and other European-style dishes and wines. Live music after 8pm. Daily 12pm–12am. Metro Taganskaya.

Dzhokonda, in Rossiya Hotel. Tel. 298-5361. Sicilian dishes. Open terrace with view of Kremlin and live music Tues–Sun after 8pm. Metro Kitai-Gorod.

Il Pomodoro, 5 Bolshoi Golovin Per. Tel. 924-2931. Italian dishes and wines. Daily 12–11pm. Metro Tsvetnoi Bulvar.

Italiya, 49 Arbat. Tel. 241-4342. Italian chef. Bottled and draft beer and live music after 8pm. Daily 12pm–2am. Metro Smolenskaya.

La Peria, 6 Barykovsky Per. Tel. 203-6865. Italian dishes and live music after 6pm. Daily 12–11:30pm. Metro Kropotkinskaya.

Le Stelle del Pescatore, 7 Pushechnaya Ul. Tel. 924-2058. Italian/Russian food, draft beer, Italian wines and piano music. Daily 12pm–1am. Metro Kuznetsky Most.

Patio Pasta, 3/1st Tverskaya Yamskaya, has a wide variety of pasta dishes. Express lunch from 12–3pm. Mon–Fri 12pm–12am. Metro Mayakovskaya.

San Marko, 25 Arbat. Tel. 291-7089. Daily 12–11pm. Metro Arbatskaya.

Spago, 1 Bolshoi Zlatoustinsky Per. Tel. 921-3797. Italian food and wines. Daily 12–11pm. Metro Lubyanka.

JAPANESE

Fuji, 32 Dmitrovka Ul. Tel. 200-0717. Prepares food flown in from Japan.

Sapporo, 14 Prospekt Mira. Tel. 207-0198. Authenic Japanese cuisine and sushi, karaoke and live music after 6pm. Daily 12–11pm; closed 4–6pm. Metro Prospekt Mira.

Tokyo, in the Rossiya Hotel. Tel. 298-5707. Beer, wine and live music. Daily 12–11pm. Metro Kitai-Gorod.

Tosahan, 12 Rozhdestvenka Ul. Tel. 925-6990. Karaoke bar. Daily 12:30–11pm; closed 3–6pm. Bar open 6pm–1am. Metro Kuznetsky Most.

JEWISH

U Yuzefa, 11 Dubininskaya Ul. Tel. 238-4646. Jewish and Russian dishes, and live music. Daily 12–11pm. Metro Paveletskaya.

KOREAN

Arirang Seoul, 5 Strelbishchensky Proyezd. Tel. 256-0897. South Korean cooking. Daily 12–11pm. Metro Ulitsa 1905 Goda.

Koreisky Dom (Korean House), 26 Volgogradsky Prospekt. Tel. 270-9070. Korean food and beer, karaoke and live music after 7:30pm. Daily 11–1am. Metro Volgogradsky.

Ozake-Okryu, 4/26 Ulitsa Bakinskikh Komissarov. Tel. 433-2201. Live music after 7pm. Daily 12–11pm. Metro Yugo-Zapadnaya.

Pkhenyan, 23 Sretenka Ul. Tel. 208-0654. Korean specialties and music. Daily 1–11pm. Metro Sukharevskaya.

MEXICAN

Azteca, 3 Tverskaya Ul. 2nd fl. Intourist Hotel. Tel. 956-8490. Authentic Tex-Mex and live music after 7pm. Daily 12pm–5am. Metro Teatralnaya.

El Kokodrilo, 30 Myasnitskaya Ul. Tel. 924-1986. Mexican, Cuban and Italian. Tequila Smash Bar. Daily 4–11pm. Metro Chistiye Prudy.

Sante Fe, 5 Mantulinskaya Ul. Tel. 256-1487. Mexican-American, margaritas and live music; disco after 8pm. Metro Ulitsa 1905 Goda.

RUSSIAN

Arkhitektor, 7 Granatny Per. Tel. 291-7738. Located in the Architect's House. Russian food and draft beer brewed on the premises. Mon–Sat 1–10pm. Metro Barrikadnaya.

Atrium, 44 Leninsky Prospekt. Tel. 137-3008. Greek-style interior and serves Russian and European food. Daily 12–11pm. Metro Leninsky Prospekt.

Danilovsky, 5 Starodanilovsky Lane (at the monastery). Tel. 954-0503. Russian food, draft beer, light music and breakfast from 10 to noon. Daily 8am–11pm. Metro Tulskaya.

Dom Kinematografistov, 13 Vasilevskaya Ul. Tel. 251-8320. In the House of Cinematographers. Live music after 8pm. Daily 2pm–12am. Metro Mayakovskaya.

Grand Imperial, 9 Gagarinsky Per. Tel. 291-6063. Russian and European specialties. French wines and piano music in the afternoon. Daily 12pm–12am. Metro Kropotkinskaya.

Karetny Ryad, 2 Karetny Ryad. Tel. 299-3021. Located in an old mansion; serves Russian-European food and wines. Jazz and blues music after 7pm. Metro Chekovskaya.

Kitai-Gorod, 14 Varvarka Ul. Tel. 298-4672. Russian and European dishes and live music after 7pm. Daily 11–12am. Metro Kitai-Gorod.

Klub 27, 27 Malaya Nikitskaya St. Tel. 202-5650. Russian-European and light music. Daily 12:30pm–12am. Metro Barrikadnaya.

Klub Pisateley (Writers Club), 50 Povarskaya Ul. Tel. 291-1515. Old Russian and European-style dishes. Daily 11am–11pm. Metro Leninsky Prospekt.

Kropotkinskaya 36, 36 Prechistenka Ul. Tel. 201-7500. One of Moscow's first cooperative restaurants, has traditional Russian food and live piano music. Metro Kropotkinskaya.

Margarita, 28 Malaya Bronnaya Ul. (near Patriarch's Pond). Tel. 299-6534. Daily 1pm–12am. Metro Pushkinskaya.

Moskovsky, in the National Hotel. Tel. 258-7000. Traditional Russian dishes and folklore ensemble. Daily 6:30–11pm. Metro Okhotny Ryad.

Russky Okhotnichky Klub (Hunter's Club), 31 Bukhvostova Ul. Tel. 962-0677. Old-style Russian cooking prepared from 18th–19th-century recipes. Wines and beer. Daily 2–11pm. Metro Preobrazhenskaya Ploshchad.

Russky Souvenir, 23 Petrovka Ul. Tel. 200-5626. Russian specialties; waiters in traditional costumes. Light music. Daily 12–11pm. Metro Pushkinskaya.

Russky Traktir, 44 Arbat. Tel. 241-9853. Scores of traditional specialties and draft beer. Live music, cossack ensemble and Gypsy entertainment. Daily 12pm–5am. Metro Smolenskaya.

Samovar, 13 Myasnitskaya Ul. Tel. 921-4688. Fine decor of old samovars.

Stanislavskovo 2, 26 Bolshaya Nikitskaya Ul. Tel. 291-8689. Russian dishes and classical piano and violin music. Open 6pm–2am; closed Mondays.

Strastnoi 7, 7 Strastnoi Bulvar. Tel. 299-0498. Italian wines and live music. Daily 12–11pm. Metro Chekhovskaya.

U Babushki, 42 Bolshaya Ordynka. Tel. 230-2797. Homemade Russian specialties, European wines and live music 7–11pm. Daily 12–11pm. Metro Tretyakovskaya.

Yakor, 2 Mamonovsky Per. Tel. 299-2951. Russian seafood dishes. Interior modeled as a ship. Live music 6–10pm. Daily 12–11pm. Metro Tverskaya.

SPANISH AND CUBAN

Don Quixote, 4 Pokrovsky Bulvar. Tel. 917-4757. Spanish food and wines. Daily 12pm–12am. Metro Kitai-Gorod.

Ispansky Ugolok (Spanish Corner), 13 Bolshaya Dmitrovka Ul. Tel 229-7023. Spanish chef. Live music and shows from 8pm. Daily 12pm–12am. Metro Okhotny Ryad.

Kashtan, 40 Taganskaya Ul. Tel. 912-6242. Cuban-style food and has music. Mon–Sat 12–11pm. Metro Marksistskaya.

Taverna Miramar, 30 Myasnitskaya Ul. Tel. 924-2094. Cuban and Mexican dishes and wines, and live music. Daily 9–6am. Metro Turgenevskaya.

SOUTH AMERICAN

Buldog, 10 Rozhdestvensky Bulvar. Tel. 928-2800. Peruvian fare, beer and live music. Daily 12pm–12am. Metro Kuznetsky Most.

El Gaucho, 3 Kozlovsky Lane. Tel. 923-1098. Argentine cooking and French wines. Live music. Daily 12pm–12am. Metro Krasniye Vorota.

SUNDAY BRUNCH

Metropole Hotel, the Metropole provides a huge breakfast buffet, live jazz band and elegant decor. Open 7–11am; Sunday brunch 12–4pm. The Boyarksky Zal serves traditional Russian cuisine. Sunday brunch 12–4pm; other days 7–10:30am, and daily 7pm–1am. Metro Tealtralnaya.

Sofitel-Iris Hotel, the Elisyskie Polya provides a European Sunday brunch; other days open 7pm–12am, offering classical French cuisine. The France serves Sunday brunch (October–May) 12–4pm. 10 Korovinskoye Highway. Metro Petrovsko-Razumovskaya.

Radisson-Slavyanskaya Hotel, the Skandia Restaurant, a Swedish table. Metro Kievskaya.

National Hotel, has Sunday brunch and breakfasts (7–11am) at the Slavyansky. Metro Okhotny Ryad. And the **Intourist Hotel** offers buffet-style breakfasts every morning.

Sante Fe, 5 Mantulinskaya Ul., has American-Mexican fare. Sunday brunches 12–5pm. Metro Ulitsa 1905 Goda.

Planet Hollywood, an American-style Sunday brunch. Open daily 11–1am. 23b Krasnaya Presnya. Metro Krasnogvardeiskaya.

THAI
Bangkok, 10 Bolshoi Strochenovsky Per. Tel. 237-3074. Classic Thai dishes, live music after 8pm and shows on Saturday nights. Daily 1–11pm. Metro Paveletskaya.

TURKISH
Almateya, 28 Stremyanni Lane. Turkish specialties, wines and draft beer. Live music and Eastern dancers. Daily 11–12am. Metro Serpukhovskaya.

Petrovsky Dvorik, 17 Preobrazhensky Val. Tel. 161-1806. Turkish food and Russian appetizers, Turkish music and a variety show. Daily 7pm–2am. Metro Preobrazhenskaya Ploshchad.

Vitosha-Nostalgiya, 35 Khoroshevskoye Shosse. Tel. 195-4114. Turkish and European food. Daily 12pm–12am; closed 4–5pm. Metro Taganskaya.

UZBEKISTAN
Navruz, 36 Begovaya Ul. Tel. 945-0457. Uzbek dishes, wine and beer, and live music. Daily 12pm–12am. Metro Begovaya.

Uzbekistan, 29 Neglinnaya Ul. Tel. 924-6053. Wines and Gypsy entertainment. Daily 12–11pm. Metro Kuznetsky Most.

VIETNAMESE
Dolina, 18a Koptevskaya Ul. Tel. 459-4423. Vietnamese cuisine, German beer, and music. Daily 12–11pm. Metro Voykovkskaya.

Hanoi, 20 60th Oktybrsky Prospekt. Tel. 125-1438. Live chamber music in the evenings. Daily 12pm–12am. Metro Akademicheskaya.

Kuilong 9 Dragons, 7 Litovsky Bulvar. Tel. 425-1111. Vietnamese chef, and live music. Open 4pm–12am; closed Mondays. Metro Yasenevo.

Shopping

ANTIQUES

Before purchasing an antique made prior to World War II, always check to see if you need special permission to take it out of the country—particularly icons, artwork and samovars; otherwise it could be confiscated at customs upon departure. Beware of fake icons, artwork and lacquer boxes.

Antiques on Myasnitskoi, 13 Myasnitskaya Ul. Closed Sundays. Metro Pushkinskaya.

Metropole Antiques, alongside Metropole Hotel. Open daily at 11am. Metro Teatralnaya.

Antiques on Bronnaya, 27/4 Bolshaya Bronnaya. Mon–Sat 12–7pm. Metro Pushkinskaya.

Antonika, 4 Arbat. Closed Sundays. Metro Arbatskaya. (On Arbat, also check out shops at numbers 6, 11, 18, 31, 36.)

Galleriya Shon, 12 Nikitsky Bulvar. Open daily. Metro Arbatskaya.

House of Books, 8 Novy Arbat, has a collection of icons and other old items on the first floor. (On the same street, check out number 21.)

Izmailovsky Market, on the weekends has a large selection of old items from icons to coins. Metro Izmailovsky Park.

Moskva, 8 Tverskaya. Closed Sundays. Metro Okhotny Ryad.

Starina, 24 Petrovka Ul. Closed Sundays. Metro Pushkinskaya.

ART GALLERIES

In the Arbat check out premises at numbers 1, 4, 6, and 55.

Art Gallery, 14 Zemlyanoi Val. Open daily.

ASTI, 5 Tverskaya Ul. Closed Sun/Mon. Metro Okhotny Ryad.

Dom-A, 5 Starosadsky Lane. Closed Sun/Mon. Metro Kitai-Gorod.

Future Classic, 58 Gilyarovskaya Ul. Closed Sundays. Metro Prospekt Mira.

Intercolor, 24/2 Malaya Dmitrovka. Closed Mondays. Metro Mayakovskaya. (Another, **Lasta**, is at number 18.)

Kitai-Gorod, 14 Varvarka Ul. Closed Sundays. Metro Kitai-Gorod.

Les Oreades and Ir-Art, 10/14 Krymsky Val. Closed Mondays. Metro Oktyabrkskaya.

Moscow Fine Art Gallery, 3/20 Sadovaya Ul. Closed Sundays. Metro Smolenskaya.

Universal Art Gallery, 29/14 Neglinnaya Ul. Closed Mondays. Metro Tsvetnoi Bulvar.

ARTS AND HANDICRAFTS

Azhur, 5 Zabelina Ul. Closed Saturdays and Sundays. Metro Kitai-Gorod.

Arbatskaya Lavitsa, 27 Arbat. Closed Sundays. Metro Arbatskaya. (**Souvenirs** is at number 23, and **Mziuri** at number 42.)

Iskusstvo (Art), 52/54 Ul. Bolshaya Yakimanka. Closed Sundays. Metro Oktybrskaya.
Salon on Pyatnitskoi, 16/2 Pyanitskaya Ul. Closed Sundays. Metro Tretyakovskaya.

BOOKSTORES
Biblio-Globe, 6 Myasnitskaya. Literature in foreign languages. Closed Sundays. Metro Lubyanka.
Foreign Books, 16 Malaya Nikitskaya Ul. Closed Sundays. Metro Barrikadnaya.
House of Books, 8 Novy Arbat. This is the place to go for books, posters, cards. Closed Sundays. Metro Arbatskaya.
Moskva, 8 Tverskaya. Now the largest bookstore in Moscow. Closed Sundays. Metro Pushkinskaya.
Progress, 17 Zubovsky Bulvar. Open daily. Metro Park Kultury.
Zwemmer Bookshop, 18 Kuznetsky Most. Books in English. Metro Kuznetsky Most.

CARPETS AND RUGS
Many department and commission stores carry new and antique rugs. Check also at outdoor markets and the Izmailovsky weekend market.
Antikvariat, 54 Frunzenskaya Nab., has antique and modern rugs. Closed Sun. Metro Park Kultury.
Dina-T, in the Radisson-Slavyanskaya Hotel. Open daily. Metro Kievskaya.
Fortuna, 6 Poklonnaya Ul. Closed Sundays. Metro Kutuzovskaya.
Kovroy Oazis (Carpet Oasis), 7 Kuznetsky Most. Closed Saturdays and Sundays. Metro Kuznetsky Most.
Kovry (Rugs), in Petrovsky Passazh Store. 10 Petrovka Ul. Metro Okhotny Ryad.
Kommissiony (Commission), 16/1st Tverskaya-Yamskaya, sell old and special rugs. Closed Sundays. Metro Mayakovskaya.
Moskovskaya Kovrovaya Kompaniya (Moscow Carpet Co.), in the Olympic Sports Complex, 16 Olympisky Prospekt. Open daily. Metro Prospekt Mira.

DEPARTMENT STORES
Over 100 department stores are scattered throughout the city. These are the largest and most popular and centrally located.
GUM, 3 Red Square. Mon–Sat 8am–8pm; Sun 11am–6pm. Metro Ploshchad Revolutsii.
Petrovsky Passazh, 10 Petrovka Ul. Mon–Sat 10am–8pm; Sun 11am–6pm. Metro Kuznetsky Most.
TsUM, 2 Petrovka Ul. Mon–Sat 8am–8pm; Sun 10am–6pm. Metro Teatralnaya.
Underground Shopping Mall, in front of the Moskva Hotel by Red Square; Metro Okhotny Ryad. Open daily.

FURS

Fur auctions are held three times a year in January, May or June, and October. The best prices for fur hats are found at markets and department stores.

Arbat-28, 28 Arbat. Closed Sundays. Metro Arbatskaya.

Mekhovoy Kholodilnik, 11 Bolshaya Dmitrovka Ul. Closed Saturdays and Sundays. Metro Pushkinskaya.

Universal-Moda, 26 Novy Arbat. Closed Saturdays and Sundays. Metro Arbatskaya.

GIFTS AND SOUVENIRS

Many souvenir shops and kiosks are located throughout the city; stroll down the Arbat, through Izmailovsky weekend market, or the underground shopping center in front of the Moskva Hotel near Red Square. Also wander through the larger department stores such as GUM or Passazh. Traditional stores called *Beriozka* carry a variety of Russian gift items, such as *matryoshka* dolls, handpainted pottery, lacquerware and boxes, samovars, amber jewelry and handicrafts; these are found in many hotel and city locations. Most stores are open daily from about 11am–7pm and are closed on Sundays.

On the Arbat, shops can be found at no. 27 (**Arbatskaya Lavitsa**), no. 29 and 36 (**Skazki Strarovo Arbata**—Fairy Tales of old Arbat) no. 31 (**Russkaya Vyshivka**—Russian Embroidery), and no. 42 (**Mziuri**). At 16 Petrovka Ul. are both **Kleopatra** and **Russkiye Uzory** (Russian Ornaments).

Gzhel, 2 Sadovaya-Samotechnaya Ul., has national handpainted pottery at Metro Mayakovskaya.

Master, 31 Povarskaya Ul., also carries Gzhel and Khokhloma lacquerware. This address is also the **Research Industry of Art** which carries additional pottery and Palekh lacquer boxes. Metro Barrikadnaya.

Iskusstvo (Art), 52 Yakimanka Ul., has paintings, graphics and handicrafts. Metro Oktyabrskaya.

Podarki (Gifts), 4 Tverskaya Ul., and 7/1st Tverskaya-Yamskaya. Carries souvenir items, ceramics and jewelry.

Russkiye Suveniry (Russian Souvenirs), 25 Malaya Pirogovskaya Ul. Metro Sportivnaya. Another branch is at 9 Kutuzovsky Pr. Metro Kievskaya.

Salon na Pyatnitskoi, 16 Pyatnitskaya Ul. Metro Novokuznetskaya.

JEWELRY

Many department stores, markets and higher-class hotels have jewelry for sale. In addition, check gift and souvenir shops which may carry items made from amber, malachite, lacquerware, etc.

The Arbat district is teeming with jewelry shops. **Novoye Zoloto** is at number

2, **Stefaniya** at number 20, **Sekunda** at number 29, **Emerald** at number 34, **Samotsvety** at number 35, and **Sady Seramidy** at number 36.

Almaz (Diamond) has gold and silver jewelry at four branches: 24 Petrovka, 22 Bolshaya Nikitskaya, 49 Komsomolsky Prospekt, and 35 Kuzutovsky Prospekt. Closed Sundays.

Brilliantovy Mir (World of Diamonds) and **Shakh** are at 2 Okhotny Ryad. Closed Sundays.

Kameya, 1 Novinsky Bulvar. Open daily. Metro Smolenskaya.

Karl Fabergé, 20 Kuznetsky Most. Closed Sundays. Metro Kuznetsky Most.

Mir Samotsvetov (World of Semiprecious Stones) is in the Vernadksy Museum, 11 Mokhovaya Ul. Closed Sundays. Metro Okhotny Ryad.

On lst Tverskaya-Yamskaya Ul., at number 6 is **Zodiak**, number 18 **Russkoye Zoloto**, and number 20 is **Jewelry Palata**. Metro Mayakovskaya.

MUSIC

Lira-1, 24 Bolshaya Nikitskaya. Closed Sundays. Metro Arbatskaya.

Melodiya, 22 Novy Arbat. Closed Sundays. Metro Arbatskaya.

Muzykalny Mir, 13 Nikitinskaya Pl. Open daily. Metro Arbatskaya.

RUSSIAN PRODUCTS IN THE USA

To order a catalog of unique Russian products from Catherine the Great goblets to a Russian MIG pilot's high-altitude helmet set, contact **Sovietsky Collection**, tel. in the US (800) 442-0002, international (619) 294-2000; fax (619) 294-2500; web-site: http://www.sovietski.com; e-mail: fulcrum@sovietski.com.

Russian Collection has a large collection of Russian lacquer boxes, *matryoshka* dolls and jewelry. In the US to order a catalog, tel. (800) 575-8049; fax (603) 356-5540; e-mail: Russian@NCIA.Net.

FARMERS' MARKETS OR RINOK

The markets are usually open Mon–Sat 8am–7pm; Sun 8am–4pm. A better selection is usually found in the mornings. Here people sell their fresh vegetables, fruit, flowers and other wares. Bring a few empty bags to carry your purchases in.

Arbat Market runs along Stary Arbat, a pedestrian street. Filled with souvenir-type articles to buy.

Cheryomushkinsky Rinok, 1 Lomonovsky Prospekt. Along with food and plants, this market also sells homemade crafts. Metro Universitet.

Kalitnikovsky, 42a Kalitnikovsky Ul., is the pet market and is a sight in itself; best on weekends. Here also is the **Ptichi Rinok**, the Bird Market. Animals for sale include dogs, cats, rabbits, and an assortment of birds and fish. Metro Marksistskaya/Taganskaya.

Kiosk Markets line the streets of Moscow, selling a wide variety of goods and souvenirs for rubles and hard currency.

Izmailovsky, in Izmailovsky Park (near Metro stop of same name). Best flea market to visit on weekends. Thousands of people sell everything imaginable. Bargaining is all part of the fun of shopping!

Tsentralny, 15 Tsvetnoi Bulvar, near the Old Circus. One of the best-stocked food markets in Moscow. Metro Tsvetnoi Bulvar.

MUSEUMS

There are over 100 museums in Moscow; this is a partial listing.

Information on museums and exhibition halls, tel. 975-9144.

Aircraft Exhibition, Khodynskoe Field, 24a Leningradsky Pr. Tel. 155-6619. Daily 10am–6pm. Metro Aeroport. (History of Russian aircraft industry.)

Andrei Rublyov Museum of Old Russian Art, Spaso-Andronikov Monastery, 10 Andronevskaya Pl. Tel. 278-1467. Open 11am–6pm; closed Wed. Metro Ploshchad Ilicha.

Armed Forces Central Museum, 2 Ul. Sovyetskoi Armii. Tel. 281-4877. Open 10am–4:30pm; closed Mon/Tues. Metro Novoslobodskaya.

Bakhrushin Theater Museum, 31/12 Bakhrushina Ul. Tel. 233-4470. Open 1–6pm; closed Tues. Metro Paveletskaya.

Battle of 1812 Borodino Museum, 38 Kutuzovsky Pr. Tel. 148-1967. Open 10:30am–6pm, Sat/Sun 10:30am–4pm; closed Fri. Metro Kutuzovskaya.

Boyar Romanov House-Museum, 10 Varvarka Ul. Tel. 298-3706. Open 10am–5pm, Wed 11am–6pm; closed Tues. Metro Kitai-Gorod.

Church of the Virgin Intercession in Fili (branch of Andrei Rublyov Museum), 6 Novozavodskaya Ul. Tel. 148-4552. Open 11am–6pm; closed Tues/Wed. Metro Fili.

Chambers of Old English Yard, 4a Varvarka Ul. Concerts held last Saturday of month. Tel. 298-3952. Open 10am–6pm, Wed/Fri 11am–7pm; closed Mon. Metro Kitai-Gorod.

Chekhov House Museum, 6 Sadovaya-Kudrinskaya Ul. Tel. 291-3837. Open 11am–6pm; Wed/Fri 2–7pm; closed Mon. Metro Barrikadnaya.

Children's Theater Museum, 12 Ul. Sovyetskoi Armii. Tel. 289-1554. Open 10am–6pm; closed Sat/Sun. Metro Rizhskaya.

Cosmonauts Memorial Museum, 111 Prospekt Mira. Tel. 286-3714. Open 10am–7pm; closed Mon. Metro VDNKh.

Decorative and Folk Art Museum, 3 Delegatskaya Ul. Tel. 923-1741. Open 10am–6pm; Sat/Sun 10am–4pm; closed Fri. Metro Mayakovskaya.

Defense of Moscow Museum, 3 Michurinsky Pr. Tel. 430-0549. Open 10am–6pm; closed Sun/Mon. Metro Yugo-Zapadnaya.

Dostoevsky Memorial-Apartment, 2 Ul. Dostoevskovo. Tel. 284-3148. Open 11am–6pm, Wed/Fri 2–6:30pm; closed Mon/Tues. Metro Novoslobodskaya.

Folk Art Museum, 7 Leotevsky Per. Tel. 290-5222. Open 11am–5:30pm; closed Sun/Mon. Metro Arbatskaya.

Glinka Music Culture Museum, 4 Ul. Fadeeva. Tel. 250-5891. Open 11am–6:30pm; closed Mon. Metro Mayakovskaya/Novoslobodskaya.

Gorky Literary Museum, 25a Povarskaya Ul. Tel. 291-2385. Open 10am–4:30pm, Wed/Fri 12–6:30pm; closed Sat/Sun. Metro Arbatskaya/Barrikadnaya.

Gorky Memorial Apartment, 6 Malaya Nikitskaya Ul. Tel. 290-5130. Open 10am–4:30pm, Wed/Fri 12–6pm; closed Mon/Tues. Metro Arbatskaya.

Great Patriotic War Museum (WWII), 11 Ul. Fonchenko Bratev (Park Pobedy). Tel. 148-5550. Open 10am–5pm; closed Mon. Metro Kutuzovskaya.

Herzen Memorial House, 27 Sivtsev Vrazhek Per. Tel. 241-5859. Open 11am–5:30pm, Wed/Fri 1–5:30pm; closed Mon. Metro Kropotkinskaya.

History of Moscow Museum, 12 Novaya Pl. Tel. 924-8490. Open 10am–6pm, Wed/Fri 11am–7pm; closed Mon. Metro Kitai-Gorod/Lubyanka.

Krasnya Presnya Museum, 4 Bolshoi Predtechensky Per. Tel. 252-3035. Open 10am–6pm, Wed 11am–7pm; closed Mon. Metro Krasnopresnenskaya.

Kremlin Museums Red Square, open 10am–6pm (ticket office 10am–4:30pm); closed Thursdays. **Armory Museum and Diamond Fund**, tel. 921-4720, 229-2036. Open 10am–4:30pm. Metro Borovitskaya/Aleksandrovsky Sad.

Kutuzov Hut, 38 Kutuzovsky Pr. Tel. 148-1875. Open 10am–5pm; closed Mon/Wed/Fri. Metro Kutuzovskaya.

Lermontov Memorial House (Poet), 2 Malaya Molchanovka Ul. Tel. 291-5298. Open 11am–5pm, Wed/Fri 2–5pm; closed Mon/Tues. Metro Arbatskaya.

Lights of Moscow Museum, 3 Armyansky Per. Tel. 924-7374. Open 9am–4pm; closed Sat/Sun. Metro Kitai-Gorod/Lubyanka.

Literary Museum, 28 Petrovka Ul. Tel. 921-7395. Open 11am–5:30pm, Wed/Fri 2–7pm; closed Mon/Tues. Metro Pushkinskaya.

Mayakovsky Museum, 3 Lubyansky Proyezd. Tel. 921-9560. Open 10am–5pm, Thurs 1–8pm; closed Wed. Metro Lubyanka.

Moscow Metro Museum, 36 Khamovnichesky Val (in Metro Sportivnaya). Tel. 222-7833. Open 9am–4pm, Mon 11am–6pm; closed Sat/Sun. Metro Sportivnaya.

Museum of Books, 3/3 Ul. Vozdvizhenka. Tel. 222-8672. Open 10am–5pm, Sat 10am–4pm; closed Sun. Metro Borovitskaya.

Museum of Fashion, 21 Novy Arbat. Tel. 202-3875. Open 10am–6pm; closed Sat/Sun. Metro Arbatskaya.

Museum of Folk Graphics, 10 Maly Golovin Per. Tel. 208-5182. Open 10am–6pm; closed Sun/Mon. Metro Sukharevskaya.

Museum of Military Regiments, 1/1st Krasnokursantsky Proyezd. Tel. 261-5576. Open 10am–5pm; closed Sun/Mon. Metro Baumanskaya.

Museum of Private Collections (branch of Pushkin Museum), 14 Volkhonka Ul. Tel. 203-1546. Open 10am–4pm, Sat/Sun 12–6pm; closed Mon/Tues. Metro Kropotkinskaya.

Nemirovich-Danchenko Memorial Apartment, 5 Glinishchevsky Per./5th floor. Tel. 209-5391. Open 11am–4pm; closed Mon. Metro Okhotny Ryad/Pushkinskaya.

Novodevichy Convent, 1 Novodevichy Per. Tel. 245-3168. Open 10am–5pm; closed Sun/Tues. Metro Sportivnaya.

Operetta Theater Museum, 6 Bolshaya Dmitrovka Ul. (inside Operetta Theater) Tel. 292-6377. Metro Okhotny Ryad.

Oriental Museum, 12a Nikitsky Bul. Tel. 291-0212. Open 11am–7pm, Mon 11am–4pm. Metro Arbatskaya.

Ostrovsky Museum Center (author N A), 14 Tverskaya Ul. Tel. 229-3134. Open 11am–7pm; closed Mon. Metro Pushkinskaya.

Ostrovsky Memorial House (playwright A N), 9 Malaya Ordynka Ul. Tel. 233-8684. Open 1–7pm; closed Tues. Metro Novokuznetskaya/Tretyakovskaya.

Paleontology Museum, 123 Profsoyuznaya Ul. Tel. 339-4544. Open 11am–6pm; closed Mon/Tues/Fri. Metro Tyoply Stan.

Politechnical Museum, 3 Novaya Pl. Tel. 923-0756. Open 10am–6pm; closed Mon. Metro Kitai-Gorod/Lubyanka.

Pushkin Memorial Apartment, 53 Arbat. Tel. 241-9295. Open 11am–5pm; closed Mon. Metro Smolenskaya.

Pushkin Museum of Fine Arts, 12 Volkhonka Ul. Tel. 203-9376. Open 10am–7pm; closed Mon. Metro Kropotkinskaya.

Revolution Museum, 21 Tverskaya Ul. Tel. 299-8515. Open 10am–6pm; closed Mon/Wed. Metro Tverskaya.

Shalyapin Memorial House, 25 Novinsky Bul. Tel. 252-2530. Open 11:30am–4pm; Tues/Sat 10am–6pm. Metro Barrikadnaya.

Skryabin Memorial Museum, 11 Bolshoi Nikolopeskovsky Per. Tel. 241-5156. Open 10am–4:30pm, Wed/Fri 12–6:30pm; closed Mon/Tues. Metro Arbatskaya/Smolenskaya.

St Basil's Cathedral, 2 Red Square. Tel. 298-3304. Open 10am–4:30pm; closed Tues. Metro Kitai-Gorod/Okhotny Ryad.

Stanislavsky Memorial Museum, 6 Leontevsky Per. Tel. 229-2855. Open 11am–5pm, Wed/Fri 2–8pm; closed Mon/Tues. Metro Pushkinskaya.

Tetris Wax Museum, 14 Tverskaya Ul. Tel. 229-8552. Open 11am–7pm; closed Mon. Metro Pushkinskaya.

Tolstoy Country Estate Museum, 12 Pyatniktskaya Ul. Tel. 231-7402. Open 11am–5pm; closed Mon. Metro Novokuznetskaya.

Tolstoy Museum, 11 Ul. Prechistenka. Tel. 202-9338. Open 11am–5pm; closed Mon. Metro Kropotkinskaya.

Tolstoy Museum, 21 Ul. Lva Tolstovo. Tel. 246-9444. Open 10am–6pm, winter 10am–4pm; closed Mon. Metro Park Kultury.

Tolstoy Museum (this is not Leo Tolstoy, but another writer A H who lived here 1942–1945), 2/6 Spiridonovka Ul. Tel. 290-0956. Open 1–8pm; closed Mon/Tues. Metro Pushkinskaya.

Tropinin Museum, 10 Shchetininsky Per. Tel. 231-1799. Open 12–6pm Sat/Sun 10am–4pm; closed Tues/Wed. Metro Polyanka/Tretyakovskaya.

Tretyakov Gallery, 10 Lavrushinsky Per. Tel. 231-1362. Open 10am–6:30pm; closed Mon. Metro Tretyakovskaya.

Vasnetsov Memorial Apartment (artist), 6 Furmanny Per. Tel. 208-9045. Open 11am–5pm, Wed/Fri 12–6pm; closed Sun/Mon. Metro Chistiye Prudy.

Vasnetsov Memorial House (branch of Tretyakov), 13 Pereulok Vasnetsova. Tel. 281-1329. Open 10am–5pm; closed Mon/Tues. Metro Sukharevskaya.

Yermolova Memorial House, 11 Tverskoi Bul. Tel. 290-4661. Open 1–8pm, Sat/Sun 12–7pm; closed Tues. Metro Tverskaya/Pushkinskaya.

Zoological Museum of Moscow University, 6 Bolshaya Nikitskaya Ul. Tel. 203-3569. Open 10am–6pm; closed Mon. Metro Aleksandrovsky Sad/Okhotny Ryad.

Zoo, 1 Bolshaya Gruzinskaya Ul. Tel. 255-5375. Rennovated in 1996. Open 9am–8pm, in winter 9am–4pm; closed Mon. Metro Barrikadnaya.

LIBRARIES

There are 15 major libraries in Moscow where one can browse through books in reading rooms, but not take books out.

Library of Foreign Literature, 1 Nikoloyamskaya Ul. Tel. 915-3636. Mon–Fri 9am–7:45pm; Sat/Sun 9am–6pm. Metro Kitai-Gorod.

Russian Library (formerly Lenin Library), 3 Vozdvizhenka Ul. Tel. 202-4056. Open 9am–6pm, Wed/Fri 12–8pm; closed Sundays. Metro Biblioteka Imeni Lenina.

Russian Art Library, 8/1 Bolshaya Dmitrovka. Tel. 200-4190. Mon–Fri 11am–6:45pm; Sat 11am–5:45pm. Metro Teatralnaya.

Russian Historical Library, 9 Starosadsky Per. Tel. 925-6514. Mon–Fri 9am–8pm; Sat/Sun 10am–6pm. Metro Kitai-Gorod.

Russian Science and Technical Library, 21/5 Kuznetsky Most. Tel. 921-2373. Mon–Fri 8:30am–5pm. Metro Kuznetsky Most.

PLACES OF WORSHIP

After the fall of Communism every type of religious denomination has taken root in Russia.

RUSSIAN ORTHODOX

There are over 100 Orthodox places of worship in Moscow. These are a few that hold regular religious services. Usual time of services: Mon–Sat 8am and 6pm. Sundays and holidays: 7am, 10am and 6pm. Women should dress modestly and men not wear hats.

■CATHEDRALS

Cathedral of Christ the Redeemer, 15 Volkhonka Ul. Tel. 203-3823. Metro Kropotkinskaya.

Cathedral of the Epiphany in Elokhovo, 15 Spartakovskaya Ul. Tel. 267-7591. Metro Baumanskaya.

Kazansky Cathedral, 8 Nikolskaya Ul. Red Square. Tel. 298-0131. Metro Okhotny Ryad.

St Basil's Cathedral, 2 Red Square. Tel. for excursions 298-3304. Metro Kitai-Gorod.

■CHURCHES

Assumption Church in Novodevichy Convent, 1 Novodevichy Per. Daily 7am–7pm. Metro Sportivnaya.

Church of All Saints in Sokol, 73a Leningradsky Pr. Tel. 158-2952. Metro Sokol.

Church of All Sorrows, 20 Bolshaya Ordynka. Daily 7am–8pm; services held at 8am. Tel. 231-1300. Metro Tretyakovskaya.

Church of the Deposition of the Robes, Donskoi Monastery. Tel. 954-1531.

Church of the Epiphany, 15 Spartakovskaya Ul. Seat of Russian Patriarch from 1943–1988. Daily 8am–8pm. Tel. 267-7591. Metro Baumskaya.

Church of the Nativity of Christ, 28 Izmailovsky Passage. Daily 9am–9pm. Tel. 164-2877. Metro Izmailovskaya.

Church of St Ilya the Prophet, 6/2nd Obydensky Per. Tel. 203-1951. Open 8–11am; closed Tues/Thurs. Metro Kropotkinskaya.

Church of St John the Warrior, 46 Yakimanka Ul. Tel. 238-2056. Metro Okyabrskaya.

Church of St Nicholas, 2 Ul. Lva Tolstovo. Daily 7:30am–8pm. Tel. 246-6952. Metro Park Kultury.

Church of Saints Peter and Paul in Kulishki, 4 Petropavlosky Per. Tel. 917-2975. Metro Kitai-Gorod.

Church of the Trinity on Sparrow Hills, 30 Ul. Kosygina. Daily 8am–5pm. Tel. 939-0046. Metro Oktyabrskaya.

OTHER ORTHODOX DENOMINATIONS

Armenian Apostolic Church of the Resurrection, 10 Ul. Sergeya Makeeva. Services Sundays at noon; open daily 10am–6pm. Tel. 255-5019. Metro Ulitsa 1905 Goda.

Greek Orthodox Church of Archangel Gabriel/Church of Martyz Fedor, 15a Arkhangelsky Per. Daily 8am–7:30pm. Metro Turgenevskaya.
Metropolitan Old Believers Church/Cathedral of the Intercession, 29 Rogozhsky Poselok. Tel. 361-0921. Mon–Fri 10am–5pm; services at 7:30am and 4pm. Metro Taganskaya.
Ostozhenskaya Old Believers Commune, 4 Turchaninov Per. Tel. 245-3029. Services Saturdays, Sundays and holidays at 8am and 3pm. Metro Park Kultury.

ROMAN CATHOLIC
Church of St Louis, 12 Malaya Lubyanka. Daily 7:30am–8pm. Masses in Latin, English, French, Polish and Russian. Tel. 925-2034. Metro Lubyanka.
Church of Our Lady of Hope and Catholic Chaplaincy, 7 Kutuzovsky Pr. Tel. 243-9621. Masses in English on Sat at 6pm and Sun at 6pm. Metro Kutuovskaya.
Christian Science Group, 14 Sushchevsky Val. Tel. 158-6096. Services Sundays at 11am. Metro Novoslobodskaya.

OTHER CHRISTIAN CHURCHES
Baptists of Russia, Kamerny Hall, Olympic Village. 11 Michurinsky Prospekt. Sunday services.
Bible Society of Russia, 51/14 Pyatnitskaya Ul. Mon–Fri 10:30am–4pm. Metro Novokunetskaya.
Church of Evangelical Christian-Baptists, 3 Maly Trekhsvyatitelsky Per. Tel. 917-5167. Daily 10am–6pm; services Tues/Thurs/Sat/Sun. Metro Chistiye Prudy.
International Christian Assembly, in concert hall of Central House of Artists. 2 Ul. Akademinka Vargi. Tel. 338-1150. English services Sundays at 10:30am. Metro Tyoply Stan.

PROTESTANT DENOMINATIONS
The Anglican Church of St Andrews, 9 Voznesensky Per. Tel. 245-3837. Metro Okhotny Ryad.
Calvary Church, 31 Ul. Usievicha. 3rd floor. Tel. 156-5679. Metro Sokol.
Mormons/Church of Jesus Christ of Latter Day Saints, 2 Chistoprudny Bul. Tel. 925-0398. Metro Chistiye Prudy; and 37 Donskaya Ul. Metro Shabolovskaya. Services Sundays at 10am.
Seventh-Day Adventists, 3 Maly Trekhsvyatitelsky Per. Tel. 917-0568. Services on Wed and Sat at 10am and 6pm. Metro Chistiye Prudy.
United Methodist Church, 50/7 Fruzenskaya Nab.

OTHER DENOMINATIONS

Religious Adminstration of Buddhists in Russia, 49 Ostozhenka Ul. Tel. 245-2289. Metro Park Kultury.

Temple for the Realization of Krishna, 8 Khoroshchevskoye Shosse. Tel. 945-3316. Services at 7am, 1:30pm and 7pm. Metro Begovaya.

JEWISH

Chabab Lubavitch Polyakova Synagogue, 6 Bolshaya Bronnaya. Tel. 202-4530. Services on Fridays after sunset and Saturdays at 10am; open 8am–9pm. Metro Pushkinskaya.

Choral Synagogue, 8 Bolshoi Spasoglinishchevsky Per. Tel. 923-4788. Services Mon–Fri at 8am, Sat and holidays at 9am, and evening after sunset. Metro Kitai-Gorod.

Marina Rostcha Moscow Jewish Commune, 5a 2nd Vysheslavtsev Lane. Tel. 289-9423. Services Wed–Fri at 9am. Metro Rizhskaya.

Representatives of World Council of Progressive Judaism, 14/2 Solyanka.

MOSLEM

Mosque, 7 Vypolzov Lane. Tel. 281-3866. Main service Friday at 1pm. Metro Prospekt Mira.

Bayt-Allah Religious Society, 28 Bolshaya Tatarskaya Ul. Tel. 231-1781. Daily 9am–6pm. Metro Novokuznetskaya.

Islamic Cultural Center, 5 Maly Tatarsky Per. Tel. 231-8856. Mon–Fri 10am–6pm. Metro Novokuznetskaya.

ENTERTAINMENT

THEATERS

There are over 100 theaters and concert halls in Moscow. A partial listing of main theaters and halls is included here. Theater, concert and circus performances begin on weekdays between 6pm and 8pm with matinée performances on weekends, with an earlier evening show. Each theater usually has its own box office; in addition, tickets can often be reserved through a travel/service bureau in your hotel, or purchased from street/Metro theater kiosks. Some main ticket/concert ticket offices are at 2, 19, 29 Tverskaya Ul; open 9am–8pm. And Arba is at 22 Tverskoi Bulvar; open 10am–7pm. For information on theater repertoires, call 975-9122 or look for the free addition of the *Moscow Times* in English which has listings of theater, concert, circus and cinematic events.

Bat Cabaret, 10 Bolshoi Gnezdikovsky Per. Tel. 229-7087/8661. Metro Pushkinskaya.

Bolshoi Opera and Ballet Theater, 1 Teatralnaya Pl. Tel. 292-3319/292-0050/9986. Metro Teatralnaya.

Buff Theater, 59 Lesnaya Ul. Tel. 251-3257. Metro Mendelyeevskaya.

Chekhov Academic Art Theater, 3 Kamergersky Per. Tel. 229-5370/292-6748. Metro Teatralnaya.

Chekhov Theater, 5 Novozykovsky Proyezd. Tel. 214-6669/212-8211. Metro Dynamo.

Children's Fairy Tale Theater, 15 Taganskaya. Tel. 912-5206. Metro Marksistskaya.

Children's Musical Theater, 17 Nikolskaya Ul. Tel. 929-1320/1326. Metro Lubyanka.

Children's Puppet Theater, 9 Ul. Bazhova. Tel. 181-0193/2044. Metro VDNKh.

Children's Variety Theater, 6 Bolshaya Sadovaya. Tel. 299-5941/8137. Metro Mayakovskaya.

Classical Ballet Theater, 3 Skakovaya Ul. Tel. 251-3221. Metro Dynamo.

Gogol Drama Theater, 8a Ul. Kazakova. Tel. 261-5528/262-9214. Metro Kurskaya.

Gorky Academic Art Theater, 22 Tverskoi Bul. Tel. 203-6222/8773. Metro Tverskaya.

Gypsy Theater Roman, 32 Leningradsky Pr. Tel. 250-7353/7334. Metro Dynamo.

Hermitage Theater, 3 Karetny Ryad. Tel. 209-2076. Metro Pushkinskaya.

Jewish Chamber Music Theater, 12/4 Taganskaya. Tel 912-5651. Metro Taganskaya.

Jewish Drama Theater Shalom, 71 Varshovsky Shosse. Tel. 110-3758/113-2753. Metro Varshavskaya.

Lencom Opera Theater, 19 Bolshaya Nikitskaya. Tel. 290-1256/6592. Metro Arbatskaya.

Lencom Theater, 6 Malaya Dmitrovka Ul. Tel. 299-1992/0708. Metro Tverskaya.

Maly Theater, 1/6 Teatralnaya Pl. Tel. 924-4083/923-2621. Metro Teatralnaya.

Maly Theater Branch is at 60 Bolshaya Ordynka. Tel. 237-3181. Metro Dobryninskaya.

Marrionette Theater, 7 Maly Kharitonevsky Per. Tel. 924-3651. Metro Chistiye Prudy.

Mayakovsky Theater, 19 Bolshaya Nikitskaya. Tel. 290-2725/4658. Metro Arbatskaya.

Mayakovsky Theater Branch is at 21 Pushkarev Ul. Metro Sukharevskaya.

Moscow Drama Theater, 4 Malaya Bronnaya. Tel. 290-6731/4093. Metro Tverskaya.

Moscow Operetta Theater, 6 Bolshaya Dmitrovka. Tel. 292-5982/1237. Metro Okhotny Ryad.

Moscow Theater School of Dramatic Arts, 20 Povarskaya Ul. Tel. 291-4339. Metro Arbatskaya.

Moscow Theater of Mimicry and Gesture, 39/41 Izmailovsky Bul. Tel. 163-8140. Metro Pervomaiskaya.

Mosoviet Theater, 16 Bolshaya Sadovaya. Tel. 299-2035/200-5943. Metro Mayakovskaya.

Obraztsov Puppet Theater, 3 Sadovaya Samotechnaya Ul. Tel. 299-3310/5373. Metro Mayakovskaya.

Old Arbat Theater, 11 Filippovsky Per. Tel. 291-1546. Metro Arbatskaya.

Puppet Theater, 26 Spartakovskaya Ul. Tel. 261-2197. Metro Baumanskaya.

Pushkin Drama Theater, 23 Tverskoi Bul. Tel. 203-8587/8582. Metro Pushkinskaya.

Russian Army Academic Theater, 2 Suvorovskaya Pl. Tel. 281-2110/5120. Metro Novoslobodskaya.

Satircon Theater, 8 Sheremetyevskaya Ul. Tel. 289-7844. Metro Rizhskaya.

Satire Theater, 2 Triumphfalnaya Pl. Tel. 299-6305/3642. Metro Mayakovskaya.

Sovremennik Theater, 19 Chistoprudny Bul. Tel. 921-2543/6473. Metro Chistiye Prudy.

Stanislavsky Drama and Arts Theater, 23 Tverskaya Ul. Tel. 299-7621/7224. Metro Mayakovskaya.

Stanislavsky and Nemirovich-Danchenko Musical Theater, 17 Bolshaya Dmitrovka Ul. Tel. 229-8388/2835. Metro Pushskinskaya.

Taganka Drama and Comedy Theater, 76 Zemlyonoi Val. Tel. 915-1015/1217. Metro Taganskaya.

Vakhtangov Academic Theater, 26 Arbat. Tel. 241-0728/1679. Metro Smolenskaya.

Variety Theater, 20/2 Bersenevskaya Nab. Tel. 959-0550/0456. Metro Polyanka.

Yermolova Drama Theater, 5 Tverskaya Ul. Tel. 203-7952/9063. Metro Okhotny Ryad.

CONCERT HALLS

Central House of Tourists Concert Hall, 149 Leninsky Pr. Tel. 434-9492. Metro Yugo-Zapadnaya.

Gnesin Institute Concert Hall, 1 Maly Rzhevsky Per. Tel. 290-2422. Metro Arbatskaya.

House of Unions Concert Hall, 1 Bolshaya Dmitrovka. Tel. 292-0956. Metro Okhotny Ryad.

Izmailovo Concert Hall, 71 Izmailovo Hgwy. Tel. 166-7953. Metro Izmailovsky Park.

Kremlin Palace of Congresses, the Kremlin (entrance through Borovitsky Gate). Tel. 917-2336. Metro Aleksandrovsky Sad.

Moscow Philharmonia, 31 Tverskaya Ul. Tel. 299-3957. Metro Mayakovskaya.

Olympic Village Concert Hall, 1 Michurinsky Pr. Tel. 437-5650. Metro Yugo-Zapadnaya.

Rossiya Concert Hall, Rossiya Hotel. Tel. 298-4350. Metro Kitai-Gorod.

Sadko, 3a Litovsky Bulvar. Tel. 427-6100. Metro Yasyenevo.

Tchaikovsky Concert Hall, 4/31 Triumphfalnaya Pl. Tel. 299-3957/0378. Metro Mayakovskaya.

Tchaikovsky Conservatory Bolshoi Hall, 13 Bolshaya Nikitskaya Ul. Tel. 229-9436. Metro Arbatskaya. Rachmaninov Hall is next door at number 11. Tel. 229-0294.

CIRCUSES

Bolshoi New Circus, 7 Vernadsky Pr. Tel. 930-2815/9809. Metro Universitet.

Clown Theater of Teresa Durova, 6 Pavlovskaya Ul. Metro Tulskaya.

Durov Animal Theater, 4 Durov Ul. Tel. 971-3047/281-9812. Metro Prospekt Mira.

Kuklachyov's House of Cats, 25 Kutuzovsky Pr. Tel. 249-2907. Metro Kievskaya.

Moscow Delfinary, 27 Mironovskaya Ul. Tel. 369-7966. Metro Semyonovskaya.

Moscow Ice Ballet, 24 Luzhnetskaya Nab. Tel. 201-1679. Metro Sportivnaya.

Old Circus, 13 Tsvetnoi Bul. Tel. 200-6889. Metro Tsvetnoi Bulvar.

Summer Circus, Nyeskuchny Gardens. Tel. 236-1462. Metro Oktybrskaya.

Tent Circus Raduga (Rainbow), Druzhba Park. (May–Sept) Metro Vodnyy Stadion.

Tent Circus Rus, 31 Ul. Novinki. Tel. 116-5676. (May–Sept) Metro Kolomenskaya.

Tent Circus, 9 Paromnaya Ul. Tel. 342-5928. (spring/summer) Metro Kashirskaya.

CINEMAS

Moscow has more than 100 cinemas. Most show movies in Russian; some screen foreign films in original language with subtitles, or with simultaneous translation.

Illusion, 1/15 Kotelnicheskaya Nab. Tel. 915-4353. Metro Kitai-Gorod.

Kino Center at Krasny Presnye, 15 Druzhinnikovskaya Ul. Tel. 255-9692.

Kodak Movie Theater, 2 Nastasinsky Per. Tel. 209-4359. Metro Pushkinskaya.

Moscow Business Plaza, 2 Berezhkovskaya Nab., Radison-Slavyanskaya Hotel. Tel. 941-8020. American films with simultaneous translations. Metro Kievskaya.

Oktyabr, 24 Novy Arbat. Tel. 291-2263. Metro Arbatskaya.

Zaryadye, Rossiya Hotel. Tel. 298-5686. Metro Kitai-Gorod.

BLUES, JAZZ AND ROCK

Arbat Blues Club, 1 Filippovsky Per. Tel. 291-1546. Fri/Sat 8:30pm–6:00am. Metro Arbatskaya.

Artos, 3 Karetny Ryad. Tel. 209-4524. Open 24 hours. Club (dancing after 10pm; disco and live music), restaurant and bar. Metro Chekhovskaya.

Bedniye Ludy (Poor People), 11/6 Bolshaya Ordynka. Tel. 231-3342. Artistic club. Open daily 7pm–5am. Restaurant and concerts after 10pm. Metro Novokuznetskaya.

Blues Club B B King, 4/2 Sadovaya-Samotechnaya Ul. Tel. 299-7549. Daily 12pm–2am. Live music and restaurant. Metro Sukharevskaya.

Jazz Art Club, 5 Begovaya Ul. Tel. 946-0165. Open Fri/Sun 7:30–11pm. Jazz concerts, exhibits, art for sale. Metro Begovaya.

Max-club, 75a Udaltsova Ul. Tel. 431-4690. Open 11pm–5am; closed Mon. Shows, disco and bar. Metro Prospekt Vernadskovo.

Vermel, 4/5 Raushskaya Nab. Tel. 959-3303. Open daily 12pm–5am. Restaurant, live music after 10pm, and dancing Thurs–Sat after midnight. Metro Tretyakovskaya.

Woodstock, 3 Kamergersky Per. Tel. 292-0934. Open daily 12pm–5am. Musical club with theater evenings on Mon, jam sessions on Wed, and concerts Thurs–Sun. Metro Okhotny Ryad.

NIGHTCLUBS AND CASINOS

Moscow is said to now have more casinos than Las Vegas! Many of these places also take credit cards. Some have cover charges.

Alexander's Club No. 1, 1 Bolshaya Dmitrovka in House of Unions. (Times have changed; people now gamble where they once stood and paid last respects to Stalin!) Tel. 292-7123. Casino and slots. Disco, bar and restaurant. Open daily 8pm–8am. Metro Okhotny Ryad.

Arbat, 21/2 Novy Arbat. Tel. 291-1134. Open daily 2pm–6am. Casino, restaurant and bar. Metro Smolenskaya.

Arlecchino, is next to the restaurant at 15 Druzhinnikovskaya. Tel. 255-9465. Open Thurs–Sun 11pm–5am. Live music and dancing, restaurant and bar. Metro Krasnopresnenskaya.

Beverly Hills, Chuck Norris Enterprise Club, 1 Kudrinskaya Pl. Tel. 255-4228. Open daily 8pm–6am. Casino, restaurant, evening musical numbers. Metro Barrikadnaya.

Club Restaurant on Neglinnoi, 8/10 Neglinnaya Ul. Tel. 924-5655. Restaurant and disco (some live music). Open daily 10pm–5am. Metro Kuznetsky Most. In the same complex is Korrida, open 12pm–6am with disco and bar.

Kosmos, 150 Prospekt Mira. Tel. 234-1155. Open 24 hours. Casino, Solaris nightclub, restaurant and bar. Metro Prospekt Mira.

Gabriella, Intourist Hotel, 3/5 Tverskaya. Tel. 956-8451. Open 24 hours. Casino, slots and bar. Metro Okhotny Ryad.

Golden Palace, 15/3rd Yamskovo Polya. Tel. 212-3909. Casino with American roulette, poker, blackjack. Restaurant and bar. Open 24 hours. Metro Belorusskaya.

Gvozdy Radio Club, 19 Bolshaya Nikitskaya Ul. Tel. 290-2254. Open daily 12pm–5am. Restaurant and bar, live music and disco. Metro Pushkinskaya.

Karo, 2 Pushkinskaya Pl. Tel. 229-0003. Open daily 5pm–5am. Casino; restaurant and bar, disco and variety shows. Metro Pushkinskaya.

Luxe, 4/1 Michurinsky Pr. Tel. 430-3763. Open 24 hours. Casino with roulette, blackjack and poker. Thurs/Sat musical nights. Metro Yugo-Zapadnaya.

Manhattan Express, in Rossiya Hotel. Tel. 298-5355. Open 8pm–5am. Dancing, disco and variety shows, restaurant and bars. Metro Kitai-Gorod.

Metelitsa, Mirazh and Arbat, 21 Novy Arbat. Tel. 291-1130/1423. Open 7pm–5am. Casino, shows, live music, disco, restaurants and bars. Metro Arbatskaya.

Metropole, in Metropole Hotel. Tel. 927-6950. Casino and bar. Metro Teatralnaya. Also in the Metropole is the **Luxor**, a sushi bar and disco. Tel. 927-6091. Open 7pm–5am.

Moskva, in Hotel Leningradskaya. Tel. 975-1967. Casino and bar. Metro Komsomolskaya.

Night Flight, 17 Tverskaya Ul. Tel. 229-4165. Open 9pm–5am. Nightclub, live music and disco, restaurant and bar. Metro Pushkinskaya.

Royale, 22/1 Begovaya Ul. (in Hippodrome Stadium). Tel. 945-1963. Open daily 10pm–5am. Casino with roulette, blackjack, poker. Restaurant, bar and disco. Metro Begovaya.

Tabula Rasa, 28 Berezhkovskaya Nab. Tel. 240-9289. Open daily 7pm–7am. Restaurant and bar, live music and disco. Metro Kievskaya.

Up and Down, 4 Zubovsky Bul. Tel. 201-4876. Open daily 8pm–5am. Casino, restaurant and bar, variety show programs after 10pm. Metro Park Kultury.

Vinso-Grand, 12 Taganskaya Pl. Tel. 912-5726. Open 24 hours. Casino and restaurant. Metro Taganskaya.

MISCELLANEOUS

TRAVEL AGENCIES AND TOUR COMPANIES

Hundreds of travel companies have opened throughout the city. If you have a touring question, inquire at a hotel service desk; they can also direct you to a specialty agency.

Academservice, 49 Ul. Arkhitektura Vlasova. Tel. 120-9005; fax 755-8855; e-mail: acs@acase.ru; web-site: http://www.acase.ru

American Express, 21a Sadovaya-Kudrinskaya. Tel. 755-9000; fax 755-9004. Metro Mayakovskaya.

Apex Travel World, 14/19 Novoslobodskaya Ul. Tel. 978-6189; fax 973-2756. Metro Park Kultury.

Barry Martin Group, 3/9 Malaya Kommunisticheskaya Ul. Tel. 911-2609. Travel in Russia and CIS. Metro Taganskaya.

Gemma Expedition, 18 Streletskaya Ul. Tel. 289-9166; fax 289-0512. Tours around Russia. Metro Savelovskaya.

Intourbureau, 146 Leninsky Pr. 3rd fl., Rm 350. Tel. 434-9032; fax 434-9082. Excursions around Moscow, hotels, tickets. Metro Yugo-Zapadnaya.

Intourist, 13/1 Milutinsky Per. Tel. 923-8575; fax 234-3778. Travel in Russia and CIS.

Intourservice, in Rossiya Hotel. Visa and hotel support, Moscow excursions, travel in Russia and CIS. Tel. 7-503-232-6194/6264; fax 7-503-232-6193; e-mail: intour@ocean.ru; web-site: http://www.ocean.ru/dl_int/intour_r.htm

IRO-Traveller's Guest House, 50 Bolshaya Pereyaslavskaya Ul.,10th fl. Tel. 974-1781; fax 280-6066. Visa support, travel, theater tickets. Metro Prospekt Mira.

Moscow Excursion Bureau, 5 Ul. Rozhdestvenka. Tel. 921-1508; fax 923-7459. Excursions around Moscow and Golden Ring area. Metro Kuznetsky Most.

Mos-Tourism, 4 Petroverigsky Per. Tel. 928-3118/3386. Metro Kitai-Gorod.

Moscow Tourist Sports Club, 4 Sadovaya-Kudrinskaya. Tel. 203-1094. Mon–Fri 9:30am–6pm. Sports-related excursions. Metro Barrikadnaya.

Patriarchi Dom—American/Russian Cultural Center, Tel. 926-5680; international-al tel/fax 7-502-220-3680; in the US tel. (202) 363-9610 for more information. Provides Russian heritage tours. Schedules a wide variety of Moscow city tours, special interest programs from art and architecture to history, politics and religion, and further excursions around the Golden Ring area. They have something scheduled for each day!

Russia Travel, 9/13 1st Yamskovo Polye. Tel. 956-6446; fax 234-3406; e-mail: rustav@glas.apc.org. Metro Belorusskaya.

Smart Travel, 6 Leninky Pr. Tel. 236-9798. Historical tours through Russia. Metro Leninsky Prospekt.

Sputnik Moscow, 6 Maly Ivanovsky Per. Tel. 925-9278; fax 230-2787. Moscow and Golden Ring tours. Metro Kitai-Gorod.

BOAT EXCURSIONS AND RIVER CRUISES

See Down the Moskva River section, page 197, for river cruises available.

Capital Navigation Company, tel. 277-6678. Ticket counter: 1 Leningradsky Pr. Tel. 257-7109. River cruises from Moscow to Golden Ring area, Nizhny Novgorod, Rostov-on-the-Don, Tver, St Petersburg and as far away as Astrakhan. Boat trips on Moskva River and canal.

River Terminals: Northern Terminal is at 51 Leningradsky Shosse; Metro Rechnoi Vokzal. Connects Moscow with the Volga. Southern Terminal is at 11 Andropov Pr; Metro Kolomenskoye. Routes to Kolomenskoye and Brateyevo. From 11am to 8pm, the riverboat *Moskva* departs about every half hour for cruises along the Moskva River. For longer cruises, the Passenger Port boards at 6 Proektiruemy Prospekt. Metro Kolomenskaya.

BUS EXCURSIONS—INTERNATIONAL AND LOCAL

Avtotur-Sputnik, 125b Varshavskoye Shosse. Tel. 381-7325. Metro Yuzhnaya. Bus tours around Russia and abroad.

Central Bus Station, 75/2 Shchelkovskoye Shosse. Tel. 468-4370. Metro Shchelkovskaya. Buses to Vladimir, Ivanovo, Kostroma, Rybinsk, Suzdal, Yaroslavl, Nizhny Novgorod and other towns.

Priltravel, 9/1 Smolenskaya Pl., 3rd fl., Rm 10. Tel. 241-5640. Travel to Finland and Sweden. Metro Smolenskaya.

CAR RENTALS

Moscow now has nearly 50 car rental agencies scattered around the city offering everything from compact cars to minibuses. Inquire if rental car comes with or without driver. Check your insurance coverage; most policies do not cover Russia. (Make sure coverage is provided for break-ins and theft.) Since most Muscovites drive without insurance, and driving in Moscow can be a nightmare, it is recommended not to rent a car, unless excursions into the countryside are planned. If none of the following fit your budget, ask at your hotel service desk—they can recommend a local company in town that may offer a better bargain. If you do not know the city, it is really easier to get around with public transport.

Alamo, 49 Prospekt Mira. Tel. 284-4391. Mon–Fri 9am–7pm. Metro Prospekt Mira.

Avis Car Rental, Sheremetyevo-II Airport. Tel. 578-5646. Daily 8am–10pm.

Budget, 16 Verx Radishchevskaya Ul. Tel. 915-0870. Metro Taganskaya. Mon–Fri 9am–6pm. Sheremetyevo-II Airport. Tel. 578-7344. Daily 12–10pm.

EuroDollar, tel. 298-6146, 911-0947. Mon–Fri 9am–6pm. Tel. 578-7534; 911-0959. Daily 12–11pm.

Europcar, 64 Leningradsky Pr. Tel. 151-6276. Mon–Fri 9am–6pm. Metro Aeroport. 12 Krasnopresnenskaya Nab. (Mezh Hotel). Tel. 253-1369. Daily 8am–11pm. Sheremetyevo-II. Tel. 578-3878. Daily 9am–8pm.

Hertz, 4 Ul. Chernyakhovskovo. Tel. 151-5426. Daily 10am–7pm. Metro Aeroport. Sheremetyevo-II. Tel. 578-5646. Daily 11am–11pm.

HEALTH CLUBS AND SAUNAS (*BANYAS*)

Most high-end hotels offer fitness club facilities; you can pay a daily entrance fee if not staying at the hotel. Some of those with workout rooms, sauna and pool are at the Radisson-Slavyanskaya, Mezhdunarodnaya, Metropole and Renaissance. Scores of health clubs have opened throughout the city and Muscovites are taking up everything from aerobics to yoga, and paying to be pampered. Call first to find out what is offered; some may only take members. Check at hotel service desk for local swimming pool locations.

Olympic Water Sport Center, 25 Mironovskaya St. Tel. 369-1086. Outdoor and indoor pools. Daily 7am–10pm. Metro Semyonovskaya. (The Dynamo and Olympic stadiums also have large indoor pools.)

Chaika Sports Complex (pool), 1/2 Korobeinikov Per. Tel. 202-0670. Metro Park Kultury. Daily 7am–11pm.

Gold's Gym, 31 Leningradsky Pr. Tel. 931-9616. Mon–Fri 9am–11pm; Sat/Sun 9am–10pm. Metro Dynamo.

Greenway (pool), 39 Leningradsky Pr. Tel. 967-6812. Open 24 hours. Metro Dynamo.

Moscow Beach Club, 6 Malaya Dmitrovka. Tel. 299-7353. Mon–Fri 7am–10pm; Sat/Sun 9am–9pm. Metro Pushkinskaya.

Nosorog Fitness and Health Club, 16 Maly Kazyenny Per. Tel. 913-6473. Daily 9am–10:30pm. Metro Kurskaya.

Luzhniki Sports Complex, near Sparrow Hills and Central Stadium. Metro Sportivnaya.

Olympic Sports Complex (pool), 16 Olimpisky Pr. Tel. 288-1545. Daily 7am–11pm. Metro Prospekt Mira.

World Class (pool), 14 Zhitnaya Ul. Tel. 239-1994. Mon–Fri 7am–10pm; Sat/Sun 9am–9pm. Metro Oktybrskaya.

Saunas/*Banyas*: Many hotels offer sauna facilities. Some favorite Russian *banyas* or bathhouses (see Special Topic on page 340) are at: **Sandunovskiye Bani**, 14 Neglinnaya Ul. Tel. 925-4631. Open 8am–10pm; closed Tues. Metro Teatralnaya. **Bani na Presnye**, 7 Stolyarny Per. Tel. 253-8690. Open 8am–10pm; Mon 2–9pm. Metro Ulitsa 1905 Goda. **Luxe**, 19 Starovagankovsky. Tel. 203-0232. Daily. Metro Biblioteka Imeni Lenina.

SPORTS

Arm Wrestling Assoc. is at 8 Luzhnetskaya Nab. Tel. 201-1214. Mon–Sat 10am–6pm. Metro Sportivnaya. Also found here is the **Badminton Club**, tel. 201-1435; the **Basketball Federation**, tel. 201-1349; and the **Water Polo Federation**, tel. 201-0771. To check on locations for alpine and cross-country skiing, contact the

Skiing Federation at 201-1771. To check on soccer games, call the Soccer Union, tel. 201-0834.

Bowling can be found in the Kosmos Hotel and at the Bowling Club, 71 Izmailovskoye Shosse. Tel. 166-7418. Daily 12pm–6am. Metro Izmailovsky Park. Glowbowling is at 1 Ostrovityanova Ul. Tel. 434-1255. Mon–Thurs 12pm–2am; Fri–Sun 12pm–3am. Metro Konkovo.

Baseball Federation is at 18 Milyutinsky Per. Tel. 924-1067. Metro Turgenevskaya. Also at this location is the Vollyball Federation, tel. 924-1067, and the Fencing Association, tel. 924-9826. To check on ice hockey games, call the Ice Hockey Federation, tel. 924-9826. Matches are held year-round at Dynamo and Central stadiums.

Bicyling Clubs: Caravan has excursions to as far away as the Golden Ring and St Petersburg. 3 Serpov Per. Tel. 390-4915. Metro Park Kultury. Russian Bicycle Club has excursions around Russia. 1 Trekhsvyatitelsky Bolshaya Per. Tel. 916-8894. Metro Chistiye Prudy.

Checkers can be played at Izmailovsky Park, 17 Narodny Pr. Tel. 166-7909. Daily 10am–7pm. Metro Izmailovsky Park.

Chess Russian Federation is at tel. 291-9584. Chess clubs are held around the city.

Golf: Moscow Country Club has Russia's first pro-18 hole/par-72 course, designed by Robert Trent Jones II (see Vicinity section on page 209). Located 30 kilometers (18 miles) from Moscow in Nahabino. Also has driving range and pro shop. The Country Club also has a fitness center and tennis club. Tel. 926-5911/5927/5924. The Moscow City Golf Club is at 1 Dovzhenko Ul. Tel. 147-5480/8330. Metro Kievskaya. It has a golf course, winter golf center and tennis courts.

Horseback Riding: horses can be rented in Tsaritsyno Park and by the Zoo. The Equestrian Sports Club (Bittsa) is at 33 Balaklavsky Pr.; has show jumping and indoor riding school. Tel. 318-5744. Metro Kaluzhskaya. See Hippodrome, below, where you can ride the grounds during winter months.

Horse Racing: the Hippodrome is at 22 Begovaya Ul. Tel. 945-0437/4516. Metro Begovaya. Includes flat racing, *kachalki-in* lightweight carriages and occasional troika in winter. Much betting and drinking. Main races Sat/Sun at 12 noon.

Hunting and Fishing: the Moscow Society of Hunting and Fishing is at 6 Stroiteley Ul. Tel. 930-4978. Offers a choice of over 100 hunting lodges. Mon–Fri 9am–6pm. Metro Universitet. Old Fox organizes hunting and fishing throughout Russia. Tel. 452-0946. Safary-Expeditions also organizes expeditions throughout Russia and the CIS. Tel. 215-7792. See also Mos-Tourism, page 335.

Ice-Skating: in Gorky Park in winter months; has skate rentals and troika rides. You can also skate at Chistoprudny Blvd (Metro Chistiye Prudy) and Patriarch's Pond (Metro Mayakovskaya). Sokolniki Park has skating and rental facilities. Metro

Sokolniki and Izmailovsky Park. Indoor rinks are at: Dynamo, 36 Leningradsky Pr; Crystal, 24 Luzhnetyskaya Nab; and Sokolniki at 16 Sokolnichesky Val.

Karate/Martial Arts Club is at 9/2 Spiridonovka Ul. Tel. 291-0825. Metro Pushkinskaya.

Skiing: the parks Sokolniki, Bittsa and Luzhniki offer cross-country skiing rentals and trails. Cross-country skiing is also popular in nearby Peredelkino. If you have your own gear, practically any park allows skiing in winter.

Soccer: the teams Asmaral, Dynamo, Lokomotiv, Spartak and Torpedo all have their own stadiums. The season is from March to November.

Tennis: Moscow has many tennis facilities. Call the **Tennis Association** at tel. 201-1249. Some of the main facilities with indoor and outdoor courts are at: **Dynamo**, 26 Petrovka. Tel. 200-5836. Metro Tealtralnaya. Daily 7am–9pm. **Druzhba** at 24 Luzhnetskaya Nab. Tel. 247-0343. Metro Park Kultury. Daily 7am–11pm. **Petrovsky Park**, 36 Leningradsky Pr. Tel. 212-7956. Daily 6am–12am. Metro Dynamo. **Chaika Sports Club**, 1/2 Korobeinikov Per. Tel. 202-0670. Daily 7am–11pm. Metro Park Kultury; and at **Luzhniki Sports Complex**, Metro Sportivnaya.

Water Skiing Club, 73 Volokolamskoye Shosse. Tel. 491-0593. Metro Tushinskaya.

Windsurfing Association is at tel. 478-2386.

BANYAS

Nothing gives a better glimpse into the Russian character than a few hours spent in a Russian bathhouse or *banya*. This enjoyable sauna tradition has been a part of Russian culture for centuries. Traditionally each village had its own communal bathhouse where, at different times, males or females would stoke wood-burning stoves and spend hours sitting, sweating and scrubbing. The Greek historian Herodotus reported from Russia in the fifth century BC: 'They make a booth by fixing in the ground three sticks inclined toward one another, and stretching around them wooden felts, which they arrange so as to fit as close as possible; inside the booth a dish is placed upon the ground, into which they put a number of red hot stones; then they take some hemp seed and throw it upon the stones; immediately it smokes, and gives out such a vapor that no Grecian hot mist can exceed; they are immediately delighted and shout for joy, and this hot steam serves them instead of a water bath.' Later, many homes even had their own private *banyas* and during winter naked bodies could be seen rolling in the snow after a well-heated sweat. Today the *banya* ritual is still a much favored pastime; this invigorating washing process has proudly been passed down from generation to generation.

Banya complexes are located throughout Russian cities and towns. Some of the most popular in Moscow are the Sandunovskiye and Krasnopresnenskaya, and in St Petersburg the Nevskiye Bani. For a minimal price the bather can spend many a pleasurable hour in the company of fellow hedonists. No *banya* is complete without a bundle of dried birch branches with leaves, called *veniki*, usually sold outside the complex. *Berioza* (birch) has always been a popular symbol of Russia, which claims more birch than any other country in the world. Buy a switch of birch and enter to pay the *banya* fee; the cashier can then point you in the right direction—*muzhchina* (men) or *zhenshchina* (women). Once inside, an attendant is there to assist you.

Many older *banyas* are housed in splendid prerevolutionary buildings; marble staircases, mirrored walls and gilded rooms, though somewhat faded, are filled with steam and cold pools. The best *banyas* even offer massage, facials, and a café. Bring along a towel, soap, shampoo, head-cap and flip-flops; otherwise you can often rent them there. It is recommended to leave valuables behind, or give them to the attendant for safe-keeping if there is no place to lock them up.

There are three main parts of the *banya*: the sitting and changing room, the bathing area and the sauna itself. The bathing area is usually one immense room filled with large benches. Soak your *veniki* in one bucket filled with warm water (it prevents the leaves from falling off), while using another to rinse yourself. Then carry the wet branches into the hot *banya* (start out on the bottom level then slowly work your way up). The custom is to lightly hit the body with the birch branch; this is believed to draw out toxins and circulate the blood. It is also traditional to whack each other, and since you will easily blend in like a native, you may find your *banya* buddy asking if you would like your own back gently swatted!

An old Russian folk-saying claims that 'the birch tree can give life, muffle groans, cure the sick and keep the body clean'. Cries of *oy oy, tak khorosho* (how wonderful) and *s lyokim parom* (have an enjoyable sweat) emanate from every corner. When someone, usually one of the *babushki* (grandmothers) or *dyedushki* (elderly men), get carried away with flinging water on the heated stones, moans of *khavatit* (enough) resound from the scorching upper balconies, when lobster-red bodies come racing out of the hot steamy interior. (Even though temperatures are lower than in Finnish or Turkish saunas, the humidity makes it feel hotter.) Back in the washroom, the bather rinses alternately in warm and cold water or plunges in the cold pool and then uses a loofah for a vigorous rubdown. Go in and out of the steam as often as you like. Afterwards, wrapped in a crisp sheet or towel, your refreshed body returns to the sitting room to relax and sip tea, cold juices, or even beer or vodka. With skin glowing and soul rejuvenated, it is time to take an invigorating walk about the city!

ST PETERSBURG

St Petersburg

The Neva is clad in granite
Bridges stand poised over her waters
Her islands are covered with dark green gardens
And before the younger capital, ancient Moscow
Has paled, like a purple clad widow
Before a new Empress...

Alexander Pushkin

Illuminated by the opalescent White Nights of summer, when the sun hardly sets, then sunk into gloomy darkness in winter, St Petersburg's history is equally juxtaposed with great artistic achievement and violent political upheaval. This paradoxical place has long inspired a flood of poetry, arts and revolutions, and combines the personality of three unique cities into one. It was Petersburg for the czars, Petrograd for a nation at war, and Leningrad for the followers of the Bolshevik Revolution. A visitor today cannot help but get swept into the remarkable vortex of all three distinctly different atmospheres.

St Petersburg initially sprang from a collision of two very different cultures and adapted the tastes of both East and West to the far northern latitudes. Situated only 800 kilometers (500 miles) south of the Arctic Circle, the population grew up along the shores of the Neva River that winds around the 44 islands which comprise the city, and flows 74 kilometers (46 miles) from Lake Ladoga into the Gulf of Finland. The swift-flowing Neva, contrasted with the wide prospekts and unique architecture, all add to the city's mystery, character and charm.

Strolling along the enchanted embankments at any time of year, the first thing one notices is the incredible light that washes over the city. Joseph Brodsky, the Nobel prize-winning poet who was born in St Petersburg, wrote: 'It's the northern light, pale and diffused, one in which memory and eye operate with unusual sharpness. In this light... a walker's thoughts travel farther than his destination.'

It was Peter the Great who brought the majesty of the West to this isolated northern region. He called his new creation Sankt Pieterburkh, from the Dutch, and named it after Christ's first apostle, his patron saint. The city was one of the first in the world built according to preconceived plans, drawn up by the most famous Russian and European architects of the day. Only nine years after its inception in 1703, Peter the Great moved out of Moscow and proclaimed his beloved city the capital of the Russian Empire; it remained so for 206 years.

Over the next 150 years, sparked by the reigns of two great women—Peter's daughter, Elizabeth I, and then Catherine the Great—St Petersburg became the host to Russia's Golden Age and a Mecca to some of the world's greatest composers, writers, artists and dancers. As the catalyst for Russia's Renaissance, St Petersburg flowered in the music of Tchaikovsky, Glinka and Rimsky-Korsakov; the Ballets Russes of Diaghilev, Pavlova and Nijinsky; in the arts and crafts of Repin, Benois and Fabergé; and in the literature and poetry of Gogol, Dostoevsky and Akhmatova. St Petersburg's first two centuries were forged on beauty, innovation and progress.

But the city, born of a forceful will and determined vision, was also destined to become the cradle of turbulent revolutions. Around the time its name was Russianized to Petrograd during World War I, political and philosophical ideas flourished. By February 1917 the monarchy of Nicholas II had been toppled, and on October 24, 1917, Lenin gave the command for the start of the great October Revolution. The battleship *Aurora* fired a blank shot at the Hermitage—the signal for the beginning of what American writer John Reed termed 'the ten days that shook the world'. Red Army troops stormed the Winter Palace and the Bolsheviks seized control of the new Soviet State.

Practically overnight, Leninist and Communist ideals took the place of czars and the aristocracy. Czar Nicholas II and his family were executed in 1918 to thwart the hopes of a return to Romanov rule. Amidst all this turmoil, Lenin transferred the capital of the new Soviet Union back to Moscow. When Lenin died in 1924, ironically (he had hated the place) the city of Petrograd was renamed Leningrad in his honor.

But an even greater tragedy lurked in the shadows. Hitler invaded the USSR in 1941 and laid siege to the city for 900 days. In three years alone, more than half a million residents died from starvation or in the defense of their city. Then, during the subsequent years of Stalin's Great Terror, many of the city's finest were executed or sentenced to gulags and never heard from again. St Petersburg's monuments not only immortalize its crowning achievements, but also serve as testaments to thousands of persecuted souls.

Much has happened to St Petersburg over the past three centuries. She has lived through revolutions and repression, sieges and purges, isolation and humiliations. But through all of this, the city has retained its propensity for courage and change. The White Nights of her spirit have always shown through the darkness as on a midsummer's night. Subdued for many years by tragedy and war, the fairytale Sleeping Beauty has reawoken to find her glorious past, prolific poetry and dedicated subjects intact.

Today there is much to behold. One day of sightseeing brings you to the former palaces of Peter the Great, from his first modest cottage on the banks of the Neva River, to his stunning summer palace at Peterhof, modeled on Versailles. The

(following pages) On the small beach in front of the Peter and Paul Fortress, two swimmers look out on the Hermitage during Navy Day (the last Sunday in July) when part of the Russian fleet is paraded down the Neva River.

fabulous Hermitage, created by Catherine the Great as her own personal museum, now contains one of the largest and most valuable art collections in the world. The center of Senate Square is marked by the celebrated statue of Peter the Great, known as the Bronze Horseman.

Another day of touring re-creates past splendors and revolutions as you stand in the Winter Palace or onboard the battleship *Aurora*. Nevsky Prospekt, the city's most popular thoroughfare, stretches five kilometers (three miles) from the golden-spired Admiralty to Alexander Nevsky Monastery, one of the largest Russian Orthodox centers in the country. A stroll along the Nevsky and adjoining side streets or a boat trip through the numerous canals leads you past former palaces of aristocrats and on to the Mariinsky (Kirov) Ballet, where Balanchine and Baryshnikov once danced, or the Maly Theater to hear opera and music written by Stravinsky, Tchaikovsky and Shostakovich.

In 1991, as a grand gesture to honor its historic foundation, the country's second largest city of five million people won the battle to change its name from Leningrad back to St Petersburg. The new 'Pieter', as residents lovingly call their city, is rising forth to embrace its past and reclaim its heritage. In 1998, the remains of the executed family of Nicholas II were ceremoniously reburied in the Peter and Paul Cathedral. Even though Moscow is still the capital, St Petersburg residents resoundingly prefer their own city. At the Baby Palace, each newborn is honored with a ceremony and medal that proudly reads, Born in St Petersburg.

Few cities in the world can compare with St Petersburg—in its vast beauty, turbulent history and remarkable endurance of the human spirit. Today, as it prepares to celebrate its tricentennary in 2003, the city pushes forward with renewed faith and optimistic vigor. As we embark on our timeless journey through this extraordinary place, let us recall the words of Alexander Pushkin, a long-time resident of the city:

> *Be beautiful, city of Peter*
> *Stay as unshakable as Russia*
> *And let no vain wrath*
> *Ever trouble the eternal dream of Peter.*

History

The delta at the mouth of the Neva River was settled long before the founding of St Petersburg. The Neva was an important trading route between Northern Europe and Asia. Finns, Swedes and Russians established settlements there at one time or another and frequently fought over the land. In the early 17th century, Russia's Time of Troubles, the nation's military power was so debilitated that Mikhail, the first of the Romanov czars, was forced to sign a treaty ceding the land to Sweden in 1617.

After Peter the Great returned from his tour of Holland, England and Germany, one of his first actions was to oust the Swedes from the Neva delta. In the winter of 1702–3, Russian forces attacked and captured Swedish forts at Nyenshatz, a few miles upstream from the river's mouth, and Noteborg on Lake Ladoga. Peter ordered that the keys to these forts be nailed to their gates. Two keys hanging from a sailing ship became the symbol representing the future of St Petersburg. On May 16, 1703, seven weeks after ousting the Swedes, Peter the Great lay the foundation stone of the Peter and Paul Fortress on an island near where the Neva divides into its two main branches. The primary role of the new settlement was as a military outpost, but right from the beginning Peter had greater designs.

While the construction of the fortress was under way, Peter lived in a rough log cabin nearby and from it planned his future capital. He decided that the hub of the new city was to be on the opposite bank of the Neva, at the present site of the Admiralty. Here he founded Russia's first great shipyard, where he built his navy. But Peter's project was hampered from the start by the occasional flooding of the Neva and by the lack of workers willing to move to the cold and isolated swamp. With typical ruthlessness, he ordered the conscription of 40,000 laborers to lay the foundations and dig the canals. It is estimated that approximately 100,000 people died from disease, exhaustion and floods during the first few years. 'The town is built on human bones,' the saying goes. The construction of the city began along the banks of the river and radiated inland along broad avenues from the shipyards.

In 1712, three years after the Swedes were finally and decisively defeated, Peter the Great decreed that St Petersburg was now the capital of the Russian Empire. Unfortunately, the aristocracy and merchants did not share his enthusiasm. Peter did not have the patience to persuade them, so he simply commanded the 1,000 leading families and 500 of the most prominent merchants to build houses in the new capital. Aside from the Peter and Paul Fortress and Peter's cabin, the notable buildings of this era still standing are the Menschikov and Kikin palaces,

St Petersburg in the early 1800s. A view of the Strelka and lighthouse with the Peter and Paul Fortress in the distance. The city was a busy port even then. In one summer month alone, contrary to the impression given by this painting, over 19,000 ships anchored here from all over the world.

the Alexander Nevsky Monastery and the Monplaisir Palace at Petrodvorets. The construction of St Petersburg was the first time—but certainly not the last—that the hand of the State intervened on a national scale in the lives of the Russian masses.

By 1725, the year of Peter's death, St Petersburg had a population of 75,000 unwilling subjects. For the next few years the future of the new capital was shaky due to the lack of Peter's strong hand. The council which then ruled Russia under the 12-year-old Peter II moved the imperial court back to Moscow and thousands of people thankfully left the half-built city. They stayed away until Peter II's early death, after which Empress Anna took the reins and in 1732 decreed that the capital would return to St Petersburg. Under Anna, the second great phase of the construction of St Petersburg began. She hired Bartolomeo Rastrelli, the son of an Italian sculptor hired by Peter the Great, to build her a Winter Palace (no longer standing), the first permanent imperial residence in the city. She also ordered the construction of a 24-meters-long (80-feet) and 10-meters-high (33-feet) ice palace complete with rooms and ice furniture on the frozen Neva. This was built for a courtier who had been unfaithful to her and was forced to marry an ugly Kalmyk tribeswoman from Central Asia in a mock ceremony. They were stripped naked and had to spend the night in the ice palace with only each other for warmth.

Anna died the same winter, and after the brief rule of another child czar, Ivan VI, the Empress Elizabeth, daughter of Peter the Great, took the throne and built many of the most important buildings in St Petersburg. At this time (1741–61), Rastrelli and other imported European architects had developed a style that later became known as Elizabethan rococo. Like a wedding cake, the basic structures disappeared underneath an ornate icing of pilasters, statuary and reliefs. The other recurrent theme was size. These buildings did not reach for the heavens like the churches of the Moscow Kremlin; they sprawled across acres of flat countryside. Huge architectural clusters like the Winter Palace and the Hermitage and the palaces at Peterhof and Pushkin, all painted an ethereal turquoise, were testament mostly to Elizabeth's power to do as she pleased. By the end of her rule, St Petersburg looked more like a stage set than a working city, with broad avenues built for parades and palaces like props for some grandiose drama.

After Elizabeth's death another weak czar, Peter III, took the throne and soon died after forging an unpopular alliance with Prussia. The scepter was handed to his wife, Catherine II, an independently-minded German princess who ruled the empire for 34 years. Under Catherine, later dubbed 'the Great', St Petersburg solidified its position as the artistic and political center of the empire, as intellectuals flocked to the now-thriving academies of arts and sciences. The latest political ideas from Western Europe were hotly debated among the aristocracy, and the streets and squares of the city were dotted with sculptures crafted by the finest European artists, including the enormous Bronze Horseman sculptural portrait of Peter the Great cast by the Frenchman Falconet. At the end of Catherine's reign in 1796, there was a profound sense of achievement in St Petersburg; in less than a century it had become one of the leading cities in the world. But there was also unease: the winds of change were blowing, and no one knew how to reconcile the new political ideas of St Petersburg with the profoundly conservative and deeply religious Russian countryside.

Catherine's son, the mentally unstable Paul I, built a fortress variously known as the Mikhailovsky or Engineer's Palace to protect himself from conspirators against the throne (see page 426). His paranoia proved justified, because in 1801, just 41 days after he moved in, his own courtiers strangled him to death. His successor was Alexander I, whose liberal reforms during the first half of his reign were wildly popular among the aristocracy and intelligentsia. In 1861, when he emancipated the serfs, thousands of freed families flocked into the capital to try and earn a living. By 1862 St Petersburg had a population of 532,000 and was the fourth largest city in Europe after Paris, London and Constantinople. The latter half of Alexander's rule was less successful, and a number of revolutionary cells were formed within the aristocracy to overthrow the imperial system. When Alexander died in December 1825, these cells were violently opposed to the accession of his anointed successor, his younger brother Nicholas, who was known to be a conservative and sympathetic to the Prussians. A group of guard officers, later known as Decembrists, took over the Senate Square and demanded a constitutional government. Nicholas ordered the army's cannons to fire on them, and the Decembrists fled in confusion. The main plotters were arrested and interned in the Peter and Paul Fortress (see page 382), where five of them were executed and 115 were sent to Siberia. Later, in 1849, this fortress was also the prison for the writer Fyodor Dostoevsky and the rest of the Petrashevsky Circle of socialist revolutionaries. Under Nicholas' orders they were sentenced to death, led before a firing squad and then reprieved at the last minute and exiled to Siberia.

The period from Nicholas I through the Russian Revolution in 1917 was an era of more or less constant political repression of the aristocracy and intelligentsia. Paradoxically, in St Petersburg it was the time of a great flowering of creativity that gave us some of the masterpieces of world literature, music and ballet, with writers like Pushkin, Gogol and Dostoevsky; the Mighty Band of the composers Rimsky-Korsakov, Mussorgsky and Borodin; and the choreographers of the Mariinsky Ballet, whose dances are still performed today.

Political turmoil proceeded apace with the artistic ferment during the latter half of the 19th century. St Petersburg was at the center, and a number of prominent revolutionary theorists, including the anarchist Mikhail Bakunin, and the writer Nikolai Chernyshevsky, spent time in the Peter and Paul Fortress. In March 1881, these activities finally bore fruit when a terrorist cell called the People's Freedom Group succeeded in mortally wounding Czar Alexander II with a bomb on the banks of the Ekaterininsky Canal. This led to more decades of oppression under Alexander III and Nicholas II, which only served to heighten the political unrest. By this time the imperial system was not only unpopular among the St Petersburg elite but throughout Russian society.

In 1905, Russia was given a portent of its future when a series of strikes by soldiers and workers led to a huge demonstration in St Petersburg. A radical priest named Father Gapon led thousands of workers in a march to the Winter Palace to present a petition to Nicholas II (see page 450). As they entered Palace Square, soldiers opened fire and hundreds of unarmed protesters were killed. 'Bloody Sunday' shocked the nation and galvanized the revolutionary movement. Socialist intellectuals and workers formed mass parties for the first time and demanded a share of the power. Nicholas gave them a weak advisory body named the Duma, which was accepted by the moderates but not by the extreme left, and arrested as many revolutionary rabble-rousers as he could. Trotsky went to jail and Lenin escaped to Switzerland.

When Russia went to war against Germany in 1914, St Petersburg's name was changed to Petrograd to avoid the Germanic implications of having a 'burg' at the end of its name. World War I was disastrous for the Russian Empire. The long and bloody war in the trenches sapped the economically and politically weak nation. Back in St Petersburg, the czar and the Duma fought for power, while the charismatic priest Rasputin played mind games with the czarina and her circle, and the people starved. On March 12, 1917, the people of the capital rioted. They killed policemen, broke open the jail and set the courthouse on fire. The soldiers stationed in the city refused to quell the rioters; instead they joined them. Three days later the czar abdicated, and Russia was ruled by the Provisional Government led by the socialist leader Alexander Kerensky.

In April 1917, Vladimir Lenin arrived in Petrograd's Finland Station (see page 447) after a decade of exile and plotting and was met by a cheering mass of thousands. From the top of an armored car in front of the station Lenin gave a speech rallying his Bolshevik Party and their allies, the Soviets of Workers and Soldiers, against Kerensky's government. There followed months of agitation and attempted revolution which culminated in the events of the night of November 7, 1917.* The battleship *Aurora*, under the control of the Bolsheviks, fired one blank shell at the Winter Palace giving the signal for the Bolshevik troops to storm the palace and the other principal government buildings. The party of Lenin, Trotsky and Stalin was in command of the Russian Empire. A month later Lenin ordered the formation of the Extraordinary Commission for the Suppression of Counterrevolution, the Cheka—later known as the KGB.

For the next three years civil war raged through the nation. The Soviets were attacked first by the Germans, then the White Russian army and the British Royal Navy. During that time Petrograd's population dropped from 2,500,000 to 720,000, due to hardship. In March 1918, Lenin moved the Soviet Government to Moscow because Petrograd was vulnerable to German attack—and perhaps also because of his distaste for the artificial imperial city.

On July 17, 1918, under Lenin's orders, the former Czar Nicholas II, his family and four servants were secretly executed by a Bolshevik firing squad in the town of

*In 45 BC Julius Caesar introduced the Julian calendar to the Western world. A new reformed calendar was introduced by Pope Gregory XIII in 1582 which calculated time more accurately. By the 20th century the difference between the Julian and Gregorian calendars was 13 days. Russia continued to use the old Julian calendar until February 1, 1918. This is why the October Revolution came to be celebrated at the beginning of November.

Yekaterinburg where they had been held in exile after Nicholas' abdication. Their unmarked graves were not discovered until 1991; the remains were reburied in 1998 in the Peter and Paul Cathedral (see page 383).

On Lenin's death in 1924, Petrograd was renamed Leningrad after a man who publicly despised the city and spent less than a year of his life there. Ominously, that same year, there was a great flood in his namesake city. During the next two decades MOSCOW became the center of cultural and political life, while Leningrad became identified as a center of shipbuilding and industry. Its tradition of political assassination nevertheless continued with the 1934 shooting of Leningrad Party leader Sergei Kirov at the Smolny Institute. Some say that Stalin was behind the, shooting, and he certainly used it

as the excuse to start the purges of 1934–6 in which thousands of Communist Party members were killed.

Leningrad received its next great blow during World War II. For 900 days, from September 1941 to January 1944, the German army laid siege to the city and hundreds of thousands of inhabitants died, adding more bones to the foundations. By 1944 there were fewer than 600,000 people left, compared to a 1939 population of 3,100,000. The poet Mandalstam wrote, 'living in St Petersburg is like sleeping in a coffin.' (See pages 464 and 467.)

Adding further to the city's misery, Stalin instigated another purge in 1948–9, known as the Leningrad Affair, in which many of the city's artists and top Party members vanished forever or were sent to Siberia. In this purge it was apparent that the Moscow leadership remained suspicious of the Leningrad Party hierarchy because they retained some of the idealism of the original revolutionaries.

The years following the war were devoted to reconstruction of the city center and the development of huge satellite suburbs to the south. Thankfully, the government banned high-rises in the center, sustaining Catherine the Great's edict that no building should be higher than the Winter Palace.

Under Khrushchev and Brezhnev, Leningrad became even more of a second-rate provincial city. It was forced to concentrate on military matters and industrial accomplishments. By the mid-1970s the population had increased significantly to 4,500,000 people. In the stagnant atmosphere of these ensuing decades the city still nurtured a reactionary climate; this time it was between the suppressed artistic community and the brainwashed bureaucrats. It was no accident that the first major post-Stalinist trial of an artist (the Jewish writer Joseph Brodsky) took place in Leningrad. In 1964, Brodsky was sentenced to Siberian exile (and later expelled from the country); his crime—not having official permission to write poetry. Brodsky wrote about his beloved city: '...during the White Night, let your immovable earthly glory dawn on me, a fugitive.'

Members of the intellectual community were forced to reject professions not officially recognized. Thus to earn a living they had to take on such menial jobs as night-watchmen, janitors, furnace stokers and dock workers, while secretly pursuing their passions. Despite this ironclad curtain, forbidden works were secretly circulated in underground *samizdat* publications. The up-and-coming rock pioneers began *magnitizdat* where homemade music tapes were circulated like manuscripts. The poet Gorgovsky recalled the 1970s in Leningrad as 'dead, inert times, and fatal for art's breathing'.

The stifling censorship and cruel punishment drove many Leningrad artists to alcoholism, madness and even suicide. On top of all this, the unchecked industrial pollution of the city added further to the suffocation of the population.

(previous pages) On May 9 Russia marks Victory Day with a holiday, commemorating the end of World War II which Russians call the Great Patriotic War. Many veterans dress in uniform and wear their medals while marching in parades and visiting war memorials.

THE OLD GUARD

*A*n old man of eighty-four attracted my attention in the Mikhailovsky gardens. He brandished a sabre-shaped walking-stick as he strode down the paths, his war medals dangled in ranks at his chest, and his features showed bellicose above a mist of white beard. He looked like God the Father peering over a cloud.

'I'm an Old Bolshevik,' he announced to me. 'One of the original Revolutionaries!'

A ghost from the twenties, he still exulted in the people's common ownership. He patted the tree trunks possessively as he marched by and frequently said 'This is my tree, and this is my tree.'

In 1907 he had become a revolutionary, and had been sent in chains to Siberia. But a fellow-prisoner, he said, had concealed a file in the lapel of his coat, and together they had cut through the manacles and fled back to Leningrad. Those were the days when Siberian exiles and prisoners—Trotsky, Stalin and Bakunin among them—escaped from Siberia with laughable ease and slipped over frontiers with the freedom of stray cats.

Then the old man had joined the Revolution and fought for the three years against the Whites. He settled into a military stride as he spoke of it, and thrust out his beard like a torpedo, while all the time his gaze flashed and fulminated over the gardens. 'Get off the grass, comrade!' he bellowed. A young mother, seated on the sward beside her pram, looked up in bewilderment. 'Get off our motherland's grass!'

He embodied the intrusive precepts of early Communism, whose zealots were encouraged to scrutinize, shrivel and denounce each other. He was the self-proclaimed guardian and persecutor of all about him, and he entered the 1980s with the anachronism of a mastodon. Farther on a girl was leaning in the fork of one of his precious trees. 'Keep away from there!' he roared. 'Can't you see you're stopping it grow? Get off!' She gaped at him, said nothing, did not move. He marched on unperturbed. He even anathematized a mousing cat. 'What are you looking for, comrade?

Leave nature alone!' He did not seem to mind or notice that nobody obeyed him.

We rested under a clump of acacias. 'When I was a boy,' he said, 'I saw these trees planted.' He pointed to the largest of them, which bifurcated into a gnarled arm. 'That tree was no taller than a little lamp-post then. The garden was private, of course, but as a boy I often squeezed in over the railings. The tsar and tsaritsa used to walk here in the summer.' His voice dwindled from an alsatian growl to purring reminiscence. 'Once, while I was hiding in the shrubs, I saw them myself... What were they like? It's hard to recall exactly. But she was a beautiful woman, I remember. She had her hand on his arm. And he seemed very large and handsome, and...' But he never finished. The lurking commissar in him erupted again. 'What are you doing, comrade?' Beneath us, a man was raking weeds out of an ornamental pond. 'How can you weed a lake?'

The gardener looked up stoically. 'I'm at work.'

Work. The magic syllable.

Immediately, as if some benedictory hand had passed its grace across the old man's brow, his expression changed to a look of benign redress. 'Fine,' he murmured, 'work.' For him the word had the potency of 'revolution' or 'collective.' The mousing cat, too, had been at work, I thought, but had been unable to voice this watchword.

Before we parted he said: 'I'll give you my address, not the real one. That's secret. You see,' he repeated, 'I'm one of the Old Bolsheviks.'

I wondered then if he were not deranged. He scribbled out his address on the back of a newspaper, in enormous handwriting. It was only as he was leaving me that I realized from his age that the history he had given me was nonsense. The tsars did not send lone boys of eleven to Siberia.

'How old did you say you were?' I asked. For he looked timeless.

'I know what you're thinking,' he answered. His eyes twinkled at me collusively. 'You Estonians, you're a clever lot. You're thinking that I can't have been sent to Siberia aged eleven. But actually I'm ninety-four...'— and he strode away through the trees.

Colin Thubron, Among the Russians

PERIOD OF PERESTROIKA

With the advent of Gorbachev and his new policy of perestroika (restructuring), the harsh totalitarian regime that had ruled Leningrad for more than seven decades began to crack. In the 1980s the most popular and controversial TV program in the country, *600 Seconds*, was broadcast from Leningrad. Its brazen reporter Alexander Nevzorov exposed the corruption and misery of the old socialist system; he was hailed as the Russian 'Robin Hood'. The State also allowed long-banned and shelved works to officially appear—everything from film, prose and poetry to music, art and ballet. In the spring of 1987, almost half a century after their completion, Anna Akhmatova's poems *Requiem* and *Poem Without a Hero* were published. Other Leningrad authors such as Mandalstam, Zoshchenko and Nabokov were widely read for the first time. The two émigrés, composer Stravinsky and choreographer Balanchine, were allowed to return and visit the city of their birth, and their creations were played and staged in the Kirov Theater's repertoire.

In 1990, the economic law professor Anatoly Sobchak was elected Leningrad city council chairman. Later, as mayor, he brought about sweeping changes to crumbling Soviet dogma. During the August attempt to overthrow Gorbachev, Mayor Sobchak lead the city back into the political arena, and personally stopped putsch plotters from a planned military takeover of the city. Sobchak had allied himself with Captain Melnikov, the commander of the nearby Kronstadt naval base, and Melnikov had offered to protect Sobchak and the city council within the fortress. Instead of hiding, Sobchak rallied 250,000 residents into Palace Square (the site of past revolutions) in support of Yeltsin. When the coup failed, Sobchak became a national hero, second only to Yeltsin.

In the early years of glasnost (openness), a democratic movement pushed to change the city's name back to St Petersburg. On October 31, 1991 (two months after the attempted coup), Leningrad was officially renamed Sankt Pieterburg. The Nobel prize-winning writer Joseph Brodsky, living in New York, was pleased: 'It is much better for them to live in a city that bears the name of a saint than that of a devil!' By December 1991, the Soviet Union had collapsed.

ST PETERSBURG TODAY

After the Baltic States broke away from the Soviet Union in May 1991, St Petersburg's presence as a major port increased sharply. The city was once again becoming the country's 'window to the West'. Even though hard-liners appeared (calling themselves everything from pro-communists to imperialists and ultra-nationalists), the city continued democratic reforms in earnest. St Petersburg was the first city in the new Russia to sell government-owned shops to private enterprises and create a private banking sector. A stock and commodities market opened in the original 18th-century Stock Exchange. In March 1997, two centuries after the original city patrols were created, the new *gorodovoys* ceremoniously marched down Nevsky Prospekt; these patrolmen, whose sole duty it is to make foreigners welcome, have extensive knowledge of the city and environs. The mayor also returned many of the churches and religious buildings to the Orthodox Church. St Petersburg is slowly evolving back into the cultural and spiritual capital of her former years.

This magnificent and soulful city seems to have always been balanced between order and chaos. With newfound freedoms, the artistic and business communities are thriving. But a grimmer reality, formed by the many changes and market reforms, also exists. With escalating inflation many residents, especially the elderly, struggle day to day merely to survive, and crime is on the rise. Over 15,000 historic palaces, mansions, museums and theaters have massively deteriorated over time. But with no federal funding the city counts on advice and investments from the West to help preserve these landmarks and solve its ecological woes. But despite the difficulties the residents remain hopeful. 'Considering the conditions that were overcome to even build this city,' observed the mayor, 'the St Petersburg tradition will surely guide us.'

The cradle to revolutions, St Petersburg stands at the forefront of determination and progress. Legend has it that as long as the statue of the Bronze Horseman remains in its place overlooking the Neva, St Petersburg will never falter.

> *And high above him all undaunted*
> *Deaf to the storm's rebellious roars*
> *With hand outstretched, the Idol mounted*
> *On steed of bronze, majestic soars.*

Alexander Pushkin (see page 510)

PETER THE GREAT (1672–1725)

Peter the Great, one of Russia's most enlightened and driven rulers, pulled his country out of her dark feudal past into a status equal with her European neighbors. Possessing an intense curiosity toward foreign lands, he opened Russia's window to the West and became the first ruler to journey extensively outside Russia. Standing at six feet seven inches, with a passionate will and temper to match his great size, Peter I, against all odds, also built a city that became one of the most magnificent capitals in all of Europe.

Peter's father, Czar Alexei, ruled the Empire from 1645 to 1676. Alexei's first wife had 13 children; but only two, Fyodor and Ivan, were destined to inherit the throne. Natalya Naryshkin became Alexei's second wife and gave birth to a son named Peter in 1672.

When Alexei died, his son, Fyodor III, succeeded to the throne and reigned from 1676 to 1682. During this time, his half-brother, Peter, along with ill-favored Natalya, were sent away from Moscow to live in the country. Instead of the usual staunch upbringing within the Kremlin walls, Peter had the freedom to roam the countryside and make friends with peasant children. When Fyodor died, a rivalry broke out between the two families as to which son would gain the throne. Peter won the first battle and was proclaimed czar at the age of ten. But soon Ivan's side of the family spread rumors to the Streltsy, or Musketeers (the military protectors of Moscow), that the Naryshkins were plotting to kill Ivan. The Streltsy demanded that Peter's half-brother be crowned, too. So, for a time, the throne of Moscovy was shared by the two boys, the feeble-minded Ivan V and the robust Peter I. In actuality, however, it was Sophia, Peter's older half-sister, who ruled as Regent for seven years with the help of her lover, Prince Golitsyn.

Peter spent most of this time back in the country, mainly engaged in studies that had a practical use. One fateful day, on his father's estate in Izmailovo, the young boy discovered a wrecked English boat that could sail against the wind. He had the boat repaired and learned how to sail it. In 1688, Peter built a flotilla on Plescheyevo Lake at Pereslavl-Zalessky to practice his ideas for a future navy. Infatuated now with sailing, he also immersed himself in the study of mathematics and navigation and tried to instill a maritime spirit into the whole of society. Naval training courses and marine sports clubs were offered to nobles, and jobs as seamen opened to the lower classes. Later, St Petersburg became one of the most important trading ports on the Baltic.

In addition, the young czar worked well with his hands and became an accomplished carpenter, blacksmith and printer; he even mended his own clothes. As a child, he loved to play soldiers, and drilled his companions in military maneuvers, eventually staging mock battles with weapons and in uniforms supplied by the Royal Arsenal. Peter was also fascinated with the techniques of torture. Later in his reign, fearing an assassination attempt, he would torture his first son, Alexei, to death.

Sophia was eventually removed from court affairs and sent off to live in Novodevichy Convent outside Moscow. When Ivan died, Peter I, at the age of 22, assumed the throne as the sole czar and took up his imperial duties with earnest. On the throne, his first real battle was against the Turks. His plan was to take the Sea of Azov at the mouth of the Don in order to gain access to the Black Sea. Peter built a fleet of ships, and for the first time in her history, Russia led a surprise attack from the water. The Turks were defeated and Russia had her first southern outlet to the sea.

After this successful campaign, Peter set off on a long journey to the West. He traveled to England, France, and Germany, and worked as a shipbuilder in Holland. Back home, the Streltsy, with the help of Sophia, began to organize a secret revolt to overthrow the czar. Peter caught wind of their plans; upon his return, he captured and tortured almost 2,000 men and dissolved the corps. By this time, the now cultured ruler had lost interest in his first wife and sent her off to a convent in Sergiyev Posad, the equivalent of divorce.

Peter was greatly impressed by Western ways and, to him, change symbolized Russia's path to modernization. Knee-length coats became the new fashion. One of the new State laws prohibited the growing of beards. Since the Church taught that man was created in God's image (ie with a beard), many believed Peter I to be the Antichrist.

But Peter was as determined as ever to pull Russia out of her isolation. He tolerated new religions, allowing the practices of Catholics,

Peter the Great in England, painted by Sir Godfrey Kneller in 1698

Lutherans and Protestants, and even approving of the sacrilegious scientific stance taken by Galileo. He exercised State control over the Russian Orthodox Church by establishing the Holy Synod. This supremacy of the czar over the Russian Church lasted from 1721 until 1917. In 1721, Peter also declared himself Emperor of All Russia.

During the Great Northern Wars, while trying to chase the Swedes out of the Baltic, Peter organized the building of the first Russian fleet on the Gulf of Finland. After conquering the Swedes in 1709, the Russian navy returned to the city where thousands of citizens lined the Neva River embankments to cheer the victorious ships. (To this day, St Petersburg celebrates Navy Day, the last Sunday in July, when the naval fleet is paraded down the Neva.) Engravings of the city filled with ships decorated the proud czar's palaces. It was during this time that Peter met and fell in love with a good-natured peasant girl named Catherine, whom he later married; Empress Catherine ruled for two years after his death.

In 1703, Peter began the fanatic building of a new city in the north at a point where the Neva River drained into Lake Ladoga. The city was constructed on a myriad of islands, canals and swamps. The conditions were brutal and nearly 100,000 perished the first year alone. But within a decade, St Petersburg was a city of 35,000 stone buildings and the capital of the Russian Empire. Peter commissioned many well-known foreign architects: the Italian Rastrelli, the German Schlüter, the Swiss Trezzini and the Frenchman Leblond, who created Peter's Summer Palace of Petrodvorets. Montferrand later designed St Isaac's Cathedral, which took over 100 kilos of gold and 40 years to build. Peter brought the majesty of the West to his own doorstep. It was no small wonder that St Petersburg was nicknamed the Venice of the North.

Peter died looking out from his window to the West. Today in St Petersburg stands a monument to the city's founder, a statue of Peter the Great as the Bronze Horseman. The statue, made by the French sculptor, Falconet, shows Peter rearing up on a horse that symbolizes Russia, while trampling a serpent that opposes his reforms. Pushkin wrote that Peter 'with iron bridle reared up Russia to her fate'. By a great and forceful will, Peter the Great had successfully led Russia out of her darkness into the light of a Golden Age.

Culture

A political and social history tells only half the story of St Petersburg. Of equal consequence are the literary and artistic creations set in St Petersburg, because in them writers and artists have created a parallel city that lives just as much in the minds of the inhabitants as today's crowded, slightly faded metropolis. Since the reign of Elizabeth, the realms of fiction, poetry, symphony, opera and ballet have all collaborated to produce an intellectual St Petersburg that is one of the great artistic creations of humankind.

Literature

In the earliest years of St Petersburg, Peter the Great emphasized the practical sciences, particularly engineering, and his image of the city as a glorified barracks left little room for the arts. St Petersburg's first great contributor to Russian culture, Mikhail Lomonosov, arrived in the city in 1736 and went on to become the director of the Academy of Sciences.

Lomonosov was a kind of Russian Benjamin Franklin—a chemist, physicist, geologist, educator, historian and poet. He had also studied in the West and was a friend of the French philosopher Voltaire. Lomonosov devoted his life to bringing the ideas of the European Enlightenment to Russia and at the same time tried to advance Russia's cultural thought in distinctly Russian ways. His greatest achievement in the cultural sphere was his Russian grammar, which codified and encouraged the use of the language of the common people in Russian literature.

If Lomonosov was the genius of the 18th century, then Alexander Pushkin was the soul of the 19th century. Pushkin was born into an aristocratic family; his mother was the granddaughter of Peter the Great's Abyssinian general, Hannibal, and the poet was proud of his nobility and African blood. In 1811, Pushkin was sent to the school at Tsarskoye Selo (also called Pushkin, see page 486) where he began to write light romantic poetry. In his 20s he led a life of aristocratic dissoluteness in the salons and bordellos of the imperial capital. Many of his friends were politically active young officers associated with the Decembrist group, which Pushkin was never asked to join because they considered him too frivolous for their revolutionary mission. Nevertheless, he wrote some mildly seditious poems; one of them, *Ruslan and Ludmilla*, caused such a stir with the younger generation that it was censored by Alexander I, who also exiled the poet to the Caucasus in 1820.

During his exile from St Petersburg he wrote some of his most famous works, including his epic *Boris Godunov*, the story of the pretender to the Russian throne at the start of the Time of Troubles in the early 17th century. At the end of his exile he began his masterpiece *Eugene Onegin*, a novel in verse about two star-crossed lovers, Onegin and Tatyana. His famous novel *Queen of Spades* came out in 1833; the gambler Ghermann symbolized the secret craving of the people to take a hand in the gamble of winning freedom during an opportunistic age. That same year Pushkin completed his last narrative poem *The Bronze Horseman*, revered as one of the greatest works about St Petersburg (see page 510). In it a young government clerk watches a huge storm cause a flood in St Petersburg which destroys most of the city and kills thousands, including his fiancée. Driven

mad by grief, he comes upon Falconet's statue of Peter the Great, the Bronze Horseman, and he associates Peter's terrible imperial power with the destructive force of the flood. The mad clerk shakes his fist at the statue, and the horseman comes to life in a rage and chases him out of the square with a great clattering of bronze hoofs. In 1836, Pushkin was mortally wounded in a pistol duel over his wife's honor and died in January 1837 at the age of 36. Immediately upon his death he was lionized as the greatest Russian writer and that acclaim continues to this day.

Pushkin's mantle was inherited by Nikolai Gogol, a Ukrainian-born writer, whose work is difficult to classify. At

Statue of Alexander Pushkin in St Petersburg's Arts Square.

A bronze bust of Fyodor Dostoevsky (1821–81) graces his tomb in the cemetery of St Petersburg's Alexander Nevsky Monastery.

times, as in his play *The Inspector General*, he satirized the vast bureaucratic state that had taken over the Russian Empire. His famous short story *The Overcoat* is more enigmatic. A petty government clerk in St Petersburg invests all his savings in a new overcoat, but as he is returning home late at night he loses it to a band of robbers. After he discovers that none of his superiors will help him find his coat he dies of grief, only to reappear on the streets of St Petersburg as an avenging ghost. Gogol followed *The Overcoat* with *Dead Souls* (see Excerpt on page 173), which was to be the first volume of a projected trilogy envisioned as a sort of Russian divine comedy about sin, atonement and salvation. As he wrote the second volume he began to go mad, thinking that the flames of hell were licking at his heels, and eventually threw the pages into the fire. He died in 1852 after doctors applied leeches and bled him to death.

The next great St Petersburg writer was Fyodor Dostoevsky, who although anguished and epileptic managed to live a full lifespan. Dostoevsky studied to be a military engineer and fell in with the Petrashevsky Circle of socialist revolutionaries in St Petersburg. After being condemned to death and reprieved at the last minute, Dostoevsky was exiled to Omsk in Siberia for four years. When he returned he wrote *Memories from the House of the Dead* about his Siberian experiences, and the acclaim at its publication in 1860 launched his career as a writer. Most of Dostoevsky's novels were written in serial form for magazines so he could stay one step ahead of his many creditors. He took his subject matter from popular melodramas and sensational newspaper stories and wrote about them with the methods of psychological realism, a form that he pioneered. His greatest novel, *Crime and Punishment*, tells the story of Raskolnikov, an impoverished former student who murders an old woman—a pawnbroker, and feels such guilt that by the time he is finally brought to justice he welcomes it.

Late in life Dostoevsky became a devout believer in Orthodox Christianity. Luckily for world literature he never lost his commitment to artistic realism, so his novels show the passionate struggle of trying to reach, but never attain, an ideal goal. When Dostoevsky died in 1881, thousands of Russians, ordinary citizens and fellow writers alike, accompanied his coffin to the Alexander Nevsky Monastery for a hero's burial.

Anton Chekhov (1860–1904), famous for such plays as *The Cherry Orchard* and *The Seagull*, had his first stories published in St Petersburg magazines. As a realist, he expressed human drama in plain and simple words. He also loved contributing to the city's monarchist daily newspaper *Novoye Vremya* (*New Times*), which even the czar read. From 1885 to 1888, Chekhov wrote more than 300 stories for the St Petersburg weekly magazine *Fragments*.

In 1906, the twenty-six-year-old writer and poet Alexander Blok was published in the St Petersburg weekly periodical *Niva*. He soon ignited the new Symbolist movement that heralded Russia's Silver Age of Literature. After many years of classical and realist prose, readers regained an interest in poetry, not popular since the era of Pushkin. Many of the symbolists looked upon the Revolution as an event that would purge Russia of its sins and bring on a new era of wholesome equality. Poets readily participated in political and spiritual themes that thrived in the dissident and decadent atmosphere of the times.

Blok's poems were also filled with erotic and romantic motifs, and the handsome blonde poet soon had a massive cult following among the female population. But soon frustrated with the new regime, Blok wrote the narrative epic poem *The Twelve*, about an army patrol who transform into the twelve apostles while walking through ruined Petrograd after the Revolution; led by Christ, they hope for redemption. A year later, Blok was arrested by the Cheka police for participating in anti-Soviet conspiracies. He was eventually released, but as he later wrote to a friend: 'I'm suffocating... and the old music is gone.' Broken, Blok never again picked up his pen. When he died in Leningrad in 1921 at the age of 40, his friends knew that the lack of creative freedom had stifled his spirit. The obituary in *Pravda* for one of the greatest poets of the 20th century was composed of one sentence: 'Last night the poet Alexander Blok passed away.'

Two weeks after Blok's funeral Nikolai Gumilyov, the ex-husband of the poet Anna Akhmatova, was arrested on false charges by Bolshevik police for participating in anti-Soviet propaganda. Before his arrest Gumilyov had written a poem called *The Streetcar Gone Astray*, about the outcome of the Revolution. He was executed by firing squad without a trial. Prior to the Revolution he had founded a new poetry movement in St Petersburg known as Acmeism. Their idea was to reject the ethereal aspects of symbolism and write about the direct and tangible 'salty skin of the earth'.

The cofounder of the Acmeist movement, Osip Mandalstam, possessed a prophetic understanding of the country's suffering and fate as expressed in his three collections of poetry: *Stone, Tristia* and *Poems*. Mandalstam also did not escape persecution under Stalin, and was eventually sentenced to five years hard labor for counterrevolutionary activities. He died in 1938 from heart failure in a freezing transit camp in Vladivostok, Siberia. His widow Nadezhda Mandalstam wrote an incredibly moving memoir about her life with Osip. It was published in two large volumes entitled *Hope Against Hope* and *Hope Abandoned*.

With these quintessential St Petersburg poets dead, the new regime severely underscored the fact that the cultural elite would be under their control. Not able to live with his own disillusionment, the futurist poet Vladimir Mayakovsky shot himself while playing Russian roulette at the age of 36. His suicide stunned an already desolate nation. It was Anna Akhmatova who took up the poetic reins during these times of terror. (See Special Topic on page 498.)

Her contemporary, Vladimir Nabokov, made his debut as a poet in St Petersburg, though he emigrated to Europe in 1919 and then in 1940 to America. Born in the city in 1899, Nabokov frequently used St Petersburg as a theme for his stories. Some of his classic works include *Pale Fire, Pnin, Laughter in the Dark* and *Lolita*—later made into a film by Stanley Kubrick. Nabokov's brilliant autobiography *Speak, Memory* was one of the first contemporary books to introduce the city of St Petersburg to an international audience.

With Akhmatova's death in 1966, the one heroic figure that had connected the three eras of St Petersburg, Petrograd and Leningrad was gone. Joseph Brodsky, born on Vasilyevsky Island in 1940, was considered the heir apparent to both Nabokov and Akhmatova. But, in 1964, the writer and poet was sentenced to five years hard labor in the Arctic Circle for writing poetry without official permission. Interrogated at the trial about where his poetry came from, he replied: 'I thought that it came from God.' After being imprisoned three times and twice thrown into a madhouse for his writings, Brodsky was finally expelled from the Soviet Union in 1972. The old regime tried to erase his existence from history, but Brodsky received international acclaim when he won the Nobel Prize for Literature in 1987. He became an American citizen in 1980 and died in New York in 1995. In Brodsky, Leningraders felt that the Nobel prize also honored the other literary geniuses who were never recognized by their own country.

In 1964, shocked by Brodsky's trial, the writer Andrei Bitov began work on his novel *Pushkin House*, a requiem for the disillusioned St Petersburg intelligentsia. The novel's hero works at Leningrad's Pushkin House, the research academy of Russian literature. Bitov uses this theme to interweave writings by many of the city's past respected authors—from Pushkin to Akhmatova. It was published in 1978 by an American publishing house, but was not allowed past Soviet censors until 1987, when it immediately became a sensation during Gorbachev's glasnost era.

By 1990 many long-banned works by authors such as Nabokov, Akhmatova and even Solzhenitsyn were allowed to be published and distributed among a new generation of Russian readers. Many foreign authors were also translated into Russian for the first time. But ironically, with the demise of socialism, the Writers' Union and most State-subsidized publishing also collapsed. Post-perestroika Russia appeared just as devastated as its corrupt Communist shadow; this time however, instead of for political reasons, contemporary writers were stifled out of economic needs.

After a period of crisis, Russian literature soon began to recover with a new exuberance and freshness of vision. In the early 1990s the International Booker Prize Committee instituted a special Booker Russian-novel prize to annually recognize a new generation of Russian writers. The quarterly periodical *GLAS* publishes contemporary Russian writers, translated into English, to stimulate wider knowledge of modern Russian fiction and poetry abroad (see Recommended Reading, page 572).

BALLET

The first *balli*, or *balletti*, originated in Italy during the Renaissance, when dance became an important social function in court life. Men would entertain at court festivities in routines combining music, dancing, singing and acting; women, on the other hand, were forbidden to dance openly in public. By the late 15th century, it was the vogue for court entertainment to be combined with banquets—each course was accompanied by a new scene in the story. Menus still list the entrées as they did five centuries ago. The French soon copied the Italians by staging their own *ballets de cour*. Their courts brought in Italian dancing masters, and many outstanding French painters and poets collaborated in the elaborate displays. These staged spectacles were set up to glorify the power and the wealth of the monarchy.

King Louis XIV of France was an avid dancer himself and was to take the part of the sun in the *Ballet de la Nuit*. Later in life, when Louis could no longer dance, he established the first *Académie Royale de Musique* (now the Paris Opera) a dancing school was added that set the foundation of classical ballet.

As the Italians invented the idea of the *balli* as a combination of all the arts, the French developed this new vision of dance into a professional school, the *danse d'école*. A style of classical dancing was born with its own vocabulary of individual steps, the five positions of the feet (fashioned from court ballroom dance moves) and synchronized group movements. French terminology is still used today.

This form of ballet-dance was first staged in Moscow in 1672 by a German ensemble for Czar Alexei I. The theatrical performance, lasting ten hours, was based on the Bible's Book of Esther. Alexei's daughter, Sophia (the future regent), was very fond of dancing herself and composed comedy ballets, such as *Russalki* (the Mermaids). Sophia's half-brother, Peter the Great, encouraged Western dance and later, as czar, brought in many French, English and Polish companies for lavish productions in his new city of Sankt Pieterburkh. Later the St Petersburg Imperial Ballet was founded in 1738.

During the reigns of Elizabeth (1741–61) and Catherine the Great (1762–96), many French and Italian masters took up residence in St Petersburg and Moscow. By the turn of the century St Petersburg was approaching the peak of its cosmopolitan fame. It had four separate opera houses with permanent companies, all fully supported by the czarinas and czars. While ballet grew in popularity and artistic importance in Russia, it declined throughout the rest of Europe.

One of the most influential characters of the early Russian ballet scene was the Frenchman Charles Didelot, who arrived in Russia in 1801. He taught at the St Petersburg Imperial Ballet School for more than 25 years and wove French classical and Russian folk themes through the new romantic style of the times. He was the first to translate Pushkin's poems, *The Prisoner of the Caucasus* and *Ruslan and Ludmilla*, into the physical world of ballet. Under his direction, the ballet was made into a grand spectacle, incorporating the entire *corps de ballet*, costumes, scenery, and even special effects—dancers were fitted with wings and live pigeons flew across the stage.

Another of St Petersburg's well-known dancers was the Frenchman Marius Petipa, who came to Russia in 1847. Petipa was the master of the grand spectacle and produced an original ballet for the opening of each new season. During his 56-year career on the Russian stage, Petipa choreographed over 60 ballets for the Imperial Ballet, highlighting solos within each performance. In the early 1890s this grand master worked almost exclusively with Tchaikovsky, choreographing *Sleeping Beauty*, *The Nutcracker*, and *Swan Lake*. It was Petipa who brought the Imperial Ballet to the pinnacle of the ballet world.

All the St Petersburg ballets premièred at the Mariinsky Theater. Built by Albert Kavos in 1860, it was named after Maria, wife of Czar Alexander II. In 1935, it was renamed the Kirov, after the prominent Communist leader under Stalin; but in 1992, the original name was restored. The Mariinsky remains one of the most respected names in the ballet world. It is situated in St Petersburg along Glinka and Decembrists streets on Ploshchad Teatralnaya (Theater Square; see page 457). This section of land was once the location for St Petersburg carnivals and fairs. (In the 18th century, it was known as Ploshchad Karusel, Merry-Go-Round Square.) This gorgeous 1,700 seater, five-tiered theater is decorated with blue velvet, gilded stucco, ceiling paintings and chandeliers.

By the end of the 19th century the Mariinsky Theater had almost 200 permanently employed dancers, graded in rank. Each graduate of the Imperial Ballet

(following pages) Dancers of the Mariinsky (Kirov) Theater. (bottom right) Ballet slippers of the famous ballerina Anna Pavlova in the Vagonova Ballet School Museum.

School was placed into the *corps de ballet*; only a few rose to coryphée, *sujet*, prima ballerina and lastly *prima absoluta* (or, for a man, soloist to the czar). They were employed by the czar for 20 years and retired with full pensions. Ballet dancers were often invited to court banquets, and favorites received many luxurious presents from admirers and the royal family themselves. Nicholas II bestowed large gifts of diamonds and emeralds upon his jewel *danseuse* Kchessinskaya, which she often wore during performances.

As the spirit of revolution hung in the air, the Imperial Ballet's conventional classical style plunged into decline. It was the St Petersburg artistic entrepreneur Sergei Diaghilev (1872–1929), who revived the stagnating Imperial Ballet with the individual and innovative style of the Ballets Russes. Diaghilev brought Russia's best dancers, choreographers, musicians and artists together to create some of the most stunning spectacles that the world had ever known. His dancers were Pavlova, Karsavina and Nijinsky; his choreographers Fokine, Massine, Nijinskaya (Nijinsky's sister) and later Balanchine; musicians Tchaikovsky, Chopin, Stravinsky and Rimsky-Korsakov; and artists Benois, Bakst, Goncharova and even Picasso. During the first season abroad in Paris in 1909, the repertoire of the Ballets Russes consisted of Borodin's *Polovtsian Dances* from *Prince Igor*, Chopin's *Les Sylphides* and *The Banquet*, with music by Tchaikovsky, Mussorgsky and Rimsky-Korsakov. The programs were designed by the French writer Jean Cocteau and posters painted by Moscow artist Valentin Serov. Even Erik Satie joined the group of musicians. In the center of all this furor were two of the most magnificent dancers of the 20th century, Anna Pavlova and Vaslav Nijinsky.

Born the illegitimate daughter of a poor laundress, Pavlova did not seem destined for the stage. But in 1891, at the age of ten, this petite dark-eyed beauty was accepted into the St Petersburg Imperial Ballet School. When she graduated in 1899, the stunning performer leaped right into solo roles in the Mariinsky Theater. Anna then left to dance with the Ballets Russes; after her first performance in Paris, a French critic exuberantly claimed: 'She is to dance what Racine is to poetry, Poussin to painting, Gluck to music.' Pavlova was known for her dynamic short solos, filled with an endless cascade of jumps and pirouettes as in *The Dying Swan* and *The Dragonfly*.

Nijinsky was heralded as the greatest male dancer of his day—dancing was in his blood. For generations his family worked as dancers, acrobats, and circus performers. Vaslav was born in Kiev, Russia, in 1888, where his Polish parents were performing. When he was 11, his mother enrolled him in the St Petersburg Imperial Ballet School, where he studied for eight years. His graduation performance so impressed the *prima absoluta* ballerina Matilda Kchessinskaya that he immediately began his career at the Mariinsky Theater as a principal soloist.

His full genius emerged at the Ballets Russes' 1909 Paris debut. One spectator felt that 'his was the victory of breath over weight, the possession of body by the soul.' In 1911, Nijinsky was fired from the Imperial Ballet for not wearing the required little pair of trunks over his tights when he danced *Giselle*; this did not go down well with the dowager empress, who witnessed with crimson face the entire performance. His range in roles was astonishing. Everywhere he went, Nijinsky captured the hearts and adoration of the critics and audiences. One American critic noted, 'few of us can view the art of Nijinsky without emotion... he completely erased the memory of all male dancers that I had previously seen.'

Nijinsky danced with Pavlova in *Cleopatra* and as the ethereal spirit in *Le Spectre de la Rose*. Jean Cocteau, who saw his first performance in Paris, exclaimed that Nijinsky's jumps 'were so poignant, so contrary to all the laws of flight and balance, following so high and curved a trajectory, that I shall never again smell a rose without this unerasable phantom appearing before me.' Fokine choreographed up a storm of innovative and dynamic ballets and stressed strong male dancing; Nijinsky danced in almost all his creations, including *Le Pavillion d'Armide*, *Sheherazade*, *The Firebird*, *Narcisse*, *Daphnis and Chloe*, and *Le Dieu Bleu* (The Blue Clown). In his diary, Nijinsky wrote 'I am beginning to understand God. Art, love, nature are only an infinitesimal part of God's spirit. I wanted to recapture it and give it to the public... If they felt it, then I am reflecting Him. The world, in turn, would regard him as *Le Dieu de la Danse*.

His first choreographic work, *L'Après-Midi d'un Faune*, was performed in 1912. Even though only eight minutes long, it managed to cause a scandal that rocked even Paris. With his natural faun-like eyes, waxed pointed ears and horns, and dressed only in tights with a curly golden wig, Nijinsky danced around seven lively nymphs. At the end of the ballet, each nymph fled as she dropped her veil. During this flight of passage, he caught up with each nymph and swept down under her in one convulsive, erotic movement. The audience gasped audibly.

Nijinsky's *Le Sacre du Printemps*, performed a year later on May 29, 1913, stopped just short of causing a riot in Paris; even the composer, Igor Stravinsky, had to flee the theater. The story of the ballet weaves around the ritual of the pagan rites of spring. The dancers' movements were not traditional gentle swayings and graceful turns, but asymmetrical rhythms and gestures, twists and jerks. By the time the first act was completed, many spectators were already hissing and screaming; the music was barely audible over the cries of emotional insults.

Nijinsky gave his last dance in Switzerland in 1919, at the age of 31, ten years after his first performance. By then he had already embarked on his voyage into madness; his memory became a blank. Prophesying in his diary, he had written, 'people will leave me alone, calling me a mad clown.' Nijinsky lived out the rest of his days in an asylum; his body died in 1950.

On the night of March 15, 1917, the day Nicholas II abdicated the throne to the Provisional Government, *Sleeping Beauty* was performed at the Mariinsky Theater in Petrograd. This parable, about a kingdom plunged into a century-long sleep on the whim of an evil witch, prophetically foretold the fate of an entire nation.

MUSIC

The development of Russian music in St Petersburg followed the same patterns as literature, only later. In the 1830s and 40s Mikhail Glinka, a close friend of Pushkin, composed many symphonies and two operas based on Russian folk songs from his childhood. Glinka put these folk themes together with many of Pushkin's poems and produced some of the first distinctly Russian musical works. One of his most famous pieces is *Ruslan and Ludmilla,* an opera based on Pushkin's mock-romantic epic about the court of Kievan Russia.

Glinka's patriotic opera *A Life for the Czar* (later renamed *Ivan Susanin*) is about a peasant who saved the first Romanov czar from a Polish invasion. Another of his popular works, *Farewell to Petersburg,* is composed of a kaleidoscope of sounds that mixes Spanish boleros, Jewish songs and Italian barcaroles. *Travel Song* depicts images in sound of the first Russian railway, built between St Petersburg and the czar's palace in Tsarskoye Selo. Russians consider Glinka to be the father of their national music.

By the mid-19th century St Petersburg had become a major musical center and Berlioz, Verdi, Strauss and Wagner conducted their works there. In response to this invasion of Western talent, particularly Wagner, whom they believed had imperial aspirations, a group of Russian composers banded together to promote their own 'Russian' music. Known as the Mighty Band, they included Nikolai Rimsky-Korsakov, Alexander Borodin and Modest Mussorgsky. The Band followed Glinka's example and composed music based on folk songs and themes from Russian literature. Borodin's most famous work was the opera *Prince Igor,* which was based on an old Russian heroic song and included the famous Eastern dance number *The Polovtsian Dances.* Rimsky-Korsakov also wrote a number of operas based on mythic-historical themes from early Russian history and folklore. Mussorgsky, an epileptic like Dostoevsky, was the most artistically ambitious of the Band. He began by writing works based on Gogol's stories, which he considered were the closest to the Russian soul. Another piece tried to reproduce musically the babble in the marketplace at Nizhny Novgorod. Mussorgsky's two greatest works are the opera *Boris Godunov,* based on Pushkin's poem, and *Pictures from an Exhibition,* inspired by the drawings of his friend Viktor Hartman. *Khovanshchina*, the first part of an unfinished trilogy, is a kind of tone poem rendition of Russian-style chaos and social anarchy set at the end of the Time of Troubles just before Peter took the throne. While Mussorgsky was finishing this piece he went mad, and died a few weeks after Dostoevsky in 1881. He was buried near the writer in the Alexander Nevsky Monastery (see page 446).

As the Mighty Band was striving to lead Russia back to her roots, another faction, led by Anton Rubenstein, preferred the influence of European-oriented music. Rubenstein, a piano prodigy, organized state sponsorship for musical training; the St Petersburg Conservatory became the first of its kind in Russia. The talented performer and composer charmed audiences with his piano pieces that included *Kamenny Island* and *Soirées à St Petersburg*.

In 1862, Peter Tchaikovsky, then aged 22, was accepted as part of the first group of students into the St Petersburg Conservatory, having earlier received a degree in law. During his time St Petersburg was a melting pot of sounds—everything from French waltzes and Italian arias to military marches and Gypsy songs. Their effect can be recognized in his first three symphonies, and in the *Slavonic March* and *1812 Overture*. In his popular opera *Queen of Spades*, based on Pushkin's novella, Tchaikovsky rekindled a patriotic theme. The talented musician also composed for the Mariinsky Ballet; some of his most evocative works include *The Nutcracker*, *Sleeping Beauty* and *Swan Lake*.

Alexander III was enraptured with the composer's genius and in 1888 granted him a lifetime annual pension of 3,000 rubles. In 1891, Tchaikovsky was even invited to conduct at the grand opening of New York's Carnegie Hall. Tchaikovsky's most popular symphony is considered to be the Sixth (*Pathétique*), written shortly before his death. Peter Tchaikovsky became one of the world's most popular composers.

The Bolshevik revolution put a serious damper on experimentation in Russian music. Many composers such as Prokofiev, Rachmaninov and Stravinsky later fled Russia for the West. Igor Stravinsky, who had composed the music for some of the finest Mariinsky ballets, eventually settled in America where he helped score Walt Disney's animated film *Fantasia* in 1940. Abroad, Stravinsky also began a close collaboration with Diaghilev and the Ballet Russes, where *The Firebird*, *Petrouchka* and *Le Sacre du Printemps* became phenomenal successes. In 1937, the New York Metropolitan opera staged *Apollon Musagète* and *Le Baiser de la Fée*—the composer's special tribute to Tchaikovsky.

Leningrad's greatest musical resident after the Revolution was Dmitri Shostakovich. The première of his First Symphony triumphantly took place in the Leningrad Philharmonic in 1926, when the composer was just 19 years old. Boxed in by the demands of socialist realism, Shostakovich soon found an outlet by experimenting with constructionist principles and the avant-garde. His new Second Symphony was named *Dedication to the October Revolution*. His Third Symphony was dedicated to May Day, the official holiday of the proletariat.

In 1930, tiring of this nonsensical propaganda, Shostakovich followed with an experimental opera entitled *The Nose*, based on Gogol's unsettling 1836 novel about a St Petersburg aristocrat. Even though Shostakovich called it 'a satire on the era of Nicholas I', the innate message of the story was not lost on Soviet censors. It was removed from the repertoire and not restaged again for more than 40 years.

Saved by the patriotic events of World War II, Shostakovich fervently began to compose his famous Seventh Symphony, dedicated to the fate of Leningrad. It was broadcast throughout the country on March 5, 1942 during the German blockade. On April 11, Shostakovich was bestowed with the country's highest cultural award, the Stalin Prize. (The composer later declared that the symphony was written as a protest against both Hitler and Stalin.) Shostakovich was also internationally honored with the Sibelius Prize and, in 1958, with an honorary doctorate from Oxford University.

Today both Russians and foreign visitors alike enjoy performances by these and other contemporary composers in the theaters and philharmonic halls of Moscow and St Petersburg. UNESCO named 1989 as the year of the composer Modest Mussorgsky. In the spring of 1990, the renowned cellist and conductor Mstislav Rostropovich and his opera singer wife were allowed to return and visit Russia after 16 years of exile.

ART

During Russia's Golden Age in the 19th century, the arts strove to portray the realistic aspects of Russian life. Russian art grew beyond the depiction of spiritual realms, as symbolized by frescoes and icons, to encompass the whole contemporary world of the common man with his hopes, sufferings and desire for change. In 1827, Karl Bryullov's masterpiece *The Last Days of Pompeii* was exhibited in St Petersburg. The public compared the Italian romantic upheaval to their own city's tendency to natural disaster. Another meaning—of citizens forced to flee their burning city—symbolized the Decembrist uprising that had taken place only two years before.

The painter Ilya Repin greatly influenced the artistic developments of the late 19th century. Repin's arrival at the St Petersburg Academy of Arts in 1863 coincided with one of the most significant events of the city's artistic life: a small group of art students led by Ivan Kramskoi rebelled against the strict academic standards and were soon forced to resign. In 1870, this group formed their own artistic movement known as the Peredvizhniki or the Wanderers. In his last year at the academy, Repin painted *The Barge Haulers*, symbolizing the heavy burdens borne by the Russian people (see page 250); after graduation he joined the Wanderers. In 1887, while living in Moscow, Repin also frequented the art salons of Pavel Tretyakov and Savva Mamontov. These circles included other well-known painters as Serov, Korovin and Vrubel.

When Repin witnessed the public execution of five people who had taken part in the assassination of Alexander II, it had a great impact on his artistic life. Soon after, he moved back to St Petersburg and explored revolutionary ideas. Like his literary contemporaries, Repin strove to capture the moral and philosophical issues of the time. His paintings *Arrest of a Propagandist*, *They Did Not Expect Him* (concerning the unexpected return of a political exile to his home) and *Ivan the Terrible and his Son—16 November 1581* (the date Ivan IV killed his son in a fit of rage; see picture on page 238) can now be seen along with many of his other works in Moscow's Tretyakov Gallery.

In 1899, Repin bought an estate (now a museum, see page 483) outside St Petersburg that he named the Penates, after the Roman gods who protected home and family, and continued to live and paint there until his death in 1930, aged 86. St Petersburg's Repin Institute of Painting, Sculpture and Architecture is one of the largest art schools in the world (see page 397).

In 1898, Diaghilev, Bakst and Benois created Russia's first art magazine *Mir Iskusstva* (World of Art), which caused an immediate sensation throughout St Petersburg. The innovative journal introduced art concepts from around the world: Postimpressionism, pointillism, cubism and art nouveau. These artists wanted to free Russia from the old artistic standards established by such groups as the Wanderers. By 1910, the avant-garde maximalists and futurists were at the center of design and art. They welcomed the Revolution—believing it would serve as a hotbed for their own radical ideas.

The abstract painter Casimir Malevich was renowned in St Petersburg for his theatrical costumes and scenery, along with his innovative paintings that included *Victory Over the Sun*. His *Black Square*, which Malevich thought to represent the universality of existence, became the icon of Russian abstract art. The painter believed that this pure simple style of color and shape would act as a catalyst to the unconscious and open a way to spiritual transcendence.

In 1988, Sotheby's held the first auction of Russian art, with one painting selling for over $400,000. Today the art scene is booming and scores of exhibition halls and galleries, displaying and selling the works of contemporary artists, grace the streets of Moscow and St Petersburg.

Getting Around

ORIENTATION

St Petersburg is 660 kilometers (410 miles) north of Moscow on the same latitude as Helsinki and Anchorage. The city lies at the mouth of the Neva River as it flows into the Gulf of Finland. The city is divided into several districts and islands, and a few moments with a map familiarizing oneself with these will make a visit to St Petersburg more enjoyable.

The eastern bank of the Neva is known as the Vyborg Side (see Finland Station on page 447). At the tip of Vasilyevsky Island the river splits into two main branches; the Bolshaya and Malaya Neva. Here the right or northern bank is known as Petrogradskaya or the Petrograd Side (see Across the Kronverk Strait on page 388), and includes the islands of Zayachy, Petrogradsky, Aptekarsky and Petrovsky. To the northwest are the Kirov Islands (see page 391). Many of the city's sights are to be found on the left (or south) bank of the Neva, known as the mainland.

St Petersburg was originally spread over 101 islands. Today, because of redevelopment, there are 44 islands that make up one-sixth of the area of the city. These are connected by 620 bridges which span 100 waterways and canals. St Petersburg is a cultural treasure-house with over 60 museums, 50 theaters and concert halls, 2,500 libraries and hundreds of well-preserved palaces and monuments.

ARRIVAL

See Getting There section, page 52, for details of international arrivals.

Arrivals at the nearby domestic airport, Pulkovo I, can choose between a taxi or the frequent express bus into town. The bus picks up and drops off at 13 Bolshaya Morskaya Ulitsa. There is also a local bus (number 39) which runs between the airport and Moskovskaya Metro station.

Those arriving in St Petersburg by train will find the main stations located around the city center. If you are carrying a modest amount of luggage, try riding the Metro to your destination.

The St Peter and Paul Cathedral inside the Peter and Paul Fortress. When it was constructed in 1732 the spire, topped with an angel holding a cross, was the highest structure in Russia. Peter the Great purposely made it taller that the Bell Tower in Moscow's Kremlin (see picture on page 103). Its gilded spire was scaled and camouflaged by mountain climbers during the Siege of Leningrad to protect it from German bombing raids.

Sights

Peter and Paul Fortress

The origins of the city can be traced back to the Peter and Paul Fortress, known as Petropavlovskaya Krepost in Russian. Peter the Great was attracted to Zayachy Ostrov (Hare Island), situated between the Neva and the Kronverk Strait, because of its small size and strategic position in the area. On May 16, 1703, the first foundation stone of the fortress, named after the apostles Peter and Paul, was laid by Peter himself. The fortress was designed to protect the city from the invading Swedes, and was built as an elongated hexagon with six bastions that traced the contours of the island. Over 20,000 workers were commissioned and within only six months the earthen ramparts were set in place. Work continued on the fortress, replacing the wooden buildings with brick and stone until its completion in 1725. The new walls were over 12 meters (39 feet) thick and 300 guns were installed. Soon after its completion the fortress lost its military significance and over the next 200 years it served instead as a political prison. In 1922, the fortress was opened as a museum. The museum is open 11am–5pm; closed Wednesdays.

Ironically, the first prisoner was Peter's son, Alexei, who was suspected of plotting against the czar. Peter supervised his son's torture and Alexei died here in 1718. (Peter had Alexei buried beneath the staircase of the cathedral, so he would always be 'trampled upon'.) An outer fortification built to cover an entrance into the fort is known as the **Alexeyevsky Ravelin** (Bastion), after Peter's son. The history of the fortress is also closely connected with revolutionary movements. Catherine the Great locked up Alexander Radishchev, who criticized the autocracy and feudal system in his book *Voyages from St Petersburg to Moscow*. In 1825, the Decembrists were placed in the Alexeyevsky Bastion, a special block for important prisoners. Five were executed on July 13, 1826, and hundreds of others were sentenced to hard labor in Siberia. Members of the Petrashevsky political movement, including Dostoevsky, were sent here in 1849 and sentenced to death. Only at the last minute did Nicholas I revoke the sentence. Nikolai Chernyshevsky wrote his influential novel *What Is To Be Done?* while imprisoned here for two years in 1862. In the 1880s many members of the Narodnaya Volya (Peoples' Freedom Group) were placed in solitary-confinement cells in the Trubetskoi Bastion. In 1887, five prisoners were executed for the attempt on the life of Alexander III, including Lenin's brother, Alexander Ulyanov. The writer Maxim Gorky was incarcerated for writing revolutionary leaflets.

During the October 1917 Revolution, when the fortress' last stronghold was captured by the Bolsheviks and the political prisoners set free, a red lantern was hung in the Naryshkin Bastion signaling the battleship *Aurora* to fire the first shot of the Revolution. Every day at noon a blank cannon shot is fired from the Naryshkin Bastion (be prepared!). It has been sounded every day (except during the Siege of Leningrad) since a similar salute in 1721 proclaimed the end to the Great Northern War. Locals also call it the Admiral's Hour; according to tradition the cannon was fired daily after an admiral drank his glass of noon-day vodka. The shot also let the townspeople know the time.

The nearest Metro stop to the fortress is Gorkovskaya. The visitor's entrance to the fortress is at **St John's Gate**, on the east side of the island not far from Kamennoostrovsky (formerly Kirov) Prospekt. After crossing St John's Bridge you come to **St Peter's Gate** (1718), the main entrance and oldest unchanged structure of the fort. Hanging over the archway is a double-headed eagle, the emblem of the Russian Empire, along with bas-reliefs of the apostle Peter. The carver Konrad Osner gave the apostle the features of the czar. Beyond the gate is His Majesty's Bastion, used as a dungeon for Peter's prisoners.

A straight path leads to **St Peter and Paul Cathedral**, built between 1712 and 1732 in the Dutch style by the architect Trezzini. Peter the Great laid the corner-stone. The cathedral, with its long slender golden spire topped with an angel holding a cross, is the focal point of the square. The belfry, 122.5 meters (402 feet) high, used to be the highest structure in the whole country; Peter purposely had the spire built higher than the Ivan the Great Bell Tower in Moscow's Kremlin. (During the Siege mountain climbers courageously scaled the spire in order to camouflage and protect it from German bombing raids.)

Inside, the gilded wooden iconostasis was carved between 1722 and 1726, and holds 43 icons. The cathedral is the burial place for over 30 czars and princes, including every czar from Peter I to Alexander III. There are no tombs for Peter II and Ivan IV, both of whom were murdered. The last czar, Nicholas II, along with his murdered family and friends were finally given an official burial in the cathedral on July 17, 1998 (80 years to the day after they were shot by a 12-man Bolshevik firing squad). They were buried in the Grand Ducal Burial Vault, where generations of Romanovs lie. Positive DNA identifications had been made on the nine skeletons exhumed in 1991 from unmarked graves in the Ural Mountains, near Yekaterinburg, 1,450 kilometers (900 miles) east of Moscow. They belonged to Nicholas II, his wife, three children and four servants. (In a breach of tradition, the servants were also allowed burial in the vault.) In January 1998, after much controversy, the Russian Government announced an official and final verification of each of the bodies. (The missing bodies of the

Peter and Paul Fortress

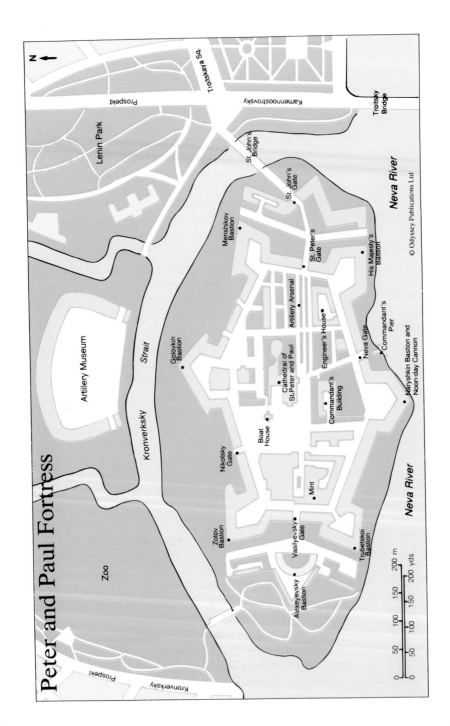

Zoo

Kronverksky Prospekt

Lenin Park

Kronverksky Prospekt

Artillery Museum

Strait

Kronverksky

Troitskaya Sq.

Prospekt

Kamennoostrovsky

Troitsky Bridge

Neva River

St. John's Bridge

St. John's Gate

Menshikov Bastion

Golovkin Bastion

Nikolsky Gate

Boat House

Cathedral of St. Peter and Paul

Artillery Arsenal

St. Peter's Gate

Engineer's House

His Majesty's Bastion

Commandant's Pier

Neva Gate

Commandant's Building

Naryshkin Bastion and Noon-day Cannon

© Odyssey Publications Ltd

Mint

Zotov Bastion

Vasilyevsky Gate

Alexeyevsky Bastion

Trubetskoi Bastion

Neva River

0   50   100   150   200 m
0   50   100   150   200 yds

N

czar's fourth daughter Maria and son Alexei are believed to have been burned by the Bolshevik executioners.) The sarcophagi of Alexander II and his wife took 17 years to carve from Altai jasper and Ural red quartz. Peter the Great himself chose his resting place to the right of the altar. In 1994, Queen Elizabeth II paid a visit here to her ancestors' tombs. This was the first visit by a British monarch to Peter and Paul Fortress in over 75 years.

Outside the cathedral entrance is a small pavilion with a statue of the Goddess of Navigation. The **Boat House** was erected in 1761 to house a small boat that was built by Peter the Great. Today, this Grandfather of the Russian Fleet is on display at the Central Naval Museum at 4 Birzhevaya Square on Vasilyevsky Island. Directly in front of the cathedral is the yellow-white building of the **Mint** (1800–1806). In 1724, Peter the Great transferred the Royal Mint from Moscow to St Petersburg. The first lever press in the world was used here in 1811. The Mint still produces special coins, medals and badges. Beyond the Mint are the Alexeyevsky, Zotov and Trubetskoi Bastions, where many of the revolutionaries were imprisoned. The latter houses an exhibit which traces the history of prisoners who stayed in the cells.

As you leave the Cathedral look for the **Statue of Peter the Great**, a life-size figure of the czar seated in an armchair. Unveiled on June 7, 1991, it was sculpted and donated by St Petersburg artist Mikhail Chemiakin (who now lives in the US), just before the city regained its historical name. The statue is an interpretation of Peter I's wax effigy (now in the Hermitage collection) made by Carlo Rastrelli (father of the famous architect) in 1725, right after the czar's death. The head is an actual cast from the life mask of Peter the Great (also in the Hermitage) made by Rastrelli in 1719.

The next structure is the stone Commandant's Building, built as the commander's headquarters and the interrogation center for prisoners. It now houses the **Museum of History of St Petersburg and Petrograd from 1703 to 1917**. Next door, the old Engineer's House is now the **Architectural Museum of St Petersburg**, displaying many original drawings and drafts of the city. Both are closed on Wednesdays. Behind these stands the **Neva Gate**, once known as the Gate of Death, because prisoners were led through it to the execution site. Now it leads to the beach area (with a spectacular view of the city) that is quite crowded in summer with sunbathers. The Walrus Club gathers here in winter to swim between the ice floes of the Neva.

As you pass through the gate notice the plaques that record the city's many floods. In the disastrous flood of 1824, the entire Vasilyevsky Island across to both the Petrograd Side and the mainland were underwater. Nikolai Gogol wrote, 'Now the belfry spire is alone visible from the sea.'

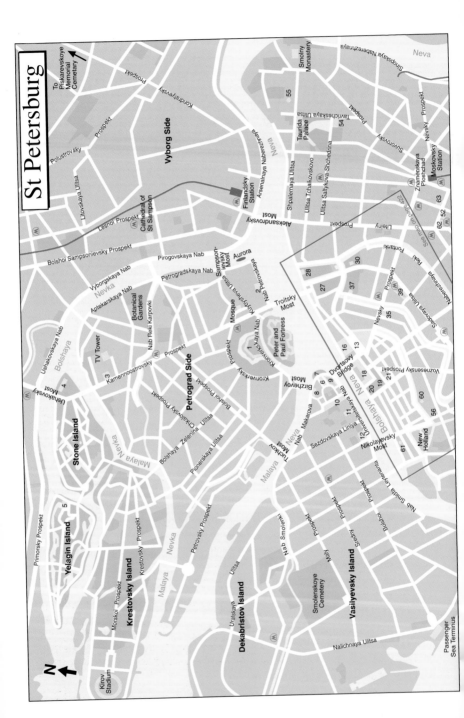

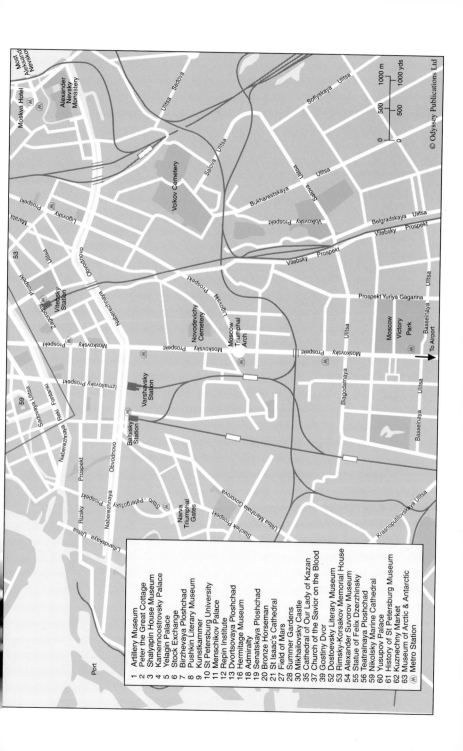

© Odyssey Publications Ltd

1000 m
1000 yds
500
500
0
0

Moskva Hotel

Most Aleksandr Nevskov

Alexander Nevsky Monastery

Ulitsa Sedova

Volkov Cemetery

Sofiyskaya Ulitsa

Sadova Ulitsa

Ulitsa

Bukharestskaya

Sadova Ulitsa

Volkovsky Prospekt

Belgradskaya Ulitsa

Vitebsky Prospekt

Vitebsky Prospekt

Ligovsky Prospekt

Marata Prospekt

Prospekt

53

Ulitsa

Prospekt

Obvodnovo

Naberezhnaya

Vitebsky Station

Zagorodny

Ligovsky Prospekt

Novodevichy Cemetery

Moscow Triumphal Arch

Prospekt Yuriya Gagarina

Basseinaya Ulitsa

To Airport

Moscow Victory Park

Prospekt

Moskovsky Ulitsa

Moskovsky Prospekt

Prospekt

Moskovsky Prospekt

Blagodatnaya

Ulitsa

Basseinaya

Ulitsa

Prospekt

Izmaylovsky Prospekt

Varshavsky Station

59

Sadovaya Ulitsa

Naberezhnaya Reki Fontanki

Baltiisky Station

Prospekt

Obvodnovo

Staro-Petergofsky

Narva Triumphal Gates

Siachek Prospekt

Ulitsa Marshala Govorova

Krasnoputilovskaya Ulitsa

Naberezhnaya

Prospekt

Rizhsky Prospekt

Liflandskaya Ulitsa

Port

1 Artillery Museum
2 Peter the Great Cottage
3 Shalyapin House Museum
4 Kamennoostrovsky Palace
5 Yelagin Palace
6 Stock Exchange
7 Birzhevaya Ploshchad
8 Pushkin Literary Museum
9 Kunstkammer
10 St Petersburg University
11 Menschikov Palace
12 Repin Institute
13 Dvortsovaya Ploshchad
16 Hermitage Museum
18 Admiralty
19 Senatskaya Ploshchad
20 Bronze Horseman
21 St Isaac's Cathedral
27 Field of Mars
28 Summer Gardens
30 Mikhailovsky Castle
35 Cathedral of Our Lady of Kazan
37 Church of the Savior on the Blood
39 Gostiny Dvor
52 Dostoevsky Literary Museum
53 Rimsky-Korsakov Memorial House
54 Alexander Suvorov Museum
55 Statue of Felix Dzerzhinsky
56 Teatralnaya Ploshchad
59 Nikolsky Marine Cathedral
60 Yusupov Palace
61 History of St Petersburg Museum
62 Kuznechny Market
63 Museum of Arctic & Antarctic
Ⓜ Metro Station

Across the Kronverk Strait

Exiting the fortress by way of St John's Bridge takes you back to Kamennoostrovsky Prospekt. To the right is the **Troitsky Most** (formerly Kirov Bridge), with a splendid view of the fortress. This is the city's longest bridge, built between 1897 and 1903 from French designs, to commemorate the silver wedding anniversary of Alexander III. Gorkovskaya Metro station is a short walk north along the prospekt. The small path to the left of St John's Bridge circles around the Kronverk Strait. This path leads to a small obelisk, a monument to the Decembrist revolutionaries, erected on the spot where Nicholas I executed the five leaders of the 1825 uprising. A witness described the execution: 'The hangmen made them stand on a bench and put white canvas hoods over their heads. Then the bench was knocked from under their feet. Three men whose ropes had broken fell on the rough boards of the scaffold bruising themselves. One broke his leg. According to custom, in such circumstances the execution had to be canceled. But in an hour, new ropes were brought and the execution carried through.'

Past the obelisk is a large building that was once the artillery arsenal. Today it is the **Kronverk Artillery, Engineers and Signals Museum**, established by Peter the Great to display the history of Russian weaponry. Today it houses more than 50,000 exhibits of artillery, firearms, engineering equipment and military paintings; there is also an outdoor display of tanks. Open 11am–5pm; closed Mondays and Tuesdays. Behind the museum is **Lenin Park**, stretching from the Strait to Kronverksky (formerly Maxim Gorky) Prospekt, where the writer lived at number 23 from 1914 to 1921. Inside the park is the **St Petersburg Zoo** and gardens, with over 1,000 animals (open daily 10am–7pm in summer, and 10am–6pm in winter, but it is in a neglected state and not really worth a visit). Nearby, at 4 Aleksandrovsky Park, is the **Planetarium**, open 10.30am–7pm Tuesday–Sunday. The **Amusement Park** just north of the zoo has roller coasters, bumper cars and other rides. Nearby is the **Baltiisky Dom Theater** which in summer months throws wild all-night parties for ex-Communist youthful party animals. At 7 Kronverksky Prospekt is a working **mosque**, modeled on Samarkand's magnificent Gur Emir Mausoleum where Tamerlaine is buried.

Sergei Kirov (1886–1934), regional head of the Leningrad Party before he was murdered, lived not far from Leo Tolstoy Square at 26–28 Kamennoostrovsky Prospekt. The **Kirov Museum** on the fourth floor (open 11am–5.30pm; closed Wednesdays) displays his possessions including many great examples from Soviet 1920s technology (including a hotline to the Kremlin). At number 10 is Lenfilm Studios, founded in 1918.

Opposite St John's Bridge on Kamennoostrovsky Prospekt is **Troitskaya Ploshchad** (Troitsky Square, formerly Revolution Square) where many of the first buildings of the city once stood. These included the Senate, Custom House and Troitsky Cathedral, where Peter was crowned emperor in 1721. Today the square is a large garden. At the northern end of the square, at 4 Ulitsa Kuybysheva, is the art-nouveau style mansion (built between 1902 and 1906 by the architect Gogen) formerly belonging to Matilda Kchessinskaya, a famous ballerina and mistress of Nicholas II before he married. It now houses the **Museum of Political History** (open 10am–5.30pm; closed Thursdays) with exhibits of Russian political parties from 1905 to the 1990s. There are also frequent concerts held in the chamber music hall.

The **Lidval Building** (1–3 Kamennoostrovsky Prospekt), an apartment block built in 1902, is named after the city's favorite architect of the moderne, Fyodor Lidval; look closely and you will see a menagerie of figures that jump out of the stone: fish, owls, spiders and webs.

Continuing along Petrovsky Embankment (Naberezhnaya Petrovskaya), you pass the two-ton granite figures of Shih-Tze, brought from Manchuria in 1907, poised on the steps by the Neva. In China these sculptures guarded the entrances to palaces (see picture on pages 14–15). Behind them is the **Cottage of Peter the Great**, one of the oldest surviving buildings of the city. It was constructed, in a mere three days in May 1703, out of pine logs painted to look like bricks. One room was a study and reception area and the other was used as a dining room and bedroom. The largest door was 1.75 meters (five feet, nine inches) high—Peter stood at 2 meters (six feet seven)! From here Peter directed the building of his fortress, which was in view across the river. Once his summer palace was completed, Peter stopped living here altogether. In 1784, Catherine the Great encased the tiny house in stone to protect it. The cottage is now a museum, displaying his furniture, household utensils, a cast of his hand and a small boat with which Peter is supposed to have saved a group of fishermen on Lake Ladoga in 1690. A bronze bust of Peter can be found in the garden. The cottage, at 6 Petrovsky Embankment, is open 10am–5pm; closed Tuesdays.

The beautiful blue building of the **Nakhimov Naval School**, at number 4 is a short walk farther east, where young boys learn to carry on the traditions of the Russian fleet. The battleship *Aurora* is anchored in front of it. The cruiser originally fought during the Russo-Japanese War (1904–05). In October 1917, the sailors mutinied and joined in the Bolshevik Revolution. On the evening of October 24, following the orders of Lenin and the Military Revolutionary Committee, the *Aurora* sailed up the Neva and at 9.45pm fired a blank shot to signal the storming of the Winter Palace. In 1948, it was moored by the Naval School and later opened as a museum. Displays include the gun that fired the legendary shot and the radio room where Lenin announced the overthrow of the Provisional Government to the citizens of Russia. The battleship is open 10.30am–4pm; closed Mondays and Fridays.

The **St Petersburg Hotel** can be reached by crossing the bridge over the Bolshaya Neva. Here you can have a quick coffee, buffet lunch or dinner at the cafeteria-type restaurant on the ground floor.

To the northeast, across the Karpovka River, were once special gardens growing medicinal plants and herbs for the city's apothecaries. This is how the island got its nickname of Aptekarsky (Apothecary). The **Botanical Gardens** are now located here (not far from the TV Tower), along with the **Botanical Museum**, at 2 Ulitsa Professora Popova, filled with over 80,000 plants and seeds. The museum is open 10am–5pm Wednesday, Saturday and Sunday. The nearest Metro station is Petrogradskaya. Try the LDM Complex Hotel at number 47 for a meal in the restaurant/bar.

Today the 50,000-watt **TV Tower**, standing at 321 meters (1,053 feet), is the tallest structure in St Petersburg. It is located in the northeast corner of the Petrograd Side and is open for tours offering great views of the city; a café is on the second deck. Contact Peter TIPS Travel, at 86 Nevsky Prospekt (tel. 279-0027) for more information.

On the other side of the TV Tower, at 26 Graftio Ulitsa, is the **Shalyapin House Museum** with exhibits on the life of the famous Russian opera singer who lived here from 1915 to 1922. Open 11am–6pm; closed Mondays and Tuesdays. It also has occasional chamber music performances.

An artist paints Peter the Great's first residence in St Petersburg, built in 1711 by Domenico Trezzini. The simple two-story stone building and steep Dutch-tiled roof is now a museum.

Kirov Islands

The northernmost islands are collectively called the Kirov Islands, the largest of which are known as Krestovsky, Yelagin and Stone. They lie between the Malaya, Srednaya and Bolshaya (Small, Middle and Large) Nevka, which are tributaries of the Neva.

Stone Island Bridge leads from the end of Kamennoostrovsky Prospekt on the Petrograd Side (about a 15-minute walk north of Petrogradskaya Metro station) to **Stone Island**, a popular summer resort area in the days of Peter the Great. (Peter is said to have planted the large oak tree found on Krestovky River Embankment (Naberezhnaya Reki Krestovki) in 1718. It is just west of the intersection with 2-ya Berezovaya Alleya.) In 1765, Catherine the Great bought the lands for her son, and the following year erected the classically designed **Kamennoostrovsky (Stone Island) Palace** on the eastern tip of the island; it is now an off-limits military sanitarium (though one can visit the small Gothic chapel on the grounds).

Today the 107-hectare (265-acre) island is filled with holiday centers and beautiful old dachas—some of the finest wooden buildings in Russia originally constructed by wealthy aristocratic families at the turn of the century. (Many have guarded gates and are now owned by businessmen and mafia.) A wonderful

During the cold winter months members of the Walrus Club chop through the ice to swim in the freezing waters of the Neva. They believe that this activity promotes health and a hardy disposition.

example on the northwest shore is the lavish mansion of Senator Polovtsev who barely escaped when the Bolsheviks took possession of it. Another is the Dolgoruky Mansion, which stands on the southern embankment near Kamennoostrovsky Prospekt. The Danish Consulate, at 13 Bolshaya Alleya, is a fairy-tale castle built in art nouveau style. On the other side of the island is the wooden **Kamenny Island Theater**, a classical giant with an eight-column portico, erected in just 40 days in the early 1820s, and now used as a TV studio.

Another interesting site is the equine cemetery for the steeds of Mad Czar Paul I. A large park fills the southwest corner and the western footbridge leads to Yelagin Island. For a bite to eat stop at the Askur Hotel (once a dacha compound for high-ranking Party officials) at 7/1-ya Berezovaya Alleya. You can also reach Kamenny Island from Chornaya Rechka Metro station and then walk south across the Ushakovsky Bridge.

Yelagin Island is connected by three bridges: from Kamenny Island to the west, Krestovsky Island to the south and Primorsky Prospekt to the north. It was once owned in the late-18th century by the wealthy aristocrat Ivan Yelagin. After his death it became the summer residence of the czars. In 1817, Alexander I bought the island for the summer residence of his mother Maria Fedorovna; he then had Carlo Rossi build the elegant **Yelagin Palace** (completed in 1822) near the northeastern shore, Rossi's first commission in the city. Today, along with beautifully restored furnishings, it houses an exhibit of decorative and applied arts. Open 10.30am–5pm, Wednesday to Sunday. Besides the main palace, there are also three outdoor pavilions and the kitchen and stable buildings. Rossi went on to replan the entire island, adding parks, ponds and shady tree-lined pathways. Today the **Kirov Central Park of Culture and Rest** takes up most of the western half of the island; carnivals are held here, especially during the White Nights in June. (In winter a 25-acre skating rink is opened.) It has also long been a tradition to watch the sunset over the Gulf of Finland from the western tip of the island. Row boats can be rented at the north end by the bridge.

Just across the northern bridge, at 91 Primorsky Prospekt, is the **Buddhist Datsun** or Temple. Open daily 9am–7pm with services at 9am. It was built between 1909 and 1915 by Pyotr Badmaev, Buddhist physician to Nicholas II, combining Tibetan and art-nouveau styles. Donations were given by the Dalai Lama and Nikolai Roerich, a leading figure of the spiritual and occult in the city. Having been shut down after the Revolution, the buildings were returned to the Buddhist community in 1990. The temple and monastery are run by monks from the Buryatia Republic, Russia's largest Buddhist area, situated along Lake Baikal in southern Siberia.

Krestovsky, the largest island in the group, houses the 65,000-seat **Kirov Stadium** on its western side. Nearby is the place where Alexander Pushkin fought his duel; a small obelisk marks the spot where he was mortally wounded. The main attraction is **Seaside Victory Park** (built after the war in 1945), with artificial lakes and swimming pools. Leningrad poet Anna Akhmatova wrote: 'Early in the morning, the people of Leningrad went out. In huge crowds to the seashore, and each of them planted a tree up on that strip of land, marshy, deserted. In memory of that Great Victory Day.' Within two weeks, 45,000 oaks, birch, maples and other trees, and 50,000 shrubs were planted over 450 acres. The easiest way here is to get off at Petrogradskaya Metro station, and then board bus 71 or 71a to Krestovsky Island; the latter runs the whole four-kilometer (2.5-mile) length of the island to the stadium.

The Strelka of Vasilyevsky Island

Vasilyevsky is the largest island in the Neva Delta, encompassing over 4,000 acres. At the island's eastern tip, known as the Strelka (arrow or spit of land), the Neva is at its widest and branches into the Bolshaya and Malaya Neva. The Dvortsovy Most (Palace Bridge) spans the Bolshaya Neva to the left bank and the Birzhevoy Most (Commerce Bridge) crosses the Malaya Neva to the Petrograd Side.

At first Peter chose to build his city, modeled after Venice, on Vasilyevsky Island. But when the Neva froze over in winter, the island was cut off from the rest of Russia. By the mid-18th century it was decided instead to develop the administrative and cultural centers on the left bank of the Neva. However, many of the original canals are still present on the island, whose streets are laid out as numbered lines (where canals were planned) and crossed by three major avenues.

After the Peter and Paul Fortress was completed, vessels docked along the Strelka. The first wooden Exchange Building was built near the fortress by Peter I for foreign merchants only. According to tradition Russian traders made their deals at the local fairs, until the end of the 18th century when they, too, were participating in stock exchange deals. Between 1805 and 1816 the present **Stock Exchange** was erected according to the designs of Thomas de Thomon. Thousands of piles were driven into the riverbed to serve as the foundation for a granite embankment with steps leading to the Neva, flanked on each side by two large stone globes. The Exchange has 44 white Doric columns, and the sea-god Neptune in a chariot harnessed to sea horses stands over the main entrance. This building, at 5 Birzhevaya Ploshchad, still serves as the city's stock exchange and also houses the **Central Naval Museum**, the largest naval museum in the world. Peter the Great originally opened this museum in the Admiralty in 1709 to store models and blueprints of Russian ships. His collection of models numbered over 1,500, and today the museum contains a half million items on the history of the Russian fleet.

Included is the *Botik*, Peter's first boat. Open 10.30am–4.45pm; closed Mondays and Tuesdays.

Birzhevaya Ploshchad (Commerce Square) lies in front of the Exchange. The dark red **Rostral Columns**, 32 meters (105 feet) high, stand on either side. These were also built by de Thomon from 1805 to 1810. The Romans erected columns adorned with the prows of enemy ships, or rostrals, after naval victories. These rostral columns are decorated with figures symbolizing the victories of the Russian fleet. Around the base of the columns are four allegorical figures, representing the Neva, Volga, Dnieper and Volkhov rivers. The columns also acted as a lighthouse; at dusk hemp oil was lit in the bronze bowls at the top. Nowadays gas torches are used, but only during festivals. This area is one of the most beautiful spots in all St Petersburg, offering a large panoramic view of the city. Imagine the days when the whole area was filled with ships and sailboats. The Frenchman Alexandre Dumas was obviously captivated with the area on his first visit over a century ago: 'I really don't know whether there is any view in the whole world which can be compared with the panorama which unfolded before my eyes.'

Two gray-green warehouses, built between 1826 and 1832, stand on either side of the Exchange. The northern warehouse is now the **Museum of Soil Science**. Opened in 1904, it displays soil collections and exhibits (open 10am–5pm; closed weekends). The southern building is the **Zoological Museum** which has a collection of over 40,000 animal species, including a 44,000-year-old stuffed baby mammoth nicknamed Dima, discovered in the Siberian permafrost in 1902. (See page 538 for web-site.) Open 11am–6pm; closed Fridays.

The eight-columned **Customs House** (1829–32) at 4 Makarova Embankment (Naberezhnaya Makarova) is topped with mounted copper statues of Mercury (Commerce), Neptune (Navigation) and Ceres (Fertility). The cupola was used as an observation point to signal arriving trade ships. It is now the **Pushkin House Literary Museum**, open 11am–5pm, Wednesday to Sunday. In 1905, the museum purchased Pushkin's library. (See also Pushkin House Museum on page 410.) Other rooms contain exhibits devoted to many famous Russian writers.

The baroque-style green and white **Kunstkammer** (1718–34), nicknamed the Palace of Curiosities, is located at the beginning of the University Embankment (Universitetskaya Naberezhnaya) which extends west along the Bolshaya Neva. Nearly every building in this district is a monument of 18th-century architecture. Kunstkammer, stemming from the German words *kunst* (art) and *kammer* (chamber), was the first Russian museum open to the public (see picture on pages 14–15). Legend has it that Peter the Great, while walking along the embankment, noticed two pine trees entwined around each other's trunks. The czar decided to cut down the trees and build a museum on the spot to house 'rarities, curiosities and

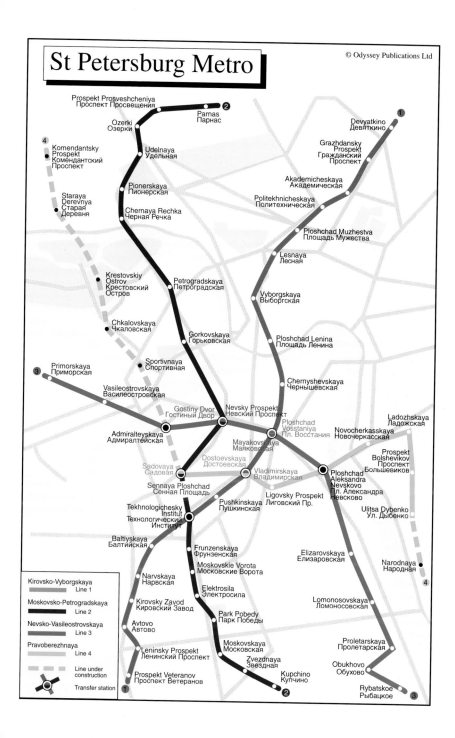

monsters'. The tree was also in the museum. In order to attract visitors, admission was free and a glass of vodka was offered at the entrance. The building became known as the 'cradle of Russian science' and was the seat of the Academy of Sciences, founded by Peter in 1724. The famed scientist and writer Mikhail Lomonosov worked here from 1741 to 1765. Today the Kunstkammer is made up of the **Museum of Anthropology and Ethnography** (open 11am–5pm; closed Fridays), and the **Lomonosov Museum** (open 11am–6pm; closed Thursdays). The first Russian astronomical observatory was installed in the museum's tower. The large globe had a model of the heavens in its interior where a mechanism was regulated to create the motion of the night sky, a forerunner of the planetarium. It is three meters (nine feet) in diameter—large enough for 12 people to fit inside. The Kunstkammer soon became too small and a new building was constructed next to it for the Academy of Sciences. Completed in 1788, it was designed by Giacomo Quarenghi. A statue of Mikhail Lomonosov stands outside the Academy.

Peter commissioned the architect Trezzini to build the Twelve Collegiums (1722–42) next to the Kunstkammer (along Mendeleyevskaya Liniya) for his Senate and colleges, which replaced more than 40 governmental departments. By the beginning of the 19th century the colleges had been replaced by ministries. After governmental orders were announced, they were posted outside the colleges for the public to read. The St Petersburg University, founded in 1819, moved into the buildings of the Twelve Collegiums in 1838, where it continues to operate today. Many prominent writers and scholars studied here; Lenin passed his bar examinations and received a degree in law. Some of the teachers were the renowned scientists, Popov and Pavlov, and Dmitri Mendeleyev (periodic law and tables) worked here for 25 years; the apartment where he lived at 7/9 Mendeleyevskaya Liniya is now a museum, open 10am–5pm, closed weekends. The red and white buildings are now part of St Petersburg University, which has more than 20,000 students.

Not far from the university at 15 University Embankment is the yellow baroque-style **Menschikov Palace**. Prince Alexander Menschikov was the first governor of St Petersburg and did much for its development. Peter the Great presented his close friend with the whole of Vasilyevsky Island in 1707 (but later took it back). The palace, built between 1710 and 1714, was the first stone residential structure on the island. It was the most luxurious building in St Petersburg and known as the Ambassadorial Palace. After the death of Peter the Great in 1725, Menschikov virtually ruled the country until he lost a power struggle and was exiled to Siberia, where he died two years later. The First Cadet Corps took over the palace as their Military College in 1831. This palace is one of the few private houses preserved from the first quarter of the 18th century. Today the restored palace is part of the

Hermitage Museum and exhibits collections of 18th-century Russian culture. Open 10.30am–4pm; closed Mondays. Chamber music concerts are frequently held in the evenings.

Peter the Great had the idea to create a Russian artistic school. A year before his death an engraving school was opened in the Academy of Sciences. It was Count Ivan Shuvalov who created the idea for an Academy of Fine Arts in 1757; the construction of the building, the first in the city with classical designs, took place between 1765 and 1788. Over the entrance is a bronze inscription: 'To Free Arts. The year—1765.' Many of Russia's most renowned artists and architects graduated from here. Today it is the largest art school is the world, and known as the **Repin Institute of Painting, Sculpture and Architecture** (named after the renowned Russian painter). Part is also a museum that depicts the educational history of Russian art and architecture; open 11am–5pm, Wednesday to Sunday.

When the Academy was built, the city's seaport was still situated here along the Neva. The river was only navigable 200 days a year (the rest of the time it was frozen). In one month alone, in May 1815, this port area received 19,327 ships— among them, 182 English, 7 American, 36 Scandinavian and 69 German. In 1885, the port was transferred to Kronstadt, and later moved to Gutuevsky Island (southwest of the city) where it remains today.

In front of the Academy two pink-granite **Egyptian Sphinxes**, over 3,500 years old, flank the staircase leading down to the water; they were brought to the city in 1832, and each weighs 23 tons. They were discovered in the early 1800s during an excavation of ancient Thebes and personify the Pharaoh Amenkhotep III, who once ruled Egypt.

The **Nikolayevsky Bridge** (formerly Most Leytenanta Shmida) crosses the Bolshaya Neva from University Embankment; it was once also named after a hero of the 1905 Revolution. Constructed between 1843 and 50, it was originally called Annunciation after the neighboring Cathedral, and was the first permanent bridge across the Neva. Later the bridge was renamed Nikolayevsky after Nicholas I; in the middle of the bridge was a chapel with the mosaic image of St Nicholas, the patron saint of navigators. Today it is also the last bridge before the river flows into the Gulf of Finland. During the White Nights, at around 2am, it is quite lovely to watch the numerous bridges of the city open from this vantage point. (They open and shut at different times throughout the night.) The rest of Vasilyevsky Island is largely residential and industrial. Vasileostrovskaya is the closest Metro station to the Strelka.

The **Pribaltiiskaya Hotel** is at the western end of the island, not far from Primorskaya (Maritime) Metro station. After shopping in the large Admiral Gallery, watch a sunset over the Gulf from the embankment behind the hotel. A few

minutes walk down the road from the hotel is the International Seaman's Club, near the Morskoi Vokzal (Marine Terminal), where most cruiseboats dock. Marine Glory Square is in front with permanent glass pavilions that house international exhibitions. The Dekabristov (Decembrist) Island lies farther to the north.

For the next 320 kilometers (200 miles), the Gulf of Finland off Vasilyevsky Island is known as Cyclone Road. Cyclones traveling west to east create what is known as the long wave. It originates in the Gulf during severe storms and then rolls toward St Petersburg. Propelled by high winds, it enters between the narrow banks of the Neva with great speed. The city has experienced over 300 floods in its 300-year history. A 29-kilometer (18-mile) barrier has been built across a section of the Gulf to control the flooding. Much controversy surrounds the barrier, since many scientists believe that it is changing the ecological balance of the area.

The view from the Winter Palace across Palace Square. In the center stands the Alexander Column commemorating the defeat of Napoleon in 1812. The General Staff Building and

Palace Square (Dvortsovaya Ploshchad)

Palace Square was the heart of Russia for over two centuries and is one of the most striking architectural ensembles in the world. Carlo Rossi was commissioned to design the square in 1819. The government bought up all the residential houses and reconstructed the area into the Ministries of Foreign Affairs and Finance, and the General Staff Headquarters of the Russian Army. These two large yellow buildings curve around the southern end of the Square and are linked by the **Triumphal Arch** (actually two arches), whose themes of soldiers and armor commemorate the victories of the War of 1812. It is crowned by the 16-ton Winged Glory in a chariot led by six horses, which everyone believed would collapse the arch. On opening day Rossi declared: 'If it should fall, I will fall with it.' He climbed to the top of the arch as the scaffolding was removed.

the Guard's Headquarters curve around the far side of the square and are linked by the Triumphal Arch, which is crowned by Carlo Rossi's 16-ton sculpture of the Winged Glory.

The Square was not only the parade ground for the czar's Winter Palace, but a symbol of the revolutionary struggle as well, and was in fact the site of three revolutions: the Decembrists first held an uprising near here in 1825. On Sunday January 9, 1905, over 100,000 people marched to Palace Square to protest intolerable working conditions. The demonstration began peacefully as the families carried icons and pictures of the czar. But Nicholas II's troops opened fire on the crowd and thousands were killed in the event known as Bloody Sunday. After the massacre, massive strikes ensued. In October of the same year, the St Petersburg Soviet of Workers' Deputies was formed. Twelve years later, in February 1917, the Kerensky Government overthrew the autocracy. At 1.50am on October 26, 1917, the Bolshevik Red Guards stormed through Palace Square to capture the Winter Palace from the Provisional Government. John Reed, the famous American journalist, wrote of the Revolution that on that night 'on Palace Square I watched the birth of a new world.'

In 1920, the anniversary of the Revolution was celebrated by thousands of people rushing through the square to dramatically reconstruct the storming of the Winter Palace. (Eisenstein's famous film *October* immortalized this embellished image.) In actuality, only one blank shot was fired by the *Aurora*, and one soldier killed—the Provisional Government surrendered virtually without a fight. For decades thereafter, parades and celebrations were held on May Day and Revolution Day. Palace Square remains the heart of the city. But today you will see anything but Socialist parades—just some die-hard nationalists. There is now everything from heavy-metal pop concerts to Hare Krishnas dancing around the square.

As you enter Palace Square from Bolshaya Morskaya Ulitsa, an unforgettable panorama unfolds. The **Alexander Column** stands in the middle of the square, symbolizing the defeat of Napoleon in 1812. Nicholas I had it erected in memory of Alexander I. The 700-ton piece of granite took three years to be extracted from the Karelian Isthmus and brought down by barges to the city. Architect Auguste Montferrand supervised the polishing in 1830, and by 1834 the 14.5 meter-high (47.5-feet) column was erected by 2,500 men using an elaborate system of pulleys. The figure of the angel (whose face resembles Alexander I) holding a cross was carved by sculptor Boris Orlovsky. The Guard's Headquarters (to the right of the column facing the Palace) was built by Bryullov (1837–43) and now serves as an administrative building.

The main architectural wonder of the Square is the **Winter Palace**, standing along the bank of the Neva. This masterpiece by Rastrelli was commissioned by the Czarina Elizabeth, daughter of Peter, who was fond of the baroque style and desired a lavish palace decorated with columns, stucco and sculptures. It was built between 1754 and 1762, as Rastrelli remarked, 'solely for the glory of all Russia'. At this time,

Inside the Hermitage Museum. (bottom) The Throne Room of Peter the Great was built to honor the czar in the early 1800s. The throne was crafted by a Huguenot silversmith and embroidered with a double-headed eagle. The czar's portrait with a woman (representing Minerva or the Spirit of Russia) was painted in 1730 for the Russian Ambasssador to London (see also pictures on pages 404–5).

the Winter Palace cost two and a half million rubles, equal to the value of 45 tons of silver. The Palace remained the czars' official residence until the February 1917 Revolution. The magnificent Palace extends over eight hectares (20 acres) and the total perimeter measures two kilometers (over a mile). There are 1,057 rooms (not one identical), 1,945 windows, 1,886 doors and 117 staircases. The royal family's staff consisted of over 1,000 servants. At 200 meters (656 feet) long and 22 meters (72 feet) high, it was the largest building in St Petersburg. After the 1837 fire destroyed a major portion of the Palace, architects Bryullov and Stasov restored the interior along the lines of Russian classicism, but preserved Rastrelli's light and graceful baroque exterior. The blue-green walls are adorned with 176 sculpted figures. The interior was finished with marble, malachite, jasper, semiprecious stones, polished woods, gilded moldings and crystal chandeliers. In 1844, Nicholas I passed a decree (in force until 1905) stating that all buildings in the city (except churches) had to be at least two meters (six feet) lower than the Winter Palace. During World War II the Winter Palace was marked on German maps as Bombing Objective number 9. (See Special Topic on pages 464.) Today the Winter Palace houses the **Hermitage Museum**—the largest museum in the country, exhibiting close to 2,800,000 items and visited by more than three million people annually. It contains one of the largest and most valuable collections of art in the world, dating from antiquity to the present.

Peter the Great began the city's first art collection after visiting Europe. In 1719, he purchased Rembrandt's *David's Farewell to Jonathan*, a statue of Aphrodite (*Venus of Taurida*), and started a museum of Russian antiquities (now on display in the Hermitage's Siberian collection).

In 1764, Catherine the Great created the Hermitage (a French word meaning secluded spot) in the Winter Palace for a place to display 225 Dutch and Flemish paintings she had purchased in Berlin. Her ambassadors were often sent to European countries in search of art; in 1769, she purchased the entire collection of Count de Bruhl of Dresden. The Hermitage held almost 4,000 paintings at the time of her death. Subsequent czars continued to expand the collection: Alexander I bought the entire picture gallery of Josephine, wife of Napoleon, and Nicholas I even purchased pictures from Napoleon's stepdaughter. Until 1852, the Hermitage was only open to members of the royal family and aristocratic friends. Catherine the Great wrote in a letter to one of her close friends that 'all this is admired by mice and myself'. A small list of rules, written by Catherine, hung by the Hermitage's entrance (see page 406). In 1852, Nicholas I opened the Hermitage on certain days as a public museum (but still closed to common people), and put it under the administrative direction of curators. After the 1917 Revolution, the Hermitage was opened full-time to the whole public.

The Hermitage occupies several other buildings in addition to the Winter Palace. The **Little Hermitage** housed Catherine's original collection in a small building next to the Palace; it was constructed by Vallin de la Mothe between 1764 and 1767. Stackenschneider's Pavilion Hall is decked with white marble columns, 28 chandeliers, the four Fountains of Tears and the Peacock Clock. The royal family would stroll in the Hanging Gardens in the summer, along with peasants and peacocks. In winter, snow mounds were built for sledding. The **Old Hermitage** (or Large Hermitage) was built right next to it to provide space for Catherine's growing collection. The **Hermitage Theater**, Catherine's private theater, is linked to the Old Hermitage by a small bridge that crosses the Winter Ditch canal. The theater was built by Quarenghi in 1787 and modeled after the amphitheaters of Pompeii. The **New Hermitage** (1839–52), located behind the Old Hermitage, houses additional works of art. Its main entrance off Millionnaya Ulitsa is composed of the ten large and powerful **Statues of Atlas**. They were designed by the sculptor A Terebenyev who personally participated in the carvings of these huge blocks of polished gray marble. The first figure took a year and a half to complete. Three more years were spent cutting the other nine. The figures of Atlas became the official emblem of the Hermitage.

The Hermitage collection spans a millennium of art and culture. As the current director of the museum stated: 'The Hermitage is a symbol of not only Russian but human civilization.' It is said that if a visitor spent only half a minute at each exhibit, it would take nine years to view them all! A map of the layout can be purchased inside, from which you can select places of interest. Plan to spend at least three hours here. Enter at the ground floor by the Neva entrance. As you pass through Classical Antiquities, walk left through the Rastrelli Gallery and up the Jordan Staircase to the first floor. Here are the State Rooms of the Winter Palace. On this floor you will also find the Field Marshal's Room and Peter's Throne Room; the Armorial Hall leads to the magnificent Alexander Hall, designed to commemorate the Napoleonic Wars. On the other side of the staircase are Nicholas Hall, the Malachite Room and the White Dining Room, where Kerensky's Provisional Government was overthrown in 1917. Other areas of interest are the Golden Room, Vatican Room and Hall of St George. Where the Imperial Throne once stood in the Hall of St George now hangs an enormous mosaic map of the former Soviet Union, covered with 45,000 semiprecious stones. Moscow is marked by a ruby star and St Petersburg is written in letters of alexandrite. The 19-ton Kolyvan Vase was made from Altai jasper and took 14 years to carve. An entire wall in the Hermitage was knocked down to bring it inside.

Other exhibits on the first floor delineate the history of Russian culture; primeval art (over 400,000 objects) is covered on the ground floor; oriental art and

Inside the Hermitage Museum. (opposite page) The Jordan Staircase (named after Jesus' baptism in the River Jordan) leads the visitor up marble steps from the Rastrelli Gallery, entrance to the museum's many halls including the Throne Room of Peter the Great (see picture on page 401); (left) The ceiling of the Gallery is decorated with a painting of the gods of Mt Olympus; (below) the Siberian green jasper Kolyvan Vase.

CODE OF THE EMPRESS CATHERINE

*A*t the entrance of one hall, I found behind a green curtain the social rules of the Hermitage, for the use of those intimate friends admitted by the Czarina into the asylum of Imperial Liberty.

I will transcribe, verbatim, this charter, granted to social intimacy by the caprice of the sovereign of the once enchanted place: it was copied for me in my presence:-

RULES TO BE OBSERVED ON ENTERING

ARTICLE I
On entering, the title and rank must be put off, as well as the hat and sword.

ARTICLE II
Pretensions founded on the prerogatives of birth, pride, or other sentiments of a like nature must also be left at the door.

ARTICLE III
Be merry; nevertheless, break nothing and spoil nothing.

ARTICLE IV
Sit, stand, walk, do whatever you please, without caring for anyone.

ARTICLE V
Speak with moderation, and not too often, in order to avoid being troublesome to others.

ARTICLE VI

Argue without anger and without warmth.

ARTICLE VII

Banish sighs and yawns, that you may not communicate ennui, or be a nuisance to anyone.

ARTICLE VIII

Innocent games, proposed by any members of the society, must be accepted by the others.

ARTICLE IX

Eat slowly and with appetite; drink with moderation, that each may walk steadily as he goes out.

ARTICLE X

Leave all quarrels at the door; what enters at one ear must go out at the other before passing the threshold of the Hermitage.

If any member violates the above rules, for each fault witnessed by two persons, he must drink a glass of fresh water (ladies not excepted); furthermore, he must read aloud a page of the Telemachiad *(a poem by Trediakofsky). Whoever fails during one evening in three of these articles, must learn by heart six lines of the* Telemachiad. *He who fails in the tenth article must never more re-enter the Hermitage.*

Marquis Astolphe Louis Leonard de Custine, Russia, 1854–5

culture (a quarter of a million pieces) from Egypt, Babylon, Byzantium, the Middle East, Japan, China and India occupy the second and ground floors; antique culture and art from Greece, Italy and Rome are also on the ground floor. Over 650,000 items in the collection of the art of Western Europe are found on the first and second floors. This includes paintings by da Vinci, Raphael, Titian, El Greco, Rubens, Rembrandt, and a fine impressionist collection by Monet, Lautrec, Van Gogh and Picasso. In addition there are numerous displays of sculpture, tapestries, china, jewelry, furniture, rare coins and handicrafts. The museum has room to display only 20 percent of its incredible treasures. In 1995, the Hermitage ran a highly controversial exhibition entitled Hidden Treasures Revealed, composed entirely of art confiscated by the Red Army from private German collections when it swept across Eastern Europe into Berlin at the end of World War II. The paintings, estimated to be worth several million dollars, are by impressionist and Postimpressionist artists. The centerpiece was Degas's 1875 painting *Place de la Concorde*, believed to have been destroyed during the war. Stored secretly for over half a century in a small room on the museum's second floor, the unveiled collection included many other paintings by Monet, Renoire, Gauguin, Cézanne, Matisse and Picasso. In all, during the war, the two countries pilfered from each other an estimated five million artworks. The dispute over who is the rightful owner of these paintings continues.

IBM is installing several computerized touch-screen information terminals to help visitors find their way around. A recommended book to buy at the Hermitage store is *Saved for Humanity*, tracing the history of the museum; available in several languages. A catalog of the Hidden Treasures is also on sale (and also available through the publisher Harry Abrahms in New York). The museum is open 10.30am–6pm; closed Mondays. Admission tickets are sold both inside the main entrance on the river side, and in summer, outside at ticket kiosks at the west end of the Palace. Tours can be booked through a hotel, city travel agency, or at the Hermitage itself, which also offers tours to the Museum's Special Collections, including Scythian art, Siberian goldwork and church ornaments. (See Practical Information section for museum and tour agency listings and web-site.)

Leaving the Hermitage through Palace Square and left past the Guard's Headquarters takes you through the Choristers' Passage and across a wide bridge known as Pevchesky Most (Singers' Bridge). This bridge crosses the lovely **Moika Canal** and leads to the former Imperial Choristers' Capella (1831), now the Glinka Academy Capella. At 12 Moika Embankment, to the left of the Capella, is the **Pushkin House Museum** where the poet, considered the fountainhead of Russian literature, lived from October 1836 until his death in January 1837. Alexander

(previous pages) The Hermitage on the Neva River. On the right the golden dome of St Isaac's Cathedral stands behind the spire of the Admiralty.

Pushkin died following a duel on Krestovsky Island with a French soldier of fortune named George D'Anthés, who had been publicly flirting with Pushkin's beautiful wife Natalia. The affair was said to have been instigated by Nicholas I, who was tired of the famous poet's radical politics; the czar was Pushkin's personal censor. A statue of Pushkin stands in the courtyard. The rooms have all been preserved and contain his personal belongings and manuscripts. The study is arranged exactly as it was when Pushkin died on the divan from a wound he received in the duel. The clock is even set to 2.45am, the moment of his death. The next room displays the clothes worn during the duel and his death mask. Since Pushkin is still one of the most popular figures in Russia, museum tickets are often sold out; it may be necessary to buy them a few days in advance. The museum is open 11am–5pm; closed Tuesdays.

The Area of Senate Square (Senatskaya Ploshchad)

Walking west of the Winter Palace along the Neva, you come to another chief architectural monument of the city, the **Admiralty**, recognizable by its tall golden spire topped by a golden frigate, the symbol of St Petersburg after Peter the Great. The best views of the building are from its southern end. A beautiful fountain stands in the middle of Alexandrovsky Garden surrounded by busts of Glinka, Gogol and Lermontov. In 1704, Peter the Great ordered a second small outpost constructed on the left bank of the Neva, opposite the main town. This shipyard was later referred to as the Admiralty. Over 10,000 peasants and engineers were employed to work on the Russian naval fleet. By the end of the 18th century the Navy had its headquarters here. Whenever the Neva waters rose during a severe storm, a lantern was lit in the spire to warn of coming floods. In 1738, the main building was rebuilt by the architect Ivan Korobov, who replaced the wooden tower with a golden spire. From 1806 to 1823, the building was again redesigned by Zakharov, an architectural professor at the St Petersburg Academy. The height of the spire was increased to 72.5 meters (238 feet) and decorated with 56 mythological figures and 350 ornamentations based on the glory of the Russian fleet. The scene over the main-entrance archway depicts Neptune handing over his trident to Peter the Great, a symbol of Peter's mastery of the sea. In 1860, many of the statues were taken down when the Orthodox Church demanded the 'pagan' statues removed. Today the Admiralty houses the Higher Naval School.

Across the street from the Admiralty, at 6 Admiralty Prospekt, is the building known as the All Russia Extraordinary Commission for Combating Counterrevolution, Sabotage and Speculation—the Cheka. Felix Dzerzhinsky, the first chairman of the Cheka Police Force (forerunner of the KGB), had his office here. His best-remembered words were that a member of the Cheka 'must have clean hands, a warm heart and a cold head'. A memorial museum dedicated to Dzerzhinsky has been here since 1974.

Beside the Admiralty is the infamous **Senate Square**, formerly known as Decembrists' and Peter Square. In 1925, to mark the 100-year anniversary of the Decembrist uprising, the area was renamed Decembrists' Square. (In 1992, its name reverted to Senate.) After the Russian victory in the Patriotic War of 1812 and the introduction of principles from the French Enlightenment, both the nobility and peasants wanted an end to the monarchy and serfdom. An opportune moment for insurrection came on November 19, 1825, when Czar Alexander I died suddenly. A secret revolutionary society, consisting mainly of noblemen, gathered over 3,000 soldiers and sailors who refused to swear allegiance to the new czar, Nicholas I. The members compiled the Manifesto to the Russian People, which they hoped the Senate would approve. (What they did not know was that the Senate had already proclaimed their loyalty to Nicholas.) They decided to lead an uprising of the people in Senate Square on December 14, 1825, and from there to capture the Winter Palace and Peter and Paul Fortress. But Nicholas I discovered the plan and surrounded the square with armed guards. The Decembrists marched to an empty Senate, and moreover, Prince Trubetskoi, who was elected to lead the insurrection, never showed up! Tens of thousands of people joined the march and prevented the guards from advancing on the main parties. But Nicholas I then ordered his guards to open fire on the crowd. Hundreds were killed and mass arrests followed. In addition, over 100 people were sentenced to serve 30 years in penal servitude. Five leaders of the rebellion were

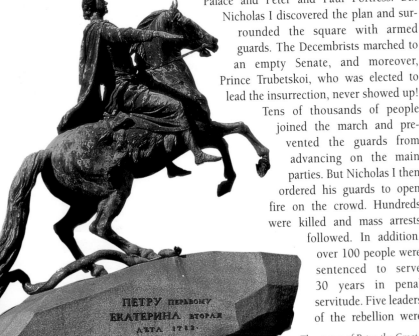

The statue of Peter the Great known as the Bronze Horseman (Medny Vsadnik)

Pushkin House Museum (see page 410). (top) Sketch of Alexander Pushkin. (bottom left) The writer's study and library of over 4,000 books. It is arranged exactly as it was when Pushkin died on the divan from a wound received in a duel. The clock is set to the moment of his death, 2.45am, on January 29, 1837. (bottom right) The inkstand on Pushkin's desk is decorated with an Ethiopian figure which reminded him of his great-grandfather, Abram Hannibal, an African officer who became Peter the Great's chief military engineer in St Petersburg.

hanged in Peter and Paul Fortress. Others received such ludicrous sentences as having to run a gauntlet of a thousand soldiers 12 times, amounting to 12,000 blows by rod; if they survived, they would be set free! Even though the 1825 uprising was unsuccessful, 'the roar of cannon on Senate Square awakened a whole generation', observed the revolutionary writer Alexander Herzen.

In 1768, Catherine the Great commissioned the sculptor Etienne Falconet to build a monument to Peter the Great. For 12 years Falconet worked 'to create an alive, vibrant and passionate spirit'. He successfully designed a rider on a rearing horse, crushing a serpent under its feet. Instead of a molded pedestal, Falconet wanted to place his monument atop natural stone. A suitable rock was found about ten kilometers (six miles) from the city. It had been split by lightning and was known as Thunder Rock. Peter the Great was said to have often climbed the rock to view his emerging city. With the help of levers, the 1,600-ton rock was raised on a platform of logs and rolled to the sea on a system of copper balls; it took a year to get it to St Petersburg. The rock bears the outlines of crashing waves. Marie Collot, Falconet's pupil and future wife, sculpted the head, and the Russian sculptor, Gordeyev, the snake. The bronze inscription on the base, written in Russian and Latin, reads: 'To Peter I from Catherine II, 1782', the date the monument was unveiled—the 100th anniversary of Peter's ascension to the throne. The monument to Peter became known as the **Bronze Horseman**, after the popular poem by Pushkin (see page 510). Today the statue is looked on as the symbol of St Petersburg, a sign of its splendor and endurance; it has remained a constant through nearly three tumultuous centuries. Legend has it that as long as the Bronze Horseman remains, St Petersburg will never perish.

The first governing Senate was established by Peter the Great in 1711 and ruled the country while the czar was away. Peter put the Church and ecclesiastical members under State control in 1721 by founding the Holy Synod. Carlo Rossi supervised the construction of the yellow-white Senate, Synod and Supreme Court buildings between 1829 and 1836. They are joined by an arch, symbolizing Faith and Law. Today they house the Historical Archives. Take a stroll down the small Galernaya Ulitsa that lies beyond the arch; this was the area of the galley shipyards. The two Ionic columns standing at the start of the next boulevard bear the Goddesses of Glory. These monuments commemorate the valor of Russia's Horse Guards during the war against Napoleon. The building that looks like an ancient Roman temple is the Horse Guard Manège, where the czar's horse guards were trained. It was built between 1804 and 1807 from designs by Quarenghi. In front of the portico are marble statues of the mythological heroes Castor and Pollux. Today the building is used as an exhibition hall for the Union of Artists.

St Isaac's Square (Isaakiyevskaya Ploshchad)

The whole southern end of Senate Square is framed by the grand silhouette of **St Isaac's Cathedral**. In 1710, the first wooden church of St Isaac was built by Peter, who was born on the day which celebrated the sainthood of Isaac of Dalmatia; it was replaced in 1729 by one of stone. At that time the church was situated nearer to the banks of the Neva and it eventually began to crack and sink. In 1768, it was decided to build another church farther away from the riverbank. But, on its completion in 1802, the church was not deemed grand enough for the growing magnificence of the capital. After the War of 1812, Czar Alexander I announced a competition for the best design of a new St Isaac's. The young architect Montferrand presented an elaborate album filled with 24 different variations, from Chinese to Gothic, for the czar to choose from. Montferrand was selected for the monumental task in 1818, and the czar also assigned the architects Stasov, Rossi and the Mikhailov brothers to help with the engineering.

The cathedral took 40 years to build. In the first year alone, 11,000 serfs drove 25,000 wooden planks into the soft soil to set a foundation. Each of the 112 polished granite columns, weighing 130 tons, had to be raised by a system of pulleys. The system was so efficient that the monolithic columns were each installed in a mere 45 minutes. The domed cathedral has a total height of 101.5 meters (333 feet). An observation deck along the upper colonnade (562 steps to climb) provides a magnificent view of the city. The State spared no expense—the cathedral cost ten times more than the Winter Palace. Nearly 100 kilograms of pure gold were used to gild the dome, which in good weather is visible 40 kilometers (25 miles) away. The interior is faced with 14 different kinds of marble, and 43 other types of stone and minerals. Inside the western portico is a bust of Montferrand, made from each type of marble. (Montferrand died one month after the completion of the cathedral. He had asked to be buried within its walls, but Czar Alexander II refused. Instead, Montferrand was buried in Paris.) The cathedral can hold 14,000 people and is filled with over 400 sculptures, paintings and mosaics by the best Russian and European masters of the 19th century. Twenty-two artists decorated the iconostasis, ceilings and walls. The altar's huge stained-glass window is surrounded by frescoes by Bryullov, who also painted the frescoes in the ceiling of the main dome. A St Petersburg newspaper wrote that the cathedral was 'a pantheon of Russian art, as artists have left monuments to their genius in it'. On May 29, 1858, St Isaac's was inaugurated with much pomp and celebration as the main cathedral of St Petersburg. In 1931, it was opened by the government as a museum. Open 11am–6pm; closed Wednesdays. Services are sometimes held during special religious holidays.

CATHERINE THE GREAT (1729–1796)

Peter the Great propelled Russia into the 18th century; Catherine II completed it by decorating his creation in European pomp and principle. Born Sophie Frederika Augusta in 1729 to the German prince of Anhalt-Zerbst, she was chosen as the future bride, at the age of 14, to Peter III, the half-wit grandson of Peter the Great. When Peter III ascended the throne in 1762, he threatened to get rid of Catherine by imprisoning her in a nunnery (and marrying his pockmarked mistress). This only fueled Catherine's ambitions; she said, 'either I die or I begin to rule'. That same year a secret coup, headed by her lover Grigory Orlov and his brothers, overthrew the unpopular Peter. When he was killed by drunken guards a week later, Catherine became the first foreigner ever to sit upon the Russian throne; she would rule for 34 years. Catherine was clever and adventurous and had fallen deeply in love with her new homeland (instead of with her husband). She immersed herself in the problems of politics and agriculture and worked toward basing the government on philosophic principles rather than on religious doctrines or hereditary rights. Because of her European roots, Catherine held a fascination for France and avidly worked to link French culture with that of her adopted nation. She read Voltaire, Montesquieu and Rousseau and sent emissaries to study in foreign lands; she also began the education of noblewomen. The Russian aristocracy soon incorporated French culture into their daily lives, giving the noblemen a common identity. The French language also set them apart from the Russian peasantry. In 1780, she further initiated the Declaration of Armed Neutrality, helping the American colonies in their struggle for independence.

Catherine described her reign as the 'thornless rose that never stings'. Along with autocratic power, she ruled with virtue, justice and reason. By the publication of books and newspapers, and instruction by Western-trained tutors, education spread throughout the provinces, where before much of the learning originated from the Church. This allowed Russian culture to cut loose from its religious roots. Paper money was introduced,

St Isaac's Cathedral on St Isaac's Square was designed by August Montferrand in 1818 and took 40 years to build. Over 100 kilograms of gold were used to gild the dome, which is visible over 40 kilometers (25 miles) away.

along with vaccinations; the day of Catherine's smallpox vaccination became a national feast day.

Scientific expeditions were sent to Far Eastern lands and hundreds of new cities were built in Russia's newly conquered territories. Along the coast of the Black Sea, the cities of Odessa, Azov and Sevastopol were constructed on the sites of old Greek settlements. With the formation of the Academy of Sciences, Russia now contributed to the Renaissance Age and would never again stand in the shadows. One of the most important figures of the time, Mikhail Lomonosov, scientist, poet and historian, later helped to establish Moscow University.

Catherine spared no expense to redecorate St Petersburg in the classical designs of the time. Wanting a home for the art that she began collecting from abroad, Catherine built the Hermitage. It was connected to her private apartments and also served as a conference chamber and theater. Besides the exquisite treasures kept within, the Hermitage itself was constructed of jasper, malachite, marble and gold. The Empress' extravagant reputation filtered into her love life as well. She had 21 known favorites, and loved being exceedingly generous to them—during her rule she spent nearly 100 million rubles on them. (Russia's annual budget, at the time, was 40 million rubles.) Among Catherine's ladies-in-waiting was a *probolshchitsa*, whose sole task was to test the virility of the Czarina's potential admirers. Platon Zubov, at age 22, was the Empress' lover when she was well into her sixties.

Unfortunately it became increasingly difficult for Catherine to maintain her autocratic rule while at the same time implement large-scale reform. Her sweeping plans for change planted the seeds for much more of a blossoming than she bargained for. The education of the aristocracy created a greater schism between them and the working class and her reforms further worsened the conditions of the peasantry. As the city took the center of culture away from the Church, more and more Old Believers were left disillusioned with her rule. Catherine tore down monasteries and torched the old symbols of Moscovy. In an Age of Reason, she had a deep suspicion of anything mystical.

Huge sums of money were also spent on constructing elaborate

The young German Princess Catherine II arrived in St Petersburg to marry Peter III. She went on to become the first foreign woman to rule Russia, and later received the title of Catherine the Great for her many accomplishments during her 34-year reign.

palaces for her favorite relations and advisors. One of these was Prince Grigory Potemkin, her foreign minister, commander-in-chief and greatest love for almost two decades. It was he who organized a trip for Catherine down the Dnieper River to view the newly accessed Crimean territories. The prince had painted façades constructed along the route to camouflage the degree of poverty of the peasants. These 'Potemkin villages' were also to give the appearance of real towns in the otherwise uninhabited areas. Finally in 1773, Pugachev, a Don cossack, led a rebellion of impoverished cossacks, peasants and Old Believers against the throne and serfdom. Pugachev was captured and sentenced to decapitation, but ended up exiled in Siberia.

It was not only the peasantry and the Church that felt alienated. The aristocracy too grew dissatisfied with the new European truths and philosophies. Those who yearned for more considered themselves a new class, the intelligentsia. Searching for their own identity amidst a surge of French principles, the intelligentsia proceeded not only to understand Voltaire's logic but to incorporate its heart and spirit as well.

By grasping the ideals of a foreign Enlightenment, Catherine II unknowingly gave birth to Russia's own. The catalyst of change, along with teaching people to think for themselves, brought despotism into deeper disfavor and paved the road to revolution. After the fall of the Bastille, Catherine turned her back on France. In a panic, she tried to dispose of all that she had helped create. Censorship was imposed throughout Russia, and Catherine attempted to slam shut the window to the West less than a century after Peter had opened it. But from this period of discontent and new search for meaning, Russia would give birth to some of the greatest writers and thinkers of all time. The West would be captivated by the works of Pushkin, Dostoevsky and Tolstoy, and Lenin would later lead Russia out of five centuries of autocratic rule. Peter the Great had built the wheels and Catherine set them in motion; there was to be no turning back.

St Isaac's Square, in front of the cathedral, was originally a marketplace in the 1830s. At its center stands the bronze **Statue of Nicholas I** constructed by Montferrand and Klodt between 1856 and 1859. The czar, who loved horses and military exploits (nicknamed Nicholas the Stick), is portrayed in a cavalry uniform wearing a helmet with an eagle. His horse rests only on two points. The bas-reliefs around the pedestal depict the events of Nicholas' turbulent rule. One of them shows Nicholas I addressing his staff after the Decembrist uprising. The four figures at each corner represent Faith, Wisdom, Justice and Might, and depict the faces of Nicholas' wife and three daughters, who commissioned the statue.

The two buildings on each side of the monument were built between 1844 and 1853 and now house the Academy of Agricultural Sciences. Behind the monument is the **Blue Bridge** (1818), which is painted accordingly. It is the broadest bridge in the city and even though it appears to be a continuation of the square, it is actually a bridge over the Moika River. There was a slave market here before the abolition of serfdom in 1861. Many of St Petersburg's bridges were named after the color they were painted; up river are the Green and Red bridges. On one side of the bridge is an obelisk crowned by a trident, known as the Neptune Scale. Five bronze bands indicate the level of the water during the city's worst floods. The Leningrad poet Vera Inber wrote of this place:

> Here in the city, on Rastrelli's marble
> Or on plain brick, we see from time to time
> A mark: 'The water-level reached this line'
> And we can only look at it and marvel.

Beyond the bridge stands the former Mariinsky Palace. It was built between 1839 and 1844 for Maria, the daughter of Nicholas I. In 1894, it was turned into the State Council of the Russian Empire. The artist Repin painted the centennial gala of the council in 1901, entitled *The Solemn Meeting of the State Council*; it can be viewed at the Russian Museum. In 1917, the Palace was the residence of the Provisional Government. It now houses the St Petersburg City Assembly (the city parliament).

The gray and orange seven-story **Astoria Hotel** on the northeast side of the square was built in 1910 and became the grandest hotel in the city. Hitler even sent out engraved invitations for a banquet to be held at the Astoria on November 7, 1942, as soon as he had captured the city. Of course, this never took place. The hotel has been remodeled and is a very popular place to stay. In front of it is the Lobanov-Rostovsky Mansion. Montferrand built this for the Russian diplomat between 1817 and 1820. Pushkin mentioned the marble lions in front of the house in the *Bronze Horseman*, when the hero climbed one of them to escape the flood. The mansion is referred to as the House with Lions.

Central St Petersburg

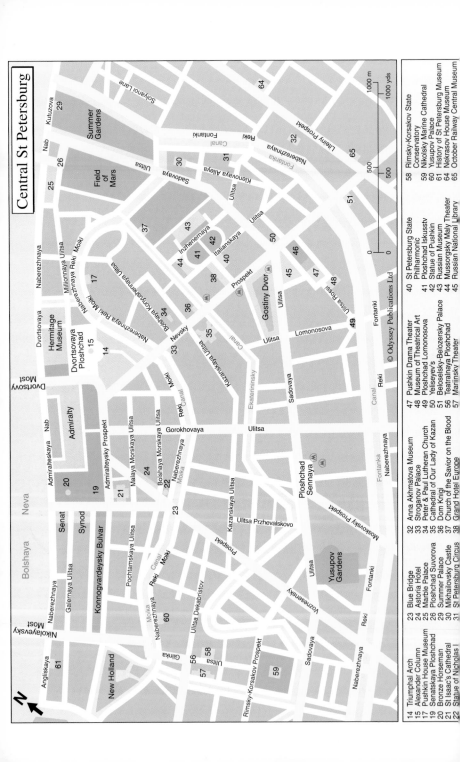

© Odyssey Publications Ltd

14 Triumphal Arch
15 Alexander Column
17 Pushkin House Museum
19 Senatskaya Ploshchad
20 Bronze Horseman
21 St Isaac's Cathedral
22 St Petersburg Circus

23 Blue Bridge
24 Astoria Hotel
25 Marble Palace
26 Ploshchad Suvorova
29 Summer Palace
30 Mikhailovsky Castle
31 Statue of Nicholas I

32 Anna Akhmatova Museum
33 Stroganov Palace
34 Peter & Paul Lutheran Church
35 Cathedral of Our Lady of Kazan
36 Dom Knigi
37 Church of the Savior on the Blood
38 Grand Hotel Europe

40 Pushkin Drama Theater
41 Museum of Theatrical Art
42 Ploshchad Lomonosova
43 Yeliseyev's
45 Russian Museum
46 Beloselsky-Belozersky Palace
56 Teatralnaya Ploshchad
57 Mariinsky Theater

47 Pushkin Drama Theater
48 Museum of Theatrical Art
49 Ploshchad Lomonosova
50 Yeliseyev's
51 Beloselsky-Belozersky Palace
56 Teatralnaya Ploshchad
57 Mariinsky Theater

58 Rimsky-Korsakov State Conservatory
59 Nikolsky Marine Cathedral
60 Yusupov Palace
61 History of St Petersburg Museum
64 Nekrasov House Museum
65 October Railway Central Museum

The **Museum of Musical Instruments**, at 5 St Isaac's Square, has one of the largest collections (3,000) in the world. Some of the items on display are the grand pianos of Rimsky-Korsakov, Glinka and Rubenstein. Open 12–5.30pm; closed Mondays and Tuesdays. In front of the museum stands Myatlev's House. Built for the poet by Rinaldi in 1760, it is one of the oldest structures on the square.

On the west side of the square is the Intourist Building, originally built in 1910 to accommodate the new German Embassy. It was designed by German architect Berens, who became one of the founders of the new *jugendstil* style. Behind this building, at 47 Bolshaya Morskaya Ulitsa, is the **Nabokov House Museum**; the famous writer was born here in 1899. Nabokov's works include *Speak, Memory, Pale Fire, Laughter in the Dark* and *Lolita*—the immensely controversial novel written in 1955. At 4 Pochtamskaya Ulitsa is the **Popov Central Communication Museum**, which traces the history of communications in the former USSR; open 12–6pm; closed Mondays. At 9 Pochtamskaya Ulitsa is the General Post Office (1782–89), with the Clock of the World mounted on its archway. Dostoevsky lived at 23 Malaya Morskaya Ulitsa before his imprisonment at Peter and Paul Fortress. Here he wrote *Netochka Nezvanova* and *The White Nights*. Dostoevsky's main museum is located at 5/2 Kuznechny Pereulok, near Vladimirskaya Metro station.

Field of Mars (Polye Marsovo)

A short walk east from the Hermitage, along Millionnaya Ulitsa (Millionaire's Row), brings you to the **Marble Palace**. In 1768, Catherine the Great commissioned Antonio Rinaldi to build a palace for her favorite, Count Grigory Orlov. But Orlov died before its completion in 1785, and it was turned over to a grand duke. This was the only building in St Petersburg faced both inside and outside with marble—32 different kinds. In 1937, the Marble Palace opened as the Leningrad branch of the Central Lenin Museum, with over 10,000 exhibits in 34 rooms relating to Lenin's life and work. In the former Leningrad alone, over 250 places were associated with Lenin. (In a small garden at the main entrance stood an armored car with the inscription, 'Enemy of Capital'. It was removed to the Artillery Museum in 1992.) After the February 1917 Revolution, Lenin returned to St Petersburg from exile in Europe in this armored car, and upon his arrival at Finland Station on April 3 delivered a speech from the turret proclaiming: 'Long live the Socialist Revolution!' After the 1991 failed coup, the Lenin Museum was removed from the Marble Palace which now, as a branch of the Russian Museum, displays a permanent exhibit entitled Foreign Painters in Russia. Open 10am–6pm; closed Tuesdays.

Right in front of the Troitsky Bridge is **Suvorov Square** (Ploshchad Suvorova), with the statue of the Russian generalissimo Alexander Suvorov depicted as Mars, the God of War. The square opens on to one of the most beautiful places in St Petersburg, the **Field of Mars**. Around 1710, Peter the Great drained the marshy field and held parades after military victories. The festivities ended in fireworks (known as amusement lights), so the square was called Poteshnoye Polye (Amusement Field). By the end of the 18th century the area was used as a routine drill field, which destroyed the grass; for a while the field was nicknamed the St Petersburg Sahara. When in 1801 the monument to Field Marshal Suvorov was placed here, the area became known as Marsovo Polye (Field of Mars). It was moved to its present location, Suvorov Square, in 1818. The 12-hectare (30-acre) field is bordered on the west by the **Barracks of the Pavlovsky Regiment**. Because of their heroic deeds this regiment was rewarded with a magnificent barracks, built between 1817 and 1820. The Pavlovsky Grenadier Regiment was the first among the czar's armies to take the side of the people during the February 1917 Revolution. It is now the St Petersburg Energy Commission. The southern side is bordered by the Moika River and Ekaterininsky Canal, and the eastern side by the Swan Canal (Lebyazhya Kanavka).

The **Memorial to the Fighters of the Revolution** stands in the center of the field. On March 23, 1917, 180 heroes of the February uprising were buried here in mass graves. The next day the first granite stone was laid in the monument foundation, which was unveiled in 1920. On each of the eight stone blocks are words by the writer Anatoly Lunacharsky. One reads: 'Not victims, but heroes, lie beneath these stones. Not grief, but envy, is aroused by your fate in the hearts of all your grateful descendants.' During the 40th anniversary of the Revolution in 1957, the eternal flame was lit in memory of those killed.

The eastern side of the field opens up on the lovely Letny Sad or **Summer Garden** with over 250 sculptures made by 17th and 18th century Italian masters. The main entrance to the garden is from the Kutuzova Embankment. A beautiful black and golden grille (1770–84 by Yuri Felten) fences it. The open railing, decorated with 36 granite columns and pinkish urns, is one of the finest examples of wrought-iron work in the world. The Summer Garden, the city's oldest, was designed by Leblond in Franco-Dutch style in 1704. Peter the Great desired to create a garden more exquisite than Versailles. On 25 acres of land he planted trees and had hothouses, aviaries, grottos and sculptures placed within. Some of the original statues remain, such as *Peace and Abundance*, the busts of John Sobiesky (a Polish king), Christina (a Swedish queen), the Roman empress Agrippina, and Cupid and

Psyche. The Swan Canal dug on the western side was filled with swans and had a tiny boat for Peter's favorite dwarf jester. The garden also had many fountains depicting characters from Aesop's *Fables*.

The water for the fountains was drained from a river on its east side; the river was named **Fontanka**, from the Russian *fontan* (fountain). Pipes made from hollowed logs ran from the Fontanka to a city pool, from which a 1.6-kilometers (one-mile) pipeline brought water to the gardens. The Fontanka formed the southern border of the city in the mid-18th century. At this time the first stone bridge was built where the Fontanka flows into the Neva. It is still known as **Prachechny Most** (Laundry Bridge) because it was located near the Royal Laundry. The gardens received their name from the many festivals that Peter the Great loved to hold in summer; the area became the center of social life in St Petersburg.

Many of the fountains, pavilions and statues were destroyed during the 1777 and 1824 floods. The Summer Garden was open only to nobility until, in the mid-19th century, Nicholas I issued a decree stating that it would be 'open for promenading to all military men and decently dressed people. Ordinary people, such as *muzhiks* (peasants) shall not be allowed to walk through the garden.' After the Revolution the garden was opened fully to the public.

After the garden was designed, Peter had his Letny Dvorets or **Summer Palace** built at the northern end by the Neva. Following its completion in 1714 by Trezzini, Peter moved from his cottage into the palace. The modest stone building was decorated with 29 terracotta figures and a weather vane of St George slaying the dragon. There are 20 rooms, ten on each floor. Peter lived on the ground floor, and his wife Catherine on the second. The czar received visitors in the reception room, and the empress enjoyed baking Peter's favorite pies in the kitchen. Nearby stood one of Peter's favorite statues, the *Venus of Taurida* (now in the Hermitage); the czar purchased it from the Pope. The House is open 11am–6pm; closed Tuesdays.

Behind the Summer Palace is an interesting bronze **Monument to Ivan Krylov** by the sculptor Klodt, dedicated to the popular Russian fabulist. There is also a playground for children with subjects from Krylov's fables. Nearer to the fountain are the Chainy Domik or **Tea House**, built in 1827 by Ludwig Charlemagne, and the **Coffee House** built by Rossi in 1826 (it is also known as Rossi's Pavilion). Recitals are now held here. The outside sculpture of *Peace and Abundance* symbolizes the peace treaty made with Sweden in 1721. It was a gift to Nicholas I from the Swedish king, Karl Johann. Nearby, across the Fontanka at 9 Solyanoi Pereulok, is the **Defense and Siege of Leningrad Museum** with exhibits concerning the 900-day blockade of the city. Open 10am–5pm; closed Wednesdays.

Engineer's (Mikhailovsky) Castle

Crossing the Moika and continuing along the banks of the Fontanka leads to the Mikhailovsky Castle, built between 1797 and 1800 by the architects Bazhenov and Brenna for Czar Paul I. Paul did not like his mother Catherine the Great's residence in the Winter Palace, and fearing attempts on his life, he ordered the castle constructed as an impregnable fortress. The Mikhailovsky Castle (the archangel Michael was Paul's patron saint) was bordered in the north by the Moika Canal and the east by the Fontanka Canal. Two artificial canals, the Resurrection and Church, were dug on the other sides creating a small island (they have since been filled in). Drawbridges, protected by cannons, were raised at 9pm when the czar went to bed. In spite of all this, 40 days after he moved in Paul was strangled in his sleep by one of his guards on March 11, 1801. Today the Mikhailovsky Castle is part of the Russian Museum, and houses a walk-through history of Russia. Open 10am–6pm; closed Mondays and Tuesdays.

In 1822, after a military engineering school was opened in the building, it became known as Engineer's Castle. Dostoevsky went to school here from the age of 16, from 1837 to 1843. It also contains a scientific and naval library. In front of the castle's main entrance is a **Statue of Peter the Great**, commissioned by Rastrelli while Peter was still alive. It was supposed to be erected near the Twelve Collegiums on Vasilyevsky Island. However, it was not completed until 1746, during the reign of Elizabeth I, and since the empress did not particularly like the statue it ended up in storage. In 1800, the monument was placed in its current location. Paul I ordered the inscription placed upon its base: 'To Great-Grandfather—From Great-Grandson. The Year 1800.' On the sides of the pedestal are bronze reliefs depicting major victories of Peter the Great.

Not far from the Mikhailovsky Castle at 3 Fontanka Embankment (Naberezhnaya Reki Fontanki) is the **St Petersburg Circus**. The circular building of the circus was constructed in 1877 by Kenel, making it one of the oldest permanent circus buildings in the world. During the intense revolutionary years, some of Russia's finest artists, such as Chekhov, Gorky, Eisenstein and Stanislavsky, focused their attention on the circus, so much so that the Soviet Government decided not to abolish it. Inside there is also the **Museum of Circus History and Variety Art** (established in 1928), with over 100,000 circus-related items (closed on Saturdays and Sundays). The circus has daily performances, except on Thursdays. Nearby is the **Klenovaya Alley Art Market**, a great outdoor arts and crafts emporium.

Further down the canal at 34 Fontanka Embankment, in a wing of the former Sheremetyev Palace, is the **Anna Akhmatova Museum**. (The entrance is from

A view looking east over St Petersburg from the top of St Isaac's Cathedral. The blue-domed cathedral in the distance is that of St Nicholas, known as the Sailor's Church (St Nicholas is the patron saint of sailors), built in 1762.

Liteiny Prospekt). The famous St Petersburg poet (see page 498) lived in the Fountain House from 1924 to 1941 and 1944 to 1954 in a small apartment on the third floor of the south wing. Open 12–6pm; closed Mondays. The palace was constructed between 1720 and 40 by the aristocratic Sheremetyev family. The gates are decorated with the family's gilded coat-of-arms.

Akhmatova wrote of St Petersburg:

> *But not for anything would we exchange this splendid*
> *Granite city of fame and calamity,*
> *The wide rivers of glistening ice,*
> *The sunless, gloomy gardens,*
> *And, barely audible, the Muse's voice.*

Nevsky Prospekt

In the words of Nikolai Gogol: 'There is nothing finer than the Nevsky Prospekt.... In what does it not shine, this street that is the beauty of the capital.' Nevsky Prospekt, which locals refer to as Nevsky, is the main thoroughfare of the city and the center of business and commercial life. A stroll down part of it during any time of day is a must, for no other street like it exists anywhere in the world. It is a busy, bustling area, filled with department stores, shops, cinemas, restaurants, museums, art studios, cathedrals, mansions, theaters, libraries and cafés. The Nevsky is made even more interesting and beautiful by the stunning architectural ensembles that line the 4.8-kilometer- (three-mile-)long route that stretches from the Admiralty to Alexander Nevsky Monastery. It also brims with history; you can find the spot where Pushkin met his second on the day of his fatal duel, where Dostoevsky gave readings of his works, and where Liszt and Wagner premiered their music.

Shortly after the Admiralty was completed, a track was cut through the thick forest, linking it with the road to Novgorod and Moscow. This main stretch of the city was known as the Great Perspective Road. The road took on the name of Neva Perspectiva in 1738, when it was linked to another small road that ran to Alexander Nevsky Monastery. In 1783, the route was renamed Nevsky Prospekt. Peter the Great had elegant stone houses built along the Nevsky and ordered food sold in the streets by vendors dressed in white aprons. The first buildings went up between the Admiralty and the Fontanka Canal. The area, nicknamed St Petersburg City, was a fashionable place to live, and it became the center for banks, stores and insurance offices. The architects desired to create a strong and imposing central district and constructed the buildings out of granite and stone brought in from Sweden.

Beginning at the Admiralty, where the street is at its narrowest—25 meters (82 feet), walk along to 9 Nevsky. On the corner you will find Vavelberg's House, which was originally a bank but is now the Aeroflot ticket office. The large stone house was built in 1912 by the architect, Peretyatkovich, to resemble the Doge's Palace in Venice and the Medici in Florence. Here the Nevsky is intersected by Malaya Morskaya Ulitsa (formerly Gogol Street), where the writer Nikolai Gogol lived at number 17 from 1833 to 1836. Here he wrote *Taras Bulba*, *The Inspector General* and the first chapters of *Dead Souls*. At 10 Malaya Morskaya is the Queen of Spades residence, the house of the old countess on whom Pushkin based his story of the same name. Tchaikovsky lived at 13 Malaya Morskaya for many years up until his death in 1893 (see Klin, page 204).

The next intersection on the Nevsky is Bolshaya Morskaya Ulitsa (formerly Herzen Street); Herzen lived at number 25 for a year in 1840. The main telephone and telegraph center is on the left by the Triumphal Arch of the General Staff. Fabergé had its main studios at number 24 (see Special Topic page 121). The architect Carlo Rossi laid out the street along the Pulkovo Meridian (which was the meridian on old Russian maps) so that at noon the buildings cast no shadows on the street.

The oldest buildings are at 8 and 10 Nevsky. Built between 1760 and 1780, they are now exhibition halls for work by St Petersburg artists. The house at number 14 (built in 1939) is a school. A pale blue rectangular plaque on its wall still reads: 'Citizens! In the event of artillery fire, this side of the street is the most dangerous!'

The house with columns at number 15 was built in 1768 as a stage site for one of Russia's first professional theaters. Later a small studio was connected to the theater where Falconet modeled the Bronze Horseman. It is now the **Barrikada Movie Cinema** with cafés and shops. The building at number 18 was known as Kotomin's House (1812–16), after the original owner. Pushkin often frequented the confectioner's shop that used to be in the bottom story; he lived nearby at 12 Moika Embankment (Naberezhnaya Reki Moiki). It was here on January 27, 1837, that Pushkin met up with his second on the way to his fatal duel with George D'Anthés. The shop is now the **Literaturnoye Café**, a popular spot to eat that offers piano and violin music. Outside the café, you can have your portrait drawn by one of the numerous artists.

The section on the left side of the Nevsky beyond the Moika Canal was once reserved for churches of non-Orthodox faiths. The Dutch church at number 20 was built between 1834 and 1836 by Jacquot and is now a library. The central part functioned as a church and the wings housed the Dutch Mission. Opposite at number 17 is the baroque **Stroganov Palace**, built by Rastrelli in 1754. The Stroganov family owned and developed vast amounts of land in Siberia (yes, one member of the family invented the well-known beef dish), and their coat-of-arms, depicting two sables and a bear, lies over the gateway arch. Alexander Stroganov was the president of the Academy of Fine Arts at the end of the 18th century. The palace, now a branch of the Russian Museum, displays items from the Stroganov collection. The Palace Art Salon Shop is on the first floor.

At 22–24 Nevsky is the Romanesque-style **Peter and Paul Lutheran Church** (1833–38). In the yard behind the church was the Peterschule, one of the oldest schools in the city (1710). The architect Rossi and musician Mussorgsky graduated from here. After the Revolution it housed a swimming pool. Today, services are held in the Spartak movie house on Sunday mornings.

Across the street from the church is the large, majestic, semicircular colonnade of the **Cathedral of Our Lady of Kazan**. The Kazansky Sobor was named after the famous icon of Our Lady of Kazan that used to be here. It is on view at the Russian Museum. The architect Voronikhin faced two challenges in 1801. First, Czar Paul I wished the cathedral modeled after St Peter's in Rome, and second, the Orthodox Church required that the altar must face eastwards, which would have had one side of the cathedral facing the Nevsky. Voronikhin devised 96 Corinthian columns to fan out toward the Nevsky. The bronze Doors of Paradise, which were replicas of the 15th-century Baptistery doors in Florence, opened on the Nevsky side. The structure took ten years to build and at that time was the third largest cathedral in the world. The brick walls are faced with statues and biblical reliefs made from Pudostsky stone, named after the village where it was quarried. The stone was so soft when dug

The Kamenny or Stone Bridge, one of the oldest bridges in St Petersburg, crosses the Ekaterininsky Canal.

out that it was cut with a saw. It later hardened like rock when exposed to air. In niches around the columns are statues of Alexander Nevsky, Prince Vladimir, St John the Baptist and the Apostle Andrew. The interior was decorated by the outstanding painters Bryullov, Borovikovsky and Kiprensky. There are 56 pink granite columns and polished marble and red-stone mosaic floors. Field Marshal Mikhail Kutuzov is buried in the northern chapel. The general stopped to pray at the spot where he is now buried before going off to the War of 1812. Many trophies from this war, like banners and keys to captured fortresses, hang around his crypt. In 1837, the two statues of Kutuzov and Barclay de Tolly were put up in the front garden.

To the right of the main entrance is a small square surrounded by a beautiful wrought-iron grille called Voronikhin's Railing. In 1876, the first workers' demonstration took place in front, with speeches by the Marxist, Georgi Plekhanov. A square and fountain were later added to prevent further demonstrations. But the area remains to this day a popular spot for gatherings and, since perestroika, political and religious demonstrations as well. Today the cathedral holds religious services at 9am and 6pm, Mondays to Fridays. The old Museum of Atheism has been converted into the **History of Religion Museum** which includes exhibits on Siberian shamanism and Buryat Buddhism. Open 11am–5pm (weekends 12–6pm); closed Wednesdays. The nearest Metro to the cathedral is Nevsky Prospekt.

Walking behind the cathedral and turning left leads to the **Ekaterininsky Canal** (formerly Griboedov) and lovely footbridge of **Bankovski Most** (Bank Bridge), adorned with winged lion-griffins (see picture on pages 440–1). At the time it was built in 1800, the bridge led to the National Bank; according to Greek mythology, griffins stood guard over gold. On the other side of Nevsky, also on the canal, is **Dom Knigi** (House of Books). This polished granite building topped by its distinguishing glass sphere and globe, was originally built in art-nouveau style between 1902 and 1907 by the architect Suzor for the American Singer Company. The first two floors now make up one of the largest bookstores in the country. Posters, calendars and postcards are sold on the second floor.

The Kazansky Most crosses the canal and was built by Ilarion Kutuzov, the father of the military leader. A few minutes' walk along the canal to the north stands the 17th-century Russian-style building known as the **Church of the Savior on the Blood** (Spasa Na Krovi). It was modeled on St Basil's in Moscow and erected on the spot where Czar Alexander II was assassinated by a member of Peoples' Will, a group of revolutionaries pushing for more liberal reforms. On March 1, 1881, the czar was returning from a military parade to the Winter Palace in a special armored coach built in Paris. (There had been six previous attempts on his life.) When it reached the embankment of the Ekaterininsky Canal, a terrorist jumped out and tossed a bomb beneath the hooves of the galloping horses. The emperor leapt out of the burning carriage unharmed. But another man then threw a second bomb. This time the czar was mortally wounded, both legs torn off. Ironically, the czar had planned to sign the draft of long-awaited constitutional reforms on that very day. His successor, Alexander III, ordered architect Alfred Parland to build the altar where the former czar's blood fell on the cobblestones. After many years of restoration, the cathedral is now open to visitors. The walls inside are decorated with mosaics in the style of both Byzantine and modern icon painting. Four jasper columns still stand on the spot where the czar was murdered. Outside, the narrow **Bridge of Kisses** (Most Polseluyev) crosses the Moika Canal.

The building at 30 Nevsky Prospekt was that of the Philharmonic Society, where Wagner, Liszt and Strauss performed. Today it is the **Hall of the Glinka Maly Philharmonic**. The **Church of St Catherine**, built between 1763 and 1783 in baroque-classical design by Vallin de la Mothe, is at 32–34 Nevsky. It is the oldest Catholic Church in St Petersburg. Stanislas Ponyalovsky, the last king of Poland and one of the many lovers of Catherine the Great, is buried inside. Religious services are also held here. In front of the church is a vibrant art market, filled with paintings and portrait artists. The **Armenian Church**, at 40–42 Nevsky, was built by Felten between 1771 and 1779. It was returned to followers for worship in 1990. So many churches were opened on Nevsky Prospekt in the 18th century that it was nicknamed the Street of Tolerance.

The corner building at 31–33 was known as Silver Row. Built between 1784 and 1787 by Quarenghi, it was used as an open shopping arcade, where silver merchants would set up their display booths. In 1799, the structure was made into the Town Hall or City Duma, and in 1802, a European Rathaus tower was installed. This served as a fire watchtower, and part of a 'mirror telegraph' that linked the residences of the czar in the city to Tsarskoye Selo. A beam of light was flashed along other aligned towers to announce the ruler's arrival or departure.

The art-nouveau **Grand Hotel Europe** is on the corner of Nevsky and Mikhailovskaya Ulitsa. Built in the 1870s, it was completely renovated between 1989 and 1991 by a Russian-Swedish joint venture. It has many antiques including one of Catherine the Great's carriages (available for guests). The hotel has a number of bars, restaurants and an American Express office. Across the street at number 35 is the **Bolshoi Gostiny Dvor** (Big Guest Yard) department store. Visiting merchants used to put up guest houses, *gostiniye dvori*, which served as their resident places of business. From 1761 to 1785 the architect Vallin de la Mothe built a long series of open two-tiered arcades, where merchants had their booths. It was not only a commercial center; representatives of all the estates of the capital were also found here. The Duke of Wellington, invited to Russia by Alexander I, loved to stroll past the many galleries. Pushkin and Dostoevsky shopped here as well and mentioned the Dvor in their works. In 1917, the Bolsheviks threw out the merchants and made the space into a State-run store. But some merchants, not believing the Revolution would actually last, stashed 128 kilograms of gold inside the walls of the store. It was found by workers in 1965. Today the newly renovated two-story building is the largest department store in the city and a popular place for shopping. Opposite Gostiny Dvor is the **Passazh** arcade, another shopper's delight. The small building that stands between the hall and Gostiny Dvor was built as the portico, and now holds the Central City Theater Booking Office.

Just off Nevsky, at 2 Mikhailovskaya Ulitsa, is the **St Petersburg State Philharmonic** (Shostakovich Grand Hall), built in 1839 by Jacquot for the Club of the Nobility. The St Petersburg Philharmonic Society was founded in 1802. The works of many Russian composers, such as Glinka, Rachmaninov, Rimsky-Korsakov and Tchaikovsky, were first heard at the Society. Wagner was the official conductor during the 1863 season. The Philharmonic Symphony Orchestra performs worldwide. The Philharmonic was named after Dmitri Shostakovich in 1976.

Shostakovich lived in Leningrad during the 900-day siege. In July 1941, he began to write his Seventh Symphony, while a member of an air-defense unit. Hitler boasted that Leningrad would fall by August 9, 1942. On this day, the Seventh Symphony, conducted by Karl Eliasberg, was played in the Philharmonic and broadcast throughout the world. 'I dedicate my Seventh Symphony to our struggle with

Vaganova Ballet School Museum on Ulitsa Rossi. Portraits of former students such as Rudolph Nureyev, Natalia Makarova and Mikhail Baryshnikov grace the walls.

fascism, to our forthcoming victory over the enemy, and to my native city, Leningrad.'

The square in front of the Philharmonic is called **Arts Square** or Ploshchad Iskusstvo. In the mid-18th century Carlo Rossi designed the square and the areas in between the Ekaterininsky Canal, the Moika Canal and Sadovaya Ulitsa. The center of the square is dominated by the **Statue of Alexander Pushkin**, sculpted by Mikhail Anikushin in 1957. Along Italianskaya Ulitsa, not far from the Philharmonic, is the Theater of Musical Comedy, the only theater in the city that stayed open during the siege. Next to it is the Komissarzhevskaya Drama Theater. Headed by Russian actress Vera Komissarzhevskaya from 1904 to 1906, the company staged plays (including Gorky's) around the political mood of the times.

Behind the square on Inzhenernaya Ulitsa (Engineer's Street) stands the majestic eight-columned building of the **Russian Museum**, second largest museum of art in the city. Alexander I had architect Carlo Rossi build this palace (1819–27) for his younger brother Mikhail; it was called the Mikhailovsky Palace. In 1898, Alexander III bought the palace and decided to convert it into an art museum. March 19, 1998 marked the 100th anniversary of the museum's opening. A splendid wrought-iron fence (embossed with the double-headed eagle) separates the palace from the square. The courtyard allowed carriages to drive up to the front portico, where a granite staircase lined with two bronze lions still leads to the front door. The Hall of White Columns was so admired by the czar that he ordered a wooden model made for King George IV of England. Rubenstein opened the city's first music school in the hall in 1862. The Mikhailovsky Gardens are situated behind the museum. The 1,000-year history of Russian art is represented by over 300,000 works of art in the museum's 130 halls (open 10am–6pm; closed Tuesdays). To the right of the museum is the **Museum of Ethnography** (open 10am–5pm; closed Mondays). The nearest Metro is Gostiny Dvor.

In Arts Square, the statue of Pushkin gestures to the building known as the **Mussorgsky Maly Theater of Opera and Ballet**. Built in 1833 by Bryullov, it was known as the Mikhailovsky Theater, and housed a permanent French troupe. Today it is 'the laboratory of opera and ballet', presenting 360 performances a year in a daily alternating repertory of opera and ballet. Subsidized by the government, it employs 800 people, including an orchestra of 100 and a chorus of 65. It is the second most popular theater (next to the Mariinsky) in St Petersburg.

The building next door, at number 5, was the site of the Stray Dog, a favorite cellar hangout for the artistic elite of St Petersburg where they gathered around midnight and did not leave until dawn. Opened on New Year's Eve 1912, the club was the country's greatest bohemian meeting spot until it was closed down in the spring of 1915. After the Revolution and Stalinist terrors, Russia would never again know such a free and vibrant artistic period. The ballerina Tamara Karsavina danced works by Michel Fokine; Mayakovsky, Blok and Mandalstam read their poetry; and Anna Akhmatova and her husband Nikolai Gumilyov formed a new movement of poetry known as Acmeism. Later, after Stalin took control of the country, many of these artists, writers and musicians died in Siberian gulags or ended their lives abroad.

The **Brodsky House Museum** at 3 Arts Square exhibits many items on the life of Joseph Brodsky, who won the Nobel Prize for Literature in 1987—the second youngest writer in history to do so (see page 369). The museum is open 11am–7pm; closed Mondays.

Continuing down the Nevsky, the **Russian National Library** stands on the corner of Nevsky and Sadovaya Ulitsa. Built in 1801 by Yegor Sokolov, it opened in 1814 as the Imperial Public Library. In 1832, Carlo Rossi built further additions. The statue of Minerva, Goddess of Wisdom, stands atop the building. It is one of the largest libraries in the world with over 25 million books! A reading room is inside, but no books can be taken out.

The library faces **Aleksandriiskaya Ploshchad** (Aleksandriisky Square). Up until 1992 it was known as Ostrovsky Square, after the playwright Alexander Ostrovsky. A **Statue of Catherine the Great** graces the center; Catherine, dressed in a long flowing robe, stands on a high rounded pedestal that portrays the prominent personalities of the time: Potemkin, Suvorov, Rumyantsev and Derzhavin, to name a few. To the left are two classical pavilions, designed by Rossi, in the Garden of Rest.

Behind the square is the **Pushkin Drama Theater**, a veritable temple to the arts. Flanked by Corinthian columns, the niches are adorned with the Muses of Dance, Tragedy, History and Music. The chariot of Apollo, patron of the arts, stands atop the front facade. The yellow building, erected by Rossi in 1828, was first known as the Aleksandrinsky Theater (after Alexandra, the wife of Nicholas I), and housed Russia's first permanent theater group. Today, as the oldest drama theater in Russia, it has a varied repertoire of classical and modern plays. Behind the theater is the **Museum of Theatrical Art**, exhibiting the history of Russian drama and musical theater. It is open 11am–6pm; closed Tuesdays. Also here is the Lunacharsky National Library with more than 350,000 volumes.

The famous **Ulitsa Rossi** (named after the architect) stretches from Aleksandriisky Square to Lomonosov Square (Ploshchad Lomonosova). The street has perfect proportions: 22 meters wide, the buildings are 22 meters high and the length is ten times the width. The world-renowned **Vagonova Academy of Ballet** is the first building on the left. Twelve boys and 12 girls (children of court servants) were the city's first ballet students, attending a school started by

Empress Anna in 1786, the same year that she founded the St Petersburg Imperial Ballet. The choreography school now bears the name of Agrippina Vagonova, who taught here between 1921 and 1951. Some famous pupils of the Imperial Ballet and Vagonova have been Pavlova, Ulanova, Petipa, Nijinsky, Fokine and Balanchine. Over 2,000 hopefuls apply to the school each year; about 100 are chosen. The school's 500 pupils hope to go on to a professional ballet company such as the Mariinsky. A museum inside the school to the left contains many magical displays, for example Pavlova's ballet shoes and Nijinsky's costumes. Posters and pictures trace the history of ballet from Diaghilev to Baryshnikov who, along with Natalia Makarova, attended the Vagonova School. (The museum is closed to the general public—but if you express an interest in ballet, you may get in.)

Back on Nevsky Prospekt in the corner building across the street is the impressive **Yeliseyev's**, once one of the most luxurious food stores in St Petersburg. The well-known Russian merchant Yeliseyev had this imposing art-nouveau structure built in 1903. Today, even though the food supplies have dwindled, it is well worth seeing the interior of the store (see Special Topic on page 442). The Marionettes Theater, started in 1918, is at 52 Nevsky, and the Comedy Theater, founded in 1929, is at number 56. In between is the popular Petersburg Antique Store. At the corner of Nevsky and the Fontanka Canal is the House of Friendship and Peace. A former residence built in the 1790s, it is now a society that promotes friendship and cultural relations with over 500 organizations in 30 countries.

The area around the Fontanka Canal (the old southern border of the city) was first developed by an engineering team headed by Mikhail Anichkov. He built the first bridge across the Fontanka here in 1715 and it is still named after him. In 1841, a stone bridge with four towers replaced the wooden structure. Peter Klodt cast the tamed-horse sculptures a century ago and today they give the bridge its distinguishing mark. During World War II the sculptures were buried in the Palace of Young Pioneers across the street. The **Anichkov Most** (Bridge) is a popular

hangout, and boats leave frequently for a city tour of the canals and waterways. A kiosk by the dock provides times of departure and tickets.

The first palace built on the Nevsky was named after Anichkov. Empress Elizabeth (Peter's daughter) commissioned the architects Dmitriyev and Zemtsov to build a palace on the spot where she stayed on the eve of her coronation. In 1751, Elizabeth gave the Anichkov Palace to her favorite, Count Alexei Razumovsky. Later, Catherine the Great gave it to her own favorite, Count Grigory Potemkin, who frequently held elaborate balls here. After that it was a part of His Majesty's Cabinet. The **Anichkov Palace** houses several concert halls. At 41 Nevsky is a mansion built in the 1840s by the architect Stackenschneider for a prince. The **Beloselsky-Belozersky Palace** is now a concert hall and special guided tours are given on the history of the palace. It is also home to the **Wax Museum** with a lifelike collection of figures; open daily 11am–7pm. The Gostiny Dvor/Nevsky Prospekt Metro station brings you right out on Nevsky Prospekt by the department store and Dom Knigi.

The red Beloselsky-Belozersky Palace, built in 1848 in rococo-style by Andrei Stackenschneider, stands beside the Fontanka Canal. Atlantes support the columns of the façade. In the foreground, stallions sculpted by Peter Klodt over a century ago adorn the Anichkov Bridge.

HOLIDAY SEASON

*F*orgive the triviality of the expression, but I am in no mood for fine
language... for everything that had been in Petersburg had gone or
was going away for the holidays; for every respectable gentleman of dignified appearance who took a cab was at once transformed, in my eyes,
into a respectable head of a household who after his daily duties were
over, was making his way to the bosom of his family, to the summer villa;
for all the passersby had now quite a peculiar air which seemed to say to
every one they met: 'We are only here for the moment, gentlemen, and in
another two hours we shall be going off to the summer villa.' If a window
opened after delicate fingers, white as snow, had tapped upon the pane,
and the head of a pretty girl was thrust out, calling to a street-seller with
pots of flowers—at once on the spot I fancied that those flowers were
being bought not simply in order to enjoy the flowers and the spring in
stuffy town lodgings, but because they would all be very soon moving into
the country and could take the flowers with them. What is more, I made
such progress in my new peculiar sort of investigation that I could distinguish correctly from the mere air of each in what summer villa he was living. The inhabitants of Kamenny and Aptekarsky Islands or of the
Peterhof Road were marked by the studied elegance of their manner, their
fashionable summer suits, and the fine carriages in which they drove to
town. Visitors to Pargolovo and places further away impressed one at first
sight by their reasonable and dignified air; the tripper to Krestovsky
Island could be recognized by his look of irrepressible gaiety. If I chanced
to meet a long procession of wagoners walking lazily with the reins in
their hands beside wagons loaded with regular mountains of furniture,
tables, chairs, ottomans and sofas and domestic utensils of all sorts,
frequently with a decrepit cook sitting on the top of it all, guarding her
master's property as though it were the apple of her eye; or if I saw boats
heavily loaded with household goods crawling along the Neva or
Fontanka to the Black River or the Islands—the wagons and the boats

were multiplied tenfold, a hundredfold, in my eyes. I fancied that every-thing was astir and moving, everything was going in regular caravans to the summer villas. It seemed as though Petersburg threatened to become a wilderness, so that at last I felt ashamed, mortified and sad that I had nowhere to go for the holidays and no reason to go away. I was ready to go away with every wagon, to drive off with every gentleman of respectable appearance who took a cab; but no one—absolutely no one—invited me; it seemed they had forgotten me, as though really I were a stranger to them!

I took long walks, succeeding, as I usually did, in quite forgetting where I was, when I suddenly found myself at the city gates. Instantly I felt lighthearted, and I passed the barrier and walked between cultivated fields and meadows, unconscious of fatigue, and feeling only all over as though a burden were falling off my soul. All the passersby gave me such friendly looks that they seemed almost greeting me, they all seemed so pleased at something. They were all smoking cigars, every one of them. And I felt pleased as I never had before. It was as though I had suddenly found myself in Italy—so strong was the effect of nature upon a half-sick townsman like me, almost stifling between city walls.

There is something inexpressibly touching in nature round Petersburg, when at the approach of spring she puts forth all her might, all the pow-ers bestowed on her by Heaven, when she breaks into leaf, decks herself out and spangles herself with flowers ...

Fyodor Dostoevsky, White Nights, 1918

YELISEYEV'S

This store, whose nickname was the Temple of Gluttons, has a long and fascinating history. In Moscow the building was originally the personal mansion of Catherine the Great's State Secretary, Prince Kozitsky, whose wife was the heiress of a Siberian goldmine. The mansion was the largest and grandest in the city.

In the 1820s, their granddaughter Princess Volkonskaya turned the drawing room into one of Russia's most prestigious salons. All the great literary figures gathered here, including Pushkin, who presented his latest poems. But in 1829, when the princess left for Italy, the mansion fell into other hands.

By the mid-1850s, the dreaded Princess Beloselskaya-Belozerskaya, a relative of Volkanskaya, was living in the mansion; she was a total recluse and only left it to attend church on Sundays. She was not popular at home since she had her servants beaten every Saturday (it was a common practice in that era to single out a few for reprimand). Not surprisingly, some of these servants ran away and eventually banded together in the house across the street. Many Muscovites believed the dark house to be haunted, claiming to see devils and ghosts, and would not even walk by, especially at night. The bandit-servants decided to lend credence to this belief. One night they dressed up like ghosts and spooked the old princess right out of her house. Some time afterwards, an animal trainer took up residence in the mansion with his black panther.

A number of years later, Grigory Grigoryevich Yeliseyev bought the vacant building. Grigory's grandfather Pyotr had won his freedom in 1813, when his master rewarded him for discovering how to produce strawberries in winter. Pyotr went off to open a wine store in St Petersburg where he soon became a member of the merchant class. His sons in turn founded the Yeliseyev Brothers Trading House, which specialized in foreign wines and other goods from tea and spices to rum and tobacco. The firm established links with the largest trading houses across Europe from Britain to Spain, and to ship the many foreign wares, several Dutch steamships were purchased.

(previous pages) Bank Bridge spans the Ekaterininsky Canal near Nevsky Prospekt. This lovely footbridge is adorned with lion-griffins; in ancient Greece griffins were said to stand guard over gold. At the time this bridge was built, around 1800, it led to the National Bank.

The Yeliseyev business reached its heyday with the third generation. It was Grigory who opened the popular chain of food emporiums from St Petersburg to Kiev. The firm also built spacious warehouses, butcheries, fish canneries and chocolate factories. The shops were filled with mouth-watering delicacies, such as Belgian Oostende oysters, smoked sturgeon, stuffed turkeys, beluga caviar, exotic fruits and Swiss and French cheeses. Its wine cellars were scattered around the world; at one point the Yeliseyevs purchased entire grape harvests in some French provinces. For promoting Russia's national trade industry, Grigory Yeliseyev was ennobled. He was also honored with France's highest award, the Legion of Honor.

Throngs of people turned out for the Moscow Yeliseyev's grand opening in 1899. There was one unexpected hitch—the liquor department turned out to be less than 50 yards from the neighboring church, which contravened the sacred law. So builders had to do a quick restructuring and move it one yard further away. The popular writer Vladimir Gilyarovsky, who lived in the area, wrote in *Moscow and Muscovites*: 'Passers-by stared at the mountains of imported fruits which looked like cannon balls, a pyramid of coconuts each the size of a child's head, bunches of tropical bananas so large you could not get your arms around them and unknown inhabitants of the ocean depths. Overhead, electric stars on tips of wine bottles flashed in enormous mirrors, the tops of which were lost somewhere up in the heights....' The store was a huge success. The Yeliseyevs even dreamed of cornering the American market and opened a chain of shops in the United States.

In his fifties, Grigory fell in love with the wife of a prominent St Petersburg jeweler. The millionaire's children and grandchildren opposed a divorce and his broken-hearted wife succeeded with suicide on her third attempt. When World War I broke out, Grigory married his lover and fled to France where he died in Paris in 1942. After this scandal, Yeliseyev's sons renounced their heritage, which included the store. This was probably just as well since the family would have lost everything anyway during the Bolshevik Revolution which broke out soon after.

The saga does not end there. Under Brezhnev, the director of Gastronom #1 (as the store was now called) was Yuri Konstantinovich Sokolov. As a friend of Brezhnev's daughter Galya, Sokolov was quite well-connected. At the store, Sokolov made up quotas and took many choice picks for himself; he also wrote a lot of food off as spoiled or sold it even more profitably on the black market. Of course, Sokolov became popular and wealthy, and was known for throwing great parties. But when Brezhnev died in 1982 and Andropov took over, the glorious days of corruption and stagnation were numbered. The head of Moscow Trade received a 15-year prison sentence, the director of another Gastronom six years, and Sokolov found himself sentenced to death—he was executed by firing squad in 1984. The police found gold, jewelry and huge bundles of rotting rubles buried in his backyard.

Today the new owners of the shops have renamed them Yeliseyev's, hoping to capitalize on their intriguing past. In the Moscow shop, a bust of Grigory Yeliseyev stands in the entrance hall, put up in 1989 to celebrate the store's 90th anniversary—the store marked its centennial jubilee with further celebrations in 1999. The Moscow store is located at 14 Tverskaya, and in St Petersburg the lavish art-nouveau building is at 58 Nevsky Prospekt.

A trolleybus on Nevsky Prospekt near Aleksandriisky Square passes Yeliseyev's Food Emporium, which celebrated its centenary in 1999.

Following the Nevsky a bit farther you come to **Znamenskaya Square** (Ploshchad Znamenskaya), formerly Vosstaniya (Uprising) Square. It was so named when troops of the czar refused to shoot a group of unarmed demonstrators during the February 1917 uprising.

One of the interesting buildings on the Square is **Moskovsky Vokzal** (Moscow Railway Station). It was built by the architect Thon in 1847. The St Petersburg–Moscow railway line opened on November 1, 1851. The word *vokzal* (derived from the English Vauxhall Station) is used for a station and now St Petersburg has five major *vokzals* in the city: Moskovsky, Finlandsky, Varshavsky (Warsaw), Baltiisky (Baltic) and Vitebsky. The last was known as Tsarskoye Selo, the station connecting Russia's first railroad line to the czar's summer residence in Pavlovsk. Overlooking the Square, the Hotel Oktyabrskaya dates from the 1890s. The Ploshchad Vosstaniya/Mayakovskaya Metro station is near the Square; the Mayakovskaya exit is close to the junction of Nevsky Prospekt and Marata Ulitsa.

A few blocks down Marata Ulitsa from Nevsky is the **Nevsky Banya Complex**, open 8am–10pm, Wednesday–Sunday, where one can experience Russian baths. (See Special Topic on page 340.) At 24 Marata is the **Museum of the Arctic and Antarctic** (in the Church of St Nicholas); open 10am–5pm, Wednesday–Sunday.

A few minutes walk away, at 5/2 Kuznechny Pereulok, is the **Dostoevsky Literary Museum**, open 10.30am–5.30pm; closed Mondays (Vladimirskaya Metro Station). Dostoevsky lived here from 1878 until his death on 9 February 1881. His novel *The Brothers Karamazov* was written in this apartment. In his novel *The*

The tomb of composer Alexander Borodin (1833–87) in Tikhvinskoye Cemetery at the Alexander Nevsky Monastery. Borodin is best known for his patriotic opera Prince Igor, *based on an epic Slavic text of the 12th century.*

Adolescent, Dostoevsky wrote of his own vision of St Petersburg and the Bronze Horseman: 'A hundred times amid the fog I had a strange but persistent dream: "What if, when this fog scatters and flies upward, the whole rotten, slimy city goes with it, rises with the fog and vanishes like smoke, leaving behind the old Finnish swamp, and in the middle of it, I suppose, for beauty's sake, the bronze horseman on the panting, whipped horse?"' At number 3 is the **Kuznechny Market**, one of the best in the city, which has a wide variety of produce and household goods at bargain prices.

A short walk away, at 28 Zagorodny Prospekt, is the **Rimsky-Korsakov Memorial House**, home of the great 19th-century Russian composer. Open 11am–6pm, Wednesday–Sunday. Chamber music concerts are also held on Wednesdays at 7pm, and weekends at 4pm. A few blocks south stands a statue of the writer Alexander Griboedov in Pionerskaya Ploshchad (Square). Here on December 22, 1949, members of the Petrashevsky political movement, including the writer Dostoevsky, were lined up to be shot for revolutionary activities. After spending eight months in the Peter and Paul Fortress, they were led out to the square and dressed in white canvas robes and hoods. The squad aimed their rifles at the men. 'I was in the second row, and had less than a minute to live,' Dostoevsky recalled in horror. But instead of hearing gunshots, a drum roll sounded. Nicholas I had decided to commute the death sentences to exile in Siberia. Dostoevsky was sent to Omsk Prison, where he spent four years shackled day and night; he would not write again for over ten years.

Walking north and crossing the Nevsky will bring you to the **Nekrasov House Museum**, at 36 Liteiny Prospekt, displaying the writer's works; open 11am–5pm; closed Tuesdays. The **October Railway Central Museum** is at number 62, exhibiting the history of the Russian railway. Open 11am–5.30pm; closed Saturdays.

The modern **Moskva Hotel** (with restaurants and a *Beriozka*—a variety store selling souvenirs, food and liquor) stands at the end of Nevsky Prospekt on Alexander Nevsky Square (Ploshchad Aleksandra Nevskovo). Across the street is the **Alexander Nevsky Monastery** (Lavra). This is the oldest monastery, or *lavra*, in St Petersburg. Peter the Great founded the monastery in 1710 and dedicated it to the Holy Trinity and military leader Alexander Nevsky, Prince of Novgorod, who won a major victory on the Neva against the Swedes in 1240. In Russia the name *lavra* was applied to a large monastery. Another *lavra* is the Trinity-Sergius Monastery in the Golden Ring town of Sergiyev Posad (see page 229).

The **Holy Trinity Cathedral** or Troitsky Sobor is the main church of the complex. The Church of Alexander Nevsky is also here. In 1724, the remains of Alexander Nevsky were transferred to the monastery from the Golden Ring town of Vladimir. Nevsky's sarcophagus, cast from one and a half tons of silver, is now in the Hermitage. The Blagoveshchensky Sobor (Annunciation Church) is the oldest church in the complex, and was built by Trezzini in 1720. It now houses the **Museum of Urban Sculpture**; open 10am–5pm, closed Thursdays. Peter the Great buried his sister Natalie in the **Lazarevskoye Cemetery** (to the left of the main entrance), St Petersburg's oldest cemetery. To the right of the main entrance is the **Tikhvinskoye Cemetery**. Both open 11am–7pm; closed Thursdays. Here are the carved gravestones of many of Russia's greatest figures such as Tchaikovsky, Glinka, Rimsky-Korsakov, Mussorgsky, Stasov, Klodt and Dostoevsky. Another entrance is across the street from the Moskva Hotel. The cathedral holds services, and on Alexander Nevsky Day, September 11–12, huge processions take place. Near the monastery is the Theological Seminary, reestablished in 1946, which trains 440 students for the clergy. About 100 women are taught to be teachers or choir conductors. Seven cathedrals, over 20 Russian Orthodox churches, and 15 other religious denomination's currently hold services in St Petersburg. (See church listings in Practical Information section.)

The Alexander Nevsky Bridge (Most Aleksandra Nevskovo), largest bridge in the city, crosses the Neva from the monastery. Ploshchad Aleksandra Nevskovo Metro station brings you right to the Moscow Hotel and the Monastery complex.

Finland Station (Finlandsky Vokzal)

The Finland Railway Station is located on the right bank of the Neva (the Vyborg Side), a little east of where the cruiser *Aurora* is docked. It is a short walk from the Petrograd Side across the **Sampsonievsky Most**, over the Bolshaya Nevka, to the Finland Station. The station dates back to 1870. It was from here that Lenin secretly left for Finland in August 1917, after he was forced into hiding by the Provisional Government. A few months later he returned on the same locomotive to direct the October uprising. This locomotive, engine number 293, is on display behind a glass pavilion in the back of the station by the platform area. A brass plate on the locomotive bears the inscription: 'The Government of Finland presented this locomotive to the Government of the USSR in commemoration of journeys over Finnish territory made by Lenin in troubled times. June 13, 1957.'

A towering monument to Lenin stands in Lenin Square (Ploshchad Lenina) opposite the station. After the February 1917 Revolution overthrew the czarist monarchy, Lenin returned to Petrograd from his place of exile in Switzerland on April 3, 1917. He gave a speech to the masses from the turret of an armored car. Originally the Lenin monument was erected on the spot where he gave the speech. But during the construction of the square the statue, portraying Lenin standing on the car's turret addressing the crowd with an outstretched hand, was moved closer to the Neva embankment, where it stands today. It was unveiled on November 7, 1926. Ploshchad Lenina Metro station is also at the Finland Station.

Farther north, near Vyborgskaya Metro station, at 41 Bolshoi Sampsonievsky Prospekt, stands the **Cathedral of St Sampson—Host of Wanderers**. Peter the Great defeated the Swedes in the Battle of Poltava (1709) on the feast day of St Sampson. To commemorate the victory a wooden church was built. Later, between 1728 and 1733, this five-domed stone church replaced it. A lovely gilded iconostasis crowns the altar; the church is currently under restoration. Many of the city's preeminent architects such as Rastrelli, Leblond and Trezzini are buried in the neighboring cemetery.

In Vyborg's northeast region lies **Piskarevskoye Memorial Cemetery**. Here are the common graves of nearly half a million Leningraders who died during the 900-day siege, marked only by somber mounds of dirt and their year of burial (see pages 464 and 467). The central path of the cemetery leads to the **Statue of the Mother Country**, holding a wreath of oak leaves, the symbol of eternal glory. Two museum pavilions are on either side of the entrance, where one realizes the horrors that faced the citizens of this city. The cemetery register is open at a page with the entries: 'February, 1942: 18th—3,241 bodies; 19th—5,569; 20th—10,043.' Another

Cadets from St Petersburg's Nakhimov Naval School on the battleship Aurora *which fired the blank shot to signal the storming of the Winter Palace during Lenin's 1917 October Revolution.*

display shows a picture of 11-year-old Tanya Savicheva and pages from her diary: 'Granny died 25 January, 1942 at 3pm. Lyoka died 17 March at 5am. Uncle Vasya died 13 April at 2am. Uncle Lyosha 10 May at 4pm. Mama died 13 May at 7.30am. The Savichevs are dead. Everyone is dead. Only Tanya remains.' Tanya later died after she was evacuated from the city. The cemetery is located at 74 Nepokorennikh Prospekt, and open daily 10am–6pm. The nearest Metro station is Ploshchad Muzhestva. (It takes about 40 minutes to get here from the center of town.) A memorial day to the Siege of Leningrad is held here every year on September 8.

Crossing the **Aleksandrovsky Most**, with its beautiful railings decorated with mermaids and anchors, over the Neva to the left bank leads to Shpalernaya Ulitsa and the **Taurida Palace** at number 47. The neoclassical-style palace was built by Ivan Stasov between 1783 and 1789 for Prince Grigory Potemkin-Tavrichesky as a gift from Catherine the Great. Potemkin was commander-in-chief of the Russian Army in the Crimea during the Turkish Wars. The Crimean peninsula was called Taurida, and Potemkin was given the title of Prince of Taurida. One party Potemkin held in the palace used 140,000 lamps and 20,000 candles. After both he and Catherine the Great died, the new czar, Paul I (who disliked his mother Catherine and her favorites), converted the palace into a riding house and stables. It was later renovated and became the seat of the State Duma in 1906. On February 27, 1917, the left wing of the palace held the first session of the Petrograd Soviet of Workers. Today the mansion is known as the Taurida or Tavrichesky Palace, and houses the Interparliamentary Assembly of CIS countries. It is closed to tourists, but one can still stroll in the Tavrichesky Gardens or Children's Park; in the 18th century they were considered the best in St Petersburg. Intricate pavilions, small bridges and carved statues dotted the landscape, and Venetian gondolas and boats sailed on the enormous pond.

Behind the gardens is the **Museum to Alexander Suvorov**, the great 18th-century Russian military leader; open 11am–6pm; closed Wednesdays. Across the street from the front of the palace is the **Kikin Palace**. Built in 1714 and one of the oldest buildings in the city, it belonged to the Boyar Kikin, who plotted, along with Peter's son Alexei, to assassinate Peter the Great. After Kikin was put to death, Peter turned the palace into Russia's first natural science museum. The collections were later moved to the Kunstkammer on Vasilyevsky Island. Today the yellow-white palace is a children's music school. The closest Metro station is Chernyshevskaya.

On Tavricheskaya Ulitsa stands one of the last remaining statues of Felix Dzerzhinsky, founder of the infamous Cheka that later became the KGB. The **Bolshoi Dom** (Big House), at 4 Liteiny Prospekt, used to be KGB headquarters; today it is part of the Interior Ministry. While you are in the neighborhood, on the corner of Potemkinskaya and Shpalernaya is the **Indoor Flower Market**. Throw a coin in the wishing well! Open 11am–7pm; closed Mondays and Thursdays.

THE PETITION OF JANUARY 9, 1905

A Most Humble and Loyal Address of the Workers of St Petersburg Intended for Presentation to HIS MAJESTY on Sunday at two o'clock on the Winter Palace Square.

SIRE:

We, the workers and inhabitants of St Petersburg, of various estates, our wives, our children, and our aged, helpless parents, come to Thee, O SIRE, to seek justice and protection. We are impoverished; we are oppressed, overburdened with excessive toil, contemptuously treated. We are not even recognized as human beings, but are treated like slaves who must suffer their bitter fate in silence and without complaint. And we have suffered, but even so we are being further pushed into the slough of poverty, arbitrariness, and ignorance. We are suffocating in despotism and lawlessness. O SIRE, we have reached that frightful moment when death is better than the prolongation of our unbearable sufferings.

Hence, we stopped work and told employers that we will not resume work until our demands are fulfilled. We did not ask much; we sought only that without which there is no life for us but hard labor and eternal suffering. Our first request was that our employers agree to discuss our needs with us. But even this we were refused. We were prohibited even from speaking of our needs, since no such right is given us by law. The following requests were also deemed to be outside of the law: the reduction of the work day to eight hours; our manual participation in determining the rates for our work and in the settlement of grievances that might arise between us and the lower managerial staff; to raise the minimum daily wages for unskilled workers, and for women as well, to one ruble; to abolish overtime work; to give our sick better medical attention without insults; and to arrange our workshops so that we might work there without encountering death from murderous drafts, rain, and snow.

According to our employers and managers, our demands turned out to be illegal, our every request a crime, and our desire to improve our conditions an insolence, insulting to them. O SIRE, there are more than 300,000 of us but we are human beings in appearance only, for we, with the rest of the Russian people, do not possess a single human right, not even the right to speak, think, gather, discuss our needs, and take steps to improve our conditions. We are enslaved, enslaved under the patronage and with the aid of Thy officials. Anyone of us who dares to raise his voice in defense of the working class and the people is thrown into jail or exiled. Kindheartedness is punished as a crime. To feel sorry for a worker as a downtrodden, maltreated human being bereft of his rights is to commit a heinous crime! The workers and the peasants are delivered into the hands of the bureaucratic administration, comprised of embezzlers of public funds and robbers, who not only care nothing for the needs of the people, but flagrantly abuse them. The bureaucratic administration brought the country to the brink of ruin, involved her in a humiliating war, and is leading Russia closer and closer to disaster. We, the workers and people, have no voice whatsoever in the spending of huge sums collected from us in taxes. We do not even know how the money, collected from the impoverished people, is spent. The people are deprived of the opportunity to express their wishes and demands, to participate in the establishment of taxes and public spending. The workers are deprived of the opportunity to organize their unions in order to defend their interests.

O SIRE, is this in accordance with God's laws, by the grace of which Thou reignest? Is it possible to live under such laws? Would it not be preferable for all of us, the toiling people of Russia, to die? Let the capitalists—exploiters of the working class and officials, the embezzlers and plunderers of the Russian people, live and enjoy their lives.

Translated by Walter Sablinsky

The Smolny

Several years after the Peter and Paul Fortress was founded, the tar yards, *smolyanoi dvori*, were set up at the Neva's last bend before the gulf to process tar for the shipyards. Empress Elizabeth I founded the monastery and convent in 1748; she had intended to take the veil at the end of her rule. The baroque (combined with Russian traditional), five-domed, turquoise and white Smolny complex is truly one of Rastrelli's greatest works. After Elizabeth died the complex was still not fully complete. (The empress lavishly spent State funds—she had over 15,000 gowns, and at her death only six rubles remained in the Treasury.) Vassily Stasov later completed the structure, adhering to Rastrelli's original design. (When the new classicism vogue in architecture replaced baroque, Rastrelli fell into disfavor under Catherine II and was asked to leave the country.)

In 1746, Catherine the Great set up the Institute for Young Noble Ladies in the **Smolny Convent**, Russia's first school for the daughters of nobility; they were educated here from the age of six to 18. Afterwards many of the women became maids-of-honor in the court. A series of portraits of the first graduates can be found in the Russian Museum. Between 1806 and 1808, the architect Quarenghi erected additional buildings, known as the **Smolny Institute**, to educate girls of lower estates. Today the Church of the Resurrection and the former convent is a small museum and additional parts of the complex serve as concert halls.

In August, 1917, the girls were dismissed and the institute closed. The building became the headquarters for the Petrograd Bolshevik Party and the Military Revolutionary Committee. On October 25, 1917, Lenin arrived at the Smolny and gave the command for the storming of the Winter Palace. On October 26, the Second All-Russia Congress of Soviets gathered in the Smolny's Assembly Hall to elect Lenin the leader of the world's first Socialist Government of Workers and Peasants, and to adopt Lenin's Decrees on Peace and Land. John Reed wrote in his book *Ten Days That Shook the World* that Lenin was 'unimpressive, to be the idol for a mob, loved and revered as perhaps few leaders in history have been. A leader purely by virtue of intellect; colorless, humorless, uncompromising and detached, without picturesque idiosyncrasies—but with the power of explaining profound ideas in simple terms...he combined shrewdness with the greatest intellectual audacity.' (See page 100 for further extract.) Lenin lived at the Smolny for 124 days before transferring the capital to Moscow. In 1925, two porticoes were built at the main entrance with the inscriptions: 'The first Soviet of the Proletarian Dictatorship and Workers of the World, Unite!' A bronze monument of Lenin was set up on the tenth anniversary of the Revolution. Today some of the rooms where Lenin lived are part of the Lenin Museum. The rest of the buildings house the Mayor's offices.

LENIN AND THE RUSSIAN REVOLUTION

Lenin, founder of the first Soviet State, was born Vladimir Ilyich Ulyanov, on April 22, 1870. Vladimir, along with his five brothers and sisters, had a strict but pleasant childhood in the small town of Simbirsk (now Ulyanovsk) on the Volga River. On March 1, 1887, when Vladimir was 17, a group of students attempted to assassinate Czar Alexander III in St Petersburg. Vladimir's older brother, Alexander, was one of five students arrested. They were imprisoned in Peter and Paul Fortress in St Petersburg, and on May 8 were hung in the Fortress of Schlüsselburg (Kronstadt).

As a marked family of a revolutionary, the Ulyanovs left Simbirsk for Kazan, where Vladimir attended Kazan University. In December 1887, after the local papers reported the news of student riots in Moscow, 99 Kazan students protested against the strict rules of their university. Ulyanov, one of them, was immediately expelled, exiled to the town of Kokushkino and kept under police surveillance. Here Vladimir began to study the works of Karl Marx (*Das Kapital*, and the *Communist Manifesto*) and Chernyshevsky (*What Is To Be Done?*). Thereupon, he decided to devote his life to the revolutionary struggle. Lenin wrote that 'my way in life was marked out for me by my brother'.

Since he was refused permission to enter another university, the young Ulyanov covered the four-year law course independently, in a little over a year. He then journeyed to St Petersburg and passed the bar exam with honors. With his law degree, Ulyanov moved to the Asian town of Samara, where he defended the local peasants and secretly taught Marxist philosophy.

In 1893, he left again for St Petersburg, where he formed the revolutionary organization, the League of Struggle for the Emancipation of the Working Class. At 24, in 1894, Vladimir Ulyanov published his first book, *What Are the Friends of the People?* During a secret meeting of the League of Struggle, Ulyanov decided to publish an underground newspaper called the *Workers' Cause*. That same day he was arrested by the police, along with hundreds of other people from the League. Ulyanov was exiled to Siberia, as was Nadezhda Konstantinovna Krupskaya. They were married in the small village of Shushenskoye on July 22, 1898.

While in exile, the League planned the first party newspaper, called *Iskra* (*Spark*), inspired by words from a Decembrist poem, 'A spark will kindle a flame'. After the Ulyanovs' release, they settled in the town of Pskov outside St Petersburg (see page 495). Since it was illegal to disseminate any print media criticizing the government, they eventually moved abroad. The first issues of *Iskra* were published in Leipzig, Germany. During these years abroad, Ulyanov wrote books on politics, economics and the revolutionary struggle. In December 1901, Vladimir Ulyanov began signing his writings with the name of Lenin.

In 1903, the Russian Party Congress secretly gathered in London. During this meeting, the Social Democratic Workers Party split into two factions: the Bolsheviks (Majority) and the Mensheviks (Minority). After the session, Lenin led the Bolsheviks to the grave of Karl Marx and said, 'Let us pledge to be faithful to his teachings. We shall never give up the struggle. Forward, comrades, only forward.'

By 1905, widespread unrest was sweeping across Russia. A popular May Day song was often sung: 'Be it the merry month of May. Grief be banished from our way. Freedom songs our joy convey. We shall go on strike today.' Workers at the Putilov factory in St Petersburg began a strike that triggered work stoppages at over 350 factories throughout the city. On Sunday, January 9, 1905, thousands of workers lined the streets of St Petersburg. In a peaceful protest, the crowd carried icons and portraits of the czar. The procession walked toward the Winter Palace and congregated in Decembrists' Square (now known as Senate Square—see page 412). The palace guards opened fire. More than 1,000 demonstrators were massacred in what is known today as Bloody Sunday. Not long afterward, sailors manning the Potemkin, largest battleship in the Russian Navy, also protested against their miserable working conditions. In a mutiny headed by Afanasy Matyushenko, the sailors raised their own revolutionary red flag on June 14, 1905.

The Geneva newspapers carried the news of Bloody Sunday and Lenin decided to return to St Petersburg. He wrote in his newspaper *Vperyod* (*Forward*): 'The uprising has begun force against force. The Civil War is blazing up. Long live the Revolution. Long live the Proletariat.' But it was still too dangerous for Lenin to remain in Russia. Two years later he left again for the West, and over the next ten years, lived in Finland, Sweden, France and Switzerland.

Accounts of a new Russian Revolution were published throughout the West in February, 1917. Lenin immediately took a train to Finland and on April 3 proceeded in an armored car to Petrograd (the city had been renamed in 1914). Today the train's engine is displayed at St Petersburg's Finland Station, where Lenin first arrived (see page 447).

In Petrograd, Lenin lived on the banks of the Moika River and started up the newspaper *Pravda* (*Truth*), which was outlawed by the new Kerensky Provisional Government. Lenin was later forced into hiding outside the city on Lake Razliv (see page 483). The hut and area where he hid out has been made into a museum. With his beard shaved off and wearing a wig, Lenin was known as Konstantin Ivanov.

On the grounds of the Smolny Cathedral (see page 452), a finishing school served as headquarters for

the Petrograd Workers Soviet, which organized the Red Guards. During the summer of 1917, more than 20,000 workers in Petrograd were armed and readied for a Bolshevik uprising. Lenin gave the command for attack from the Smolny on October 24, 1917. To signal the beginning of the Great

Vladimir Ilyich Lenin, father of the 1917 October Socialist Revolution and leader of the Bolshevik Party. This statue used to stand on one of the highest spots in the Kremlin gardens in Moscow, known as Kremlin Hill, but was removed in 1997.

October Socialist Revolution, the battleship *Aurora* fired a blank shot near the Hermitage. The Red Guards stormed the Winter Palace and almost immediately defeated the White Guards of the Provisional Government; the Moscow Kremlin was taken two days later.

On October 25, the Second Congress of Soviets opened in the Smolny and Lenin was elected chairman of the first Soviet State; Trotsky was his Foreign Minister. Sverdlov, Stalin, Bobnov and Dzerzhinsky (later to head the Cheka, which authorized police to 'arrest and shoot immediately all members of counterrevolutionary organizations') were elected to the Revolutionary Military Committee. Lenin introduced a Decree on Land, proclaiming that all lands become State property. At the end of the Congress, all members stood and sang the Internationale, the proletarian anthem: 'Arise ye prisoners of starvation. Arise ye wretched of the earth. For Justice thunders condemnation. A better world's in birth.' On March 11, 1918, Lenin moved the capital from Petrograd to Moscow. He lived in a room at the National Hotel across from Red Square. The Bolsheviks, known as the Communist Party, had their offices in the Kremlin.

During the last years of Lenin's life, the country was wracked by war and widespread famine. He implemented the NEP (New Economic Policy) that allowed foreign trade and investment, but he did not live long enough to bear witness to its effects. Lenin died at the age of 54 on January 21, 1924. The cause of death was listed as cerebral sclerosis, triggered, as stated in the official medical report, by 'excessive intellectual activity'. (It's suspected he really died of syphilis.) In three days a wooden structure to house his body was built on Red Square. Later, it was replaced by a mausoleum of red granite and marble. For decades, thousands lined up daily to view his embalmed body and witness the changing of the guards. Soon after his death, Petrograd's name was changed to Leningrad in his honor; it bore this epithet until 1991, when the city's name reverted back to St Petersburg. Today, even though the Red Square mausoleum is still opened to visitors (without the long lines), the changing of the guards was stopped. The current government is reviewing proposals to close the mausoleum and give Lenin's body a burial elsewhere, either on Kremlin grounds or in a city cemetery.

Theater Square (Teatralnaya Ploshchad)

In the southwest part of the city along Glinka and Decembrists streets lies Theater Square or Teatralnaya Ploshchad. This section of land was once the location for St Petersburg carnivals and fairs. In the 18th century it was known as Ploshchad Karusel (Merry-Go-Round Square). A wooden theater was built here and later, in 1783, it was replaced by the Bolshoi Stone Theater with over 2,000 seats. In 1803, the drama troupe moved to the Aleksandrinsky Theater and the opera and ballet remained at the Bolshoi. In 1860, Albert Kavos completed the **Mariinsky Theater** (which replaced the Bolshoi Stone Theater), named after Maria, the wife of Alexander II. (It was named the Kirov Theater, after a prominent Communist leader, from 1935 to 1992.) The five-tiered theater is decorated with blue velvet chairs, gilded stucco, ceiling paintings and chandeliers.

In the 19th century St Petersburg was the musical capital of Russia. At the Mariinsky Theater premiers of opera and ballet were staged by Russia's most famous composers, dancers and singers. Under Petipa, Ivanov and Fokine, Russian ballet took on worldwide recognition (see page 370). The Fyodor Shalyapin Memorial Room, named after the great opera singer, is open during performances. (The Shalyapin House Museum is located at 26 Graftio Ulitsa on the northern Petrograd Side near the TV Tower; see page 390.) The Mariinsky Theater of Opera and Ballet continues to stage some of the world's finest ballets and operas; its companies tour many countries throughout the world.

Opposite the Mariinsky stands the **Rimsky-Korsakov State Conservatory**, Russia's first advanced school of music. The founder of the conservatory was the composer Anton Rubenstein. Some of the graduates include Tchaikovsky, Prokofiev and Shostakovich. On either side of the conservatory stand the monuments to Mikhail Glinka and Rimsky-Korsakov (whose museum is not far from the Vladimirskaya Metro station, at 28 Zagorodny Prospekt, open 11am–6pm, Wednesday–Sunday). At the west end of Ulitsa Dekabristov at number 57, by the Pryazhka Canal, is the **Blok Museum** and former home of the great Russian poet during the last eight years of his life. Open 11am–5pm; closed Wednesdays.

A short walk south down Glinka Ulitsa leads to the **Nikolsky Marine Cathedral**, built between 1753 and 1762 by Chevakinsky in honor of St Nicholas, the protector of seamen. Naval officers once lived in the area, thus the full name of Nikolsky Morskoi (Marine). Standing at the intersection of the Ekaterininsky and Kryukov canals, the blue and white church combines the old Russian five-dome tradition with the baroque. A lovely carved wooden iconostasis is inside and a four-tiered bell tower stands by itself in the gardens. It has daily church services. Thousands came

here to attend the funeral of the famous poetess Anna Akhmatova on March 10, 1966. (She is buried in the village of Komarovo northwest of the city, near Repino. See page 483.)

At the opposite end of Glinka Ulitsa, at 94 Moika Embankment (Naberezhnaya Reki Moiki), is the **Yusupov Palace**. The last owner of the palace was the wealthy Prince Yusupov, who was responsible for the assassination of Grigory Rasputin (the priest who exerted much influence in the court of Nicholas II) in 1916. Rasputin was first given poisoned cakes in the palace's basement. Nothing happened—the sugar in the cakes was thought to have neutralized the poison. In desperation Yusupov shot the priest. Later, however, Rasputin came back to life and managed to walk into the courtyard, where the conspirators shot him once more. Finally, they tied up Rasputin's body and threw it through a hole in the ice of the river. Later, after his body was found floating under the ice downstream, an autopsy showed that Rasputin had water in his lungs and rope burns on his wrists, proving he had still been alive after all the attempts to kill him. Yusupov later fled Russia. The palace houses the **Rasputin Museum** and you can actually stand in the small basement room where Rasputin was poisoned. Open daily 11am–3pm.

Crossing the Moika and continuing towards the Neva, you will see a number of brick buildings on a small triangular island. These were the storehouses for ship timber during the time of Peter the Great. Manmade canals created the small island known as **New Holland** or Novaya Gollandiya. The New Admiralty Canal, dug in 1717, once connected the island with the Admiralty. Konnogvardeysky (formerly Trade Union) Boulevard was laid partly along the route of the canal.

Pass through Annunciation Square (Blagoveshchenskaya Ploshchad) and turn left at the Neva. At number 44 Angliskaya Embankment (Angliskaya Naberezhnaya) is the branch **Museum of the History of St Petersburg** (in the Soviet era). It is located in the former Rumyantsev Palace, built in Empire style in 1827 and named after the son of a famous Field Marshal, who bought it from a British merchant. Open 11am–4pm; closed Wednesdays.

Moscow Avenue (Moskovsky Prospekt)

Moskovsky Prospekt runs for nearly 16 kilometers (10 miles) in a straight line from **Sennaya Square** (and Sennaya Ploshchad Metro station) to the airport. The avenue follows the line known as the Pulkovo Meridian (zero on old Russian maps) that led to the Pulkovo Astronomical Observatory. The square was known even in czarist times as Sennaya Ploshchad or Haymarket, the underbelly of St Petersburg and a place used for public punishment of serfs. The area was the residence of many

(previous pages) The funeral of St Petersburg's famous poet Anna Akhmatova was held at St Nicholas Cathedral in 1966. The cathedral's four-tiered baroque bell tower stands beside the Kryukov Canal.

of Dostoevsky's characters—including *Crime and Punishment's* Sophia Marmeladova. Today the neighborhood remains a bit seedy, and it is still easy to imagine how the place fueled Dostoevsky's creative imagination. In Dostoevsky's time Stolyarny Alley was filled with drunkards and prostitutes, and brazen crowds bustled through the night in the Haymarket district. At 9 Przhevalskovo Ulitsa is the **Rodion Raskolnikov House**, where Dostoevsky's character from *Crime and Punishment* lived. (On the fifth floor is Russian graffiti that reads, 'Don't Kill, Rodya!') Dostoevsky described this house and yard in detail—Rodion stole the murder ax from the basement, and it was 730 paces between the murderer's house and his victim's. Even the stone under which Raskolnikov hid the stolen goods was real. Raskolnikov later knelt on Sennaya Square repenting his crime.

Off Przhevalskovo is Kaznachevskaya Ulitsa. Dostoevsky lived at number 1 from 1861 to 1863 and at number 7 he wrote his famous novel *Crime and Punishment*. Imagine Dostoevsky as Raskolnikov, leaving his house and walking south down toward the Griboedov (now Ekaterininsky) Canal. Crossing the Kokushkin Bridge, he turns right onto Sadovaya Ulitsa and continues past the Yusupov Gardens. He then turns right into Rimsky-Korsakov Prospekt, walking several blocks until arriving at Srednaya Podyacheskaya. The entrance to the old-lady moneylender's house (approximately 730 paces from Dostoevsky's doorstep) is at 104 Canal Embankment. Head through the tunnel to block 5 (apartments 22–81). Look for the brass balls placed at the corners of the banisters by the residents; they lead to the pawnbroker's apartment, number 74, just after the third floor. (Dostoevsky's museum is actually located at 5/2 Kuznechny Pereulok, close to Vladimirskaya Metro station; see page 445.)

Back on Moskovsky Prospekt, continue south past the Obvodnovo Canal and Novodevichy Cemetery to the **Moscow Triumphal Arch**. It was built between 1834 and 1838 by Vassily Stasov to commemorate the Russian victories during the Russo-Turkish War (1828–9), and was the largest cast-iron structure in the world in the mid-19th century. Modeled on the Brandenburg Gate in Berlin, the arch was decorated with figures representing Winged Victory, Glory and Plenty. It once marked the end of the city where a road toll was collected. In 1936, Stalin had it taken down; but the Arch was put back up during the Siege of Leningrad when it was hoped that it would serve as a barricade. The closest Metro station is Moskovskiye Vorota (Moscow Gates).

South of the Arch, past the Elektrosila Factory, is the 70-hectare (170-acre) **Moscow Victory Park**, through which runs the Alley of Heroes. The park was laid out by tens of thousands of Leningraders after World War II. The 20,000-seat Sports and Concert Complex is located in the park at 8 Prospekt Yuriya Gagarina, near Park Pobedy Metro Station.

Farther down Moskovsky Prospekt is the stone Gothic-style **Chesme Church and Palace**, (near Moskovskaya Metro station on Lensoveta Ulitsa). Catherine the Great commissioned Felten to build the palace in 1770. It was named after the Russian victory over the Turkish fleet in Chesme Bay. It became a rest stop for the empress between the city and Tsarskoye Selo. It was here too that Rasputin's body lay in state after his murder in 1916. Today part of the palace serves as a hospital. The church, built between 1777 and 1780, appears as a red and white fairy-tale concoction with fancy Russian-style *kokoshniki* (named after a Russian woman's headdress) decorating the archways that outline the five-domed roof. It is also known as the Church of Nativity of John the Baptist. Daily services are held at 10am.

The **Monument to the Heroes of the Defense of Leningrad** (unveiled 30 years after the Siege on May 9, 1975) is the focal point of **Victory Square**. The heroic black sculpted figures, called *The Victors*, look out on where the front once ran. (Notice how close the Germans came to capturing the city.) Pink granite steps lead down to an obelisk (dated 1941–45) that stands inside a circle symbolizing the breaking of the blockade ring. An eternal flame burns at the base. Here you will find the **Siege of Leningrad Museum**, open 10am–6pm; Tuesdays and Fridays 10am–5pm; closed Wednesdays. Moskovskaya Metro station.

The **Green Belt of Glory** is a memorial complex that stretches 230 kilometers (143 miles) along the front line of 1941–44. At **Moscow Square** (Moskovskaya Ploshchad), Stalin tried to transplant the heart of the old city to beat anew in these

The beautiful ensemble of St Nicholas' Naval Cathedral (Nikolsky Morskoi Sobor) was built in honor of St Nicholas, the protector of seamen; the area was once inhabited by naval officers. Built in 1762, it combines old Russian traditions of a five-domed church with baroque decorations.

The Rocket hydrofoil takes tourists on trips along the Neva River and out to Peterhof Palace on the Gulf of Finland.

concrete suburbs; he built up the entire eastern side with gloomy apartment blocks and the House of Soviets with a Statue of Lenin at its center.

Moskovsky Prospekt was built in the early 18th century to connect the royal residences in St Petersburg to Tsarskoye Selo. Later the road was continued all the way to Moscow. Today, on the way to Tsarskoye Selo, the prospekt passes the famed **Pulkovo Astronomical Observatory**, which once served as part of a 'mirror telegraph' that linked the residences of the czar. After crossing the Kuzminka River, you come to the **Egyptian Entrance Gates** of the city. The gates were built in 1830 and designed by the British architect Adam Menelaws, who incorporated motifs from the Egyptian temples at Karnak. A **Statue of Alexander Pushkin** stands to the left of the gates.

To the northwest, not far from the Baltic (Baltiisky) Railway Station at Narvskaya Metro station, are the Narva Triumphal Gates which mark the successful outcome of the War of 1812. In 1814, the first gates were erected at the Narva outpost to meet the Russian Guards returning from France. Two decades later, the present gates were designed by Stasov and built of bricks covered with copper sheets, and placed (farther south) at the city's then boundary. The Chariot of the Goddess of Victory crowns the arch; the palm and laurel branches symbolize peace and glory. Four Russian armored warriors decorate the bottom; gold letters describe the regiments and places of battle. Words inscribed on the arch in both Latin and Russian read: 'To the victorious Russian Emperor Guard. Grateful Motherland. On 17 August, 1834.'

THE SIEGE OF LENINGRAD

It's now the fifth month since the enemy has tried to kill our will to live, break our spirit and destroy our faith in victory.... But we know that victory will come. We will achieve it and Leningrad will once again be warm and light and even gay.

Olga Bergholts, Leningrad Poet

For 900 days between 1941 and 1944, Leningrad was cut off from the rest of the Soviet Union and the world by German forces. During this harsh period of World War II, the whole city was linked to the outside world only by air drops and one dangerous ice road, The Road of Life (opened only in winter), that was laid across the frozen waters of Lake Ladoga.

The invading Nazis were determined to completely destroy Leningrad, and Hitler's goal was to starve and bombard the city until it surrendered. The directive issued to German command on September 29, 1941 stated: 'The Führer has ordered the city of St Petersburg to be wiped off the face of the earth.... It is proposed to establish a tight blockade of the city and, by shelling it with artillery of all calibers and incessant bombing, level it to the ground.' Hitler was so certain of immediate victory that he even printed up invitations to a celebration party to be held in the center of the city at the Hotel Astoria.

But the Germans did not plan on the strong resistance and incredible resilience of the Leningrad people. For almost three years, the Nazis tried to penetrate the city. All totaled, over 100,000 high-explosive bombs and 150,000 shells were dropped on the city. The suffering was immense: almost one million people starved to death. At one point, only 125 grams (four ounces) of bread were allocated to each inhabitant per day. The winters were severe with no heat or electricity. There are many stories, for example, of mothers collecting the crumbs off streets or scraping the paste off wallpaper and boiling it to feed their hungry children. Tanya Savicheva, an 11-year-old girl who lived on Vasilyevsky Island, kept a diary that chronicled the deaths of her entire family. It ended with the words: 'The Savichevs died. They all died. I remained alone.' Tanya was later evacuated from Leningrad, but died on July 1, 1944 (see Piskarevskoye Memorial Cemetery, page 448).

Damage to the city was extensive. More than half of the 18th- and 19th-century buildings classified as historical monuments were destroyed; over 30 bombs struck the Hermitage alone. Within one month of the German invasion in June 1941, over one million works of art were packed up by the Hermitage staff and sent by train to Sverdlovsk in the Urals for safekeeping. Other works of art and architecture that could not be evacuated were buried or secretly stored elsewhere within the city. Over 2,000 staff members and art scholars lived in 12 underground air-raid shelters beneath the Hermitage in order to protect the museum and its treasures. Boris Piotrovsky, the Hermitage's former director, lived in one of these shelters and headed the fire brigade. He noted that 'in the life of besieged Leningrad a notable peculiarity manifested itself—an uncommon spiritual strength and power of endurance... to battle and save the art treasures created over the millennia by the genius of humanity.' Architect Alexander Nikolsky, who also lived in an air-raid shelter, sketched the city during the entire blockade. His pencil and charcoal drawings can be seen today in the Hermitage Department of Prints and Drawings.

The city's outskirts were the worst hit. The palaces of Peter the Great, Catherine II, and Elizabeth I were almost completely demolished. Peter's Palace of Petrodvorets was put to use as a Nazi stable. The Germans sawed up the famous Sampson Fountain for wood and took rugs and tapestries into the trenches.

The Soviet author, Vera Inber, was in Leningrad during the Siege. She wrote the narrative poem *Pulkovo Meridian* about the Pulkovo Astronomical Observatory outside Leningrad, where many scientists were killed when it was struck by an enemy bomb.

Dmitri Shostakovich's Seventh Symphony was composed in Leningrad during the siege and broadcast from the city around the world on August 9, 1942. Shostakovich was a member of the fire-defense unit housed in the Leningrad Conservatory. During bomb attacks, Shostakovich would hurriedly write the Russian letters BT, which stood for air raid, on his score before running to his post on the roof of the conservatory.

On January 27, 1944, Leningraders heard the salute of 324 guns to celebrate the complete victory over German troops. Even though most of the buildings, museums, and palaces have now been restored, the citizens of St Petersburg will never forget the siege, during which every fourth person in the city was killed. May 9, a city holiday, is celebrated as Liberation Day. Schoolchildren take turns standing guard at cemeteries.

Over half a million of the people who died between 1941 and 1943 are buried in mass graves at Piskarevskoye Cemetery outside St Petersburg. Inside the pavilion is a museum dedicated to the Siege of Leningrad. Outside, the Statue of the Motherland stands over an eternal flame. At the base of the monument are inscribed words by Olga Berggolts. The end of the inscription reads: 'Let no one forget. Let nothing be forgotten.'

The Tomb of the Unknown Soldier outside the Kremlin walls in Moscow. The eternal flame honors the memory of the 20 million Russians who died during World War II. It was moved to this site from the Field of Mars in St Petersburg in 1967.

STATE OF SIEGE

What an incredible thing is this feeling of hunger. One can get used to it as to a chronic headache. For two successive days I have been waiting with blind resignation for one glutinous piece of bread, without experiencing acute hunger. That means the disease (ie hunger) has gone over from the acute stage to the chronic.

It's dark. I couldn't stop myself getting out that precious candle-end, hidden away in case of dire emergency. The darkness is terribly oppressive. Mila's dozing on the sofa. She is smiling in her sleep, she must be dreaming of a sandwich with smoked sausage or of thick barley soup. Every night she has appetizing dreams, which is why waking up is particularly tormenting for her.

The entire flat is appallingly cold, everywhere is frozen, stepping out into the corridor involves putting on one's coat, galoshes and hat. The bleakness of desolation everywhere. The water supply is non-existent, we have to fetch water from more than three kilometres away. The sewage system is a thing of the distant past—the yard is full of muck. This is like some other city, not Leningrad, always so proud of its European, dandy-ish appearance. To see it now is like meeting a man you have become accustomed to seeing dressed in a magnificent, thick woollen overcoat, sporting clean gloves, a fresh collar, and good American boots. And here you suddenly meet that same man completely transformed—clothed in tatters, filthy, unshaven, with foul-smelling breath and a dirty neck, with rags on his feet instead of boots.

Yesterday's Leningradskaya Pravda published an article by the chairman of the Leningrad Soviet, comrade Popov, entitled 'On the Leningrad Food Situation'. After calling on all citizens to summon their courage and patience, comrade Popov goes on to speak of the very real problems of theft and abuse in Leningrad's food distribution network.

My candle-end has almost burnt down. Soon darkness will descend upon me—until morning...

17th January. *Old age. Old age is the fatigue of the well-worn components that are involved in the working of a human body, an exhaustion of man's inner resources. Your blood no longer keeps you warm, your legs refuse to obey you, your back grows stiff, your brain grows feeble, your memory fades. The pace of old age is as unhurried as the slow combustion of the almost burnt-out logs in a stove: the flames die away, lose their colour, one log disintegrates into burning embers, then another—and now the last flickering blue flames are fading—it will soon be time to shut off the flue.*

We are, all of us, old people now. Regardless of age. The pace of old age now governs our bodies and our feelings.... Yesterday at the market I saw a little girl of about nine, wearing enormous felt boots which were full of holes. She was bartering a chunk of dubious-looking brawn—probably made from dog meat—for 100 grammes of bread. Her eyes, hardly visible beneath a pair of heavy lids, looked terribly tired, her back was bent, her gait slow and shuffling, her face puckered and the corners of her mouth turned down. It was the face of an old woman. Can this ever be forgotten or forgiven?

23rd January, 11a.m. *Slowly, laboriously, like emaciated people toiling up a hill, the days drag by. Monotonous, unhealthy, withdrawn days in a now silent city. Leningrad's nerve centres, which have until recently kept the life of the city going, fed it vital impulses—the power-stations—have ceased to function. And all the nerve fibres extending over the city lie dormant, inactive. There is no light, no trams or trolley-buses are running, the factories, cinemas, theatres have all stopped working. It is pitch black in the empty shops, chemists', canteens—their windows having been boarded up since autumn (as protection from shell fragments). Only the feeble, consumptive flame of a wick-lamp flickers on every counter.... Thickly coated in snow, the tram, trolley-bus and radio cables hang listlessly above the streets. They stretch overhead like an endless white net, and there is nothing to make them shed their thick snow cover.*

The great city's nervous system has ceased its function. But we know that this is not death, but only a lethargic sleep. The time will come when the sleeping giant will stir, and then rouse himself...

Alexander Dymov, Winter of 1942, *translated by Hilda Perham*

Vicinity of St Petersburg

If you have time, go on a few excursions outside of St Petersburg. Day trips to Peter the Great's Summer Palace on the Gulf of Finland, or to the towns of Tsarskoye Selo and Pavlovsk are highly recommended. Here are 13 areas from which to choose.

Peterhof or Petrodvorets   (Петродворец)

Peterhof is located 30 kilometers (20 miles) west of the city, on the shores of the Gulf of Finland. Peter the Great named his imperial residence Peterhof; but during World War II its name was dutifully Russianized to Petrodvorets (Peter's Palace). Even though the name reverted back to Peterhof in 1992, many still refer to the area as Petrodvorets.

While Peter the Great was supervising the building of the Kronstadt fortress, he stayed in a small lodge on the southern shore of the Gulf of Finland. After Russia defeated the Swedes in the Battle of Poltava in 1709, Peter decided to build his summer residence, Peterhof, so that it not only commemorated the victory over Sweden (and of gaining access to the Baltic), but also the might of the Russian Empire. Peterhof was designed to resemble Versailles in France.

Architects were summoned from around the world: Rastrelli, Leblond, Braunstein, Michetti and the Russian, Zemtsov. Over 4,000 peasants and soldiers were brought in to dig the canals, gardens and parks in the marshy area. Soil, building materials and tens of thousands of trees were brought in by barge. Peter helped to draft the layout of all the gardens and fountains. The fountains were built by Vasily Tuvolkov, Russia's first hydraulics engineer. Over 20 kilometers (12 miles) of canals were constructed in such a way that 30,000 liters (7,926 US gallons) of water flowed under its own pressure to 144 fountains.

The great **Cascade Fountain** in front of the palace has 17 waterfalls, 142 water jets, 66 fountains (including the two cup fountains on either side), 29 bas-reliefs and 39 gilded statues, including the famous Sampson—the Russians won the Battle of Poltava on St Sampson's Day. The five-ton Sampson, surrounded by eight dolphins, is wrestling open the jaws of a lion, from which a jet of water shoots over 20 meters (65 feet) into the air.

Approaching the back of the palace from St Petersburg Prospekt, the first fountain is known as the **Mezheumny**, with a dragon in the center pool. The **Neptune Fountain** was brought to Russia from Nuremberg, Germany. The Square Ponds are right by the walls of the palace in the Upper Park.

The northeast path leading to **Alexander Park** takes you by the Gothic Court Chapel (with 43 saints along the outer walls), the **Cottage** (built in 1829 by Adam Menelaws, who designed it to resemble an aristocratic Englishman's cottage), and the **Farmer's Palace**. This was also built by Menelaws as a storage house, but was later turned into a small summer palace by Alexander II. Following the path back around to the palace, you will come upon the **Conservatory**, used as a greenhouse. Nearby is the **Triton Fountain**, which shows Neptune's son wrestling with a sea monster. **Chess Hill**, with a checkerboard design, contains some of the best water-falls, cascading over bronzed dragons. The two **Roman Fountains** (modeled after those at the Cathedral of St Peter in Rome) stand at the bottom of the hill and were designed by Karl Blank.

Following the path around to the right of the palace brings you to the **Pyramid Fountain**. Peter the Great designed this water pyramid, made up of seven tiers and 505 jets. A circular seat is positioned under the **Little Umbrella Fountain**. If you are tempted to have a short rest on the bench under the umbrella, be ready to scramble—as 164 jets spray out water as soon as anyone sits down! As you scamper away, you will approach the **Little Oak Fountain**, which has dozens of hidden jets (as do the artificial tulips) that spray as any weight approaches the oak tree. When you run off to the nearby bench to catch your breath, you will now get drenched by 41 more jets! Beware of the three fir trees!

Approaching Monplaisir, the Sun Fountain shoots out from a rectangular pond as 16 golden dolphins swim around shiny disks. Jets of water sprinkle out from the center column, creating the golden rays of the sun. The **Adam and Eve Fountains** (the statues were done by the Venetian sculptor Bonazza) stand on either side of the path leading to the Gulf from the Palace.

While the Grand Palace was under construction, Peter designed and lived in the smaller Dutch-style villa that he called **Monplaisir** (My Pleasure), right on the Gulf of Finland on the eastern side of the lower park. Even after the larger palace was completed, Peter preferred to stay here while he visited Peterhof. Today it houses a small collection of 17th- and 18th-century European paintings.

In 1762, when Catherine the Great's husband, Czar Peter III threatened divorce (he planned to send her off to a nunnery), the empress came here to live in the Tea House. A few days after Catherine's lover Count Orlov picked her up from Peterhof on July 28, 1762, the day of their planned and secret coup, Czar Peter mysteriously died, strangled in his sleep. The whole army came out to pledge its allegiance to Catherine when she returned to the Winter Palace in the city. (See Special Topic on Catherine the Great on page 417.)

The two-story house by the water on the western side of the lower park, is known as the **Château de Marly**, built in 1714 in Louis XIV style—Peter had visited a French

In front of the Peterhof Palace the five-ton Sampson Fountain wrestles open the jaws of a lion from which a jet of water shoots over 20 meters (65 feet) into the air.

king's hunting lodge in Marly. Behind it flows the **Golden Hill Cascade**. The other quaint two-story structure is known as the **Hermitage Pavilion**. It was built by Johann Friedrich Braunstein. The retreat was surrounded by a moat and had a drawbridge that could be raised to further isolate the guests. The first floor consisted of one room with a large dining room table that could be lifted from or lowered to servants on the ground floor; the guests placed a note on the table, rang a bell, and the table would shortly reappear with their orders. The **Lion Cascade Fountains** stand in front of the Hermitage, which houses over 100 paintings by 18th-century European artists.

The original palace was built between 1714 and 1724, designed in the baroque and classical styles. It stands on a hill in the center of the Peterhof complex and over-looks the parks and gardens. Rastrelli enlarged it (1747–54) for Empress Elizabeth. After Peter's death the palace passed on to subsequent czars and was declared a muse-um after the Revolution. The palace is three stories high with wings that contain the galleries. The central part contains the Exhibition Rooms, Peter the Great's Oak Study and the Royal Bedchamber. The rooms have magnificent parquet floors, gilded ceil-ings and crystal chandeliers, and are filled with exquisite objets d'art from around the world. The **Crimson Room** has furniture by Chippendale; the walls of the Oak Study are adorned with portraits of Empress Elizabeth, Catherine the Great and Alexander I; the **Partridge Chamber**, so named for the silk ornamental partridges that covered the walls, is decorated with French silk-upholstered furniture, porcelain and clocks.

The **Portrait Gallery**, in the central hall of the palace, is filled with portraits by such painters as Pietro Rotari (the whole collection was acquired by Catherine the Great) and serves as an interesting catalog of period costumes. The **White Dining Hall**, used for State dinners, is decorated in classical style with white molded figures on the walls and a crystal and amethyst chandelier. The table is ceremoni-ously laid out for 30 people with 196 pieces of English porcelain. Rastrelli built the adjacent **Throne Room** for official receptions. A portrait of Catherine the Great on horseback hangs over Peter's first throne.

The **Chesme Room** commemorated the battles between the Russian and Turkish fleets in Chesme Bay in the Aegean Sea. The German artist Hackert was commis-sioned to paint the victory scenes in the room. Count Orlov (a squadron com-mander at Chesme) checked the artist's sketches and was dissatisfied with one that depicted an exploding ship. Hackert mentioned that he had never seen such a thing. Orlov ordered a 60-cannon Russian frigate, anchored off the coast of Italy, to be packed with gunpowder. Hackert had to journey to Italy to see the ship exploding. The rest of the palace is joined by numerous galleries and studies. At the east end is a Rastrelli rococo chapel with a single gilded cupola.

When visiting the palace itself it is customary to join a group tour. They are held in different languages. If you cannot find one in English, join any tour and once inside you can slip away from the group and go off on your own. Tickets are sold in the lobby where you pick up your *tapochki* (slippers) to put over your shoes.

The **Benois Museum**, to your right as you leave the palace, exhibits over 1,000 works by the famous set designer and several generations of the Benois family. Open daily 10.30am–5pm. Nearby is the **Apothecary Museum and Herbarium** (open daily 8am–8pm; closed Saturdays), once the center for growing medicinal herbs for the royal family. (It also serves as a functioning pharmacy and a staff member can whip up a herbal drink for you.) The five-domed **Peter and Paul Cathedral**, at 32 St Petersburg Prospekt, was built in the 1890s, and is slowly being restored (it was a Soviet-era movie cinema). Today religious services are usually held at 5pm. Listen to the church bells play at 9.45am and 4.45pm.

Hitler invaded Russia on June 22, 1941. When the Nazis reached Peterhof on September 23, many of the art pieces and statues had still not been evacuated. The German army spent 900 days here and destroyed the complex. Monplaisir was an artillery site, used to shell Leningrad. The Germans cut down 15,000 trees for firewood, used tapestries in the trenches, plundered over 34,000 works of art and made off with priceless objects, including the Sampson statue, which were never recovered. After the war massive restoration work began, and on June 17, 1945, the fountains flowed once again. The head of the Hermitage, Joseph Orbelli, who lived in the Hermitage during the siege, remarked: 'Even during our worst suffering, we knew that the day would come when once again the beautiful fountains of Petrodvorets would begin to spray and the statues of the park flash their golden gleam in the sunlight.' There are black-and-white photographs on display in the Exhibition Room that show the extensive damage to the palace.

Leningrad poet Olga Bergholts visited Peterhof after the siege and wrote:

> *Again from the black dust, from the place*
> *of death and ashes, will arise the garden as before.*
> *So it will be. I firmly believe in miracles.*
> *You gave me that belief, my Leningrad.*

The upper and lower parks and gardens cover about 121 hectares (300 acres), stretching around the palace to the Gulf of Finland. When warm, it is wonderful to have a picnic on the grounds or beach, stroll in the gardens, and spend the entire day. In June during the White Nights, a variety of festivals and musical concerts are held on the palace grounds. One can grab a quick bite at numerous cafés on the grounds; the Gallery Café, in the Grand Palace's western gallery is open daily 10am–8pm. Or try one of the following restaurants: the Emperor's Table is at 2 Razovodnaya Ulitsa (tel. 427-9106), open daily 10.30am–6pm; Peterhof, at

(following pages) The great Cascade Fountain stands in front of Peterhof, Peter the Great's Summer Palace. Its 66 fountains, 17 waterfalls and 142 water jets all flow without the aid of a single pump.

3 Ulitsa Morskovo Desanta (tel. 427-9884), open daily 10am–8pm; Trapeza (Refectory) Restaurant located at 9 Pravlenskaya Ulitsa (tel. 427-9393), open daily 1pm–10pm.

GETTING THERE

The most enjoyable and convenient way to Peterhof is by hydrofoil. From May to September (from about 9.30am–7pm daily), the *Rocket* jets across the Gulf of Finland to the Marine Canal in less than 45 minutes. Catch one at the pier right in front of the Hermitage Museum, or at the jetty in front of the Bronze Horseman in Senate Square. Both have hydrofoils that depart about every half hour and drop you off right by the palace grounds. In summer try buying your ticket ahead of time as queues tend to be long. Besides your boat ticket, you will also be issued a separate ticket to enter the palace grounds when you arrive.

At Peterhof, check to see if you still need to purchase an entrance ticket to the palace from the small kiosk situated by the end of the dock. (Sometimes, you are made to walk all the way back to purchase one!) From here it is a good ten-minute walk up to the palace. It is also a good idea to buy your return hydrofoil ticket at the dock as soon as you arrive. If you wait until the last minute on a busy day, all tickets for the time you want may be sold out. (The ticket kiosks are to your left across the bridge as you get off the dock.) A hydrofoil number will be stamped on the back of your ticket; for the return, line up on the dock by the sign that shows this number. (Ferries also depart for Tuchkov Bridge.)

You can also travel on commuter trains from Baltic (Baltiisky) Railway Station to Novy Peterhof; they depart every half hour or so, and the trip takes 40 minutes. From Peterhof station take any bus numbered 350–356 (not 357); it is then a ten-minute ride to the palace grounds (get off at Fontana, the fifth stop). Tickets for a bus tour can be booked at the excursion booth in front of Gostiny Dvor on Dumskaya Ulitsa. Coaches also leave from in front of the Cathedral of Our Lady of Kazan on Nevsky Prospekt; usually a person with a megaphone is selling tickets. Ask at your hotel about other travel companies that provide tours to Peterhof, such as Peter TIPS and St Petersburg Travel.

The palace grounds are open daily 9am–9pm, and the fountains operate from May to September. The Grand Palace (tel. 427-9527) is open 10.30am–5pm Tuesday–Sunday, and closed on the last Tuesday of the month. The Cottage Palace is open 10.30am–4pm. Monplaisir, the Hermitage, Château de Marly and the Catherine Wing Museum are usually open daily 10.30am–4pm Monday–Saturday. (In summer months everything is generally open at least one hour later; in winter months some of the smaller palaces may be closed.) Art Peterhof at 4 Pravlenskaya Ulitsa (in the Orangerie near the Hermitage) has a wax museum and art exhibitions; open daily

11am–7pm. Banks for currency exchange are at 12 and 13/17 St Petersburg Prospekt behind the palace. Nearby at number 15 is a telephone calling center. To stay overnight, see the Accommodation section, page 523, for hotel listings.

On the way to Peterhof from St Petersburg is the baroque Grand Palace at Strelna, the residence of Alexander II's younger brother Konstantin Nikolayevich. Restored after World War II, its present condition has deteriorated. With its parks running down to the sea, it looks like a faded version of Peterhof. Nearby is the Trinity-Sergius Monastery, also known as the Czar's Monastery. The recently restored interior is modeled after St Catherine's at Sinai. It also contains many aristocratic graves including that of Zinaida Yusupova, the mother of Count Yusupov who participated in the murder of Rasputin.

Lomonosov or Oranienbaum   (Ломоносов)

Lomonosov, once called Oranienbaum, is situated only 10 kilometers (six miles) west of Peterhof on the Gulf of Finland. In 1707, while Peter the Great was building Monplaisir, he gave these lands to his close friend Prince Alexander Menschikov to develop. Menschikov was the first governor-general of St Petersburg and supervised the building of the nearby Kronstadt Fortress. (For his palace in the city see page 396) He wanted to turn the estate into his summer residence. Since the prince planted orange trees in the lower parks (first grown in hothouses), he named his residence Oranienbaum, German for wild orange trees.

Unfortunately Menschikov never fully enjoyed his product—he ended up in exile three years after Peter I's death. The property was briefly made into a hospital before Peter III preferred living here to the Winter Palace. After his mysterious death, Catherine the Great expanded the buildings and grounds in the style of the times and made it her private pleasure abode. Until the 1917 Revolution it was used by members of the Romanov family. In 1948, the name was changed to Lomonosov after the great Russian scientist who had a glassworks and mosaic factory nearby. (For Lomonosov Museum see page 396.)

The estate escaped major shelling during the war and is beautifully preserved. The two-story Grand Palace (1725, by architects Fontana and Shedel) stands atop a hill overlooking parks and gardens that were originally designed by Antonio Rinaldi, who also built the two pleasure pavilions, the **Chinese Palace** and **Katalnaya Gorka** (Sliding Hill). Visitors could glide on sleds along a wooden path from the third story of the pavilion and ride down through the lower parks. Oranienbaum became the center of masked balls and parties that entertained Russian royalty and foreign diplomats. The park is open daily 9am–10pm (closed Tuesdays), but closes earlier

Peter the Great's Palace, Peterhof, was designed to resemble the French palace of Versailles. The rooms have magnificent parquet floors, painted ceilings and even Chippendale furniture.

The entrance gate to Catherine's Palace (Yekaterinsky Dvorets) is decorated with the Russian czarist crest of the double-headed eagle, adopted by Ivan the Great in the 15th century.

The 18th-century Catherine's Palace in Tsarskoye Selo, designed by Rastrelli, is over 300 meters (980 feet) long. At the time it was the longest palace in the world. Two forms of garden make up Catherine Park, the naturalistic and formal. In front of the palace beds of symmetrical red and black arabesque shapes gradually lead into a wilder area of wooded paths and fish-filled ponds.

in winter. The estate is now a museum, and the buildings are open 11am–5pm, Wednesday–Sunday (many are closed in winter from November to April). The Grand Palace (tel. 423-1635) is usually closed to visitors. In summer there are also boat rentals and carnival rides on the grounds. The **Wax Museum Workshop**, at 37a Krasny Partizan (9am–6pm, Monday–Friday), manufactures figures for the wax museum in the Beloselsky-Belozersky Palace in the city (see page 437). On Komsomolskaya Ulitsa is the **Lomonosov History Museum**.

The easiest way to get to Lomonosov is by *elektrichka* train from the city's Baltic (Baltiisky) Station to the Oranienbaum stop (four stops after Novy Peterhof). This takes one hour. It is a five-minute walk (head toward the green-domed Cathedral of the Archangel Michael) to the park. There is also a ferry from Kronstadt, or a local bus from Peterhof (the bus stop is next to the railway station). Some bus tour companies in the city also offer excursions. It is advisable to bring your own food and drink. The few cafés are located in the railway station (open daily 7.30am–9pm): Lana 2nd floor, 5 Manezhnaya Ulitsa (open daily 8am–8pm); Baltika Restaurant near the post office and bank on Ulitsa Pobedy; and a cafeteria at 1 Privokzalnaya Ulitsa (open daily 7.30am–9pm). There is also a small café near the Chinese Palace.

Kronstadt   (Кронштадт)

When Peter the Great founded St Petersburg in 1703, the Great Northern War (1700–21) with the Swedes was in its early stages. To protect the gulf approach to his city, Peter began building the Kronstadt Fortress in 1704; its construction was overseen by Prince Menschikov (see Lomonosov, page 477). The fortress, on the island of Kotlin, also contained the shipyards. Monuments on the island are linked to the history of the Russian fleet.

From April 25 through November 10, a hydrofoil leaves daily from Tuchkov Bridge (next to Hotelship Peterhof) from 6.20am–9.30pm; the trip takes 30–40 minutes. (Check, you may still need to get admission permits before departing, tel. 218-2223.) Or try taking a local *elektrichka* train from Finland Station to Gorskaya, on the north shore of the Gulf of Finland, and the ferry to Kronstadt. An *elektrichka* also leaves from the Baltic (Baltiisky) Train Station to Oranienbaum in Lomonosov, where ferries depart for the island. From Peterhof, there is a local bus or train to Oranienbaum. (Remember to find out times of returning transport.)

On the way, notice the 29-kilometer (18-mile) barrier built across a section of the Gulf of Finland to control the floods (over 300 in St Petersburg's history). Tidal waves sweep inland during severe storms. In 1824, the water level rose over four meters (13 feet), killing 569 people.

A CULTURAL EXTRAVAGANZA

*I*n the season of 1903–4 Petersburg witnessed concerts in the grand manner. I am speaking of the strange, never-to-be surpassed madness of the concerts of Hoffmann and Kubelik in the Nobility Hall during Lent. I can recall no other musical experiences, not even the premiere of Scriabin's Prometheus, *that might be compared with these Lenten orgies in the white-columned hall. The concerts would reach a kind of rage, a fury. This was no musical dilettantism: there was something threatening and even dangerous that rose up out of enormous depths, a kind of craving for movement; a mute prehistorical malaise was exuded by the peculiar, the almost flagellant zeal of the halberdiers in Mikhaylovsky Square, and it whetted the Petersburg of that day like a knife. In the dim light of the gas lamps the many entrances of the Nobility Hall were beset by a veritable siege. Gendarmes on prancing horses, lending to the atmosphere of the square the mood of a civil disturbance, made clicking noises with their tongues and shouted as they closed ranks to guard the main entry. The sprung carriages with dim lanterns slipped into the glistening circle and arranged themselves in an impressive black gypsy camp. The cabbies dared not deliver their fares right to the door; one paid them while approaching, and then they made off rapidly to escape the wrath of the police. Through the triple chains the Petersburger made his way like a feverish little trout to the marble ice-hole of the vestibule, whence he disappeared into the luminous frosty building, draped with silk and velvet.*

The orchestra seats and the places behind them were filled in the customary order, but the spacious balconies to which the side entrances gave access were filled in bunches, like baskets, with clusters of humanity. The Nobility Hall inside is wide, stocky, and almost square. The stage itself takes up nearly half the area. The gallery swelters in a July heat. The air is filled with a ceaseless humming like that of cicadas over the steppe.

Osip Mandelstam, The Noise of Time

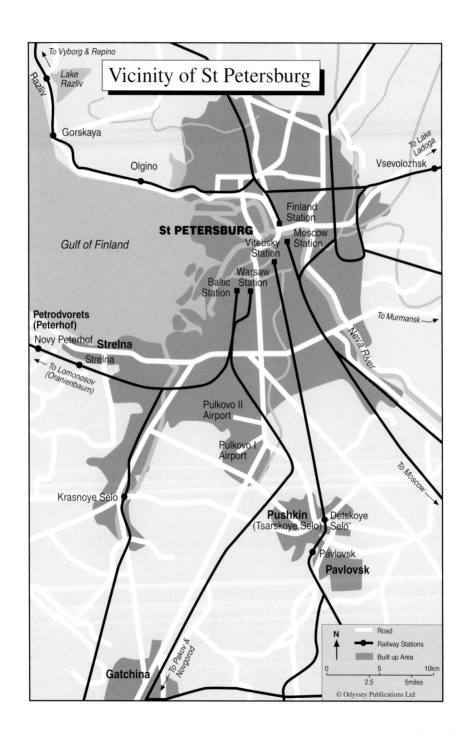

Vicinity of St Petersburg

To Vyborg & Repino

Razliv

Lake Razliv

Gorskaya

Olgino

To Lake Ladoga

Vsevolozhsk

Finland Station

St PETERSBURG

Moscow Station

Vitebsky Station

Gulf of Finland

Warsaw Station

Baltic Station

To Murmansk

Neva River

Petrodvorets (Peterhof)

Novy Peterhof

Strelna

Strelna

To Lomonosov (Oranienbaum)

Pulkovo II Airport

Pulkovo I Airport

To Moscow

Krasnoye Selo

Pushkin (Tsarskoye Selo)

Detskoye Selo

Pavlovsk

Pavlovsk

N

Road

Railway Stations

Built up Area

0   5   10km

2.5   5miles

To Pskov & Novgorod

Gatchina

© Odyssey Publications Ltd

West of the City—Northern Gulf

Razliv (Разлив)

The village of Razliv lies 35 kilometers (22 miles) northwest of the city on the Karelian Isthmus, near the former Finnish border. Lenin fled here in 1917 to hide from the Provisional Government. Agents were searching everywhere for him and advertised a reward of 200,000 rubles in gold. Shaving off his trademark beard and wearing a wig, he ventured out in the darkness of night from the Finland Railway Station to the village, and stayed in a barn owned by the Yemelyanov family. The barn is now the **Sarai Museum**, housing some of the things Lenin used. A few days later Nikolai Yemelyanov rowed Lenin across Lake Razliv and built a hut out of hay for a more secretive shelter. Lenin lived and wrote articles in a *shalash*, or thatched hut, by the lake. The **Shalash Museum**, near the hut, exhibits Lenin's personal documents and belongings. A tourist boat takes visitors across the lake. The museum and grounds are open 11am–5pm; closed Wednesdays. The easiest way to get there is by *elektrichka* train from Finland Station (about an hour) along the northern shore of the Gulf of Finland toward Sestroretsk; the stop is Razliv.

Repino (Репино)

The road from Razliv along the Karelian Isthmus leads to Repino about 45 kilometers (30 miles) northwest of St Petersburg. Repino is a small town in the resort area once known as Kurnosovo. It now bears the name of the celebrated painter Ilya Repin (1844–1930), who bought a cottage in the settlement in 1899 and made it his permanent residence. All his friends and students gathered there every Wednesday and Repin painted the rest of the week. Repin named his estate the Penates, after the Roman gods of home and well-being. Repin is buried on the grounds. His grave lies atop a hill. The Penates burned down during World War II, but was totally reconstructed and is now a museum, displaying Repin's art and personal belongings. The house containing his studio is at 411 Primorskoye Shosse (open 10am–6pm, groups after 4pm, closed Tuesdays). Take an *elektrichka* train from Finland Station (or if already in Razliv, it is only about 15 minutes further west) in the direction of Zelenogorsk/Vyborg to Repino. From the station head towards the water. To stay overnight, see the Accommodation section, page 523. One train stop west of Repino brings you to the village of **Komarovo** (once a part

The interior splendors of Catherine's Palace in Tsarskoye Selo. (above) The opulent Great Hall was designed by Rastrelli for Empress Elizabeth I (daughter of Catherine I and Peter the Great). On the ceiling is the painting Triumph of Russia.

of Finnish territory) where the famous poet Anna Akhmatova is buried near the dacha where she lived for many years. Her funeral was held in the city's Nikolsky Marine Cathedral on March 10, 1966. In 1963, at the age of 74, Akhmatova wrote of Komarovo:

> This land, although not my native land,
> Will be remembered forever,
> And the sea's lightly iced,
> Unsalty water.
>
> The sand on the bottom is whiter than chalk
> The air is heady, like wine,
> And the rosy body of the pines
> Is naked in the sunset hour,
>
> And the sunset itself on such waves of ether
> That I just can't comprehend
> Whether it is the end of the day, the end of the world,
> Or the mystery of mysteries in me again.

South of the City

Tsarskoye Selo or Pushkin   (Царское Село)

If you plan to visit Tsarskoye Selo and Pavlovsk in one day, come on Wednesday, Saturday or Sunday, when both are open.

The town of Tsarskoye Selo, the Czar's Village, is located 24 kilometers (15 miles) south of St Petersburg. City residents used to flock here in summer for the beneficial effects of the climate. After the Revolution the name was changed to Detskoye Selo (Children's Village), because of the large number of orphanages in town; many of the buildings were turned into schools. Pushkin studied at the Lyceum from 1811 to 1817. In 1937, to commemorate the 100-year anniversary of the poet's death, the town was renamed Pushkin. Today the town is referred to either as Tsarskoye Selo or Pushkin, but the train station is still called Detskoye Selo.

Peter the Great won the region between the Neva and the Gulf of Finland during the Great Northern War. He later presented these lands to his wife Catherine I who built parks and gardens and the **Yekaterinsky Dvorets**, Catherine's Palace. In 1752, the Empress Elizabeth commissioned Rastrelli to renovate the palace. The beautiful baroque building stretches 300 meters (980 feet) and is lavishly decorated.

Catherine the Great built additions to the palace. During her reign many renowned architects, such as Cameron, Rinaldi and Quarenghi, worked in the neo-classical style on the palace. Cameron's **Green Dining Room** and **Chinese Blue Room** are breathtaking. The walls of the Blue Room are decorated with Chinese blue silk and the Empress Elizabeth is portrayed as Flora, Goddess of Flowers. The white marble staircase leading into the palace was built in 1860 by Monighetti. On the inside walking tour, you pass through Rastrelli's **Cavalier Dining Room** and **Great Hall**. Peter the Great presented 248 personal guards to a Prussian king and in return received panels of amber. Rastrelli built the **Amber Room** using those panels in 1755. During World War II, the Nazis made off with the panels, which were never found.

The **Picture Hall** stretches the entire width of the building; of the 130 French, Flemish and Italian canvasses that were here before the war, 117 were evacuated and can be seen today. The palace chapel was begun by Rastrelli and completed by Stasov. The northeast section of the palace, in the chapel wing, contains the **Pushkin Museum**, made up of 27 halls displaying his personal belongings and manuscripts.

The **Lyceum** is linked to the Palace by an archway. It was originally built by Catherine the Great as the school for her grandsons and was expanded in 1811 for the children of the aristocracy. The classrooms were on the second floor and the dormitory on the third. The Lyceum's first open class consisted of 30 boys between 11 and 14. One of these students was Alexander Pushkin. The Lyceum is now a museum and the classrooms and laboratories are kept as they were during Pushkin's time. In the dormitory is a plaque which reads: 'Door no. 14 Alexander Pushkin'. Pushkin read aloud his poem 'Recollections of Tsarskoye Selo' on June 9, 1817, in the school's assembly hall. The statue of Pushkin outside was sculpted by Robert Bach in 1900. In the old royal stables is the **Carriage Museum**. The neighboring **Church of the Sign** (1734) is the oldest building in town; services are held here. Nearby is also **Pushkin's Dacha** where he lived from May to October, 1831.

Catherine's parks consisted of three types: the French one was filled with statues and pavilions, the English had more trees and shrubs and the Italian contained more sculpted gardens. The grounds stretch over 567 hectares (1,400 acres). Rastrelli built the Orlov column in the middle of the lake as a monument to the victory at the Battle of Chesme.

The Hermitage structure was built between 1744 and 1756 to entertain the guests. No servants were allowed on the second floor. The guests wrote requests on slates; the tables were lowered and raised with the appropriate drinks and dishes, including such things as elk lips and nightingale tongues! The adjacent fish canal provided seafood for the royal banquets. The upper bathhouse was used by the royal family and the lower by the visitors. Other buildings on the estate include the Admiralty (with a boat collection), the Grotto (once decorated with over 250,000 shells), the Cameron Gallery, the Hanging Gardens, the Agate Rooms, the Granite Terrace, Marble Bridge (made from Siberian marble), Turkish Baths (resembling a mosque) and the Milkmaid Fountain (built in 1816 by Sokolov from a fable by La Fontaine). Pushkin wrote a poem based on the fable about the sad girl who holds a piece of her milk jug that lies broken at her feet. The Alexander Palace was built by Catherine the Great (1792–96 by Quarenghi) for her grandson, the future Alexander I. Nicholas II lived here after the 1905 Revolution in St Petersburg.

The first Russian railway was constructed between Tsarskoye Selo and Pavlovsk in 1834. By 1837 the line had been extended all the way to St Petersburg. (A model of the inaugural train which took Czar Nicholas I and his family to the summer palace in Tsarskoye Selo stands at the end of the platform in Vitebsky Station in St Petersburg; check out the Royal Waiting Room.) One of the passengers who rode the first train to St Petersburg on October 31, 1837, wrote, 'The train made almost one *verst* (kilometer) a minute... 60 *versts* an hour, a horrible thought! Meanwhile, as you sit calmly, you do not notice the speed, which terrifies the imagination, only the wind whistles, only the steed breathes fiery foam, leaving a white cloud of steam in its wake....' The line between St Petersburg and Moscow was later built between 1843 and 1851.

A 19th-century ball is held annually at Catherine's Palace.
Dressed in turn-of-the-century aristocratic costume,
city folk gather to celebrate their historical roots.

Catherine's Palace (tel. 466-5308) and the National Park are open 10am–5pm; closed Tuesdays. The ticket office and entrance is at the side of the courtyard. Russian-language tours are given at set hours all day. (In crowded months buy a ticket immediately, before they are sold out for the day!) If you cannot find a tour in English, follow a Russian group and once inside you can wander off on your own. From St Petersburg there are also foreign language excursions (to both Pushkin and Pavlovsk), each lasting about four hours.

The Lyceum is open 10.30am–5pm; closed Tuesdays. The nearby Carriage Museum is closed Tuesdays and Wednesdays. The hours for Pushkin's Dacha are 10.30am–4pm; closed Mondays and Tuesdays. Chistyakov's

The beautiful baroque-style Catherine's Palace, built by Peter the Great for his wife and future Empress, Catherine I, in the town of Tsarskoye Selo

Country House, 23 Moskovskoye Prospekt, is open 10am–5pm, Wednesdays and weekends. The City of Pushkin History Museum, at 28 Leontevskaya Ulitsa, is open 10am–5pm; closed Thursdays and Fridays. The Tsarskoye Selo Collection Museum, 40 Magazeynaya Ulitsa, is open 11am–3pm, Thursday–Sunday. In winter, cross-country skis and sledges are for rent in the semicircular wing of Catherine's Palace.

The quickest way to Tsarskoye Selo is by *elektrichka* train from Vitebsky Railway Station to Detskoye Selo; the journey takes half an hour. Buses 371 and 382 run from the station to Catherine's Palace in about ten minutes. To get to Pavlovsk, continue on the train one stop farther to Pavlovsky Station. Bus 370 also runs from near the Palace directly to Pavlovsk, only five kilometers (three miles) away. Many cafés dot the area. Restaurants are located at: 7 Sadovaya (Admiralty), open daily 12pm–8pm; 4 Novoderevenskaya (Duke), open daily 12pm–midnight; 8 Malaya (Milena), open daily 1pm–11pm; 1 Privokzalnaya Ploshchad (Tsarskoye Selo), open daily 11am–midnight (café: 8am–midnight). (To stay overnight, see hotel listings under Accommodation, page 523.) For a bus tour from the city, see Bus Excursion listings on page 546. Check out Alexander's Palace web-site: http://www.alexanderpalace.org/palace/index.html

Pavlovsk   (Павловск)

The flamboyant court life of Tsarskoye Selo scared away most of the wildlife, so the royal family went into the nearby area of **Pavlovskoye** (about four kilometers/two and a half miles away) to hunt. Two wooden hunting lodges were known as Krik and Krak. In 1777, Catherine the Great presented the villages, along with the serfs, to her son Pavel (Paul), whose first son Alexander had just been born. The village was renamed Pavlovsk when Paul became czar. The Scottish architect Cameron began building the palace in the 1780s and Paul turned it into his official summer residence. **Pavlovsk Park** was created by Pietro Gonzaga (who lived here from 1803 to 1838) and covers over 1,500 hectares (3,700 acres), making it one of the largest landscaped parks in the world, with designs such as the **Valley of the Ponds** and the **White Birchtree**. Cameron also designed the **Pavilion of Three Graces**, the **Temple of Friendship** (1782) and the **Apollo Colonnade** (1783). Other structures include the **Twelve Paths** (and 12 bronze statues), **Pavilion of the Monument to My Parents** (of Paul I's wife), and the **Mausoleum of Paul I** (the murdered czar is buried in the Peter and Paul Fortress).

Many famous architects such as Brenna, Cameron, Quarenghi, Rossi and Voronikhin worked on the construction of the palace, with its 64 columns and yellow façade. The palace contains an Egyptian vestibule, a library, French, Greek and Italian halls, orchestral chambers, billiard and ball rooms, and the dressing rooms of Empress Maria Fyodorovna and Paul I. Paul had his suites along the north side that included the **Hall of War** (he was obsessed with the military; see Engineer's Castle, page 426). Maria created the **Hall of Peace**. In the south block are Paul's **Throne Room** and the **Hall of the Maltese Knights of St John** of which he was the Grand Master. A very lovely part of the park is known as the Big Star where rows of birch trees radiate out from the center.

The palace and grounds were virtually destroyed during the war (over 70,000 trees were cut down for firewood), but were impressively restored by 1970; luckily nearly 14,000 pieces of furniture and art were evacuated before the occupation, and later returned to their original places. The **Monument to the Defenders of Pavlovsk**, on the grounds north of the palace, is dedicated to all those who died clearing the park of mines after the war. The palace is opened 10am–5pm Saturday–Thursday; if you can only enter by group tour, buy a ticket for one in Russian (which operate frequently), and this will at least get you inside. There is also boating in summer and cross-country skiing in winter.

Pavlovsk is located 30 kilometers (19 miles) south of St Petersburg. To get here, take an *elektrichka* train from Vitebsky Railway Station; they leave every half hour, and the trip takes 35–40 minutes. It is also only one stop from Tsarskoye Selo (station name Detskoye Selo). The entrance to the park is opposite Pavlovsk station. (To get to the front of the palace, you can take bus 370 or 383 from the station or walk 15 minutes.) From the stop by the palace, bus 370 returns to the station and continues on to Tsarskoye Selo near Catherine's Palace only five kilometers (three miles) away. (See Bus Excursions on page 546 for a bus tour from the city.) Cafés are located in the train station, and the Café of Pavlovsk Museum is at 20 Ulitsa Revolutsii, open 11am–5pm Saturday–Thursday. On the road to Pavlovsk, at 16 Filtrovskoye Shosse, Tyarlevo, is the Podvorye Restaurant (tel. 465-1399/1499), open daily 12pm–11pm. It is in a lovely old wooden-style building and serves hearty Russian food and an assortment of wines. At times, a wild cossack ensemble performs.

Gatchina   (Гатчина)

The village of Gatchina, 43 kilometers (27 miles) southwest of St Petersburg, was first mentioned in 15th-century chronicles. In the early 18th century Peter the Great presented his sister Natalya Alekseevna with a farm in the area. In 1765, Catherine the Great acquired the land and gave the estate as a gift to her lover Count Grigory Orlov. Between 1766 and 1781 a palace was built by Rinaldi and a park laid out. After Orlov's death Catherine passed the estate on to her son and heir Paul, who later redesigned the palace into a medieval castle. During his reign Paul I was a terribly paranoid czar (and for good reason—he was later murdered); he had the architect Brenna add sentry boxes, toll-gates and a military parade ground, and build a moat, fortress and drawbridges around the castle. After Paul's death the estate remained neglected until Alexander III made Gatchina his permanent residence. (Alexander was terrified of revolutionary elements and felt safe here after his own father was assassinated.) The grounds were badly damaged during World War

II—the area was occupied by German forces for two years—and have not yet been fully restored. Here one can really get some idea of the havoc caused by the intense German shelling to Leningrad and the environs.

Gatchina Park surrounds **White Lake**. The park lands were mainly designed by a pair of Englishmen: Mr Sparrow and Mr Bush. At the end of the lake there is a lovely little **Temple to Venus** on the Island of Love. Behind Long Island is **Silver Lake**, which never freezes over; the first Russian submarine was tested here in 1879. On the northeastern shore of White Lake is **Birch Cabin** which looks just that from the outside; but inside is an unexpected suite of palatial rooms lined with mirrors. The **Palace** (tel. (271) 13492), with over 500 rooms, is still being renovated, and only a few rooms (with exquisite porcelain collections) are open for a tour 11am–6pm, Tuesdays–Sundays; closed first Tuesday of the month. There is also an exhibit of old weaponry, and a secret underground passage leads to a grotto on the edge of Silver Lake. Near the Pavlovsky Cathedral on Chekhov Ulitsa is the **Shcherbakov Literary Museum**, open 10am–6pm weekends.

Gatchina is a lovely place to spend a day. Pack a picnic; the only place to eat on the estate is in a café near Birch Cabin. Two restaurants (Gatchina and Mercury) are

Russian folk singers perform in front of Catherine's Palace at Tsarskoye Selo. The woman wears a traditional peasant costume—sarafan jumper, embroidered blouse and tall kokoshniki headdress.

The Palace of Paul I, Pavlovsk, is filled with statues, tapestries and hand-painted ceramics. (top left) The Empress' Bedroom was modeled after a state bedroom in Versailles. The bed was crafted in Paris by the Jacob studio. The floor is inlaid with arabesque designs that mirror the painted ceiling. (bottom left) The royal family's private chapel.

located at 10 Krasnaya Ulitsa (near the Cathedral of the Assumption), open daily 12pm–5pm, and at 10 Ulitsa Konstantinova, open daily 12pm–midnight. The easiest way here is by commuter train (about an hour's ride) from Baltiisky Railway Station to Gatchina; from there it is only another ten-minute walk to the grounds. To stay overnight, see hotel listings under Accommodation, page 523.

Novgorod   (Новгород)

Novgorod is one of the oldest towns in all Russia, founded almost 1,200 years ago. The first Varangian leader Rurik settled here by the shores of Ilmen Lake. The northern Slavs named the town Novgorod, meaning New Town. The town served as the main northern trading center between the Varangians and the Greeks. As it grew it became known as Novgorod the Great. The city was one of the few places that escaped the Mongol occupation in the 12th century, while other areas of the country were totally destroyed. There were over 200 churches here. The golden age of Novgorod lay between the 12th and 15th centuries, when wealthy nobles built the kremlin and Byzantine churches, including the **Churches of Saints Boris and Gleb, St Theodore Stratelates** and **Church of Our Transfiguration Savior** which still stand. The city remained a center for trade and religion well into the 16th century. When Novgorod refused to give up its independence, it is said that Ivan the Terrible built a wall around the town, preventing anyone from leaving. Then, after the population still refused his subjugation, he had thousands of people tortured and killed in front of him.

The old town is divided by the River Volkhov. The right bank is known as the Commercial Side where the merchants lived and the markets were held. The left bank, the Sofia Side, is the area of the kremlin and fortress; the prince once governed from within these walls. Novgorod is an excellent example of an old Russian town with its ancient architecture (over 50 old churches and monasteries remain), paintings (icons, frescoes and mosaics) and history (birch-bark manuscripts).

The original wall of the kremlin was laid in about 1000 AD. At this time it was still common practice in Russian towns to lay the first stone over a living child, thought to bring prosperity to the future town. The most famous structure inside the kremlin is the five-domed **Cathedral of St Sophia** (1045–50). The son of Yaroslavl the Wise modeled it after the great cathedral in Kiev, which his father had built.

The **Museum of History, Architecture and Art** is the largest building inside the kremlin; it was built as administrative offices in the 1800s. It is located south of the cathedral. The museum has 35 halls and over 8,000 exhibitions. To the west of the cathedral is the 15th-century **Clock Tower**, whose bell was carried away by the father of Ivan the Terrible. Alongside the tower is the **Faceted Chamber** and on the other side of the cathedral is **St Sophia's Belfry**. The **Millennium Monument** was erected in 1862 to commemorate the 1,000th anniversary of Rurik's arrival in Novgorod.

Across the river on the Commercial Side remains part of a 17th-century arcade, which boasted 1,500 stalls in its heyday. Behind it is **Yaroslavl's Court** and one of the largest surviving churches, **Church of St Nicholas**, built in 1113. Take a number 7 bus three kilometers (two miles) south to the **Yurev Monastery** and the **Open Air Museum of Wooden Architecture**.

In 1998, Novgorod town lawmakers voted to change the city's name back to Novgorod Veliky or Novgorod the Great, bestowed in the 12th century to recognize the town's special status. Today, the town has a population of 234,000. Novgorod is about a three-hour drive (190 kilometers/118 miles) south of St Petersburg on the M20 highway. If you have no access to a car, try going to the Terminal at 36 Obvodnovo Canal Embankment (Ligovsky Prospekt Metro station), where buses depart for Novgorod and Pskov about every two hours; remember to check the departure time of returning buses. Although trains to Novgorod run from the city's Moskovsky Station in the evenings Monday to Saturday, the best time to travel is on the Sunday morning train. (Check, schedules frequently change; see Railways, page 517.) The bus and train stations in Novgorod are located next to each other. A local bus takes you directly to the kremlin. To stay overnight, see the Accommodation section, page 523, for hotel listings. Check with HOFA in St Petersburg for a stay with a private family.

Pskov   (Псков)

Pskov is a few hours farther southwest of Novgorod. Another of Russia's most ancient towns—it was first mentioned in a chronicle in 903. Pskov began as a small outpost of Novgorod and later grew into a commercial center and developed its own school of icon painting. It is still filled with many beautiful churches and icons. Ivan the Terrible tried to annex Pskov, but the town resisted for many years before being subjugated. Rimsky-Korsakov later wrote an opera based on the uprisings called *The Maid of Pskov*. Nicholas II abdicated the throne while in his train at the Pskov station on March 15, 1917. Near Pskov, in the cemetery of the Svyatogorsk Monastery, lies buried the famous poet Alexander Pushkin. For information on getting to Pskov, see Novgorod.

The oldest part of town stands where the Pskova and Velikaya rivers join. Here the 17th-century white **Trinity Cathedral**, the main church, towers above the other wooden buildings of the town. In the early 12th century the stone Mirozhsky Monastery was constructed by the Mirozh River and, in 1150, its **Spas-Transfiguration Cathedral** was consecrated by the Archbishop of Novgorod and Pskov; the monks of the monastery painted all the interior frescoes. One Pskov monk also penned the famous 12th-century epic chronicle, *The Lay of Igor's Host*, based on the fighting campaigns of Prince Igor of Novgorod. (In 1795, Prince Musin-Pushkin discovered these chronicles in Yaroslavl's Savior Monastery (see page 252). To the north lies the **Ivanovsky Monastery** and the white **Predtechensky Church**. Many of the town's churches were named according to their location, such as **St Basil's-on-the-Hill**, **Assumption Church-by-the-Ferry** and **St Nicholas-at-the-Stone Wall**.

East of the City—Lake Ladoga Area

Petrokrepost or Schlüsselburg   (Петрокрепост)

Peter's Fortress, or Petrokrepost, on a small island near the southwestern shore of Lake Ladoga, was founded by Slavs in 1323 to protect the trade waterways linking Novgorod with the Baltic. At that time, the small outpost was known as Oreshek (Nut). When Peter the Great captured the tiny fortress from the Swedes in 1702 (they took control of the lands in the 17th century), he renamed it Schlüsselburg, the Key Fortress. The town of Schlüsselburg sprang up along the left bank of the Neva, where it flows out of the lake. After the Great Northern War ended in 1721, Peter converted the fortress into a prison. He had his sister Maria and first wife Evdokia Lopukhina imprisoned here, and many Russian revolutionaries suffered similar fates. On May 8, 1887, Lenin's brother Alexander Ulyanov, along with four others who attempted to assassinate Czar Alexander III, were hung in the prison yard. The German name of Schlüsselburg was changed to Petrokrepost in 1944 during World War II. If you would like to make a day trip to Petrokrepost, check at your hotel; they can direct you to travel companies which offer bus trips, taking about 45 minutes each way. For more information on bus excursions, try the Intercity Bus Terminal at 36 Obvodnovo Canal Embankment, tel. (814) 166-5777. Open daily 7am–9pm. Ligovsky Prospekt Metro station. By car, take the M18 Highway east. (See also Valaam for boat tours.)

Valaam Island

The Valaam Archipelago (made up of over 50 islands) lies in northwestern Lake Ladoga. Valaam Island is the largest, with 600 residents. The main attraction is the 14th-century **Transfiguration Monastery** which is thought to have first been built as a fortress to protect the area from the Swedes. After it was destroyed by Swedish armies in 1611, Peter the Great later rebuilt it and had the monastery double as a prison. When the territory reverted to Finnish rule between 1918 and 1940, many of the treasures were removed to Finland. Today the inhabitants are mixed with monks, army personnel and restoration workers, and get around by horse and boat. The buildings are protected architectural landmarks and are slowly being renovated; but many remain in a state of neglect.

The most common excursion to Lake Ladoga is by boat from St Petersburg. Cruises leave at night, arrive the next morning and then tour the islands and lake, returning the following morning. If you add Kizhi, the trip becomes four nights/five days. Boats run from mid-May to mid-September, depending when the area is navigable. (For a list of boat companies that tour Lake Ladoga, see Boat Excursions and River Cruises on page 545.)

Kizhi Island

This island lies about 150 kilometers (93 miles) northwest of Lake Ladoga in Lake Onega. Its first settlers arrived in the sixth millennium BC, and ancient petroglyphs are still discernible on some of the rock formations. Between the tenth and 12th centuries inhabitants of Novgorod set out to colonize their own lands along the shores of the lake. The **Church of the Resurrection of Lazarus**, on the islet of Mooch, is one of the oldest buildings in Russia. The main attraction on the island is the wooden 22-domed **Cathedral of the Transfiguration**, built in 1714. It is protected and being slowly restored by UNESCO. Nearby is the 18th-century nine-domed **Church of Intercession**, where icons from the cathedral are displayed. (Other items can be found in the Museum of Fine Arts in the neighboring town of Petrozavodsk.) A climb to the top of the church belfry provides a great panoramic view of the island. Bells of the **Chapel of Archangel Michael** are played in summer. A **Museum of Wooden Architecture** hosts a collection of 19th-century wooden architecture from all around the country. (See Valaam for boat excursions here.) For a virtual tour of Kizhi Island, check out the web-site: http://mars.uthscsa.edu/Russia/

ANNA AKHMATOVA (1889–1966)

In 1889, the Gorenko family of Odessa added a new daughter, Anna. She was destined to become one of Russia's greatest 20th-century lyric poets.

When Anna was one year old, the family moved north to Tsarskoye Selo near St Petersburg, where she lived until she was 16. 'My first memories are those of Tsarskoye Selo,' she later wrote, 'the green grandeur of the parks, the groves where nanny took me, the hippodrome where small, mottled ponies jumped, and the old train station....' (See page 486.)

She wrote her first poem at the age of 10. But poetry was a licentious pastime, according to her father, and he admonished her not to 'befoul his good and respected name.' So, Anna, while still in her teens, changed her surname to Akhmatova, honoring her maternal great-grandmother's Tartar heritage which, supposedly, was traced back to the last khan of the Golden Horde in Russia, Achmat Khan, a descendant of Genghis.

Her first book of poetry, *Evening*, appeared in 1912, and was an immediate success. 'Those pathetic verses of an empty-headed girl,' the astonished author wrote, 'have, no one knows why, been reprinted 13 times.' And yet every young person of the time could recite her *Gray-Eyed King*. Prokofiev later set the lyrics to music.

> Hail to thee, everlasting pain!
> The gray-eyed King died yesterday...
> I will wake up my daughter now.
> And look into her eyes of gray.
> And outside the window the poplars whisper.
> 'Your King is no more on this earth.'

Her second collection, *The Rosary*, was published in 1914. With the publication of Akhmatova's *White Flock* collection, Russian poetry hit the 'real' 20th century. Her recurrent themes of romance and love and the wounded heroine of these poems speaks with intimacy and immediacy.

There is a sacred boundary between those who are close,
And it cannot be transcended by passion or love
Though lips on lips fuse in dreadful silence
And the heart shatters to pieces with love...
Those who strive to reach it are mad, and those
Who reach it are stricken with grief...
Now you understand why my heart
Does not beat faster beneath your hand.

In 1910, Anna married the talented poet Nikolai Gumilyov, who had begun to court her when she was 14. Together they traveled to Italy and then to France where Modigliani made a series of drawings using Anna as his model. Along with her talent, she had tremendous physical beauty. Anna was five-foot-eleven-inches tall, dark-haired, lithe and feline; someone once compared her light green eyes to those of a snow leopard. Positively stunning, she caught the eye of many an artist and sculptor. In addition, a whole volume could be filled with poetry and prose written just about her.

Recollections of the years with Gumilyov echoed many times throughout her poetry.

He loved three things in the world,
Singing at night, white peacocks
and old maps of America.
He hated when children cried,
He hated tea with raspberry jam
And women's hysterics.
...and I was his wife.

Anna was 28 and at the center of Petersburg's artistic world of cabarets and intellectuals when the Romanov dynasty was ousted during the 1917 Revolution. She was 32 when, under Stalin, Gumilyov (by then her ex-husband) was arrested on a charge of plotting against the Soviet Government. He was executed soon afterwards. Her only son, Lev, was later twice arrested and sentenced to many years in a labor camp.

Anna Akhmatova's name began to disappear from the literary scene and from 1925 until 1940 there was an unofficial ban on the publication of all her poetry. In 1935, her second husband Nikolai Punin, an art critic and historian of Western art, was arrested; he soon died in prison. The disappearance and death of friends, harassment by officials, no place to live, hours of waiting in lines for news of her arrested son, all took their voice in her prose-poem *Requiem*, dedicated to those times. Not daring to write anything down on paper, her friends memorized the verses. She wrote it between 1935 and 1940, but it wasn't allowed to be published in Russia until 1987.

> In the terrible years of the Yezhov horrors, I spent 17 months standing in prison lines in Leningrad. One day somebody recognized me. There standing behind me was a woman with blue lips. She had, of course, never heard of me, but she suddenly came out of her stupor so common to us all and whispered in my ear (everybody there spoke only in whispers) 'Can you describe this'? and I said 'Yes, I can.' And then a fleeting smile passed over what had once been her face ...

Even though Akhmatova had opportunities to leave the country during Stalin's Terror, she refused to emigrate. To her, being Russian meant living in Russia, no matter what the government did to her or her loved ones. 'No! Not beneath foreign skies.... I was with my people then.'

Pictures of Akhmatova show a beautiful woman with an aristocratic profile and a proudly raised head—a lioness with sad eyes. In the summer of 1936, a friend of hers wrote, 'She is extraordinary and quite beautiful. Those who have not seen her cannot consider their lives full.'

In November 1941, during the Siege of Leningrad, Akhmatova was evacuated to Tashkent. There she began writing her *Poem Without a Hero* set in the Fontanka House (off of the Fontanka Canal) in St Petersburg. The work consumed her for 22 years; she finished it in 1962. In 1946, after the war, Akhmatova returned to Petersburg, where her popularity was again immense. Because of her growing celebrity, and also possibly because of a meeting with Isaiah Berlin, she was expelled from the Writer's Union and denounced by Zhdanov, Stalin's cultural watchdog, who accused her of poisoning the minds of Soviets; he called her a 'half-nun, half-harlot'.

After this denunciation, Akhmatova was no longer published. She earned her money through translations and writing about accepted poets such as Pushkin. With no official residence, she lived off the help and kindness of friends. The West suspected that she was no longer writing poetry; many in Russia thought that she was no longer alive. But, somehow, she always knew that it was her fate to live through an epoch of interminable grief and upheaval.

In 1956, Akhmatova's son was released from the camps, and the last decade of her life became somewhat easier. She continued to live in the house on the Fontanka and was given the use of a tiny summer house in Komarovo, a writer's colony outside Petersburg. She was allowed to travel twice abroad. In 1964, Anna Akhmatova received the Etna Taormina Literary Prize in Catania, Italy; and in 1965, in England, she received an honorary doctorate from Oxford.

After her death on March 5, 1966, a memorial service was held at the Cathedral of St Nicholas the Seafarer, a 20-minute walk from her house on the Fontanka. It was said that the crowd attending her memorial looked like a human sea. The poet Joseph Brodsky, a close friend, wrote:

'At certain periods of history only poetry is capable of dealing with reality by condensing it into something graspable, something that otherwise couldn't be retained by the mind. In that sense, the whole nation took up the pen name of Akhmatova, which explains her popularity and which, more importantly, enabled her to speak for the nation as well as to tell it something it didn't know... her verses are to survive because they are charged with time....'

Anna Akhmatova (1889–1966) was one of St Petersburg's legendary poets. This portrait of her was painted by Natan Altman in 1914. Earlier, during a trip to Paris in 1910, she befriended the artist Amedeo Modigliani who, enamored with her beauty, frequently sketched her portrait.

And timelessness. She captured the sense of the eternal in her last dated poem of February 1965, at the age of 75.

> So we lowered our eyes,
> Tossing the flowers on the bed,
> We didn't know until the end,
> What to call one another.
> We didn't dare until the end
> To utter first names,
> As if, nearing the goal, we slowed our steps
> On the enchanted way.

A literary critic who visited the house on the Fontanka described her room: 'A bed, or rather a stretcher, covered with a thin, dark blanket stands by the wall: on another wall is a mirror in an ancient gilt frame. Next to it, on a shelf, is a porcelain object, not really valuable but antique. In the corner is a folding icon. By the wall next to the door stands a small rectangular table, with a simple inkstand and a blotter—the desk. There are also one or two old chairs and a worn armchair, but neither wardrobe nor bookshelves. Books are everywhere, on the desk, the chair and on the windowsill.'

Today at 34 Fontanka is the Anna Akhmatova House Museum, which displays these rooms, where she lived and wrote, along with photos, letters and her poetry (see page 426).

Akhmatova never stopped writing about life's tumultuous truths.

> These poems have such hidden meanings
> It's like staring into an abyss.
> And the abyss is enticing and beckoning,
> But never will you discover the bottom of it,
> And never will its hollow silence
> Grow tired of speaking...
>
> I know the gods transformed
> Humans into objects without killing their minds.
> So that my amazing sorrows will live forever...
>
> ...I am not allowed to forget
> The taste of the tears of yesterday.

THE FIREBIRD

*O*nce upon a time, a very long time ago, there was a beautiful girl named Marushka, who was orphaned at an early age. This maiden was capable of embroidering the most beautiful and exquisite patterns on cloths and silks; no one, on all the earth, could match her talents.

Word of her marvelous works spread far and wide, and merchants from all over the world sought Marushka, trying to lure her off to their kingdoms. 'Come away with us,' they pleaded, 'riches and fame will surely be yours.' Marushka always replied, 'I shall never leave the village where I was born. But if you indeed find my work beautiful, then I will sell it to you. If you don't have the money, you can repay me whenever you can. I get my pleasure from the work itself; the money I distribute throughout my village.'

Even though the merchants would leave the village without Marushka, they spread their stories of her incredible talent across the world. The tales finally reached the ears of Kaschei the Immortal, the most wicked of the sorcerers. Kaschei was immediately curious and enraged to think that such beauty existed somewhere that he had never seen. He learned too that Marushka was quite beautiful herself, so he turned himself into the handsomest of princes and flew out over the mountains, oceans, and almost impassable birch forests until he found Marushka's village.

'Where is the maiden who embroiders the most exquisite of patterns?' He was led to her very door, as the villagers were used to the many visitors. When Marushka answered the door herself, the disguised sorcerer asked to see all the needlework and tapestry that she had ready to show. Marushka fetched all her shirts and sashes, towels and trousers, handkerchiefs and hats. Kaschei could hardly contain his delight.

Marushka said, 'My lord, I hope my work pleases you. Anything that meets your fancy is yours to keep. If you don't have the money, you needn't pay me. My happiness comes from your delight.'

Although the great Kaschei could not believe that this girl could fashion things even better than he, he was also taken by her beauty and kindness. He decided that if he could not make such things himself, then he most possess her and take her home to his kingdom.

'Come away with me, and I will make you my queen. You shall live in my palace, all the fruits of my kingdom shall be yours, your clothes shall be covered with jewels, and birds of paradise will sing you to sleep every night. You shall even have your own chamber, containing the most exotic of threads and materials, where you will embroider for me and my kingdom.'

Marushka listened quietly to all this, then she softly replied, 'I couldn't ever leave this village where my parents are buried, where I was born. Here my heart shall always be. There is nothing sweeter than the fields and woods and neighbors of my own village. I must give my embroidery to anyone who receives joy from my work. I could never embroider for you alone.'

The Great Kaschei had never been refused, nor had he ever failed to bewitch a mere girl. Furious, his face suddenly changed from that of the handsome prince to his very own, dark and raging. At this sight, Marushka gasped and tried to flee the room. But it was too late.

'Because you will not leave your village and come to be my queen, because you dared to refuse the Great Kaschei, from this moment on I cast a spell on you. You shall be a bird! I shall make sure that you fly far, far away and never see your village again!'

As he spoke these terrible words, the beautiful Marushka turned into a magnificent, flaming red firebird. In the same moment, the Great Kaschei turned himself into a great black falcon, who swooped down on the firebird, grasping her in his enormous claws. He carried her high into the clouds so she would never return to her birthplace.

Marushka knew that she had to leave something behind. As the great falcon carried her through the sky, the firebird began to shed her flaming plumage. Soon, feather after feather floated down, dusting her beloved homeland. A rainbow of colors dotted the meadows and forests; and by the time the falcon had reached its own kingdom, all her feathers had fallen, leaving a shimmering trail right back to her cottage.

Even though the firebird died, all her magical feathers continued to live forever. The firebird's feathers carried their own spell: All those who loved and honored beauty in themselves and others, as Marushka, and who sought to create beauty for others, without expecting anything in return, would always be able to see the firebird's feathers.

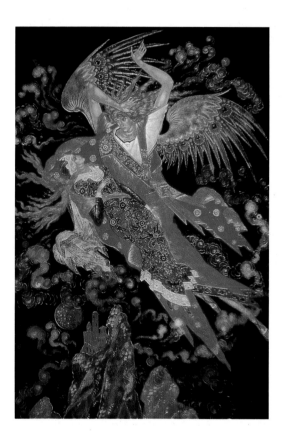

THE RUSSIAN CINEMA

In May 1996, Russia celebrated the centennial of the first movies ever shown in the country. The first motion picture or Cinématographe-Lumière in Russia was shown in St Petersburg on May 4, 1896, at the Aquarium Gardens (now St Petersburg Film Studios). Three weeks later it also opened at Moscow's Hermitage Pleasure Garden. (The first Cinéma, created by the Lumiére brothers, had been shown in Paris on December 28, 1895.) In May 1896, the coronation of the last czar, Nicholas II, was filmed at the Kremlin and Red Square by a team of Parisian filmmakers; the motion picture they produced is regarded as the world's first newsreel. Russia's first feature film, *Stenka Razin* (a popular Russian hero who led a cossack uprising in 1670), premiered on October 15, 1908, and was seven and a half minutes long. Even at this time Russian films were censored by the czar; thus the subject matter focused mainly on mystical dramas or historical costume pieces, such as *The Death of Ivan the Terrible*. Opening in Moscow on October 24, 1917 (and for only one day), *The Silent Ornaments of Life* was about the lives of aristocrat Prince Obolensky and two of his sweethearts. By the next day the Bolshevik Revolution had changed the course of history, along with the future of Russian cinema.

The world's first film school opened in the budding Soviet Union, and the new government recognized the propaganda value of filmmaking. In 1923, film student Lev Kuleshov incorporated his 'Kuleshov technique'—the first pioneering montage effects—in his film *The Strange Adventures of Mr West in the Land of the Bolsheviks*, a satire about an American visitor to Russia. Even after the Revolution, Russia put forth some of the world's most memorable cinematic classics: Pudovkin's *Mother* and Dovzhenko's *Earth* were at the core of the silent cinema. Vertov's *Man with a Movie Camera* became the forerunner to cinéma vérité.

The master of the Golden Age of Russian Cinema was Sergei Mikhailovich Eisenstein, born in 1898 to a Jewish family in Riga, Latvia. In 1914 he moved to Petrograd in order to study architecture and civil engineering. When his authoritarian father joined the White forces in 1918, Sergei rebelled by serving in the Red Army where he studied arts and theater and worked as a poster artist in the psychological action division. By 1920 he was attending classes with leading stage director Vsevolod Meyerhold and working with avant-garde theater groups. As part of a theater production, Eisenstein made his first film in 1923, called

Glumov's Diary, a five-minute interlude for a play by Alexander Ostrovsky. A few years later he followed with his first feature, *Strike*, a criticism of czarist times. Here, the filmmaker created his own form of dramatic montage effects called shocks.

Eisenstein settled in Moscow's Chistoprudny District and lived at 23 Makareno Street, near the Sovremennik Theater. By the age of 27, Sergei had created one of his masterpieces, *Battleship Potemkin*, about the 1905 revolutionary events and mutiny of the battleship crew which culminated in the famous massacre scene on the Odessa steps. (At the Brussels Exhibition in 1958, this classic was voted the Best Film of All Time by a jury of film critics.) *Oktober* was made to celebrate the tenth anniversary of the 1917 Revolution. Supported completely by the government, *Oktober* became the Soviet Union's first film epic; thousands of extras and nearly 50,000 meters of film were used. But upon completion so many political changes had occurred that Eisenstein had to re-edit the film. When it premiered on March 14, 1928, the new version was only 2,800 meters long. A year later, the first sound-film theater (now Znaniye Cinema at 72 Nevsky Prospekt) was opened in Leningrad on October 5, 1929.

In 1930, Eisenstein traveled to Europe and then America where he lived in Hollywood, met Charlie Chaplin and pitched ideas to Paramount

The giant of Soviet cinema, Sergei Eisenstein, wrote, produced, directed and edited many film classics. He wrote in his A History of the Close Up *(1942–46): 'A branch of lilac. White. Double. In lush green of the leaves... it becomes the first childhood impression I can recollect. A close up!'*

Film Studios. American novelist Upton Sinclair offered to help finance Eisenstein's movie about Mexico, *Que Viva Mexico*. In 1932, when Sinclair's wealthy wife broke off their deal with Eisenstein, the director was forced to stop filming with only one episode remaining. (The first version of the Mexican film was edited in 1954, and finally reconstructed in 1979.) After returning to Moscow and suffering the strict confines of Soviet-Realism, Eisenstein suffered a nervous breakdown. For the next few years he was only allowed to make *agitkas*, or propaganda films. Then, after his first sound-speaking film, *Bezhin Meadow*, Eisenstein followed with his brilliant classic, *Alexander Nevsky*, about the Russian hero who, in 1240, defeated invading Teutonic knights. (The famous battle on the ice was shot outside Moscow in summer with artificial snow and ice.) Luckily Stalin liked the film (released in 1938 on the eve of World War II), with its anti-German tones and dramatic musical score by Prokofiev. Eisenstein fell back into favor and received the Order of Lenin. But, over the next three years (a period of Stalin's anti-Semitic stances and ruthless purges), Eisenstein was once again forbidden to practice his craft.

Finally, in 1942, the gifted filmmaker was permitted by ministers Zhdanov and Molotov to begin production on *Ivan the Terrible*, a three-part film epic. (Stalin felt a kinship with Ivan the Terrible and his Opritchniki police forces.) Part one was to be about Ivan IV's rise to power and proclamation as the first czar of all Russia. Filmed during the war years at a special studio in Central Asia, the movie was a triumphant success when it opened on January 16, 1945, and Eisenstein was awarded the Stalin Prize. But later, during the filming of part two, *The Boyars' Plot* (the last sequence was shot in color with Agfa film confiscated from the Germans at the end of the war), the mercurial Stalin staged vicious attacks and forbade the release of the film, demanding reshoots (the picture was not to be screened publicly until 1958). Under terrific strain, Eisenstein died of a heart attack on February 9, 1948, at the age of 50. Stalin allowed him to be buried in Moscow's Novodevichy Cemetery with honors. In 1998 Russia celebrated the centenary of his birth.

After World War II, one of the few themes that could pass by the censor boards of Goskino (Government controlled cinema) was that of the patriotic military. The best films of this genre usually involved the adventures of a hero struggling within the larger context of battle. The most popular included Mikhail Kalatozov's *And the Cranes are Flying* (1957); Sergei Bondarchuk's *This Man's Destiny* (1959); Grigory Chukhrai's *Ballad of a Soldier* (1960); Naum Birman's *Chronicle of the Nose-diving*

Bombardier (1968) and Andrei Tarkovsky's *Ivan's Childhood* which won the Grand Prix at the Venetian Film Festival in 1962. (Tarkovsky went on to make many other classics such as *Andrei Rublyov, Solaris, The Mirror* and *Nostalgia*. His last film *The Sacrifice* was shot in 1985.)

During the mid-1980s, another war film, *A Battlefield Romance* by Pyotr Todorovsky, was nominated for an Oscar (Best Foreign Film). It was only after perestroika that Todorovsky's next film, *Encore, Encore, Encore,* was permitted to paint a depressing portrait of Soviet military life. One of the last successful war genre films was Bodrov's 1997 *Prisoner of the Caucasus*, a realistic portrayal of the war in Chechnya.

After the fall of the Soviet Union, long-banned films were released to packed houses, including Tengiz Abuladze's *Repentence* (about Stalinist horrors); Alexander Askoldov's *The Commissar*; Alexei German's *My Friend Ivan Lapshin*; and Panfilov's *Tema*, whose hero (a censored writer forced to work as a gravedigger to earn a living) utters the memorable line, 'Death is living in a country where one cannot practice the craft that gives one life!'

Once the film censor board was disbanded, scores of realistic films flowed from the studios: *Is It Easy to Be Young?*; *Solovki Power* (about Stalin's Siberian prison island) and *The Humiliated and the Offended* (a dramatized version of Dostoevsky's classic novel with Nastasia Kinsky as the heroine). Other popular films included *Little Vera*, a candid portrayal of a young woman and her family in a small industrial town. Andrei Mikhalkov-Konchalovsky shot *The Inner Circle*, about Stalin's projectionist, and Yevtushenko made *Stalin's Funeral*. Konchalovsky's brother, Nikita Mikhalkov won a 1995 Best Foreign Film Oscar for *Burnt by the Sun*. His other films include *Oblomov* (after a novel by Ivan Goncharov), *Urga, Black Eyes* (with Marcello Mastroanni) and *The Siberian Barber*. Five other Russian films have also won an Academy Award for Best Foreign Film: the first was *Route of the German Troops* (1942); Mark Douskoi's *Rainbow* (1944); Sergei Bondarchuk's *War and Peace* (1967); the Soviet-Japanese production directed by Akiro Kurosawa, *Dersu Uzala* (1976); and Vladimir Menshov's *Moscow Does Not Believe in Tears* (1981). Foreign ventures also came to Russia to produce such feature and television projects as *The Russia House, The Saint* and *Rasputin*.

On average, Russians go to the cinema five times more often than people in the West, and at any one time over 100 features play in Moscow alone. Every alternate summer Moscow hosts a popular International Film Festival.

THE BRONZE HORSEMAN

W*here lonely waters, struggling, sought*
To reach the sea, he (Peter the Great) paused, in thought...
The haughty Swede here we'll curb and hold at bay
And here, to gall him, found a city.
As nature bids so must we do:
A window will we cut here through
On Europe, and a foothold gaining
Upon this coast, the ships we'll hail
Of every flag, and freely sail
These seas, no more ourselves restraining.
A century passed, and there it stood,
Of Northern lands the pride and beauty,
A young, resplendent, gracious city,
Sprung out the dark of mire and wood...
Now there rise great places and towers; a maze
Of sails and mastheads crown the harbor;
Ships of all ports moor here beside
These rich and people shores; the wide,
Majestic Neva slowly labors,
In granite clad, to push its way
'Neath graceful bridges; gardens cover
The once bare isles that dot the river,
Its glassy surface still and grey.
Old Moscow fades beside her rival.
A dowager, she is outshone,
Overshadowed by the new arrival
Who, robed in purple, mounts the throne...

...the weather raged wildly
The Neva swelled and roared,
Gurgling and welling up like a cauldron
Rushed on the city. Before her, all fled...
It was then on Peter's square...
Sat motionless, terribly pale,
Eugene. He was in terror, not for himself...
The widow and her daughter, his fiancée Parasha,
Had been swept away...
Eugene shuddered...above him loomed...
A brazen head in the dusk,
Him by whose fateful will
The city by the sea was founded...
Awesome is he in the surrounding gloom!...
Where are you galloping, haughty steed,
And where will you plant your hooves?
Oh, mighty potentate of fate!
Was it not thus, aloft hard by the abyss,
That with curb of iron
You reared up Russia?...
Scowling, Eugene stood before the prideful statue...
'I'll show you!' And suddenly full tilt...
He runs down the empty square...
But, all night, wherever the wretched madman
Might turn his steps,
Behind him everywhere the Bronze Horseman
Was galloping with heavy clatter...

Alexander Pushkin (1799–1837)

Everything we have comes from Pushkin. His turning to the people so early in his career was so unheard of, so astonishing, such a new and so unexpected departure it can only have been a miracle or, failing that, the fruit of the singular grandeur of genius—one, I might add, we cannot fully appreciate even today.

Fyodor Dostoevsky, A Writer's Journal, 1876

The realm of poetry is as boundless as life itself; yet every object of poetry has been set, from time out of mind, into a specific hierarchy, and to confuse the high with the low or take the one for the other is a major stumbling block. In the great poets, in Pushkin, this harmonious precision in the ranking of objects has been brought to perfection.

Leo Tolstoy, 1874

Alexander Pushkin

St Petersburg Practical Information

Telephone Numbers
Country code for Russia (7)
St Petersburg city code (812)

Emergency Services

Fire	01	Ambulance	03 (See also Medical)
Police	02	Gas Leaks	04

Telephone Information

Time	08	Intercity Information	07
Directory Enquiries	09	Weather	001
Addresses of St Petersburg residents	061	(Four-day forecast 234-1392)	

To order an international call dial 315-0012

Taxis
To order a taxi 24 hrs/day   068, 312-0022, 294-1552, 265-1333
To/from airport and railway stations (Transwell Co.)   113-7253

24-Hour Hotlines
Police Emergency, Info and Help   'KRIK' 315-0272
Report Racketeering/Organized Crime   278-2192

On-Line Services
Traveller's Yellow Pages for St Petersburg: http://www.infoservices.com
St Petersburg Page: http://www.spb.su/sppress
The Entire St Petersburg Telephone Book: http://www.spb.su
AT&T 800 Directory: http://att.net/dir800
Weather: http://www.intellicast.com/weather/led/

Express Mail/Post
DHL, Express Mail Center at 57 Nevsky Prospekt (Nevsky Palace Hotel).
Tel. 326-6400; fax 326-6410. Mon–Fri 9am–6pm; Sat. 10am–4pm.
Other drop-off points located in hotels Astoria, Grand Hotel Europe, Hotelship
Peterhof, Okhtinskaya and Pribaltiiskaya. Web-site: http://www.dhl.com

Federal Express, 2 Mayakovskaya Ul. Tel. 279-1287/1931; fax 273-2139. Mon–Fri 9am–6pm; Sat 9am–2pm. Web-site: http://www.fedex.com
TNT Express Worldwide, 12 Shturmanskaya Ul. Tel. 122-9670, 104-3840; fax 104-3684. Mon–Fri 9am–6pm.
UPS, 31 Saltykova-Shchedrina. Tel. 327-8540; fax 275-4405; web-site: http://www.ups.com

USEFUL PUBLICATIONS IN ENGLISH

Many foreign newspapers and magazines can be found in hotel shops and magazine kiosks. Russia-on-line web-site: http://win.www.online.ru/main/rnews/

Neva News was the first English language newspaper. *Pulse St Petersburg* is published monthly with city cultural news and events. *St Petersburg Times* is the best way to find out what's happening in the city. *St Petersburg Day & Night* is filled with city news. *Moscow Times* has news on Moscow, Russia and the world. *The Travellers' Yellow Pages of St Petersburg* contains over 7,000 useful addresses; on sale in stores throughout the city. Tel. 315-6412; fax 312-7341. See web-site on previous page.

MEDICAL

Most top-end hotels have a resident nurse or doctor.
Clinic Complex, 22 Moskovsky Pr. 24-hr. Tel. 316-6272, 110-1102; fax 316-5939. 24-hour emergency coverage, house calls at house or hotel, ambulance services.
American Medical Center, 10 Serpukhovskaya Ul. Tel. 325-6101; fax 325-6120. 24 hours. (Arranges medical evacuations.)
Emergency Medical Consulting, 14 Izmailovsly Pr. Tel. 112-6510/6512; fax 112-6508. 24 hours. Drug prescriptions/pharmacies can be arranged.

DENTAL

American Medical Center, see Medical, above.
ABC Dental, 2 Krasny Tekstilshchikov Ul. Tel. 271-8954; tel/fax 271-1509. Mon–Fri 9am–9pm; Sat 9am–4pm.
Clinic Complex, see Medical, above. Tel. 316-6272; 110-1273. Mon–Fri 9am–9pm; Sat 9am–3pm.

CONSULATES

Web-site: Consultates of Russia http://www.vidbros.com/consul/address.html
Australia, tel. (095) 956-6070 (in Moscow).
Austria, 43 Furshtatskaya Ul. Tel. 275-0502. Honorary consulate. Visa department in Moscow. Mon–Fri 10am–6pm; visitors 10am–1pm.

Bulgaria, 27 Ryleeva Ul. Tel. 273-7347. Mon–Fri 9am–5pm; visitors 10am–12:30pm.
Canada, 32 Malodetskoselsky Pr. Tel. 325-8448. Mon–Fri 10am–5pm; closed 1–2pm.
China, 134 Griboedova Canal Emb. Tel. 114-6230. Mon/Wed 9:30–11:30am.
Cuba, 37 Ryleeva Ul. Tel. 272-5303. Mon–Fri 9am–7pm; closed 1–2pm.
Czech Republic, 5 Tverskaya Ul. Tel. 271-0459. Mon–Fri 9–18; visa department Mon/Tues/Thurs/Fri 10am–1pm.
Denmark, 13 Bol. Alleya, Stone Island. Tel. 234-3755. Mon–Fri 10am–4pm. Visa 11am–1pm.
Estonia, 14 Bol. Monetnaya Ul. Tel. 233-5548. Mon–Fri 9am–6pm.
Finland, 71 Ul. Tchaikovskovo. Tel. 273-7321. Mon–Fri 8:30am–4pm. The visa department is located nearby at 17 Chernyshevskaya Ul. Tel. 272-2082; 279-1102. Mon–Fri 9am–3:30pm; closed 11:30am–1:30pm.
France, 15 Moika River Emb. Tel. 312-1130; 311-8511. Mon–Fri 9:30am–6pm; closed 1–3pm.
Germany, 39 Furshtatskaya Ul. Tel. 327-3111. Mon–Thur 8am–4pm; Fri 8am–3pm.
Great Britain, 5 Proletarsky Diktatury. Tel. 325-6166/6036. Visas Mon–Fri, applications 9:45am–12:15pm; issued 4–5pm.
Hungary, 15 Ul. Marata. Tel. 312-6753/6458. Visas Tues/Wed/Fri 10am–12pm.
India, 35 Ryleeva Ul. Tel. 272-1731/1988. Visas Mon–Fri 10:30–12:30pm.
Italy, 10 Teatralnaya Pl. Tel. 312-3106/3217. Visas Mon–Fri 9:30am–12:30pm.
Latvia, 34 Ul. Kuibysheva. Tel. 230-3374. Visas Mon/Tues/Thurs/Fri 9:30am–12:30pm.
Lithuania, 4 Gorokhovaya Ul. Tel. 314-5857. Visas Mon–Thurs, applications 9am–1pm; issued 4–5pm and Fri 11am–12pm.
Netherlands, 118 Morisa Toreza Pr. Tel. 554-4900/4890; visas tel. 553-1691. Mon–Fri 9am–5pm.
Norway, 8 21-ya Liniya, 4th fl. Tel. 213-7610/1992. Visas Mon–Fri, applications 10am–12pm; issued 12–1pm.
Poland, 12/14 5-ya Sovetskaya Ul. Tel. 274-4170. Mon–Fri 9am–1pm.
Sweden, 11 10-ya Liniya. Tel. 218-3527; visas tel. 213-4191. Visas Mon/Tues/Wed/Fri 9am–12pm.
Thailand, 9/6 Bolshoi Pr. Tel. 325-6271. Mon–Fri 11am–1pm.
United States, 15 Furshtatskaya Ul. Tel. 274-8235; 275-1701. Mon–Fri 10am–4pm. (Visa by appointment.) Commercial Dept. 57 Bol. Morskaya. Tel. 110-6656.

AIRPORTS
Flight Schedule Information
Pulkovo-II (International). Tel. 104-3444.
Pulkovo-I (flights throughout Russia and CIS). Tel. 104-3822.

Rzhevka (east of St Petersburg, now used only for air cargo). Tel. 527-5208.
Levashovo Sports Airport is 20 kilometers (12 miles) northwest of the city. Tel. 594-9519.

AIRLINES

Web-site: train and flight schedules to/from St Petersburg:
http://www.kenga.ru/travel/index.htm

Aeroflot, Central Air Communication Agency, 7/9 Nevsky Prospekt. Tel. 315-0072. Mon–Fri 8am–8pm; Sat/Sun 8am–6pm. Reservations for Russia and CIS, tel. 311-8093. Other locations at Moskva Hotel, 27 Kamennostrovsky Pr. (tel. 272-6879) and 47 Gorokhovaya Ul. (tel. 310-0709). Web-site: http://www.aerflot.org/

Air France, 35 Bolshaya Morskaya. Tel. 325-8252. Pulkovo-II tel. 104-3433. Web-site: http://www.airfrance.com

Austrian Airlines, 57 Nevsky Pr. at Nevsky Palace Hotel. Tel. 325-3260. Pulkovo-II tel. 104-3443.

Balkan Airlines, 36 Bolshaya Morskaya Ul. Tel. 315-5030/5019. Pulkovo-II tel 104-3436.

Baltic Airlines, 9 Razezzhaya Ul. Tel. 315-3458. Helicoptor excursions to Pushkin, Pavlovsk, Novgorod, Pskov, Kizhi and Helsinki.

British Airways and Deutsche BA, 57 Nevsky Pr. at Nevsky Palace Hotel. Tel. 325-6222. Pulkovo-II tel. 104-3749. Web-site: www.british-airways.com

CSA Czech Airlines, 36 Bolshaya Morskaya. Tel. 315-5259. Pulkovo-II tel. 104-3430.

Delta Airlines, 36 Bolshaya Morskaya. Tel. 311-5819. Pulkovo-II tel. 104-3438.

El-Al, 21 Baskov Lane. Tel. 275-1720/21.

Finnair, 19 Malaya Morskaya. Tel. 315-9736; 314-3645. Pulkovo-II tel. 104-3629. Web-site: http://www.finnair.com

KLM, 5 Zagorodny Lane. Tel. 325-8989. Pulkovo-II tel. 104-3440. Web-site: http://www.klm.tnl

LOT, 1 Karavannaya Ul. Tel. 272-2982; 273-5721. Pulkovo-II tel. 104-3432.

Lufthansa, 7 Voznesensky Pr., 314-4979/5917. Pulkovo-II tel. 104-3661. Web-site: http://www.lufthansa.com

Malev, 7 Voznesensky Pr. Tel. 315-5455. Pulkovo-II tel. 104-3435.

SAS, 57 Nevsky Pr. at Nevsky Palace Hotel. Tel. 325-3255. Pulkovo-II tel. 104-3443. Web-site: http://www.sas.se

Swissair, 57 Nevsky Pr. at Nevsky Palace Hotel. Tel. 325-3250. Pulkovo-II tel. 104-3443.

Transaero, 48 Liteiny Pr. Tel. 279-1974/6463.

Railways

See Getting Around section, page 62, for more details on train travel and buying tickets. For info about trains from all stations: tel. 168-0111. Web-site for schedule of international passenger trains: http://www.relis.ru:8080/MEDIA/train/frames.html. Web-site for train/flight schedules to/from St Petersburg: http://www.kenga.ru/travel/index.htm. Ticket windows at each station sell same-day and advance (up to 45 days) tickets. Each station has both long distance and local electric/commuter trains. (The practice of foreigners having to pay for local or international tickets in foreign currency is slowly becoming obsolete. You can request to pay in rubles.) To book tickets for home delivery call 201 (takes 2–3 days; pay upon delivery).

The **Central Railway Ticket Office**, 24 Nab. Ekaterininskovo Kanala. Info. tel. 162-3344. Mon–Sat 8am–8pm; Sun 8am–4pm. Metro Nevsky Prospekt. Tickets for any station or destination.

Baltic Station (Baltiisky Vokzal), 120 Obvodnovo Kanala. Metro Baltiiskaya. Trains include those to Moscow, Peterhof, Gatchina and Oranienbaum. Tickets for the ER-200 fast train to Moscow can be bought at the ticket booth to the right of the square. Tel. 168-2859.

Finland Station (Finlyansky Vokzal), 6 Lenina Pl. Metro Ploshchad Lenina. Trains include those to Helsinki, Finland, Vyborg, Lake Ladoga, Repino, Razliv and Olgino. Tel. 168-7687.

Moscow Station (Moskovsky Vokzal), 85 Nevsky Pr. Metro Ploshchad Vosstaniya. Trains include those to Moscow, Novgorod and many other points north and south. Connection to Trans-Siberian express. Ticket windows on 2nd floor near train platforms. Commuter tickets sold on right side of station. Tel. 168-4597.

Vitebsk Station (Vitebsky Vokzal), 52 Zagorodny Pr. Metro Pushkinskaya. Trains to southwest Russia, and direct trains to Brussels. Tel. 168-5807.

Warsaw Station (Varshavsky Vokzal), 118 Obvodnovo Kanala. Metro Baltiiskaya. Trains include to western Europe and western Russia/CIS. Tel. 168-2690.

Accommodation

Useful web-site: hotels of St Petersburg: http://www.teleart.ru/ep/hotel/index.htm (For more information see Being There/Hotels section, page 66.)

DELUXE—FIVE STAR

Grand Hotel Europe, 1/7 Mikhailovsky Ul. (off Nevsky Pr.), is the former Evropeiskaya Hotel. After a lengthy restoration to its turn-of-the-century glory, the hotel was reopened in December 1991 and is now managed by Kempinski Hotels. Tel. 329-6000; fax 329-6001; e-mail: res@ghe.spb.ru or sales@ghe.spb.ru. It has 301 rooms, four restaurants, three bars, shops, a health club, billiard room, business center, AMEX office and nightclub. Sadko's Restaurant next door is one of the city's most popular hangouts. Metro Nevsky Prospekt.

Nevsky Palace Hotel, five-star hotel at 57 Nevsky Pr., has 287 rooms, five restaurants, a shopping arcade, fitness club (with pool and sauna) and business center. The hotel was built in 1861, and restored and reopened in 1993. As of 1998, run by ITT Sheraton. Tel. 275-2001; fax 301-7323. (Also contact Sheraton International for reservations.) Metro Mayakovskaya/Ploshchad Vosstaniya.

Severnaya Korona, the North Crown Hotel, on the same island as Peter and Paul Fortress, opened in the winter of 1997. It is located at 37 Karpovki River Emb., near Metro Petrogradskaya. Tel. 329-7000; fax 329-7001. It has four restaurants, a business center and fitness facilities with sauna and pool.

HIGH-END

Astoria, 39 Bolshaya Morskaya Ul., is located by St Issac's Cathedral. Restored to its art-nouveau grandeur, the four-star hotel is split in two sections, new and old (the old wing lies along the far corner of the street). It has three restaurants, bars, fitness (with sauna) and business centers, and casino. The Zimniy Sad (Winter Garden) Restaurant has good food, along with evening classical concerts. The best of the non joint venture hotels. Tel. 210-5757, 210-5132; fax 210-5133, 210-5059. Metro Nevsky Prospekt.

Askur, once a dacha for high-ranking Party officials (and formerly called the Petrodin Hotel), it is located a bit far from the center in a lovely park on Kamenny Ostrov (Stone Island) at 7/1-ya Berezovaya Alley. Seven luxury rooms with a restaurant and bar, billiards and tennis courts. Tel 234-4588. Metro Chornaya Rechka/Petrogradskaya.

Hotelship Peterhof, a Swiss venture, is located by Makarov pier near Tuchkov Bridge, by Lenin Stadium. Tel. 325-8888; fax 325-8889. (For reservations from abroad, contact I C H Management in Switzerland, tel. (41) 55-27-2755, 55-27-5617; fax (41) 55-27-2788, 55-27-3174. This four-star hotel has double and single cabins, a restaurant and bar, nightclub and casino, and a fitness center. Metro Vasileostrovskaya (across the Neva).

Pribaltiiskaya Hotel, is located at 14 Korablestroiteley way out on Vasilyevsky Island by the Gulf of Finland (a half-hour Metro ride from city center). Tel. 356-0001/3001; fax 356-4496. This three-star hotel, built in 1978, has 1,200 rooms (ask for a water view), a bowling alley, business and fitness center (with sauna), four restaurants, bars and shops. One of the city's largest department stores is across the street. Metro Primorskaya.

Pulkovskaya Hotel, 5/2 Pobedy Ploshchad. Tel. 123-5122/5022; fax 264-6396/5844, is a four-star hotel (built in 1981), with 840 rooms, two restaurants, bar, fitness (with sauna) and business centers, and tennis courts. Metro Moskovskaya (8 kilometers (5 miles) south of the center).

MODERATE

Deson-Ladoga Hotel, at 26 Shaumyana Pr., has a restaurant and bar, sauna, and business center. Tel. 528-5200/5393/5450; fax 528-5448. It is one block east of Novocherkasskaya Metro station, across the Neva from the Alexander-Nevsky Monastery.

Hotel Helen-Sovietskaya, a three-star Russian-Finnish joint venture, is at 43-45 Lermontovsky Pr., 3 kilometers (2 miles) southwest of the Hermitage, by the Fontanka. Tel. 251-6101, 329-0181, 259-2552; fax 113-0859, 329-0188, 251-8890. Reservations can also be made through Arctia Hotels in Helsinki at (358-0) 694-8022. It has a Bavarian pub, pizzeria, grill, sauna, shops, and business center. Metro Baltiyskaya.

LDM Complex Hotel, at 47 Ul. Professora Papova, has two restaurants, three bars, a business center, sauna, pool, shops and casino. Tel. 234-5341/2825; fax 234-9818. Metro Petrogradskaya, near the Karpovki River.

Mercury Hotel, at 39 Tavricheskaya Ul., near the Smolny Cathedral, originally hosted regional Party officials. Located in a quiet residential area, it has a bar and restaurant, and winter garden. Tel. 325-6444; fax 276-1977. Metro Chernyshevskaya.

Moskva Hotel, at 2 Alexander Nevsky Square, just opposite the monastery. Though a bit drab now, it has a restaurant and bar, business center and the Neva Star Shop. Tel. 274-3001; fax 274-2130/2102. Metro Ploshchad Aleksandra Nevskovo.

Neptun Hotel, managed by Best-Western, is at 93a Nab. Obvodnovo Kanala, about a ten-minute walk from Metro Baltiiyskaya on the Obvodny canal. Tel. 315-4851, 210-1707; fax 311-2270. (May be closed for renovation.)

Neva, at 17 Chaikovskovo Ul., has a restaurant, bar and souvenir kiosk. Tel. 278-0500; fax 273-2593. Centrally located near Metro Chernyshevskaya.

Okhtinskaya Hotel, a French-Russian joint venture at 4 Bolsheokhtinsky Pr. and Sverdlovsky Emb., is situtated on the Vyborg side of the river across from the Smolny Cathedral. It has 300 rooms, a restaurant and bar, fitness room and sauna, business center and great Italian deli. Tel. 227-4438; fax 227-2618. Metro Novocherkasskaya.

Oktyabrskaya Hotel, was the Grand Hotel du Nord in czarist times (1847); the terrific central location makes up for the present uninviting atmosphere still left over from Soviet occupation. Has fairly shabby rooms, a restaurant and bar, workout room and business center. At 10 Ligovsky Prospect, off Nevsky Pr. near Metro Ploshchad Vosstaniya. Tel. 277-6330; fax 315-7501.

Pallada Hotelship, at 6a Ul. Smolnovo (along the Neva), has 100 rooms, along with

a restaurant, bar and sauna. Tel. 325-1916; fax 279-8100. Metro Chernyshevskaya.
Prin Hotel, has 32 rooms and a restaurant, bar and business center. Tel. 184-3550, 185-4949; fax 185-4970. Located at 4 Vozrozhdeniya Ul., near Metro Kirovsky Zavod, south of the Baltiisky Railway Station.
St Petersburg Hotel, at 5/2 Pirogovskaya Emb., on the Vyborg Side, opposite the Aurora. A large renovation took place in 1991 after nearly burning down (a TV exploded and set fire to several floors). It has a restaurant and bar, sauna, food store and business center. Ask for a water view. Tel. 542-9101/9411; fax 248-8002. A 15-minute walk to Metro Ploshchad Lenina by the Finland Station.

INEXPENSIVE
Bolshoi Teatr Kukol, or the Big Puppet Theater Hotel, is located at 12 Nekrasov Ul. by the theatre. Tel. 273-3996. If not booked by visiting performers, you may get in. Metro Gostiny Dvor.
Druzba, or Friendship Hotel has 30 double rooms with a restaurant, bar and sauna. Tel. 234-1844; fax 234-6727. Located at 4 Chapygina Ul., at the foot of the TV Tower, a ten-minute walk to Metro Petrogradskaya.
Dvorets Molodyozy, or Palace of Youth is at 47 Professor Popova and a 20-minute walk from Metro Petrogradskaya. Soviet-style outside, with plain rooms inside, including a restaurant and grill-bar. Tel. 234-3278.
Kievskaya Hotel, at 49 Dnepropetrovskaya Ul. by the Obvodny Canal. Tel. 166-0456; fax 166-5398. Metro Ligovsky Prospekt.
Zarya Hotel, a block away from the Kievskaya Hotel at 40 Kurskaya. Tel. 316-8398, 166-5811. Metro Ligovsky Prospekt.
Mir, the Peace Hotel, at 17 Gastello Ul., is next to the Chesma Church. Tel. 108-5166; fax 108-5118. Metro Moskovskaya, south of Victory Park.
Olgino, is located 18 kilometers (11 miles) northwest of the center in pine forests at 59 Primorskoye. Very far away and inconvenient for public transport; unless heading for the Finnish border, find a hotel closer to town. It does have camp-grounds in summer (and you can rent horses to ride), but should be booked in advance; careful, crime is on the increase. Tel. 238-3550/3009.
Rechnya, at 195 Obukhovskoy Oborony Pr., has a restaurant and grill-bar. Tel. 267-3196, 262-8971. Metro Proletarskaya, near Passenger River Port.
Rossiya, located at 11 Chernyshevskovo Pl., a classic Soviet-style block hotel with a café-bar and sports center with sauna. Tel. 296-7649/7349; fax 296-3303. Metro Park Pobedy, near Victory Park.
Hotel Rus, at 1 Artilleryskaya Ul., a two-star modern hotel with café-bar, sauna and business center. Tel. 279-5003, 273-4683; fax 279-3600. Metro Chernyshevskaya.
Sputnik Hotel, in a quiet neighborhood at 34 Morisa Toreza. (Rooms with both

attached and communal baths.) Has a restaurant, nightclub and casino, and sauna. Tel. 552-5632; fax 552-8084. A ten-minute walk from Metro Ploshchad Muzhestva in the northeast part of town.

Veronika, a small and cozy hotel with 14 rooms, situated at 6 Generala Khruleva Ul., near Metro Pionerskaya in the northern part of town across the Bolshaya Neva. Tel. 395-1373.

Vyborgskaya Hotel, three buildings located at 3 Torzhkovskaya Ul., across the river, north of Petrovsky Island. Rooms have either attached or communal baths. It also has a restaurant with live music and a sauna. Tel. 246-2319/9141/9101; fax 246-8187. Metro Chornaya Rechka.

HOSTELS

HI St Petersburg Hostel, is the city's first Hostelling International member, and is run by American and Russian partners. Rooms have two to six beds; a downstairs video café shows movies! A five-minute walk from Moscow Station/Metro Ploshchad Vosstaniya to 28 3-ya Sovietskaya Ul. The Hostel also provides visa support, and has the travel agency Sindbad Travel for train and plane travel. Tel. 329-8018, 327-8384. Reservations can be made directly by fax on 329-8019, or by e-mail to: bookings@ryh.spb.suby (general e-mail: ryh@ryh.spb.su), or by contacting any HI Hostel on the IBN intl. booking system. (It also takes reservations for other Russian Youth Hostels, RYHA.) Web-site: http://www.spb.su/ryh

Hostel Holiday, became St Petersburg's second western-style hostel in 1994. Located at 1 Mikhailova Ul. (3rd floor), south of Finland Station and Metro Ploshchad Lenina. Tel/fax 542-7364. Dormitory rooms (up to five beds) with a rooftop café. (Ask for a river view.) Also provides visa invitations. One drawback is the Kresty prison next door; it is perfectly safe, but one tends periodically to hear voices of families calling to inmates inside!

Summer Hostel, at 26 Baltiiskaya Ul., about a ten-minute Metro ride from the city center south to Metro Narvskaya. There are two wings on the third floor. The building also has a health club with sauna (for a few extra dollars charge). You can book with them directly at tel. 252-7763; fax 252-4011/4019. Or you can make reservations though IBN or RYHA.

Student Dormitory, centrally located behind the Kazan Cathedral at 6 Plekhanova Ul. with comfortable singles and doubles. Try calling first; it is usually quite full in summer months. Tel. 314-7472. Metro Nevsky Prospekt.

BED & BREAKFASTS

American International Homestays, sets up homestays in numerous cities throughout Russia. PO Box 1754, Nederland, Colorado 80466. Tel. (800) 876-2048, (303)

642-3088; fax (303) 642-3365; e-mail: ash@igc.apc.org; web-site: http://www.com-merce.com/homestays/

International Bed & Breakfast, comfortable and inexpensive accommodation provided in Moscow, St Petersburg, Novgorod and other cities in Russia and Eastern Europe. English-speaking host families. Visa support. PO Box 823, Huntingdon Valley, Pennsylvania 19006. Tel. (800) 422-5283, (215) 663-1438; fax (215) 379-3363; e-mail: ibb@dca.net; web-site: http//www.ibed.com

St Petersburg Host Family Association (HOFA), places travelers with Russian families (generally professionals who speak English) in their apartments. You usually get a private room with breakfast included and a shared bathroom. Generally, the room can be rented from one day up to several weeks with a discount in price. Payment is made directly to the host family; HOFA will provide a business invitation and OVIR registration. Tel/fax 275-1992/395/1338; e-mail: alexei@hofak.hop.stu.neva.ru; web-site: http://www.spb.ru/~homestays. They are located at 5 Tavricheskaya Ul. Apt. 25, 193015. Open 9am–6pm. To receive a booklet about HOFA, in the US tel. (202) 333-9343; fax (202) 337-6090; e-mail: hofa@usa.net

Shakti, arranges similar homestays. The price also includes a business visa and OVIR registration. Tel. 279-5198; e-mail: cas@spectron.spb.su

Traveller's Guest House Moscow, can also book rooms in St Petersburg. Tel. (7-095) 971-4059; e-mail tgh@glas.apc.org

Peter TIPS, offers rooms and apartments on a daily to monthly basis and visa support. Located in Dom Aktyor (House of Actors) at 86 Nevsky Prospekt. It also offers free hotel booking and visa services. Tel. 279-0037; fax 275-0806.

PRIVATE APARTMENTS

Russian residents now approach travelers as they arrive in train stations offering a place to stay. Most of these people are professionals and just in need of some extra cash. (Many grandmothers on pension receive only $25/month.) Trust your instincts, make sure it is not too far from the city center, and do not commit yourself until you see the room. Bargain prices can be negotiated. Many train stations now have a small bureau with a dispatcher who has a list of residents with rooms to rent.

CAMPING

Because of the rising crime rates, camping is not really recommended.

Retur, Motel-Camping is 29 kilometers (18 miles) out of town at 202 Primorskoe Shosse. It offers chalets or camp sites on the Gulf of Finland. It also has a restaurant and bar, sauna and swimming pool, and tennis courts. Tel. 437-7533; fax 434-5022. Public transportation to the city center is long and tedious.

Olgino Camping (see Olgino Hotel, page 520).

VICINITY OF ST PETERSBURG
(also see listings under Bed & Breakfasts, page 521)

■GATCHINA

Gatchina Hotel, at 77 Chkalova Ul., has restaurant and bar, sauna and swimming pool. Tel. (271) 1-14-58.
Akademicheskaya, at 12 Krupskoy Ul., run by the Institute of Nuclear Physics. Tel. (271) 3-56-11/3-57-00.

■NOVGOROD

Beresta Palace Hotel, one of the first Austrian-built Marco Polo Hotels in Russia. Located on Studencheskaya Ul. Tel. (816) 34-747; fax (816) 31-707.
Sadko Hotel is less expensive at 16 Fyodorovsky Ruchey. Tel. (816) 75-366.
Intourist Hotel, located across the river from the Beresta. The rooms are standard old Soviet-fare and poorly maintained.

■PETERHOF

Chaika, or the Seagull Hotel is located at 16 Shakhmatova Ul. It has rooms and apartments, a restaurant and café. Tel. 428-6892.
Hotel Complex of St Petersburg Univ., is located at 66/4 Botanicheskaya Ul. Tel. 428-4603.

■TSARSKOYE SELO OR PUSHKIN

Chaika, or the Seagull Hotel is at 32/15 Shishkova Ul. Tel. 465-9407.

■REPINO

Repinskaya Hotel, (Repino Tour Hotel) has 40 rooms, a restaurant and bar, sauna, and winter ski and sleigh rentals. Located in the town of Repino at 428 Primorskoye Shosse. Tel. 231-6627/6530; fax 231-6621. At 427 is the **Baltiets Health Resort**, with pool, sauna and massage. Tel. 231-6221.

DINING

Surprise! St Petersburg has changed dramatically over the last several years. There are now over 1,000 eating establishments from corner take-outs to elegant dining in restored palaces; practically every street in the city center has a place that offers a bite of something. And besides Russian rubles, many now take major credit cards and/or foreign currency. The larger hotels all have their own restaurants and cafés. And most restaurants have a bar or a selection of liquors available. The city offers a wide range of dishes that include Russian, Georgian, Armenian, Uzbek, Azerbaijani, European, Asian,

Arabian, Mexican and American—with or without music and entertainment. Prices vary from cheap to extremely expensive. For the more upscale or popular eateries, reservations are recommended. (For more information, see Food section, page 73.)

So many food stores and supermarkets have opened up, from grocery stores and gastronomes to 24-hour mini-markets; just ask the staff of your hotel to direct you to the nearest one. A Westerner can now find practically everything that is available at home. (Most take rubles and some accept credit cards.) Some of the larger supermarket chains are Babylon and Kosmos; and *24-chasa* (24-hour) round-the-clock open markets dot the city. **Yeliseyev's**, at 58 Nevsky Prospekt, is the original lavish 19th-century grocery palace.

CITY CENTER

Arirang, 20/8-ya Sovetskaya Ul., tel. 274-0466. Korean fare. Daily 11am–11pm. Metro Pl. Vosstaniya.

Bagdad Café, 35 Furshtatskaya Ul., tel. 272-2355. Uzbek and European. Daily 11am–11pm. Metro Chernyshevskaya.

Bella Leone, 9 Vladimirsky Pr., tel. 113-1670. Italian cuisine and piano music. Daily 12pm–1am. Metro Vladimirskaya.

Graf (Count) Suvorov, 6 Lomonsova Ul., tel. 315-4328. European/seafood. Daily 11am–11pm. Metro Gostiny Dvor.

House of Architects Nikolai Restaurant, 52 Bol. Morskaya (five-minutes' walk from St Issac's Cathedral), tel. 311-1402. European dishes. Daily 12pm–12am. Metro Nevsky Pr.

Krasny Terem (Red Tower), 10 Razezzhaya Ul., tel. 315-9145. Chinese food. Daily 12pm–12am. Metro Vladimirskaya.

Krunk, 14 Solyanoy Lane, tel. 273-3830. Armenian and European. Daily 1–11pm. Metro Gostiny Dvor.

Metekhi, 3 Belinskovo Ul., tel. 272-3361. Georgian cooking. Daily 11am–8pm. Metro Gostiny Dovr.

Nairi, 6 Dekabristov Ul., tel. 314-8093. Armenian food. Daily 11–12am. Metro Sadovaya.

Okhotnichy Klub (Hunter's), 45 Gorokhovaya Ul., tel. 232-3694. Daily 12pm–12am. Metro Sadovaya.

Polonaise, 45 Bol. Morskaya Ul., tel. 315-0339. Russian/European in mansion. Daily 12pm–2am. Metro Sennaya Pl.

Saigon-Neva, 33 Kazanskaya Ul. tel. 315-8772. Vietnamese cooking; Asian decorated interior. Daily 12–11pm. Metro Sennaya Pl.

Shakheraezada, 3 Razezzhaya Ul., tel. 112-4271. Mid-Eastern cooking and good vegetarian selection; Oriental music. Daily 11–5am. Metro Vladimirskaya.

Sudarnaya (Lady), 28 Rubinsteina Ul., tel. 312-6380. Russian food; cozy café. Daily 12–11pm. Metro Dostoevskaya.

Tashkent 1001 Nights, 21 Millionnaya Ul., tel. 312-2265. Uzbek cuisine. Daily 12pm–12am.

Tandoori, 2 Voznensky Pr., tel. 312-3886. Indian cuisine. Daily 12–11pm. Metro Nevsky Pr.

Troika, 27 Zagordny Pr., tel. 113-5343. European with Russian decor. Variety show. Open 7:30pm–1am; closed Mon. Metro Dostoevskaya.

Vena, 13/8 Mal. Morskaya Ul., tel. 311-3227. Austrian food; soft music. Daily 12pm–12am. Metro Nevsky Pr.

Zakarpate, 14 Bol. Morskaya, tel. 315-9536. Food á la trans-Carpathian area. Cozy with live music. Daily 11am–11pm. Next door is the **Yan Dzyn Chinese Restaurant**.

CITY SOUTH

Drakon, 49 Blagodatnaya Ul., tel. 298-6000. European cuisine and piano music. Daily 12pm–12am. Metro Elektrosila.

Korean House, 2 Izmailovsky Pr., tel. 259-9333. South Korean food. Daily 1–10pm. Metro Teknologichesky Inst.

Nectar, 25/12 Malodetskoselsky Pr., tel. 316-6818. Russian/wine tasting. Daily 12–11pm. Metro Teknologichesky Inst.

Pietari, 222 Moskovsky Pr., tel. 293-1809. European food, live music and dance. Daily 12pm–2am. Metro Moskovskaya.

Sakura, 45 Narodnaya Ul., tel. 263-3594. Japanese cuisine. Daily 12–11pm. Metro Lomonovskaya.

Simona, 130 Moskovsky Pr., tel. 294-5277. European. Mon–Sat 12–11pm. Metro Moskovskiye Vorota.

Tetris Internet Café, 33 Ul. Chernyakhovskovo, tel. 164-8759. Intimate; Russian/European. Daily 12pm–12am. Metro Ligovsky Pr.

EKATERININSKY CANAL EMBANKMENT (NABEREZHNAYA EKATERININSKOVO KANALA)

Chaika German Restaurant, 14 Ekaterininsky, tel. 312-4631. German cooking and draught and bottled beer. Daily 11–3am.

Gridnitsa, 20 Ekaterininsky, tel. 310-3420. Grill bar with music. Daily 11am–11pm.

Restaurant St Petersburg, 5 Ekaterininsky, tel. 314-4947. Fine Russian and European cuisine; evening cabaret. Daily 12pm–1am. Next door is the Kafe; daily 12–11pm.

FONTANKA RIVER EMBANKMENT (NABEREZHNAYA REKI FONTANKI)

Ambassador Restaurant, 14 Fontanka, tel. 272-3791. Russian and European food. Daily 12pm–12am. Metro Gostiny Dvor. Ambassador Café next door.

Derzhavinsky, 118 Fontanka, tel. 251-1441. Russian fare and light music. Daily 12pm–12am. Metro Sadovaya.

Kioto, 77 Fontanka, tel. 310-2547. Japanese cuisine. Daily 12pm–12am. Metro Pushkinskaya.

La Cucaracha, 39 Fontanka, tel 110-4006. Mexican. Mon–Thurs/Sun 12pm–1am; Fri/Sat 12pm–5am. Metro Gostiny Dvor.

Na Fontanke, 77 Fontanka, tel. 310-2547. Russian-European with music. Daily 1–11pm.

GREAT BREAKFASTS AND SUNDAY BRUNCHES

Angleterre in the Astoria Hotel. Offers an all-you-can-eat buffet; daily 7–10:30am. Café/bar, also in the hotel, has pastries and cappuccino.

European Restaurant in the Grand Hotel Europe has a daily buffet breakfast (7–10:30am), and Sunday jazz brunch 12–3pm. The Mezzanine Café has pastries and cappuccino.

ICE CREAM PARLORS

Baskin Robbins, locations at 79 Nevsky Pr., 19 Nab. Ekaterininskovo Kanala, 31 Moskovsky Pr. and 19 Prosveshcheniya Pr. Daily 10am–10pm.

Frogs Pool, 24 Nevsky Pr. Daily 10am–9pm.

Gino Ginelli, 14 Nab. Ekaterininskovo Kanala. Italian ices. Daily 10–12am.

Morzh (Walrus), 27 Sadovaya Ul. Daily 10am–10pm.

Kafe-Morozhenoe (Ice Cream Café), at 154 Nevsky Pr., 33 Sadovaya and 32 Stachek Pr. Daily 10am–10pm.

Pingvinchik (Little Penguin), 54 Nevsky Pr. Daily 10am–10pm.

Vienna Café in the Nevsky Palace Hotel, Nevsky Pr.

MOIKA CANAL EMBANKMENT (NABEREZHNAYA REKI MOIKI)

Adamant, 72 Moika, tel. 311-5575. Traditional Russian dishes, steak and seafood. Live music at piano bar. Daily 1pm–12am. Metro Nevsky Pr.

NEVSKY PROSPEKT

Afrodite, 86 Nevsky, tel. 275-7620. Specializes in seafood. Daily 12pm–1am. Metro Mayakovskaya.

Domenicos, 70 Nevsky, tel 272-5717. Russian and European. Music and dancing nightly. Daily 12pm–6am. Metro Gostiny Dvor/Mayakovskaya.

Grand Hotel Europe, 1/7 Mikhailovsky Ul. (off Nevsky), the Brasserie, tel. 329-6000/ext 6637. Italian/Russian food in an elegant interior. Daily 12pm–12am. Chopsticks, tel. ext 6391. Cantonese and Sichuan specialties. Daily 1–11pm.

Europe, tel. ext 6630 Russian and European specialties. Breakfast 7–10:30am; dinner 7–11pm; Sunday brunch 12–3pm; closed Sunday dinner. Jacket and tie required. Mezzanine Café has coffee and pastries. Caviar Bar, daily 5pm–12am.

Fantome, 113 Nevsky, tel. 277-0097. Italian restaurant and nightclub. Daily 12pm–6am. Metro Pl. Vosstaniya.

Kafe 01, 5 Karavannaya Ul. (off Nevsky), tel. 312-1136. Popular Russian food. Daily 12–11pm. Metro Gostiny Dvor.

Literary Café, 18 Nevsky, tel. 312-6057. Dates back to czarist times (Pushkin left for his duel from here); classical music, literary and poetry readings. Daily 11–1am.

Milano, 8 Karavannaya Ul. (off Nevsky), tel. 314-7348. Italian cuisine. Daily 12pm–12am. Metro Nevsky Pr.

Nevsky Palace Hotel, 57 Nevsky, the Admiralty, tel. 275-2001. Traditional Russian. Die Bierstube, has Austrian fare and beer. Open till 1am. Imperial, dinner and breakfast buffets; Sunday jazz brunch. Landskrona, European cuisine with music and dancing in this rooftop restaurant. Café Vienna, coffee, tea and pastries.

Moskva Hotel Arbat, 2 Alexander Nevsky Pl., tel. 274-4001. European food. Daily 12pm–12am. Metro Aleksandra Nevskovo.

Nevsky Restaurant, 71 Nevsky, tel. 311-3093. Russian food and variety shows. Daily 12pm–12am. Metro Mayakovskaya.

Polyarny, 79 Nevsky, tel. 311-8589. Russian/European; live music. Daily 12pm–12am. Metro Pl. Vosstaniya.

Rioni, 136 Nevsky, tel. 277-5893. Georgian food. Daily 11am–8pm. Metro Pl. Vosstaniya.

U Kazansksovo, 26 Nevsky, tel. 314-2745. Russian/European. Daily 11am–10pm. Metro Nevsky Pr.

Warsteiner Forum, 120 Nevsky, tel. 277-5406. German cooking and beer. Daily 12–24. Metro Pl. Vosstaniya.

NORTHEAST

Aladdin, 29 Bol Sampsonievsky Pr., tel. 541-8459. Arabian cuisine. Mon–Sat 12–5pm; Sun 12–11pm. Metro Vyborgskaya.

Aragvi, 41 Ul. Marshala Tukhachevskovo, tel. 545-3451. Georgian dishes. Daily 12pm–12am. Metro Pl. Lenina.

Nobileb, 14 Bol. Sampsonievsky Pr., tel. 245-3644. Italian/European. Daily 12–11pm. Metro Lesnaya.

PETROGRAD SIDE

Antverpen Grand Kafe, 13/2 Konversky Pr., tel. 233-9746/8433. International food, live music and Belgian draught beer. Daily 12pm–12am. Metro Gorkovskaya.

Austeria, at Peter and Paul Fortress, tel. 238-4262. Traditional Russian dishes in quaint 18th-century setting. Live music after 7pm. Daily 12–11pm. Metro Gorkovskaya.

Demyanova Ukha, 53 Kronversky Pr., tel. 232-8090. Seafood. Daily 11am–10pm. Metro Gorkovskaya.

Dionis Club, 31/20 Ul. Voskova, tel. 233-3352. Russian and European. Daily 11am–11pm. Metro Gorkovskaya.

Flora, 5 Kamennoostrovky Pr., tel. 232-3400. Russian food with orchestra. Daily 1pm–2am. Metro Gorkovskaya.

Fortetsiya (Fortress), 7 Ul. Kuibysheva, tel. 233-9468. Russian and Belgian food; classical music. Daily 12pm–12am. Metro Gorkovskaya.

Imperial, 53 Kamennoostrovsky Pr., tel. 234-1742. Russian/European cuisine in court-style interior. Classical and jazz piano. Daily 12pm–12am. Metro Petrogradskaya.

Petro Star, 30 Bol. Pushkarskaya Ul., tel. 232-8760. Russian/European; old-style decor. Daily 12–10pm. Metro Petrogradskaya.

Pirosmani, 14 Bolshoi Pr., tel. 235-4666. Georgian cooking; live music. Daily 12pm–12am. Metro Petrogradskaya.

Russian Modern, 32 Ul. Lenina, tel. 232-6208. Georgian/Russian. Russian piano and violin music. Daily 12–10:30pm. Metro Petrogradskaya.

Tavern on Maly, 48 Maly Pr., tel. 235-4621. Russian food. Open 24 hours. Metro Petrogradskaya.

Tbilisi, 10 Sytninskaya Ul., tel. 232-9391. Georgian and vegetarian food; music. Daily 12–11:30pm. Metro Gorkovskaya.

Tête-à-Tête, 65 Bolshoi Pr., tel. 232-7548. French cooking; piano music. (Only tables for two.) Daily 12–11pm. Metro Petrogradskaya.

Tornado International Club, 24 Maly Pr., tel. 230-8391. Russian/European; orchestra music; catering. Daily 12pm–12am. Metro Petrogradskaya.

Troitsky Most (Trinity Bridge), 2 Mal. Posadskaya., tel. 232-6693. Hare Krishna; vegetarian and herbal teas. Mon–Sat 11am–7pm. Metro Gorkovskaya.

SADOVAYA ULITSA

Ampir, 12 Sadovaya, tel. 314-3138. Russian, European and Chinese. Daily 12pm–12am. Metro Gostiny Dvor.

Diana, 56 Sadovaya, tel. 310-9355. Russian/European with French wines. Daily 12pm–4am. Metro Sennaya Pl.

Metropol, 22 Sadovaya, tel. 310-1845. City's oldest restaurant; Russian food. Daily 12–11pm. Metro Gostiny Dvor.

Shanghai, 12/23 Sadovaya, tel. 311-2751. Chinese cooking; casino/karaoke upstairs. Daily 12–11pm. Metro Gostiny Dvor.

Shashlychnaya, 36 Sadovaya, tel. 310-7946. Shish kebab specialists. Daily 12–10pm. Metro Sennaya Pl.

SENATE SQUARE (SENATSKAYA PLOSHCHAD) AND ST ISAAC'S CATHEDRAL

Astoria Hotel, 39 Bol. Morskaya, Angleterre Restaurant, tel. 210-5906. Russian and European dishes; live music. Daily 7am–11pm. The Astoria, tel. 210-5906. Daily 7am–8pm; closed 10:30am–12:30pm. Zimny Sad (Winter Garden), Russian food; music evenings. Daily 6pm–12am.

Bistro Le Francais, 20 Galernaya Ul., tel. 315-2465. French cuisine and tea shop. Daily 11–3am. Near St Isaac's Cathedral.

Senat, 1 Galernaya Ul., in the Senate Bldg., tel. 314-9253. European cuisine, 50 kinds of Dutch and Belgian beer and selection of wines. Daily 11–5am.

Tribunal, 1 Senate Sq., tel. 311-1690. Under brick arches of Senate Bldg., European food and beers. Live music and disco. Daily 11–3am. Metro Nevsky Pr.

SOUTH

Near Metro Novocherkasskaya (across river from Alexander Nevsky Monastery).

Antaliya, 19/30 Metallistov Pr., tel. 224-0208. Azerbaijani food. Daily 1pm–12am.

Kavkaz, 5 Ul. Stakhanovtsev, tel. 221-4309. Caucasian cuisine. Daily 12pm–12am.

Polese, 4 Sredneokhtinsky Pr., tel. 310-1048. Belorussian cooking. Daily 12:30–11:30pm.

U Petrovicha, 44 Sredneokhtinsky Pr., tel. 227-2135. Russian/European; 18th-century decor. Music and dancing on Thurs/Sun. Daily 12–11pm.

ULITSA DEKABRISTOV

Dvorianskoe Gnezdo, 21 Dekabristov, tel. 312-3205. Russian/European; in restored garden pavilion. Daily 12pm–12am. Metro Sadovaya.

Restaurant 1913, 2/13 Dekabristov, tel. 315-5148. Russian food. Daily 12pm–4am.

Seul, 34 Dekabristov, tel. 114-2527. Korean cuisine. Daily 11am–11pm.

Zolotoi Drakon (Golden Dragon), 62 Dekabristov, tel. 114-8441. Chinese/South Asian cooking. Daily 12pm–12am.

VASILYEVSKY ISLAND

Breeze Café, 70 Bolshoi Pr., tel. 217-8101. Armenian cuisine. Daily 10am–11pm. Metro Vasileostrovskaya.

Delovoi Mir, 103 Bolshoi Pr., tel. 355-5123. Russian and European. Daily 12pm–12pm. Metro Primorksaya.

Fregat, 39 Bolshoi Pr., tel. 213-4923. Peter-the-Great-era cuisine with live music. Daily 11am–10pm. Metro Vasileostrovskaya.

530 MOSCOW & ST PETERSBURG

Hotelship Petership SVIR Restaurant, tel. 325-8888. International cuisine; live music. Daily 12–11pm. Metro Vasileostrovskaya.
Kalinka, 9 Sezdovskaya Liniya, tel. 213-3751. Russian food; folk music. Daily 12pm–12am. Metro Vasileostrovskaya.
Sirin, 16 1-ya Liniya, tel. 213-7282. Russian/European; intimate candlelit tables. Daily 12pm–12am. Metro Vasileostrovskaya.
Solnyshko, 8 Dekabristov Lane, tel. 350-2938. Chinese/Russian. Thurs–Sun 12–11pm. Metro Primorskaya.
Veneziya (Venice), 21 Korablestroiteley Ul., tel. 352-1432. Italian cuisine and wines; variety show. Daily 1pm–5am. (Pizza parlor below.) Metro Primorskaya.

VYBORG SIDE—NORTH
Near Metro Chornaya Rechka (across Bolshaya Nevka River).
Ryabinushka (Little Ashberry Tree), 11 Oskalenko Ul., tel. 239-4080. Meals and desserts. Thurs–Sun 11am–6pm.
Slavyanskoe Podvore (Slavic Town House), 13 Lanskoie Shosse, tel. 246-2256. Traditional Russian. Daily 12pm–12am.
Staraya Derevnya (Old Village), 72 Savushkina Ul., tel. 239-0000. Traditional Russian cooking; art-nouveau decor. Daily 1–10pm.
Uratu, 25 Rudneva Ul., tel. 558-6919. Georgian/Armenian. Daily 12–11pm. Metro Pr. Proveshcheniya.

(For restaurant locations for towns outside St Petersburg, see individual listings under Vicinity of St Petersburg.)

SHOPPING
ANTIQUES
Antik Center, 21 Nalichnaya Ul. Everything from furniture, rugs and jewelry to paintings, china and icons. Mon–Sat 11am–7pm; closed 2–3pm. Metro Primorksaya.
Antikvariat, 5 Pochtamtskaya Ul. Mon–Sat 10am–5pm; closed 2–3pm. Metro Nevsky Pr.
City Antiques, 32 Nab. Moika. Mon–Sat 10am–7pm; closed 2–3pm.
Mikhailovsky Manezh, 2 Manezhnaya Pl. International art exhibitions and auctions. Metro Gostiny Dvor.
Peterburg, 54 Nevsky Pr. Everything from art, furniture and paintings, to icons, coins and antique souvenirs. Mon–Sat 11am–7pm. Metro Nevsky Pr. (Also visit **Gelos** at 151 Nevsky. Mon–Sat 10am–7pm; Sun 10am–6pm. Metro Alek. Nevskovo. And **Na Staronevskom**, 122 Nevsky. Mon–Fri 10am–8pm; Sat/Sun 10am–6pm. Metro Pl. Vosstaniya.)

Russian Antiques, 6 Nekrasova Ul. Mon–Sat 11am–7pm; closed 2–3pm. (Nearby, at 11, is Zerkalo Gallery with displays of paintings and jewelry of the New Romantic school. Metro Chernyshevskaya.)

Secunda, 61 Liteiny Pr. (in courtyard) has posters, postcards, Soviet art and old photos. Mon–Sat 11am–7pm. Metro Mayakovskaya.

Starinnye Chasy (Old Clocks), 19 Bol. Konyushennaya Ul. Daily 10am–7pm; closed 2–3pm. Metro Nevsky Pr.

Tertia, 5 Italianskaya Ul. Antiques, art and books. Daily 11am–7pm. Metro Gostiny Dvor.

ARTS AND HANDICRAFTS

Art Shop, 2 Sadovaya at Mikhailovsky Castle. Daily 10am–7pm; wide selection. Metro Gostiny Dvor. (Another Art Shop is located at 54 Angliiskaya Emb. Daily 11am–7pm.)

Klenovaya Alleya Art Market is an outdoor arts and handicrafts market held in the Klenovaya Alley near the St Petersburg Circus.

Arts & Handicrafts, 51 Nevsky Pr. Daily 11am–7:30pm; closed 2–3pm. Includes paintings and antiques, magazines and maps. (Other shops are at 132 and 184 Nevsky.) Farfor, at 64, has a large selection of crystal and china. Mon–Sat 10am–7pm.

Aurora Plus, 33/8 Kuibysheva Ul. Daily 10am–7pm. Traditional Russian handicrafts. Metro Gorkovskaya.

Khokhlomskaya Rospis, 6/19-ya Liniya. Khokhloma painted wooden ware. Mon–Fri 10am–6pm. Metro Vasileostrovskaya.

Lavka Drevnostey (Old Curiosity Shop), 9 Morskaya Nab. Mon–Fri 10am–7pm. Arts, handicrafts and contemporary paintings. Metro Primorskaya.

Pushkinskaya, 4 Pushkinskaya. Mon–Sat 10am–7pm. Traditional wooden and ceramic crafts and jewelry. Metro Pl. Vosstaniya.

Red October, 8 Blokhina Ul. Daily 10am–6pm. Lacquer boxes, amber, *matryoshka* dolls. Metro Gorkovskaya.

Russian Art,1 Pl. Dekabristov. Tradional Russian souvenirs. Daily 10am–6pm.

Stroganov Palace Art Salonb, 17 Nevsky Pr. Daily 10am–7pm. Collectors paradise. Metro Nevsky Pr.

Vasilyevsky Island, 31 Sredny Pr. Mon–Fri 11am–7pm; closed 2–3pm. A wide selection including Palekh boxes, paintings and model ships. Metro Vasileostrovskaya.

Vesta-M, 25/5 Bolsheoktinsky Pr. Mon–Fri 11am–7pm. Sat 11am–6pm; closed 2–3pm. Khokhloma wooden items, paintings and jewelry. Metro Novocherkasskaya.

ART GALLERIES

Display and sale of paintings and graphics.

Anna, at Nevsky Palace Hotel. Daily 11am–8pm.

Borey Art Gallery, 58 Liteiny Pr. New exhibition is presented every other Tuesday. Tues–Sat 12–8pm. Metro Mayakovskaya.

Elena, 15/2 Morskaya Nab. Mon–Sat 11am–7pm. Metro Primorskaya.

Eva, 5/4 Pl. Iskusstvo. Gallery of contemporary art. Thursday lectures. Mon–Fri 12–6pm. Metro Nevsky Pr.

Galereya 10-10, 10 Pushkinskaya. Mon–Fri 12–7pm. Metro Mayakovskaya.

Gallery 102, 102 Nevsky Pr. Daily 11am–8pm. Metro Mayakovskaya. (Nearby at 82, is the Master's Guild with a wide variety of art made by well-known artists. Daily 11am–7pm. **The Independent Artists Society** is at 20 Nevsky; daily 12–8pm. Metro Nevsky Pr.)

Hiron Art Gallery, at 8/3-ya Sovetskaya, has modern figurative art.

Palitra Gallery, 166 Nevsky Pr. Contemporary art. Tues–Sat 11am–7pm. Metro Pl. Alek. Nevskovo.

Petropole Gallery, 27 Millonnaya Ul. Exhibit of Peter the Great's turnery and mammoth ivory. Daily 12–6pm.

Union of Artists, 38 Bol. Morskaya. Seven exhibition halls, including **Center of Graphic Arts**, Wed–Sun 1–7pm. Golubaya Gostinaya (Blue Drawing Room), contemporary art on 2nd floor. Tues–Sat 1–8pm; Sun 1–7pm. Metro Gostiny Dvor.

BOOKSTORES

Web-site: http://www.piter-press.ru

Bukinist (Old Books), 59 Liteiny Pr. Mon–Sat 10am–7pm; closed 2–3pm. Metro Vladimirskaya. (See also **Planeta** at 30, **MIR Bookstore** at 64, and **Na Liteynom**, 61 Liteiny Pr. Many of these have books in foreign languages.)

Dom Knigi (House of Books), 28 Nevsky Pr., the largest bookstore in the city. Great selection from books to postcards. Mon–Sat 9am–8pm. Sun 11am–7pm. Metro Nevsky Pr.

Iskusstvo (Art), 16 Nevsky Pr., has a collection of art books and souvenirs. Mon–Sat 10am–7pm; closed 2–3pm. Metro Nevksy Pr.

Knigy, Iconi (Books and Icons), 7 Doblolyubova Pr. Orthodox literature and religious supplies. Daily 10am–7pm. Metro Gorkovskaya.

Maska, 13 Nevsky Pr., offers theater goods. Daily 10am–7pm; closed 2–3pm.

Sankt-Peterburgskaya Knizhnaya Lavka Pisataley (Writer's Book Corner), 66 Nevsky Pr., has both Russian and foreign-language books, art albums and stationery. Mon–Sat 10am–7pm. (See also **Lenkniga** at 141). Metro Gostiny Dvor.

Bookstores are also within the Hermitage and Russian museums.

CITY FAIR AND FLEA MARKET
8 Yuri Gagarin Sq., tel. 264-8954. Daily 10am–7pm. Metro Park Pobedy. (See Polyushtrovsky Rinok below under Markets.)

DEPARTMENT STORES
Admiral Shopping Gallery, 15 Morskaya Nab. (near Pribaltiiskaya Hotel) Daily 10am–8pm. Metro Primorskaya.
Bolshoi Gostiny Dvor, 35 Nevsky Pr. Recently restored (dates back to 18th century); has two floors packed with shopping: clothing, jewelry, souvenirs, etc. Metro Gostiny Dvor.
Passah, 48 Nevsky Pr. Mon–Sat 10am–7pm.
Military Department Store, 6 Nepokorennykh Pr. Mon–Sat 11am–8pm; closed 2–3pm. Metro Pl. Muzhestva. Another is located at 67 Nevsky Pr., Metro Mayakovskaya. **Kollektsioner-M**, at 47 Ligovsky Pr., has old military medals and supplies. Mon–Sat 11am–7pm; closed 2–3pm. Metro Pl Vosstaniya. Another store is at 18 Aviatsionnaya Ul. Metro Moskovskaya.

FURS
Auctions are held in January, May or June, and October, where fur hats are the best buy. Selections at major department stores. See also **Lena**, 50 Nevksy Pr.; **Roma**, 46 Liteiny Pr.; **Rot-Front**, 9 Dumskaya, 34 Bol. Morskaya, 22 Zagorodny Pr.; **Russiye Mekh**, 82 Bolshoi Pr.; **Vremena Goda**, 34 Kamennoostrovsky Pr.

GIFTS AND SOUVENIRS
On Nevsky Prospekt:
Iskusstvo (Art), at 52, has art items and books. Mon–Sat 11am–7pm; closed 2–3pm. Metro Nevsky Pr.
Gildiya Masterov (Master's Guild), at 82, has paintings and graphics. Daily 11am–7pm. Metro Mayakovskaya.
Suveniry (Souvenirs), at 92, has jewelry, crystal and china. Daily 10am–8pm.
Nasledie (Heritage), at 116, has a large collection of everything from jewelry, painted boxes and samovars to ceramics, paintings and tapestries. Daily 10am–7pm; closed 2–3pm. Metro Pl. Vosstaniya.
Pole Star, at 158, has precious stones and silver. Mon–Sat 10am–8pm; closed 2–3pm. Jewelry shops are at numbers 8 (**Ring**), 23 (**Salon Bure**), 44 (**Jewelry Salon**), 69 and 130 Nevsky (**Jewelry**).
Additional jewelry stores can be found at the Grand Hotel Europe, **Ananov**; **Akvamarin** (Aquamarine), 1 Novosmolenskya Nab. Metro Primorskaya; **Almaz** (Diamond), 87 Veteranov Pr. Metro Pr. Veteranov; **Ametist** (Amethyst), 64 Bolshoi

Pr. Metro Petrogradskaya; **Gem World**, 1 Pl. Alek. Nevskovo. Metro Pl. Alek. Nevskovo.

Melodiya, 34–36 Moskovsky Pr. and 47 Bolshoi Pr. Sells records, CDs and musical instruments.
Rapsodiya, 13 Bol. Konyushennaya Ul. Everything from sheet and orchestral music to antiques. Mon–Sat 11am–7pm. Metro Nevsky Pr.
Severnaya Lira, at 26 Nevsky Pr., (Mon–Sat 11am–7pm), and Karaven at 22 Karavannaya Ul., (daily 11am–7pm) sell CDs, music literature and supplies. Metro Gostiny Dvor.
Voyazh-media Ananov, 36 Ligovsky Pr. has CDs. Daily 11am–8pm. Metro Pl. Vosstaniya.

FARMERS' MARKETS OR *RINOK*
The markets are usually open Mon–Sat 8am–7pm; Sun 8am–4pm.
Kuznechny Rinok, 3 Kuznechny Pereulok, tel. 312-7727. Closed second Monday of month. Metro Vladimirskaya.
Maltsevsky Rinok, 52 Nekrasova Ul., tel. 272-3350. Closed last Monday of month. Metro Pl. Vosstaniya.
Moskovsky Rinok, 12 Reshetnikova Ul., tel. 298-1189. Closed first Tuesday of month. Metro Elektrosila.
Narvsky Rinok, 54 Stachek Pr., tel. 185-0639. Closed third Monday of month. Metro Kirovsky Zavod.
Nevsky Rinok, 75a Obukhovskoy Oborony Pr., tel. 567-9825. Closed first Tuesday of month. Metro Yelizarovskaya.
Polyustrovsky Rinok, 45 Polyustrovsky Pr., tel. 540-3039. Pet and bird market; really busy on the weekends, best to get there early (fur, clothing and hats in back). Open daily 8am–7pm. Metro Pl. Lenina.
Sennoy (Hay) Rinok, 4/6 Moskovsky Pr., tel. 310-0618. Closed second Tuesday of month. Metro Sennaya Pl.
Svtny Rinok, (oldest market), 3/5 Sytninskaya Pl., tel. 233-2293. Closed last Monday of month. Metro Gorkovskaya.
Torzhkovsky Rinok, 20 Torzhkovskaya Ul., tel. 246-8238. Closed first Monday of month. Metro Chornaya Rechka.
Vasileostrovsky Rinok, 16 Bolshoi Pr. Vasilyevsky Island. Tel. 213-2898. Closed first Monday of month. Metro Vasileostrovskaya.
Velomarket, 13 Pestelya Ul. Tel. 279-3009. Bicycle market. Mon–Sat 10am–6pm; closed 1–2pm.

MUSEUMS

Web-site: http://www.arcom.spb.su/~anna/museums/museums.html
(*Highly recommended)

Anichkov Palace, 39 Nevsky Pr., tel 310-4395. Houses several concert halls. Metro Gostiny Dvor.

*Anna Akhmatova Museum, 34 Fontanka Emb. in the former Sheremetyev Palace (entrance from 53 Liteiny Pr.), tel. 272-1811. Daily 12–6pm; closed Mon and last Wed of month. Also here is an art gallery displaying paintings from the Silver Century period of Russian art. Metro Mayakovskaya.

Applied Arts Museum, 13–15 Solyanov Lane, tel. 273-3258. Tues–Sat 11am–5pm. Metro Chernyshevskaya.

Blok House, 57 Dekabristov Ul., tel. 113-8616. Daily 11am–5pm; closed Wed and first day of each month.

Botanical Museum, 2 Professora Popova, tel. 234-8470. Open Wed/Sat/Sun 10am–5pm. Greenhouse 11am–4pm; closed Fri.

Brodsky House, 3 Pl. Iskusstvo, tel. 314-3658. Tues–Sun 11am–7pm. Metro Gostiny Dvor.

*Cemeteries (Necropolis) of Alexander Nevsky Monastery, 1 Monastery River Emb., tel. 274-2952. Lazarevskoe is open 11am–7pm; closed Thur. Nikolskoe, open 9am–6pm; closed Sat and Sun. Tikhvinskoe, open 11am–7pm; closed Thurs. Metro Pl. Aleksandra Nevskovo. (See also Museum of Urban Sculpture.)

Communication Museum, 7 Pochtamtskaya Ul., tel. 315-4873. Tues–Sat 9:30am–6pm. Metro Nevsky Pr.

*Circus Museum, 3 Nab. Fontanka, tel. 210-4413. Mon–Fri 12–6pm. (Entrance into circus building from the side by canal; second floor.) Worth a visit before the circus performance begins.

*Cruiser *Aurora*, 4 Petrogradskaya Nab., tel. 230-8440. Open 10:30am–4pm; closed Mon and Fri. Metro Gorkovskaya.

*Defense and Siege of Leningrad Museum, 9 Solyanoi Lane, tel. 273-7647. Open 10am–5pm; closed Wed. Metro Chernyshevskaya.

Dostoevsky Literary Memorial Museum, 5/2 Kuznechny Lane, tel. 164-6950. Open 10:30am–5:30pm; closed Mon and last Wed of month. Metro Vladimirskaya.

Engineer's Castle, 2 Sadovaya Ul., tel. 210-4173. Mon 10am–5pm; Wed–Sun 10am–6pm. Metro Gostiny Dvor. (Now a branch of the Russian Museum.)

*Hermitage, 34 Dvortsovaya Nab., tel. 110-9625/311-3465. Open 10:30am–6pm; closed Mon. Metro Nevsky Pr.

Icebreaker *Krasin* **Museum**, moored near 16-ya Liniya, Vasilyevsky Island, tel. 356-2969. Daily 9am–5pm. Metro Vasileostrovskaya.

*Kazan Cathedral/Religion Museum, 2 Kazanskaya Pl., tel. 311-0495. Daily

11am–5pm; Sat–Sun 12–5pm; closed Wed. Metro Nevsky Pr.

Kirov Museum, 28 Kamennoostrovsky Pr., tel. 346-1481. Open 11am–5:30pm; closed Wed. Metro Petrogradskaya.

*Kunstkammer/Museum of Anthropology and Ethnography, 3 Universitetskaya Nab., tel. 218-0712. Sat–Thurs 11am–5pm. (Visit the nearby Zoological Museum.)

Lomonsov Museum, Kunstkammer, 3 Universitetskaya Nab., tel. 218-1211. Open 11am–6pm; closed Thurs. At 17 Universitetskaya is the Museum of the Academy of Art exhibiting works of Academy graduates. Wed–Sun 11am–7pm.

Marble Palace, 5/1 Millionnaya Ul., tel. 312-9196. Displays art exhibitions. Open 10am–6pm; closed Tues. Metro Chernyshevskaya.

Menschikov Palace, 15 Universitetskaya Nab., tel 213-1112. Hall of chamber music and exhibits on 18th-century Russian culture. Open 10am–6pm; closed Mon.

Militia Museum, 12 Poltavskaya Ul., tel. 277-7825. Mon–Fri 10am–5pm. Metro Pl. Vosstaniya.

Museum of the Arctic and Antarctic, 24a Marata Ul., tel. 311-2549. Wed–Sun 10am–5pm. Metro Vladimirskaya.

Museum of the Artillery and Military, 7 Aleksandrovsky Park, tel. 233-0382. Wed–Sun 11am–5pm. Metro Gorkovskaya.

Museum of Bread, 73 Ligovsky Pr., tel. 164-1110. Tues–Fri 9am–5pm; Sat 11am–3pm. Metro Pl. Vosstaniya.

Museum of Musical Instruments, 5 Isaakievskaya Pl., tel. 314-5394. Wed–Sun 12–5:30pm; closed last Fri of month. Metro Nevsky Pr.

Museum of Printing, 32/2 Nab. Moika, tel. 312-0977. Open 11am–5pm; closed Wed. Metro Nevsky Pr.

Museum of Urban Sculpture, on the grounds of the Alexander Nevsky Monastery, tel. 274-2635. Also an exhibit of avant-garde paintings and graphics. Open 10am–5pm; closed Thurs. Metro Ploshchad Aleksandra Nevskovo.

Naval Central Museum, 4 Birzhevaya Pl., tel. 218-2501. Open 10:30am–4:45pm; closed Mon/Tues.

Nekrasov House, 36 Liteiny Pr., tel. 272-0165. Open 11am–5pm; closed Tues. Metro Vladimirskaya.

October Railroad Central Museum, 62 Liteiny Pr., tel. 168-6891. Open 11am–5:30pm; closed Sat. Metro Vladimirskaya.

Oreshek Fortress and Memorial Center of WWII, Schlüsselburg on Orekhovy Island, tel. 238-4679/4511. Open daily 10am–5pm from May 15 to October 1.

Repin Penates Estate, 411 Primorskoye Shosse in town of Repino, tel. 231-6828. Open 10am–5pm; closed Tues. (Check first, the estate is often closed for repairs.)

*Peter and Paul Fortress/History of St Petersburg Museum, 3 Petropavlovskaya Krepost, tel. 238-4511; excursion tel. 238-4540. Open 11am–5pm; closed Wed. Metro Gorkovskaya.

*Peter the Great's House, 6 Petrovskaya Nab., tel. 232-4576. Open 10am–5pm; closed Tues. Metro Gorkovskaya.

*Piskarevskoye Memorial Cemetery, 74 Nepokorennykh Pr., tel. 247-5716. Metro Pl. Muzhestva.

Planetarium, 4 Aleksandrovsky Park, tel. 233-5312. Open 10:30am–7pm; closed Mon. Metro Gorkovskaya.

Popov's Memorial Museum, 5/33 Professora Popova, tel. 234-5900. Open 11am–5pm; closed Sat/Sun. Metro Petrogradskaya.

Pushkin House, 4 Makarova Nab., tel. 218-0502. Open 11am–5pm; closed Mon/Tues. Metro Vasileostrovskaya.

*Pushkin House Museum, 12 Nab. Moika, tel. 311-3531. Open 11am–5pm; closed Tues.

Railway Museum, 50 Sadovaya Ul., tel. 315-1476. Open 11am–5:30pm; closed Fri/Sat. Metro Sennaya Pl. (If you're a railway buff, ask here about the National Railway Bridge Museum at Krasnoye Selo, the Shushary Museum of Railway Technology in Paravozy Museum, or the Lebyazhe Railway Museum Depot in the town of Lubyaze.)

*Rasputin Museum in the Yusupov Palace, 94 Nab. Moika, tel. 314-9883. Daily 11am–3pm.

Razliv Barn (Lenin) Museum, 3 Emelyanova in town of Sestroretsk, tel. 434-6117. Also in the same town is the Razliv Hut Museum, tel. 437-3098.

Rimsky-Korsakov Memorial House, 28/3 Zagorodny Pr., tel. 113-3208. Open 11am–6pm; closed Mon/Tues. Metro Vladimirskaya.

Rumyantsevsky Mansion, 44 Angliskaya Nab., tel. 311-7544. A branch of St Petersburg City Museum. Open 11am–4pm; closed Mon.

*Russian Museum, 4 Inzhenernaya Ul., tel. 219-1615. Open 10am–6pm; closed Mon. Right next door, at 4/1, is the Russian Museum of Ethnography, open 10am–5pm; closed Mon. Metro Gostiny Dvor.

*St Isaac's Cathedral, Isaakievskaya Pl., tel. 315-9732. Open 11am–6pm; closed Wed. (Great panorama of city from its roof.) Metro Nevsky Pr.

Museum of Political History, in the former Kchessinskaya Mansion at 2/4 Ul. Kuybysheva, tel. 233-7052. Open 10am–5:30pm; closed Thurs. Metro Gorkovskaya.

*Stroganov Palace, 17 Nevsky Pr., tel. 311-2360. Metro Nevsky Pr.

Submarine Narodovolets is moored at 10 Shkipersky Protok, tel. 356-5266. Open 11am–3pm; closed Mon/Tues/Fri.

*Summer Garden and Palace of Peter the Great, tel. 312-9666/314-0456. Open 11am–6pm; closed Tues. Metro Chernyshevskaya.

Theater and Musical Arts Museum, 6 Pl. Ostrovskovo., tel. 311-2195. Open 11am–6pm; closed Tues. Metro Gostiny Dvor.

Vagonova Ballet School, 2 Rossi Ul., tel. 312-1702/311-4317. A small ballet museum is located within the school. Usually closed to public, but try calling to make an appointment.

Wax Museum, 41 Nevsky Pr., tel. 315-5636; located in the Beloselsky-Belozersky Palace, now also a concert hall. Special tours on the history of the palace are also given. Open daily 11am–7pm. Metro Gostiny Dvor.

Yelagin Palace, 1 Yelagin Island, tel. 239-0080. Open 10:30am–5pm; closed Mon/Tues.

*Zoological Museum, 1 Universitetskaya Nab., tel. 218-0112. Open 11am–6pm; closed Fri. Metro Gostiny Dvor. Here resides the 45,000-year-old Siberian baby mammoth, Dima, the unofficial city mascot! (Also try to visit the nearby Kunstkammer.) Dima web-site: http://www.museum.state.il.us/zooinst/images/

Zoo, 1 Aleksandrovsky Park, tel. 232-2839. Summer 10am–7pm. Winter 10am–6pm. Metro Gorkovskaya.

LIBRARIES

St Petersburg has more than 3,000 libraries with over 250 million volumes. The best known libraries are the **Russian National Library** at 18 Sadovaya Ul., tel. 310-7137, daily 9am–9pm, Metro Nevsky Pr.; and the **Russian Academy of Sciences Library** at 1 Birzhevaya Liniya, tel. 218-4091. Mon–Fri 9am–8pm; Sat–Sun 10am–6pm. The **American Info. Center** is at 5/1 Millionnaya Ul., tel. 311-8905; Mon–Fri 1–5pm.

PLACES OF WORSHIP

RUSSIAN ORTHODOX

■CATHEDRALS

(There are over 30 other churches located throughout the city, and over half now conduct daily religious services.) Women should dress modestly and cover heads; men remove hats.

Cathedral of Apostle St Andrew the First, 11/6-ya Liniya, tel. 213-6239. Services daily at 10am and 5pm. Metro Vasileostrovskaya.

Cathedral of the Holy Trinity, 1 Monastery River Emb. in Alexander Nevsky Monastery, tel. 274-0409. Services Mon–Sat at 10am and 5pm; Sun and religious holidays 7am, 10am and 5pm. Metro Pl. Alek. Nevskovo.

Cathedral of Prince Vladimir, 26 Blokhina Ul., tel. 233-6856. Services Mon–Fri at 9am and 6pm; Sat 10am and 6pm; Sun and religious holidays 7am, 10am and 6pm. Metro Gorkovskaya.

Cathedral of Sampson, 41 Bol. Sampsonievsky Pr., tel. 542-3377. Metro Vyborgskaya.

Cathedral of the Savior on the Blood, 2a Nab. Ekaterininskovo Kanala, tel. 314-4053. (Now open to visitors after an extensive renovation and houses an icon collection.) Metro Nevsky Pr.

Cathedral of the Transfiguration, 1 Preobrazhenskaya Pl., tel. 272-3662. Services Mon–Sat at 10am and 6pm; Sun and religious holidays at 7am, 10am and 6pm. Metro Chernyshevskaya.

Kazan Cathedral, 2 Kazanskaya Pl., tel. 311-0495. Services Mon–Fri at 9am and 6pm. (Also houses a Museum of Religion.) Metro Nevsky Pr.

Smolny Cathedral of the Resurrection of Christ, 3/1 Rastrelli Pl., tel. 271-7632. Open 11am–6pm; closed Thurs. No services. Metro Chernyshevskaya.

St Isaac's Cathdral, 1 Isaakievskaya Pl., tel. 315-9732. Open 11am–6pm; closed Wed. Beautiful panorama of the city from the top. No services.

St Nicholas Cathedral, 1/3 Nikolskaya Pl., tel. 114-6926. Services daily 6:30am and 9am. Metro Sennaya Pl.

St Peter and Paul Cathedral, in Peter and Paul Fortress, tel. 238-4540. Open 11am–5pm; closed Wed. No services.

Trinity Cathedral, 7a Izmailovsky Pr., tel. 251-8927. Open Mon–Fri 9am–5pm; Sat–Sun 8am–5pm. Services (chapel) daily at 10am and 5pm. Metro Teknologichesky Inst.

OTHER DENOMINATIONS

Armenian Church of Holy Resurrection, 29 Nab. Smolenki, tel. 350-5301. Daily 10am–6pm. Services daily 10am and 6pm; Sat at 5pm.

Armenian Orthodox Church of St Catherine, 40/42 Nevsky Pr., tel. 219-4108. Open daily 9am–11pm. Services daily 9am and 11pm; Sat at 5pm. Metro Nevsky Pr.

Baptist Church of the Gospel, 52 Borovaya Ul., tel. 166-2831. Services Wed at 6:30pm; Fri 5pm; Sun 11am and 4pm. Metro Ligovsky Pr.

Church of Evangelical Christian Baptists, 29a Bol. Ozernaya Ul., tel. 553-4578. Services Tues/Thurs at 7pm; Sat 11am; Sun at 10am and 4pm. Metro Ozerki.

Our Lady of Lourdes Roman Catholic, 7 Kovensky Pereulok, tel. 272-0442. Services Mon–Sat 9am and 7pm; Sun and religious holidays at 9am, 10:30am, 11:30am, 1:30pm, 3pm and 7pm. Metro Mayakovskaya.

Roman Catholic Church of St Catherine, 32/34 Nevsky Pr., tel. 311-5795. Services (in chapel) Mon–Fri at 8am and 6:30pm; Sat 6:30pm; Sun at 12pm and 7pm. Metro Nevsky Pr.

Evangelical Christian Church, 2 Pargolovo Polevaya Ul., tel. 594-8997. Services Wed at 7pm; Sat 6pm; Sun at 11am and 4pm.

Seventh-Day Adventist, 7 Internasionalnaya Ul., tel. 138-9811. Daily 9am–8pm.

Evangelical Lutheran Church of St Peter, 22/24 Nevsky Pr., tel. 311-2423. Services held on Sun at 10:30am in Spartak movie house, 8 Saltykova-Schedrina Ul.

Church of St Catherine, 1 Bolshoi Pr., Vasilyevsky Island, tel. 552-0816. Services Sun at 11am and 1pm.

Mormon Church of Jesus Christ of Latter Day Saints, 11 Nab. Moika, tel. 325-6148. (Services at 6 Aerodromnaya Ul. on Sun at 11am and 3pm.)

Buddhist Temple Monastery, 91 Primorsky Pr., tel. 239-0341. Open daily 9am–7pm. Services at 9am. Metro Chornaya Rechka.

Mosque of the Congregation of Moslems, 7 Kronversky Pr., tel. 233-9819. Open daily 12–4pm. Services daily at 2:20pm in summer and 1:20pm in winter. Metro Gorkovskaya.

Choral Synagogue and Jewish Religious Center, 2 Lermontovsky Pr., tel. 114-0078/1153. Open 10am–8pm; closed Sat. Services Mon–Fri and Sun at 9am, Sat at 10am. (Time of sunset determines evening services.)

Synagogue at Preobrazhenskoe Jewish Cemetery, 2 Aleksandrovsky Fermy Pr. The cemetery (tel. 262-0397) is at 66a. Daily 9am–4pm.

ENTERTAINMENT

THEATERS AND CONCERT HALLS

Theater, concert and circus performances usually begin on weekdays at 7pm, 7:30pm or 8pm with matinée performances on weekends, with an earlier evening show. Be on time, as ushers are strict about curtain time! The date and time of the performance, and your seat number are written on the ticket. It is usually required to leave your coat in the lobby cloakroom. Opera glasses are available for a small rental fee. Programs are also sold. During the intermission, drinks and snacks are served in the lobby. Each theater usually has its own box office; also tickets can often be reserved through a travel/service bureau in your hotel, or purchased from street/Metro theater kiosks. Also try the Central Ticket Office at 42 Nevsky Prospekt (open 9am–8pm; Metro Nevsky Pr.) The ticket office for the State Philharmonic is nearby at 2 Mikhailovskaya Ul. On the night of the performance you can also bargain for tickets from touts at the door.

Aleksandrinsky or Pushkin Academic Drama Theater, the oldest drama theater in Russia, at Pl. Ostrovskovo., tel. 110-4103/312-1545. Metro Nevsky Pr./Gostiny Dvor. (Performances Tues–Fri at 7pm; Sat/Sun at 11am and 6pm.)

Anichkov Palace Carnival Hall, 30 Nevsky Pr., tel. 310-4822. Metro Nevsky Pr.

Beloselsky-Belozersky Palace Mirror Hall, 41 Nevsky Pr., tel. 315-3821. Metro Nevsky Pr. Has symphonic musical concerts and theater performances.

Bolshoi Drama Theater, 65 Nab. Fontanka, tel. 310-0401. Performances Tues–Sun at 7pm. Box office open Tues–Sun 11am–7pm; Mon 11am–6pm. Metro Vladimirskaya.

Bolshoi Puppet Theater, 10 Nekrasov Ul., tel. 272-9065. Performances Wed–Sun at 11:30am, 2pm and 7pm. Metro Vladimirskaya/Mayakovskaya.

Boris Eyfman's Contemporary Ballet, 2 Lizy Chaikinoy Ul., tel. 232-0235. Metro Petrogradskaya.

Bryantsev Theater for Children, 1 Pionerskaya Pl., tel. 112-4102. Metro Pushkinskaya.

Buff Theater, 1 Narodnaya Ul., tel. 263-6767. Metro Lomonosovskaya.

Children's Ballet Theater, 4 Stachek Pr., tel. 186-2426. Metro Narvskaya.

Children's Ice Theater, 148 Ligovsky Pr., tel. 112-8625. Metro Moskovskaya.

Circus 3 Nab. Fontanka, tel. 210-4198 (museum tel. 210-4413). Closed Thurs. Metro Gostiny Dvor.

Comedian's Refuge, 27 Sadovaya Ul., tel. 310-3314. Performance at 7pm. Metro Sadovaya.

Comedy Academic Theater, 56 Nevsky Pr., tel. 312-4555. Ticket office open daily 11am–8pm. Metro Nevsky Pr.

Composer's House, 45 Bol. Morskaya, tel. 311-0262.

Drama Theater (Komissarzhevskaya), 19 Italyanskaya Ul., tel. 311-3102.

Estrady Variety Theater, 27 Bol. Konyushennaya Ul., tel. 314-7060. Metro Nevsky Pr.

Etno Folklore Theater, 3 Mokhovaya Ul., tel. 275-4226. Metro Chernyshevskaya.

Glinka Kapella Concert Hall, 20 Moika River Emb., tel. 314-1058. Metro Nevsky Pr.

Glinka Maly Zal, 30 Nevsky Pr., tel. 311-0688/7333. Chamber music.

Hall of Ancient Music, 33 Galernaya Ul., tel. 311-4311.

Hermitage Theater of Concerts and Ballets, 34 Dvortsovaya Nab. in Hermitage complex, tel. 311-9025. Metro Nevsky Pr.

House of Officers Concert Hall, 20 Liteiny Pr., tel. 278-8641. Metro Chernyshevskaya.

Jubilee Sports Palace, 18 Dobrolyubova Pr., tel. 119-5604. Popular music/rock concerts.

Litsedei Minus 4 Clown-Mime Theater, 14 Chernyshevskovo Pr., tel. 272-8879. Metro Chernyshevskaya.

Maly Drama Theater, 18 Rubinshteina Ul., tel. 113-2028. Metro Dostoevskaya.

Maly Theater of Opera and Ballet, 1 Pl. Iskusstvo. Tel. 219-1978. Metro Nevsky Pr.

Mariinsky (Kirov) Theater of Opera and Ballet, 1 Teatralnaya Pl., tel. 114-5264. Ticket office open daily 11am–7pm.

Marionettes Theater, 52 Nevsky Pr., tel. 311-2156. Ticket office daily 11am–7pm. Metro Gostiny Dvor.

Miniature Theater, 15 Mokhovaya Ul., tel. 272-0015. Metro Chernyshevskaya.

Music Hall, 4 Aleksandrovsky Park, tel. 232-0243. Metro Gorkovskaya.

Musical Comedy Theater, 13 Italianskaya Ul., tel. 219-1143. Metro Nevsky Pr.

Na Neve for Children, 5 Sovyetsky Per., tel. 259-9104. Metro Tekno. Inst.
Nikolaevsky Folklore Art and Dance Center, 4 Truda Pl., tel. 311-9304.
Open Air Theater, 12 Vladimirsky Pr., tel. 113-2191. Metro Vladimirskaya.
Oktybrsky Concert Hall, 6 Ligovsky Pr., tel. 275-1273. Metro Pl. Vosstaniya.
Osobnyak Classical Theater, Tel. 234-4794.
Petersburg Mosaic Dance Theater, 41 Nevsky Pr., tel. 274-1287. Metro
Mayakovskaya.
Petersburg Sport and Concert Complex, 8 Yuri Gagarin Pr., tel. 298-1211. Metro
Park Pobedy.
Puppet Opera for Children, 4 Tavricheskaya Ul., tel. 275-6090. Metro
Chernyshevskaya.
Puppet Theater of Fairy Tales, 121 Moskovsky Pr., tel. 298-0031. Metro
Moskovskiye Vorota.
Rimsky-Korsakov Opera and Ballet Theater, 3 Teatralnaya Pl., tel. 312-2519.
Closed Tues. Metro Sennaya Pl.
Rock Opera Theater, 36 Labutina Ul. Tel. 114-0547.
Smolny Cathedral Concert Hall, 3/1 Rastrelli Pl., tel. 271-7632. Metro
Chernyshevskaya.
St Petersburg Hotel Concert Hall, 5/2 Pirogovskaya Nab., tel. 542-9680. Metro Pl.
Lenina.
Theater of Satire, 48 Sredny Pr., tel. 213-6683. Metro Vasileostrovskaya.
Vagonova School Of Ballet, 2 Zodchedgo Rossi Ul., tel 312-1702/311-4317. (Small
ballet museum located inside; performances by pupils in Mariinsky ensembles.)
Youth Theater on Fontanka, 114 Nab. Fontanka, tel. 316-6564. Metro Tekno. Inst.
Zazerkale Music and Drama Theater, 13 Rubinsteina Ul., tel. 311-0406. Metro
Dostoevskaya.

JAZZ AND ROCK
Check *Pulse St Petersburg* and the press for listings.
The New Dzhaz-klub, 58 Bol. Morskaya, tel. 311-1504. Open Wed–Sat
9am–10pm.
Fireball, 20 Alpisky Lane, tel. 172-4424. Rock music. Fri/Sat 6pm–5:30am. Other
days 6–11pm; closed Mon. Metro Kupchino.
Kvadrat Jazz Club, 10 Pravdy Ul., tel. 164-8508. Mon 8–11pm. (Tues has live rock
and disco.) Metro Pushkinskaya.
Indi-Club, 223 Obukhovskoi Oborony Pr. Open Mon–Sat 12–8pm. Metro
Proletarskaya.
JFC Jazz Club, 23 Shpalernaya Ul., tel. 272-9850. Daily 7–10pm. Metro
Chernyshevskaya.

Money Honey Salon, 14 Apraksin Dvor, tel. 310-0147. Daily 10am–11pm. Metro Sadovaya.

Okoshki Art Café, 3 Nab. Ekaterininsky Kanala, tel. 314-5273. Daily 12–11pm. Dance parties 10pm–6am. Bohemian hangout; music groups live on Sat night.

Rock Around the Clock, at 20 Sadovaya Ul., tel. 310-1216. Metro Sennaya Pl.

St Petersburg Jazz Hall, 27 Zagorodny Pr., tel. 164-8565. Open from 8pm. Metro Vladimirskaya/Dostoevskaya.

St Petersburg Rock Club, 13 Rubinsteina Ul., tel. 312-3483. Mon–Sat 12–11pm. Metro Dostoevskaya.

Tamtam Club, 49 Maly Pr., Vasilyevsky Island, tel. 355-9740. Live rock music. Fri/Sat 8–11pm; Metro Vasileostrovskaya.

Ten Club, 60 Nab. Obvodnovo. Rock music. Metro Pushkinskaya.

Theater DDT, 10 Pushkinskaya St/Apt 37, tel. 164-4873. Mon–Fri 11am–7pm. Concerts of rock musicians. Metro Mayakovskaya.

Tunnel, Lyubansky and Zverinskaya Ul. in former bomb shelter, tel. 238-8075. Raucous rock n' roll. Thurs/Sat midnight to 6am. Metro Gorkovskaya.

Wild Side, 12 Nab. Bumazhnovo, tel. 186-3466. Disco, rock and pop music. Mon–Sat 10pm–5:30am. Metro Narvskaya.

CASINOS AND NIGHTCLUBS

Some charge a small entrance fee.

Admiral Casino, 20 Mal. Morskaya at Astoria Hotel, tel. 316-9784. High stakes; includes blackjack and roulette; tie and jacket. Daily 4pm–6am. Also located at LDM Hotel Complex.

Bambuk Casino, 12 Sadovaya Ul. above Shanghai Rest., tel. 312-7627. Includes blackjack, poker and roulette. Daily 1pm–6am. Metro Gostiny Dvor.

Candyman Nightclub, 17 Kosygina Pr., tel. 525-6313. Wed–Sun 10pm–6am. Metro Ladozhskaya.

Cleo Nightclub, 18 Stachek Pr., tel. 252-4355. Roulette, billiards, blackjack and disco. Daily 10pm–6am. Metro Narvskaya.

Domenicos Nightclub, 70 Nevsky Pr., tel. 272-5717. Daily 12pm–6am. Metro Gostiny Dvor.

Eldorado Night Club, 27/2 Tukhachevskovo Ul. in Hotel Karelia, tel. 226-3078. Daily 10–5am.

Fakel (Torch) Dance Club, 44 Sofiskaya Ul., tel. 108-7665. Live music/disco. Metro Lomonosovskaya.

Fortuna Casino, 71 Nevsky Pr., tel. 164-2087. Daily 2pm–6am. Blackjack, roulette and poker. Metro Mayakovskaya.

Hollywood Nights Disco, 46 Nevsky Pr., tel. 311-6077. Daily 10pm–6am. Metro Nev. Pr.

Joy Nightclub, 28/1 Nab. Ekaterininsky Kanala, tel. 312-1614. Dance, music, and karaoke on Fri/Sat nights.

Kunyusheny Dvor (Horse Stables), 5 Nab. Ekaterininsky Kanala, tel. 315-7607. Live music and disco. Daily 12pm–6am. Metro Nevsky Pr.

Khammer Casino, 3 Bolshevikov Pr., tel. 589-1191. Blackjack, roulette and poker. Daily 7pm–6am. Metro Pr. Bolshevikov.

Kenguru Nightclub (Kangaroo), 15/1 Kupchinskaya Ul., tel. 172-5598. Daily 6pm–6am. Metro Kupchino.

Konti Casino & Nightclub, 44 Kondratevsky Pr. at Gigant Cinema. Blackjack, roulette, poker, billiards, slots. Jacket and tie. Tel. 540-2836. Metro Pl. Lenina. Open 24 hours.

Monarkh Casino & Nightclub, 37 Stachek Pr., tel. 186-9679. Open 24 hours. Metro Narvskaya.

Nevskaya Melodiya Casino, 62 Sverdlovskaya Nab., tel. 224-2876. Daily 9–6am. Metro Novocherkasskaya.

Palace Casino, 4 Aleksandrovsky Park, tel. 232-8173. Blackjack, roulette, poker, billiards, slots. Open 24 hours. Metro Gorkovskaya.

Panda Casino, 26 Nab. Ekaterininsky Kanala, tel. 312-896. Blackjack, roulette, poker. Daily 7pm–6am. Metro Gostiny Dvor.

Planetarium Stardust Club, 4 Aleksandrovsky Park, tel. 233-4956. Live rock/disco. Thurs–Sat 11pm–6am. Metro Gorkovskaya.

Premier Casino Club, 47 Nevsky Pr., tel 315-7893. Daily 6pm–6am. Metro Vladimirskaya.

Relax Nightclub, 34 Morisa Toreza Pr., tel. 552-8344. Daily 10pm–6am. Metro Pl. Muzhestva.

Stiers Nightclub, 4 Stachek Pl, tel. 186-5429. (Very pricey.) Wed–Sun 10pm–6am. Metro Narvskaya.

Volkhov Casino, 27 Liteiny Pr. Daily 6pm–7am. Metro Chernyshevskaya.

GAY AND LESBIAN NIGHTCLUBS

Nonexistent during the Soviet era (homosexuality received up to three years imprisonment), gay culture, though no longer punishable, has barely taken root and there is still 'gay bashing'. (In Russian, the world for gay is *goluboy*, meaning blue; and the word for lesbian, *lesbianka*, has been taken from the English.)

Klub-Disco, 33 Galernaya Ul. is open on weekends.

Teatr Experiment, (downstairs) near Metro Petrogradskaya. Weekend disco.

Nightclub, 15 Mokhovaya. Open daily.

Occasionally all-night parties take place at the **Baltiisky Dom**, 4 Aleksandrovsky Park. Metro Gorkovskaya. Gay activity is also centered along Dumskaya Ul., off

Nevsky. Try calling the St Petersburg Chaikovsky Fund, a gay resource center, tel. 311-0937 or Krilya, tel. 312-3180. The Intl. Gay and Lesbian Human Rights Com. in San Francisco publishes the Rights of Lesbians and Gay Men in the Russian Federation. For a copy tel. (415) 255-8680 or fax (415) 255-8662. The Spartacus Guide (from the West) contains numerous listings about gay activities in numerous Russian cities (some may be outdated).

MISCELLANEOUS
TRAVEL AGENCIES AND TOUR COMPANIES
Sinbad Travel at Russian Youth Hostel, 3-ya 28 Sovietskaya Ul. Tel. 327-8384, 329-8018; fax 329-8019. Provides visa processing assistance, hotel bookings and other general information. Make sure to include your fax number or e-mail address. Replies take 1–2 business days. E-mail: internet:ryh@ryh.spb.su; web-site: http://www.spb.ru/ryh

Lenart Tours, 40 Nevsky Pr. Tel. 312-6824/4837; fax 110-6614. Travel services and tours in St Petersburg.

Bouziinenko, 10 Ligovsky Pr. Tel. 277-6846; tel/fax 311-5953. Visa support, hotel reservations and specialized tours.

Terra, 27 Bolshaya Konyushennaya Ul. Tel. 312-1811. Visa support and tours of St Petersburg.

Cyrion, 22 Galernaya Ul. Tel. 219-8269; tel/fax 219-8142. Full-service travel agency. (If one of the above no longer offers visa support, ask them to recommend a company that does.)

BOAT EXCURSIONS AND RIVER CRUISES
Balt Express, canal and river excursions from April to October. Trips to Kizhi and Valaam. 116 Nevsky Pr., tel. 279-0496. Mon–Fri 10am–7pm; Sat 11am–3pm. Metro Pl. Vosstaniya.

City Excursion Bureau of St Petersburg, trips on Neva and canals to Kizhi and Valaam. 56 Angliyskaya Nab., tel. 311-4019. Mon–Fri 10am–6pm. Metro Sadovaya.

Itus-Tur, boat excursions to Moscow, Kizhi and Valaam. 64 Ligovsky Pr., tel. 112-2013. Mon–Fri 10am–8pm; Sat 11am–4pm. Metro Pl. Vosstaniya.

Nord-Soyuz, city excursions on rivers and canals (April–Oct); and to Kizhi and Valaam. 9a Bol. Posadskaya Ul., tel. 238-8261. Mon–Fri 10am–6pm. Metro Gorkovskaya.

Sankt Peterburg, excurions on rivers and canals and to Petrodvorets; riverboats to Valaam; April–Oct. 60b Nab. Moika, tel. 210-0905. Metro Sennaya Pl.

St Petersburg Central Travel Bureau, excursions on rivers and canals; boat trips to Kizhi and Valaam. 27 Bolshaya Konyushennaya Ul. Tel. 315-4555. Mon–Sat 10am–6pm. Metro Nevsky Pr.

PASSENGER BOAT DOCKS

Anichkov Bridge Dock has boat tours through St Petersburg's rivers and canals. Corner of Nevsky Pr. and Fontanka River. Tel. 272-4411. Boats also leave from a pier located on the corner of Nevsky Pr./Moika Canal. Ticket window at piers; trips last about one hour. Customized canal and group trips are also available. May 25–October 10.

Hermitage Dock, hydrofoils to Petrodvorets (30 minutes) can be boarded at the pier in front of the Hermitage. (Another pier is located in front of the Statue of the Bronze Horseman in Pl. Dekabristov.) One-hour cruises along the Neva are also available. Ticket window at docks. Tel. 311-9506. May 10–October.

Tuchkov Bridge Dock, hydrofoils to Kronstadt (30–40 minutes) leave from Tuchkov Bridge (next to Hotelship Peterhof). April 25–Nov 10. Tel. 213-4486; 218-2223.

During the summer White Nights, boat tours leave at midnight from the Hermitage Dock/Anichkov Bridge and return at 5am, cruising the Neva and canals.

FERRIES

Baltic Line has cruise ships that travel to Sweden, Finland and Germany. 1 Morskoy Slavy Pl., tel. 355-1616. Metro Primorskaya.

Sea Passenger Terminal, 1 Morskoy Pl., tel. 355-1310. Tickets tel. 355-1312. Metro Primorskaya.

TOUR COMPANIES—BUS AND AIR EXCURSIONS

Information for all intercity buses: tel. 166-5777

Check with **PETER TIPS** for additional tourist info. 86 Nevsky. Tel. 279-0027.

Tourist Hotline, tel. 311-4956, provides free information on tour trip prices organized by tour firms around the world.

Paradiz, at 11 Universitetskaya Nab., tel. 238-4709 has bus tours to the palaces. **The City Excursion Bureau**, tel. 311-4019/312-0527, is located at 56 Nab. Angliskaya; it provides bus and boat tours. The **St Petersburg Tourist Company** (a restructuring of the old Intourist) is at 60b Nab. Moika (tel. 210-0905) with another office in the Astoria Hotel; offers bus tours that include Peter and Paul Fortress, the Hermitage and Yusupov Palace, as well as Peterhof, Tsarskoye Selo and Pavlovsk. Check also **St Petersburg (Intourist) Travel Company**, at 16 Nevsky Pr., tel. 312-2433. **Tetratur** offers thematic excursions around the city (such as art, architecture, history), tel. 277-7517/7316. Try also **Intourbus**, tel. 226-1800, at 3 Ekaterininsky Pr., and **Intourbureau**, tel. 315-7876, at 22 Galernaya Ul. **Davranov-Travel**, tel. 311-1629, offers tours of St Petersburg and suburbs.

(For air/helicopter excursions of the city and/or surrounding areas, see Baltic Airlines under Airlines, page 516. Check also LenAir at tel. 104-1676; 350-0760.)

EXCURSIONS TO PETROZAVODSK, NOVGOROD AND PSKOV
Bus Terminal at 36 Nab Obvodnovo, tel. 166-5777/0859. Daily 7am–9pm. Metro Ligovsky Pr. Also serves destinations in Estonia.
Resort-tur, offers bus tours around city and environs, and 1–2 day tours to Novgorod, Vyborg, Pskov and Pushkinskiye Gory. 22 Galernaya Ul. Tel. 219-8256/8442. Mon–Fri 10am–6pm. Metro Nevsky Pr.

INTERNATIONAL ROUTES
Finnord, 37 Italianskaya Ul., tel. 314-8951. To Helsinki, Finland; daily departures 2:40pm from Pulkovskaya Hotel and 3:30pm from Finnord Office, which is open Mon–Fri 10am–5pm, Sat/Sun 12–4pm. Metro Gostiny Dvor.
Gaugeamus-Tur, 1/28 Lomonosova Ul., tel. 110-5596. Routes to cities throughout Europe. Mon–Fri 10am–6pm. Metro Gostiny Dvor.
Scandinavia-Petersburg, 28 Nevsky Pr. Rm. 503, tel. 219-4990/6568. Sells tickets to Finland.
Sovavto, 1 Pobedy Pl. in Hotel Pulkovskaya, tel. 123-5125, 327-0050; daily 8am–7pm. Daily departures to Finland from hotels Astoria, Grand Hotel Europe and Pulkovskaya.

HEALTH CLUBS AND SAUNAS
Most top-end hotels have fitness centers; usually, for a fee, non-hotel members can use the facilities. (See Accommodation, page 517.)
Health Complex, 6 Tallinnskaya Ul., tel. 310-9410. Open 24 hours. Pool and sauna. Metro Novocherkasskaya.
Olympus Fitness Center, 14/6-ya Krasnoarmeiskaya Ul., tel. 110-1887. Fitness room, aerobics, massage. Mon–Sat 9am–9pm. Metro Tekno. Inst.
SKA Army Sport Club, 3 Litovskaya Ul., tel. 542-0162. Swimming pool. Metro Vyborgskaya.
World Class, 57 Nevsky Pr./Nevsky Palace (tel. 275-2001); 1/7 Mikhailovsky Ul./Grand Hotel Europe (tel. 329-6597); and 6 Vyborgskoe Shosse (tel. 554-4147). Mon–Fri 7am–10pm; Sat/Sun 11am–9pm. Workout, aerobics, massage and sauna.

Saunas/Banyas: Upmarket *banyas* usually have saunas, pools, showers, massage and private rooms. There are over 60 *banya* complexes located throughout the city. (see Special Topic on page 340).
Banya Nevsky, 5/7 Marata Ul., tel. 311-1400. Wed–Sun 8am–10pm. Metro Mayakovskaya.
Bateynenskiye Bani, 20 Aleksandra Matrosova Ul., tel. 245-2501. Tues–Sun 8am–9pm.

Krugliye Bani, 29a Karbysheva Ul., tel. 550-0985. Open 8am–9pm; closed Wed. Metro Pl. Muzhestva.

Lotsmanskiye Bani, 20 Lotsmanskaya Ul., tel. 219-5898. Open 8am–10pm; closed Tues. Metro Sennaya Pl.

Superlyuks Banya, 1 Ul. Tchaikovskovo, tel. 272-0911. Open 8am–10pm; closed Mon/Tues. Metro Chernyshevskaya.

Other *banyas* are located at:

5 Gavanskaya Ul., tel. 356-6351. Wed–Sun 8am–9pm. Metro Vasileostrovskaya.

28 Mal. Posadskaya Ul., tel. 233-5092. Wed–Sun 8am–9pm.

55 Moskovsky Pr., tel. 316-2266. Open 8am–9pm; closed Wed. Metro Fruzenskaya.

6 Olgi Forsh Ul., tel. 592-7622. Open Wed–Sun 8am–10pm. Metro Pr. Prosveshcheniya.

8/10 Voronezhskaya Ul., tel. 164-3169. Open 8am–10pm; closed Wed. Metro Ligovsky Pr.

CAR RENTALS

Many of the more expensive hotels have car rentals available. With most, you have to rent both a car and a driver. Car, minivan, truck and bus rentals can be found.

Hertz, 40 Nekrasova Ul., tel. 272-5045. Daily 9am–6pm. Web-site: http://www.hertz.com

Hertz-Interavto, 2 Aleksandra Nevskovo Sq., tel. 274-2060.

Holiday Autos, 20 Nab. Moika, tel. 312-9984. English firm. Metro Nevsky Pr.

Intour Auto Service, 5 Sedova Ul., tel. 567-8226. Metro Yelizarovskaya.

Mobil-Service, 11 Borovaya Ul., tel. 164-6066. 15 Frunze Ul. Tel. 293-2475.

Svit, 14 Korablestroiteley Ul., Vasilyevsky Island. Tel. 356-9329.

Transwell, at 63 Galernaya Ul., tel. 312-9602. Provides car and minibus rentals without drivers.

SPORTS STADIUMS

Dinamo, 44 Dinamo Pr., tel. 235-4717. Metro Petrogradskaya.

Jubilee Stadium Sports Complex, 18 Dobrolyubova Pr., tel. 119-5601. Metro Petrogradskaya.

Kirov Stadium, 1 Morskoi Pr., tel. 235-0078. Metro Petrogradskaya.

Petrovsky Stadium, 2 Petrovsky Island, tel. 119-5700.

SKA Stadium or Army Sport Club, 13 Inzhenernaya Ul., tel. 210-4237. Metro Nevsky Pr.

Zimny (Winter) Stadium, 2 Manezhnaya Pl., tel. 210-4671. Metro Nevsky Pr.

SPORTS

Bowling, at Pribaltiiskaya Hotel, tel. 356-0001. Daily 12–10pm.

Chess, Ladya (Castle) Chess Club, 3 Vladimirsky Pr., tel. 311-7160. Mon 10am–8pm. Tues 6–8pm.

Golf, the United Club is a golf and tennis club. 9 Butlerova Ul., tel. 535-0168. Call the club and arrange to play on the course at the Zenit Sports Complex. Golf clubs can be rented. Tel. 535-0168. Mon–Fri 4–9pm, Sat 10am–2pm. Metro Pl. Muzhestva. The Golf Assoc. of St Petersburg is at 22 Millionnaya Ul., tel. 225-3312.

Horse Rental, the Equestrian Sports Center at Kirov Stadium has riding lessons in an indoor ring. 1 Morskoy Pr., tel. 235-5448. Metro Petrogradskaya. Prostor, tel. 230-3988, has a riding school and stables; also has carriages for riding in downtown.

Rowing Club, Energiya at tel. 235-1544; Rowing Sport Club at tel. 234-0466; and Spartak Rowing Club at tel. 234-3644; all have rowing, sculling and canoeing.

Skating, year-round skating is at the Yubileyny Sports Palace (skates can be rented) located at 18 Dobrolyubova Pr., tel. 119-5622. Metro Petrogradskaya (great ice hockey games go on in winter). Many pond locations are flooded in winter for skating. Ice rink at 4 Yelagin Island; tel. 239-0911. Ice rink of Moscow Victory Park is at 25 Kuznetsovaya Ul., tel. 298-3411; skates for rental. Metro Park Pobedy. Ice rink of Tavrichesky Gardens is at 2–4 Potemkinskaya Ul., tel. 273-6420. Metro Chernyshevskaya. Kristall, near Metro Pl. Lenina, is at 44 Marshala Blyukhera Pr. The Kronwerk Canal, behind the Peter and Paul Fortress is also a great place if you have your own skates.

Skiing, Okhta Park Downhill Ski Center is 3 kilometers (2 miles) from Enkolovo on the road to Yukki. Tel. 238-1539. Downhill trails, ski lift and equipment rentals. Take a commuter train from Finland Station to Kuzmolovo; closed Mondays. Zolotaya Dolina (Golden Valley) has two downhill trails and a lift. Tel. 246-6302. Take a commuter train from Finland Station to Sosnovo, followed by bus 145 to Michurinskaya. The best places for cross-country skiing are in the nearby villages of Kavgolovo (also has Alpine) and Komarovo; both are less than an hour's journey by electric train from Finland Station. Other ski spots are in Pavlovsky Palace Park (in Pavlovsk), and at Tsarskoe Selo. You can rent skis/sledges in the semicircular wing of Catherine's Palace.

Tennis, the best courts in the city are at the Tennis Club, 23 Konstantinovsky Pr., tel. 235-0407; outdoor and indoor courts with equipment rentals; daily 7am–11pm. The Molniya (Lightning) Sports Club has good indoor and open courts. Located at 50 Primorsky Pr., tel. 239-7509; open 24 hours. Metro Chornaya Rechka. Other courts are at Moscow Victory Park (outdoor) and the United Club (see Golf, above). The Tennis Federation of St Petersburg is located at 22–24 Nevsky Pr., tel. 510-8515.

Useful Addresses

CONSULATES OF THE RUSSIAN FEDERATION
Web-site: http://www.vidbros.com/consul/address.html

IN THE USA
The travel advisory line at the US State Department is (202) 647-5225.
Russian Embassy, 2650 Wisconsin Ave NW, Washington DC 20007. Tel. (202) 298-5700.
Visa/Consular Office, 1825 Phelps Place NW, Washington DC 20009. Tel. (202) 939-8907.

RUSSIAN CONSULATES GENERAL
In New York: 9 East 91st Street, New York, NY 10020. Tel. (212) 348-0926.
In San Francisco: 2790 Green Street, San Francisco, CA 94123. Tel. (415) 202-9800.

AIRLINES
Aeroflot, tel. (888) 340-6400; web-site: http://www.aeroflot.org/
Air France, tel. (800) 237-2747; web-site: http://www.airfrance.com
Alaska Airlines, tel. (800) 426 0333 (flights to Siberia).
British Airways, tel. (800) 247-9297; web-site: http://www.british-airways.com
Delta, tel. (800) 241-4141; web-site: http://www.delta-air.com
Finnair, tel. (800) 950-5000; web-site: http://www.finnair.com
KLM, tel. (800) 374-7747; web-site: http://www.klm.tnl
Lufthansa, tel. (800) 645-3880; web-site: http://www.lufthansa-usa.com
SAS, tel. (800) 221-2350; web-site: http://www.sas.se

TRAVEL AGENCIES, TOUR AND SPECIALTY GROUPS
American Express Travel Services, World Financial Center, 200 Vesey Street, New York, NY 10285. Tel. (212) 640-2000. In Los Angeles, CA, tel. (310) 274-8277.
American International Homestays, PO Box 1754, Nederland, Colorado 80466. Tel. (800) 876-2048/(303) 642-3088; fax (303) 642-3365; e-mail: ash@igc.apc.org; web-site: http://www.commerce.com/homestays/
Blue Heart Tours, PO Box 16930, Alexandria, VA 22302. Tel. (703) 329-6400; fax (703) 329-6777; web-site: http://www.BlueHeart.com
Beverly International Travel, 4630 Campus Drive #205, Newport Beach, CA 92660. Tel. (310) 271-4116/(949) 474-7582; fax (949) 756-2169.

Center for Citizen Initiatives, PO Box 29912, Presidio, San Francisco, CA 94129. Tel. (415) 561-7777; fax (415) 561-7778; web-site: http://www.igc.org/cci

Council on International Exchange (CIEE), 205 East 42nd Street, New York, NY 10017. Tel. (212) 822-2600; fax (212) 822-2699; e-mail: info@ciee.org; web-site: http://www.ciee.org

Host Families Association (HOFA), tel. (202) 333-9343; fax (202) 337-6090; e-mail: hofa@usa.net (See also Practical Information sections under Accommodation).

Hostels: Contact HI Hostel on IBN Intl Booking System; many hostels provide visa processing help. (See Practical Information sections under Hostels for additional contact numbers.)

IBV Bed & Breakfast Systems and Capital Visa, 13113 Ideal Drive, Silver Spring, MD 20906. Tel. (301) 942-3770; fax (301) 933-0024

Independent Russian Travel Agencies, see Practical Information sections under Miscellaneous/Travel Agencies listings for each city; many sponsor and process visa invitations, make hotel reservations, provide tours of the city, train tickets, etc.

International Bed & Breakfast, PO Box 823, Huntingdon Valley, PA 19006. Tel. (800) 422-5283/(215) 663-1438; fax (215) 379-3363; e-mail: ibb@dca.net; web-site: http://www.ibed.com

International Cruises and Tours, 2476 N. University Pkwy #B1, Provo, Utah 84604. Tel. (888) 827-8357; web-site: http://www.cruisesandtours.com

Intourist-USA Inc., 630 Fifth Avenue, Suite 868, New York, NY 10011. Tel. (800) 556-5305/(212) 757-3884; fax (212) 459-0031; 12 South Dixie Highway, Lake Worth, Florida 33460. Tel. (561) 585-5305; fax (561) 582-1353; e-mail: info@intourist-usa.com. Moscow City Tourist office, tel. (888) 966-7269.

MIR, 85 South Washington St, Suite 210, Seattle, Washington 98104. Tel. (800) 424-7289/(206) 624-7289; fax (206) 624-7360; e-mail: mir@igc.apc.org; web-site: http://www.mircorp.com

Nicko Tours, (stay at Moscow Country Club and golf on Robert Trent Jones II designed golf course, venue of Russian Open.) Moscow: 53 Prospekt Vernadskovo. Tel. 230-6088; fax 956-8001. Information in the US: tel. (310) 306-6262; fax (310) 306-5025. (Specialty golf and tennis.)

Pioneer East-West Initiative, 203 Allstone Street, Cambridge MA 02139. Tel. (800) 369-1322/ (617) 547-1127; fax 617-547-7304. Custom designed Russian trips, and homestays.

Rail Europe, tel. (800) 848-7245; e-mail: webmaster@raileurope.com Specializing in Russian, CIS & European train travel. Can reserve and order tickets directly through them.

Russian Travel Bureau, 225 East 44th St, New York, NY 10017. Tel. (212) 986-1500; fax (212) 490-1650; e-mail: russntvl@interserv.com; web-site:

http://www.astanet.com/get?russntrvl
Russian Travel Service/Zephhr Press, 13 Robinson St., Sommerville, MA 02145. Tel. (617) 628-9726; fax (617) 776-8246.
Tour Designs, 713 Sixth Street SW, Washington DC 20024. Tel. (800) 432-8687/(202) 554-5820; fax (202) 479-0472; e-mail: tourdesigns@igc.org
Uniworld, tel. (800) 733-7820; fax (818) 382-7820; web-site: http://www.travel uniworld.com. Cruises along waterways of Russia and Ukraine.
Visa Advisors, Inc., 1819 Connecticut Ave, NW #300, Washington, DC 20009. Tel. (202) 797-7976; fax (202) 337-3019; web-site: http://www.visaadvisors.com

ADVENTURE TRAVEL
Abercrombie & Kent, tel. (800) 323-7308; fax (630) 954-3324; web-site: http://www.abercrombiekent.com
Boojum Expeditions, (Horse) tel. (800) 287-0125/(406) 587-0125; fax (406) 585 3474; web-site: http://www.boojumx.com
Geographic Expeditions, tel. (800) 777-8183/(415) 922-0448; fax (415) 346-5535; web-site: http://www.geoex.com
Mountain Travel/Sobek, tel. (800) 227-2384/(510) 527-8100; fax (510) 525-7710; web-site: http://www.MTSobek.com
Quark Expeditions, (Arctic) tel. (800) 356-5699/(203) 656-0499; fax (203) 655-6623; web-site: http://www.quark-expeditions.com
REI Adventures, tel. (800) 622-2236; fax (253) 395-8160; web-site: http://www.rei.com/travel

IN THE UK
Russian Embassy, 18 Kensington Place Gardens, London W8 4QX. Tel. (171) 229-3628; fax (171) 727-8624.
Russian Visa Consulates, 5 Kensington Place Gardens, London W8. Tel. (171) 229-8027; fax (171) 229-3215. Edinburgh, Scotland. Tel. (131) 225-7098; fax (131) 225-9587.

AIRLINES
Aeroflot, tel. (171) 491-1764.
British Airways, tel. (0345) 222-111.
Finnair, tel. (171) 408-1222.
KLM, tel. (0990) 561-000.
Lufthansa, tel. (0345) 737-747.
SAS, tel (171) 734-4020.

TRAVEL AGENCIES
Russian Tourist Information Service, tel. (0891) 516951.
Barry Martin Travel Ltd, 342–346 Linden Hall, 162/168 Regent Street, London W1. Tel. (171) 439-1271. In Moscow: 3/9 Kommunisticheskaya Nab. Tel. 271-2609/9242; fax 956-1213.
Findhorn Ecotravels, The Park, Forres, Morayshire IV36 OTZ. Tel/fax (01309) 690995.
Intourist Travel, 219 Marsh Wall, London E14 9FJ. Tel. (171) 538-8600; fax (171) 538-5967.
Progressive Tours, 12 Porchester Place, Connaught Square, London W2 2BS. Tel. (171) 262-1676.
Room with the Russians, 1–7 Station Chambers, High Street North, London E6. Tel. (181) 472-2694.
St Petersburg Travel Ltd, 196 High Road, London N22 4HH. Tel/fax (171) 249-7503.
The Russia Experience, Research House, Fraser Road, Perivale, Middx UB6 7AQ. Tel. (181) 556-8846; fax (181) 556-8843.
The Russia House, 37 Kingly Court, Kingly Street, London W1. Tel. (171) 439-1271; fax (171) 434-0813.
Visa Shop, 44 Chandos Place, London W2. Tel. (171) 379 0419.
Voyages Jules Verne/Noble Caledonia Ltd, 21 Dorset Square, London NW1 6QG. Tel. (171) 723-5066/616-1000. 11 Charles Street, London W1X 7HB. Tel. (171) 491-4752 (cruises.)

IN CANADA
Russian Embassy, 285 Charlotte Street, Ottawa, Ontario K1N 8LS. Tel. (613) 235-4341; fax (613) 236 6342.

CONSULATES
52 Range Road, Ottawa, Ontario K1N 8JS. Tel. (613) 236-7220; fax (613) 238-6158.
3655 Avenue du Musée, Montréal, Quebéc H3G 2E1. Tel. (514) 843-5901; fax (514) 842-2012.

AIRLINES
Aeroflot, tel. Montréal (514) 288-2125.
British Airways, tel. Toronto (416) 250-0880; Montréal (514) 287-9282.
Finnair, tel. Toronto (416) 222-0203/0740.
KLM, tel. (800) 225-2525.
Lufthansa, tel. Toronto (800) 563-5954.

TRAVEL AGENCIES
Canadian Gateway, 7707 Bathurst #204, Toronto, Ontario L4J 2J6. Tel. 800-668-8401; fax (416) 660-7004.
Carlson Wagonlit Travel, 4 King Street #805, Toronto, Ontario M5H 1B6. Tel. (416) 862-8020; fax (416) 862-2390.
Intourist Office, 1801 McGill College Avenue, Suite 630, Montréal H3A 2N4. Tel. (514) 849-6394; fax (514) 849-6743.
Travel Cuts, 187 College Street, Toronto M5T 1P7. Tel. (416) 979-2406.

IN HONG KONG
Russian Embassy, Room 2932, Sun Hung Kai Centre, Wanchai. Tel. 2877-7188; fax 2877-7166.

AIRLINES
Aeroflot, tel. 2537-2611.
British Airways, tel. 2868-0303.
Finnair, tel. 2926-2048.
KLM, tel. 2808-2111.
Lufthansa, tel. 2769-6048.

TRAVEL AGENCIES
Global Union Express HK Ltd, Rm 22 2/F New Henry House, 10 Ice House Street, Central. Tel. 2868-3231; fax 2845-5078. (For Aeroflot bookings tel. 2845-4232; fax 2537-2605.)
Phoenix Services, 96 Nathan Road, Milton Mansion, 6th floor Room B, Kowloon. Tel. 2722-7378.
Time Travel Service, 40 Nathan Road, Chungking Mansions, 16th floor Block A, Kowloon. Tel. 2723-9993; fax 2739-5413. (For Trans-Siberian, also try Moonsky Star at tel. 2723-1376; fax 2723-6653; e-mail: 100267.2570@compuserve.com).

IN AUSTRALIA
Russian Embassy, 78 Canberra Avenue, Griffith ACT, Canberra 2603. Tel. (06) 295-9033; fax (06) 295-1847.

Consulate, 7–9 Fullerton Street, Woollahra, Sydney, NSW 2025. Tel. (02) 9327-5065.

AIRLINES IN SYDNEY
Aeroflot, tel. 9233-7911.

British Airways, tel. 9258-3300.
Finnair, tel. 9244-2299.
KLM, tel. 1-800-505-747.

TRAVEL AGENCIES
Gateway Travel, 48 The Boulevard, Strathfield, NSW 2135. Tel. (02) 9745-3333; fax (02) 9745-3237.
Intourist, 37–49 Pitt Street, Underwood House 6th floor, Sydney, NSW 2000. Tel. (02) 9247-7652; fax (02) 9251-6196.
Red Bear Tours/Passport Travel, 320B Glenferrie Road, Melbourne, Victoria 3144. Tel. 1-800-337-031 or (03) 9824-7183; fax (03) 9822-3956.
Sundowners Adventure Travel, 600 Lonsdale Street, Lonsdale Court #15, Melbourne, Victoria 3000. Tel. 1-800-337-089 or (03) 9600-1934; fax (03) 9642-5838. The Sydney regional office is tel. (02) 9261-2927; fax (02) 9261-2907.
STA Travel, 1a Lee Street, Railway Square, Sydney, NSW 2000. Tel. (02) 9519-9866.

IN NEW ZEALAND
Russian Embassy, 57 Messines Road, Karori, Wellington. Tel. (04) 476-6113; consular department (04) 476-6742; fax (04) 476-3843.

AIRLINES
British Airways, tel. 356-8690.
Finnair, tel. 524-2526.

TRAVEL AGENCIES
STA Travel, 64 Highland Street, Auckland. Tel. (09) 309-0458.
SunTravel, 407 Great South Road (PO Box 12-424), Penrose, Auckland. Tel. (09) 525-3074; fax (09) 525-3065.

(For listings of embassies, consulates, travel agencies and other useful addresses in Moscow and St Petersburg, see Practical Information sections.)

RUSSIAN ORTHODOX CHURCH HOLIDAYS AND FESTIVALS

There are 11 fixed Orthodox Church observances that fall on the same date each year:

Jan 6	Sochelnik	Christmas Eve
Jan 7	Rozhdestvo Khristovo	Nativity of Christ
Jan 19	Bogoyavlenie Gospodne	Epiphany
Feb 15	Sretenie Gospodne	Candlemas Day
Apr 7	Blagoveshchenie Bogoroditsy	Annunciation of Our Lady
Aug 19	Preobrazhenie Gospodne	Transfiguration of Christ (Second Savior)
Aug 28	Uspenie Bogoroditsy	Assumption of the Holy Virgin
Sept 21	Rozhdestvo Bogoroditsy	Nativity of Our Lady
Sept 27	Vozdvizhenie Zhivotvoryashchevo Kresta Gospodnya	Exaltation of the Cross
Oct 14	Pokrov Bogoroditsy	Intercession of Our Lady
Dec 4	Vvedenie vo Khram Bogoroditsy	Feast of Presentation of the Blessed Virgin

The Orthodox Church celebrates numerous holidays and religious events; many of these Church holy days stem from old pagan rituals. The month of May, for example, is very significant in the Orthodox religion. The first Sunday after Easter is known as Krasnaya Gorka or Little Red Mountain. It originated as a pagan spring rite when newlyweds and their relatives celebrated fertility, both for the land and their future offspring. In May, some of Russia's most revered saints are also honored: Saint Georgy Pobedonosets (Victory-Bringer) is remembered on May 6 and Saint Nikolai Chudotvorets (the Miracle-Maker) on May 22. The Day of Slavic Language and Culture falls on May 24. This marks the birth of Saint Cyril (827–869) who helped create the first Slavic written language, based on Greek characters.

Fifty days after Easter the Church celebrates the holiday week of Pyatidesyatnitsa (50)—the feast of the descent of the Holy Spirit on the apostles. The festival is also known as Troitsa (Trinity), an honoring of the Father, Son and Holy Spirit. Centuries ago, this was merged with the old Slavonic pagan feast

Semik (Seven Days) which heralded the beginning of summer. Villagers cut down a birch tree, decorated it with ribbons and flowers, and then held parties beneath it. Afterwards they threw the garlands into the river; how they floated predicted the village's future year.

Additionally, Slavs made sure to pay an annual visit to their ancestors' graves. They believed that the dead influenced the fate of the living. The cult of the dead is also linked with the legend of the mermaid. Spirits of young women or unbaptized children who died unnatural deaths were thought to be transformed into mermaids who, each spring, roamed the riverbanks to entice victims into the water. Anyone who had a relative die in this way paid extra attention to their gravesites. Mermaids were considered the female spirits of the water, and Troitsa/Semik week is also nicknamed Rusalnaya or Mermaid.

In August the Orthodox Church celebrates three feast days connected with the life of Christ. Since both Russian farmers and Christians were concerned with their summer harvests and sowing seeds for the following year, they developed protective religious rites. Spas the First (Festival of the Savior's Cross or First Savior) falls on August 14; it is also known as Honey Day. The holiday let people know it was time to gather honey from the beehives. A large festival was held on Moscow's Trubnaya Square where peasants sold crimson honey from large vats along with *barankas* (ring-shaped rolls). On this day peasants also brought their seeds to church and the priest sprinkled the fields with holy water. In old Rus, the cleansing of the water also took place; everyone down to livestock would be baptized in the rivers and blessed by the priests. This was thought to ward off evils and cure all ills.

August 19, Transfiguration Day of Christ (or Spas the Second/Second Savior), is also known as Apple Day. On the morning of Apple Day, everyone would take their apples to local churches. They couldn't be eaten until blessed—people believed that worms would appear in their stomachs if they broke this rule. It was customary for thousands of vendors to pour into Moscow's Zamoskvorechye district across the river from the Kremlin to sell many varieties of this fruit.

Spas the Third or Third Savior-on-the-Veil falls on August 29; this is also known as Nut Day. Nuts in the woods were gathered in sacks for the winter. Everywhere throughout Russia religious processions were also held leading with the Veronika Icon. According to legend, St Veronika gave Christ, while on the way to Calvary, her handkerchief with which to wipe his face. His image was miraculously left on it; in 944, the Veronika Icon (in Greek, *eikon* means image) was purchased by Byzantine Emperor Konstantine and moved to Constantinople.

Russian Language

CYRILLIC ALPHABET

CYRILLIC	APPROXIMATE PRONUNCIATION
Аа	*a* as in 'father'
Бб	*b* as in 'book'
Вв	*v* as in 'vote'
Гг	*g* as in 'good'
Дд	*d* as in 'day'
Ее	*ye* as in 'yes'
Ёё	*yo* as in 'yonder'
Жж	*s* as in 'pleasure'
Зз	*z* as in 'zone'
Ии	*ee* as in 'meet'
Йй	*y* as in 'boy'
Кк	*k* as in 'kind'
Лл	*l* as in 'lamp'
Мм	*m* as in 'man'
Нн	*n* as in 'note'
Оо	*o* as in 'pot'
Пп	*p* as in 'pet'
Рр	*r* as in 'red' (slightly rolled)
Сс	*s* as in 'speak'
Тт	*t* as in 'too'
Уу	*oo* as in 'fool'
Фф	*f* as in 'fire'
Хх	*kh* as in 'Bach'
Цц	*tz* as in 'quartz'
Чч	*ch* as in 'chair'
Шш	*sh* as in 'short'
Щщ	*shch* as in 'fresh'
Ъъ	hard sign (silent)
Ыы	no equivalent, but close to *ee*
Ьь	soft sign (silent)
Ээ	*e* as in 'men'
Юю	*u* as in 'university'
Яя	*ya* as in 'yard'

BASIC RUSSIAN VOCABULARY

ENGLISH	RUSSIAN PHONETIC TRANSLITERATION
Hello	*zdrahst'voitye*
Good morning	*do'broye oo'tro*
Good afternoon	*do'bree dyen*
Good evening	*do'bree vye'cher*
Good night	*spakoi'ne no'chee*
Goodbye	*da sveedahn'ya*
Yes	*da*
No	*nyet*
Please, You're welcome	*pozhal'sta*
Thank you	*spasee'bah*
Okay/good	*kharoshaw'*
Excuse me	*eezveenee'tye*
My name is ...	*menyah' zavoot' ...*
What is your name?	*kahk vahs zavoot'?*
Nice to meet you	*o'chin priyat'na svah'mee paz nahko'mitsa*
How are you?	*kahk dyelah'?*
Do you speak ...?	*vii govoree'tye po ...?*
English	*ahnglee'ski*
German	*nemyet'ski*
French	*frantsooz'ski*
Russian	*roos'ski*
I speak English	*ya gavaryoo'po ahnglee'ski*
I don't speak Russian	*ya ne gavaryoo'po roos'ski*
I (don't) understand	*ya (ne) poneemah'yoo*
Speak slowly	*gavaree'tye myed'lenna*
Please repeat	*pazhal'sta paftaree'tye*
We (I) need a translator	*nam (menye) noo'zhen perevod'chik*
I'm a foreigner (male/female)	*ya eenastra'nets/eenastran'ka*
I'm from America/England	*ya eez Ahmer'eekee/ Ahn'glee ee*
I'm a tourist	*ya tooree'st*
Group	*groo'pa*
Tell me	*skazhee'tye menye'*
Show me	*pakazhee'tye menye'*
Help me	*pamaghee'tye menye'*

I (don't) want	*ya (ne) khahchoo'*
I want to rest/sleep	*ya khahchoo' ot dakhnoot'/spaht*
eat/drink	*yest/peet*
I can/can't	*ya magoo'/ne magoo'*
It (is) here/there	*e'to zdyes, tahm*
How old are you?	*skol'ka vahm lyet?*
Of course	*kahnyesh'na*
With pleasure	*soodavolst'veeyem*
Congratulations	*pazdrahvlah'yoo vahs*
where	*gedye'*
what	*shtoh*
who	*ktoh'*
when	*kagdah'*
how	*kahk*
why	*pachemoo'*
How much/many	*skol'ka*
How much does it cost?	*skol'ka stoi'eet?*
I	*ya*
he	*ohn*
she	*ahna'*
it	*ahno'*
you (informal)	*tii* (like German *du* and French *tu*)
we	*mii*
you (formal, plural)	*vii* (like German *sie* and French *vous*)
they	*ahnee'*
man	*moozhchee'na*
woman	*zhen'shcheena*
boy	*mahl'cheek*
girl	*dye'vooshka*
father	*otyets'*
mother	*maht*
brother	*braht*
sister	*sestrah'*
grandfather	*dye'dooshka*
grandmother	*ba'booshka*
husband	*moozh*
wife	*zhenah'*

AIRPORT

airplane	*samolyot'*
flight	*reys*
arrival	*prilyot'*
departure	*vylyit*
boarding	*pasad'ka*
baggage	*bagazh'*
my passport	*moy pas'port*
my visa	*maya' vee'za*
my ticket	*moy beelyet'*
suitcase(s)	*chemodahn' (ee)*
porter	*naseel'shchik*
I want to go to the airport	*ya khachoo' ∫ aeroport'*

HOTEL

I want to go to the hotel	*ya khachoo' ∫ gastee'neetsu*
Where is the hotel?	*gedye' gastee'neetsa?*
Where is Intourist?	*gedye' Intooreest'?*
floor lady	*dezhoor'naya*
maid	*gor'nichnaya*
key	*klyooch*
floor	*etazh'*
taxi	*tahksee'*
elevator	*leeft*
room	*kom'nata*
telephone	*telefon'*
lavatory	*tooalyet'*

TRANSPORT

map	*kar'ta*
street	*oo'leetsa*
crossing	*perekhot'*
Metro station	*stan'tseeya metro'*
bus stop	*astanof'ka afto'boosa*
tram stop	*astanof'ka tramva'ya*
taxi station	*stayahn'ka tahksee'*
train	*po'yezd*
station	*vokzahl'*
Must I transfer?	*na'do peresad'ku?*

Please tell me where/when	*skazheet'ye pazhal'sta gedye'/kagda'*
to get off	*na'da soy tee*
I want to go to ...	*ya khachoo' pahye'khat ʃ ...*
Stop here	*astanavee'tyes zdyes*
Wait for me	*padazhdee'tye menyah'*
entrance	*vkhot*
exit	*vy'khot*
stop	*stoi'tye*
go (on foot)	*eedee'tye*
go (by vehicle)	*payezhai'tye*
Let's go (on foot)	*pashlee'*
Let's go (by vehicle)	*paye'khelee*
attention	*vneemah'neeyah*
forbidden	*nelzya'*

THEATER

theater/ballet/opera	*teea'tr/balyet'/o'pira*
concert/cinema	*kantsert'/keeno'*
What is playing tonight?	*shto eedyot' seevod'nya vye'chiram?*
ticket office	*kas'sa*
Do you have tickets?	*oo vas yest bilye'tee?*
When does the show begin?	*kagda' nachinai'itsa predstavlyen'iye?*
museum/park/exhibition	*moozey'/Pahrk/Vees'taʃka*

DAYS OF THE WEEK

Monday	*paneedyel'nik*
Tuesday	*ʃtor'nik*
Wednesday	*sreda'*
Thursday	*chetvyerk'*
Friday	*pyat'neetsa*
Saturday	*sooboh'ta*
Sunday	*vaskresyen'ye*
today	*sevod'nya*
yesterday	*ʃcherah'*
tomorrow	*zahf'tra*
morning	*oo'trom*
day	*dyen*
evening	*ve'cherom*
night	*noch*

week	*nedehl'ya*
month	*meh'sats*
What time is it?	*kator'ee chahs?*

CHARACTERISTICS

good/bad	*kharoshaw/plo'kha*
big/small	*ballshoy'/mal'enkee*
open/closed	*otkri'to/zakri'to*
cold/warm/hot	*kho'lodno/zhar'ko/gory ach'ee*
left/right	*le'vo/prah'vo*
straight ahead	*preeyah'mo*
(not) beautiful	*(ne) krahsee'vo*
(not) interesting	*(ne) eenteres'no*
quick/slow	*bi'stra/med'lenna*
much (many)/few	*mino'ga/mah'lo*
early/late/now	*rah'no/poz'no/say chas'*
fun/boring	*vesyol'ye/skoosh'no*
(not) delicious	*(ne) fkoos'no*
possible/impossible	*mozh'no/nevozmozh'no*

NUMBERS

one	*adeen'*	nineteen	*devyatnaht'set*
two	*dvah*	twenty	*dvaht'set*
three	*tree*	thirty	*treet'set*
four	*chetir'ee*	forty	*so'rak*
five	*pyaht*	fifty	*peedesyaht'*
six	*shest*	sixty	*shestdesyat'*
seven	*syem*	seventy	*sem'desyet*
eight	*vo'syem*	eighty	*vo'semdesyet*
nine	*dye'vyet*	ninety	*dyevenos'ta*
ten	*dyes'yat*	one hundred	*sto*
eleven	*adeen'natset*	one thousand	*tis'yacha*
twelve	*dvenaht'set*		
thirteen	*treenaht'set*		
fourteen	*chetir'nahtset*		
fifteen	*pyatnaht'set*		
sixteen	*shesnaht'set*		
seventeen	*semnaht'set*		
eighteen	*vosemnaht'set*		

MAP GLOSSARY AND ABBREVIATIONS

big	*Bolshoi (Bol.)*
boulevard	*Bulvar (Bul.)*
small	*Maly/Malaya (Mal.)*
bridge	*Most*
embankment	*Naberezhnaya (Nab.)*
new	*Novy*
lane	*Pereulok (Per.)*
square	*Ploshchad (Pl.)*
passage	*Proyezd*
avenue	*Prospekt (Pr.)*
highway	*Shosse*
old	*Stary*
street	*Ulitsa (Ul.)*
rampart	*Val*

MENU VOCABULARY

APPETIZERS

mushrooms in sour cream sauce	*gribi'so smetan'oi*
caviar	*ikra'*
salmon	*lososin'a*
black olives	*maslin'i*
sardines	*sardin'i*
herring	*seld*
salad	*salat'*
crab salad in mayonnaise	*salat kra'bi pod*
cucumber salad	*salat iz ogurtsov'*
tomato salad	*salat iz pomidor'*
salad made with potatoes, mayo, small chunks of meat, pickles	*stolich'ni salat*

ZAKUS'KI

SOUP

borsch	*borshch*
bouillon	*bulyon*
meat and potato soup	*pokhlyob'ka*
cabbage soup	*shchi*
fish or meat soup	*solyan'ka-riibni* or *myas'ni*

SUP

MEAT	MYA'SO
mutton	*bara'nina*
steak	*bifshteks'*
meatballs	*bitoch'ki*
filet	*file*
beef	*govya'dina*
goulash	*gulyash*
sausage	*kolbasa'*
meat patties	*kotle'ti*
lamb patties/kebab-style	*lyul'ya kebab*
shish kebab	*shashliik'*
schnitzel	*shnit'sel*
wieners	*sosis'ki*
pork	*svini'na*
veal	*telya'tina*
ham	*vetchi'na*
tongue	*yaziik'*

FOWL	PTIITSA
chicken	*kur'iitsa*
duck	*ut'ka*

FISH	RII'BA
crab	*kra'bi*
flounder	*kambala'*
carp	*karp*
shrimp	*krevet'ki*
salmon	*lososi'na*
perch	*o'kun*
sturgeon	*osetri'na*
pike	*sudak'*
cod	*treska'*

OTHER DISHES	
blintzes	*blin'chiki*
pancakes with fillings	*blini'*
fried meat pastries	*chebur'eki*
hot cereal	*kash'a*
boiled meat dumplings	*pelmen'i*

baked dough with fillings   *pirogi*
small hot pastries with fillings   *pirozhki'*
rice   *ris*
cheese pancakes   *siir'niki*
fruit or cheese dumplings   *varen'iki*
cold cheese tarts   *vatrush'ki*

BREAD (BLACK/WHITE)   *KHLEB (CHORNI/BELII)*
rolls   *bu'lochki*
jam   *dzhem*
preserves   *varen'ye*

DAIRY PRODUCTS   *MOLOCHNIYE BLYUDA*
thick buttermilk-like yoghurt   *kefir'*
butter   *mas'lo*
yoghurt   *prostok'vasha*
cream   *sliv'ki*
sour cream   *smetan'a*
cheese   *siir*
cottage cheese   *tvorog'*
egg   *yait'so*

VEGETABLES   *OVOSHCHI*
peas   *goroshek'*
mushrooms   *griibi'*
cabbage   *kapus'ta*
potatoes   *kartofel/kartosh'ka*
onions   *luk*
carrots   *morkov'*
cucumbers   *ogurtsi'*
tomatoes   *pomidor'i*
beets   *svyok'la*

FRUIT   *FRUKTI*
oranges   *apelsi'ni*
watermelon   *arbuz'*
melon   *dii'nya*
pears   *grush'i*
strawberries   *klubnika'*

lemon	*limon'*
raspberries	*malin'a*
peaches	*per'siki*
grapes	*vinograd'*
cherries	*vish'nia*
apples	*yab'loki*
CONDIMENTS	*PREPRAVA*
garlic	*chesnok'*
mustard	*garchee'tsa*
ketchup	*ketsup*
honey	*myod*
pepper	*per'ets*
sugar	*sak'har*
salt	*sol*
DESSERT	*SLADKOYE*
candy	*konfeti*
ice cream	*orozh'noye*
nuts	*orek'hi*
small cake/cookie	*pirozh'noye*
ice cream with fruit topping	*plombir'*
chocolate	*shokolad'*
pretzels	*sukhari'*
cake	*tort*
BEVERAGES	*NAPITKI*
tea	*chai*
coffee	*kofe*
near-beer	*kvas*
seltzered soda	*limonad*
beer	*pivo*
wine	*vino*
vodka	*vodka*
water	*voda'*
mineral	*mineralnaya*
seltzered	*gaziro'vannaya*
milk	*moloko'*
cognac	*konyak'*

juice	*sok*
orange	*apelsinovi*
tomato	*tomatni*
grape	*vinogradni*
apple	*yablochni*

TERMS	TERMEN
hot	*goryach'ee*
cold	*kho'lodno*
too	*slish'kom*
sweet	*slad'kee*
dry	*sukhoi'*
fresh	*svezh'ee*
not fresh	*he svezhee*
tasty	*vkus'no*
it's very good/delicious	*eto o'chen vkusno*
not tasty	*ne vkus'no*
with sugar	*s sak'harom*
without sugar	*biz sah'kara*
with milk	*s molokom'*
without milk	*biz moloka'*
rare (meat)	*s krov'yu*
medium	*sred'ne*
well-done	*prozhar'enye*

RESTAURANT	RESTORAN'
self-service	*samaapsloo'zhevaneye*
open	*otkri'to*
closed	*zakri'to*
(lunch) break	*(obyed) pereriv'*
dinner	*oo'zhin*
breakfast	*zaf'trak*
no space available	*mest nyet*
plate	*tarel'ka*
napkin	*salfet'ka*
cup	*chash'ka*
glass	*stakan'*
knife	*nozh*
fork	*vil'ka*

spoon	*lozh'ka*
table	*stol*
chair	*stul*
cigarettes	*ceegare'tee*
matches	*speech'kee*
waiter/waitress	*ofit'siant/ka*
I want	*Ya khachu'*
I want tea	*Ya khachu' chai*
menu	*menyoo*
bill	*schot*
bring me a bottle of	*preenesee'te bootil'koo*
wine/beer	*veena'/pee'va*
give me	*dai'te menye'*
pass me	*peredai'tye menye*
please	*pozhal'sta*
thank you	*spasee'bo*

The apostrophes in the phonetic transliteration indicate that the stress falls on the preceeding syllable (eg. in *spasee'bo* the stress is on *ee*).

Genealogy of the Imperial Family

This table is only a partial listing of dynastic relatives.

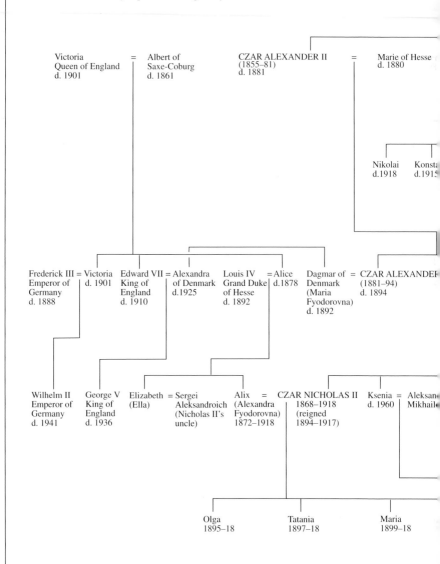

Victoria Queen of England d. 1901 = Albert of Saxe-Coburg d. 1861

CZAR ALEXANDER II (1855–81) d. 1881 = Marie of Hesse d. 1880

Nikolai d.1918   Konsta d.1915

Frederick III Emperor of Germany d. 1888 = Victoria d. 1901

Edward VII King of England d. 1910 = Alexandra of Denmark d.1925

Louis IV Grand Duke of Hesse d. 1892 = Alice d.1878

Dagmar of Denmark (Maria Fyodorovna) d. 1892 = CZAR ALEXANDER (1881–94) d. 1894

Wilhelm II Emperor of Germany d. 1941

George V King of England d. 1936

Elizabeth (Ella) = Sergei Aleksandroich (Nicholas II's uncle)

Alix (Alexandra Fyodorovna) 1872–1918 = CZAR NICHOLAS II 1868–1918 (reigned 1894–1917)

Ksenia d. 1960 = Aleksan Mikhaile

Olga 1895–18   Tatania 1897–18   Maria 1899–18

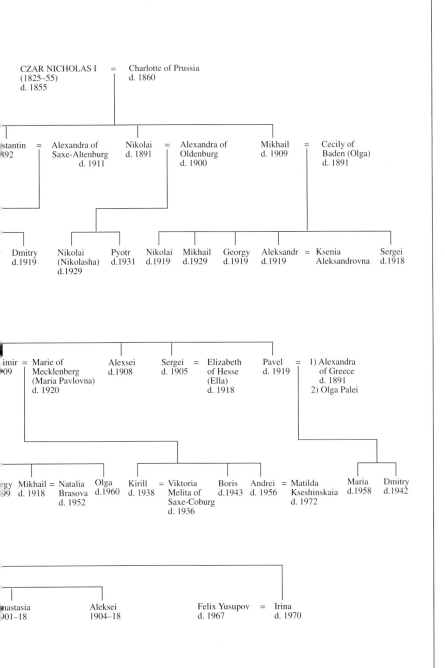

CZAR NICHOLAS I = Charlotte of Prussia
(1825–55)   d. 1860
d. 1855

stantin = Alexandra of   Nikolai = Alexandra of   Mikhail = Cecily of
)92   Saxe-Altenburg   d. 1891   Oldenburg   d. 1909   Baden (Olga)
          d. 1911   d. 1900   d. 1891

Dmitry   Nikolai   Pyotr   Nikolai   Mikhail   Georgy   Aleksandr = Ksenia   Sergei
d.1919   (Nikolasha) d.1931   d.1919   d.1929   d.1919   d.1919   Aleksandrovna d.1918
          d.1929

imir = Marie of   Alexsei   Sergei = Elizabeth   Pavel = 1) Alexandra
109   Mecklenberg   d.1908   d. 1905 of Hesse   d. 1919   of Greece
       (Maria Pavlovna)   (Ella)   d. 1891
       d. 1920   d. 1918   2) Olga Palei

rgy   Mikhail = Natalia   Olga   Kirill = Viktoria   Boris   Andrei = Matilda   Maria   Dmitry
)9   d. 1918   Brasova   d.1960   d. 1938 Melita of   d.1943   d. 1956 Kseshinskaia   d.1958   d.1942
                d. 1952   Saxe-Coburg   d. 1972
                                              d. 1936

nastasia   Aleksei   Felix Yusupov = Irina
)01–18   1904–18   d. 1967   d. 1970

Recommended Reading

CITY DIRECTORIES AND MAGAZINES

The Traveller's Yellow Pages for Moscow and St Petersburg and for Northwest Russia (from Murmansk to Novgorod). Editor Michael R Dohan. The first comprehensive business telephone book for these cities is now sold in many stores and hotels throughout Moscow and St Petersburg. For a copy, also call in the United States, Infoservices International. Tel (516) 549-0064; fax (516) 549-2032. 1 St Marks Place, Cold Spring Harbor, NY 11724.
On-Line at http://www.infoservices.com; e-mail: 71147.2275@compuserve.com
Russian Life Magazine: monthly, 89 Main St #2, Montpelier, Vermont 05602.
Tel (805) 223-4955; fax (802) 223-6105; web-site: www.rispubs.com; e-mail: sales@rispubs.com or ruslife@rispubs.com. Access Russia: For books, maps, videos, software and CD-ROMs, music, periodicals, in US, call toll free (800) 639-4301.
Passport Magazine: Business, Politics and Culture of Russia and the CIS Magazine 6 issues/year.Worldwide sales office: in New York, tel (212) 725-6700; fax (212) 725-6915. In Moscow, tel/fax (095) 158-7583/7336.
GLAS: New Russian writing, a literary journal of four book-length issues. To order a subscription contact: Zephr Press, 13 Robinson Street, Somerville, Massachusetts 02145. Tel (617) 628-9726; fax (617) 776-8246.

For a book and video catalog of Russia-related books, contact Pavlovsk Press, the Czar's Bookshop, 103 Bristol Road East, #202, Mississauga, Ontario Canada L4Z 3P4. Tel (905) 568-3522; fax (905) 568-3540. In the US and Canada, toll free call (888) 269-7721. Web-site: http://www.angelfire.com/biz/pavlovsk/bookshop.html; e-mail: czarpav@msn.com.

ON-LINE SITES ABOUT RUSSIA

Here are some of the most popular of the hundreds of Russian-related sites.
Friends and Partners: Links to many Russian-related sites and calendar events. Also contains e-mail sites of people who can answer Russian-related questions. http://solar.rtd.utk.edu/friends/home.html
REESWEL Virtual Library: Great for research; Russia listings and related links. http://www.pitt.edu/~cjp/rees.html. At University of Pittsburg.
Omri News: Russian-related on-line news service. http://www.omri.cz
Relcom Window to Russia: Moscow weather, business, travel information. http://www.kiae.su/www/wtr/

Russia Today: Russia news source and selected articles from the *Moscow Times*.
http://www.russiatoday.com/
Dazhbog's Grandchildren: Literature, art, fairy tales.
http://sunsite.unc.edu/sergei/vnuki.html
The Russian Chronicles: A fascinating photo trip across Russia.
http://www.f8.com/FP/Russia/index.html
Little Russia: Lots of useful information and CD catalog.
http://mars.uthscsa.edu/Russia/
St Petersburg Page: Information on the city and on-line version of *St Petersburg Times*. http://www.sptimes.ru
Russian National Tourist Office: http://www.interknowledge.com/russia
Russian Railways: http://pavel.physics.sunysb.edu/RR/Railroads.html
CIA City Maps: http://www.lib.utexas.edu/Libs/PCL/Map_collection/Map_collection.html
Mir Space Station: http://www.maximov.com/mir/mir2.html
Orthodox Church in America: http://www.oca.org
Russian Gifts Catalog: From Fulcrum Trading. http://www.sovietski.com

GENERAL HISTORY AND CURRENT AFFAIRS

Brewster, Hugh, *Anastasia's Album* (1996)
Channon, John, *The Penguin Historical Atlas of Russia* (1995)
Cronin, Vincent, *Catherine: Empress of All Russias* (1996)
de Jonge, Alex, *The Life and Times of Gregory Rasputin* (Dorset Press, 1987)
Duffy, J P & Ricci, V L, *Czars: Russia's Rulers for Over One Thousand Years* (1995)
Galy, Darya, *A Lifelong Passion: Nicholas and Alexandra, Their Own Story* (1997)
Halperin, Charles, *Russia and the Golden Horde* (1987)
Harford, James, *Korolev: How One Man Masterminded the Soviet Drive to Beat America to the Moon* (1997)
Kalugin, Oleg, *The First Directorate (on the KGB)*, (St Martin's Press, 1994)
Lenin, Vladimir, *What is To Be Done?* (Written 1902, published by Penguin, 1988)
Massie, Robert, *Peter the Great* (Ballantine, 1980); *Nicholas and Alexandra* (Atheneum)
Massie, Suzanne, *Land of the Firebird: The Beauty of Old Russia* (Simon and Schuster, 1980); *Pavlovsk—The Life of a Russian Palace* (Little Brown, 1990)
Morrison, John, *Boris Yeltsin: From Bolshevik to Democrat* (EP Dutton, 1991)
Oakley, Jane, *Rasputin: Rascal Master* (St Martin's Press, 1989)
Radzhinsky, Edvard, *The Last Tsar: The Life and Death of Nicholas II* (Doubleday, 1991); *Stalin: The First In-Depth Biography* (1996)

Reed, John, *Ten Days That Shook the World* (Written in 1919, published by International, 1967); *The Collected Works of John Reed* (The Modern Library, 1995)

Remnick, David, *Resurrection* (Random House, 1997); *Lenin's Tomb: The Last Days of the Soviet Empire* (Random House, 1993) (Winner of the 1993 Pulitzer Prize)

Richelson, Jeffrey, *A Century of Spies: Intelligence in the 20th Century* (1997)

Riehn, Richard, *1812: Napoleon's Russian Campaign* (McGraw Hill, 1990)

Salisbury, Harrison, *Nine Hundred Days: The Siege of Leningrad* (Avon, 1970)

Service, Robert, *A History of Twentieth Century Russia* (1998); *The Russian Revolution 1900–1927* (Macmillan, 1986)

Smith, Hedrick, *The New Russians* (Random House, 1991); (also *The Russians*)

Ulam, Adam, *The Communists: The Story of Power and Lost Illusions 1948–1991*, (Charles Scribners Sons, 1992); *Stalin: The Man and His Era* (Beacon Press, 1989); *The Bolsheviks* (Macmillan)

Yeltsin, Boris, *Against the Grain* (Summit Books, 1990); *The Struggle for Russia* (Time Books)

Yevtushenko, Yevgeny, *Don't Die Before You're Dead* (Random House) (about the 1991 coup attempt)

Volkogonov, Dmitri, *Lenin: A New Biography* (The Free Press, 1994); *Autopsy of an Empire: The Seven Leaders Who Built the Soviet Regime* (1998)

PICTURE BOOKS, ART AND CULTURE

A Day in the Life of the Soviet Union (Collins, 1987)

A Portrait of Tsarist Russia (Pantheon, 1989)

Before the Revolution: St Petersburg in Photographs 1890–1914 (Harry Abrahms, 1991)

Bird, Alan, *A History of Russian Painting* (Oxford, London, 1987)

Botkin, Gleb, *Lost Tales: Stories for the Romanov Family* (1996)

Brown, Archie, *The Gorbachev Factor* (1997)

Brumfield, William Craft, *Landmarks of Russian Architecture: A Photographic Survey*; *Lost Russia: Photographing the Ruins of Russian Architecture* (1995)

Chamberlain, Leslie, *The Food and Cooking of Russia* (Penguin, London, 1983)

Gray, Camilla, *The Russian Experiment in Art 1863–1922* (Thames & Hudson, 1984)

Maxym, Lucy, *Russian Lacquer, Legends and Fairy Tales Vols I & II* (Coral Color Process, Ltd, 1986)

McPhee, John, *The Ransom of Russian Art* (Farrar, Straus & Giroux)

Molokhovets, Elena, *Classic Russian Cooking* (1992)

Moynahan, Brian, *A Russian Century: A Photographic History of Russia's 100 Years* (Random House, 1994); *Rasputin: The Saint Who Sinned* (1997)

Murrel, Kathleen Berton, *Eyewitness: Russia* (1997)

Pokhlebkin, William, *A History of Vodka* (Verso, 1993)

Prince Michael of Greece, *Nicholas and Alexandra: The Family Albums* (Tauris Parke, 1992)

Riasanovsky, Nicholas, *A History of Russia* (5th edition, 1993)

Richmond, Yale, *From Nyet to Da* (1996, on the Russian character)

Rudnitsky, Konstantin, *Russian and Soviet Theater 1905–32* (Harry Abrahms, 1988)

Robinson, Harlow, *Sergei Prokofiev: A Biography* (Paragon, 1988)

Russian Fairy Tales (Pantheon, 1976; Collected by Alexander Afanasev)

Russian Masters: Glinka, Borodin, Balakirev, Mussorgsky, Tchaikovsky (W W Norton, 1986)

Saved for Humanity: The Hermitage During the Siege of Leningrad 1941–44 (Aurora, St Petersburg, 1985)

Shead, Richard, *Ballets Russes* (Wellfleet Press, 1989)

Shvidkovsky, Dmitri, *St Petersburg: Architecture of the Tsars* (1996)

Snowman, Kenneth, *Carl Fabergé: Goldsmith to the Imperial Court of Russia* (Crown, 1983)

Strizhenova, Tatiana, *Soviet Costume and Textiles 1917–45* (Flammarion, 1991)

Stuart, Otis, *Perpetual Motion: The Public and Private Lives of Rudolf Nureyev* (Simon & Schuster, 1995)

Thomas, D M, *Alexander Solzhenitsyn: A Century in his Life* (1998)

Townend, Carol, *Royal Russia: The Private Albums of the Russian Imperial Family* (1998)

Troitsky, Artemus, *Children of Glasnost* (1992); *Back in the USSR: The True Story of Rock in Russia* (Faber & Faber, 1987)

Volkov, Solomon, *St Petersburg: A Cultural History* (Simon & Schuster, 1995)

von Solodkoff, Alexander, *Masterpieces from the House of Fabergé* (1996)

Yermikova, Larisa, *The Last Tsar* (1995)

NOVELS, POETRY AND TRAVEL WRITING

Andreyeva, Victorya, *Treasury of Russian Love Poems* (1995)

Aitken, Gillon, *Alexander Pushkin: The Complete Prose Tales* (W W Norton, 1996)

Akhmatova, Anna, *The Complete Poems of Anna Akhmatova*, expanded edition. Translated by Judith Hemschemeyer and edited by Roberta Reeder (Zephyr Press, 1997)

Akhmatova, Anna, *My Half Century, Selected Prose* (Ardis, 1992)

Aksyonov, Vassily, *Generations of Winter* (Random House, 1994); *In Search of a Melancholy Baby* (1985)

Bulgakov, Mikhail, *The Master and Margarita; Heart of a Dog* (Penguin, 1993)

Byron, Robert, *First Russia, Then Tibet* (Penguin, 1985)

Capote, Truman, *The Muses are Heard* (from A Capote Reader, Hamish Hamilton, 1987)

Chronicles Abroad: St Petersburg, Edited by John and Kirsten Miller (Chronicle Books, 1994)

Dostoevsky, Fyodor, *Crime and Punishment* (Bantam, 1982)

Eisler, Colin, *Paintings in the Hermitage* (1990)

Erofeyev, Victor, *The Penguin Book of New Russian Writing* (1996)

Gogol, Nikolai, *Dead Souls* (Penguin)

Mandelstam, Nadezhda, *Hope Against Hope and Hope Abandoned: Memoirs* (Collins Harvill, London, 1989)

Mochulsky, K, *Dostoevsky: His Life and Work* (Princeton University Press)

Morris, Mary, *Wall to Wall* (Penguin, 1989) (A trip from Beijing across Russia on the Trans-Siberian)

Pasternak, Boris, *Dr Zhivago* (Ballantine, 1988)

The Portable Chekhov (Viking, Penguin); **Rayfield, Donald**, *Anton Chekhov: A Life* (1998)

The Portable Tolstoy, and *War and Peace* (Penguin)

Reeder, Roberta, *Anna Akhmatova: Poet and Prophet* (1995)

Rybakov, Anatoly, *Fear* (Little, Brown & Co, 1992); *Children of the Arbat* (Dell, 1988)

Rzhevsky, Nicholas, *An Anthology of Russian Literature from Earliest Writings to Modern Fiction* (1996)

Solzhenitsyn, Alexander, *One Day in the Life of Ivan Denisovich* (Bantam); *The First Circle*, and *The Gulag Archipelago* (Harper and Row); *The Red Wheel* (1994).

Steinberg, Mark & Khrustalyov, Vladimir, *The Fall of the Romanovs* (Yale University Press, 1995)

Theroux, Paul, *The Great Railway Bazaar* (A trip across Russia on the Trans-Siberian)

Thubron, Colin, *Where Nights are Longest* (Atlantic Monthly Press, 1983); *Among the Russians* (Penguin, 1985)

Tolstoya, Tatyana, *On the Golden Porch* (1988); *Sleepwalker in a Fog* (1992)

Turgenev, Ivan, *Fathers and Sons* (Penguin)

Ustinov, Peter, *My Russia* (Little, Brown & Co, 1983)

Van Der Post, Laurens, *Journey in Russia* (Penguin, 1965)

Voinovich, Vladimir, *Moscow, 2042* (Harcourt Brace Jovanovich, 1987)

Wilson, A N, *Tolstoy Biography* (Ballantine, 1988)

Index

Practical information, such as telephone numbers and opening hours, is notoriously subject to change. We welcome corrections and suggestions from guidebook users; please write to:

Odyssey Publications Ltd,
1004 Kowloon Centre,
29–43 Ashley Road,
Tsim Sha Tsui,
Kowloon, Hong Kong.
Fax: (852) 2565 8004
E-mail: odyssey@asiaonline.net